WOMEN WRITERS IN RENAISSANCE ENGLAND

LONGMAN ANNOTATED TEXTS

GENERAL EDITORS:
Charlotte Brewer, *Hertford College, Oxford*
H.R. Woudhuysen, *University College London*
Daniel Karlin, *University College London*

PUBLISHED TITLES:
Michael Mason, *Lyrical Ballads*
Alexandra Barratt, *Women's Writing in Middle English*
Tim Armstrong, *Thomas Hardy: Selected Poems*
René Weis, *King Lear: A Parallel Text Edition*
James Sambrook, *William Cowper: The Task and Selected Other Poems*
Joseph Phelan, *Clough: Selected Poems*
Douglas Brooks-Davis, *Edmund Spenser: Selected Shorter Poems*
Priscilla Bawcutt, *William Dunbar: Selected Poems*
Helen Ostovich, *Ben Jonson: Four Comedies*

WOMEN WRITERS IN RENAISSANCE ENGLAND

EDITED BY

RANDALL MARTIN

LONGMAN

London and New York

Addison Wesley Longman
Edinburgh Gate
Harlow
Essex CM20 2JE
England
and Associated Companies throughout the world.

*Published in the United States of America
by Addison Wesley Longman Inc., New York.*

First published 1997

ISBN 0 582 09621 9 CSD
ISBN 0 582 09620 0 PPR

British Library Cataloguing-in-Publication Data

A catalogue record of this book is
available from the British Library

Library of Congress Cataloging-in-Publication Data

A catalog entry for this title is available from the
Library of Congress

Set by 3 in 9½/12pt Sabon
Produced by Longman Singapore Publishers (Pte) Ltd.
Printed in Singapore

CONTENTS

ACKNOWLEDGEMENTS

It is a great pleasure to record my gratitude for the support and encouragement I have received from many people while working on this project, especially from women scholars who were gracious enough never to utter a discouraging word about what they must often have recognised as a male editor's blind spots. The following friends and colleagues took time to read various sections of the manuscript at different stages and to offer valuable suggestions for improvement. Their collaboration has been indispensable: Elizabeth Archibald, Margaret Arnold, Richard Carruthers-Zarowski, Katherine Duncan-Jones, Frances Dolan, A.S.G. Edwards, Isobel Grundy, Gwynne Kennedy, Kathy Kerby-Fulton, M.J. Mills, Andrea Sella, Lisa Surridge, Wendy Wall, and Alice Woolley.

Other people offered expert assistance and advice in particular areas. Steven Gunn of Merton College, Oxford and Diarmaid MacCulloch of the University of Bristol provided me with answers to queries about the Howard Family. Sister M. Esther Hanley, Archivist of Loretto College, Toronto, kindly furnished me with information about Mary Ward and obtained Sister Immolata Wetter's *Letters of Instruction*, containing Ward's writings, for my use. George Schner S.J. of Regius College, University of Toronto, obtained permission for me to consult Jeanne Cover's unpublished University of Toronto Ph.D. dissertation, 'The Significance of Mary Ward's Spirituality and Practice for Moral Theology Today'. I also had many enlightening discussions about Ward, the Hebrew Psalms, Old Testament heroines, and female spirituality with Walter Deller of the Logos Institute, Toronto. William Cooke of the Records of Early English Drama Project at the University of Toronto offered me meticulous help with translations of difficult and obscure Latin and Greek passages in Elizabeth Grymeston's *Miscellanea*.

My colleagues in the Departments of English at the Universities of Toronto, Victoria, and New Brunswick have continuously shown me cheerful solidarity. I am also grateful to each of these universities for providing me with funding which enabled me to visit research libraries in the United States and Britain. I should further like to thank the following persons and institutions for permission to consult and quote from material held by them: the Rt Hon. the Viscount De L'Isle, MBE; the British Library; the Bodleian Library; the Huntington Library; the Fisher Rare Book Library and John Robarts Research Library at the University of Toronto; the Centre for Kentish Studies, Maidstone; and M.E. Arnold of the Northampton Central Library. Diana Rutherford of the University of Victoria transcribed several long sections of this volume, thereby saving me considerable labour, while Misty Hazlett, Vera Zarowsky, and Jacqueline Cox of the University of New Brunswick helped me assemble the final typescript. Linda McNutt took time from a busy schedule to proof-read the entire work. Elizabeth Mann, my publisher at Longman's, has kindly sent regular messages of encouragement and been very forbearing in the face of several delays. Finally, my work has benefited hugely from the scholarly advice of Henry Woudjuysen, Renaissance general editor of this series. He has guided my handling of this project from the very beginning with shrewd intelligence, devoted more time than I deserved to making helpful suggestions, and patiently corrected my errors and omissions. Those that remain are now my own responsibility.

On a personal note, I should like to thank Peter and Betsy Newell, and Jonathan and Henrietta Freeman-Attwood, for their warm and generous hospitality during several research trips to Oxford and London.

Fredericton, New Brunswick,
28 January 1996

INTRODUCTION

In the course of preparing this volume I have repeatedly been asked two questions which came to shape my assumptions about the needs of potential readers and how they might best be served. Most frequently asked was the predictable and often incredulous, 'Were there any?' More encouraging, though still somewhat sceptical, was, 'Did Renaissance women writers adopt pseudonyms like many of their eighteenth- and nineteenth-century successors?' Though answers to both questions surprised most people, the second usually generated greater astonishment because those who asked believed they were making an informed enquiry based upon what they knew about later periods of women's literary history. But the answer was no: most Renaissance Englishwomen wrote under their own names. A few of their works appeared with initials only, and several did so anonymously (though *how* anonymously it is often difficult to say), but in terms of title-page identification the situation for women does not differ very much from men, even though in most other respects, particularly later historical visibility, disparities between early modern male and female authors are profound. Out of these two usefully mistaken suppositions emerged this volume's several aims, the most important of which is to recover and make more widely available a substantial selection of these 'lost' female writers. Doing so will enable students of English Renaissance literature, history, women's studies, and other fields to know their creative achievements first hand, in many cases after four centuries of complete silence. The rediscovery of a considerable number of early modern women writing on a wide range of subjects invites readers to re-evaluate their work from a distinct female perspective, rather than collapsing it into historical narratives governed by assumptions and interests that remain dominantly masculine. It is hoped that students of women's literary history will find this volume a useful resource for reconstructing the stories of early modern female authors, individually and collectively. The multifaceted profile of this anthology's writings may also encourage readers to study the effects of contemporary social customs and gender ideologies on the lives of these women, and allow their beliefs to be compared with those of female authors who came after in order to understand how the latter drew strength from, or broke with, the attitudes and experiences of their Renaissance foremothers. Furthermore, the recuperative nature of this project inevitably touches on the revision of the traditional Renaissance literary canon. This anthology hopes to make a strong case for greater representation of Renaissance female authors hitherto ignored or suppressed, and for a scholarly reassessment of literary and social relationships amongst writers of both sexes. Just as the territories and audiences of this volume are multiple, in the same way the writers themselves attest to culturally interconnected, though only lately recognised and still unequal, histories.

The question about pseudonyms was also valuable for the light it shed on the received picture of these authors and of female literary history generally. Sensibly enough in the absence of well-known facts about early modern women, my interlocutors applied what they knew about the celebrated travails of later English female authors retrospectively, positing a continuity of unfavourable cultural attitudes and practical resistance. Yet the approach taken by Renaissance women in this one respect indicates that their situation differed from, say, eighteenth-century female authors. The deep-seated prejudices of early modern society towards women engaging in any form of public discourse were not to be overcome by what later became the quasi-legitimate expedient of adopting male pseudonyms. All the women presented in this anthology confronted far more implacable hostility towards any kind of writing and publishing, and it was the local nature of this opposition that determined the specific strategies of self-representation they deployed to express themselves. Thus even though modern readers will identify with and perhaps be moved by these authors' efforts and aspirations, since the social obstacles they encountered do often mirror those against which women in later ages have also struggled, the reactions of early modern Englishwomen were historically conditioned and therefore need to be differentiated from those of other times and places, as do the particular forms of patriarchy ranged against them. As the material record of this group of authors becomes better known, accounts of English literary history will be rewritten accordingly, and studies of early modern gender relations will become more reliably grounded in their documentation of real social conditions.

Such accounts do not emerge by themselves, however, but are shaped by scholars who narrate the lives of these women, just as the form and direction of this anthology depends on its editor's suppositions about readers' expectations and interests. Anticipating the latter partly involves drawing on personal preferences. While reading the female-authored texts of this period and considering which ones should be included in this volume, I found myself attracted to writing that was distinctively voiced, artfully expressive, historically textured, and forward-looking in terms of female advocacy. Yet some women writers in this period seem to fall short of meeting any of these criteria; like many more of their male contemporaries, they are dull and unmemorable. In particular not all Renaissance women questioned the patriarchal ideology that restricted and oppressed them in varying degrees: many accepted it either in whole or part, some with evident satisfaction, and so to some readers these authors may appear self-defeating and even irritating in terms of what we now believe were necessary steps for women to take collectively towards achieving greater access to education, political enfranchisement, and social justice. Nonetheless our responsibility for establishing an accurate record of the lives and work of all early modern women demands that we account for these more complacent writers as well as their defiant and, in terms of our present-day values, like-minded contemporaries. Accordingly, this anthology tries to include examples of both singular and representative women writers of the time in order to represent a broad spectrum of early modern female expression. Anthologisers recognise all too well that the composition of their volumes will never be a perfect mix; but if the present selection encourages discussion or disagreement about the merits or demerits of particular writers or works, that is welcome, because at this stage no definitive canon of Renaissance female authors exists – nor (to be idealistic) perhaps should it ever – and in most cases our first impressions of these texts are still being formed. I have tried to reflect the current state of critical provisionality by recording varying interpretations (when they have occurred) as well as my own readings in the introductions and notes to individual authors and works, in the hope that readers will find the overall exchange informative and stimulating. In short, though this volume inescapably represents a critical intervention in the field, its selections and commentary are not intended to be dogmatic but critically suggestive.

An anthology that decides to include more than just conventional literary genres – now a characteristic orientation of revisionist 'literary' history and feminist scholarship – must also consider the practical question of which kinds of writing to represent, since including an example of everything set down by Renaissance Englishwomen would result in a volume that was too fragmentary and weakly discriminating. I have therefore selected a limited number of genres and authors to ensure that those texts which are represented are usefully ample. Among the genres omitted are private letters, prayers, anagrams, acrostics, medical and cookery receipts, translations (more for reasons of space than from qualms about 'originality', and with the prominent exception of Mary Sidney's version of the *Psalms*, a work which is undoubtedly original), and other minor written forms. Several texts of questionable or disputed authorship have also been excluded. Among these are apocryphal writings attributed to Mary Stuart, Queen of Scots (extensively reproduced in Travitsky 1981), verses published in the name of the Countess of Oxford in 1584 but probably written by John Southern (May 1992; Smith 1994), and the pseudonymous duo Constantia Munda and Esther Sowernam, who published *The Worming of a Mad Dog* and *Esther Hath Hanged Haman* in 1617 to counter Joseph Swetnam's *Arraignment of Lewd, Idle, Froward, and Unconstant Women* in 1615. As Diane Purkiss (1992) and others have shown, Munda and Sowernam are almost certainly men responding knowingly to Swetnam for the sake of publicity and sales, whereas Rachel Speght, who also rebutted him in 1617, responded very differently as a real woman. She is therefore the only combatant in the Swetnam controversy reproduced here. All texts related to this contention as well as Jane Anger's *Protection for Women* (1589), which I also accept as female-authored, are reproduced in the collections edited by Shepherd 1985 and (with the exception of Speght) Henderson and McManus 1985. Even more likely to be men *en travestie* are 'spinsters' Mary Tattle-well and Joan Hit-him-home, authors of *The Women's Sharp Revenge* (1640, reproduced in Travitsky 1981 and Henderson and McManus 1985). These were pugnacious responses to anti-female pamphlets by John Taylor, who may in fact have written the whole lot. Less trivially, opinion remains divided over the authorship of 'The Doleful Lay of Clorinda', published in Edmund Spenser's *Colin Clout's Come*

Home Again (1595). Waller (Sidney 1977: 54–9) and Hannay (1990: 63–7) are the most recent critics to defend attribution of the poem to the Countess of Pembroke, while others such as Michael Brennan (1988: 61–2) argue that the poem is by Spenser. Opinion at the moment seems to favour the Countess, but the debate is by no means closed.

I have also passed over certain long works if they could not be satisfactorily represented by extracts or are currently or imminently available in other modern editions. An abridged version of the First Part of Lady Mary Wroth's prose romance *Urania*, for example, appears in Paul Salzman's *Anthology of Seventeenth-century Fiction* (1991). The entire First Part has been edited by Josephine A. Roberts (Wroth 1995) with the unprinted Second Part forthcoming. Wroth's pastoral drama *Love's Victory*, on the other hand, has been edited by Michael G. Brennan (1988) but is not yet widely available because it was printed privately. I have therefore included excerpts from the prologue and third act of Wroth's play that provide a lively glimpse of the whole work and are able to stand well on their own. The complete texts of Elizabeth Cary, Lady Falkland's *The Tragedy of Mariam, the Fair Queen of Jewry* (1613) and a biography written by her daughter have recently been edited by Barry Weller and Margaret W. Ferguson (Cary 1994). The play alone has also been available in a Malone Society Reprint edited by A.C. Dunstan and W.W. Greg in 1914, with a revised version being published in 1992 edited by Marta Straznicki and Richard Rowland.

Elizabeth Cary's *Edward II* (written in *c.* 1627 but not published until 1680) is chronologically the last work presented here even though the English Renaissance is usually deemed to extend until the Restoration. This closing date is partly arbitrary, based on space available to editors in this series and the priority I have chosen to give Tudor and Jacobean writers (who have been the most superficially represented in modern anthologies of English or British female authors). To have gone much beyond Elizabeth Cary would also have meant taking account of the civil war period, which in fact saw an explosion of women's writings (Elaine Hobby reckons that 70 of the 130 texts – consisting mainly of protest pamphlets and parliamentary petitions – published in the 1650s were by women (1992: 16)). The political and religious conflicts of the 1640s and 1650s created a distinct literary culture which demands a carefully historicised context better served in a specialised volume. Female civil-war authors have been excerpted in Greer *et al.* 1988 and Otten 1992, and received detailed discussion in Hobby 1988, 1992 and Ezell 1987, 1993.

Considerations of accessibility and historic prominence also affected my decision not to represent writings by Elizabeth I. She is the one Renaissance Englishwoman whose words and deeds have been on record continuously for 400 years and are currently available in many modern volumes. While in theory she provided a model for early modern Englishwomen, in practice her position as a female ruler was viewed as anomalous, serving neither to modify traditional gender roles nor to encourage women to participate more actively in public life; indeed it may have increased social pressure on ordinary women to conform to traditional female behaviour. Moreover, pressure from male courtiers and traditional cultural prejudices led Elizabeth to subordinate aspects of her womanhood or elide them into a celebrated androgyny. She took virtually no action to promote women's literary aspirations or wider access to female education, even though she was a shining example of humanism's 'learned lady'. One can therefore argue that Elizabeth has long been disproportionately represented in relation to the lives and writings of her female subjects, and that, though it is admittedly an exception to the general principle of historical representativeness, the latter for once deserve as much space as an editor can give them. There is little danger of Elizabeth being permanently marginalised, let alone forgotten.

Early modern Englishwomen were directed to confine their literary aspirations to socially acceptable 'feminine' genres: religion, advice to children, and translation of male-authored works. These areas corresponded to traditional female moral virtues of chastity and obedience and to the domestic roles that male writers of conduct books repeatedly exhorted women to cultivate. Within the traditional literary hierarchy these 'private' genres ranked below the 'masculine' public ones such as epic poetry, tragedy, and history, which were generally dependent on a rhetorical education in ancient languages and literature unavailable to most Renaissance Englishwomen. Though a few authors such as Anne Dowriche and Elizabeth Cary ventured directly into these male preserves, others negotiated varying degrees of creative autonomy within the approved or related genres by reinscribing their structures, characters, and symbolic languages with alternative female values. To ensure their work reached a public audience after writing, especially amongst female friends and acquaintances, women either had their works printed – often with apologetic prefaces and stories of being 'pressed' to do so by male relations – or had them transcribed in fair copies for manuscript distribution (Ezell 1993: 53). As evidence for the nature of women's reading and writing in this period increases, we are beginning to recognise that proportionately it was not so much the overall number of female writings that was small but the audience of literate women amongst whom female-authored works regularly circulated. Renaissance Englishwomen sometimes wrote in the hope of attracting patronage and preferment, although not usually for direct financial gain from publishing (commercial profit motivated few Renaissance women because most came from the ranks of the gentry or nobility). There were exceptions, however, such as Isabella Whitney and Aemilia Lanyer, both of whom were middle-class women who had fallen on hard times and hoped to improve their situations by attracting potential patrons or employers with presentation copies of their work. Other women, such as the Countess of Pembroke and Lady Mary Wroth, became famous patrons in their own right and also wrote creatively to uphold their family's celebrated literary reputation. Their artistic achievements, as well as those of Elizabeth Cary, Lady Falkland, demonstrate irrefutably that women could act as autonomous artists – albeit sometimes at considerable personal cost – who were able to find intellectual and social fulfilment outside of relationships to husbands, fathers, or other male relations. In the same way Renaissance women were active in diverse areas of English public life, even though cultural attitudes overall remained hostile to such intrusions and national affairs in many areas were entirely closed to them (Amussen 1988; Warnicke 1993). Their roles included those in the royal household and court offices, legal actions, court testimony and guarantees, certain parish functions, midwifery, hospital nurses and matrons, teaching within the household and local community, and of course writing as a public service (Crawford 1993a). Gentlewomen such as Margaret, Lady Hoby and Grace, Lady Mildmay regularly wrote and collected receipts preserving medical information that had been passed down by their mothers, and they performed surgery and other healing arts for members of their local parishes. Since these women often assumed primary responsibility for the health of tenants and servants, their skills were essential to a community's welfare, and acquiring and practising them was presumably a genuine source of intellectual and creative satisfaction (Pollock 1993). Beyond medicine there was the traditional female responsibility for childbirth and infant care. Renaissance women such as the Countess of Lincoln wrote treatises in these areas based on real-life experience and accumulated female wisdom. This distinguished them from male writers who simply repeated non-empirical theories handed down by classical authorities. As the writings of Elizabeth Jocelin, Dorothy Leigh, Elizabeth Grymeston and others also show, child-rearing and education were of deep concern to Renaissance parents, who vigorously debated claims about the benefits of female education, the forms it should take, and the subjects it should include. Moreover, while most gentlewomen's lives did indeed remain centred on domestic activities, these were not exclusively private because the typical Renaissance house was not a closed space. By comparison with later periods, early modern households were relatively open sites of circulation amongst family members, guests, servants, and neighbourhood workers (all of whom remain visible in these writings, in contrast, say, to the picture of domestic settings derived from Victorian fiction). The home was permeable to involvement by the local parish and not yet sharply defined in terms of the nuclear family. Gentlewomen such as Lady Hoby and Lady Anne Clifford managed and provisioned large and complex households, often during prolonged absences by their husbands. They supervised tenants, transacted their own and their husbands' financial business, negotiated neighbourhood alliances, and exercised varying degrees of influence over political, judicial, and clerical appointments. The multiplicity of female activity documented in this anthology underlines the claims of Lois Schwoerer (1984), Diane Willen (1989), Retha Warnicke (1993), Patricia Crawford (1993a, 1993b) and other historians that modern theories about the strict gendered division of public and private spheres, and especially so-called notions of 'privatised' women restricted to family roles in 'spiritualised', emotionally barren, and despotically patriarchal households (Stone 1977), have been applied too broadly to sixteenth- and early seventeenth-century England and are not borne out either by the fluidity of the concepts themselves or the emerging material evidence of women's lives. There are, for instance, numerous accounts of local challenges by women to the repeated calls by Puritan preachers for female submission and silence (Lucas 1990), just as there are many examples of authors such as Isabella Whitney, Mary Wroth, and Elizabeth Cary opposing such strictures through literary self-representation (Jones 1987, 1990a, 1990b, 1991). Such evidence alerts us to the discrepancies between officially promulgated customs and laws that gave early modern Englishwomen few independent rights (Hogrefe 1972), and the acts of effective resistance and conditions of relative freedom negotiated by many of these women.

Like any anthology, this one is heavily indebted to the efforts of previous scholars, in particular the steadily increasing body of research by feminist literary critics and early modern social historians. Though few anthologies of Renaissance women writers have yet appeared, one issued over a decade ago was seminal insofar as it introduced specialists to a wide sampling of writings and served to define the emerging field: Betty Travitsky's *The Paradise of Women* (1981). There is no doubt that her work blazed a trail followed by this and other recent volumes. Nonetheless her anthology has proved to be unsuitable for classroom or scholarly use because its selections are too short for meaningful study. It also confines itself to reproducing only unedited extracts from printed texts, a format recently repeated by Charlotte Otten's non-fiction prose anthology *English Women's Voices, 1540–1700* (1992). By omitting many potentially important manuscript texts, both anthologies have tended to reinforce the common belief that only women who circulated printed works can be considered real authors. Yet this ignores the material conditions of Renaissance literary culture and the examples of famous male writers, such as Philip Sidney, whose most important works were never printed in their lifetimes. Harold Love (1993) has demonstrated conclusively how seventeenth-century manuscript production was a thriving industry and an undoubted means of establishing public authorship. Margaret Ezell (1987, 1993) likewise calls attention to distortions in our emerging picture of Renaissance women writers caused by the devaluation of manuscript texts. She argues this has come about partly under the influence of Woolfian paradigms privileging what only later became the predominance of commercial print culture. An exception to this thinking is *Kissing the Rod* (1988, ed. Germaine Greer *et al.*), which presents a wide range of seventeenth-century women's verse from both manuscript and printed sources with accompanying notes. Greer's anthology shows that while Woolf's memorable tale of Judith Shakespeare in *A Room of One's Own* (1928) was perhaps a necessarily provocative mythologising gesture, it had the unintentional effect of erasing, or at least deflecting scholarly study away from, pre-1700 female authors who did not reach print or write for a living. These are biases that recent, otherwise weighty anthologies of English women's literature, such as *The Norton Anthology of Literature by Women: The Tradition in English* (1985, ed. Sandra M. Gilbert and Susan Gubar), have tended to perpetuate: excerpts dating from before 1800 constitute only 7 per cent of this volume. The picture it and many other anthologies present, as Ezell observes, is one of Renaissance women as pathetically isolated eccentrics crying in the patriarchal wilderness until the publishing industry and the example of professional female authors brings salvation. Readers may decide that the present volume redraws this picture substantially.

Deeper investigation of Renaissance women writers in England seems to have been slowed by several other factors, with the result that perhaps every other major period of English literary studies may now be more 'advanced' in terms of its recovery and critical investigation of notable female authors. Besides the short-term problem of obtaining edited texts with commentary from which to teach, especially at the undergraduate level, there have also been the depressive phenomena of protracted public-spending cuts and competition from other newly emerging fields that have made it difficult to get ageing university departments and bureaucracies to revise traditional syllabuses to accommodate these 'new' writers. Jean Howard has also remarked on the preference of many female critics for re-interpreting male-authored Renaissance texts using modern theoretical discourses, particularly feminism, rather than using the rediscovered works of early modern women:

> [Existing anthologies of Renaissance women writers] are the fruits of long and patient scholarly work, often implicitly disparaged or overlooked by avant-garde critics whose preferred mode of disrupting settled paradigms of knowledge is to read familiar texts *with a difference*, to do battle on the terrain already constructed as important. (1991: 154)

As Howard observes this situation leaves existing notions about early modern English society largely unrevised and impedes the task of writing a new literary history of interrelated male and female authors.

The relative neglect of Renaissance women writing in England may also be partly owing to a modern lack of sympathy for the religious subjects that interested so many of them. In some ways this aversion is understandable given the responsibility that traditional religions bear for female subordination, which many women today feel they continue to perpetuate. Nonetheless, this is a profoundly unhistorical response to the period, it belittles the complexity of early modern women's lives, and it colludes with their silencers. The Reformation and its aftermath were certainly the most significant events in early modern England and the most far-reaching in terms of advancing female literacy and of opening spaces for greater participation by women in public life, national affairs being predominantly concerned with religious controversies. (Margaret Tyler, for example, defends her translation of *The Mirror of Princely Deeds and Knighthood*, a Spanish romance, partly on the grounds that religion is better avoided because it is an inherently volatile and immodest topic for female writers.) As Janel Mueller has aptly remarked, the paramount historical question pertaining to early modern Englishwomen is not whether they had a Renaissance, in the words of Joan Kelly's now famous but still contentious phrase (1977), but whether they had a Reformation (Mueller 1988: 15). In the same historical context but under very different conditions, networks of Catholic women took over many of the educational and pastoral roles normally exercised by priests, who were outlawed in England, and by male heads of families, who often had to conform publicly to avoid fines for recusancy. Though the details of how much freedom Englishwomen gained or lost in the Renaissance compared to earlier periods are still being researched and debated, particularly in the area of legal and property rights (e.g. Erickson 1993), the historicising work of recent scholars has shown that for most English gentlewomen the Reformation brought about changes in cultural attitudes that altered their social duties and responsibilities in important new ways. The Reformation's call for an unmediated relationship between divine atonement and personal salvation dependent upon individual agency likewise empowered women to read and write in greater numbers than ever before, often in court circles (e.g. Katherine Parr) or household groups (Aemilia Lanyer). While doing so could be defended on the grounds of moral benefit and in deference to the prevailing idealisation of chastely pious women, the practical effects were the blossoming of a subjective self-consciousness and a female-specific cultural scrutiny, as women began to rethink traditional discourses, mythologies, and supposed female capacities underpinning prescribed public behaviour and gender roles. During these moments women cleared intellectual spaces for themselves in which they began to reinvent affirming self-images reflecting newly imagined possibilities as well as their own occluded intellects and feelings. In non-fictional writings these representations may take the form of distinctive narrative personas ranging from the coolly assured (e.g. Rachel Speght) to the unshakeably defiant (Anne Askew), while in fictional works by Isabella Whitney, Mary Wroth, Elizabeth Cary and others, they become characters who voice passionate assertiveness in tones of lingering self-doubt, thereby attesting to the new and sometimes bewildering experience of improvised female self-definition.

In broad terms the impact of cultural attitudes and social habits inculcated by the Reformation's insistence on spiritual self-sufficiency superseded calls for greater access to female education made at the beginning of the sixteenth century by humanist scholars. Their ideas were based on the rejection of medieval theories that learning would aggravate the supposed tendency of womankind towards evil and prohibited knowledge, as exemplified by Eve (who accordingly becomes an object of female vindication in works by writers such as Rachel Speght and Aemilia Lanyer). Yet humanist promotion of the 'learned lady' was short-lived and restricted to a small circle of families connected to the court or government (Warnicke 1983). Early modern women in general continued to have virtually no access to institutional secondary learning, and only in certain cases would daughters and relations sent away to serve in socially superior households possibly learn languages other than English from private tutors. Very few men were as high-minded as Thomas More or Anthony Cooke (Lamb 1985; Warnicke 1983: ch. 6), whose daughters became famous for their classical learning. Most fathers regarded female education as a passing court fashion or a means of positioning their daughters in potential marriages to humanist-educated princes or noblemen, and amongst many of them strong biases remained against any programme that went beyond basic subjects in English. Moreover, such negative views seem to have deepened as Protestantism became entrenched as the national religion and Puritan values gained increasing currency (viz. studying classical literature was dangerously pagan, Latin was Popish, and schools for girls seemed like a throwback to Catholic convents). In terms of advanced formal education, therefore, the situation for women throughout this period changed very little. What did improve was their reading and writing competence in English, which by the late sixteenth and early seventeenth centuries had been socially legitimated by Protestant values, even if writing skills grew less rapidly than reading abilities, and literacy rates for women lagged behind those for men. Elaine Beilin's ground-breaking survey of English Renaissance female authors, *Redeeming Eve* (1987), has demonstrated the crucial link between the new scripture-reading culture which gave women some permission to comment authoritatively on spiritual matters, and the developing cultural awareness by women of themselves as independent subjects with literary callings, a thesis that has recently been strengthened by many of the studies of individual authors in Barbara Kiefer Lewalski's *Writing Women in Jacobean England* (1993).

Moreover, because the main discourse shared by all female readers was biblical, it is not surprising that when female writers wished to discuss any topic, whether secular or religious (or both, Renaissance culture by no means invariably separating the two realms), they often turned to scriptural analogies and commentary. A good example of this typical cross-pollination of interests is Aemilia Lanyer's *Salve Deus Rex Judaeorum*, a verse-meditation about the Passion in which Lanyer laments women's universal experience of misogyny and repression. Like many of her contemporaries she clearly found the opportunity of being able to read biblical narratives in groups with other women (as she did with Margaret and Anne Clifford) a formative intellectual experience. The socially impeccable activity of reading scripture impelled these women towards interpreting central episodes of biblical – and therefore Western – history differently from ways expounded by male divines, and then to use these re-readings to reconceptualise their lives. In the gospels, for example, Lanyer and other women discovered in Christ's 'feminine' qualities of love and nurturing and his impassive responses to victimisation a recognisably female yet irreproachable model of alternative conduct freed from gender dichotomies. In biblical stories involving women they likewise found authentic precedents for either empowered public action (Purkiss 1992: 93) or rightful complaints about patriarchal repression, precedents that sometimes became the historical subjects of their creative work (e.g. Elizabeth Cary's *Tragedy of Mariam*). From Old Testament avengers such as Jael (in Lanyer's 'To the Virtuous Reader') it is not such a great distance to Elizabeth Caldwell, who uses the language of religious conversion to denounce her husband's infidelity and financial neglect and to justify the violent extremes to which he drove her. For Caldwell to have used quasi-legal or common 'rational' language to plead her case and assert her rights would have meant attempting to use a discourse ideologically unequipped to conceptualise her gendered viewpoint as an abused wife. The prophetic language she adopts, on the other hand, allows her to speak out and differentiate herself as somebody who is not a man yet who should not be immediately dismissed or attacked as a mere woman. Modern readers should therefore not be misled into thinking that when women such as Caldwell, Rachel Speght, or Elizabeth Clinton use scriptural analysis to underpin their arguments they are pious obsessives, or in the case of radicals like Aemilia Lanyer that religion was merely camouflage for social criticism or personal gain. Such divisions are anachronistic. Early modern women used their own culturally specific discourse to express imaginations, ambitions, and frustrations as real and complex as later women. It is well to remember that over half of all the material that reached print during this period was religious in subject matter, but it does not follow that the lives of Renaissance women (or men for that matter) were correspondingly narrow in outlook. While social changes brought about by humanist theories and Reformation ideologies admittedly had little effect in achieving greater female participation in politics, government, and related areas, they did gradually encourage many women to develop a heightened awareness about their own nature and status, and to prompt a few into writing eloquently creative challenges to gender restrictions. These were pre-conditions for the collective public action that a broader spectrum of women would pursue later in the seventeenth century and beyond.

Selections presented below are edited from the original sources, with the exception of Mary Ward's *Autobiographical Papers* (see below p. 228ff.). I have identified the particular manuscript or early printed copy-text at the end of each introduction, as well as the Short Title Catalogue and Wing numbers, Early English Books microfilm reels, and modern editions and anthologies of Renaissance women writers containing full texts or excerpts. Spelling and punctuation, including titles, names, and non-sounded -ed endings, have been modernised unless it is essential to retain the original form for the sake of the metre. In general I have followed the principles set out by Stanley Wells in *Modernizing Shakespeare's Spelling* (Oxford, 1979). Quotations from contemporary sources have also been modernised unless the original spelling or punctuation is at issue. Abbreviations and initials for proper names are silently expanded. I have also introduced additional paragraphs in certain texts (e.g. Margaret Tyler's Epistle to *The Mirror of Princely Deeds and Knighthood*). Corrections of what appear to be uncontroversial copy-text errors have also been made silently. All other editorial changes are identified either by square brackets [ ] or are listed in the Textual Notes, which record substantive emendations or contestable departures from the source-texts. Original marginal comments or notes (e.g. scriptural references) are not reproduced (they do not always derive from the author herself) but in most cases have been recorded in the commentary. Quotations from the Bible are taken from the Geneva version for authors writing before 1611 and from the Authorised version after that date, unless an author shows a demonstrable preference for a particular version (e.g. Elizabeth Grymeston, being a Catholic, uses the Rheims and Douay versions).

To loosen the literary classifications that Renaissance women were themselves often at pains to resist or subvert because of their gendered associations, this anthology presents texts in three general categories: prose, prose autobiography, and verse. (An exception is Aemilia Lanyer's Epistle 'To the Virtuous Reader' from *Salve Deus Rex Judaeorum* which I have placed in the section of verse-texts immediately before Lanyer's poems.) Within each category authors appear chronologically. In addition, by way of introduction, the volume begins with a selection of epistles that preceded main works. These were an important sub-genre for women writers, for it was here that they spoke most directly (though not always guilelessly) to their readers as they disclosed the personal circumstances of their writing, invoked the solidarity of a female audience, wooed potential patrons, and defended their participation in male public discourse. These brief prologues, sometimes amounting to manifestos, set the stage for their main performances as independent (or in some cases doubtful) writing subjects.

ABBREVIATIONS

BCP	Book of Common Prayer
OED	Oxford English Dictionary
Tilley	M.P. Tilley, *A Dictionary of Proverbs in England in the Sixteenth and Seventeenth Centuries* (1950)
x^r/x^v	Refer respectively to the recto and verso of any leaf

1

PREAMBLE: WOMEN'S SELF-IMAGE AS WRITERS

MARGARET TYLER (?–*c.* 1595)

EPISTLE TO THE READER, FROM *DIEGO ORTÚÑEZ DE CALAHORRA'S THE MIRROR OF PRINCELY DEEDS AND KNIGHTHOOD*

(*c.* 1578)

Introduction

In this Epistle to the Reader Margaret Tyler affirms the intellectual equality of early modern women readers. It is the first such declaration by an Englishwoman to appear in print, and it prefaces her translation of Diego Ortúñez de Calahorra's *The Mirror of Princely Deeds and Knighthood* (*c.* 1578), the first full rendering of a Spanish prose-romance into English. In order to justify writing and publishing as a woman, Tyler uses the traditional hierarchical valuation of literary genres to her advantage. She draws attention to the derivative and supposedly less complex nature of translation (a 'matter of more heed than of deep invention or exquisite learning'), suggesting that as a creative enterprise it poses no challenge to the priority of male-authored original compositions. Her work is therefore an acceptably subordinate literary activity for a woman. Yet Tyler does not defend herself merely by adopting deferential roles. The nature of her subject was bound to arouse controversy, because instead of translating a religious text she chose a work of Continental romantic fiction, a genre routinely denounced as immoral during the sixteenth century. English Protestants were suspicious of its Catholic origins, while Renaissance humanists objected to its typical courtly-love narratives in which passionate relationships between men and women occur outside marriage – and by implication women possess considerable power over men (Krontiris 1992: 23–6). For example, Juan Luis Vives, the leading early sixteenth-century proponent of classical education for women, forbade them the reading of romances. Despite persistent attacks, the genre nonetheless grew steadily in popularity, particularly amongst female readers to whom three of the greatest English romances – John Lyly's *Euphues* (1579), Sidney's *Arcadia* (*c.* 1580) and Spenser's *Faerie Queene* (1590ff.) – were formally dedicated (Hull 1982: 75–6). Prohibitions on women *writing* romantic fiction remained unchallenged until Lady Mary Wroth published *The Countess of Montgomery's Urania* in 1621. The fact that Tyler prefixes her feminist arguments to a Spanish romance at this date, when women were restricted largely to translating devotional or classical works and romantic fiction had yet to be socially rehabilitated, makes her work courageous and prescient.

Regrettably we know little about the writer herself except for what can be gleaned from this Epistle and a Dedication to Lord Thomas Howard that precedes it. Tyler had been a member of his parents' household and may have been educated there according to humanist theories, but with the unusual addition of Spanish, a language not commonly studied in England at the time. Its inclusion in the household curriculum may owe something to family tradition, since Lord Thomas's grandfather, the Earl of Surrey, was a celebrated poet who knew Italian and Spanish and hired the distinguished scholar Hadrianus Junius to tutor his family (Williams 1964: 6). Tyler's knowledge of Spanish may also be related to the Howard family's Catholic connections. Thomas Howard's father, the 4th Duke of Norfolk, although outwardly a conforming Protestant, had been discussed as a possible husband to Mary Queen of Scots and was imprisoned for his association with the Northern Rebellion (1569) which attempted to place Mary, a Catholic, on the English throne. He was later executed for treason in 1572 for his links to the Ridolfi plot, another attempt to overthrow Elizabeth and restore Catholicism. As a result the Howard family was temporarily attainted (i.e. legally deprived of titles and status), so Tyler's published praise of Lord Thomas and his father in her Dedication could be construed as seditious. Another theory proposed by Louise Schleiner is that Tyler translated *The Mirror of Princely Deeds* during readings aloud for the Duke's second wife, Margaret (Audley) Howard, who employed her until 1564 or 1567. Schleiner has also discovered a short will written in 1595 by a 'Margaret Tyler late of Castle Campes' near Cambridge. While it seems likely to be the translator's, the document unfortunately does not shed much additional light on her life (Schleiner 1992: 1–6). Finally, Moira Ferguson (1985: 51) suggests that Tyler's real name may have been Tyrrell, changed to disguise her religion (or, if she was related to the Howards by marriage, to suppress obvious links to them).

After these somewhat unsatisfactory personal speculations, one turns with greater confidence to the Epistle itself, which boldly sets out to vindicate Tyler's rights as a female reader and writer. Besides strengthening her position by praising Ortúñez's ingenuity and moral integrity, she defends her choice of a work dealing largely with chivalry on the grounds that it represents a legitimate exercise of the creative imagination in which first-hand experience is no more necessary for men than for women. Besides, she argues, the impact of war on both sexes gives them a mutual – if grim – interest in the subject. Moreover, though Tyler could have chosen a merely entertaining text from among the many issued by men, this would be an empty justification of her own skills and intelligence. Instead her defence 'is by example of the best' authors: men habitually dedicate books to women on all kinds of subjects, sacred and secular; if they may do so, then women may read in any of these areas without reproach. And if reading is permissible, why not also deeper study of them, through the art of translation? Indeed, Tyler concludes, if women's opinions and reputations can be valued by men in their dedications, 'it is all one for a woman to pen a story as for a man to address his story to a woman'. Meanwhile Tyler tempers her possible over-assertiveness in several ways. She claims that translating secular material was essential to avoid being drawn into theological controversy (traditionally another male domain), and that the socially questionable step of printing her work is excused by her age (she writes as a mature woman, and has been reading Ortúñez for some time). She likewise reassures her readers that this is her only attempt to publish, and that close friends or relations had urged her to make public use of her talents. While male authors often used the last of these pretexts to signal conventional literary modesty, for women it became almost an obligatory element of their prefatory defences when venturing into the restrictive zone of masculine print culture.

Editions:
The Mirror of Princely Deeds and Knighthood (*c.* 1578). STC 18859, reel 1029. *The Paradise of Women*, ed. Betty Travitsky (Westport, Conn., 1981, brief excerpts). *First Feminists: British Women Writers 1578–1799*, ed. Moira Ferguson (Bloomington, 1985).

MARGARET TYLER

FROM *THE MIRROR OF PRINCELY DEEDS AND KNIGHTHOOD*

(c. 1578)

MARGARET TYLER TO THE READER:

Thou hast here, gentle reader, the history of Trebatio an emperor in Greece: whether a true story of him indeed or a feigned fable, I wot not, neither did I greatly seek after it in the translation; but by me it is done into English for thy profit and delight. The chief matter therein contained is of exploits of wars, and the parties therein named are especially renowned for their magnanimity and courage. The author's purpose appeareth to be this: to animate thereby and to set on fire the lusty courages of young gentlemen to the advancement of their line by ensuing such like steps. The first tongue wherein it was penned was the Spanish (in which nation by common report the inheritance of all warlike commendation hath to this day rested), the whole discourse in respect of the end not unnecessary, for the variety and continual shift of fresh matter very delightful, in the speeches short and sweet, wise in sentence, and wary in the provision of contrary accidents. For I take the grace thereof to be rather in the reporter's device than in the truth

1. *history of Trebatio*: the title-page reads: '*The Mirror* ... Wherein is showed the worthiness of the Knight of the Sun, and his brother Rosicleer, sons to the great Emperor Trebatio, with the strange [i.e. foreign] love of the beautiful and excellent Princess Briana, and the valiant acts of other noble Princes and Knights.'
2. *wot*: know
3. *I ... after*: concern myself about
4. *profit and delight*: *utile et dulce*, moral instruction and aesthetic pleasure, the conventional Renaissance formula for good art deriving from Horace, *Ars Poetica*, 343
7. *thereby*: i.e. by the related exploits
   lusty: vigorous
8. *line ... ensuing*: lineage (through fame) by following
10. *inheritance ... commendation*: reputation for complete renown in warfare
11. *the ... unnecessary*: i.e. the conclusion justifies the events that precede it
12. *shift ... matter*: devising of new plot developments
13. *sentence*: pithy sayings, maxims
   wary ... accidents: mindful of not introducing too many unexpected reversals of fortune
14. *reporter's device*: the story-teller's design

of this report, as I would that I could so well impart with thee the delight which myself findeth in reading the Spanish; but seldom is the tale carried clean from another's mouth.

Such delivery as I have made I hope thou wilt friendly accept, the rather for that it is a woman's work, though in a story profane and a matter more manlike than becometh my sex. But as for the manliness of the matter, thou knowest that it is not necessary for every trumpeter or drumsler in the war to be a good fighter. They take wage only to incite others, though themselves have privy maims and are thereby recureless. So, gentle reader, if my travail in Englishing this author may bring thee to a liking of the virtues herein commended, and by example thereof in thy prince's and country's quarrel to hazard thy person and purchase good name, as for hope of well deserving myself that way, I neither bend myself thereto nor yet fear the speech of people if I be found backward. I trust every man holds not the plough which would the ground were tilled, and it is no sin to talk of Robin Hood though you never shot in his bow; or be it that the attempt were bold to intermeddle in arms (so as the ancient Amazons did, and in this story

16–17. *seldom ... mouth*: i.e. good news may be spoilt in the telling. Proverbial (Tilley T38). This may also refer to a translator's difficulty in conveying the full sense of the original language.

18. *delivery*: translation

18–19. *rather for that*: more readily because

19. *woman's work*: and therefore more excusable if found faulty. Tyler pre-empts criticism by recontextualising supposed female weakness as modesty, desirable in both male and female authors.

21. *drumsler*: drummer, sixteenth-century variant form of *drumslager*, from Ger. *drummeschläger*

22. *take wage*: receive payment

23. *privy maims*: private or personal permanent injuries
recureless: incurable

26. *quarrel*: cause

27. *bend ... thereto*: direct my course to 'quarrelling' on behalf of king and country

28. *backward*: not actively or sufficiently partisan

28–9. *holds ... plough*: does not take up farming

29. *which would*: who desires that

30. *in*: with
be it: if it be

30–1. *were ... intermeddle*: presumed to take part

31. *Amazons*: mythical nation of female warriors, originally counterparts to the classical heroes, living in a closed, all-female society. They were viewed as either wondrously admirable or abominably freakish – more often the latter – for challenging 'natural' masculine supremacy. Tyler here disclaims Amazonian 'intermeddling' in male activities such as warfare.

Claridiana doth, and in other stories not a few), yet to report of arms is not so odious but that it may be borne withal not only in you men which yourselves are fighters, but in us women to whom the benefit in equal part appertaineth of your victories, either for that the matter is so commendable that it carrieth no discredit from the homeliness of the speaker, or for that it is so generally known that it fitteth every man to speak thereof, or for that it jumpeth with this common fear on all parts of war and invasion. The invention, disposition, trimming, and what else in this story is wholly another man's, my part none therein but the translation, as it were only in giving entertainment to a stranger, before this time unacquainted with our country guise. Marry, the worst perhaps is this: that among so many strangers as daily come over – some more ancient and some but new set forth, some penning matters of great weight and sadness in divinity or other studies (the profession whereof more nearly beseemeth my years), other some discoursing of matters more easy and ordinary in common talk wherein a gentlewoman may honestly employ her travail – I have notwithstanding made countenance only to this gentleman, whom neither his personage might sufficiently commend itself unto my sex, nor his behaviour

33. *withal*: at the same time
35, 36, 37. *for that*: because
36. *carrieth … from*: is no discredit or reproach to
homeliness: plainness, good intent
37. *fitteth*: is appropriate for
38. *jumpeth*: coincides with
39. *trimming*: furnishing (with elegant phrases)
40–1. *only … entertainment*: the metaphor suggests Tyler restricts herself to a domestic female role of providing hospitality
41. *stranger*: foreigner
42. *country guise*: native customs
Marry: indeed
43. *strangers*: foreign books
43–4. *new set forth*: recently written or published
44. *sadness*: gravity
45. *profession*: concern
48. *made … gentleman*: favoured only this male author with my attention; i.e. this is my only published translation. The courtship metaphor implies self-display, but by limiting herself to a single 'suitor' Tyler preserves feminine decorum. Because male critics habitually equated female circulation in print with sexual promiscuity, women writers often deployed such rhetorical gestures of modesty. It also explains why Tyler draws attention to her (middle) age: because she is no longer sexually 'available', her 'liaison' with a male writer is less improper.
49. *personage … sex*: presumably because of Ortúñez's lower social rank

(being light and soldierlike) might in good order acquaint itself with my years.

So the question now ariseth of my choice, not of my labour, wherefore I preferred this story before matter of more importance. For answer whereto, gentle reader, the truth is that as the first motion to this kind of labour came not from myself, so was this piece of work put upon me by others, and they which first counselled me to fall to work took upon them also to be my taskmasters and overseers lest I should be idle; and yet because the refusal was in my power, I must stand to answer for my easy yielding and may not be unprovided of excuse, wherein if I should allege for myself that matters of less worthiness by as aged years have been taken in hand, and that daily new devices are published in songs, sonnets, interludes, and other discourses and yet are borne out without reproach only to please the humour of some men, I think I should make no good plea therein; for besides that I should find thereby so many known enemies as known men have been authors of such idle conceits, yet would my other adversaries be never the rather qui-

50. *light*: merry, sexually active

52. *So … labour*: Tyler is again anticipating potential criticism, since women were expected to restrict themselves to devotional writing or translating moral or philosophical texts by men. Romances, on the other hand, were virtually synonymous with sexual immorality.

54. *motion*: encouragement

55–7. *so … idle*: Renaissance women nearly always claimed that friends or relations had encouraged them to publish. Elizabeth Cary later mocked what she took to be the formulaic use of such pretexts in the introduction to her translation of *The Reply of the Most Illustrious Cardinal of Perron to the Answer of the Most Excellent King of Great Britain* (1630). Nonetheless composition and translation were normal parts of a gentlewoman's upbringing (see Lady Mildmay below, pp. 215–16), which male authors of conduct books approved of as remedies against idleness. 'Avoiding idleness' could thus be turned round by women to defend writing and publication, as Anne Wheathill does in the preface to her *Handful of Wholesome (though homely) Herbs* (1584).

57. *refusal*: presumably of choosing to publish. In her dedication to Lord Thomas Howard, Tyler states 'easing my sufficiency' [= means to pay debts] as a further reason for publishing. She may have planned to use the book's earnings to pay off fines for recusancy, if she was in fact a Catholic. Louise Schleiner finds a record of 'Margaret Tiler, spinster' paying such a fine in 1588–89 at Benacre in Suffolk, and suggests it may refer to the translator (1992: 5).

60. *by as*: by (persons) of such

61. *devices*: clever pieces of work

62. *humour*: fancy

65. *idle conceits*: trifling or silly inventions, perhaps recalling the masculine complaint (l. 57 above) that women are idle by nature: Tyler counters that men are far more actively 'idle'

eted: for they would say that as well the one as the other were all naught, and though peradventure I might pass unknown amongst a multitude, and not be the only gaze or the odd party in my ill doing, yet because there is less merit of pardon if the fault be excused as common, I will not make that my defence which cannot help me and doth hinder other men. But my defence is by example of the best, amongst which many have dedicated their labours – some stories, some of war, some physic, some law, some as concerning government, some divine matters – unto divers ladies and gentlewomen. And if men may and do bestow such of their travails upon gentlewomen, then may we women read such of their works as they dedicate unto us; and if we may read them, why not farther wade in them to the search of a truth? And then much more why not deal by translation in such arguments, especially this kind of exercise, being a matter of more heed than of deep invention or exquisite learning? And they must needs leave this as confessed: that in their dedications they mind not only to borrow names of worthy personages but the testimonies also for their further credit, which neither the one may demand without ambition nor the other grant without overlightness. If women be excluded from the view of such works as appear in their name, or if glory only be sought in our common inscriptions, it mattereth not whether the parties be men or women, whether alive or dead. But to return, whatsomever the truth is – whether that women may not at all discourse in learning (for men lay in their claim to be sole possessioners of

66. *naught*: worthless
67. *peradventure*: perhaps
68. *gaze*: public spectacle
69. *merit*: recompense
71. *best*: (authors)
72. *physic*: healing, medicine
73. *divers*: various
76. *wade in*: go through
78. *heed*: careful attention (to immediate details)
79. *exquisite*: consummate, long-perfected; abstruse
80. *confessed*: acknowledged
mind not: do not scruple
borrow: assume the credit that comes from association with
81. *testimonies*: in this context, commendatory writings such as epistles or introductory verses
82. *the one ... other*: authors ... patrons or well-wishers
83. *overlightness*: appearing too easy or cheaply had
view: reading
84. *inscriptions*: dedications (to women)
86. *whatsomever*: whatever

knowledge), or whether they may in some manner (that is by limitation or appointment in some kind of learning) – my persuasion hath been thus: that it is all one for a woman to pen a story as for a man to address his story to a woman. But amongst all my ill-willers, some I hope are not so strait that they would enforce me necessarily either not to write or to write of divinity. Whereas neither durst I trust mine own judgement sufficiently if matter of controversy were handled, nor yet could I find any book in the tongue which would not breed offence to some.

But I perceive some may be rather angry to see their Spanish delight turned to an English pastime: they could well allow the story in Spanish, but they may not afford it so cheap, or they would have it proper to themselves. What natures such men be of I list not greatly dispute, but my meaning hath been to make other partners of my liking, as I doubt not, gentle reader, but if it shall please thee after serious matters to sport thyself with this Spaniard, that thou shalt find in him the just reward of malice and cowardice, with the good speed of honesty and courage, being able to furnish thee with sufficient store of foreign example to both purposes. And as in such matters which have been rather devised to beguile time than to breed matter of sad learning he hath ever borne away the prize which could season such delights with some profitable reading, so shalt thou have this stranger an honest man when need serveth, and at other times either a good companion to drive out a weary night, or a merry jest at thy board.

And thus much as concerning this present story, that it is neither unseemly for a woman to deal in, neither greatly requiring a less staid age than mine is. But of these two points, gentle reader, I thought to give thee warning, lest perhaps understanding of my name and years, thou mightest be carried into a wrong suspect of my boldness and rashness, from which I

88. *may*: may (discourse)
limitation: allotted sphere or boundaries
91. *strait*: inflexible
93. *divinity*: theology
98. *afford … cheap*: want it to be made so commonly accessible (in English)
proper: exclusively
99. *list not greatly*: do not like greatly to
102. *just*: i.e. morally just (as opposed to the common view that romances allow wickedness to go unpunished)
105. *sad*: serious, grave
106–7. *season … reading*: see n. to l.4
109. *board*: table (where reading aloud during meals was a customary diversion)
110–11. *neither … neither*: neither … nor
114. *suspect*: apprehension
boldness and rashness: i.e. for appearing in print

would gladly free myself by this plain excuse; and if I may deserve thy good favour, by like labour when the choice is mine own I will have a special regard of thy liking.

So I wish thee well.
Thine to use, Margaret Tyler.

116. *like labour*: way of return goodwill
117. *regard*: consideration

ANNE DOWRICHE (?–1638)

EPISTLE TO THE READER, FROM *THE FRENCH HISTORY*

(1589)

Introduction

Anne Dowriche cites a well-known passage from Corinthians to justify her enterprise: 'What is to be done then, brethren? when ye come together, according as every one of you hath a psalm, or hath doctrine, or hath a tongue, or hath revelation, or hath interpretation, let all things be done unto edifying' (14.26). 'Edify' means to build up, and Dowriche implies that her verse-histories will deepen her readers' moral knowledge and fortify their community. What is perhaps less obvious to us but Dowriche is certain to have known is that this same chapter of Corinthians contains St Paul's endlessly repeated prohibition on female public speech: 'Let your women keep silence in the churches: for it is not permitted unto them to speak, but they ought to be subject' (14.34). Many modern scholars now regard this verse as a post-Pauline interpolation, but for Dowriche it created a dilemma, contradicting the liberating exhortation to edify. From a wider perspective, therefore, this Epistle addresses a cultural paradox faced by all female writers during this period, the implications of which extend Dowriche's 'only purpose' beyond its narrowly stated aims. On the one hand, male authorities barred women from exercising their intellectual and prophetic gifts in clerical or many secular offices. On the other hand, Renaissance theologians affirmed their equal capacity for moral growth and spiritual insight, which spurred Protestant female reformers to assert their right to interpret scripture as their consciences guided them, and publicly to defend – and die for – Reformation doctrines. Dowriche's solution is similar to that arrived at by other women of the time: to subordinate Pauline-inspired restrictions on female speech (while never being free to ignore them) and to foreground the larger context of Corinthians which authorises both women and men to act for worthy common causes. As her main work unfolds we receive a strong impression of her passionate delight in being able to write in support of militant Protestantism.

We begin to sense a measure of this personal commitment here as Dowriche outlines her reasons for versifying prose accounts of Huguenot (French Protestant) sufferings during the sixteenth-century wars of religion. Though she at first depreciates her skill and experience, this is token modesty, since her ambition to raise the moral standard of poetry is hardly compatible with shrinking amateurism. As Elaine Beilin observes, 'hesitantly ... [Dowriche] presents herself as a poet; yet her artistic goals are no less than to write God's truth, to regenerate poetry, and to move a wide audience with [its] power' (1987: 102). In putting forward her work as a model for imitation, Dowriche hopes that it will establish her public reputation and grant her an authoritative speaking-position comparable to male writers such as Christopher Marlowe, whose *Massacre at Paris* (*c.* 1592) depends upon the same sources and sectarian viewpoint as *The French History*. Dowriche makes it clear she is aware of what is at stake when towards the end of her Epistle she promises the reader 'more excellent actions' if her present work finds approval. Her final arguments for writing again begin unassumingly but develop important implications: using re-creations of topical speeches and events to engage readers' imaginative and emotional sympathies, while offering solidarity to those persecuted for their religious beliefs. Given the continuing material involvement of the Elizabethan government and certain powerful families such as the Sidneys in Continental religious conflicts, Dowriche's subject inevitably touches on national policies, though she does not explicitly offer political advice – conventionally an exclusively masculine discourse – until the end of her volume, where she exhorts the Queen to heed Huguenot pleas for aid and to repel Catholic attempts to undermine English interests.

(For further discussion see the selection from *The French History* below.)

Editions:
The French History (1589). STC 7159, reel 289. *The Paradise of Women*, ed. Betty Travitsky (Westport, Conn., 1981, brief excerpts).

ANNE DOWRICHE

FROM *THE FRENCH HISTORY*

(1589)

EPISTLE TO THE READER

Amongst many excellent precepts which St Paul gave unto the church, this is to be considered: let all things be done unto edifying. If this had been of all men well considered, many things which now fly abroad might well have been spared. That my only purpose in collecting and framing this work was to edify, comfort, and stir up the godly minds unto care, watchfulness, zeal, and ferventness in the cause of God's truth, you shall easily perceive by the choosing and ordering of these singular examples which hereafter ensue....

The causes why I have described [this *French History*] in verse are three. First for mine own exercise, being a learner in that faculty. Secondly to restore again some credit if I can unto poetry, having been defaced of late so many ways by wanton vanities. Thirdly for the more novelty of the thing, and apt facility in disposing the matter framed to the better liking of some men's fantasies, because the same story in effect is already translated into English prose. Many of these orations that are here fully and amply expressed were in the *French Commentaries*, but only in substance lightly touched, and the sum set down without amplifying the circumstance; and

3. *things ... fly abroad*: writings ... are publicly printed
4. *framing*: designing, ordering
10. *exercise*: in an accompanying dedicatory epistle to her brother, Piers Edgecombe, Dowriche says that writing 'hath been my ordinary exercise for recreation at times of leisure for a long space together'. This echoes remarks by other women such as Grace Mildmay and Anne Clifford and allows us to assume that composition was a widespread activity for gentlewomen, even though many did not have their work printed.
12. *wanton vanities*: trifling or lasciviously barren writings (chiefly by men). Dowriche proffers her own talents for the sake of improving the moral value of contemporary poetry. Margaret Tyler makes similar claims (above pp. 21–2).
13. *apt facility*: natural or willing dexterity (or courtesy)
    framed: artfully rendered
14. *fantasies*: fancies, likings
    translated: *The Three Parts of Commentaries ... of the Civil Wars of France* by Jean de Serres, were translated by Thomas Tymme in 1574. Book Ten, on which Dowriche bases the Third Part of *The French History*, is actually a reprint of *A True and Plain Report of the Furious Outrages of France* by 'Ernest Varamund' (pseudonym of François Hotman, 1573).
17. *touched ... sum*: drawn upon ... gist

yet here is no more set down than there is signified. I have also, for the more terror unto the wicked, diligently collected the great plagues and just judgements of God showed against the persecutors in every several history, and have set them down so in order, and amplified them by the like judgements against sinners out of the word and other histories, that every proud persecutor may plainly see what punishment remaineth due unto their wicked tyranny. To speak truly without vainglory, I think assuredly that there is not in this form anything extant which is more forcible to procure comfort to the afflicted, strength to the weak, courage to the faint-hearted, and patience unto them that are persecuted, than this little work, if it be diligently read and well considered, so wishing that all the excellent and rare wits that now flourish in England and show themselves many times in vain devices would all learn to consecrate their singular gifts to the glory of God, the edifying of his church, and the salvation of the souls of God's chosen. Then would the Lord still bless their labours, and give their names a perpetual memory.

So I commit thee to God's protection, and commend this my pleasant exercise to thy good liking, which if I perceive to be accepted, thou shalt encourage me to proceed to make thee acquainted with more excellent actions. Honiton in Devon this xxv of July 1589.

Anne Dowriche.

To the reader that is friendly to poetry

What so thou be that read'st my book,
  Let wit so weigh my will;
That due regard may here supply
  The want of learned skill.

A. D.

20. *in ... history*: suggesting that Dowriche uses authors other than de Serres and Hotman in *The French History*

21–2. *amplified ... histories*: alluding to Dowriche's practice of using biblical (especially Old Testament) and historical figures to allegorise modern opponents in France (e.g. Huguenots as Israelites, Catholics as Egyptians, etc.)

22. *word*: Bible

25. *form*: arrangement (i.e. modern and biblical (universal) history)

27. *persecuted*: for their religious beliefs, in England and abroad. Again Dowriche claims her work has the power to transform public opinion, here in the political sphere.

28. *rare*: splendid (spoken ironically)

30. *devices*: writings
singular: in both positive and negative senses: uniquely remarkable; limited

31. *chosen*: people; the elect

36–7. *more ... actions*: i.e. future writings

RACHEL SPEGHT (*c.* 1597–1630+)

EPISTLE DEDICATORY, FROM *MORTALITY'S MEMORANDUM, WITH A DREAM PREFIXED*

(1621)

Introduction

In this epistle addressed to her godmother, Mary Moundeford, Rachel Speght reveals her thoughts about writing several years after the publication of her first work, *A Muzzle for Melastomus* (1617), which responded to attacks against women by a male pamphlet-writer. She here repudiates the earlier negative reactions of certain male readers as well as their attempts to deny her the authorship of her own writing. The experience of such hostility and threatened erasure prompts Speght to reflect briefly on her position as a female author and to articulate reasons for venturing into print a second time.

Like Margaret Tyler and others, Speght defends a woman's fundamental right to read and learn freely on the grounds of fostering personal growth and contributing meaningfully to society. She invokes the moral authority of several well-known precepts from Matthew to justify writing for the public good, in the service of which gender distinctions ought to be irrelevant. And though formal education was not widely available to seventeenth-century women, Speght implies that if they have been fortunate enough to acquire it, its benefits should not be hoarded but shared generously with those who hunger for intellectual and spiritual nourishment, regardless of conventional but false restrictions on female speech.

Yet Speght also acknowledges the pain of having been attacked for assuming such liberty as to publish her work. On one level her comments relate to cultural anxieties shared by both men and women about the risks of appearing in print, since male authors often echoed her lament that 'censure' was 'inevitable to a public act'. But unlike men, women faced uniquely gendered opposition, and in Speght's case we possess actual evidence of this. A Yale library copy of *A Muzzle for Melastomus* contains copious comments written by an unidentified male reader (van Heertum 1987). Many of his remarks are crudely sexist, and most malicious in some way. They illustrate fully what Speght means by 'critical readers' and demonstrate her courage in daring to face this audience again, though admittedly here in a less controversial genre and a less commercially competitive context (Purkiss 1992: 90).

As writing became a more common activity for Renaissance women, they also encountered attempts by readers or publishers to impugn their integrity by attributing their work to male ghost-writers. In addition to Speght's own testimony, we again have direct evidence of this in the form of the 1570 title-page of Justin's *Abridgement of the Histories of Trogus Pompeius*, which names Arthur

Golding as the translator. He was the most prolific and famous Elizabethan translator of classical authors, whose works were used extensively by Shakespeare and others. The volume opens, however, with an eloquent epistle by his wife, 'Ursula Golding to the Reader', in which she states unapologetically that the translation is hers. Yet in later editions the title is changed to 'To the Reader' and Ursula's name is dropped (Duncan-Jones 1992). Evidently Arthur Golding decided it was unwise to credit a translator whose gender might make male readers doubt the quality of 'his' scholarship, and whose learning and skill might call into question received assumptions about inferior female intelligence. Speght faced a similar situation when certain male readers claimed that her father, a London clergyman, actually wrote *A Muzzle*. But unlike Ursula Golding (whose circumstances we do not know), Speght decided to speak up, vigorously denying the misappropriation of her work. By doing so she provided other Renaissance women with a positive example of naming and displaying their intellectual property.

These adverse conditions led Speght to develop a defensive strategy seen also in other women writers of the time: defining the value of her work in relation to female lives and networks of support. As she reveals in her *Dream*, *Mortality's Memorandum* was occasioned by the death of her mother and is dedicated to her godmother; it therefore represents Speght's personal negotiation of grief as well as her tribute to both these women for their physical, emotional, and intellectual nurture. Moreover, as Simon Shepherd observes, it is perhaps telling that when Speght married soon after publishing this work, she passed on her Christian name to her first daughter (1985: 58). As in the case of the present 'offspring', as she calls it, Speght evidently wished to associate her creative powers – in all senses of the phrase – primarily with a matrilineal heritage.

(For further discussion see the selections from *Mortality's Memorandum* and *A Muzzle for Melastomus* below.)

Editions:
Mortality's Memorandum, with a Dream Prefixed (1621). STC 23057, reel 1220. *The Paradise of Women*, ed. Betty Travitsky (Westport, Conn., 1981, brief excerpts). *Kissing the Rod*, ed. Germaine Greer *et al.* (London, 1988, excerpts from *A Dream*).

RACHEL SPEGHT

FROM *MORTALITY'S MEMORANDUM, WITH A DREAM PREFIXED, IMAGINARY IN MANNER, REAL IN MATTER*

(1621)

THE EPISTLE DEDICATORY TO THE WORSHIPFUL AND VIRTUOUS GENTLEWOMAN, HER MOST RESPECTED GODMOTHER MRS MARY MOUNDEFORD,* WIFE UNTO THE WORSHIPFUL DOCTOR MOUNDEFORD, PHYSICIAN.

Amongst diversity of motives to induce the divulging of that to public view which was devoted to private contemplation, none is worthy to precede desire of common benefit. Corn kept close in a garner feeds not the hungry; a candle put under a bushel doth not illuminate an house; none but unprofitable servants knit up God's talent in a napkin. These premisses have caused the printing press to express the subsequent *Memorandum of Mortality*, by which if oblivious persons shall be incited to premeditation of and preparation against their last hour (when inevitable death seizing on them shall cease their being upon earth), I shall with Jacob say, 'I have

* *Moundeford*: her husband had been Bursar of King's College, Cambridge before moving to London, where he became President of the Royal College of Physicians (Shepherd 1985: 58)

2. *precede*: take precedence over

4. *candle ... house*: Matthew 5.15, but also alluding to verse 16, which many Renaissance women cited to authorise public use of their knowledge and abilities: 'Let your light so shine before men, that they may see your good works'

4–5. *none ... napkin*: alluding to the parable of talents (Matthew 25.14–30), another favourite enabling text for Renaissance women. A master goes away, giving three of his servants five, two, and one talent(s) respectively. The first two servants put their talents to use and increase their holdings, but the third buries his talent because he is timid. When the master returns, he praises the first two servants for their industry but condemns the third for gaining nothing. Speght refers to the parable again in *A Dream*, ll. 133–4.

6. *express*: a pun on (printing) press

8. *against*: in expectation of

9–10. *Jacob ... enough*: Genesis 45.28

enough'. I level at no other mark, nor aim at other end, but to have all sorts to mark and provide for their latter end. I know these populous times afford plenty of forward writers and critical readers; myself hath made the number of the one too many by one, and having been touched with the censures of the other by occasion of my *Muzzling Melastomus*, I am now, as by a strong motive induced (for my right's sake), to produce and divulge this offspring of my endeavour to prove them further futurely who have formerly deprived me of my due, imposing my abortive upon the father of me, but not of it. Their variety of verdicts have verified the adagy, *quot homines, tot sententiae*, and made my experience confirm that apophthegm which doth affirm censure to be inevitable to a public act.

Unto your worthy self do I dedicate the sequel as a testimony of my true thankfulness for your fruitful love (ever since my being, manifested toward me), your actions having been the character of your affection; and that

10. *level … mark*: aim … goal
11. *populous*: perhaps with an underlying sense of 'popular' = common, vulgar. Because Speght's earlier *Muzzle for Melastomus* (1617) was associated with the popular press (despite its pro-female position), this passage suggests a further attempt 'to distance herself from the realm into which she once ventured' (Purkiss 1992: 91).
12. *forward*: eager, bold
14. *Muzzling Melastomus*: Speght's first publication defending women against misogynist attacks made by Joseph Swetnam's *Arraignment of Lewd, Idle, Froward, and Unconstant Women* (1615). See below p. 126ff.
15. *right's*: the original spelling can be read alternatively as 'rights' '; i.e. for the sake of my rights (as a woman, writer, etc.)
15. *offspring*: the metaphor suggests that the relationship between Speght and her work is as culturally privileged as that of a mother and child – a valuation echoed by other Renaissance women writers. Less conventionally, Speght rewrites the patriarchal model, in which a male heir legitimises transmission of his father's property, by leaving her own 'child' ungendered, and in the next paragraph she characterises her intellectual and emotional heritage as primarily matrilinear. The 'offspring' thus supports her claims to be an autonomous creator – a role traditionally assigned to men – capable of generating her own poetic lineage without male mediation.
16. *futurely*: in the future
17. *abortive*: the shift from 'offspring' to this negative term is explained by the altered context of misassigned 'parentage' to her father: in this case the work has no future value either of its own or for its true 'parent', and its potential to confirm an ability to generate intellectual heirs comes to nothing, in contrast to the fruitful love of Speght's godmother (see l. 22ff.)
18. *not of it*: i.e. not deprived me of the 'offspring' itself
    adagy: maxim

18–19. *quot … sententiae*: there are as many opinions as there are men

19. *apophthegm*: maxim
21. *sequel*: i.e. this second work, which follows

hereby the world may witness that the promise you made for me when I could make none for myself, my careful friends (amongst whom I must repute your ever esteemed self) have been circumspect to see performed. I would not have anyone falsely to think that this *Memorandum* is presented to your person to imply in you defect of those duties which it requires, but sincerely to denote you as a *paradigma* to others; for what it shows to be done shows but what you have done. Yet ere I leave, give me leave to put you in mind of Paul's precept: 'be not weary of well-doing, for in due time you shall reap if you faint not'. Thus presenting unto God my supplication and unto you my operation, the former to him for your safety, the latter to you for your service, I ever remain

Your goddaughter in duty obliged,
Rachel Speght.

24. *promise*: by her godmother at her baptism, to ensure she is raised according to Christian principles
29. *paradigma*: example
31. *Paul's . . . not*: Galatians 6.9

ELIZABETH JOCELIN (1596–1622)

EPISTLE DEDICATORY, FROM *THE MOTHER'S LEGACY TO HER UNBORN CHILD* (1624)

Introduction

Elizabeth Jocelin's *Mother's Legacy to her Unborn Child* is a book of conventional moral advice set out in the form of a single day's ideal conduct. It was written during her first pregnancy to anticipate the possibility of dying in childbirth – highly likely in this age – and thus being prevented from guiding her child's upbringing. Unfortunately her fears were justified, as she died nine days after giving birth to a daughter on 12 October 1622. Her manuscript (still extant though unfinished, and which provides the text for the Epistle presented below) was published in 1624 by Thomas Goad, who had known Elizabeth from childhood and was presumably a family friend. He prefaced her main work with a brief 'Approbation' of her life, and by including this moving personal letter from Jocelin to her husband.

Goad's 'Approbation' fashions a portrait of the author very different from the impression we receive of her in the Epistle. His high praise for her learning, piety, and modesty was probably intended, among other things, to anticipate male readers' objections to a woman assuming the unconventional role of moral teacher. Jocelin also gains legitimacy from the context of imminent personal danger in which she wrote; for pregnancy was recognised as a culturally privileged time granting women limited entitlement to offer public counsel. And if, as in Jocelin's case, a woman's writing was published after she had died in such circumstances, it became a self-defining act of near heroic value – though predicated, ironically, on the woman's physical non-existence (Wall 1991: 37–8). Jocelin is just one of several women (e.g. Dorothy Leigh, Elizabeth Grymeston) who rely on the mediating pre-texts of impending death and/or maternal solicitude to justify writing and publishing. Aside from Queen Elizabeth's writings, *The Mother's Legacy* was the most widely reproduced original work by a Renaissance Englishwoman. It was reissued eleven times between 1622 and 1674, translated into Dutch in 1699, and reprinted in the eighteenth and nineteenth centuries.

Jocelin's Epistle opens by explaining the necessity of ensuring that her children will be raised according to godly principles. Yet what is striking is the display of self-depreciation the author feels obliged to make for venturing to write and circulate her thoughts. Her apologies go well beyond conventional gestures of modesty deployed by male and female authors and surpass even the strategically magnified diffidence of certain authors such as Isabella Whitney. Moreover, nothing she mentions hints at the intellectual achievements praised by Goad – her prodigious memory or her extensive knowledge of history, theology, classical and foreign languages, 'not without a taste and faculty in poetry' (a3^{r}) – any of which would have been enough to validate a man's writing. Even Goad notes with some surprise that the *Legacy* contains hardly a trace of her 'secular learning'. Instead Jocelin laments various inadequacies which patriarchal society attributed to 'natural' female weakness. Although she manages on this occasion to overcome these 'disabilities', she does so on the solemn assurance that what she has to say arises from, and will remain limited to, her private domestic sphere (Beilin 1987: 272–3). Her self-presentation thus remains scrupulously non-threatening. Nonetheless we note that in the *Legacy*'s published form, which Jocelin may or may not have foreseen, Goad's 'Approbation' claims that the benefits of her advice extend beyond her household to the 'common kindred of Christianity'. And when by the end of the Epistle she repeats her disavowals of literary skill, they may seem to protest too much, hinting at her real anticipation of a wider audience.

Ultimately, however, any questions about the sincerity of Jocelin's feelings must remain speculative, as we do not know at what point her Epistle was written or the precise nature of its relationship to the *Legacy*. Yet there is little doubt that gendered distinctions are central to her ideas of child-rearing and social occupations. In certain areas of conduct such as swearing there is no differentiation between girls and boys: day-to-day behaviour should be guided by vigilant parental discipline. But in terms of education and career, the divergence between sons and daughters becomes stark. Given Jocelin's moderately Puritan values, it is not surprising that she hopes her son may become a minister. She states this matter-of-factly, because for boys such goals are normative and can be realised through well-established institutions. Girls, on the other hand, received their education almost exclusively in private households at the discretion of parents or guardians, hence the need for an explicit list of recommended subjects. Moreover, at the time the question of how much education a woman ought to receive was vigorously contested. In the light of her own reportedly advanced level, which she acquired in the household of her grandfather William Chaderton, Bishop of Lincoln and Master of Queens' College Cambridge, it is extraordinary that Jocelin prescribes such a restrictive 'curriculum': Bible-reading, writing competency, and essential domestic and social skills; 'other learning a woman needs not'. These abilities will complement but not burden 'wisdom', which, though not explicitly defined, seems in the context of Jocelin's remarks about 'a poor man's wife' to signify attracting a husband and appearing not to challenge his authority. Her metaphor of the ideal learned-but-wise woman as 'a well-balanced ship that may bear all her sail' quietly implies the need for a captain.

In fact as Jocelin goes on to discuss the workings of humility and pride, particularly in relation to daughters, we sense anxiety about the very idea of female education. From a historical perspective Jocelin's opinions mirror the reactions of seventeenth-century reformers against the earlier ideas of Christian humanists (while bearing in mind the latters' own restrictions on proper areas of female endeavour). Sixteenth-century theorists such as Sir Thomas More and Juan Luis Vives argued that education was socially and ethically ameliorating for both sexes. They based their optimism on a belief in the perfectibility of human nature under the right conditions, which included the possibility of social mobility, since education could prepare men and women for new roles considered unthinkable within traditional, ostensibly static hierarchies. Jocelin herself had clearly benefited from such humanist thinking in her own education. By the early seventeenth century, however, these more progressive ideas (which in any case remained confined largely to court and upper-class circles) had become devalued, at least as they concerned women. Various commentators, especially those influenced by Puritanism's more pessimistic view of human nature as irremediable, issued warnings against the dangers of female learning (Jones 1987: 60–3). Jocelin apparently shares this view, implying that anything more than a functional education will aggravate female tendencies towards vanity, and she reiterates many preachers' doubts about the ability of learning – as opposed to divine grace – to instil ethical virtue (Sizemore 1981: 63–4).

Such scepticism about the value and effects of education also explains the oppositional counsel Jocelin puts forward at the end of her letter to counter the practical and even calculating advice Renaissance parents regularly offered their children. For Jocelin, there appears to be virtually no distinction between healthy self-esteem and virulent pride, and thus little desire to promote any kind of female empowerment through widened educational or occupational horizons. Her views, which have to be taken as partly representative of her particular generation, class, and religion, also remind us of the shift in mental attitudes that needed to precede real material progress for women in terms of gaining approved access to advanced learning.

Manuscript:
BL Add. MS 27467 (source for text presented here).

Edition:
The Mother's Legacy to her Unborn Child (1624). STC 14624, reel 745.

ELIZABETH JOCELIN

FROM *THE MOTHER'S LEGACY TO HER UNBORN CHILD*

(1624)

EPISTLE DEDICATORY TO MY TRULY LOVING AND MOST DEARLY LOVED HUSBAND, TURRELL JOCELIN.

Mine own dear love, I no sooner conceived an hope that I should be made a mother by thee, but with it entered the consideration of a mother's duty, and shortly after followed the apprehension of danger that might prevent me from executing that care I so exceedingly desired, I mean in religious training our child. And in truth, death appearing in this shape was doubly terrible unto me. First in respect of the painfulness of that kind of death, an[d] next of the loss my little one should have in wanting me. But I thank God these fears were cured with the remembrance that all things work together for the best to those that love God, and a certain assurance that he will give me patience according to my pain.

Yet still I thought there was some good office I might do for my child more than only to bring it forth (though it should please God to take me). When I considered our frailty, our apt inclination to sin, the devil's subtlety, and the world's deceitfulness from these, how much I desired to admonish it! But still it came into my mind that death might deprive me of time if I should neglect the present. I knew not what to do. I thought of writing, but then mine own weakness appeared so manifestly that I was ashamed and durst not undertake it. But when I could find no other means to express my motherly zeal, I encouraged myself with these reasons:

First, that I wrote to a child, and though I were but a woman, yet to a child's judgement what I understood might serve for a foundation to better learning.

Again, I considered it was to my own, not to the world, and my love to my own might excuse my errors.

6. *that … death*: i.e. in childbirth

9. *certain*: steadfast

14. *from … I desired*: (that arises) from … The 1624 edition substitutes 'against … desired I'.

23. *own*: (family)
not … world: not intended for publication; 'and in private sort' (1624 edn)

And lastly but chiefly, I comforted myself that my intent was good, and that I was well assured God was the prosperer of good purposes.

Thus resolved, I writ this ensuing letter to our little one, to whom I could not find a fitter hand to convey it than thine own, which mayest with authority see the performance of this my little legacy, of which my child is executor.

And, dear love, as thou must be the overseer, for God's sake, when it shall fail in duty to God or to the world, do not let thy fondness wink at such folly but severely correct it. And that thy trouble may be little when it comes to years, I pray thee be careful when it is young. First, to provide it a religious nurse – no matter for her complexion. As near as may be, choose a house where it may not learn to swear or speak scurrilous words. I know I may be thought too scrupulous in this, but I am sure thou shalt find it a hard matter to break a child of that it learns so young. It will be a great while ere it will be thought old enough to be beaten for evil words, and by that time it will be so perfect that blows will not mend it. And when some charitable body reproves or corrects it for these faults, let nobody pity it with the loss of the mother, for truly I should use it no better.

Next, good sweetheart, keep it not from school, but let it learn betimes. If it be a son, I doubt not but thou wilt dedicate it to the Lord as his minister, if he will please of his mercy to give him grace and capacity for that

26. *God was*: 'God is' (1624 edn)
29. *performance*: circulation (in manuscript, not necessarily print)
31. *overseer*: legal term: one who supervises or assists the executor of a will
it: the child. Originally 'he or she' in the MS but struck out.
32. *do not let*: 'let not' (1624 edn)
fondness: 'indulgence' (1624 edn)
wink: connive at
34. *I ... careful*: 'take the more care' (1624 edn)
to provide: 'in providing' (1624 edn)
35. *religious nurse*: wet-nurse with firm religious convictions; 'nurse' (1624 edn)
no matter: 'O make choice, not so much' (1624 edn)
complexion: physical constitution, temperament. The 1624 edn adds: 'as for her mild and honest disposition. Likewise if the child be to remain long abroad after weaning.' 'abroad' = away from home, following the common practice among middle- and upper-class parents of sending their children to serve and/or be raised in the households of better-off or better-connected relations or friends.
40. *perfect*: 1624 edn adds 'in imperfections'
41. *body*: person
42. for ... better: omitted 1624 edn. 'use' = treat.
43. *betimes*: early in life

great work. If it be a daughter, I hope my mother Brooke (if thou desirest her) will take it among hers and let them learn one lesson. I desire her bringing up may be learning the Bible, as my sisters do, good housewifery, writing, and good work; other learning a woman needs not. Though I admire it in those whom God hath blessed with discretion, yet I desire it not much in my own, having seen that sometimes women have greater portions of learning than wisdom, which is of no better use to them than a main-sail to a fly-boat, which runs it under water. But where learning and wisdom meet in a virtuous-disposed woman, she is the fittest closet for all goodness. She is like a well-balanced ship that may bear all her sail. She is – indeed I should but shame myself if I should go about to praise her more.

But my dear, though she have all this in her, she will hardly make a poor man's wife. Yet I will leave it to thy will. If thou desirest a learned daughter, I pray God give her a wise and religious heart that she may use it to his glory, thy comfort, and her own salvation.

But howsoever thou disposest of her education, I pray thee labour by all means to teach her true humility, though I much desire it may be as humble if it be a son as a daughter. Yet in a daughter I more fear that vice, pride, being now rather accounted a virtue in our sex worthy praise than a vice fit for reproof. Parents read lectures of it to their children, how necessary it is, and they have principles that must not be disputed against. As first: 'Look how much you esteem yourself, others will esteem of you'. Again: 'What you give to others, you derogate from yourself'. And many more of these kind. I have heard men accounted wise that have maintained this kind of pride under the name of generous knowing or understanding themselves. But I am sure that he that truly knows himself shall know so much evil by himself, that he shall have small reason to think himself better than another man.

46–7. *mother Brooke ... among hers*: unidentified. Elizabeth Jocelin's father was Sir Nicholas Brooke. Her mother, Joan Chaderton, had died when she was six, so perhaps this refers to her old nurse (mother *OED* 4a).

47. *them*: 'them all' (1624 edn)
learn one lesson: i.e. learn together

49. *work*: needlework. 'works' (1624 edn) is less gender-specific.

50. *desire it*: 'desired' (1624 edn)

52–3. *no ... water*: 'fly-boat' = small vessel for coastal transport. 'which ... water' = presumably because a main-sail would overpower such a vessel, causing it to capsize.

54. *closet*: private repository, non-public domain

65. *Parents*: 'Many parents' (1624 edn)
read ... of: give ... on

66–70. *Look ... themselves*: reminiscent of maxims found in conventional Renaissance advice books for daughters or sons (e.g. Elizabeth Grymeston's *Miscellanea* (below p. 97ff.), or Polonius in *Hamlet*)

69. *kind*: 'kinds' (1624 edn)

Dearest, I am so fearful to bring thee a proud, high-minded child that, though I know thy care will need no spur, yet I cannot but desire thee to double thy watchfulness over this vice; it is such a crafty, devilish, insinuating sin, it will enter little children in the likeness of wit, with which their parents are delighted, and that is sweet nourishment to it.

I pray thee, dear heart, delight not to have a bold child: modesty and humility are the sweetest groundworks of all virtue. Let not thy servants give it any other title than the Christian name, till it have discretion to understand how to respect others. And I pray thee be not profuse in the expense of clothes for it. Methinks it is a vain delight in parents to bestow that cost upon one child which would serve two or three. If they have them not of their own, *pauper ubique iacet*.

Thus, dear, thou seest my belief. If thou canst teach thy little one humility, it must needs make thee a glad father.

But I know thou wonderest by this time what the cause should be that, we two continually unclasping our hearts one to another, I should reserve this to write. When thou thinkest thus, dear, remember how grievous it was to thee but to hear me say, 'I may die', and thou wilt confess this would have been an unpleasing discourse to thee, and thou knowest I never durst displease thee willingly, so much I love thee. All I now desire is that the unexpectedness of it make it not more grievous to thee. But I know thou art a Christian, and therefore will not doubt thy patience.

And though I thus write to thee as heartily desiring to be religiously prepared to die, yet, my dear, I despair not of life, nay, I hope and daily pray for it, if so God will be pleased. Nor shall I think this labour lost though I do live; for I will make it my own looking-glass wherein to see when I am too severe, when too remiss, and (in my child's fault through this glass) to discern mine own error. And I hope God will so give me his grace that I shall more skilfully act than apprehend a mother's duty.

My dear, thou knowest me so well, I shall not need to tell thee I have written honest thoughts in a disordered fashion, not observing method. For thou knowest how short I am of learning and natural endowments to take

76–7. *devilish … sin*: 'insinuating devil' (1624 edn)

80. *of*: 'for' (1624 edn)

83. *for*: 'upon' (1624 edn)

84–5. *If … own*: 'If they have not children enow [= enough] of their own to employ so much cost upon' (1624 edn)

85. *pauper … iacet*: a marginal manuscript note in the Bodleian Library copy of 1624 glosses this: 'There wants not poor at every door'

89. *another*: 'the other' (1624 edn)

90. *write*: 'writing' (1624 edn)

92. *unpleasing*: 'unpleasant' (1624 edn)

99. *looking-glass*: mirror

102. *act … apprehend*: put directly into action rather than be fearful of performing

such a course in writing. Or if that strong affection of thine have hid my weakness from thy sight, I now profess seriously my own ignorance; and though I did not, this following treatise would betray it. But I send it only to the eyes of a most loving husband, and a child exceedingly beloved, to whom I hope it will not be altogether unprofitable.

Thus humbly desiring God to give thee all comfort in this life and happiness in the life to come, I leave thee and thine to his most gracious protection.

Thine inviolable,
Eliza.

109. *and a*: 'and of a' (1624 edn)
115. *Eliza*: 'Eliza:[beth] Jocelin' (1624 edn)

2

PROSE

KATHERINE PARR, QUEEN OF ENGLAND (1512–48)

FROM *THE LAMENTATION OF A SINNER* (1547)

Introduction

Katherine Parr's *Lamentation of a Sinner*, 'a classic of Tudor devotional literature' (McConica 1965: 251), is one of only three statements of faith published by Englishwomen before the civil war, the others being the eponymous *Book of Margery Kempe* (*c.* 1433–38) and the *Examinations* of Anne Askew (1545–46) (Warnicke 1983: 95). Though Parr and Askew were friends, their responses to the new Bible-centred theology of the English Reformation differed markedly, illustrating divergent strains seen elsewhere in religious writings by Renaissance women. Askew's attitude to external authority in matters of faith was uncompromising: a self-authorising vision grounded in Protestantism's egalitarian spirituality and its shift of responsibility for gaining salvation on to the individual through her personal knowledge of scripture. Parr did not advocate such radical self-sufficiency; rather, she wished to balance traditional respect for social hierarchy with a commitment to popular spiritual renewal through wider scriptural literacy. The English Reformation – and female readers and writers – benefited from the example of both women, but in the long term Parr's views became more representative of mainstream culture, partly owing to their impression on the young Princess Elizabeth, whose education she directed.

Parr is perhaps best known as the wife who managed to survive Henry VIII. Her parents served in the royal household, where she was tutored by the humanist educational reformer Juan Luis Vives. Upon becoming Queen in 1543 Parr decisively influenced government policy. She persuaded the King to restore Mary and Elizabeth to the royal succession, from which they had been excluded as bastards, and to drop plans for plundering the universities as he had the monasteries. Her household attracted a circle of brilliant reform-minded humanists, several of whom she assigned as royal tutors to Prince Edward and Princess Elizabeth. She also gathered friends and divines for readings from the new English Bible, and debated church reforms with her more conservative husband. Parr's growing influence alarmed religious reactionaries at court, who, sensing Henry's impatience with his wife's growing independence, decided to incriminate Parr by attacking the outspoken Anne Askew. The latter was interrogated several times in 1545–46 before finally being tortured and executed. Though no damning evidence against Parr emerged, her rooms were searched for unorthodox books and heresy charges were drawn up which Henry seemed to approve. Learning of these developments (and no doubt mindful of the fate of her predecessors), Parr saved herself only by publicly submitting to Henry's supreme authority (McConica 1965: 215–30).

Parr wrote *The Lamentation* prior to 1547 (it was circulating in manuscript at court by November 1545) but delayed publishing it until after Henry's death in

January that year. Previously she had issued a collection of non-sectarian *Prayers* (1545) based on Thomas à Kempis's fifteenth-century *Imitation of Christ*, a traditional meditative work. *The Lamentation* is more personal, 'an unfolding of the momentous significance [Parr] discerned in her Protestant conversion' (Mueller 1988: 15). It moves purposefully from confession and repentance to conversion and prophecy (a pattern reminiscent of the Psalms). Though the narrator refers to herself as 'I' and recounts events pertaining to Parr's own religious experiences, she includes few topical or autobiographical details. Her voice is therefore personal but universalised (Mueller 1988: 25), designed to impress the reader with its human other-relatedness and authenticity, but only fleetingly achieving any sense of gendered subjectivity. Doctrinally Parr's prose-treatise stresses the primacy of scripture in Christian life, thus clearly marking it as a Reformation document. Yet she is careful to avoid extremes. Having disclosed her own faults and gained self-assurance towards the end of her work, she criticises the narrow self-righteousness of 'vain gospellers' (anticipating complaints against Puritans in later years) as well as patriarchal Catholic authorities who considered any public discussion of the Bible in English to be heretical. Nonetheless, her criticisms are never personally directed, so that *The Lamentation*'s dominant impulse remains conciliatory exhortation rather than Askew's principled defiance.

Editions:
The Lamentation of a Sinner (1547). STC 4827, reel 29. Reprinted in Thomas Bentley, *The Monument of Matrons* (1582). STC 1892, reel 174. *The Female Spectator*, ed. Mary R. Mahl and Helene Koon (Bloomington, 1977, brief excerpts). *The Paradise of Women*, ed. Betty Travitsky (Westport, Conn., 1981, brief excerpts).

KATHERINE PARR, QUEEN OF ENGLAND

FROM *THE LAMENTATION OF A SINNER*

(1547)

When I consider (in the bethinking of mine evil and wretched former life) mine obstinate, stony, and untractable heart to have so much exceeded in evilness that it hath not only neglected – yea condemned and despised – God's holy precepts and commandments, but also embraced, received, and esteemed vain, foolish, and feigned trifles, I am (partly by the hate I owe to sin, who hath reigned in me, partly by the love I owe to all Christians, whom I am content to edify even with the example of mine own shame) forced and constrained with my heart and words to confess and declare to the world how ingrate, negligent, unkind, and stubborn I have been to God my creator, and how beneficial, merciful, and gentle he hath been always to me his creature, being such a miserable, wretched sinner. Truly I have taken no little small thing upon me, first to set forth my whole stubbornness and contempt in words, the which is incomprehensible in thought (as it is in the psalm: who understandeth his faults?). Next this, to declare the excellent beneficence, mercy, and goodness of God, which is infinite, unmeasurable; neither can all the words of angels and men make relation thereof, as appertaineth to his most high goodness. Who is he that is not forced to confess the same, if he consider what he hath received of God, and doth daily receive? Yea, if men would not acknowledge and confess the same, the

2. *stony ... heart*: common image among early Protestant reformers, signifying the inherent sinfulness of human nature, which depends on divine grace alone for redemption (Lewalski 1979: 195–6)
5. *feigned trifles*: i.e. traditional but spurious devotions
7. *edify*: instruct morally (1 Corinthians 14.26). Anne Dowriche cites the same text to justify writing *The French History* (above p. 27).
   even ... shame: Parr will use her own life to exemplify common personal struggles and shortcomings. 'The combination of universalism and personalism that energized early Protestants – the conviction that all souls are equal before God and that every soul is individually accountable to God' – is modelled on the self-referential mode of Paul's epistles, which Parr draws on throughout *The Lamentation* (Mueller 1988: 25, 31–2).
9. *ingrate*: unfriendly, ungrateful
11. *creature*: i.e. created being (as elsewhere below)
13. *incomprehensible*: limitless
14. *psalm*: 19.12
   his: his own

stones would cry it out. Truly I am constrained and forced to speak and write thereof to mine own confusion and shame, but to the great glory and praise of God. . . .

I professed Christ in my baptism when I began to live, but I swerved from him after baptism in continuance of my living, even as the heathen which never had begun. Christ was innocent and void of all sin, and I wallowed in filthy sin and was free from no sin. Christ was obedient unto his father even to the death of the cross, and I disobedient and most stubborn even to the confusion of truth. Christ was meek and humble in heart, and I most proud and vainglorious. Christ despised the world with all the vanities thereof, and I made it my god because of the vanities. Christ came to serve his brethren, and I coveted to rule over them. Christ despised worldly honour, and I much delighted to attain the same. Christ loved the base and simple things of the world, and I esteemed the most fair and pleasant things. Christ loved poverty, and I wealth. Christ was gentle and merciful to the poor, and I hard-hearted and ungentle. Christ prayed for his enemies, and I hated mine. Christ rejoiced in the conversion of sinners, and I was not grieved to see their reversion to sin.

By this declaration all creatures may perceive how far I was from Christ and without Christ – yea, how contrary to Christ although I bare the name of a Christian. Insomuch that if any man had said I had been without Christ, I would have stiffly withstood the same. And yet I neither knew Christ, nor wherefore he came. As concerning the effect and purpose of his coming, I had a certain vain, blind knowledge, both cold and dead, which may be had with all sin, as it doth plainly appear by this my confession and open declaration. . . .

I know, O my Lord, thy eyes look upon my faith. St Paul saith, 'We be justified by the faith in Christ, and not by the deeds of the law. For if right-wiseness come by the law, then Christ died in vain.' St Paul meaneth not

20. *stones ... out*: 'But [Jesus] answered and said unto [the Pharisees], I tell you, that if these [disciples, rejoicing at Jesus's entry into Jerusalem] should hold their peace, the stones would cry [out]' (Luke 19.40)

23. *professed*: acknowledged openly (my acceptance of)

23–4. *live ... living*: in spirit ... material or worldly way of life

25. *begun*: to live spiritually

42. *wherefore*: why

46–7. *We ... law*: 'Therefore we conclude that a man is justified by faith without the works of the law' (Romans 3.28). The contrast is between Old Testament laws and observances, and New Testament belief, traditionally believed to supersede them.

47–8. *For ... vain*: Galatians 2.21

47–8, 57, 61. *right-wiseness*: righteousness, moral virtue

here a dead, human, historical faith gotten by human industry, but a supernal, lively faith which worketh by charity, as he himself plainly expresseth. This dignity of faith is no derogation to good works, for out of this faith springeth all good works. Yet we may not impute to the worthiness of faith or works our justification before God, but ascribe and give the worthiness of it wholly to the merits of Christ's passion, and refer and attribute the knowledge and perceiving thereof only to faith; whose very true, only property is to take, apprehend, and hold fast the promises of God's mercy, the which maketh us right-wise, and to cause me continually to hope for the same mercy, and in love to work all manner of ways allowed in the scripture, that I may be thankful for the same. Thus I feel myself to come, as it were, in a new garment before God, and now, by his mercy, to be taken just and right-wise, which of late without his mercy was sinful and wicked. . . .

Christ hath not only overcome sin, but rather he hath killed the same, inasmuch as he hath sacrificed for it himself with the most holy sacrifice and oblation of his precious body, in suffering most bitter and cruel death. Also after another sort: that is, he giveth to all those that love him so much spirit, grace, virtue, and strength, that they may resist, impugn, and overcome sin, and not consent neither suffer it to reign in them. He hath also vanquished sin because he hath taken away the force of the same; that is, he hath cancelled the law which was in evil men the occasion of sin. Therefore sin hath no power against them that are with the Holy Ghost united to Christ. In them there is nothing worthy of damnation. And although the dregs of Adam

49. *dead . . . industry*: besides Old Testament customs, this includes the Church's accumulation of traditional but non-scriptural beliefs and practices over the centuries *supernal*: heavenly

50. *charity . . . expresseth*: charity = Christian love (1 Corinthians 13; see King James version)

51–2. *faith . . . good works*: touching on one of the main theological disputes of the Reformation. Protestants maintained that salvation could be gained only through faith in the once-for-all-time benefits of Christ's passion. Good deeds appropriately express this faith, but add no value to it. Catholics believed that emulating Christ's life, receiving the sacraments, and performing charitable works, increased one's worthiness to enjoy the merits of Christ's redemption. In her moderate statement Parr assigns priority to justification by faith while approving the practice of good works that extreme protestants rejected. 'is no derogation to' = does not diminish the value of.

56–8. *take . . . same*: 'Parr's scripturalism manifests itself as an immediate and subjective response, the first impulsion of her soul under justifying faith' (Mueller 1988: 22)

60. *new . . . God*: 'I put on justice, and it covered me: my judgement was as a robe and a crown' (Job 29.14)

64. *oblation*: offering

69. *the law*: of Moses, and the Old Testament penalties on mankind resulting from the fall of Adam and Eve

71. *dregs of Adam*: effects of original sin

do remain (that is our concupiscences, which indeed be sins), nevertheless they be not imputed for sins if we be truly planted in Christ. It is true that Christ might have taken away all our immoderate affections, but he hath left them for the greater glory of his Father, and for his own greater triumph. As for an example: when a prince fighting with his enemies (which sometime had the sovereignty over his people) and subduing them, may kill them if he will, yet he preserveth and saveth them. And whereas they were lords over his people, he maketh them after to serve whom they before had ruled. Now in such a case the prince doth show himself a greater conqueror (in that he hath made them which were rulers to obey, and the subjects to be lords over them to whom they served) than if he had utterly destroyed them upon the conquest. For now he leaveth continual victory to them whom he redeemed, whereas otherwise the occasion of victory was taken away where none were left to be the subjects. Even so in like case, Christ hath left in us these concupiscences to the intent they should serve us to the exercise of our virtues, where first they did reign over us to the exercise of our sin....

Truly it may be most justly verified that to behold Christ crucified, in spirit, is the best meditation that can be. I certainly never knew mine own miseries and wretchedness so well, by book, admonition, or learning, as I have done by looking into the spiritual book of the crucifix. I lament much I have passed so many years not regarding that divine book, but I judged and thought myself to be well instructed in the same. Whereas now I am of this opinion: that if God would suffer me to live here a thousand year, and should study continually in the same divine book, I should not be filled with the contemplation thereof, neither hold I myself contented, but always have a great desire to learn and study more therein. I never knew mine own

72. *concupiscences*: excessive desires for carnal or material things

76ff. *when* ... : 'A similitude' (original marginal note)

84. *occasion*: sign

89–90. *behold ... be*: 'For I esteemed not to know anything among you, save Jesus Christ, and him crucified' (1 Corinthians 2.2)

92. *spiritual ... crucifix*: the underlying opposition is between scripture and visual images as devotional aids. As Mueller observes (1988: 25), Parr reworks traditional terminology for new doctrinal purposes: the book of the crucifix 'is not a physical object [associated with Catholic worship]. Rather, it is a lively image which the inward eye of the Christian is enabled to see through knowledge of the Gospel.'

97–8. *I ... therein*: perhaps alluding to the historical context of Parr's promotion of the English Bible, which received royal approval in Coverdale's translation in 1537 but had been unofficially available since 1525 in Tyndale's version. The latter was finally approved in 1547 – only several months after Henry VIII sent Tyndale to the stake as a heretic. In the final years of Henry's reign Parr became celebrated (or to religious conservatives, notorious) for organising Bible-reading groups for her female friends and male scholars.

wickedness, neither lamented for my sins truly, until the time God inspired me with his grace, that I looked in this book. Then I began to see perfectly that mine own power and strength could not help me, and that I was in the Lord's hand even as the clay is in the potter's hand. Then I began to cry and say: alas, Lord, that ever I have so wickedly offended thee, being to me from the beginning so gracious and so good a father, and most specially now hast declared and showed thy goodness unto me when in the time I have done thee most injury, to call me, and also to make me know, and take thee for my saviour and redeemer. Such be the wonderful works of God to call sinners to repentance and to make them to take Christ his well-beloved son for their saviour; this is the gift of God and of all Christians to be required and desired. For except this great benefit of Christ crucified be felt and fixed surely in man's heart, there can be no good work done, acceptable before God. . . .

The example of good living is required of all Christians but especially in the ecclesiastical pastors and shepherds, for they be called in scripture workmen with God, disbursers of God's secrets, the light of the world, the salt of the earth, at whose hands all other should take comfort in working knowledge of God's will and sight to become children of the light, and taste of seasonable wisdom. They have or should have the holy spirit abundantly, to pronounce and set forth the word of God in verity and truth. If ignorance and blindness reign among us, they should, with the truth of God's word, instruct and set us in the truth, and direct us in the way of the Lord. But thanks be given unto the Lord that hath now sent us such a godly and learned king in these latter days to reign over us, that, with the virtue and force of God's word, hath taken away the veils and mists of errors, and

101–2. *I . . . hand*: Jeremiah 18.6

110–11. *For . . . done*: 'For [Parr], the Passion becomes the vital meeting point of private religious feeling and public enactment, or, more simply, of the faith and works that English Protestants remained so intent on uniting' (Mueller 1988: 37). Aemilia Lanyer focuses on the same event as a nexus of spiritual and social action in *Salve Deus Rex Judaeorum* (below p. 368ff).

114–15. *workmen . . . God*: Ephesians 2.10

115. *disbursers . . . secrets*: 1 Corinthians 4.1. 'disbursers' = paymasters

115–16. *light . . . earth*: Matthew 5.14, 13

117. *children . . . light*: John 12.36

118. *seasonable*: timely, opportune

119–21. *If . . . Lord*: the pre-Reformation clergy's ignorance and worldliness were major complaints of Christian humanists and the theme of famous reformers such as Hugh Latimer, who preached in Parr's household and was aided by her close friend and fellow populariser of classical and scriptural learning, Catherine Brandon, Duchess of Suffolk (King 1985: 55–7). Parr credits her on the title-page with encouraging *The Lamentation*'s publication.

124. *errors*: i.e. of certain Catholic practices

brought us to the knowledge of the truth by the light of God's word, which was so long hidden and kept under that the people were nigh famished, and hungered for lack of spiritual food (such was the charity of the spiritual curates and shepherds). But our Moses and most godly, wise governor and king hath delivered us out of the captivity and bondage of Pharaoh. I mean by this Moses King Henry the Eighth, my most sovereign favourable lord and husband, one (if Moses had figured any more than Christ) through the excellent grace of God, meet to be another expressed verity of Moses's conquest over Pharaoh. And I mean by this Pharaoh the bishop of Rome, who hath been and is a greater persecutor of all true Christians than ever was Pharaoh of the children of Israel. For he is a persecutor of the gospel and grace, a setter-forth of all superstition and counterfeit holiness, bringing many souls to hell with his alchemy and counterfeit money, deceiving the poor souls under the pretence of holiness. But so much the greater shall be his damnation because he deceiveth and robbeth under Christ's mantle. The Lord keep and defend all men from his jugglings and sleights, but specially the poor, simple, unlearned souls....

The regenerated by Christ are never offended at the works of God because they know by faith that God doeth all things well, and that he cannot err neither for want of power, nor by ignorance nor malice. For they know him to be almighty, and that he seeth all things, and is most abundantly good. They see and feel in spirit that of that will most highly perfect cannot but proceed most perfect works. Likewise they be not offended at the works of men; for if they be good, they are moved by them to take occasion to follow them, and to re-knowledge the goodness of God with giving of thanks and praising his name, daily the more. But if they be indifferent, and such as may be done with good and evil intents, they judge the best part, thinking they may be done to a good purpose, and so they be edified; but if they be so evil that they cannot be taken in good part by any means, yet they be not offended, although occasion be given; nay, rather

128. *curates*: deputy clergy, not likely to be zealous in their duties, as opposed to 'pastors' (l. 114 above) who had greater responsibility and better incomes

128–9. *Moses ... Pharaoh*: The preface to Coverdale's 1537 English Bible praised Henry VIII ' "for being our Moses" ' and delivering England-as-Israel from ' "the cruel hands of our spiritual Pharaoh" ', the Pope (Haugaard 1969: 357)

132. *meet ... verity*: worthy of being a latter-day figure repeating the action

137. *counterfeit money*: perhaps referring to the selling of indulgences, notes promising the purchaser remission of sins or punishment in the afterlife

140. *jugglings and sleights*: trickery and cunning deceptions

149. *re-knowledge*: acknowledge

150. *indifferent*: morally neutral

151–3. *they ... they ... they*: works ... the regenerated ... works

153. *if they*: works

154. *yet they*: yet the regenerated

they be edified, inasmuch as they take occasion to be better, although the contrary be ministered unto them. Then begin they to think and say thus: 'If God had not preserved me with his grace, I should have committed this sin, and worse. O how much am I bound to confess and knowledge the goodness of God!' They go also thinking and saying further: 'He that hath sinned may be one of God's elect; peradventure the Lord hath suffered him to fall, to the intent he may the better know himself. I know he is one of them that Christ hath shed his blood for, and one of my Christian brethren. Truly I will admonish and rebuke him, and, in case I find him desperate, I will comfort him and show him the great goodness and mercy of God in Christ, and with godly consolations I will see if I can lift him up.' And thus ye may see how the men regenerated by Christ of everything win and receive fruit.

And contrary the younglings and unperfect are offended at small trifles, taking everything in evil part, grudging and murmuring against their neighbour. And so much the more as they show themselves fervent in their so doing, they are judged of the blind world, and of themselves, great zeal-bearers to God. If this were the greatest evil of these younglings, it were not the most evil; but I fear they be so blind and ignorant that they are offended also at good things, and judge nothing good but such as they embrace and esteem to be good, with murmuring against all such as follow not their ways. If there be any of this sort, the Lord give them light of his truth that they may increase and grow in godly strength. I suppose if such younglings and unperfect had seen Christ and his disciples eat meat with unwashed hands, or not to have fasted with the Pharisees, they would have been offended, seeing him a breaker of men's traditions. Their affections dispose their eyes to see through other men, and they see nothing in themselves; where charity (although it be most fullest of eyes to see the faults of others whom it coveteth to amend) thinketh none evil, but discreetly and rightly interpreteth all things, by the which more justly and truly everything is taken.

158. *knowledge*: acknowledge

160. *elect*: chosen (probably not in the Calvinist sense of *the* elect)

163. *desperate*: reckless, self-destructive

167. *fruit*: spiritual benefits

168. *younglings*: new converts to Protestantism

169. *grudging ... murmuring*: grumbling ... whispering rumours

178–9. *eat ... hands*: 'For out of the heart come evil thoughts, murders, adulteries ... These are the things which defile the man: but to eat with unwashen hands defileth not the man' (Matthew 15.19–20)

179. *not ... Pharisees*: 'Moreover, when ye fast, look not sour as the hypocrites: for they disfigure their faces, that they might seem unto men to fast' (Matthew 6.16)

180. *affections*: inclinations, state of mind

182. *fullest of eyes*: quick to observe

Now these superstitious weaklings, if they had been conversant with Christ and seen him lead his life sometime with women, sometime with Samaritans, with publicans, sinners, and with the Pharisees, they would have murmured at him. Also if they had seen Mary pour upon Christ the precious ointment, they would have said with Judas, 'This ointment might have been sold and given to the poor'. If they also had seen Christ with whips drive out of the temple those that bought and sold, they would forthwith have judged Christ to have been troubled and moved with anger, and not by zeal of charity. How would they have been offended if they had seen him go to the Jews' feast, heal a sick man upon the sabbath day, practise with the woman of Samary, yea, and show unto her of his most divine doctrine and life? They would have taken occasion to have hated and persecuted him as the scribes and Pharisees did. And even so should Christ, the saviour of the world have been to them an offence and ruin....

Now I will speak with great dolour and heaviness in my heart of a sort of people which be in the world that be called professors of the gospel, and by their words do declare and show they be much affected to the same. But I am afraid some of them do build upon the sand, as Simon Magus did, making a weak foundation. I mean, they make not Christ their chiefest foundation, professing his doctrine of a sincere, pure, and zealous mind. But either for because they would be called gospellers to procure some credit and good opinions of the true and very favourers of Christ's doctrine (either to find out some carnal liberty, either to be contentious disputers, finders, or rebukers of other men's faults), or else finally to please and flatter the world, such gospellers are an offence and a slander to the word of God, and make the wicked to rejoice and laugh at them, saying, 'Behold, I pray you, their fair fruits!' What charity? What discretion? What godliness, holiness, or purity of life is amongst them? Be they not great avengers, foul gluttons, slanderers, backbiters, adulterers, fornicators, swearers, and blasphemers? Yea, and wallow and tumble in all sins? These be the fruits of their doctrine.

186. *weaklings*: 'timid or time-serving souls' (Mueller 1988: 26)
188. *publicans*: tax-gatherers (then as now, loathed)
189–91. *Mary ... poor*: Mary Magdalene: John 12.3–5
191–2. *Christ ... sold*: Matthew 21.12
195. *heal ... day*: Matthew 12.10–12
195–6. *practise ... Samary*: reveal himself (as the Messiah) to the woman of Samaria (Samaritans regularly had no dealings with Jews)
196–7. *show ... life*: John 4.4–30
200–1. *sort of people*: 'Vain gospellers' (original marginal note)
202. *affected*: inclined, attached
203–4. *build ... foundation*: Matthew 7.24–5
206. *credit*: good report
215. *tumble*: toss about (as on a bed, possibly in sexual terms)

And thus it may be seen how the word of God is evil spoken of through licentious and evil living; and yet the word of God is all holy, pure, sincere, and godly, being the doctrine and occasion of all holy and pure living. It is the wicked that perverteth all good things into evil; for an evil tree cannot bring forth good fruit. And when good seed is sown in a barren and evil ground, it yieldeth no good corn. And so it fareth by the word of God; for when it is heard and known of wicked men, it bringeth forth no good fruit. But when it is sown in good ground (I mean the hearts of good people), it bringeth forth good fruit abundantly, so that the want and fault is in men and not in the word of God. I pray God all men and women may have grace to become meet tillage for the fruits of the gospel, and to leave only the jangling of it; for only speaking of the gospel maketh not men good Christians but good talkers, except their facts and works agree with the same. So then their speech is good because their hearts be good.

And even as much talk of the word of God without practising the same in our living is evil and detestable in the sight of God, so it is a lamentable thing to hear how there be many in the world that do not well digest the reading of scripture, and do commend and praise ignorance, and say that much knowledge of God's word is the original of all dissension, schisms, and contention, and maketh men haught, proud, and presumptuous by reading of the same. This manner of saying is no less than a plain blasphemy against the Holy Ghost. For the spirit of God is the author of his word, and so the Holy Ghost is made the author of evil, which is almost great blasphemy and (as the scripture saith) a sin that shall not be forgiven in this world, neither in the other to come. It were all our parts and duties to procure and seek all the ways and means possible to have more knowledge of God's words set forth abroad in the world, and not allow ignorance, and

219–20. *evil ... fruit*: Matthew 7.19–20

220–5. *And ... God*: paraphrasing the parable of the good and bad seed, Matthew 13.24–39

226. *meet*: fit
tillage: fertile ground; i.e. receptive to
jangling: noisy babbling, wrangling

228. *except*: unless

234–5. *much ... contention*: the argument of some Catholics against making the Bible accessible in vernacular translations; original = origin

235. *haught*: haughty

238–40. *Holy ... come*: 'But he that blasphemeth against the Holy Ghost shall never have forgiveness, but is culpable of eternal damnation' (Mark 3.29)

241–6. *more ... them*: as King (1985) and McConica (1965: ch. 7) observe, Parr was the leading facilitator of a new mid-century generation of Protestant humanists who worked towards making the newly translated Bible and reformist interpretations widely available to new readers, including women

242. *abroad*: currently available

discommend knowledge, of God's word (stopping the mouths of the unlearned with subtle and crafty persuasions of philosophy and sophistry, whereof cometh no fruit but a great perturbation of the mind to the simple and ignorant, not knowing which way to turn them). For how is it not extreme wickedness to charge the holy sanctified word of God with the offences of man? To allege the scriptures to be perilous learning, because certain readers thereof fall into heresies? These men might be forced by this kind of argument to forsake the use of fire because fire burned their neighbour's house, or to abstain from meat or drink because they see many surfeit. O blind hate, they slander God for man's offence, and excuse the man whom they see offend, and blame the scripture which they cannot improve. Yea, I have heard of some that have very well understood the Latin tongue, that when they have heard learned men persuade to the credit and belief of certain unwritten verities (as they call them) which be not in scripture expressed and yet taught as doctrine apostolic and necessary to be believed, they have been of this opinion: that the learned men have more epistles written by the apostles of Christ than we have abroad in the canon of the Old and New Testament, or known of any but only to them of the clergy. Which belief I did not a little lament in my heart to hear, that any creature should have such a blind ignorant opinion. Some kind of simplicity is to be praised, but this simplicity without the verity I can neither praise nor allow.

And thus it may be seen how we that be unlettered remain confused (without God of his grace lighten our hearts with a heavenly light and knowledge of his will), for we be given of ourselves to believe men better than God. I pray God send all learned men the spirit of God abundantly, that their doctrine may bring forth the fruits thereof....

I pray God our own faults and deeds condemn us not at the last day, when every man shall be rewarded according to his doings. Truly if we do not redress and amend our living according to the doctrine of the gospel, we shall receive a terrible sentence of Christ the son of God, when he shall come

252. *surfeit*: indulge to excess

255. *persuade ... credit*: urge strongly in favour of upholding

256. *unwritten verities*: non-biblical but traditional doctrines declared necessary for salvation by the Catholic Church. Protestants insisted that the Bible alone prescribed all things necessary to be believed.

257. *apostolic*: pertaining to the Pope's authority, based on the association of apostles Peter and Paul with Rome

259. *apostles*: not Christ's original apostles but their later imitators. 'Forged writings' (marginal note).

265. *unlettered*: lacking formal or extensive book-learning (normally available only through the grammar schools and universities, open only to boys and men)

270. *last*: i.e. Judgement

to judge and condemn all transgressors and breakers of his precepts and commandments, and to reward all his obedient and loving children. We shall have no man-of-law to make our plea for us, neither can we have the day deferred, neither will the just judge be corrupted with affection, bribes, or reward, neither will he hear any excuse or delay, neither shall this saint or that martyr help us (be they never so holy), neither shall our ignorance save us from damnation. But yet wilful blindness and obstinate ignorance shall receive greater punishment, and not without just cause. Then shall it be known who hath walked in the dark, for all things shall appear manifest before him. No man's deeds shall be hidden, no, neither words nor thoughts. The poor and simple observers of God's commandments shall be rewarded with everlasting life as obedient children to the heavenly father. And the transgressors, adders, and diminishers of the law of God shall receive eternal damnation for their just reward.

I beseech God we may escape this fearful sentence and be found such faithful servants and loving children, that we may hear the happy, comfortable, and most joyful sentence ordained for the children of God, which is: 'Come hither ye blessed of my father, and receive the kingdom of heaven prepared for you before the beginning of the world'. Unto the Father, the Son, and the Holy Ghost, be all honour and glory, world without end. Amen.

277. *affection*: emotional pleading

278–9. *saint* ... *us*: alluding to the practice of invoking the aid of departed saints and martyrs, a devotion repudiated by Protestants

283. *him*: Christ

286. *adders*: i.e. of non-scriptural customs and beliefs

291–3. *Come* ... *world*: Matthew 25.34

ANNE ASKEW (*c.* 1520–46)

THE EXAMINATIONS

(1546, 1547)

Introduction

Anne Askew was born into a landed, politically active Lincolnshire family and was evidently well-educated. When her elder sister Martha died about 1540, she was forced by her father Sir William Askew to take her sister's place in an arranged marriage with Thomas Kyme. It was a deeply unhappy relationship, with the authoritarian Kyme eventually turning Anne out of the house because of her Protestant beliefs. Yet far from crushing her, Kyme's action catalysed Anne's sense of personal autonomy and religious self-assurance. She discarded her married name (perhaps her family too, if the two children she had borne survived) and travelled to London to seek a divorce. The courts did not accept her argument (based on 1 Corinthians 7.15) that her husband had no legal claim on her because he was an 'unbeliever'. But Anne never again lived with Kyme and remained in London, turning for support to friends such as Queen Katherine Parr and members of her household who were sympathetic to Protestantism.

Unfortunately the times were reactionary. Though Henry VIII had broken with Rome (1533–34), dissolved the monasteries (1539), and approved English translations of the Bible (1537), England otherwise remained Catholic. By the mid-1540s conservatives in the government, capitalising on the ageing King's resistance to change, tried to stamp out nascent religious reform, which then mainly took the form of a relatively small number of renegade clergy and secret groups operating in London (Dickens 1989: 220). Askew belonged to one of the latter and may have been its leader. After being spied on by government informers, she was arrested in March 1545 and questioned by church and local authorities about her religious views, chiefly transubstantiation. *The First Examination* records the events of this inquisition, which ended in June with her forced signature of a statement of faith prepared by Bishop Bonner of London – though not before she made equivocating alterations which infuriated her male accusers who assumed women like Askew could be easily manipulated. Publication of Bonner's statement, along with pressure from friends at court and perhaps Queen Katherine herself, secured Askew's acquittal.

The interest of the *Examinations* lies not only in her struggle for freedom of belief but also in the government's arbitrary exercise of institutional power over a non-conforming woman. For Henry VIII's self-declared supremacy in Church matters had made religious dissent a political crime. Trials and executions for heresy, often without due process, served to enforce and publicise broader government policy (Davis 1983: 18). The intertwining of religious and state power is well illustrated at one point when one of Askew's inquisitors equates exposition of the sacrament (which Protestants rejected) with public displays of 'his majesty's honour', the more it 'is set forth, the more commendable it is'. When Askew was brought to trial a second time in Greenwich on charges of heresy in June 1545, the political dimension of her dissent became more obvious. At the beginning her antagonists were mainly clerics, but by the end of *The Latter Examination*, which relates the progress of this inquest and the last events of Askew's life, she is being tortured at the hands of two of Henry's most ruthless government ministers (torture was little known in England before Henry VIII). It is in these sections especially that the *Examinations* can seem depressingly modern to readers familiar with coercive methods used by twentieth-century regimes to impose doctrinal purity.

No less does Askew's clash with hierarchical authority involve defying gender barriers. Halfway through *The First Examination*, for example, when the examiners become frustrated by her shrewdly evasive replies, they give up on rational argument and fall back on silencing her, citing traditional Pauline-inspired prohibitions on female public speech. What emerges is their patriarchal insecurity: Askew is a unhusbanded woman meddling in religious matters reserved to men. After she had been condemned to death Anne was removed to the Tower and racked. Such unprecedented treatment of a gentlewoman indicated the high stakes of a plot that sought to wrest information out of her in order to incriminate Katherine Parr, whose independent attitudes and patronage of humanist reformers was resented by Henry's male councillors. Nonetheless, even when Askew's tormenters became appallingly vicious, they failed to break her stillness and got nothing from her. But she was so crippled that she had to be carried to her execution in a chair.

News of Askew's racking in the Tower became known within days, and then became grist for an energetic polemicist named John Bale, 'one of the stranger human creations of early academic Protestantism' (Dickens 1989: 194). He obtained Askew's writings as well as eye-witness reports, writing them up with his own furious 'elucidations'. The persona that emerges from Bale's editorial material is diametrically opposed to Askew's own: where she is quick-witted, terse, and subtle, he lays on personal and pedantic abuse with a trowel. As Leslie Fairfield has shown, Bale uses – perhaps exploits – Askew to serve his wider objective of defining female Protestant martyrdom, comparing her to biblical and early Christian women who were 'naturally' tender but became indomitably strong through their faith in God (1976: 129–33). The question of whether Bale has altered or even invented some of Askew's words to make her fit this stereotype must therefore always remain a possibility, though scholars generally agree her *Examinations* (published independently during the sixteenth century as well as in Bale's editions) seem authentic. As for female 'weakness', Askew often self-consciously plays up this quality in order to confound her male accusers, but otherwise the details of her life render such a notion absurd.

With or without Bale, Askew's actions came to inspire later women. Joan Bocher claimed during her well-publicised heresy trial in 1549, for example, that she had known Askew and drawn strength from her heroic resistance. Evidently so did other female reformers. Of the 60–70 Protestant martyrs during Henry

VIII's reign, only four or five were women. But during the Marian persecutions (1553–58) this number rose to over 60 of the nearly 300 people burnt in Smithfield, and included many lower-class women from clandestine groups such as the one Anne Askew had belonged to in London (Crawford 1993b: 30–3). Her life and writings would later enable the seventeenth-century feminist educator Bathusa Makin to claim, 'Our very Reformation of Religion, seems to be begun and carried on by Women'.

Editions:
The First Examination (1546). STC 848, reel 21. *The Latter Examination:* (1547). STC 850, reel 21. *Select Works of John Bale, D.D. Containing The Examinations of ... Anne Askew*, ed. Henry Christmas, Parker Society (Cambridge, 1849, some silent emendations). *The Paradise of Women*, ed. Betty Travitsky (Westport, Conn., 1981, excerpts).

ANNE ASKEW

THE FIRST EXAMINATION

(1546)

To satisfy your expectation, good people, this was my first examination in the year of our Lord 1545 and in the month of March. First Christopher Dare examined me at Sadlers' Hall, being one of the quest, and asked if I did not believe that the sacrament hanging over the altar was the very body of Christ really. Then I demanded this question of him: wherefore St Stephen was stoned to death? And he said he could not tell. Then I answered that no more would I assoil his vain question.

Secondly, he said that there was a woman which did testify that I should

1. *good people*: Askew's fellow reformers. Her sense of an audience implies some degree of self-consciousness in constructing a public persona

1–2. *first ... 1545*: Foxe's *Acts and Monuments* (1563) reprints the full (but now non-extant) statement she was made to sign by Bishop Bonner (partly recalled below at ll. 233ff.), as well as Bonner's (still extant) register-entry, both dated 20 March 1544 (Foxe 1843: vol. 5, 542–3). Under the old-style calendar (when the new year began on Lady Day, 25 March) this would mean 1545 by modern dating (not an earlier inquest by Bonner in 1544 prior to the events of *The First Examination*, as some writers have supposed).

2–3. *Christopher Dare*: professional London inquisitor

3. *quest*: inquest

4–5. *sacrament ... really*: the main theological issue in *The Examinations* and one of the Reformation's main controversies: the nature of the consecrated bread and wine at the Eucharist. The Catholic belief, transubstantiation, held that the entire material reality or substance of the bread and wine changed into the real body and blood of Christ, while retaining the outward appearance of bread and wine. Protestants rejected this doctrine in varying degrees. Askew's view appears to follow Luther's: the bread and wine are only symbolic of Christ's body and blood, which is present spiritually but not materially. According to Davis (1983: 96) Askew affirmed this view before the Lord Mayor (below ll. 43ff.), then upheld transubstantiation in her first meeting with Bishop Bonner, and finally changed back.

4. *hanging ... altar*: consecrated bread and wine reserved after mass

5–6. *St Stephen ... tell*: see n. to ll. 9–10 below

7. *assoil*: resolve, answer

8–9. *should read*: had claimed

read how God was not in temples made with hands. Then I showed him the seventh and the seventeenth chapter of the Apostles' Acts, what Stephen and Paul had said therein. Whereupon he asked me how I took those sentences. I answered that I would not throw pearls among swine, for acorns were good enough.

Thirdly, he asked me wherefore I said that I had rather to read five lines in the Bible, than to hear five masses in the temple. I confessed that I said no less, not for the dispraise of either the epistle or gospel, but because the one did greatly edify me and the other nothing at all, as St Paul doth witness in the fourteenth chapter of his first epistle to the Corinthians, whereas he doth say, 'If the trump giveth an uncertain sound, who will prepare himself to the battle?'

Fourthly, he laid unto my charge that I should say, if an ill priest ministered, it was the devil and not God. My answer was that I never spake such thing, but this was my saying: that whatsoever he were which ministered unto me, his ill conditions could not hurt my faith, but in spirit I received nevertheless the body and blood of Christ.

Fifthly, he asked me what I said concerning confession. I answered him my meaning, which was as St James saith, that every man ought to acknowledge his faults to other, and the one to pray for the other.

Sixthly, he asked me what I said to the King's Book. And I answered him that I could say nothing to it, because I never saw it.

Seventhly, he asked me if I had the spirit of God in me. I answered, if I had not, I was but a reprobate or cast-away. Then he said he had sent for a priest to examine me which was there at hand. The priest asked me what I said to the sacrament of the altar, and required much to know therein my meaning. But I desired him again to hold me excused concerning that matter. None other answer would I make him because I perceived him a papist.

9–10. *God ... Acts*: Acts 7.48, part of an oration made by Stephen before the Sanhedrin, or supreme Jewish Council, which became enraged at his call for Christian conversion and allowed him to be stoned to death. He thus became the first Christian martyr. Askew identifies herself with his story of public questioning and violent death. Paul reiterates Stephen's words in Acts 17.24: 'God that made the world ... dwelleth not in temples made with [human] hands'.

12. *throw ... swine*: Matthew 7.6

19–20. *If ... battle*: 1 Corinthians 14.8. The context is Paul's argument that preaching is more effective in known rather than foreign languages. Askew equates the latter with the Latin mass (ll. 16–17).

21–2. *ill ... God*: i.e. the priest's personal morals directly affect the spiritual value of his actions (especially when he presides at the eucharist)

27–8. *St James ... other*: James 5.16. Anne rejects the Catholic practice of confessing to a priest to receive divine absolution.

29. *King's Book*: written by a commission of bishops in 1543, it upheld traditional doctrines such as transubstantiation while denouncing the financial abuses of the papacy

Eighthly, he asked me if I did not think that private masses did help souls departed. And I said, it was great idolatry to believe more in them than in the death which Christ died for us.

Then they had from thence unto my lord Mayor. And he examined me as they had before, and I answered him directly in all things as I answered the quest afore.

Beside this, my lord Mayor laid one thing unto my charge which was never spoken of me but of them, and that was whether a mouse eating the host received God or no. This question did I never ask, but indeed they asked it of me, whereunto I made them no answer, but smiled. Then the bishop's chancellor rebuked me and said that I was much to blame for uttering the scriptures. For St Paul, he said, forbade women to speak or to talk of the word of God. I answered him that I knew Paul's meaning so well as he, which is (1 Corinthians 14) that a woman ought not to speak in the congregation by the way of teaching. And then I asked him how many women he had seen go into the pulpit and preach. He said he never saw none. Then I said he ought to find no fault in poor women except they had offended the law. Then my lord Mayor commanded me to ward. I asked him if sureties would not serve me. And he made me short answer, that he would take none. Then was I had to the Counter and there remained twelve days, no friend admitted to speak with me.

But in the meantime there was a priest sent to me, which said that he was commanded of the bishop to examine me and to give me good counsel (which he did not). But first he asked me for what cause I was put in the Counter. And I told him I could not tell. Then he said it was great pity that I should be there without cause, and concluded that he was very sorry for me.

Secondly, he said it was told him that I should deny the sacrament of the altar. And I answered him again, that that I had said, I had said.

37–8. *masses ... departed*: i.e. to shorten their time in purgatory

44–6. *whether ... smiled*: A contemporary reformer, John Loud, reports the exchange thus (J. Strype, *Ecclesiastical Memorials* (Oxford, 1822), vol. 1, pt. 1, 599):

Lord Mayor: What if a mouse eat [the consecrated bread] after the consecration? What shall become of the mouse? What sayest thou, thou foolish woman?

Anne Askew: What shall become of her, say you, my Lord?

Lord Mayor: I say, that that mouse is damned.

Anne Askew: Alack poor mouse!

49–51. *I ... teaching*: 'Let your women keep silence in the Churches: for it is not permitted unto them to speak' (1 Corinthians 14.34; some modern theologians argue this passage is not by Paul)

54. *ward ... sureties*: prison ... bail

56. *Counter*: London prisons in Poultry and Bread Streets

64–5. *deny ... altar*: i.e. transubstantiation

Thirdly, he asked me if I were shriven. I told him no. Then he said he would bring one to me for to shrive me. And I told him, so that I might have one of these three, that is to say Dr Crome, Sir Gyllam, or Huntington, I was contented, because I knew them to be men of wisdom. 'As for you or any other, I will not dispraise because I know ye not.' Then he said, 'I would not have you think but that I or another that shall be brought you shall be as honest as they, for if we were not ye may be sure the King would not suffer us to preach'. Then I answered by the saying of Solomon: 'By communing with the wise I may learn wisdom; but by talking with a fool I shall take scathe' (Proverbs 1).

Fourthly, he asked me if the host should fall and a beast did eat it, whether the beast did receive God or no. In answered, 'seeing ye have taken the pains to ask this question, I desire you also to take so much pain more so as to assoil it yourself, for I will not do it because I perceive ye come to tempt me'. And he said it was against the order of schools that he which asked the question should answer it. I told him I was but a woman, and knew not the course of schools.

Fifthly, he asked me if I intended to receive the sacrament at Easter or no. I answered that else I were no Christian woman and that I did rejoice that the time was so near at hand. And then he departed thence with many fair words.

And the twenty-third day of March my cousin Brittain came into the Counter to me and asked there whether I might be put to bail or no. Then went he immediately unto my lord Mayor, desiring of him to be so good lord unto me that I might be bailed. My lord answered him and said that he would be glad to do the best that in him lay; howbeit, he could not bail me without the consent of a spiritual officer, so requiring him to go and speak with the Chancellor of London. For, he said, like as he could not commit me to prison without the consent of a spiritual officer, no more could he bail me without consent of the same. So, upon that he went to the chancellor, requiring of him as he did afore of my lord Mayor. He answered him that the matter was so heinous that he durst not of himself do it without my lord of London were made privy thereunto. But he said he would speak unto my

66, 67. *shriven, shrive*: had confessed to a priest and received absolution on condition of performing some penance

68. *Dr Crome … Huntington*: Crome was a well-known reformist preacher who at the time of Askew's second *Examination* was forced publicly to recant his views. Huntington was a reforming minister in Norfolk. Nothing is known of Sir Gyllam (Sir = priest's title).

72–3. *King … preach*: public preachers were officially licensed

73–5. *By … scathe*: Proverbs 1.5–7; take scathe = receive harm

80. *order of schools*: i.e. rules of academic debate

93. *Chancellor*: the Bishop of London's chancellor

97. *lord*: bishop

lord in it, and bade him repair unto him the next morrow and he should well know my lord's pleasure.

And upon the morrow after, he came thither and spake both with the Chancellor and with my lord Bishop of London. My lord declared unto him that he was very well contented that I should come forth to a communication, and appointed me to appear afore him the next day after at three of the clock at afternoon. Moreover, he said unto him that he would there should be at that examination such learned men as I was affectioned to, that they might see and also make report that I was handled with no rigour. He answered him that he knew no man that I had more affection to than other. Then said the bishop, 'Yes, as I understand, she is affectioned to Dr Crome, Sir Gyllam, Whitehead and Huntington, that they might hear the matter, for she did know them to be learned and of a godly judgement'. Also he required my cousin Brittain that he should earnestly persuade me to utter even the very bottom of my heart. And he swore by his fidelity that no man should take any advantage of my words, neither yet would he lay aught to my charge for anything that I should there speak; but if I said any manner of thing amiss, he, with other more, would be glad to reform me therein with most godly counsel.

On the morrow after, my lord of London sent for me at one of the clock, his hour being appointed at three. And as I came before him, he said he was very sorry of my trouble, and desired to know my opinion in such matters as were laid against me. He required me also in any wise boldly to utter the secrets of my heart, bidding me not to fear in any point, for whatsoever I did say within his house, no man should hurt me for it. I answered, 'For so much as your lordship appointed three of the clock, and my friends shall not come till that hour, I desire you to pardon me of giving answer till they come'. Then said he that he thought it meet to send for those four men which were afore named and appointed. Then I desired him not to put them to the pain, for it should not need, because the two gentlemen which were my friends were able enough to testify that I should say. Anon after, he went

99. *repair*: return

102. *Bishop of London*: though he was vilified by Protestant writers such as Bale and Foxe, Edmund Bonner (*c.* 1550–69) was initially sympathetic to religious reform prior to Henry VIII's death, and tried, after his own fashion, to help Anne during her first examination

103. *communication*: interview

106. *affectioned*: sympathetically disposed

107. *rigour*: harsh or severe proceeding

114. *advantage … words*: i.e. to incriminate me
aught: anything

116. *other*: other persons

126. *four men*: 'More lambs to devour' (Bale's marginal note)

128. *the pain*: torture

into his gallery with Master Spelman and willed him in anywise that he should exhort me to utter all that I thought.

In the meanwhile he commanded his archdeacon to commune with me, who said unto me, 'Mistress, wherefore are ye accused?' I answered, 'Ask my accusers, for I know not as yet'. Then took he my book out of my hand and said, 'Such books as this is hath brought you to the trouble ye are in. Beware', saith he, 'beware, for he that made it was burnt in Smithfield.' Then I asked him if he were sure that it was true that he had spoken. and he said he knew well the book was of John Frith's making. Then I asked him if he were not ashamed for to judge of the book before he saw it within, or yet knew the truth thereof. I said also that such unadvised and hasty judgement is a token apparent of a very slender wit. Then I opened the book and showed it him. He said he thought it had been another, for he could find no fault therein. Then I desired him no more to be so swift in judgement till he thoroughly knew the truth. And so he departed.

Immediately after came my cousin Brittain in with divers other, as Master Hawe of Gray's Inn, and such other like. Then my lord of London persuaded my cousin Brittain as he had done oft before, which was that I should utter the bottom of my heart in anywise.

My lord said after that unto me, that he would I should credit the counsel of my friends in his behalf, which was that I should utter all things that burdened my conscience; for he ensured me that I should not need to stand in doubt to say anything, for like as he promised them, he said, he promised me, and would perform it, which was that neither he nor any man for him should take me at advantage of any word I should speak. And therefore he bade me say my mind without fear. I answered him that I had nought to say, for my conscience, I thanked God, was burdened with nothing. Then brought he forth this unsavoury similitude: that if a man had a wound, no

130. *gallery*: covered passage or balcony open to one side

130, 148. *anywise*: by any means possible

134–44. *Then ... departed*: '[Askew] gives [her inquisitor] every opportunity to reconsider before he goes on to incriminate himself for hastily assuming and drawing conclusions without examining the evidence ... The archdeacon's sheepish reply and his exit ... indicate how completely her dialogue has ... [asserted] her own ability to assume his role and language' (Beilin 1991: 319)

136. *Smithfield*: in north-west London, where heretics were burnt

138. *John Frith's*: Protestant martyr (1505–33) who helped Tyndale translate the English Bible and wrote a treatise against purgatory

146. *Gray's Inn*: one of the Inns of Court for students of Common Law

149. *would*: desired
credit: believe

151. *ensured*: assured

157. *similitude*: comparison

wise surgeon would minister help unto it before he had seen it uncovered. 'In like case', saith he, 'can I give you no good counsel unless I know wherewith your conscience is burdened.' I answered that my conscience was clear in all things, and for to lay a plaster unto the whole skin, it might appear much folly. 'Then ye drive me', saith he, 'to lay to your charge your own report, which is this: ye did say, he that doth receive the sacrament by the hands of an ill priest or a sinner, he receiveth the devil and not God.' To that I answered that I never spake such words, but as I said afore both to the quest and to my lord Mayor, so say I now again, that the wickedness of the priest should not hurt me, but in spirit and faith I received no less the body and blood of Christ. Then said the bishop unto me, 'What a saying is this! In spirit? I will not take you at that advantage.' Then I answered, 'My lord, without faith and spirit I cannot receive him worthily'.

Then he laid unto me that I should say that the sacrament remaining in the pyx was but bread. I answered that I never said so, but indeed the quest asked me such a question, whereunto I would not answer, I said, till such time as they had assoiled me this question of mine: wherefore Stephen was stoned to death? They said they knew not. Then said I again, no more would I tell them what it was.

Then laid it my lord unto me that I had alleged a certain text of the scripture. I answered that I alleged none other but St Paul's own saying to the Athenians in the seventeenth chapter of the Apostles' Acts, that God dwelleth not in temples made with hands. Then asked he me what my faith and belief was in that matter. I answered him, 'I believe as the scripture doth teach me'. Then enquired he of me, 'What if the scripture doth say that it is the body of Christ?' 'I believe', said I, 'like as the scripture doth teach me.' Then asked he again, 'What if the scripture doth say that it is not the body of Christ?' My answer was still, 'I believe as the scripture informeth me'. And upon this argument he tarried a great while, to have driven me to make him an answer to his mind. Howbeit, I would not, but concluded thus with him, that I believed therein and in all other things as Christ and his holy apostles did leave them.

Then he asked me why I had so few words. And I answered, 'God hath given me the gift of knowledge but not of utterance. And Solomon saith that a "Woman of few words is a gift of God" ' (Proverbs 19).

Thirdly, my lord laid unto my charge that I should say that the mass was idolatry. I answered him, 'No, I said not so. Howbeit', I said, 'the quest did

167. *spirit . . . faith*: i.e. spiritually, symbolically (see n. to ll. 4–5). Askew cleverly applies her words to the condition of the communicant, rather than the nature of the sacrament.

172. *pyx*: vessel in which the sacrament is kept

177–80. *certain . . . hands*: see ll. 9–10 above and n.

192. *Proverbs 19*: actually = the apocryphal book of Ecclesiasticus or Sirach, 26.14, although Proverbs 19.14 states 'a prudent wife cometh from the Lord'

193. *should say*: had said

ask me whether private masses did relieve souls departed or no. Unto whom then I answered, "O Lord, what idolatry is this, that we should rather believe in private masses than in the healthsome death of the dear son of God".' Then said my lord again, 'What an answer was that!' 'Though it were but mean', said I, 'yet was it good enough for the question.' Then I told my lord that there was a priest which did hear what I said there before my lord Mayor and them. With that the chancellor answered, 'Which was the same priest? So she spake it in very deed', said he, 'before my lord the Mayor and me'. Then were there certain priests, as Dr Standish and other, which tempted me much to know my mind. And I answered them always thus, 'That I have said to my lord of London, I have said'. And then Dr Standish desired my lord to bid me say my mind concerning that same text of St Paul. I answered that it was against St Paul's learning that I, being a woman, should interpret the scriptures, specially where so many wise learned men were. Then my lord of London said he was informed that one should ask of me if I would receive the sacrament at Easter, and I made a mock of it. Then I desired that mine accuser might come forth, which my lord would not. But he said again unto me, 'I sent one to give you good counsel, and at the first word ye called him papist'. That I denied not, for I perceived he was no less, yet made I none answer unto it. Then he rebuked me and said that I should report that there were bent against me threescore priests at Lincoln. 'Indeed', quoth I, 'I said so. For my friends told me, if I did come to Lincoln, the priests would assault me and put me to great trouble, as thereof they had made their boast. And when I heard it, I went thither indeed, not being afraid, because I knew my matter to be good. Moreover, I remained there six days to see what would be said unto me. And as I was in the minster reading upon the Bible, they resorted unto me by two and by two, by five and by six, minding to have spoken to me. Yet went they their ways again, without words speaking.' Then my lord asked if there were not one that did speak unto me. I told him, yes, that there was one of them at the last which did speak to me indeed. And my lord then asked me what he said. And I told him his words were of so small effect, that I did not now remember them. Then said my lord, 'There are many that read and know the scripture and yet do not follow it nor live thereafter'. I said again, 'My lord, I would wish that all men knew my conversation and living in all points, for I am so sure of myself this hour, that there are none able to prove any dishonesty by me. If you know any that can do it, I pray you bring them forth.'

Then my lord went away and said he would entitle somewhat of my

196–8. O ... *God*: see ll. 37–8 above and n.
206. *same text*: i.e. Acts 17 (above ll. 9–10)
207–9. *I ... were*: see n. to ll. 49–51
216. *Lincoln*: Askew came from Stallingborough near Grimsby, Lincolnshire
233. *entitle*: organise under different headings in a prepared statement for Askew to sign

meaning. And so he writ a great circumstance; but what it was I have not all in memory, for he would not suffer me to have the copy thereof. Only do I remember this small portion of it: 'Be it known', saith he, 'to all men that I, Anne Askew, do confess this to be my faith and belief, notwithstanding my reports made afore to the contrary. I believe that they which are houselled at the hands of a priest, whether his conversation be good or not, do receive the body and blood of Christ in substance really. Also I do believe it, after the consecration, whether it be received or reserved, to be no less than the very body and blood of Christ in substance. Finally I do believe in this and in all other sacraments of holy Church, in all points according to the old Catholic faith of the same. In witness thereof I, the said Anne, have subscribed my name.' There was somewhat more in it, which because I had not the copy, I cannot now remember.

Then he read it to me and asked me if I did agree to it. And I said again, 'I believe so much thereof as the holy scripture doth agree to. Wherefore I desire you that ye will add that thereunto.' Then he answered that I should not teach him what he should write. With that he went forth into his great chamber and read the same bill afore the audience, which inveigled and willed me to set to my hand, saying also that I had favour showed me. Then said the bishop, I might thank other and not myself of the favour that I found at his hand. For he considered, he said, that I had good friends, and also that I was come of a worshipful stock. Then answered one Christopher, a servant to Master Denny, 'Rather ought ye, my lord, to have done it in such case for God's sake, than for man's'.

Then my lord sat down and took me the writing to set thereto my hand. And I writ after this manner: 'I Anne Askew do believe all manner things contained in the faith of the Catholic Church'. Then, because I did add unto it 'the catholic church', he flung into his chamber in a great fury. With that my cousin Brittain followed him, desiring him for God's sake to be good

234. *circumstance*: contextual narrative relating to the main facts

239. *houselled*: receive communion. Bale's marginal gloss: 'Holy lechery'.

241. *it ... it*: the sacrament

253–4. *I ... friends*: influential people intervened on Anne's behalf on this occasion, as she states at the end of *The Latter Examination* (l. 226). They were probably friends of Katherine Parr who supported religious reform.

259ff. *And ...* : an entry in Bonner's register, written after Anne's death, claims she altered nothing. As Fairfield observes (1976: 134–5), Bonner may have been seeking to justify her punishment by demonstrating that she was a relapsed heretic (and to clear himself of having released Askew in the first place). The theory that Bonner would not have let her go without a plain submission is undermined by the pressure Anne's friends at court exerted to set her free.

260–1. *Catholic ... catholic*: the Church of Rome ... the universal or ancient church (to whose practices reformers wished to return)

lord unto me. He answered that I was a woman and that he was nothing deceived in me. Then my cousin Brittain desired him to take me as a woman and not to set my weak woman's wit to his lordship's great wisdom.

Then went in unto him Dr Weston and said that the cause why I did write there 'the catholic church' was that I understood not 'the Church' written afore. So with much ado they persuaded my lord to come out again and to take my name with the names of my sureties, which were my cousin Brittain and Master Spelman of Gray's Inn. This being done, we thought that I should have been put to bail immediately, according to the order of the law. Howbeit, he would not so suffer it, but committed me from thence to prison again until the next morrow. And then he willed me to appear in the Guildhall, and so I did. Notwithstanding, they would not put me to bail there neither, but read the bishop's writing unto me as before, and so commanded me again to prison.

Then were my sureties appointed to come before them on the next morrow in Paul's church, which did so indeed. Notwithstanding, they would again have broken off with them because they would not be bound also for another woman at their pleasure, whom they knew not, nor yet what matter was laid unto her charge. Notwithstanding, at the last, after much ado and reasoning to and fro, they took a bond of them of recognisance for my forthcoming. And thus I was, at the last, delivered.

Written by me, Anne Askew.

263–5. *He ... wisdom*: Katherine Parr made similar arguments to Henry VIII to extricate herself from a plot by religious conservatives to charge her with heresy. This was preceded by the torture of Anne Askew in an effort to gather incriminating evidence against Katherine (reported in the *Latter Examination*).

266–8. *Weston ... afore*: Weston persuades Bonner to accept 'catholic' as implying the Roman Church. Whereas Askew could claim her clause qualified the statement, Bonner could claim it conformed to the definition of transubstantiation in the 1539 Act of Six Articles (Trollope 1862: 123).

272. *he*: presumably Bonner

278. *Paul's*: St Paul's cathedral

278–9, 282. *they ... them*: church authorities ... Brittain and Spelman

282. *recognisance*: legal pledge to observe conditions laid down by the inquest

ANNE ASKEW

THE LATTER EXAMINATION

(1547)

THE SUM OF MY EXAMINATION AFORE THE KING'S COUNCIL AT GREENWICH

Your request, as concerning my prison fellows, I am not able to satisfy because I heard not their examinations. But the effect of mine was this: I, being before the council, was asked of Master Kyme. I answered that my lord Chancellor knew already my mind in that matter. They with that answer were not contented, but said it was the King's pleasure that I should open the matter to them. I answered them plainly that I would not so do, but if it were the King's pleasure to hear me, I would show him the truth. Then they said it as not meet for the King with me to be troubled. I answered that Solomon was reckoned the wisest king that ever lived, yet misliked not he to hear two poor common women, much more his Grace a simple woman and his faithful subject. So, in conclusion, I made them none other answer in that matter.

Then my lord Chancellor asked me of my opinion in the sacrament. My answer was this: 'I believe that so oft as I, in a Christian congregation, do

1. *Your*: presumably the same audience of fellow reformers addressed in *The First Examination*
3. *being ... council*: Askew was summoned on 24 May 1546, and appeared on 17 or 18 June. According to Trollope (1862: 124), she was betrayed by her brother Sir Francis Askew after passing heretical books to Queen Katherine Parr.
   of ... Kyme: about Askew's estranged husband, who rejected her reformist beliefs. She discarded his name and tried unsuccessfully to obtain a divorce after he turned her out of their house. During Anne's trial Kyme charged her with deserting him and claimed that she had refused to live with him without just cause. Anne in turn asked to put her case before the King – presumably because Henry would be sympathetic to the idea of divorce – but was told her request was improper (Trollope 1862: 124).
4. *lord Chancellor*: Thomas Wriothesley (1505–50), rigorous persecutor of reformers
9–10. *Solomon ... women*: In 1 Kings 3.16 two women come before Solomon to settle a dispute after having each borne a child. One child has died and its mother has exchanged it for the living one, which she then claims as her own. Solomon orders the surviving child to be cut in half. The true mother willingly offers to give up the child as long as it is spared, whereas the false mother does not object to the child being divided.
13. *opinion ... sacrament*: see *First Examination*, ll. 4–5 and n.

receive the bread in remembrance of Christ's death, and with thanksgiving according to his holy instruction, I receive therewith the fruits also of his most glorious passion.' The Bishop of Winchester bade me make a direct answer. I said I would not sing a new song to the lord in a strange land. Then the bishop said I spake in parables. I answered, it was best for him, 'for if I show the open truth', quoth I, 'ye will not accept it'. Then he said I was a parrot. I told him again I was ready to suffer all things at his hands, not only his rebukes but all that should follow besides, yea, and that gladly. Then had I divers rebukes of the council because I would not express my mind in all things as they would have me. But they were not in the meantime unanswered for all that (which now to rehearse were too much), for I was with them there above five hours. Then the clerk of the council conveyed me from thence to my Lady Garnish.

The next day I was brought again before the council. Then would they needs know of me what I said to the sacrament. I answered that I already had said that I could say. Then, after divers words, they bade me go by. Then came my Lord Lisle, my Lord of Essex, and the Bishop of Winchester, requiring me earnestly that I should confess the sacrament to be flesh, blood, and bone. Then said I to my Lord Parr and my Lord Lisle that it was great shame for them to counsel contrary to their knowledge. Whereunto, in few words, they did say that they would gladly all things were well.

Then the bishop said he would speak with me familiarly. I said, 'So did Judas when he unfriendlily betrayed Christ'. Then desired the bishop to speak with me alone. But that I refused. He asked me why. I said that in the mouth of two or three witnesses every matter should stand, after Christ's and Paul's doctrine (Matthew 18 and 2 Corinthians 13).

15. *in remembrance*: i.e. symbolically. See next n.

16. *according ... instruction*: 'And [Jesus] took bread, and when he had given thanks, he brake it and gave to them, saying, This is my body which is given for you; do this in the remembrance of me' (Luke 22.19)
fruits: spiritual benefits

17. *Winchester*: Stephen Gardiner (*c.* 1483–1555), doctrinal conservative

18. *sing ... land*: Psalm 137.4

23. *divers*: various

30. *go by*: leave (them)

31. *Lisle ... Winchester*: John Dudley, Viscount Lisle, and William Parr, Lord Essex and brother of Queen Katherine Parr; both men, like the Queen, were sympathetic to Askew's opinions and joined with Gardiner to try a final time to change her mind (Redworth 1990: 236)

35. *would*: wished

36. *familiarly*: informally, in a friendly or private way

38–40. *I said ... doctrine*: 'But if [a brother who wrongs someone] hear thee not, take yet with thee one or two, that by the mouth of two or three witnesses every word may be confirmed' (Matthew 18.16, 2 Corinthians 13.1)

Then my lord Chancellor began to examine me again of the sacrament. Then I asked him how long he would halt on both sides. Then would he needs know where I found that. I said in the scripture (3 Kings 18). Then he went his way.

Then the bishop said I should be burnt. I answered that I had searched all the scriptures yet could I never find there that either Christ or his apostles put any creature to death. 'Well, well', said I, 'God will laugh your threatenings to scorn' (Psalm 2). Then was I commanded to stand aside.

Then came Master Paget to me with many glorious words, and desired me to speak my mind to him. 'I might,' he said, 'deny it again if need were.' I said that I would not deny the truth. He asked me how I could avoid the very words of Christ, 'Take, eat, this is my body which shall be broken for you'. I answered that Christ's meaning was there, as in these other places of scripture: 'I am the door' (John 10), 'I am the vine' (John 15), 'Behold the Lamb of God' (John 1), 'The rock-stone was Christ' (1 Corinthians 10), and such other like. 'Ye may not here', said I, 'take Christ for the material thing that he is signified by, for then ye will make him a very door, a vine, a lamb, and a stone, clean contrary to the Holy Ghost's meaning. All these indeed do signify Christ, like as the bread doth his body in that place. And though he did say there, "Take, eat this in remembrance of me", yet did he not bid them hang up that bread in a box, and make it a god, or bow to it.'

Then he compared it unto the king, and said that the more his majesty's honour is set forth, the more commendable it is. Then said I, that it was an abominable shame unto him to make no better of the eternal word of God than of his slenderly conceived fantasy. A far other meaning requireth God therein than man's idle wit can devise, whose doctrine is but lies without his heavenly verity. Then he asked me if I would commune with some wiser man. 'That offer', I said, 'I would not refuse.' Then he told the council. And so went I to my lady's again.

Then came to me Dr Coxe and Dr Robinson. In conclusion, we could not

43. *3 Kings*: = 1 Kings 18.21: 'And Elijah came unto all the people, and said, How long halt ye between two opinions? If the Lord be God, follow him: but if Baal be he, then go after him. And the people answered him not a word'

48. *Psalm 2*: 4

49. *Paget*: Sir William, later Lord Paget Secretary of State. When Henry VIII was safely dead, he became a Protestant.

54. *John 10 ... John 15*: 7–9 ... 1

55. *John 1*: 29
1 Corinthians 10: 4

61. *hang ... it*: box = pyx. Protestants objected to the sacrament being ceremonially displayed or worshipped.

62. *he*: Paget

63. *set forth*: displayed publicly

65. *far*: more profound

agree. Then they made me a bill of the sacrament, willing me to set my hand thereunto, but I would not. Then on the sunday I was sore sick, thinking no less than to die. Therefore I desired to speak with Latimer. It would no[t] be. Then was I sent to Newgate in my extremity of sickness, for in all my life afore was I never in such pain. Thus the Lord strengthen you in the truth. Pray, pray, pray.

THE CONFESSION OF ME ANNE ASKEW, FOR THE TIME I WAS IN NEWGATE, CONCERNING MY BELIEF

I find in the scriptures that Christ took the bread and gave it to his disciples saying, 'Eat, this is my body which shall be broken for you', meaning in substance his own very body, the bread being thereof an only sign or sacrament. For after like manner of speaking, he said he would break down the temple and in three days build it up again, signifying his own body by the temple, as St John declareth it (John 2), and not the stony temple itself. So that the bread is but a remembrance of his death, or a sacrament of thanksgiving for it, whereby we are knit unto him by a communion of Christian love, although there be many that cannot perceive the true meaning thereof. For the veil that Moses put over his face before the children of Israel, that they should not see the clearness thereof (Exodus 34 and 2 Corinthians 3), I perceive the same veil remaineth to this day. But when God shall take it away, then shall these blind men see. For it is plainly expressed in the history of Bel in the Bible that God dwelleth in nothing material. 'O king', saith Daniel, 'be not deceived' (Daniel 14), 'for God will be in nothing that is made with hands of men' (Acts 7). O what stiff-necked people are these, that will always resist the Holy Ghost! But as their fathers have done, so do they, because they have stony hearts.

Written by me, Anne Askew, that neither wish death nor yet fear his might, and as merry as one that is bound towards heaven. 'Truth is laid in

71. *bill of*: prepared statement about

73. *Latimer*: reforming Bishop of Gloucester, preacher in Katherine Parr's household. He had recently been examined by the Council and was kept in custody for the remainder of Henry VIII's reign.

74. *Newgate*: London prison for the condemned

79–80. *sign or sacrament*: one classic definition is: 'an outward and visible sign of an inward and spiritual grace' (*BCP*)

82. *John* 2: 19–21

87. *clearness*: luminousness (from seeing God directly)

87–8. *Exodus 34 ... 2 Corinthians 3*: 33 ... 13

90. *Bel*: or Baal and the Dragon, story in the Apocryphal 14th chapter of Daniel

91. *Daniel 14*: 7

92. *Acts 7*: 48

prison' (Luke 21). 'The law is turned to wormwood' (Amos 6). 'And there can no right judgement go forth' (Isaiah 59)....

THE SUM OF THE CONDEMNATION OF ME, ANNE ASKEW, AT GUILDHALL

They said to me there that I was an heretic, and condemned by the law if I would stand in my opinion. I answered that I was no heretic, neither yet deserved I any death by the law of God. But as concerning the faith which I uttered and wrote to the council, I would not, I said, deny it, because I knew it true. Then would they needs know if I would deny the sacrament to be Christ's body and blood. I said, 'Yea, for the same son of God that was born of the Virgin Mary, is now glorious in heaven, and will come again from thence at the latter day, like as he went up (Acts 1). And as for that ye call your God, is but a piece of bread. For a more proof thereof (mark it when ye list) yet it lie in the box but three months, and it will be mould and so turn to nothing that is good. Whereupon I am persuaded that it cannot be God.'

After that they willed me to have a priest, and then I smiled. Then they asked me if it were not good. I said I would confess my faults to God, for I was sure that he would hear me with favour. And so we were condemned, without a quest.

My belief which I wrote to the council was this: that the sacramental bread was left us to be received with thanksgiving in remembrance of Christ's death, the only remedy of our souls' recover[y], and that thereby we also receive the whole benefits and fruits of his most glorious passion.

Then would they needs know whether the bread in the box were God or no. I said, 'God is a spirit, and will be worshipped in spirit and in truth' (John 4). Then they demanded, 'Will you plainly deny Christ to be in the

97. *Luke 21*: 12
Amos 6: 12; wormwood = gall, figuratively anything that is bitter to the soul
98. *Isaiah 59*: 8
106. *Acts 1*: 11
113. *we*: Askew was condemned with three others: John Hemley, an Essex priest; John Hadlam, a tailor; and John Lascells, follower of John Frith, servant in the King's household, and radical Protestant (Dickens 1959: 11, 33; see below l. 202ff.). It is uncertain whether Lascells or Askew headed their clandestine London group of reformers. Bale says it was Lascells but is contradicted by the Jesuit Robert Parsons. Gardiner, although obviously an interested party, also claimed that Bale's accounts were 'utterly misreported' (Redworth 1990: 232). Since Bale presents Askew to fit a particular type of female martyr (physically and socially meek but spiritually bold), it is possible that he misrepresented her position and/or her words to suit his own views.
121. *John 4*: 24

sacrament?' I answered that I believed faithfully the eternal Son of God not to dwell there. In witness whereof I recited again the history of Bel, and the ninth chapter of Daniel, the seventh and seventeenth of the Acts, and the twenty-fourth of Matthew, concluding thus: I neither wish death, nor yet fear his might, God have the praise thereof with thanks.

MY LETTER SENT TO THE LORD CHANCELLOR

The Lord God, by whom all creatures have their being, bless you with the light of his knowledge. Amen.

My duty to your lordship remembered, etc.

It might please you to accept this my bold suit as the suit of one which upon due considerations is moved to the same, and hopeth to obtain. My request to your lordship is only that it may please the same to be a mean for me to the king's majesty, that his Grace may be certified of these few lines which I have written concerning my belief; which when it shall be truly conferred with the hard judgement given me for the same, I think his Grace shall well perceive me to be weighed in an uneven pair of balances. But I remit my matter and cause to almighty God, which rightly judgeth all secrets. And thus I commend your lordship to the governance of him, and fellowship of all saints. Amen.

By your handmaid,
Anne Askew.

MY FAITH BRIEFLY WRITTEN TO THE KING'S GRACE

I Anne Askew, of good memory, although God hath given me the bread of adversity and the water of trouble, yet not so much as my sins have deserved, desire this to be known to your Grace: that forasmuch as I am by the law condemned for an evildoer, here I take heaven and earth to record that I shall die in my innocency. And, according to that I have said first and will say last, I utterly abhor and detest all heresies. And as concerning the supper of the Lord, I believe so much as Christ hath said therein, which he confirmed with his most blessed blood. I believe also so much as he willed me to follow and believe, and so much as the catholic church of him doth

125. *twenty-fourth of Matthew*: in which Jesus enumerates the cataclysms that will take place at the end of time

131. *moved*: pressed

132. *mean*: agent

142. *good memory*: i.e. mentally sound

teach; for I will not forsake the commandment of his holy lips. But look what God hath charged me with his mouth, that have I shut up in my heart. And thus briefly I end, for lack of learning.

Anne Askew.

THE EFFECT OF MY EXAMINATION AND HANDLING SINCE MY DEPARTURE FROM NEWGATE

On Tuesday I was sent from Newgate to the sign of the Crown, whereas Master Rich and the Bishop of London with all their power and flattering words went about to persuade me from God. But I did not esteem their glozing pretences. Then came there to me Nicholas Shaxton, and counselled me to recant as he had done. Then I said to him, that it had been good for him never to have been born, with many other like words.

Then Master Rich sent me to the Tower, where I remained till three of the clock. Then came Rich and one of the council, charging me upon my obedience to show unto them if I knew man or woman of my sect. My answer was that I knew none. Then they asked me of my Lady of Suffolk, My Lady of Sussex, my Lady of Hertford, my Lady Denny, and my Lady Fitzwilliams. I said, if I should pronounce anything against them, that I were not able to prove it. Then said they unto me that the King was informed that I could name, if I would, a great number of my sect. Then I answered that the King was as well deceived in that behalf, as dissembled with in other matters.

Then commanded they me to show how I was maintained in the Counter, and who willed me to stick by my opinion. I said that there was no creature that therein did strengthen me. And as for the help that I had in

151–2. *look what*: whatever

153. *learning*: i.e. knowledge of formal closing formulas or elegant phrases

156. *Rich*: Sir Richard Rich (*c.* 1497–1567), Solicitor-General, had prosecuted Bishop Thomas Fisher and Sir Thomas More by dubious legal means and zealously persecuted reformers

157. *glozing*: specious

158. *Nicholas Shaxton*: Bishop of Salisbury, was interrogated with Latimer over transubstantiation and condemned for heresy, but saved himself by recanting. He was ordered to preach a sermon at Askew's execution on 16 July 1546.

159–60. *that* ... *born*: '... woe be to that man by whom the Son of man is betrayed: it had been good for that man if he had never been born' (Matthew 26.24)

161ff. *Then* ... : 28 June 1546

164–6. Suffolk ... Fitzwilliams: associated with Katherine Parr's household, known for its reformist discussions of the English Bible

171. *maintained*: prisoners were responsible for providing themselves with food, money, and other basic comforts if they wished to avoid the very worst conditions

the Counter, it was by the means of my maid; for as she went abroad in the streets, she made to the prentices, and they by her did send me money. But who they were I never knew.

Then they said that there were divers gentlewomen that gave me money. But I knew not their names. Then they said that there were divers ladies which had sent me money. I answered that there was a man in a blue coat which delivered me ten shillings, and said that my Lady of Hertford sent it me, and another in a violet coat did give me eight shillings, and said that my Lady Denny sent it me. Whether it were true or no, I cannot tell, for I am not sure who sent it me, but as the men did say.

Then they said there were of the Council that did maintain me. And I said no. Then they did put me on the rack because I confessed no ladies nor gentlewomen to be of my opinion, and thereon they kept me a long time. And because I lay still and did not cry, my lord Chancellor and Master Rich took pains to rack me at their own hands, till I was nigh dead.

Then the Lieutenant caused me to be loosed from the rack. Incontinently I swooned, and then they recovered me again. After that I sat two long hours reasoning with my lord Chancellor upon the bare floor, whereas he with many flattering words persuaded me to leave my opinion. But my Lord God (I thank his everlasting goodness) gave me grace to persevere, and will do (I hope) to the very end.

Then was I brought to an house and laid in a bed with as weary and painful bones as ever had patient Job, I thank my Lord God thereof. Then my lord Chancellor sent me word, if I would leave my opinion, I should want nothing; if I would not, I should forth to Newgate and so be burned. I sent him again word that I would rather die than to break my faith. Thus the Lord open the eyes of their blind hearts, that the truth may take place. Farewell, dear friend, and pray, pray, pray.

175. *prentices*: apprentices

179–81. *blue ... violet*: colours typical of servants' livery

182. *Denny*: Joan Denny, wife of Sir Anthony, aid to Henry VIII

184. *Council*: the Privy Council

189. *Lieutenant*: of the Tower of London, Sir Antony Knevet. Wriothesley and Rich judged him to be too lenient when racking Askew. When they asked her whether she was pregnant before turning the screws themselves, she is said to have replied, 'Ye shall not need to spare for that, but do your wills upon me' (Foxe 1843: vol. 5, 547). *Incontinently*: immediately

196. *Job*: suffers long but innocently in the Old Testament book bearing his name

ANNE ASKEW'S ANSWER UNTO JOHN LASCELLS'S* LETTER

O friend, most dearly beloved in God, I marvel not a little what should move you to judge in me so slender a faith as to fear death, which is the end of all misery. In the Lord I desire you not to believe of me such wickedness, for I doubt it not but God will perform his work in me, like as he hath begun.

I understand the council is not a little displeased that it should be reported abroad that I was racked in the Tower. They say now, that they did there was but to fear me, whereby I perceive they are ashamed of their uncomely doings, and fear much lest the king's majesty should have information thereof; wherefore they would no man to noise it. Well, their cruelty God forgive them. Your heart in Christ Jesu. Farewell, and pray.

I have read the process which is reported (of them that know not the truth) to be my recantation. But as sure as the Lord liveth, I never meant thing less than to recant. Notwithstanding this I confess that in my first troubles I was examined of the Bishop of London about the sacrament. Yet had they no grant of my mouth but this, that I believed therein as the word of God did bind me to believe. More had they never of me.

Then he made a copy, which is now in print, and required me to set thereunto my hand. But I refused it. Then my two sureties did will me in no wise to stick thereat, for it was no great matter, they said. Then, with much ado, at the last I wrote thus: 'I Anne Askew do believe this (if God's word do agree to the same) and the true catholic church'.

Then the bishop, being in great displeasure with me because I made doubts in my writing, commanded me to prison where I was awhile. But afterwards, by the means of friends, I came out again. Here is the truth of that matter. And as concerning the thing that ye covet most to know, resort to the sixth of John, and be ruled always thereby. Thus fare ye well, quoth Anne Askew.

* *John Lascells's*: see n. to l. 113

208. *abroad*: publicly

209–11. *fear ... thereof*: because torturing a woman was illegal

211. *noise*: rumour

213. *process*: legal proceedings

219. *he*: Bishop Bonner

221. *stick*: hesitate

228. *sixth of John*: 'Verily, verily, I say unto you, he that believeth in me hath everlasting life. / I am the bread of life' (John 6.47–8). The *Latter Examination* ends with a brief Confession of Faith reiterating Askew's views, notably on the mass: 'I do say and believe it to be the most abominable idol that is in the world' (B3^{r}).

JANE ANGER (*fl.* 1589)

FROM *JANE ANGER HER PROTECTION FOR WOMEN* (1589)

Introduction

The occasion of Jane Anger's *Protection* was a contemporary pamphlet attacking women, and hers is the first full-length defence alleged to have been written by an English female author. Anger is audacious but self-possessed, making none of the disabling gestures other women feel obliged to offer for transgressing conventional gender roles. Though in her brief opening letter 'To the Gentlewomen of England' she worries about appearing too heated in her defence, she trusts her readers' understanding of the nature of the provocation will overlook any indecorousness. In a second letter 'To all Women in General' her tone changes, however. No longer a 'defendant', she seizes the role of clamorous avenger, and it is this combative persona, as the *Protection* proceeds, that constitutes much of its immediate appeal.

Nonetheless, the work's authorship and purpose raise certain questions. Jane Anger may be the pseudonym of a male author, perhaps the same man who wrote *Book his Surfeit in Love, a Farewell to the Follies of his own Fantasy*, to which the *Protection for Women* replies. Though no copy of the Surfeiter's *Book* has survived, it was entered in the Stationers' Register on 27 November 1588 and apparently printed soon after. The *Protection*'s derivative quality suggests the possibility of male authorship, since in many ways it remains bound by the discourse of the male-dominated *querelle des femmes*, or controversy over the nature of women. This was a bookish sixteenth-century debate in which male writers presented formal arguments praising or denouncing women (and sometimes both). Their 'evidence' consisted of lists of historical 'good' and 'bad' women, as well as opinions derived from classical authorities. The genre had no basis in the real lives of early modern women, though one cannot say it did not reinforce cultural stereotypes and so make it more difficult to reform the restrictions under which they lived (Woodbridge 1984: 3–6). Pamela Joseph Benson has argued that the *Protection* remains undifferentiated from other interventions in the *querelle* because it relies largely on the traditional issue of sexual behaviour to evaluate woman's moral nature. Seen in this light, Jane Anger's efforts may go no further than trying to gain greater sexual autonomy for women while defending their slandered reputations; the male-determined parameters of the *querelle* remain, and no 'feminist program' or new idea of woman seems to emerge (Benson 1992: 224).

Other evidence, however, suggests Jane Anger may be a real woman rather than a ventriloquising man, and that her work does manage to break free of certain gender and genre limitations. Simon Shepherd notes that there were five or six women with this name living in southern England when the *Protection* was published in

1589 (1985: 30); one of these could have been the author. The volume was issued by Thomas Orwin and Richard Jones, printers who accepted other works by female writers. Orwin published Anne Dowriche's *French History* in the same year, while Jones had printed Isabella Whitney's poetry. Furthermore, Lynne Magnusson has identified Pierre de la Primaudaye's *Academie françoise*, translated into English as *The French Academy* by Thomas Bowes (1586), as a main source of the *Book his Surfeit*. Since the latter borrowed heavily from la Primaudaye, Magnusson is able to compare *The French Academy* with the *Protection*, and in turn demonstrates how Anger deliberately reworked her opponent's misogynist arguments to establish a distinct female viewpoint which partly transcends the boundaries of the *querelle* genre (Magnusson 1989, 1991).

Like other works governed by the rhetorical form of *controversia* or disputations, Anger's argument proceeds mainly by compilation: allusions, sayings, and examples matching *Book his Surfeit* are mustered to refute her antagonist. Many of the traditional proverbs she cites imply female inferiority; so her usual strategy is to turn these inside out, showing that their negative implications apply equally well if not more so to men. But if this were all, her *Protection* would remain largely a tit-for-tat exercise typical of the *querelle*. Instead it goes further by calling into 'question that now which hath ever been questionless'. This means reprehending obvious male double standards and deceit, and fostering in women a 'conviction of their own intellectual and moral worth' through her own example of speaking out; in doing so Anger laid the imaginative foundations for a later, more socially active feminism (Henderson and McManus 1985: 31). Her arguments also anatomise the patriarchally encoded nature of everyday language, in which 'woman' is a discourse constructed from masculine moral and aesthetic values that denies real women any authentic sense of agency. By exposing the mono-gendered basis of the Surfeiter's 'objective' or 'natural' commonplaces and assertions, she begins the forward-looking task of language reform in which female life experiences will take their place in a bi-gendered, genuinely human epistemology.

Editions:

Jane Anger her Protection for Women (1589). STC 644, reel 165. *The Paradise of Women*, ed. Betty Travitsky (Westport, Conn., 1981, brief excerpts). *First Feminists*, ed. Moira Ferguson (Bloomington, 1985). *Half Humankind: Contexts and Texts of the Controversy about Women in England, 1540–1640*, ed. Katherine Usher Henderson and Barbara F. McManus (Urbana and Chicago, 1985). *The Women's Sharp Revenge*, ed. Simon Shepherd (New York, 1985).

JANE ANGER

FROM *JANE ANGER HER PROTECTION FOR WOMEN TO DEFEND THEM AGAINST THE SCANDALOUS REPORTS OF A LATE SURFEITING* LOVER, AND ALL OTHER LIKE VENERIANS† THAT COMPLAIN SO TO BE OVERCLOYED WITH WOMEN'S KINDNESS.*

(1589)

TO THE GENTLEWOMEN OF ENGLAND, HEALTH:

Gentlewomen, though it is to be feared that your settled wits will advisedly condemn that which my choleric vein hath rashly set down, and so perchance Anger shall reap anger for not agreeing with diseased persons, yet, if with indifferency of censure you consider of the head of the quarrel, I hope you will rather show yourselves defendants of the defender's title than complainants of the plaintiff's wrong. I doubt judgement before trial, which were injurious to the law; and I confess that my rashness deserveth no less, which was a fit of my extremity. I will not urge reasons because your wits are sharp and will soon conceive my meaning, ne will I be tedious lest I prove too too troublesome, nor over-dark in my writing for fear of the name of a riddler. But in a word, for my presumption I crave pardon because it was Anger that did write it, committing your protection and myself to the protection of yourselves, and the judgement of the cause to the censures of your just minds.

Yours ever at commandment,
Jane Anger.

* *surfeiting*: sickened by sensual over-indulgence

† *Venerians*: followers of Venus, and thus of sexual desire

1. *settled wits*: calm rationality

2. *choleric vein*: angry temper. Choler or bile was one of four 'humours' or body fluids believed to determine human temperament.

3. *diseased*: i.e. by 'surfeiting'

4. *indifferency*: impartiality
head: main topic (perhaps implying 'chief instigator')

6. *doubt*: suspect, fear

9. *ne*: nor

10. *over-dark*: obscure

TO ALL WOMEN IN GENERAL, AND GENTLE READER* WHATSOEVER:

Fie on the falsehood of men, whose minds go oft a-madding and whose tongues cannot so soon be wagging but straight they fall a-railing. Was there ever any so abused, so slandered, so railed upon, or so wickedly handled undeservedly, as are we women? Will the gods permit it, the goddesses stay their punishing judgements, and we ourselves not pursue their undoings for such devilish practices? O Paul's steeple and Charing Cross! A halter hold all such persons. Let the streams of the channels in London streets run so swiftly as they may be able alone to carry them from that sanctuary. Let the stones be as ice, the soles of their shoes as glass, the ways steep like Etna, and every blast a whirlwind puffed out of Boreas his long throat, that these may hasten their passage to the devil's haven. Shall surfeiters rail on our kindness? You stand still and say naught. And shall not Anger stretch the veins of her brains, the strings of her fingers, and the lists of her modesty, to answer their surfeitings? Yes truly. And herein I conjure all you to aid and assist me in defence of my willingness, which shall make me rest at your commands. Fare you well.

Your friend,
Jane Anger.

* *Reader*: *sic*

1. *a-madding*: carried away by wild foolishness

2. *tongues*: a key word illustrating Anger's inversion of traditional gendered attributes. When discussing the nature of woman, Renaissance male writers habitually equated unruly female tongues with innate moral inferiority. Female public speech is always frivolous yet threatening to masculine order, so the 'good' woman is silent. Here, however, by making the unruly tongue 'her synecdoche for the omnipresence and power of the male word, Anger turns back against its maker a discursive practice that itself rationalizes and preserves [public] discourse as a male prerogative' (Magnusson 1991: 273–4).

3–5. *handled ... undoings*: one of many sexual puns throughout the *Protection*

6. *Paul's ... Cross*: London landmarks and gathering places. Paul's = St Paul's cathedral. Charing Cross stood at the western end of the Strand at the junction of Whitehall.

7. *halter*: noose or gallows

7ff. *Let ...*: invocations of calamities suggesting righteous indignation, but perhaps playfully deflated by the use of local details; channels = gutters or runnels, for carrying away rubbish and fouled water

10. *Etna*: active volcano in Sicily
Boreas: the north wind

11. *devil's haven*: perhaps alluding to Cuckhold's Haven east of London on the south bank of the Thames, named after the post that stood there bearing a pair of horns (= sign of a cuckholded husband)

12. *kindness*: i.e. in granting loving favours

13. *lists*: limits

A PROTECTION FOR WOMEN, ETC.

The desire that every man hath to show his true vein in writing is unspeakable, and their minds are so carried away with the manner as no care at all is had of the matter. They run so into rhetoric as oftentimes they overrun the bounds of their own wits and go they know not whither. If they have stretched their invention so hard on a last as it is at a stand, there remains but one help, which is to write of us women. If they may once encroach so far into our presence as they may but see the lining of our outermost garment, they straight think that Apollo honours them in yielding so good a supply to refresh their sore over-burdened heads (through studying for matters to indite of). And therefore, that the god may see how thankfully they receive his liberality (their wits whetted and their brains almost broken with botching his bounty), they fall straight to dispraising and slandering our silly sex. But judge what the cause should be of this their so great malice towards simple women: doubtless the weakness of our wits and our honest bashfulness, by reason whereof they suppose that there is not one amongst us who can or dare reprove their slanders and false reproaches. Their slanderous tongues are so short, and the time wherein they have lavished out their words freely hath been so long, that they know we cannot catch hold of them to pull them out, and they think we will not write to reprove their lying lips. Which conceits have already made them cocks and would (should they not be cravened) make themselves among themselves be thought to be

1. *unspeakable*: inexpressible in words

2–3. *manner ... matter*: the respective merits of form and content were argued in a sixteenth-century debate about whether writing in English should be artfully elegant or plain and direct. The stylistic standard once set by Cicero's polished, ornamental Latin was increasingly regarded as too flowery and artificial for English prose. Anger takes an anti-Ciceronian position against the Surfeiter's rhetoric.

5. *last*: wooden model of a foot used to shape shoe-leather; the implication is that the Surfeiter can 'cobble together' only middling-quality work
stand: halt

8. *Apollo ... them*: women's verse was not authorised, as men's was, by the Renaissance theory of poetic discourse as a patriarchal heritage stretching back through classical authors to Apollo and Orpheus: '[male] poets experience no problem of origin: all the ancient mythology exists to reassure them of the divine origin of their inspiration and activity, and of their deserved place in the ... mythical Platonic chain of poetic transmission' (Sankovitch 1986: 229)

10. *indite*: write

11–12. *wits ... bounty*: the alliteration mocks the Surfeiter's taste for highly wrought prose. botching = ineptly patching.

13. *silly*: plain, simple, innocent

20–1. *should ... cravened*: if they are not exposed as real cowards

of the game. They have been so daintily fed with our good natures that like jades (their stomachs are grown so queasy) they surfeit of our kindness. If we will not suffer them to smell on our smocks, they will snatch at our petticoats; but if our honest natures cannot away with that uncivil kind of jesting, then we are coy. Yet if we bear with their rudeness and be somewhat modestly familiar with them, they will straight make matter of nothing, blazing abroad that they have surfeited with love, and then their wits must be shown in telling the manner how.

Among the innumerable number of books to that purpose of late unlooked for, the new *Surfeit of an Old Lover* (sent abroad to warn those which are of his own kind from catching the like disease) came by chance to my hands; which, because as well women as men are desirous of novelties, I willingly read over. Neither did the ending thereof less please me than the beginning, for I was so carried away with the conceit of the gentleman as that I was quite out of the book before I thought I had been in the midst thereof, so pithy were his sentences, so pure his words, and so pleasing his style. The chief matters therein contained were of two sorts: the one in the

22. *game*: cock-fighting, a metaphor for male sexual prowess. The passage probably alludes through *Boke His Surfeit* to Lyly's 'Cooling Card for Philautus and All Fond Lovers' (1578), in which Euphues, having sworn off love, contrasts himself with a lusty youth named Curio: 'Though [Curio] be a cock of the game, yet [Euphues] is content to be craven and cry creak' (*Euphues the Anatomy of Wit*, ed. Croll and Clemens, 1964: 92).

23. *jades*: knackered horses; an abusive male term for women, which Anger characteristically reverses

25. *away*: do away

27. *nothing*: possible sexual meaning

28. *blazing abroad*: boasting publicly

31. *sent abroad*: published

31–2. *warn ... disease*: as Magnusson observes, this links *Boke His Surfeit* to a literary stereotype, the reformed libertine, who publishes seduction-romances on the pretext of warning younger men about the dangers of alluring women. An example which *Book his Surfeit* draws on is Lyly's 'Cooling Card for Philautus', a loose paraphrase of Ovid's *Remedia Amoris*. Anger recognises the self-interest in this genre, in that it boasts male writers' familiarity with 'the game': '[Anger] exposes the Surfeiter's repentant posture as a rhetorical ploy, a contrivance enabling him to pass off titillating and self-aggrandizing tales as godly and self-effacing sermons' (1991: 277).

35–8. *carried ... style*: If this is not ironic, Anger admits that the Surfeiter's fluency, as well as the interest of his stories, lulled her into non-critical enjoyment. Such an admission is strategic, demonstrating that she is not superior to her female readers and so may speak on their behalf. As for the Surfeiter's subject, Magnusson suggests it may have consisted partly of seduction narratives designed to illustrate his double theme: man's folly and women's guile (1991: 276–7). Anger omits discussion of the stories themselves to concentrate on refuting his misogynist commentary.

dispraise of man's folly, and the other invective against our sex; their folly proceeding of their own flattery joined with fancy, and our faults are through our folly, with which is some faith....

The greatest fault that doth remain in us women is that we are too credulous, for could we flatter as they can dissemble, and use our wits well as they can their tongues ill, then never would any of them complain of surfeiting. But if we women be so so perilous cattle as they term us, I marvel that the gods made not Fidelity as well a man as they created her a woman, and all the moral virtues of their masculine sex as of the feminine kind, except their deities knew that there was some sovereignty in us women which could not be in them men. But lest some snatching fellow should catch me before I fall to the ground, and say they will adorn my head with a feather (affirming that I roam beyond reason, seeing it is most manifest that the man is the head of the woman and that therefore we ought to be guided by them), I prevent them with this answer. The gods, knowing that the minds of mankind would be aspiring, and having throughly viewed the wonderful virtues wherewith women are enriched, lest they should provoke us to pride and so confound us with Lucifer, they bestowed the supremacy over us to man, that of that coxcomb he might only boast, and therefore for God's sake let them keep it. But we return to the *Surfeit*.

Having made a long discourse of the gods' censure concerning love, he leaves them (and I them with him) and comes to the principal object and general foundation of love, which he affirmeth to be grounded on women. And now beginning to search his scroll wherein are taunts against us, he beginneth and saith that we allure their hearts to us. Wherein he saith more truly than he is aware of; for we woo them with our virtues and they wed

45. *so so*: *sic*
perilous cattle: harmful contemptuous creatures or property
46. *93*: 'most of the moral virtues were traditionally represented as female figures' (Shepherd 1985: 47)
48. *deities*: mock deferential address: 'deity-ships'
50. *fall ... ground*: i.e. safely disappear
51. *feather*: perhaps of a peacock, symbol of pride, or alternatively the sign of a fool
52. *man ... woman*: 1 Corinthians 11.3: 'Christ is the head of every man: and the man is the woman's head: and God is Christ's head.' 'Head' may mean 'source' (alluding to the creation of woman in Genesis 2) rather than 'authority'.
53. *prevent*: forestall
54. *minds ... aspiring*: alluding to Prometheus, who stole fire from heaven after Zeus had taken it away from humans
54. *throughly*: thoroughly
56. *confound us ... Lucifer*: turn us into ... arch-angel who rebelled against heaven and was overthrown; a type of pride
57. *coxcomb*: the cock's comb, but also a fool's cap, thereby suggesting deluded self-conceit
62. *scroll*: body of evidence

us with vanities; and men, being of wit sufficient to consider of the virtues which are in us women, are ravished with the delight of those dainties which allure and draw the senses of them to serve us, whereby they become ravenous hawks who do not only seize upon us but devour us. Our good toward them is the destruction of ourselves; we being well-formed are by them foully deformed. Of our true meaning they make mocks, rewarding our loving follies with disdainful flouts. We are the grief of man, in that we take all the grief from man; we languish when they laugh, we lie sighing when they sit singing, and sit sobbing when they lie slugging and sleeping. *Mulier est hominis confusio*, because her kind heart cannot so sharply reprove their frantic fits as those mad frenzies deserve. *Aut amat aut odit, non est in tertio*: she loveth good things and hateth that which is evil; she loveth justice and hateth iniquity; she loveth truth and true dealing and hateth lies and falsehood; she loveth man for his virtues and hateth him for his vices. To be short, there is no *medium* between good and bad, and therefore she can be *in nullo tertio*. Plato his answer to a vicar of fools which asked the question, being that he knew not whether to place women among those creatures which were reasonable or unreasonable, did as much beautify his divine knowledge as all the books he did write; for knowing that women are the greatest help that men have (without whose aid and assistance it is as possible for them to live as if they wanted meat, drink, clothing, or any other necessary), and knowing also that even then in his age (much more in those ages which should after follow) men were grown to be so unreasonable, as he could not decide whether men or brute beasts were more reasonable. Their eyes are so curious as, be not all women equal with Venus for beauty, they cannot abide the sight of them; their stomachs so queasy as, do they taste but twice of one dish, they straight surfeit and needs must a new diet be provided for them. We are contrary to men because they are contrary to that which is good. Because they are spurblind they cannot see into our natures, and we too well, though we had but half an eye, into their conditions because they are so bad; our behaviours alter daily because men's virtues decay hourly.

71. *flouts*: jeers
73. *slugging*: idling
74. *Mulier ... confusio*: proverbial (Tilley W656): woman is the ruin of man
75–6. *Aut ... tertio*: proverbial (Tilley W651): either she loves or she hates, there is no third way
80. *in ... tertio*: in nothing a third way (i.e. in between)
Plato ... fools: probably Socrates responding to Glaucon on the equal capacities of men and women in *The Republic*, V, 451–6
84. *greatest help*: Genesis 2.18 (see below ll. 225–6).
85. *wanted*: lacked
89. *curious*: particular
93. *spurblind*: obtuse (literally, wholly or partly blind)

If Hesiodus had with equity as well looked into the life of man as he did precisely search out the qualities of us women, he would have said that if a woman trust unto a man it shall fare as well with her as if she had a weight of a thousand pounds tied about her neck and then cast into the bottomless seas. For by men are we confounded, though they by us are sometimes crossed. Our tongues are light because earnest in reproving men's filthy vices, and our good counsel is termed nipping injury in that it accords not with their foolish fancies. Our boldness rash for giving noddies nipping answers, our dispositions naughty for not agreeing with their vile minds, and our fury dangerous because it will not bear with their knavish behaviours. If our frowns be so terrible and our anger so deadly, men are too foolish in offering occasions of hatred, which shunned, a terrible death is prevented. There is a continual deadly hatred between the wild boar and tame hounds; I would there were the like betwixt women and men unless they amend their manners, for so strength should predominate where now flattery and dissimulation hath the upper hand. The lion rageth when he is hungry, but man raileth when he is glutted. The tiger is robbed of her young ones when she is ranging abroad, but men rob women of their honour undeservedly under their noses. The viper stormeth when his tail is trodden on, and may not we fret when all our body is a footstool to their vile lust? Their unreasonable minds which know not what reason is make them nothing better than brute beasts. . . .

Euthydemus made six kind of women, and I will approve that there are

97. *Hesiodus*: seventh-century BC Greek poet, proverbial for misogyny. He related the myth of Pandora, the first woman, whom Zeus sent with a jar of evils to punish man for Prometheus's theft of fire.

98. *precisely*: scrupulously; a word often derogatively applied to Puritans

100–1. *thousand . . . seas*: Luke 17.2

102–6. *Our . . . behaviours*: passage closely resembling Thomas Bowes's translation of Pierre de la Primaudaye's *The French Academy* (1586, p. 483, e.g. light, nipping, rash, boldness), a work which *Book his Surfeit* has 'slavishly' imitated (Magnusson 1989: 312). Anger evidently did not know *The French Academy* itself.

102. *light*: Anger recontextualises the usual male insult (= wanton) to bring out pro-female meanings: nimble, swift

103. *nipping*: biting

104. *noddies nipping*: fools decisively refuting

109–16. *There . . . lust*: again close to *The French Academy* (505), which cites (but does not endorse) such 'proofs' of woman's 'natural' irascibility. Anger recycles them to show man's inversion of natural relationships.

111–12. *strength . . . hand*: Anger 'prefers the clarity of openly aggressive relations between the sexes' (Shepherd 1985: 48) to unnatural deceit

119. *Euthydemus*: opponent of Socrates in an early Platonic dialogue on education named after him. *The French Academy* (238–40) quotes part of their debate but does not mention his list.

so many of men, which be: poor and rich, bad and good, foul and fair. The great patrimonies that wealthy men leave their children after their death make them rich, but dice and other marthrifts, happening into their companies, never leave them till they be at the beggar's bush, where I can assure you they become poor. Great eaters, being kept at a slender diet, never distemper their bodies but remain in good case; but afterwards, once turned forth to liberty's pasture, they graze so greedily as they become surfeiting jades and always after are good for nothing. There are men which are snout-fair whose faces look like a cream-pot, and yet those not the fair men I speak of; but I mean those whose conditions are free from knavery, and I term those foul that have neither civility nor honesty. Of these sorts there are none good, none rich or fair long. But if we do desire to have them good, we must always tie them to the manger and diet their greedy paunches, otherwise they will surfeit. What shall I say? Wealth makes them lavish, wit knavish, beauty effeminate, poverty deceitful, and deformity ugly. Therefore of me take this counsel:

Esteem of men as of a broken reed,
Mistrust them still, and then you well shall speed.

I pray you then, if this be true (as it truly cannot be denied) have not they reason who affirm that a goose standing before a ravenous fox is in as good case as the woman that trusteth to a man's fidelity? For as the one is sure to lose his head, so the other is most certain to be bereaved of her good name, if there be any small cause of suspicion. The fellow that took his wife for his cross was an ass, and so we will leave him; for he loved well to swear on an ale-pot, and because his wife, keeping him from his drunken vein, put his nose out of his socket, he thereby was brought into a mad mood in which he did he could not tell what.

When provender pricks, the jade will winch, but keep him at a slender

122. *marthrifts*: spoilers of thrifty ways
123. *beggar's bush*: a London tavern in St Giles notorious for its shady clientele
128. *snout-fair*: fair-faced
cream-pot: pallid (and therefore suggesting cowardice, as in *Macbeth* 5.3.11–12: 'The Devil dam thee black, thou cream-faced loon: / Where got'st thou that goose-look?')
132. *diet*: slim
136. *broken reed*: perhaps a riposte to the traditional idea of woman as a broken rib (Genesis 2.21)
143. *cross*: penance (alluding to Christ's exhortation to follow his example of taking up the cross, i.e. finding spiritual strength in adversity; Matthew 16.24)
swear on: i.e. live life dependent on
147. *provender pricks*: (the need for) fodder urges (him on)
winch: kick impatiently

ordinary and he will be mild enough. The dictator's son was crank as long as his cock was crowing, but proving a craven he made his master hang down his head.

Thales was so married to shameful lust as he cared not a straw for lawful love, whereby he showed himself to be endued with much vice and no virtue; for a man doth that oftentimes standing of which he repenteth sitting. The Roman could not, as now men cannot, abide to hear women praised and themselves dispraised, and therefore it is best for men to follow Alphonso his rule: let them be deaf and marry wives that are blind, so shall they not grieve to hear their wives commended nor their monstrous misdoing shall offend their wives' eyesight.

Tibullus, setting down a rule for women to follow, might have proportioned this platform for men to rest in and might have said: every honest man ought to shun that which detracteth both health and safety from his own person, and strive to bridle his slanderous tongue. Then must he be modest and show his modesty by his virtuous and civil behaviours, and not display his beastliness through his wicked and filthy words. For lying lips and deceitful tongues are abominable before God. It is an easy matter to entreat a cat to catch a mouse, and more easy to persuade a desperate man to kill himself. What nature hath made, art cannot mar, and (as this surfeiting lover saith) that which is bred in the bone will not be brought out of the flesh. If we clothe ourselves in sackcloth and truss up our hair in dish-

148. *ordinary*: = regular diet; literally, a set-price meal in a public house
dictator's son: unidentified
crank: cocky, self-confident

151. *Thales*: seventh-century BC Greek philosopher. In *The French Academy* (481) when asked why he never married, Thales explains it was too soon when he was young and too late when he was old. Anger reinterprets the story from a woman's viewpoint, exposing Thales's 'wisdom' as sexual self-interest.

153. *standing ... sitting*: presumably, seeking public attention versus quietly ruminating

154. *The Roman*: in *The French Academy* Marius the Roman rejects Metellus's beautiful and virtuous daughter: '*I had rather be mine own than hers*' (482)

156. *Alphonso*: (so-called) the Wise (1221–84), King of Leon and Castile (Aragon in *The French Academy*, 484), to whom this opinion is attributed

159. *Tibullus*: sexually ambivalent Roman poet (*c.* 55–19 BC) claimed women were deceivers in his *Elegies* III.4.60 (Shepherd 1985: 48). In *The French Academy* he commends female 'shamefastness' (516).

160. *platform*: plan, counsel

168–9. *that ... flesh*: proverbial (Tilley F365); 'brought out' = removed from

169–70. *sackcloth ... dish-clouts*: traditional apparel signifying repentance and mourning (and therefore sexual unavailability). *clouts* = cloths

clouts, Venerians will nevertheless pursue their pastime. If we hide our breasts it must be with leather, for no cloth can keep their long nails out of our bosoms.

We have rolling eyes and they railing tongues; our eyes cause them to look lasciviously, and why? because they are given to lechery. It is an easy matter to find a staff to beat a dog, and a burnt finger giveth sound counsel. If men would as well embrace counsel as they can give it, Socrates's rule would be better followed. But let Socrates, heaven and earth say what they will, 'man's face is worth a glass of dissembling water'. And therefore to conclude with a proverb: 'write ever, and yet never write enough of man's falsehood' (I mean those that use it). I would that ancient writers would as well have busied their heads about deciphering the deceits of their own sex as they have about setting down our own follies; and I would some would call in question that now which hath ever been questionless. But sithence all their wits have been bent to write of the contrary, I leave them to a contrary vein, and the Surfeiting Lover, who returns to his discourse of love.

Now while this greedy grazer is about his entreaty of love (which nothing belongeth to our matter) let us secretly, ourselves with ourselves, consider how and in what they that are our worst enemies are both inferior unto us and most beholden unto our kindness.

The creation of man and woman at the first (he being formed *in principio* of dross and filthy clay) did so remain until God saw that in him his workmanship was good, and therefore, by the transformation of the dust which was loathsome unto flesh, it became purified. Then, lacking a help for him, God making woman of man's flesh (that she might be purer than he) doth evidently show how far we women are more excellent than men. Our bodies are fruitful, whereby the world increaseth, and our care wonderful, by which man is preserved. From woman sprang man's salvation. A woman

173. *rolling*: sexually provocative

176. *Socrates's rule*: at his trial, as elsewhere in Plato's writings, Socrates claimed the only wisdom he possessed was knowledge of his own ignorance

178. *dissembling water*: proverbial (Tilley W86): as false, unstable, as water

179–80. *man's falsehood*: proverbial (Tilley F34)

183. *questionless*: taken as certain
sithence: since

185. *returns*: Anger has presumably been refuting the Surfeiter's argument point by point. She now skips his 'entreaty of love', which does not attack women directly, returning to his text at l. 282.

187. *ourselves ... ourselves*: women to women

190–1. *he ... clay*: Genesis 2.7; *in principio* = in the beginning

196. *fruitful ... increaseth*: fulfilling the divine injunction in Genesis 1.28.

197. *woman*: the virgin Mary

was the first that believed, and a woman likewise the first that repented of sin. In woman is only true fidelity; except in her there is no constancy, and without her no housewifery. In the time of their sickness we cannot be wanted, and when they are in health we for them are most necessary. They are comforted by our means, they [are] nourished by the meats we dress, their bodies freed from diseases by our cleanliness, which otherwise would surfeit unreasonably through their own noisomeness. Without our care they lie in their beds as dogs in litter, and go like lousy mackerel swimming in the heat of summer. They love to go handsomely in their apparel and rejoice in the pride thereof; yet who is the cause of it, but our carefulness to see that everything about them be curious? Our virginity makes us virtuous, our conditions courteous, and our chastity maketh our trueness of love manifest. They confess we are necessary, but they would have us likewise evil. That they cannot want us I grant; yet evil I deny, except only in the respect of man who, hating all good things, is only desirous of that which is ill (through whose desire, in estimation of conceit, we are made ill).

But lest some should snarl on me, barking out this reason, that none is good but God, and therefore women are ill, I must yield that in that respect we are ill, and affirm that men are no better, seeing we are so necessary unto them. It is most certain that if we be ill they are worse, for *malum malo additum efficit malum peius*; and they that use ill worse than it should be are worse than the ill. And therefore if they will correct *Magnificat*, they must first learn the signification thereof. That we are liberal they will not deny, sithence that many of them have, *ex confessio*, received more kindness

198. *first ... repented*: the Samaritan Woman in John 4 who is 'the first character in the Gospel to engage in serious theological conversation with Jesus' (*Women's Bible Commentary* 1992: 296) ... Mary Magdalene, the woman who annoints Jesus and is traditionally (though erroneously) identified as a prostitute in Western Christian tradition

201. *wanted*: lacking

202. *meats we dress*: food we prepare

204. *noisomeness*: capacity for self-injury

208. *curious*: just right

210. *necessary ... evil*: proverbial (Tilley W703)

213. *in ... conceit*: by fanciful or self-flattering thoughts

214–15. *none ... God*: the Calvinist belief that human nature is deeply sinful and utterly dependent upon divine grace for reclamation

217–18. *malum ... peius*: evil added to evil makes a worse evil

219. *Magnificat*: first word in the Latin version of Mary's hymn of thanksgiving (Luke 1.46–55) upon learning she has been chosen to bear Christ. 'Correcting Magnificat' is proverbial for finding fault on the basis of false knowledge; 'here Anger applies the proverb literally, since men who learn the signification of [the] *Magnificat* ... will of necessity realize the worth of women' (Henderson and McManus 1985: 181).

221. *ex confessio*: by their own admission

in one day at our hands than they can repay in a whole year; and some have so glutted themselves with our liberality as they cry 'no more'. But if they shall avow that women are fools, we may safely give them the lie; for myself have heard some of them confess that we have more wisdom than need is, and therefore no fools, and they less than they should have, and therefore fools. It hath been affirmed by some of their sex that to shun a shower of rain and to know the way to our husband's bed is wisdom sufficient for us women; but in this year of '88 men are grown so fantastical that unless we can make them fools we are accounted unwise....

And now, seeing I speak to none but to you which are of mine own sex, give me leave like a scholar to prove our wisdom more excellent than theirs (though I never knew what sophistry meant).

There is no wisdom but it comes by grace; this is a principle, and *contra principium non est disputandum*. But grace was first given to a woman, because to our Lady; which premisses conclude that women are wise. Now *primum est optimum*, and therefore women are wiser than men. That we are more witty, which comes by nature, it cannot better be proved than that by our answers men are often driven to a *non plus*; and if their talk be of worldly affairs, with our resolutions they must either rest satisfied or prove themselves fools in the end....

Now sithence that this overcloyed and surfeiting lover leaveth his love and comes with a fresh assault against us women, let us arm ourselves with patience and see the end of his tongue which explaineth his surfeit. But it was so lately printed as that I should do the printer injury should I recite but one of them, and therefore, referring you to *Boke His Surfeit in Love*, I come to my matter. If to enjoy a woman be to catch the devil by the foot, to obtain the favour of a man is to hold fast his dam by the middle, whereby the one may easily break away and the other cannot go without he carries the man with him. The properties of the snake and of the eel are the one to sting and the other not to be held; but men's tongues sting against nature and therefore they are unnatural. Let us bear with them as much as may be, and yield to their wills more than is convenient; yet if we cast our reckon-

229. *fantastical*: absurdly irrational
234. *grace*: divine grace
234–5. *contra ... disputandum*: there is no arguing against principle
236. *Lady*: the virgin Mary
237. *primum ... optimum*: the first is the best
238. *witty*: wise, prudent; clever
239. *non plus*: nonplus, inability to reply
245. *lately printed*: entered in the Stationers' Register on 27 November 1588 and evidently published soon after
247–8. *devil ... dam*: proverbial combination (Tilley D225)
249. *without*: but that
253. *cast ... reckoning*: balance our accounts

ing at the end of the year we shall find that our losses exceed their gains, which are innumerable. The property of the chameleon is to change himself; but man always remaineth at one stay and is never out of the predicaments of dishonesty and unconstancy. The stinging of the scorpion is cured by the scorpion, whereby it seems that there is some good nature in them. But men never leave stinging till they see the death of honesty. The danger of pricks is shunned by gathering roses glove-fisted, and the stinging of bees prevented through a close hood. But naked dishonesty and bare inconstancy are always plagued through their own folly.

If men's folly be so unreasonable as it will strive against nature, it is no matter though she rewards them with crosses contrary to their expectations; for if Tom Fool will presume to ride on Alexander's horse, he is not to be pitied though he get a foul knock for his labour. But it seems the gentleman hath had great experience of Italian courtesans, whereby his wisdom is showed; for *experientia praestantior arte*, and he that hath experience to prove his case is in better case than they that have all unexperienced book cases to defend their titles.

The smooth speeches of men are nothing unlike the vanishing clouds of the air, which glide by degrees from place to place till they have filled themselves with rain, when breaking, they spit forth terrible showers. So men gloze till they have their answers, which are the end of their travail, and then they bid modesty adieu and, entertaining rage, fall a-railing on us which never hurt them. The rankness of grass causeth suspicion of the serpent's lurking, but his lying in the plain path at the time when woodcocks shoot, maketh the patient passionate through his sting because no such ill was suspected. When men protest secrecy most solemnly, believe them least, for then surely there is a trick of knavery to be discarded; for in a friar's habit an old fornicator is always clothed.

It is a wonder to see how men can flatter themselves with their own conceits. For let us look, they will straight affirm that we love, and if then lust

256. *at ... stay*: in the same state

259. *pricks*: thorns

265. *Alexander's*: one of the traditional nine worthies or heroes

267. *Italian courtesans*: in Lyly's 'Cooling Card for Philautus', Euphues worries about betraying his former lover, an Italian courtesan named Lucilla, by writing against love. As in the case of *The French Academy*, Anger seems to rework details which the Surfeiter borrowed directly from Lyly but does not consult Lyly herself (Kahin 1947: 33).

268. *experientia ... arte*: experience surpasses art (theory)

274. *gloze*: flatter

276. *rankness*: coarse overgrowth
serpent's: snake's (proverbial; Tilley S585)

277–8. *shoot ... passionate*: dart (i.e. at dusk) ... suffer painfully

283. *look*: i.e. with any interest

pricketh them, they will swear that love stingeth us; which imagination only is sufficient to make them essay the scaling of half a dozen of us in one night, when they will not stick to swear that if they should be denied of their requests, death must needs follow. Is it any marvel though they surfeit, when they are so greedy? But is it not pity that any of them should perish, which will be so soon killed with unkindness? Yes truly. Well, the onset given, if we retire for a vantage they will straight affirm that they have got the victory. Nay, some of them are so carried away with conceit that, shameless, they will blaze abroad among their companions that they have obtained the love of a woman unto whom they never spake above once, if that. Are not these froward fellows? You must bear with them because they dwell far from lying neighbours; they will say *mentiri non est nostrum*, and yet you shall see true tales come from them as wild geese fly under London bridge. Their fawning is but flattery, their faith falsehood, their fair words allurements to destruction, and their large promises tokens of death, or of evils worse than death. Their singing is a bait to catch us, and their playings plagues to torment us; and therefore take heed of them, and take this as an axiom in logic and a maxim in the law: *nulla fides hominibus*. There are three accidents to men which, of all, are most unseparable: lust, deceit, and malice (their glozing tongues the preface to the execution of their vile minds, and their pens the bloody executioners of their barbarous manners). A little gall maketh a great deal of sweet sour, and a slanderous tongue poisoneth all the good parts in man. . . .

At the end of men's fair promises there is a labyrinth, and therefore ever hereafter stop your ears when they protest friendship, lest they come to an end before you are aware, whereby you fall without redemption. The path which leadeth thereunto is man's wit, and the miles-ends are marked with these trees: folly, vice, mischief, lust, deceit, and pride. These to deceive you shall be clothed in the raiments of fancy, virtue, modesty, love, true-meaning, and handsomeness. Folly will bid you welcome on your way and tell you his fancy concerning the profit which may come to you by this journey,

286. *stick*: hesitate
289. *killed . . . unkindness*: variant of the 'to kill with kindness' (proverbial; Tilley K51)
290. *vantage*: superior or secure position
294. *froward*: perverse
294–5. *bear . . . neighbours*: spoken sarcastically (it's the neighbours who are dishonest, never oneself)
295. *mentiri . . . nostrum*: we are not liars
296–7. *geese . . . bridge*: 'London Bridge was made for wise men to go over and fools to go under' (Tilley L417)
301. *nulla . . . hominibus*: there is no truth in men (Tilley F34)
302. *accidents*: attributes
304. *pens*: a sexual pun
310. *miles-ends*: posts marking miles

and direct you to vice who is more crafty. He, with a company of protestations, will praise the virtues of women, showing how many ways men are beholden unto us; but our backs once turned, he falls a-railing. Then mischief, he pries into every corner of us, seeing if he can espy a cranny that, getting in his finger into it, he may make it wide enough for his tongue to wag in. Now, being come to lust, he will fall a-railing on lascivious looks and will ban lechery, and with the collier will say, 'the devil take him', though he never means it. Deceit will give you fair words and pick your pockets, nay, he will pluck out your hearts if you be not wary. But when you hear one cry out against lawns, drawn-works, periwigs, against the attire of courtesans, and generally of the pride of all women, then know him for a wolf clothed in sheep's raiment, and be sure you are fast by the lake of destruction. Therefore take heed of it, which you shall do if you shun men's flattery, the forerunner of our undoing. If a jade be galled, will he not winch? And can you find fault with a horse that springeth when he is spurred? The one will stand quietly when his back is healed and the other go well when his smart ceaseth. You must bear with the old *Lover his Surfeit* because he was diseased when he did write it; and peradventure hereafter, when he shall be well amended, he will repent himself of his slanderous speeches against our sex and curse the dead man which was the cause of it and make a public recantation. For the faltering in his speech at the latter end of his book affirmeth that already he half repenteth of his bargain, and why? because his melody is past. But believe him not, though he should out-swear you, for although a jade may be still in a stable when his gall-back is healed, yet he will show himself in his kind when he is travailing; and man's flattery bites secretly, from which I pray God keep you and me too. Amen.

Finis.

318. *cranny*: sexual pun

321. *ban*: curse
collier … him: 'Like will to like, quoth the devil to the collier' (Tilley L287)

324. *lawns, drawn-works*: fine linens, ornamentally patterned fabrics

326. *fast*: close

328. *galled*: chafed by a harness or over-work (proverbial; Tilley H700)

333–6. *repent … repenteth*: another indication of Anger's perception that the Surfeiter's hand-wringing over the dangers of love is simply a prelude to his 're-conversion' in future romance narratives (Magnusson 1991: 277–8)

337. *melody*: (sexual) performance

339. *gall-back*: chafed back, rubbed sore
kind: true colours
travailing: toiling (at seduction); alternatively, 'travelling'

ELIZABETH GRYMESTON (before 1563–*c.* 1603)

FROM *MISCELLANEA, MEDITATIONS, MEMORATIVES*

(1604, 1605–6)

Introduction

Elizabeth Grymeston's *Miscellanea* was published posthumously from papers she wrote either close to her death *c.* 1603 or (perhaps more likely) over a longer period preceding it. Though we cannot be certain about the identity of her editor, it was probably her husband, since the second edition (1605–6) prominently displays the family arms and also expands the first edition's original fourteen chapters to twenty. These additions are composed in the same way as her earlier chapters and seem to be authentic (Hughey and Hereford 1934: 90–1). As its title suggests, the volume is made up of mixed genres, and insofar as we can take it to represent what Grymeston calls a 'true portraiture' of her mind, its composite nature reflects the diversity of her intellectual interests. These included classical literature, theology, Latin, Italian, and some Greek, the last being exceptional for an Elizabethan woman who had no access to grammar schools or the universities. In attempting to comment briefly on the chapters selected here, it may be helpful to consider each of Grymeston's genres by discussing the title's three terms in reverse order. We thereby move from conventional to more innovative literary forms.

The opening Epistle supplies most of the biographical information we have about Grymeston. It was written when she was gravely ill, and declares the main purpose of her work to be the instruction of her only surviving son, Bernye. Framing the volume as its first and last chapters, the *Memoratives* serve this didactic purpose most directly. They adopt a popular contemporary genre, the advice book, consisting of precepts and adages presented as guides to proper conduct (some of this material also appears in the Epistle). Grymeston's counsel is very similar to that passed on by other Elizabethan parents (e.g. Lord Burghley, *Advice to a Son*, ed. Wright 1962), with the same strong emphasis on godly living and a characteristic mingling of religious advice and worldly wisdom without any modern sense of their customary separation. One sees precisely the same features in other advice books by seventeenth-century women such as Elizabeth Jocelin and Dorothy Leigh (Sizemore 1976). Grymeston's *Memoratives* are therefore wholly representative of efforts by early modern parents to instil traditional values in their children (though women of course faced obstacles to *publishing* their advice – of which more below).

Other sections of the volume are devoted to prayers and religious *Meditations* (Chapters 7 and 9 presented here). These provide Grymeston with greater opportunities for creative self-expression as she seeks to present spiritual counsel in an imaginatively engaging way. Collectively her meditations develop a central theme:

'He that liveth well, shall maketh a good end'; that is, since life focuses in the terminal events of death and judgement, one should live as though these were imminent, detaching oneself from worldly concerns while looking upon misfortunes as tests of faith. These interests relate her work to another popular Renaissance genre, that of holy dying or *ars moriendi*. This too attracted female authors such as Mary Sidney (see Lamb 1986). Yet Grymeston individualises these sections according to her own Catholic sensibility. Her exhortations are developed through elaborate metaphors and vividly sensual descriptions, a practice she learns partly from Counter-Reformation writers such as Robert Southwell. Ultimately it derives from meditative techniques developed by Ignatius Loyola, whose *Spiritual Exercises* strongly influenced English Metaphysical writers. Thus as Fletcher and Sizemore observe (1981: 56), Grymeston's own ruggedly material expression of abstract principles sometimes reminds one of the Metaphysical poets.

This brings us to her 'miscellaneous' chapters. Several of these (omitted here) consist of other writers' work: a madrigal by her son (Chapter 12), poems from Robert Southwell's *Peter's Complaint* (Chapter 11) and Richard Rowland's *Odes in Imitation of the Seven Penitential Psalms* (Chapter 13). But there is also original work (in the Renaissance sense of the term as well as the modern, each of which Grymeston defines in her Epistle by comparing the respective activities of the spider and the bee). She achieves a notable degree of dramatic and visual immediacy in Chapter 3, for instance, a prose soliloquy spoken by Dives (the rich man in Luke 16 who ends his life tormented in hell, while the beggar he had always spurned, Lazarus, goes to heaven). What is remarkable about this portrait is how Grymeston's artistic identification with her subject allows Dives's voice to resonate with an emotional urgency that invites us to recognise his suffering, despite the moral viewpoint that condemns him for failing to share his wealth. Indeed, the whole relation of this speech to the biblical passage is curious, for in Luke Dives is pointedly denied both the relief he begs from Lazarus when their situations are reversed and the request for a warning to be sent to his rich brothers to beware his fate. Grymeston's monologue grants his belated concern for others a voice forbidden by scripture, thereby reinterpreting Abraham's judgement less harshly, perhaps even subversively. She likewise partly rehabilitates Dives's moral authority by personalising the parable's application, representing him as an exemplum to her son and her comfortable readers.

While Grymeston's opening Epistle prepares the reader for the moral instruction she offers her son, it does not anticipate some of the other *Miscellanea* added to the second edition: political authority and treason, murder, and the qualities of judges (the second of these, Chapter 17, presented here). These topics are mainly civil in nature, and so were traditionally considered to be the preserve of male writers. This may be why they were excluded from the first edition: they strayed from the 'proper' female subjects of maternal affection and pious advice, topics about which women writers could better hope to gain public acceptance as authoritative counsellors, especially if they were ill, dying, or dead (cf. Wall 1991, Leigh, Jocelin). Having proved to be a profitable commodity for her male editor(s) in 1604, however, by 1605–6 'Grymeston' could risk venturing into culturally dangerous waters. Accordingly these chapters display a more self-conscious sense of addressing and attempting to influence public opinion, as the author delineates her topics in pithy observations and historical illustrations drawn from a range of classical and Christian sources. Generically, these chapters are essays, similar in subject and form (e.g. the aphoristic lines and parallel structures) to those Francis Bacon first published in 1597 (as *Essays, Religious Meditations, Places of Persuasion and Dissuasion*). Grymeston's *Miscellanea*, however, do not follow Bacon's practice of rigorously separating civil and religious concerns. The reasons for this (supposing that she had in mind his example) may reflect her culturally 'marked' status as a Catholic woman. Being thus doubly marginalised in English society, she knew that such a division between private belief and public conduct was theoretically as well as practically impossible: Catholicism was illegal (her cousin Robert Southwell had been executed as a priest in 1595), and women had little claim to free utterance except for those acts that could be controlled or mediated by male authority. Grymeston therefore had no real scope to be 'objective' when considering various social topics, again unlike Bacon's celebrated forensic explorations of 'purely human' knowledge. Nonetheless, given her work's popularity (four editions, as well as long passages copied in a contemporary commonplace book kept by Thomas Chaffyn), her essays mark significant historical contributions to this relatively new form before it became fully 'naturalised' as another characteristically male genre.

Editions:
Miscellanea, Meditations, Memoratives (1604). STC 12407, reel 1068. 2nd edn 1605–6, STC 12407.5, reel 1272. *The Female Spectator*, ed. Mary R. Mahl and Helene Koon (Bloomington, 1977, excerpts). *The Paradise of Women*, ed. Betty Travitsky (Westport, Conn., 1981, Epistle to Bernye Grymeston and brief excerpts). *English Women's Voices, 1540–1700*, ed. Charlotte F. Otten (Miami, 1992, excerpts).

ELIZABETH GRYMESTON

From *MISCELLANEA, MEDITATIONS, MEMORATIVES* (1604, 1605–6)

THE EPISTLE TO HER LOVING SON BERNYE GRYMESTON:

My dearest son, there is nothing so strong as the force of love, there is no love so forcible as the love of an affectionate mother to her natural child, there is no mother can either more affectionately show her nature or more naturally manifest her affection than in advising her children out of her own experience to eschew evil and incline them to do that which is good. Out of these resolutions, finding the liberty of this age to be such as that *quicquid libet licet* (so men keep themselves from criminal offences), and my mother's undeserved wrath so virulent as that I have neither power to resist it nor patience to endure it but must yield to this languishing consumption to which it hath brought me, I resolved to break the barren soil of my fruitless brain to dictate something for thy direction. The rather for that as I am now a dead woman among the living (so stand I doubtful of thy father's life, which albeit God hath preserved from eight several sinister assaults by which it hath been sought, yet for that I see that *quem saepe transit casus, aliquando invenit*), I leave thee this portable *veni mecum* for thy counsellor, in which thou mayest see the true portraiture of thy mother's mind, and find something either to resolve thee in thy doubts or comfort thee in thy distress, hoping that, being my last speeches, they will be better kept in the

6–7. *quicquid ... licet*: whatever pleases is lawful

7–8. *mother's ... virulent*: possibly owing to a family disagreement over the will of Grymeston's father, Martin Bernye. In 1586 he left his property to his wife Margaret (Flint) for her lifetime and thereafter to his heirs. But in 1595 he altered this arrangement, settling his estate after his own death and his wife's on Elizabeth and her husband Christopher Grymeston, thereby cutting out the direct family heir, Thomas, son of his deceased eldest son Francis (Hughey and Hereford 1934: 74).

13. *eight ... assaults*: the Grymestons were Catholics, and the 'assaults' may be related to Christopher's religious activism. He attended Caius College, Cambridge, known for its Catholic sympathies, and became a fellow there (which may have obliged him to keep his marriage secret, since fellows were required to be bachelors; Hughey and Hereford 1934: 80–1).

14–15. *quem ... invenit*: whom mischance often passes over, it comes upon now and again

15. *veni mecum*: come with me: a book of ready reference (like *vade-mecum*)

conservance of thy memory, which I desire thou wilt make a register of heavenly meditations.

For albeit if thou provest learned (as my trust is thou wilt, for that without learning, man is but as an immortal beast) thou mayest happily think that if every philosopher fetched his sentence, these leaves would be left without lines. Yet remember withal that, as it is the best coin that is of greatest value in fewest pieces, so is it not the worst book that hath most matter in least words:

> The gravest wits, that most grave works expect,
> The quality, not quantity, respect.

And the spider's web is neither the better because woven out of his own breast, nor the bee's honey the worse for that gathered out of many flowers; neither could I ever brook to set down that haltingly in my broken style which I found better expressed by a graver author:

> God send thee, too, to be a wit's chameleon
> That any author's colour can put on.

I have prayed for thee that thou mightest be fortunate in two hours of thy lifetime: in the hour of thy marriage, and at the hour of thy death. Marry in thine own rank, and seek especially in it thy contentment and preferment. Let her neither be so beautiful as that every liking eye shall level at her, nor yet so brown as to bring thee to a loathed bed. Defer not

19. *conservance*: keeping (not in *OED*, but related to *conservancy*)
22. *immortal beast*: i.e. in God's image only in terms of possessing a soul but in no other faculties
23. *fetched ... sentence*: called back the words (I have borrowed)
leaves: sheets (for writing)
24. *withal*: at the same time
27–8. *The ... respect*: as Hughey and Hereford observe (1934: 84), all of Grymeston's quoted verse is derivative, most of it deriving with minor alterations from *England's Parnassus* (1600, though this passage apparently does not). Her Latin phrases are likewise mainly conventional classical tags, when they are not taken from the Vulgate (Latin Bible).
31. *brook*: bear
37–9. *Marry ... bed*: traditional advice. Compare Lord Burghley to his son Robert Cecil: 'If thy estate be good, match near home and at leisure ... Let her not be poor how generous soever, for a man can buy nothing in the market with gentility. Neither choose a base and uncomely creature altogether for wealth, for it will cause contempt in others and loathing in thee' (Wright 1962: 10).
38. *preferment*: advancement in family or social status
39. *level*: aim
brown: i.e. swarthy; considered by Elizabethans to be less attractive or fashionable than fair skin (e.g. Shakespeare sonnet 127: 'In the old age, black was not counted fair')

thy marriage till thou comest to be saluted with a 'God speed you sir', as a man going out of the world after forty, neither yet to the time of 'God keep you sir', whilst thou art in thy best strength after thirty; but marry in the time of 'You are welcome sir', when thou art coming into the world. For seldom shalt thou see a woman out of her own love to pull a rose that is full blown, deeming them always sweetest at the first opening of the bud. It was Phaedra her confession to Hippolytus, and it holds for truth with the most: *Thesei vultus amo illos priores quos tulit quondam iuvenis*. Let thy life be formal, that thy death may be fortunate, for he seldom dies well that liveth ill. To this purpose, as thou hast within thee reason as thy counsellor to persuade or dissuade thee, and thy will as an absolute prince with a *fiat vel evitetur* (with a 'Let it be done or neglected'), yet make thy conscience thy *censor morum* and chief commander in thy little world. Let it call reason to account whether she have subjected herself against reason to sensual appetites. Let thy will be censured whether her desires have been chaste or, as a harlot, she have lusted after her own delights. Let thy thoughts be examined. If they be good, they are of the spirit (quench not the spirit); if bad, forbid them entrance, for once admitted, they straightways fortify and are expelled with more difficulty than not admitted:

Crush the serpent in the head,
Break ill eggs ere they be hatched.
Kill bad chickens in the tread,
Fledge, they hardly can be catched.
In the rising, stifle ill,
Lest it grow against thy will.

40. *saluted*: greeted
41. *going*: on the way
43. *when … world*: i.e. late teens or twenties
44–5. *woman … bud*: interesting reversal of conventional gender roles: the female actively chooses according to appearance, while the male is passive. Roses traditionally represent virginity.
45. *full blown*: fully bloomed
47. *Thesei … iuvenis*: I still love those looks in Theseus which as a young man he bestowed on me
48. *formal*: regular and proper
52. *censor morum*: judge of customs, habits. In ancient Rome the *censor morum* was an official charged with maintaining public manners and morals.
53–4. *reason … will*: gendered feminine as in Latin
58. *fortify*: grow strong
59–64. *Crush … will*: verbatim from Robert Southwell's 'Loss in Delays' in his *Peter's Complaint* (1595; ed. McDonald and Brown, Oxford 1967, p. 59)
59. *serpent*: snake, referring to Genesis 3.14–15
62. *fledge*: having grown up

For evil thoughts are the devil's harbingers; he never resteth but where they provide his entertainment. These are those little ones whose brains thou must dash out against the rock of true judgement, for

As a false lover that thick snares hath laid
T'entrap the honour of a fair young maid,
(When she, though little, listening ear affords
To his sweet, courting, deep-affected words,
Feels some assuaging of his freezing flame)
And soothes himself with hope to gain his game,
And rapt with joy, upon this point persists:
That parleying city never long resists;
Even so the serpent that doth counterfeit
A guileful call t'allure us to his net,
Perceiving us his flattering gloze digest,
He prosecutes, and jocund doth not rest
Till he have tried foot, hand, and head, and all,
Upon the breach of this new-battered wall.

I could be content to dwell with thee in this argument, but I must confine myself to the limits of an epistle, *quae non debet implere sinistram manum*. To which rule I do the more willingly submit myself for that the discourses following are motives to the same effect, which I pray thee, use to peruse even in that my affectionate love which, diffused amongst nine children which God did lend me, is now united in thee, whom God hath only left for my comfort. And because God hath endued thee with so violent a spirit, as that *quicquid vis valde vis*, therefore by so much the more it behoveth thee to deliberate what thou undertakest; to which purpose my desire is that thou mightest be seasoned with these precepts in thy youth, that the practice of thy age may have a taste of them. And because that it

66–7. *little ... judgement*: 'Blessed is he that shall hold, and shall dash thy [Babylon's] little ones against the rock' (Psalm 137.9, Douay 1609)

68–81. *As ... wall*: Joshuah Sylvester, 'The Imposture' (*England's Parnassus*, p. 64)

69. *maid*: again, Grymeston's excerpt places her son in the passive position conventionally assigned to women

72. *assuaging*: abating
freezing flame: oxymoron typical of Petrarchan poetry, signifying a lover's volatile emotional state

79. *prosecutes*: pursues (to a conclusion)

83–4. *quae ... manum*: which is not bound to engage the left hand (i.e. a letter should be short enough to occupy only one sheet and the right hand, rather than – in classical times – a longer scroll also requiring the use of the left. I am indebted to Dr W.G. Cooke for this explanation).

86–7. *nine ... thee*: i.e. you are the only survivor of my nine children

89. *quicquid ... vis*: whatever you desire, you desire greatly

is incident to quick spirits to commit rash attempts, as ever the love of a mother may challenge the performance of her demand of a dutiful child, be a bridle to thyself to restrain thee from doing that which indeed thou mayest do, that thou mayest the better forbear that which in truth thou oughtest not to do. For *haud cito progreditur ad maiora peccata, qui parva reformidat*: he seldomest commits deadly sin that makes a conscience of a venial scandal.

Thou seest my love hath carried me beyond the list I resolved on, and my aching head and trembling hand have rather a will to offer than ability to afford further discourse. Wherefore with as many good wishes to thee as goodwill can measure, I abruptly end, desiring God to bless thee with sorrow for thy sins, thankfulness for his benefits, fear of his judgements, love of his mercies, mindfulness of his presence; that living in his fear, thou mayest die in his favour, rest in his peace, rise in his power, remain in his glory for ever and ever.

Thine assured loving mother,
Elizabeth Grymeston.
En ma foi je souffre tout

*TOTA VITA, DIES UNUS**
CHAPTER 1
A SHORT LINE HOW TO LEVEL YOUR LIFE

When thou risest, let thy thoughts ascend, that grace may descend. And if thou canst not weep for thy sins, then weep because thou canst not weep.

Remember that prayer is the wing wherewith thy soul flieth to heaven, and meditation the eye wherewith we see God, and repentance the *supersedeas* that dischargeth all bond of sin.

Let thy sacrifice be an innocent heart. Offer it daily at set hours with that devotion that well it may show thou both knowest and acknowledgest his greatness before whom thou art. So carry thyself as worthy of his presence.

93. *incident*: natural

97–8. *haud ... reformidat*: whoever shuns venial sins avoids rushing into mortal ones

100. *list*: limit (i.e. length appropriate to an epistle)

103. *abruptly*: i.e. without a drawn-out or elegant conclusion

110. *En ... tout*: I suffer everything for my faith. The same tag appears on the flyleaf of a manuscript miscellany once belonging to Elizabeth Grymeston's husband (Hughey and Hereford 1934: 82).

* *Tota ... unus*: a whole life in one day

1. *grace*: divine grace

2. *not weep*: i.e. not be moved to repent

4. *supersedeas*: you shall desist: the name of a common legal writ that stays a judge's proceedings

Where thou owest, pay duty. Where thou findest, return courtesy. Where thou art known, deserve love. Desire the best. Disdain none but evil company. Grieve, but be not angry at discourtesies. Redress but revenge no wrongs. Yet so remember pity as you forget not decency.

Let your attire be such as may satisfy a curious eye, and yet bear witness of a sober mind.

Arm yourself with that modesty that may silence that untemperate tongue, and control that unchaste eye, that shall aim at passion.

Be mindful of things past, careful of things present, provident of things to come.

Go as you would be met. Sit as you would be found. Speak as you would be heard. And when you go to bed, read over the carriage of yourself that day. Reform that is amiss, and give God thanks for that which is orderly, and so commit thyself to him that keeps thee.

Teach me, O Lord, to number my days and to
order my life after this thy direction.

CHAPTER 3
A PATHETICAL* SPEECH OF THE PERSON OF DIVES, IN THE TORMENTS OF HELL

O death, how sudden was thy arrest unto me! How unexpected! While my body was strong, while my entrails were full of fat and my bones were watered with marrow, while I had rest in my substance, and peace in my riches, in one night my soul was taken from me and all my joy was turned into mourning:

Like as the sacred ox that careless stands
With gilded horns and flowery garlands crowned,

13. *curious*: particular, careful

15. *untemperate*: intemperate

17–18. *Be … come*: from Robert Southwell's *Epistle … unto his Father* (1595; ed. N.P. Brown, Charlottesville 1973, p.8)

20. *carriage*: behaviour, conduct

* *pathetical*: passionate; moving

Dives: the unnamed man who is described as 'rich' in the Vulgate ('*Homo quidam erat dives …*', Luke 16.19–31) and is suffering in hell. A beggar at his gate named Lazarus had died and gone to heaven, where Dives begged to him to relieve his pains. But Abraham refused Dives's request, pointing out that he had once lived in material comfort, ignoring Lazarus, and that the gulf between them is now unbridgeable.

1. *arrest*: seizure (of my life)

6–14. *Like … shore*: Spenser's *The Faerie Queene* (III.4.17.1–8) taken from *England's Parnassus* (pp. 453–4)

6. *sacred*: sacrificial

Proud of his dying honour and dear bands,
Whilst theatres fume with frankincense around:
All suddenly with mortal blow astoned
Doth grovelling fall, and with his steaming gore
Distain the pillars and the holy ground,
And the fair flowers that decked him afore;
So down I fell on wordless precious shore.

I saw my friends forsake me in a moment. I felt how hard a thing it was to sever two such old acquaintances as my soul and body. I wanted no view of the vanities wherein I had delighted. On the one side hung a register of my sins committed, on the other side lay a catalogue of good deeds omitted. Within me boiled my conscience confessing and accusing me; before me stood the judgements of God denounced against sin, so mustered in rank, as I might well perceive my dangers were certain, and destruction imminent. In this ecstacy, while I desired but one hour's delay, I was carried with a motion *torrenti simili*, as swift as the torrent, before the tribunal seat of God:

Under whose feet, subjected to his grace,
Sat Nature, Fortune, Motion, Time, and Place.

To this tribunal seat attended me my evil works, where Christ, showing himself, laid open unto me the benefits he had bestowed upon me, the rewards he promised me, the torments he suffered for me. All which the devil confessing, concluded me to be his, for that though he never loved me, yet I served him; though he never gratified me, yet I obeyed him; without wooing he won me, performing what he suggested, embracing what he preferred, affecting everything he cast in my way; all which my conscience acknowledging censured me to this bottomless depth, to this profound lake, to this sink of the world, whither all the afflictions and unpleasant things in the world drain and unite themselves to take revenge of sin:

A deadly gulf where naught but rubbish grows,
Which up in th'air such stinking vapour throws,

9. *theatres*: open-air amphitheatre for viewing spectacles. *Faerie Queene* reads 'th'altars'.
10. *astoned*: stunned
12. *Distain*: stain
14. *wordless ... shore*: the sense is odd because Grymeston has altered the last line of Spenser's original ('So fell proud *Marinell* upon the pretious shore')
16. *wanted*: lacked
20. *denounced*: proclaimed
25–6. *Under ... Place*: Tasso, *Clorinda*, trans. Edward Fairfax (*England's Parnassus*, p. 115)
33. *affecting*: inclining eagerly towards
37–40. *A ... arise*: Thomas Sackville, Induction, *Mirror for Magistrates* (*England's Parnassus*, p. 133)

That over there may fly no bird but dies,
Choked with the pestilent savours that arise.

To this chaos of confusion, to this well of perdition wherein I am coarcted, to this burning lake of fire and brimstone wherein I lie burning but not consuming, lamenting but not pitied; where I vomit out the riches which I devoured, in pain without ease, in torture without intermission; where my lascivious eyes are afflicted with most ugly and fearful sights of grisly devils. My ears that once were delicate are laden now with the hideous noise of damned spirits. My nose that once was dainty is cloyed with the stink of unsupportable filth. My taste that sometimes was curious and surfeited with plenty is now tormented with want. My imagination is vexed with apprehension of pains present, my memory grieved with the loss of pleasures past, my understanding affected with the consideration of felicity lost and misery found. Thus comparing senses' pleasure with incumbent joy, I find my joys abortive, perished ere they bud, my pains everlasting, during beyond eternity:

Your fond preferments are but children's toys,
And as a shadow all your pleasures pass.
As years increase, so waning are your joys,
Your bliss is brittle, like a broken glass,
Or as a tale of that which never was.

Wherefore, as one past cure, dejected beyond hope of redemption into endless perdition (rather condoling my misfortune than expostulating my mishap whereof myself was author), I call to you, the glory of your age, the meat of time, who, proud in your errors, tread the path of worldly pleasures wherein I was impathed: *Frustra, O frustra haec alio properanti*:

What in this life we have or can desire
Hath time of growth and moment of retire;

41. *coarcted*: confined
47. *dainty*: fastidious
48. *surfeited*: overfed, cloyed
52. *incumbent*: imagined, approaching
53. *during*: enduring
55–9. *Your ... was*: Michael Drayton (*England's Parnassus,* p. 230). The original has 'our' instead of 'your', and the last two lines read 'And beauty crazed, like a broken glass, / A pretty tale of that which never was'.
63. *meat of time*: food for (devouring) time; or perhaps an error for 'mate'
64. *impathed*: placed (not in *OED*)
Frustra ... properanti: paraphrase of Horace: *Frustra vitium vitaveris illud si te alio pravum detor seris*: 'It is vain for you to shun one vice, if in your depravity you rush into another'
65–6. *What ... retire*: Thomas Lodge (*England's Parnassus*, p. 168). retire = withdrawal

So feeble is man's state as sure it will not stand,
Till it disordered be from earthly band.

It was a condition annexed to our creation: *Intrasti ut exires*; thou wert born to die. Nothing more sure than thy dissolution; no time more uncertain than thy time of separation. Be always ready to prevent that enemy that is always in readiness to take advantage. *Qui non vult in vita praevidere mortem, non potest in morte videre vitam.* Who while he lives will not prevent eternal death, shall never after death inherit eternal life:

Let every one do all the good he can,
For never cometh ill of doing well.
Though just reward it wants here, now and then,
Yet shame and evil death it doth expel....
Wretched is he that thinks by doing ill
His evil deeds long to conceal and hide,
For though the voice and tongues of men be still,
By fowls and beasts his sin shall be descried.
And God oft worketh by his secret will
That sin itself the sinner so doth guide,
That of his own accord, without request,
He makes his wicked doings manifest.
Shame follows sin never so closely done;
Shame always ends what wickedness begun.

Hoc est momentum temporis unde pendet aeternitas. The carriage of thyself in this life is the beam whereof thy welfare for ever dependeth. Defer not thy amendment:

67–8. *So ... band*: Spenser (*England's Parnassus*, p. 179 [= 169]). The original reads: 'So feeble is man's state, and life unsound, / That in assurance it may never stand, / Till it dissolved be ...' (= *Faerie Queene* II.xi.30.3–5).

68. *disordered ... band*: severed ... ties

69. *Intrasti ut exires*: you came in (to the world) so that you might go out

71. *prevent*: guard against, forestall

75–88. *Let ... begun*: identified by Hughey and Hereford (1934: 86) as an extract from Sir John Harington's translation of *Orlando Furioso* (*England's Parnassus*, pp. 120–1). The last two lines, however, paraphrase Daniel's *Complaint of Rosamund* (*England's Parnassus*, p. 265).

76–7. *For ... then*: the original reads: 'For seldom cometh harm of doing well, / Though just reward it wanteth now and then'

79–88. *Wretched ... begun*: Grymeston supplies the original passage in Italian (not reproduced here) from *Orlando Furioso* (in *England's Parnassus*) prior to this translation

89. *Hoc ... aeternitas*: from Cicero: *Tempus est quaedum aeternitatis*: 'Moments constitute eternity'
carriage: moral conduct

God is best when soonest wrought,
Lingering thoughts do come to naught.
O suffer not delay to steal the treasure of that day,
Whose smallest minute lost, no riches render may.

Turpe est eo statu vivere, in quo non statuas mori. In vain thou livest in that estate of life in which thou meanest not to die. Make, O make your salvation sure unto you by good works. Incline your heart to do good, for the reward thereof is infinite; for he is coming and cometh quickly, and brings his reward with him to distribute to everyone as he hath deserved, even according to his works. Omission and commission brought my confusion.

Cautior exemplo tu. Let my example provoke you to detest that wherein I took delight, lest you also come hither to be tormented not only with oppression of eternal punishment, but with omission of everlasting joys, which I admire now, *carendo, non fruendo*; which if I might redeem by suffering all the torments that either tyrants have invented or martyrs suffered; if with my tongue I might lick out the print of my feet out of the way of sinners; if with tears of blood and water I might purge my uncleanness to work my redemption: *ecce Domine paratum aegrum haberes in omnem medicinam*; behold, O Lord, thou shouldest have a patient fit for any cure. I would wring my drained eyes, *ut facile sentires paratum ad omne supplicium ipsum habitum orantis Christiani*. But since my glass is run and my sun set; since death hath overshadowed me and that there is no pleading after sentence; since that *sero ducit suspiria, qui non expectat remedium*; since my affecting what I should have desired is turned into a feeling of that I lost, *quia ex inferno nulla redemptio, quia poenarum nullus finis, suppliciorum nulla defectio*; because there is no end for my hell, nor satisfaction for my punishment; therefore to you I call, to you that careless live, that feel not with what sense I speak. Consider whence you came, where you are, and whither you go. You are parts of that God that created all things for you,

94–5. *O ... may*: Spenser, *Faerie Queene*, IV.9.14 (*England's Parnassus*, p. 55)

97–8. *Make ... works*: Grymeston probably intends the Catholic belief that good works contribute to achieving salvation

99–101. *he ... works*: alluding to Christ's second coming and last judgement (which traditionally was supposed to be imminent): 'Behold I come quickly, and my reward is with me, to render to every man according to his works (Revelation 22.12, Rheims 1582)

101. *commission*: act of committing (offences, crimes)

105. *carendo ... fruendo*: in deprivation, not enjoyment

111–12. *ut ... Christiani*: that you might easily perceive the very disposition of a praying Christian, ready for any entreaty

112. *glass*: hourglass

114. *sero ... remedium*: too late he draws breath who does not await (hope for) a remedy

116. *quia poenarum ... finis*: (unlike the Latin clauses before and after, not translated by Grymeston): because there is no end to my punishments

and you for himself. You live on the stage of the earth, *ubi spectaculum facti estis Deo, angelis, et hominibus*; where you are in the view of God, angels and men. And you are going, O look to your going, *non est vitae momentum sine motu ad mortem*; there is no moving of life without a motion to death. You go and are always going to make your appearance before the tribunal seat of God, where every man shall receive according to his works. *Qualis vita, finis ita: ut cecideris, ita eris.* As you fall, so he finds you; as he finds you, so he censures you; and as he censures you, so he leaves you for ever and ever. Wherefore, *Quia arbor ad eam partem moriens cadit, ad quam partem vivens ramos extenderat*; because as a tree falls that way it sways while it is in growing, if you desire to fall right, learn while you are in your growth to sway the right way. Judge yourselves that you be not judged, *ut sementem feceris, ita metes*. What you sow, that you reap, either a crown of glory, *quam nemo scit nisi qui accepit*, or a chaos of confusion, *in qua sempiternus horror habitat*, whose worth cannot be expressed but of him that enjoys it, or a mass of confusion in which eternal horror doth inhabit.

CHAPTER 7
*IUGUM MEUM SUAVE**

It is well observed by one that the rod of the root of Jesse flowered that the sweetness of the flower might mitigate the severity of the rod. The devil is never suffered to punish us farther than is for our benefit; for either he corrects us for our former offences or else to prevent our future infirmities. Neither is every one that spareth a friend, nor every one that striketh an enemy, but the words of a friend are better than the flatterings of a foe, and he that loves with austerity is better than he that kills with delicacy. It is the devil's common course to kill our soul while he flatters our fancy. For as the thief that cannot by open violence catch his booty seeketh by shrouding himself in valleys and bushes to take the travellers unprovided, so the devil,

127. *Qualis ... ita*: as the life (is), so is (its) ending
134. *quam ... accepit*: = 'whose worth ... enjoys it'
135. *in ... habitat*: = 'in which ... inhabit'

* *Iugum ...*: My yoke is easy (Matthew 11.30, Vulgate)
1. *one*: unidentified
Jesse: father of David and founder of the royal line from which Christ derived his human heritage (Isaiah 11.10). In Christian iconography Jesse appears as the root or at the base of a family tree whose branches extend to flowers representing Christ or the Virgin and child.
2–3. *rod ... suffered*: tree-shoot or branch (continuing the tree of Jesse image) ... allowed
4. *infirmities*: (moral) diseases
7. *delicacy*: sensual indulgence

when by open pursuit he cannot prevail, he coucheth himself in briars and shadows of worldly vanities, entrapping us before we prevent his trains. For albeit with a smooth flight and even wing he lessen himself into the clouds as an eagle delighted to view the sun, yet is he but a ravening kite, soaring in the air the better to see how to seize upon his prey. God borroweth not the Siren's voice when he would sting with a scorpion's tail, and when he bites with the tooth of a lion he useth not the tears of a crocodile. But as the husbandman lops his vine lest the juice should be spent in leaves, so (lest our minds should be employed in vain and superfluous pleasures) our wits, which without profit would be diffused, are by him kept in compass by tribulation. For where he purposeth to heal, he spareth not to lance. And if he see thou be fostered by the world thy natural nurse, he can anoint her teat with the bitterness of discontent to wean thee from her. For he that binds the frantic and awakes the lethargy is troublesome but friendly to both:

> If aught can touch us aught, affliction's looks
> Makes us to look into ourselves so near,
> Teach us to know ourselves beyond all books
> Or all the learned schools that ever were.
> This makes our senses quick and reason clear,
> Resolves our will and rectifies our thoughts;
> So do the winds and thunder cleanse the air,
> So lopped and pruned trees do flourish fair.

Be not discouraged, thou art a Christian, whose captain is a crucifix, whose standard the cross, whose armour patience, whose battle persecution, whose victory death. Whether God fostereth thee as a weakling, or exercise thee as one stronger, or check thee as one unruly, yet he tendereth

13. *lessen*: lift
14. *eagle ... sun*: proverbially, eagles could look into the sun without blinking
    kite: hawk-like bird of prey
16. *Siren's*: mythological monster in Homer's *Odyssey*, part woman, part bird, whose enchanted singing lured sailors to destruction
18. *juice*: sap
21. *heal ... lance*: i.e. a wound
22–3. *fostered ... thee*: alluding to the Nurse's bawdy speech in *Romeo and Juliet* 1.3.26–32
24. *binds ... frantic*: 'Go bind that man, for he is frantic too' (*Comedy of Errors* 4.4.113) = lunatic
    lethargy: lethargic or sleepy person (*OED* first citation 1634)
26. *aught ... aught*: anything ... in any way. Sir John Davies, 'Nosce Teipsum' (*England's Parnassus*, p. 8).
33. *lopped*: topped

all as his own children. Behold thy Saviour with his head full of thorns, his eyes full of tears, his ears full of blasphemies, his mouth full of gall, his body full of wounds, his heart full of sorrow. And blame him not if, ere thou find him, he give thee a sip of the chalice whereof he drunk so full a cup. Thy love must be great when his sorrow is more at thy ingratitude than at his own affliction, when he lost himself to win thee – a work without example, a grace beyond merit, a charity surpassing measure. Wherefore, whether he set thee to seek him in the poverty of the crib and manger, or in the agony of his bloody sweat in the garden, or in the midst of reproaches and false accusations before the tribunal, or in the torments of a shameful death, yet think thyself as deep in his favour for being tried by the torments of his passion as those that are called by the testimony of his glorious transfiguration.

ABSIT MIHI GLORIARI NISI IN CHRISTO *
CHAPTER 9
THAT AFFLICTION IS THE COAT OF A CHRISTIAN

If we be Christians, affliction is our coat and the cross our cognisance: *in hoc signo vinces*. Christ's clouts comfort not those that walk in side robes. The stable and manger are no refreshings to such as love the highest rooms

38–40. *Behold ... sorrow*: from Robert Southwell's *Mary Magdalene's Funeral Tears* (1591): 'she saw thee her only hope, hanging on a tree, with thy head full of thorns, thy eyes full of tears, thy ears full of blasphemies, thy mouth full of gall, thy whole person mangled and disfigured' (G3[v])

41. *chalice*: cup, alluding to Christ's ordeal in Gethsemane (see below l. 46): 'Father, if thou wilt, transfer this chalice from me. And being in an agony, he prayed the longer. And his sweat became as drops of blood trickling down upon the earth' (Luke 22.42–4, Rheims 1582)

43. *lost himself*: i.e. died

44. *charity*: 'divine love' as well as 'generosity'

45. *poverty ... manger*: i.e. the humble conditions of Christ's birth

46. *garden*: Gethsemane (see n. to l. 41 above)

47. *tribunal*: i.e. the high priests and Pontius Pilate

49. *transfiguration*: i.e. transformed human nature after the resurrection

* *Absit ... Christo*: Vulgate, Galatians 6.14: 'But God forbid that I should glory, saving in the cross of our Lord Jesus Christ' (Rheims 1582)

1. *cognisance*: badge

1–2. *in ... vinces*: by virtue of this sign you will overcome (sin). Eusebius's *Life of Constantine* reports that the Roman emperor Constantine (AD 280–337) saw a cross over the sun with this motto whilst preparing for the battle of Milvian bridge. That night Christ told him in a dream to paint crosses on his soldiers' shields.

2. *clouts*: ragged clothes
side robes: long robes (suggesting sumptuousness)

3. *highest rooms*: gathering-place of the high priests (Luke 20.46)

in the synagogue. Our ark lieth not *in papyrionibus* but *in praesepio*. If we be members of that head which was pricked with thorns, let the rest of the parts sympathise with it. Let the Mount Calvary be our school, the cross our pulpit, the crucifix our meditation, his wounds our letters, his lashes our commas, his nails our full points, his open side our book, and *scire Christum crucifixum* our whole lesson. By his nakedness, learn to clothe thee; by his crown of thorns, how to adorn thee; by his vinegar and gall, how to diet thee; by his praying for his murderers, how to revenge thee; by his hanging on the cross, how to repose thee. Here learn that death reviveth, sorrow solaceth, an eclipse enlighteneth; that out of the devourer there came meat, and out of the stronger issueth sweetness. And since our sins, like fierce Samson's, have murdered the lion of the tribe of Judah, let our repentant thoughts, like bees, suck at the flowers of his passion and make honey to delight ourselves and provoke others. Let us seek Christ not *inter cognatos et natos*, nor with the spouse in the Canticles *in lectulo meo quaesivi quem amavi*, nor with them in Hosea that look him *in gregibus et armentis*, but seek him with Moses in the desert, with Daniel in a fiery throne. His delight is to see Nineveh in sackcloth, Job on the dunghill. He expects a perfect demonstration of a serviceable mind, for an *Eamus et nos, ut moriamur cum illo*; for loss of felicity searcheth the force of affection. It is neither

4. *ark*: or basket among the reeds in which the baby Moses was found (Exodus 2.5), and thus representing deliverance and safety (recalling Noah's ark)
 in praesepio: in papyrus reeds but in the manger (i.e. Jesus, the New Testament type of Moses)

6. *sympathise*: respond in agreement

6–8. *Mount ... book*: as Fletcher and Sizemore observe (1981: 56), Grymeston uses material analogies linking the transcendent to the homely in ways often resembling the practice of later Metaphysical poets. Calvary = site of the crucifixion.

8. *points*: stops

8–9. *scire ... crucifixum*: to know Christ crucified (1 Corinthians 2.2)

11. *diet*: govern, regulate

14. *meat*: food (i.e. the spiritual sustenance Christ brings back after being 'devoured' by hell)

15. *Samson ... Judah*: Judges 14.5–8 in which Samson kills a lion bare-handed and finds honey in its carcass (a figure for the image in l. 16)

17–18. *inter ... natos*: among relations and family members

18–19. *in lectulo ... amavi*: 'In my little bed in the nights I have sought him, whom my soul loveth' (Song of Solomon 3.1, Douay 1609). W.G. Cooke points out to me that the Vulgate reads '*quem diligit anima mea*', 'whom my soul loveth', whereas Grymeston changes this to *amavi*, 'I have loved', substituting the more erotic *amare* for *diligere*.

19. *look*: search for
 in ... armentis: in flocks and herds (Hosea 5.6, Vulgate)

20. *Daniel ... throne*: Daniel 7.9

22–3. *Eamus ... illo*: Let us go also, that we may die with him (John 11.16, Vulgate)

prosperity that tries a friend nor adversity that concealeth an enemy. This is that true God, that chief life, in whom, by whom, and from whom all things do flow, from whom to revolt is to fall, to whom to return is to rise, in whom to stay is to stand sure, from whom to depart is to die, to whom to repair is to revive, in whom to dwell is to live; that God whom none loseth but deceived, none seeketh but admonished, none findeth but are cleansed. Whatever is not of God is not good. Give me thyself, and take all things else from me.

CHAPTER 17
OF WILFUL MURDER

As I entreated formerly of high treason, which was the sin of Adam, who thought by eating of an apple to have equalled himself with God, so now I will write of murder, which was the sin of Cain, who killed his brother Abel, which as it is the next in place, so it is the nearest in degree to the former.

For if we respect the majesty of God himself, what can be more odious unto him than to see his own image defaced in his own presence, or what can be more contemptuous than to destroy one in his view that is so dear unto him, as he hath numbered the hairs of his head, and suffers not a sparrow to fall on the ground before him without his providence? *Non sinet neglecte perire quod est, qui quod non fuit creavit ut esset ... deus totus occulus est: sic te gere tanquam illo inspiciente.*

If we regard the commandment of so great a commander, how can we break it more than, when he hath ordained that generations should succeed by propagation, for man to interrupt his course by taking away the means? If we look to the obedience due to our prince (who as he is God's deputy on earth, is to be respected accordingly) when his honour consists in the multitude of obedient hearts, what greater dishonour than to diminish the number?

23. *searcheth*: tests
28. *repair*: return
29. *deceived*: (those who are) deceived

1. *entreated formerly*: wrote about in ch. 16: 'That Majesty is the daughter of Honour and Reverence; Against Traitors'
3. *Cain ... Abel*: Genesis 4
4. *place*: sequence of the Genesis narrative
8–9. *numbered ... providence*: Matthew 10.29-31
9–11. *Non ... inspiciente*: 'He will not carelessly leave to perish what is, who created what was not that it might exist ... God is completely hidden; therefore bear yourself as if he were watching.' The ellipsis marks a Greek phrase in the original text that has been misprinted and is unreadable.

If we leave the light of religion and take a view with our natural eyes, what stirs her more to wrath than the sight of blood? What works her confusion more readily than discord? *Parum progrediuntur in bona via qui in obvios quosque arietant.*

If we survey the sin itself, it carries this note with it: that it is never kept secret. For anger, the harbinger of revenge, cannot change his livery but either shows himself by being pale, for fear he should not revenge, or else by being red, as inflamed with desire of revenge: *condemnat se nullo accusante, prodit se arguente nullo.*

Heu, quam difficile est, crimen non prodere vultu. A sin that hath always punishment attendant on her, *cui crimen in pectore ei Nemesis a tergo, sequitur homicidas ultor a tergo deus.* And no marvel, for the very blood that issues out of the wounds of the murdered calls to heaven for vengeance, and the very soul that by that means is set at liberty, ceaseth not to cry and sound in the ears of our God, 'How long wilt thou, O Lord, defer thy judgement, and stay revenge against them that murdered us?' The same spirit that testifieth this, the same spirit saw it, and saith, *Vidi spiritus interfectorum clamantes ad dominum, usque quo domine non das iudicium et vindicas sanguinem nostrum de interfectoribus nostris.*

This brought in that *lex tallionis animam pro anima, occulum pro occulo*, and that old law, *homicida quod fecit idem expectat*, both which are warranted by that of Peter: *Qui gladio ferit, gladio peribit.*

Now in divinity, as there is *homicidium manuale* (of which I have

21–2. *Parum ... arietant*: They make too little progress in the good way who run into all the obstacles (they meet)

26–7. *condemnat ... nullo*: he condemns himself when nobody is accusing him, he gives himself up when nobody is charging him

28. *Heu ... vultu*: Alas, how hard it is not to betray a crime by (the appearance) of one's countenance

29–30. *cui ... deus*: to whom a crime (is) in the breast, to him Nemesis (is right) behind; God (the) avenger follows murders from behind

33–7. *How ... nostris*: loose rendering of the Vulgate version of Revelation 6.9–10: 'I saw under the altar the souls of them that were slain for the word of God, and for the testimony which they had. And they cried with a loud voice, saying, How long Lord, holy and true, judgest thou not and revengest thou not our blood of them that dwell on the earth?' (Rheims 1582)

38–9. *lex ... occulo*: Vulgate, Deuteronomy 19.21: law of retaliation: 'life shall go for life, eye for eye'

39. *homicida ... expectat*: Vulgate, Numbers 35.18–19: 'If he cast a stone, and he that is strooken die, he shall be punished in like manner' (Douay 1609)

40. *Qui ... peribit*: Vulgate, Matthew 26.52: 'For all that take the sword, shall perish with the sword'; Jesus addressing Peter, who cut off the ear of the high priest's servant (Rheims 1582)

41. *homicidium manuale*: physical murder

spoken), so is there also *homicidium linguae*, and that is committed either by bearing false witness in trial of causes, or by detracting and taking away one's good name. And in this sense the detractors' tongues are called by the Fathers *dentes, a demendo, quia corrodunt hominum aestimationem, quis potest maligni dentes vitare* (Augustine, *Soliloquies*).

A magistrate, though he be God's deputy here on earth, yet he is no Cardiagnostes to search the corners of the heart. He must judge *secundum allegata et probata*. As things appear upon him, so must he deem them. The means he hath to search the truth is by oath, which is *vinculum animae*, a course warranted by Abraham's example (Genesis 24) and out of the word itself, which is *hiphill* in Hebrew, in Greek *orcos*. So that not only the body but *anima* also *est potestatibus subiecta* (Romans 13). For *ut corpus traditur carceri ne quo aufugeat, sic anima traditur iureiurando ne quo subter-fugeat*. Now if the deponent will swear amiss, he calls God to witness a falsehood; he deceives the judge (who is God's deputy) and murders the cause of the poor plaintiff, lamenting his cause so murdered by false witness. And then, having the rule of nature before his face, *quod tibi fieri nolis, alteri ne feceris*, it will manifest unto him what an execrable thing it is to spill either the blood, fame, or fortune of the innocent, in which three consists the whole discourse of wilful murder.

42. *homicidium linguae*: verbal murder

45–6. *dentes ... vitare*: teeth (are so called) from going down, because they eat away at persons' worth; who can avoid the teeth of an evil man? (this passage does not appear to derive from Augustine's *Soliloquies*, despite Grymeston's attribution)

48. *Cardiagnostes*: one who knows the heart (*OED* first citation 1652, cardiognostic 1640)

48–9. *secundum ... probata*: in accordance with the allegations and the (legal) proofs

49–50. *him ... he hath*: the accused ... the judge

50. *vinculum animae*: bond of the soul

51. *Abraham's example*: in Genesis 24.2ff, Abraham makes his servant swear not to seek a Canaanite wife for his son Isaac

53. *anima ... subiecta*: Vulgate, Romans 13.1: 'Let every soul be subject to higher powers; (for there is no power but of God)' (Rheims 1582)

53–5. *ut ... subter-fugeat*: as the body is delivered up to prison (so) that it may not escape by any route, so the soul is bound by an oath (so) that it may not in any way evade (telling the truth)

58–9. *quod ... feceris*: do not do to another what you do not wish done to you

DOROTHY LEIGH (?–1616)

FROM *THE MOTHER'S BLESSING* (1616)

Introduction

Like Elizabeth Jocelin and Elizabeth Grymeston, Dorothy Leigh justifies writing her *Mother's Blessing* by invoking the uniquely permissive circumstances of approaching death, in which she may set aside normal prohibitions on female public speech. She 'forgets' the 'usual custom of women' – instructing her own children orally within the confines of her husband's household – and instead composes a written legacy of (largely conventional) religious advice. Leigh's view of herself as a writer, however, differs markedly from that of Jocelin. She is burdened with far less of the latter's sense of shame on account of her sex and makes no pretence about writing exclusively for her immediate family; for although her counsel is intended above all for her three sons, the book itself is aimed at parents, as the full title indicates:

> The Mother's Blessing, or The Godly Counsel of a gentlewoman not long since deceased, left behind her for her children, containing many good exhortations and godly admonitions, profitable for all parents to leave as a legacy to their children, but especially for those who, by reason of their young years, stand most in need of instruction.

Leigh thus offers her maternal experience as a public service, and this leads to greater self-consciousness than Jocelin in her strategies for addressing an audience.

The reader's reception of the main work, for example, is carefully prepared for by an introductory poem, 'Counsel to my Children' (a little allegory contrasting the 'laborous bee' who works industriously 'to do her Country good' with the 'Idle Bee' whose laziness imperils the community) and by two dedications (not reproduced here). In the first of these dedications Leigh seeks public support for her project and protection from potential critics from Princess Elizabeth, eldest daughter of James I and Anne of Denmark. Elizabeth was a likely patron because of her strong Protestant beliefs and marriage to the equally zealous Prince-Elector Palatine, Frederick V, in 1613. She became a focus for promoting more vigorous Protestant policies abroad, in opposition to the wishes of James I who desired peaceful relations with Catholic powers. By appealing to Elizabeth, Leigh draws attention to the fact that her work seeks to change public attitudes and that her own moderately Puritan views dissent from official government and church policies. The fact that her volume was reissued nineteen times between 1616 and 1640 perhaps indicates the reach of that dissent, as well as the general approval of her parental advice. Leigh also relates her writing to a wider cultural context in the magnificent periodic sentence that opens her first chapter, in which she denounces a broad range of social and domestic abuses. Enumerating these announces her determination to broaden the scope of legitimate discussion open to a female author (Beilin 1987: 280) and to emphasise the national consequences of individual approaches to child-rearing and education. She makes the same point in Chapter 2, urging parents to teach their children to read from an early age, since reading manifests a will to serve God, 'their king and country'.

Leigh's title-page and her second dedication to her sons reveal that *The Mother's Blessing* fulfils a charge by her late husband to instruct their children in godly knowledge and 'temporal good'. She thereby justifies her work as the dutiful fulfilment of her husband's will, an imperative that overrides or at least mitigates the threat of censure for circulating her ideas. Leigh also argues the necessity of publishing on the grounds of treating her sons equally, for if she were to leave her counsel 'with the eldest, it is thus likely the youngest should have but little part in it'. Though her concern is an intellectual and moral legacy rather than a financial one, and no daughters are involved, Leigh ignores the custom of primogeniture which privileges eldest sons as the main inheritors of dynastic and economic power. As Wendy Wall observes, the cultural subtext of Leigh's and other women's spiritual legacies to their children is their actual *inability* to bequeath material wealth (a situation that several contemporary women contested legally; see Clifford p. 249ff., Mildmay, p. 222ff.): 'In these mothers' "wills," we see the way in which the form of the last testament allowed women to participate in generational transmission as well as affording them an arena in which the legal/economic power denied by the culture could be simulated.' The effect was to substitute 'proprietorship in another realm' (1991: 45–6) in which a female writer's 'power of bestowal' could serve to constitute herself as an authoritative subject – or 'public monument', to use Thomas Goad's terms when describing Elizabeth Jocelin.

Other interesting differences between Leigh and Jocelin emerge in several chapters of the main work selected here. Chapter 11 displays their contrasting approaches to child-rearing. Whereas Jocelin approves of the need for beatings to suppress bad behaviour, Leigh, while being equally concerned about moral formation, recommends patience and gentleness. We have already noted how Leigh links reading to social and patriotic duties. She likewise does not place any restrictions on what may be read (although the Bible is first in priority), nor does she differentiate between sexes in terms of a 'curriculum' or set limitations on a child's choice of vocation. Elsewhere in her book, when she is addressing her sons directly, she expresses the hope that one of them may become a clergyman, but when speaking here about 'all [readers'] children' she is open-minded. Her preference is that they may advance to 'the schools of learning' if they are gifted, but if this is not practicable they should at least be taught to read the Bible (the minimum educational standard for English Protestants) and fit themselves to some 'trade of life'.

Chapters 12 and 13 reinterpret contemporary ideas about the so-called companionate marriage from a female viewpoint. Though Leigh upholds traditional ideas about woman being the 'weaker vessel', she turns the dominant focus of marriage away from female obedience (which male preachers habitually emphasised) to male reciprocity (which they downplayed). Leigh tries to bring the ideal of mutuality, which Protestant ideology conceded in theory, into line with actual social practice, in which male authority regularly operated as if it was absolute rather than contingent (Lucas 1990: 229). She forcefully urges her sons to love their wives, and never to forget that the latter enter marriage as real persons with meaningful histories, highly valued networks of friends, and dignity of feelings which must not be abrogated by their change in status. She also anticipates Mary Wollstonecraft's famous complaint about wives being no better than 'upper-servants', and, by laying stress on woman's goodness, challenges deep-rooted cultural assumptions about inherent female depravity. In short, Leigh tries to shift the dominant marital paradigm away from conjugal obedience to love and respect. Given her emphasis on scripture, it seems likely that what lies behind this reorientation is a re-reading of one of the key biblical passages bearing on marital relationships, Ephesians 5 (which Leigh cites). This is the chapter containing Paul's infamous injunction that wives should submit themselves to their husbands. But what male commentators regularly passed over was the paramount responsibility of the husband to love his wife. Paul repeats this command three times, adding that the man's behaviour must live up to the standard of Christ's love for his Church. The social issue of male family headship is therefore 'radically questioned' by the alternative moral paradigm of individual self-giving love (Fiorenza 1992: 269–70). By emphasising this undervalued aspect of Paul's teaching, Leigh challenges Protestant patriarchy to live up to its word (and the Word) on the central issue of partnership in marriage.

Leigh extends her theme of respecting the value of individual personhood in the next chapter on servants. Here she portrays the Protestant family as an interdependent spiritual and social unit, whose connectedness depends fundamentally on being able to read, above all the Bible. Again this contrasts with Jocelin's reluctance to endorse literacy without hedges and qualifications. By refusing to see it as a threat to social order and instead welcoming its transformative power, Leigh anticipates what will become the historical nexus of universal literacy and evangelism, ultimately mythologised into a 'civilising' destiny that in later centuries would underwrite the expansion of British imperial power.

Editions:
The Mother's Blessing (1616). STC 15402, reel 1455. *The Paradise of Women*, ed. Betty Travitsky (Westport, Conn., 1981, brief excerpts). *English Women's Voices, 1540–1700*, ed. Charlotte F. Otten (Miami, 1992, excerpts).

DOROTHY LEIGH

FROM *THE MOTHER'S BLESSING, OR THE GODLY COUNSEL OF A GENTLEWOMAN, NOT LONG SINCE DECEASED, LEFT BEHIND HER FOR HER CHILDREN*

(1616)

CHAPTER 1
THE OCCASION OF WRITING THIS BOOK WAS THE CONSIDERATION OF THE CARE OF PARENTS FOR THEIR CHILDREN

My children, when I did truly weigh, rightly consider, and perfectly see the great care, labour, travail, and continual study which parents take to enrich their children – some wearing their bodies with labour, some breaking their sleeps with care, some sparing from their own bellies, and many hazarding their souls, some by bribery, some by simony, others by perjury, and a multitude by usury, some stealing on the sea, others begging by land portions from every poor man, not caring if the whole commonwealth be impoverished so their children be enriched (for themselves they can be content with meat, drink, and cloth, so that their children by their means may be made rich, always abusing this portion of scripture: 'he that provideth not for his own family, is worse than an infidel'), ever seeking for the temporal things of this world and forgetting those things which be eternal – when I considered these things, I say I thought good (being not desirous to enrich you with transitory goods) to exhort and desire you to follow the counsel of Christ: 'First seek the kingdom of God and his righteousness, and then all these things shall be administered unto you.'

2. *travail*: labour of childbirth; tiring travel

5. *simony*: trafficking in church offices or spiritual benefits

6–8. *begging ... enriched*: agricultural enclosure, a cause of great rural misery in the sixteenth and seventeenth centuries. Because wool was more profitable than grain, landowners converted common (or sometimes privately owned) arable land into sheep pasture, which meant it could no longer be farmed by local tenants. The result was widespread depopulation and impoverishment of the countryside, accompanied by frequent protests and rioting.

10–11. *he ... infidel*: 1 Timothy 5.8 (scriptural references derive from the original edition unless otherwise noted)

15–16. *First ... you*: Matthew 6.33. Leigh's 'administered' indicates she is using the Geneva Bible (1560) rather than the Authorised Version (1611) which reads 'added'.

CHAPTER 2
THE FIRST CAUSE OF WRITING IS A MOTHERLY AFFECTION

But lest you should marvel, my children, why I do not, according to the usual custom of women, exhort you by word and admonitions rather than by writing (a thing so unusual among us, and especially in such a time when there be so many godly books in the world that they mould in some men's studies while their masters are marred because they will not meditate upon them, as many men's garments moth-eat in their chests while their Christian brethren quake with cold in the street for want of covering), know therefore that it was the motherly affection that I bare unto you all which made me now (as it often hath done heretofore) forget myself in regard of you. Neither care I what you or any shall think of me if among many words I may write but one sentence which may make you labour for the spiritual food of the soul, which must be gathered every day out of the word, as the children of Israel gathered manna in the wilderness. By the which you may see it is a labour. But what labour? A pleasant labour, a profitable labour, a labour without the which the soul cannot live. For as the children of Israel must needs starve except they gathered every day in the wilderness and fed of it, so must your souls, except you gather the spiritual manna out of the word every day and feed of it continually.... Whereas if you desire any food for your souls that is not in the written word of God, your souls die with it even in your hearts and mouths. Even as they that desired other food, died with it in their mouths, were it never so dainty, so shall you, and there is no recovery for you.

CHAPTER 11
CHILDREN TO BE TAUGHT BETIMES AND BROUGHT UP GENTLY

I am further also to entreat you that all your children may be taught to read, beginning at four years old or before. And let them learn till ten, in which

2. *word ... admonitions*: i.e. orally, in private conversation

6. *moth-eat*: are moth-eaten

7–9. *know ... you*: Leigh stresses her nurturing instincts, which empower her to speak (Wall 1993: 289)

12. *word*: Bible

13. *children ... wilderness*: Exodus 16 (not cited in the original); manna = the miraculous substance with which God fed the Israelites in the wilderness

20–1. *Even ... mouths*: Numbers 11.3; also: '[The Israelites] were not turned from their lust, but the meat was yet in their mouths, When the wrath of God came even upon them' (Psalm 78.30–1)

2. *ten*: by which age (male) children would enter public 'schools of learning' (below l. 11). If girls were to receive further formal education, they would be tutored at home.

time they are not able to do any good in the commonwealth but to learn how to serve God, their king and country, by reading. And I desire, entreat, and earnestly beseech you and every one of you that you will have your children brought up with much gentleness and patience. What disposition so ever they be of, gentleness will soonest bring them to virtue. For frowardness and curstness doth harden the heart of a child and maketh him weary of virtue. Among the froward thou shalt learn frowardness. Let them therefore be gently used and always kept from idleness, and bring them up in the schools of learning, if you be able and they fit for it. If they will not be scholars, yet I hope they will be able by God's grace to read the Bible, the law of God, and to be brought to some good vocation or calling of life. Solomon saith, 'Teach a child in his youth the trade of his life, and he will not forget it nor depart from it when he is old'.

CHAPTER 12
CHOICE OF WIVES

Now for your wives the Lord direct you, for I cannot tell you what is best to be done. Our Lord saith, 'First seek the kingdom of God and his righteousness, and all things else shall be ministered unto you'. First you must seek a godly wife, that she may be a help to you in godliness; for God said, 'It is not good for man to be alone, let him have a helper meet for him'. And she cannot be meet for him except she be truly godly; for God counteth that the man is alone still if his wife be not godly....

'Be not unequally yoked' saith the Holy Ghost. It is indeed very unequal for the godly and ungodly to be united together, that their hearts must be both as one, which can never be joined in the fear of God and faith of Christ. Love not the ungodly. Marry with none except you love her, and be not changeable in your love. Let nothing, after you have made your choice, remove your love from her; for it is an ungodly and very foolish thing of a man to mislike his own choice, especially since God hath given a man much choice among the godly; and it was a great cause that moved God to command his [followers] to marry with the godly, that there might be a continual agreement between them.

7. *frowardness*: irascibility, unreasonable irritability
8. *curstness*: perversity, viciousness
14–15. *Teach ... old*: Proverbs 22.6
1–2. *for ... done*: i.e. in terms of a personal choice
2–3. *First ... you*: Matthew 6.33 (not marginally noted; but see Chapter 1, ll. 15–16)
5. *It ... him*: Genesis 2.18
8. *Be ... yoked*: 2 Corinthians 6.14
9. *must*: could
16. *followers*: a noun has been omitted in the original

CHAPTER 13
IT IS GREAT FOLLY FOR A MAN TO MISLIKE HIS OWN CHOICE

Methinks I never saw a man show a more senseless simplicity than in misliking his own choice, when God hath given a man almost a world of women to choose him a wife in. If a man hath not wit enough to choose him one whom he can love to the end, yet methinks he should have discretion to cover his own folly. But if he want discretion, methinks he should have policy, which never fails a man to dissemble his own simplicity in this case. If he want wit, discretion, and policy, he is unfit to marry any woman. Do not a woman that wrong as to take her from her friends that love her and after a while to begin to hate her. If she have no friends, yet thou knowest not but that she may have a husband that may love her. If thou canst not love her to the end, leave her to him that can. Methinks my son could not offend me in any thing, if he served God, except he chose a wife that he could not love to the end. I need not say if he served God, for if he served God he would obey God, and then he would choose a godly wife and live lovingly and godlily with her, and not do as some man who taketh a woman to make her a companion and fellow, and after he hath her, he makes her a servant and drudge. If she be thy wife, she is always too good to be thy servant, and worthy to be thy fellow. If thou wilt have a good wife, thou must go before her in all goodness and show her a pattern of all good virtues by thy godly and discreet life, and especially in patience, according to the counsel of the Holy Ghost: 'Bear with the woman, as with the weaker vessel.' Here God showeth that it is her imperfection that honoureth thee, and that it is thy perfection that maketh thee to bear with her. Follow the counsel of God, therefore, and bear with her. God willed a man to leave father and mother for his wife. This showeth what an excellent love God did appoint to be between man and wife. In truth I cannot by any means set down the excel-

1. *simplicity*: foolishness

5. *policy*: the art or skill to contrive a situation. This passage recalls Puritan preachers who advise husbands to assert their authority subtly so that a wife will believe she is 'freely' accepting his rule (Lucas 1990: 230). In effect the husband is advised to deceive his wife for her 'benefit' and his own interests. Whereas preachers recommend this role-playing as a general rule, Leigh's context suggests it should be adopted as a last resort only if the marriage is unharmonious.

15–17. *who ... drudge*: hath = possesses physically, legally. Christine Sizemore notes that by encouraging her sons not to treat their potential wives as servants, she implies they have sexual desires, as well as other needs and rights (1976: 47).

18. *go before*: be an example to

21. *Bear ... vessel*: 1 Peter 3.7

24–5. *God ... wife*: Genesis 2.24

26. *set down*: express

lency of that love. But this I assure you, that if you get wives that be godly, and you love them, you shall not need to forsake me. Whereas if you have wives that you love not, I am sure I will forsake you. Do not yourselves that wrong as to marry a woman that you cannot love. Show not so much childishness in your sex as to say you loved her once, and now your mind is changed. If thou canst not love her for the goodness that is in her, yet let the grace that is in thyself move thee to do it. And so I leave thee to the Lord, whom I pray to guide both thee and her with his grace, and grant that you may choose godlily, and live happily, and die comfortably through faith in Jesus Christ.

CHAPTER 14
HOW TO DEAL WITH SERVANTS

Yet one thing I am to desire you to do at my request and for my sake; and though it be some trouble to you to perform it, yet I assure myself you will do it. If God shall at any time give you or any of you a servant or servants, you shall ask them if they can read. If they cannot you shall, at my request, teach them or cause them to be taught till they can read the ten commandments of almighty God. And then you shall persuade them to practise by themselves and to spend all their idle time in reading that so they may come the better to know the will of God written in his word. Remember, your servants are God's servants as well as yours. If they be not, say as David said: 'There shall not an ungodly person dwell in my house; he that loveth or maketh lies shall depart out of my sight.'

It is not for you by any means to keep any ungodly, profane, or wicked person in your house, for they bring a curse upon the place wherein they are and not a blessing, neither will they be taught any goodness. But you must keep those that be tractable and willing to serve God, that he may bless you and your household. For God doth not delight in that master that will suffer his servant to blaspheme his name or to misspend his sabbaths. For God commanded the master that he should see his servants to keep holy the sabbath day; and if he keep that day holy, he will learn to spend all the other days in the week well, in following the duties of his calling. I pray you keep the servants of God, and then remember they are your brethren. Use them well, and be as ready to do them good as to have their service. Be not chiding for every trifle, for that will hinder good living, and nothing enrich you. Be careful that they be godly, for 'godliness hath the promise of this present

10–11. *There ... sight*: Psalm 101.7, altering Geneva's 'deceitful' to 'ungodly'

16–17. *God ... sabbaths*: Exodus 20.10

20. *keep*: a richly suggestive word: employ, preserve, provide for (materially and/or spiritually), have a regard for, look to the well-being of

24–8. *godliness ... contented*: a paraphrase of 1 Timothy 6.6–8

life and of the life to come; godliness is great riches if a man be contented with that he hath. For we brought nothing with us into this world, neither shall we carry anything out of the world; if we have food and raiment, let us therewith be contented.'

27. *raiment*: clothing

RACHEL SPEGHT (*c*. 1597–1630+)

FROM *A MUZZLE FOR MELASTOMUS*

(1617)

Introduction

Like Jane Anger's *Protection for Women* written nearly 30 years before, Rachel Speght's *Muzzle for Melastomus* responds to a misogynist attack, in this case Joseph Swetnam's *Arraignment of Lewd, Idle, Froward, and Unconstant Women* (1615). His pamphlet provoked several replies, but only Speght's, the first among them, is undoubtedly by a female author, who at the time was the nineteen-year-old daughter of a London clergyman, James Speght.

Perhaps her most important task after deciding to refute Swetnam was to develop an authentic voice which would break completely with *The Arraignment*'s misogynist discourse – or discourses, since his pamphlet is a jumble of personas and genres. Swetnam parodies contemporary domestic conduct books, for example, by exaggerating their paradoxically repressive and sentimental advice to husbands about wives (Shepherd 1985: 54–5). His orotund language and conspiratorial tone at other points echo John Lyly's 'Cooling Card for Philautus and All Fond Lovers' in *Euphues the Anatomy of Wit*, the text used by *Book his Surfeit* that provoked Jane Anger (above p. 85). Swetnam also poses as a jaded traveller who amuses himself by stringing together anecdotes of outlandish female depravity. And overall he perpetuates the anti-female harangues of the sixteenth-century *querelle des femmes*, but with a difference: his 'evidence' is not predominantly literary let alone scholarly, but drawn largely from non-textual popular culture – ballads, proverbial lore, traditional pastimes, and urban amusements. As Diane Purkiss argues (1992: 73–8), Swetnam's use of such material reflects his real purpose of generating subversive male pleasure rather than upholding established social values. *The Arraignment* signals the beginning of a pamphlet-scrum that Swetnam hopes other male writers will join for entertainment and profit. Obviously in such a context serious discussion about female nature is not the concern: 'woman' is simply the field over which Swetnam and his mates scramble to score points against each other.

Speght's approach differs, either because the intermittent *querelle* was unknown to her (Woodbridge 1984: 92) or because she recognised the futility of responding to Swetnam on his own terms. Instead she chooses moral argument grounded in scriptural interpretation – not much fun for the gamesters, but valuable to women. This form of discourse, though usually associated with theological inquiry (as other Renaissance women demonstrate), is an inventive solution to the problem of representing female agency within the masculine debate-genre. (Originality in the modern sense of novelty is not to be expected; the Renaissance considered innovation to be compatible with derivation.) While lacking in neither humour nor playfulness, Speght's *Muzzle* is a serious vindication of women, distinguished structurally from her *querelle* 'co-defendants' and intellectually from Swetnam's jejune attack. While Speght is aware that relying on the Bible means working with a text men have often used to oppress women, she also knows it possesses the crucial advantages of being an unimpeachable authority universally familiar to female readers, and the basis of a cultural discourse they could hope to make partly their own through independent reinterpretation of seminal passages. Rather than being weak 'because of [its] especially religious orientation' (Henderson and McManus 1985: 17), Speght's defence actually offers her seventeenth-century female readers 'some kind of clear and recognizable starting-point from which to speak as woman without attracting instant condemnation' (Purkiss 1992: 94), as using Swetnam's mode inevitably would have done.

In the opening Dedicatory Epistle Speght presents herself in the defiant image of Israel's young underdog-champion David, while also seeking patronage and protection from upper-class female readers. To remain silent in the face of Swetnam's defamations, she argues, would be to condone them as well as to court further abuse, since he claimed to be preparing further assaults. Speght also hopes to 'comfort' her women readers, strengthening their self-esteem by defending female moral goodness which male authorities traditionally deny. She then addresses Swetnam in a Preface, condemning him on two grounds: illiteracy, in filling his 'mingle-mangle' polemic with logical and grammatical howlers; and blasphemy, in degrading God's creation, woman, and twisting scripture to suit his opinions. After some brief remarks Speght defers the first topic to the end of her pamphlet ('Certain Queries to the Baiter of Women', not presented here), while the second occupies most of *A Muzzle* proper. It begins with a positive revaluation of Eve as God's divine gift to Adam, and thus as a forerunner of Christ to mankind. Although Speght stops short of demanding full equality between men and women in every respect, in her 'linguistic stress on balance and mutuality to neutralize hierarchical oppositions', she 'may very well be the most important unsung foremother of modern liberal feminist commentators' on the Eve story in Genesis (Nyquist 1987: 108). Speght then carefully refutes four supposedly anti-female texts from scripture cited by Melastomus ('black-mouth' or slanderer) as well as other misogynists. Most impressive is her handling of the last two which she contextualises in the light of historical events, and so dares to assert that some biblical passages are locally contingent rather than literally or universally consequential. The final section presented here stresses domestic reciprocity between married couples.

Editions:
A Muzzle for Melastomus (1617). STC 23058, reel 939. *The Paradise of Women*, ed. Betty Travitsky (Westport, Conn., 1985, brief excerpt). *The Women's Sharp Revenge*, ed. Simon Shepherd (New York, 1985).

RACHEL SPEGHT

FROM *A MUZZLE FOR MELASTOMUS, THE CYNICAL* BAITER OF, AND FOUL-MOUTHED BARKER AGAINST, EVE'S SEX, OR AN APOLOGETICAL† ANSWER TO THAT IRRELIGIOUS AND ILLITERATE PAMPHLET MADE BY JOSEPH SWETNAM AND BY HIM ENTITLED 'THE ARRAIGNMENT OF WOMEN'‡* (1617)

THE EPISTLE DEDICATORY TO ALL VIRTUOUS LADIES HONOURABLE OR WORSHIPFUL, AND TO ALL OTHER OF EVE'S SEX FEARING GOD AND LOVING THEIR JUST REPUTATION, GRACE AND PEACE THROUGH CHRIST, TO ETERNAL GLORY.

It was the simile of that wise and learned Lactantius that if fire, though but with a small spark kindled, be not at the first quenched, it may work great mischief and damage. So likewise may the scandals and defamations of the malevolent in time prove pernicious if they be not nipped in the head at their first appearance. The consideration of this, right honourable and worshipful ladies, hath incited me (though young, and the unworthiest of thousands) to encounter with a furious enemy to our sex, lest if his unjust imputations should continue without answer, he might insult and account himself a victor, and by such a conceit deal as historiographers report the

* *Cynical*: besides the usual definitions (surly, sneering) the word also means 'dog-like' (cynic = Greek for dog)

† *apologetical*: protective (not regretful)

‡ *Joseph ...Women*: *The Arraignment* (1615) was first signed 'Thomas Tel-troth', but later editions (1616, 1617) gave Swetnam's name

1. *Lactantius*: early Christian writer (third–fourth century AD), whose simile is traceable to Quintus Curtius, *De Rebus Gestis Alexandri Magni*, vi.3.11 (Shepherd 1985: 80) and is used without acknowledgement by Swetnam. Speght's identification displays her superior scholarship and intellectual honesty.

6. *young*: Speght says elsewhere that she was 19 when she wrote *A Muzzle*

9. *conceit*: opinion
historiographers: natural historians

viper to do (who in the winter time doth vomit forth her poison and in the spring time sucketh the same up again, which becometh twice as deadly as the former). And this our pestiferous enemy, by thinking to provide a more deadly poison for women than already he hath foamed forth, may evaporate by an addition unto his former illiterate pamphlet entitled *The Arraignment of Women* a more contagious obtrectation than he hath already done, and indeed hath threatened to do.

Secondly, if it should have had free passage without any answer at all (seeing that *tacere* is *quasi consentire*), the vulgar ignorant might have believed his diabolical infamies to be infallible truths not to be infringed, whereas now they may plainly perceive them to be but the scum of heathenish brains, or a building raised without a foundation (at least from sacred scripture), which the wind of God's truth must needs cast down to the ground.

A third reason why I have adventured to fling this stone at vaunting Goliath is to comfort the minds of all Eve's sex, both rich and poor, learned and unlearned, with this antidote, that if the fear of God reside in their hearts, maugre all adversaries, they are highly esteemed and accounted of in the eyes of their gracious redeemer, so that they need not fear the darts of envy or obtrectators; for shame and disgrace, saith Aristotle, is the end of them that shoot such poisoned shafts. Worthy therefore of imitation is that example of Seneca, who when he was told that a certain man did exclaim and rail against him, made this mild answer: 'Some dogs bark more upon custom than cursedness, and some speak evil of others not that the defamed deserve it, but because through custom and corruption of their hearts they cannot speak well of any'. This I allege as a paradigmatical pattern for all women, noble and ignoble, to follow, that they be not inflamed with choler against this our enraged adversary, but patiently consider of him according to the portraiture which he hath drawn of himself (his writings being the very emblem of a monster).

13. *evaporate*: exhale

15, 29. *obtrectation*: slander, detraction

18. *tacere . . . consentire*: to keep silent is as good as consenting

24–5. *fling . . . Goliath*: alluding to the young David's deliverance of Israel by killing the Philistine champion (1 Samuel 17). It is part of Speght's strategy, as Diane Purkiss notes (1992: 93), to equate 'female honour and reputation with divine honour and reputation'.

25. *comfort*: strengthen, encourage

27. *maugre*: notwithstanding

29–30. *shame . . . shafts*: possibly referring to *The Ethics*, IV.9.6 (Shepherd 1985: 80)

31. *Seneca*: famous Stoic philosopher, poet, and essayist (*c.* 4 BC–AD 65, whose emphasis on rational self-control Speght admires

33. *custom . . . cursedness*: learned habit . . . innate vicious nature

This my brief apology, right honourable and worshipful, did I enterprise not as thinking myself more fit than others to undertake such a task, but as one who, not perceiving any of our sex to enter the lists of encountering with this our grand enemy among men (I being out of all fear, because armed with the truth – which though often blamed, yet can never be shamed – and the word of God's spirit, together with the example of virtue's pupils for a buckler), did no whit dread to combat with our said malevolent adversary. And if in so doing I shall be censured by the judicious to have the victory, and shall have given content unto the wronged, I have both hit the mark whereat I aimed and obtained that prize which I desired. But if Zoilus shall adjudge me presumptuous in dedicating this my chirograph unto personages of so high rank, both because of my insufficiency in literature and tenderness in years, I thus apologise for myself, that seeing the Baiter of women hath opened his mouth against noble as well as ignoble, against the rich as well as the poor, therefore meet it is that they should be joint spectators of this encounter. And withal, in regard of my imperfection both in learning and age, I need so much the more to impetrate patronage from some of power to shield me from the biting wrongs of Momus, who oftentimes setteth a rankling tooth into the sides of truth. Wherefore I, being of Decius his mind (who deemed himself safe under the shield of Caesar), have presumed to shelter myself under the wings of you honourable personages against the persecuting heat of this fiery and furious dragon, desiring that you would be pleased not to look so much *ad opus*, as *ad animum*. And so, not doubting of the favourable acceptance and censure of all virtuously affected, I rest

Your honours' and worships'
Humbly at commandment,
Rachel Speght.

40. *enterprise*: undertake
42. *lists*: barriers marking off an enclosed area for jousting
45. *example ... pupils*: i.e. famous examples of virtuous women
46. *buckler*: shield
47. *censured*: judged
49. *mark*: target (continuing the jousting metaphor)
Zoilus: fourth-century. BC sophist and biting critic
50. *chirograph*: written bond or formal pledge (to 'do battle' with Swetnam)
54. *they*: i.e. persons of high rank
56. *impetrate*: request
57. *Momus*: god of satire
59. *Decius*: accompanied Julius Caesar to the senate on the day he was assassinated
62. *ad ... animum*: to the work itself but to its motivation

THE PREFACE NOT UNTO THE VERIEST IDIOT THAT EVER SET PEN TO PAPER, BUT TO THE CYNICAL BAITER OF WOMEN,* OR METAMORPHOSED MISOGENES,† JOSEPH SWETNAM.

From standing water, which soon putrifies, can no good fish be expected, for it produceth no other creatures but those that are venomous or noisome, as snakes, adders, and such like. Semblably, no better stream can we look should issue from your idle corrupt brain than that whereto the rough of your fury (to use your own words) hath moved you to open the sluice. In which excrement of your roving cogitations you have used such irregularities touching concordance, and observed so disordered a method, as I doubt not to tell you that a very accidence-scholar would have quite put you down in both. You appear herein not unlike that painter who, seriously endeavouring to portray Cupid's bow, forgot the string; for you, being greedy to botch up your mingle-mangle invective against women, have not therein observed in many places so much as grammar sense. But the emptiest barrel makes the loudest sound, and so we will account of you.

Many propositions have you framed which (as you think) make much against women; but if one would make a logical assumption, the conclusion would be flat against your own sex. Your dealing wants so much discretion that I doubt whether to bestow so good a name as the dunce upon you. But minority bids me keep within my bounds, and therefore I only say unto you that your corrupt heart and railing tongue hath made you a fit scribe for the devil.

In that you have termed your virulent foam 'The Bear-baiting of Women', you have plainly displayed your own disposition to be cynical, in that there appears no other dog or bull to bait them but yourself. Good had

* *Not ... women*: this mocks the wording of Swetnam's preface: 'Neither to the best nor yet to the worst, but to the common sort of women'

† *Misogenes*: misogynist

3. *Semblably*: likewise
4. *rough*: disagreeable part; the bombastic refrain 'rough of ...' recurs throughout Swetnam's piece
6. *excrement*: excretions
7. *concordance*: grammatical agreement between parts of speech
8. *accidence-scholar*: student possessing only a rudimentary knowledge of a subject; accidence = rules of grammatical inflection
11. *botch up*: patch together
15. *one would*: one (proposition) were able to
18. *minority*: i.e. being under 21
21. *Bear-baiting*: referring to Swetnam's fourth chapter, 'The Bear-baiting, or the Vanity of Widows', an invective against marriage

it been for you to have put on that muzzle which St James would have all Christians to wear: 'Speak not evil one of another'. And then had you not seemed so like the serpent Porphyrus as now you do (which, though full of deadly poison yet being toothless, hurteth none so much as himself). For you having gone beyond the limits not of humanity alone but of Christianity, have done greater harm unto your own soul than unto women, as may plainly appear. First, in dishonouring of God by palpable blasphemy, wresting and perverting every place of scripture that you have alleged, which by the testimony of St Peter is to the destruction of them that so do. Secondly, it appears by your disparaging of, and opprobrious speeches against, that excellent work of God's hands, which in his great love he perfected for the comfort of man. Thirdly and lastly, by this your hodge-podge of heathenish sentences, similes, and examples, you have set forth yourself in your right colours unto the view of the world, and I doubt not but the judicious will account of you according to your demerit. As for the vulgar sort, which have no more learning than you have showed in your book, it is likely they will applaud you for your pains.

As for your 'bugbear' or advice unto women, that whatsoever they do think of your work they should conceal it, lest in finding fault they bewray their galled backs to the world (in which you allude to that proverb, 'Rub a galled horse and he will kick'), unto it I answer by way of apology that, though every galled horse being touched doth kick, yet every one that kicks is not galled; so that you might as well have said that because burnt folks dread the fire, therefore none fear fire but those that are burnt, as made that illiterate conclusion which you have absurdly inferred.

In your title-leaf you arraign none but lewd, idle, froward, and unconstant women, but in the sequel (through defect of memory as it seemeth), forgetting that you had made a distinction of good from bad, condemning all in general, you advise men to beware of and not to match with any of

25. *Speak ... another*: James 4.6–11. Most of the scriptural references cited below derive from marginal notes in the original edition and are probably Speght's, though occasional errors may have been introduced by the printer.

26. *serpent Porphyrus*: purple snake with a white head, said by Claudius Aelianus (*De Natura Animalium* IV, 36) to come from the hottest regions of India and to lack fangs. It was capable, however, of vomiting a putrifying venom. I am indebted to Professor M.J. Mills for this information.

32–3. *testimony ... do*: 2 Peter 3.16 (original edn = 1 Peter)

38–9. *demerit ... vulgar sort*: deserts ... common people

41. *advice*: Swetnam attempts to forestall criticism by placing women in a classic double bind: if they object to his attacks they will confirm his accusations

42–3. *bewray ... galled*: betray ... chafed or diseased

48. *illiterate conclusion*: 'Criticizing Swetnam's logic is good strategy: a recurrent misogynist's allegation was that women are incapable of logic' (Woodbridge 1984: 88) *inferred*: alleged

49. *froward*: difficult to deal with

these six sorts of women; *viz.* good and bad, fair and foul, rich and poor. But this doctrine of devils St Paul, foreseeing would be broached in the latter times, gives warning of.

There also you promise a commendation of wise, virtuous, and honest women, whenas in the subsequent, the worst words and filthiest epithets that you can devise you bestow on them in general, excepting no sort of women. Herein may you be likened unto a man which upon the door of a scurvy house sets this superscription, 'Here is a very fair house to be let', whereas the door being opened, it is no better than a dog-hole and dark dungeon.

Further, if your own words be true that you wrote with your hand but not with your heart, then are you an hypocrite in print. But it is rather to be thought that your pen was the bewrayer of the abundance of your mind, and that this was but a little mortar to daub up again the wall which you intended to break down.

The revenge of your railing work we leave to him who hath appropriated vengeance unto himself, whose pen-man hath included railers in the catalogue of them that shall not inherit God's kingdom, and yourself unto the mercy of that just judge who is able to save and to destroy.

Your undeserved friend,
Rachel Speght.

A MUZZLE FOR MELASTOMUS

Proverbs 18.22: He that findeth a wife findeth a good thing, and receiveth favour of the Lord.

If lawful it be to compare the potter with his clay, or the architect with the edifice, then may I in some sort resemble that love of God towards man in creating woman unto the affectionate care of Abraham for his son Isaac, who, that he might not take to wife one of the daughters of the Canaanites, did provide him one of his own kindred.

Almighty God, who is rich in mercy, having made all things of nothing and created man in his own image (that is, as the apostle expounds it, 'In

54–5. *doctrine ... of*: that being forbidden to marry is not divine law (1 Timothy 4.3)
60. *scurvy*: diseased, wretched
65. *bewrayer*: betrayer
68–9. *him ... himself*: i.e. God (in Romans 12.19)
69–70. *pen-man ... kingdom*: St Paul in 1 Corinthians 5.11

2. *resemble*: liken
3–5. *Abraham ... kindred*: Genesis 24.4. Isaac's wife was Rebecca
6. *rich ... mercy*: Ephesians 2.4.
7. *created ... image*: 1 Colossians 3.10 (original = 30) from Genesis 1.27
7–8. *apostle ... all*: St Paul to the Ephesians 4.24

wisdom, righteousness, and true holiness', making him lord over all), to avoid that solitary condition that he was then in, having none to commerce or converse withal but dumb creatures, it seemed good unto the Lord that as of every creature he had made male and female, and man only being alone without mate, so likewise to form an help-meet for him. Adam for this cause being cast into a heavy sleep, God, extracting a rib from his side, thereof made or built woman, showing thereby that man was an unperfect building afore woman was made, and, bringing her unto Adam, united and married them together.

Thus the resplendent love of God toward man appeared, in taking care to provide him an helper before he saw his own want, and in providing him such an helper as should be meet for him. Sovereignty had he over all creatures, and they were all serviceable unto him; but yet afore woman was formed there was not a meet help found for Adam. Man's worthiness not meriting this great favour at God's hands, but his mercy only moving him thereunto, I may use those words which the Jews uttered when they saw Christ weep for Lazarus: 'Behold how he loved him'. Behold, and that with good regard, God's love, yea his great love which from the beginning he hath borne unto man; which as it appears in all things, so, next his love in Christ Jesus, apparently in this: that for man's sake, that he might not be an unit when all other creatures were for procreation dual, he created woman to be a solace unto him, to participate of his sorrows, partake of his pleasures, and as a good yoke-fellow bear part of his burden. Of the excellency of this structure (I mean of women), whose foundation and original of creation was God's love, do I intend to dilate.

Of woman's excellency, with the causes of her creation, and of the sympathy which ought to be in man and wife each toward other.

The work of creation being finished, this approbation thereof was given by

9. *commerce*: have social (or perhaps sexual) intercourse. Accent on the second syllable.
13. *heavy sleep*: Genesis 2.21
18. *before … want*: Mary Nyquist reads this phrase as Speght's 'highly provocative' reinterpretation of Eve's creation story in Genesis 2, in which Adam's need for a companion was traditionally assumed to arise from his own desire, which prompted God to create Eve from his rib. Speght instead views Adam as a passive recipient of God's independently planned gift of divine love, woman (1987: 114). She thus depicts Eve as the fulfilment of God's image in human nature.
21. *meet … Adam*: Genesis 2
24. *Behold … him*: John 11.36
26. *next*: second to (i.e. woman is below only Christ in importance as a manifestation of divine grace to humans)
27. *apparently*: openly, visibly
30. *burden*: 1 Corinthians 11.9

God himself, that 'All was very good'. If all, then woman, who, excepting man, is the most excellent creature under the canopy of heaven. But if it be objected by any:

First, that woman, though created good, yet by giving ear to Satan's temptations, brought death and misery upon all her posterity.

Secondly, that 'Adam was not deceived, but that the woman was deceived and was in the transgression'.

Thirdly, that St Paul saith, 'It were good for a man not to touch a woman'.

Fourthly and lastly, that of Solomon, who seems to speak against all of our sex: 'I have found one man of a thousand, but a woman among them all have I not found' (whereof in its due place).

To the first of these objections I answer that Satan first assailed the woman because where the hedge is lowest, most easy it is to get over, and she being the weaker vessel was with more facility to be seduced (like as a crystal glass sooner receives a crack than a strong stone pot). Yet we shall find the offence of Adam and Eve almost to parallel; for as an ambitious desire of being made like unto God was the motive which caused her to eat, so likewise was it his, as may plainly appear by that *ironia*: 'Behold, man is become as one of us'. Not that he was so indeed, but hereby his desire to attain a greater perfection than God had given him was reproved. Woman sinned, it is true, by her infidelity in not believing the word of God but giving credit to Satan's fair promises that 'she should not die', but so did the man too. And if Adam had not approved of that deed which Eve had done, and been willing to tread the steps which she had gone, he, being her head, would have reproved her and have made the commandment a bit to restrain him from breaking his maker's injunction. For if a man burn his hand in the fire, the bellows that blowed the fire are not to be blamed, but himself rather for not being careful to avoid the danger. Yet if the bellows had not blowed, the fire had not burnt; no more is woman simply to be condemned for man's transgression. For by the free will, which before his fall he enjoyed, he might have avoided and been free from being burnt or singed with that fire which was kindled by Satan and blown by Eve. It therefore served not his turn a whit afterwards to say: 'The woman which thou gavest me gave me of the

34. *All ... good*: Genesis 1.31
39–40. *Adam ... transgression*: 1 Timothy 2.14
41–2. *It ... woman*: 1 Corinthians 7.1
44–5. *I ... found*: Ecclesiastes 7.30 (Geneva; Authorised Version = 28)
48–9. *weaker ... pot*: Speght's comparison emphasises Eve's physical rather than her moral qualities (cf. 'stronger vessel' l. 72)
52. *ironia*: irony (because spoken by God)
52–3. *Behold ... us*: Genesis 3.22
56. *promises ... die*: Genesis 3.4
67–8. *The ... eat*: Genesis 3.12

tree, and I did eat'. For a penalty was inflicted upon him as well as on the woman, the punishment of her transgression being particular to her own sex and to none but the female kind; but for the sin of man the whole earth was cursed. And he, being better able than the woman to have resisted temptation because the stronger vessel, was first called to account, to show that to whom much is given, of them much is required; and that he who was the sovereign of all creatures visible should have yielded greatest obedience to God....

To the second objection I answer that the Apostle doth not hereby exempt man from sin, but only giveth to understand that the woman was the primary transgressor and not the man; but that man was not at all deceived was far from his meaning, for he afterward expressly saith, that as 'in Adam all die, so in Christ shall all be made alive'.

For the third objection ... the Apostle makes it not a positive prohibition, but speaks it only because of the Corinthians' present necessity, who were then persecuted by the enemies of the church; for which cause and no other he saith, 'Art thou loosed from a wife? Seek not a wife' (meaning whilst the time of these perturbations should continue in their heat),

> 'but if thou art bound, seek not to be loosed; if thou marriest thou sinnest not, only increasest thy care. For the married careth for the things of this world, and I wish that you were without care, that ye might cleave fast unto the Lord without separation. For the time remaineth that they which have wives be as though they had none; for the persecutors shall deprive you of them, either by imprisonment, banishment, or death.'

So that manifest it is that the Apostle doth not hereby forbid marriage but only adviseth the Corinthians to forbear a while till God in mercy should curb the fury of their adversaries. For, as Eusebius writeth, Paul was after-

69–70. *punishment* ... *sex*: the pains of childbirth (Genesis 3.16)

78. *primary*: can mean first in sequence or in importance

80. *in* ... *alive*: 1 Corinthians 15.22

81. *positive*: absolute

83. *cause*: i.e. pertaining to particular local circumstances, rather than universal principles. Speght takes the same historicising approach in her reading of Solomon's words (ll. 100ff.). Such critically contextual readings of the Bible were relatively rare at the beginning of the seventeenth century.

84–92. *Art* ... *death*: a paraphrase of 1 Corinthians 7.27–31

95. *Eusebius*: Bishop of Caesarea and earliest Church historian, AD 260–340. Speght alludes to his *Ecclesiastical History* iii.30 (Shepherd 1985: 81). Her use of Eusebius to reinterpret Paul's epistles anticipates the readings of modern feminist theologians (e.g. Fiorenza 1992: 225–6).

ward married himself, the which is very probable, being that interrogatively he saith,

> 'Have we not power to lead about a wife being a sister, as well as the rest of the Apostles, and as the brethren of the Lord, and Cephas?'

The fourth and last objection is that of Solomon.... For answer of which, if we look into the story of his life we shall find therein a commentary upon this enigmatical sentence included; for it is there said that Solomon had seven hundred wives and three hundred concubines, which number connexed make one thousand. These women, turning his heart away from being perfect with the Lord his God, sufficient cause had he to say that among the said thousand women found he not one upright. He saith not that among a thousand women never any man found one worthy of commendation, but speaks in the first person singularly, 'I have not found', meaning in his own experience. For this assertion is to be holden a part of the confession of his former follies and no otherwise, his repentance being the intended drift of Ecclesiastes....

Woman was made ... to be a companion and helper for man; and if she must be an helper, and but an helper, then are those husbands to be blamed which lay the whole burden of domestical affairs and maintenance on the shoulders of their wives. For as yoke-fellows they are to sustain part of each other's cares, griefs, and calamities. But as if two oxen be put in one yoke, the one being bigger than the other, the greater bears most weight; so the husband being the stronger vessel is to bear a greater burden than his wife. And therefore the Lord said to Adam, 'In the sweat of thy face shalt thou eat thy bread, till thou return to the dust'. And St Paul saith that 'he that provideth not for his household is worse than an infidel'. Nature hath taught senseless creatures to help one another, as the male pigeon, when his hen is weary with sitting on her eggs and comes off from them, supplies her place, that in her absence they may receive no harm, until such time as she is fully refreshed. Of small birds the cock always helps his hen to build her nest, and while she sits upon her eggs he flies abroad to get meat for her, who cannot then provide any for herself. The crowing cockerel helps his hen to defend her chickens from peril, and will endanger himself to save her and them from harm. Seeing then that these unreasonable creatures by the instinct of nature bear such affection each to other that without any grudge they willingly, according to their kind, help one another, I may reason *a*

96. *interrogatively*: rhetorically
98–9. *Have ... Cephas*: 1 Corinthians 9.5; sister = female member of the brethren; Cephas = Paul
104. *connexed*: added together
119–20. *In ... dust*: Genesis 3.19
120–1. *he ... infidel*: 1 Timothy 5.8
132–3. *a ... maius*: from smaller to greater things

minore ad maius that much more should man and woman, which are reasonable creatures, be helpers each to other in all things lawful, they having the law of God to guide them, his word to be a lantern unto their feet and a light unto their paths, by which they are excited to a far more mutual participation of each other's burden than other creatures. So that neither the wife may say to her husband nor the husband unto his wife, 'I have no need of thee', no more than the members of the body may so say each to other, between whom there is such a sympathy, that if one member suffer, all suffer with it. Therefore, though God bade Abraham forsake his country and kindred, yet he bade him not forsake his wife, who, being 'flesh of his flesh, and bone of his bone' was to be co-partner with him of whatsoever did betide him, whether joy or sorrow. Wherefore Solomon saith, 'Woe to him that is alone'; for when thoughts of discomfort, troubles of this world, and fear of dangers do possess him, he wants a companion to lift him up from the pit of perplexity into which he is fallen; for a good wife, saith Plautus, is the wealth of the mind and the welfare of the heart, and therefore a meet associate for her husband; and 'woman', saith Paul, 'is the glory of the man'....

137–8. *I ... thee*: 1 Corinthians 12.21

141. *wife*: Sarah, whose advice Abraham was commanded to heed (Genesis 21.12)

143–6. *Woe ... fallen*: paraphrasing Ecclesiastes 4.10

146. *Plautus*: Roman dramatist *c.* 254–184 BC. Shepherd suggests that the words could derive from his *Amphitryo*, 839ff. (1985: 82).

148–9. *woman ... man*: 1 Corinthians 11.7

ELIZABETH CALDWELL (?–1603)

A LETTER WRITTEN BY ELIZABETH CALDWELL TO HER HUSBAND DURING THE TIME OF HER IMPRISONMENT, FROM *A TRUE DISCOURSE OF THE PRACTICES OF ELIZABETH CALDWELL*

(1604)

Introduction

A Letter to her Husband appeared in 1604 as part of a pamphlet-collection, *A True Discourse of the Practices of Elizabeth Caldwell* by Gilbert Dugdale, relating the story of Elizabeth Caldwell's unsuccessful attempt to poison her husband with the help of her lover, Jeffrey Bownd, and a go-between, Isabel Hall. Dugdale includes reports of the conspirators' testimony during the ensuing assize trials, and of Caldwell's deep repentance in prison prior to her execution. These elements are what one would expect to find in an early modern 'true-crime' story, a highly popular genre also normally characterised by unequivocal denunciations of the wrongdoers by moralising narrators. What is unusual about this particular account is that during the course of his narration Dugdale becomes a partial advocate for the 'criminal', and that his decision to reproduce Caldwell's *Letter* allows her an opportunity to defend herself in what appears to be her own voice.

At the heart of *A True Discourse* is the crime itself: Thomas Caldwell nearly dies after breakfasting on buttered oat-cakes spiked with rat-poison, and is only saved 'by way of vomit'. One little girl, two dogs, and a cat are not so lucky. In these matters Dugdale flatly condemns the offenders. But prior to this he supplies background details about the Caldwell marriage that establish a sympathetic and surprisingly gendered defence of Elizabeth. He tells us that she came from an old county family, had received a good education, and was 'framed and adorned with all the gifts that nature could challenge' (A4^{r}). As he ascribes no comparable traits to Thomas, his statement (benefiting from hindsight) that 'the like matches do not often prove well' amounts to criticism of him rather than his wife. Dugdale also clearly holds Thomas responsible for the marital breakdown. One factor he cites was 'the continuance of [Thomas's] absence', another his financial deprivation: 'to the great discontentment of his wife, and other his friends, [Thomas left] her often times very bare, without provision of such means as was fitting for her' (A4^{r}). We know from the writings of women such as Grace Mildmay (below p. 218) that prolonged absences by husbands from home were common, and that they often left their wives short of money for maintaining themselves and their households. Thomas appears especially culpable when Dugdale reports that Elizabeth brought to the marriage 'a yearly annuity of ten pounds' as well as 'a good dower' yet mentions nothing of his contributions to the family estate (contemporary records suggest Thomas became a 'gentleman born' by marrying Elizabeth). 'Annuity' and 'dower' refer to the jointure and marriage-portion Elizabeth's family would have provided for the new couple's household. The usual ratio of portion to jointure at this time was five to one; so if one reckons the rate of return on Elizabeth's annuity at 5 per cent, then the land value of her jointure was probably about £200, and her family's (presumably cash) dowry about £1,000 – respectable sums for non-titled county gentry (Erickson 1993: 85–91). The implication is that Thomas has squandered his wife's money, for as Dugdale adds, 'Caldwell being young, and not experienced in the world, gave his mind to travel and see foreign countries, which tended rather to his loss than profit' (A4^{r}). Under these circumstances, when Jeffrey Bownd, 'a man of good wealth', becomes attracted to her, his role seems to be that of a financial saviour rather than an illicit lover.

Dugdale's account of events after Elizabeth's trial also seems to exonerate her. While awaiting execution in Chester Castle, she managed to bring about an astonishing turn-around in public support by transforming herself into a spiritual counsellor for the local community:

> And for *Elizabeth Caldwell*, from her first entrance into prison, till the time of her death, there was never heard by any, so much as an idle word to proceed out of her mouth, neither did she omit any time, during her imprisonment, in serving of GOD, and seeking pardon for her sins, with great zeal and industry, continually meditating on the Bible ... There was many of all sorts resorted to see her, as no fewer some days than three hundred persons: and such as she thought were viciously given, she gave them good admonitions. (B2^{r})

Over the course of sixteen months or so, Caldwell reinvented a heroic persona which seems to have obliterated the old 'criminal' one. She became, in Dugdale's words, a Job, 'picked out by the hand of God' as 'an example to thousands' (B2^{r-v}). Her new role included making 'known that she could teach as [well as] the preachers, for they taught as they found it in the word, and she was able to speak from a feeling heart' (D1^{v}), and also sending 'some days a dozen letters to several preachers to be resolved as touching her faith'. By offering pastoral advice to male clerics as well as to lay-people, she effectively developed a quasi-ecclesiastical function for herself. Needless to say, all these roles were extraordinary for any Renaissance woman, let alone a convicted criminal.

It is this refashioned identity that one sees represented by the *Letter*. With insistent conviction Caldwell justifies her motives from the culturally marginalised position of a wife whose husband has denied her proper material security and sexual fidelity. In the first area Caldwell seeks to relativise her official guilt by pointing to Thomas Caldwell's financial neglect and waste of their joint resources; she assigns these faults a moral value equivalent to her own actions, even though society recognises only hers as crimes. In the second area, through apparent allusions to her husband's adultery, she undercuts his position as the injured party while also condemning sexual double standards. Since her conviction by the local assize disqualifies her from launching any formal inquiry into her husband's conduct and its bearing on her actions, Caldwell uses the *Letter* to open a discursive space for herself in which she may present counter-charges against her husband and, in effect, seek a retrial in the court of public opinion.

Rhetorically Caldwell repositions herself by deploying a discourse of spiritual redemption and social reform weighty with biblical quotations, rather than ordinary public speech. By grounding her arguments in scripture, she displaces the murder-pamphlet's criminal-law focus, in which pro-female values find little scope, with a moral and remedial one that supports a wife's claim to exercise positive marital direction – in legal terms an appeal to equity. The *Letter* accordingly exhorts Thomas to embrace spiritual mourning for his past misconduct and practical behavioural reforms such as sabbath-keeping, while also challenging the dominant cultural attitudes and legal privileges that shield him.

Edition:
Gilbert Dugdale, *A True Discourse of the Practices of Elizabeth Caldwell* (1604). STC 7293, reel 955.

ELIZABETH CALDWELL

A LETTER WRITTEN BY ELIZABETH CALDWELL TO HER HUSBAND DURING THE TIME OF HER IMPRISONMENT, FROM *A TRUE DISCOURSE OF THE PRACTICES OF ELIZABETH CALDWELL ... ON THE PERSON OF MASTER THOMAS CALDWELL IN THE COUNTY OF CHESTER, TO HAVE MURDERED AND POISONED HIM WITH DIVERS OTHERS, BY GILBERT DUGDALE*

(1604)

Although the greatness of my offence deserves neither pity nor regard, yet give leave unto your poor sorrowful wife to speak unto you what out of her own woeful experience, with abundance of grief and tears, she hath learned in the school of affliction. It is the last favour that I shall ever beg at your hands, and the last office that ever I shall perform unto you. And therefore, dear husband, if you have any hope or desire to be partaker of the joys of heaven, let my speeches find acceptance and do not slightly esteem what I write unto you, but read these lines again and again, and lay them up in your heart, where I beseech almighty God they may take deep root and impression. For my witness is in heaven, that my heart's desire and earnest prayer to God is that your soul may be saved. And if the loss of my blood or life, or to endure any torments that the world can inflict upon me, might procure your true conversion, I should esteem it purchased at an easy rate.

1–4. *Although ... affliction*: Caldwell's only reference to her crime, and her only implied apology

5. *office*: service, duty

11–13. *And ... rate*: language of self-sacrifice reminiscent of sixteenth-century female martyrs such as Lady Jane Grey (*Words she spake upon the scaffold before she suffered,* 1554) and others in Foxe's *Acts and Monuments* (the popular *Book of Martyrs*, 1563 and many reprintings). Caldwell moves beyond her opening role as a remorseful penitent by reconfiguring her coming execution as a bold opportunity to assert her personal agency and catalyse her husband's rehabilitation. For a discussion of executions and scaffold-speeches as occasions for early modern women to construct subject-positions for themselves see Belsey 1985: 190–1, and Dolan 1994a.

13. *esteem ... rate*: i.e. consider it a small price to pay

But sith none can have salvation without true reformation, both inward and outward amendment in changing the affection, words, and works from evil to good (which till you feel in your soul and conscience to be effectually wrought, you have not repented), defer not time but call to God for grace of true repentance, which may be found even in this accepted time when the doors of God's mercy are open, that so he have mercy on you, lest he give you over to hardness of heart that you cannot repent....

O husband, be not deceived with the world, and think that it is in your power to repent when you will, or that to say a few prayers from the mouth outward a little before death, or to cry God mercy for fashion sake, is true repentance. No, no, 'not every one that saith Lord, Lord, shall enter into the kingdom of heaven, but he that doeth the will of my Father which is in heaven', saith our saviour. Late repentance is seldom true, and true repentance is not so easy a matter to come by, as the word doth judge. Do not presume on it, and so run on in your sinful course of life, and think to repent when you list. You cannot do it, for repentance is the rare gift of God which is given but to a very few, even to those that seek it, with many tears and very earnestly with fervent prayers. None can better speak of it, for none better knows it than myself; my sorrowful heart hath smarted for it and my soul hath been sick to the gates of hell and of death to find it, and to have it is more precious than all the world. Therefore cease not to pray day and night with the prophet: 'Turn thou us unto thee, O Lord, and we shall be turned'. And with Ephraim: 'Convert thou me, O Lord, and I shall be converted'. For except you be converted, you shall not enter into the kingdom of heaven.

And because none can be converted nor come unto Christ except the

14. *sith*: since
    reformation: spiritual or moral conversion
15. *affection*: emotional tendencies; state of mind
16. *effectually*: genuinely
18. *accepted*: because Thomas Caldwell has already received signs of divine grace such as being saved from death
21. *the world*: worldly values or beliefs
23. *cry ... sake*: publicly humble yourself when conventional expectations call upon you to do so
24–6. *not ... heaven*: Matthew 7.21
27. *word*: scripture, or perhaps a printer's error for 'world'
29. *list*: wish
31–4. *None ... it*: Rather than undercutting her own position, Caldwell claims her past experiences now authenticate her moral authority
35–6. *Turn ... turned*: Lamentations 5.21
36–7. *Convert ... converted*: Jeremiah 31.18
37–8. *except ... heaven*: Matthew 18.3

Father draw him, never leave to solicit the Father of mercy to create a new heart and renew a right spirit within you, and call to remembrance the dissoluteness of your life. I speak it not to lay anything to your charge, for I do love you more dearly than I do myself. But remember in what a case you have lived, how poor you have many times left me, how long you have been absent from me, all which advantage the devil took to subvert me. And to further his purpose, he set his hellish instruments a-work, even the practice of wicked people who continually wrought upon my weakness, my poverty, and your absence, until they made me yield to conspire with them the destruction of your body by a violent and sudden death, which God in his great mercy prevented. And on the knees of my heart, in the abundance of his compassion, I beseech him to forgive us all and wash our souls in the blood of his Christ, and to open the eyes of your understanding that you may see by my example (which the providence of God, for some secret cause best known to himself, hath appointed to come to pass), how weak and wretched we are, and how unable to stand of ourselves, when it shall please him to take his grace from us, and to leave us to ourselves. Therefore, good husband, as you tender the welfare of your soul, go no further on in your sinful race, but turn unto the Lord, and so shall you save your soul alive. If you continue in your abominations, and shut your ears against the word of exhortation, you cannot have any hope of salvation; for the book of God is full of judgements against wilful sinners, and mercy is to them that repent and turn.

Therefore I beseech you use no delay, defer no time, but presently be acquainted with the scriptures, for they will lead you to eternal life. Make haste, even before your hands part with this paper, to search therein that so you may truly understand the wretched estate and condition of those who,

41–2. *renew … life*: Caldwell adds to her theme of spiritual renewal a call to reform her husband's marital conduct; dissoluteness = wanton extravagance; profligacy of manners and morals.

42. *lay … charge*: burden you (with accusations touching your misbehaviour – what's past is past, Caldwell seems to say). Yet the phrase suggests legal indictment (see next note).

43. *case*: condition, circumstances. Again Caldwell appears to lay counter-charges against her husband: 'Although she claims not to place blame or to harbor any resentments, Caldwell's bold insistence that she is the one who has to forgive [her husband], and that she is the one able to offer spiritual and moral guidance, denigrates him as a neglectful husband and Christian and as her own inferior' (Dolan 1994a: 170).

45. *subvert*: undermine, corrupt (my character)

51. *his*: God's

53–4. *example … pass*: i.e. as an instrument of, and warning from, God for her husband's faults

58. *race*: course of life

save … alive: save your soul while you are still living

61. *and*: but

following the lusts of their eyes, wallow in all sensuality and so heap up vengeance against the day of wrath – even heavy judgements no less than condemnation both of soul and body.... Remember he spared not the angels when they sinned, but cast them down into hell, nor of the old world but eight only escaped; the rest were drowned in their sins because they would not be warned. 'Belshazzar', saith Daniel (expounding the fearful vision of the hand's writing when he was banqueting with his concubines), 'thou art weighed in the balance and are found light'....

And for the sabbath day, be ye assured that the Lord of heaven hath not in vain chosen it to himself, commanding us to sanctify it unto his holy name. No, no, if ever we desire to be partakers of the spiritual sabbath in heaven, whereof ours on earth is but a type and a figure, then must we strive to keep the same sabbath on earth as much as in us lies, which the saints keep in heaven. They are at rest from those labours that mortality is subject unto, and uncessantly sing praises unto the lamb; so should we rest that day from the labours of our calling and spend the whole day in hearing of the

68. *against ... wrath*: in certain expectation of ... final judgement

69. *he*: God

69–70. *spared ... hell*: alluding to the fall of Lucifer and the rebel angels, a traditional elaboration of Luke 10.18

70. *old*: pre-fallen

72–4. *Belshazzar ... light*: alluding to Belshazzar's feast (Daniel 5). Belshazzar, King of the Babylonians, had conquered Israel and despoiled the temple at Jerusalem. Daniel and his Jewish companions were living in exile at the Babylonian court but had remained faithful to their heritage. During a feast for Belshazzar's courtiers and concubines in which drinking vessels were used that had been plundered from the Jewish temple, hand-writing appeared on the palace wall. When called to interpret the writing Daniel condemned Belshazzar for idol-worship and prophesied his death and the seizure of Babylon by Darius and the Medo-Persians – both of which immediately came to pass. Caldwell reinterprets the passage, stressing Belshazzar's wantonness (with 'concubines', 'banqueting', and 'light' all carrying sexual meanings) rather than the dominant scriptural concern with idolatry. The shift of emphasis strongly suggests her husband has behaved in the same way as Belshazzar, thereby adding a charge of adultery to her accusations of financial abuse. The overall effect is not only to strengthen her self-defence but also to challenge sexual double standards.

75ff. *sabbath day*: from the context of her accumulated charges, it is clear that this represents not just a call for higher moral standards but also a practical means of exercising domestic control. Sabbatarianism is a scripturally authorised way of keeping her husband at home, steering him away from dissipation, and actively promoting companionship, rather than suffering abandonment and neglect.

77. *spiritual sabbath*: i.e. eternal 'rest' or peace

78. *type ... figure*: symbol or prefiguration of a future actuality

81. *uncessantly*: unceasingly
lamb: of God; an image from Revelation 5.11–12

word preached, praising the Lord publicly in the great congregation, privately at home with our families, preferring such other holy exercises as may tend to the glory of God, the comfort of our souls, and the good of others, which we are bound to perform so straitly, as that we may not that day be allowed to speak such words as concern of vocations....

O dear husband, the Lord hath long since taken his sword in his hand to execute his vengeance against all disobedient wretches who turn the sabbath of the Lord into a day of wantonness, liberty, and licentiousness; and although in his great mercy he doth yet forbear to proceed to judgement, as it were in great mercy, waiting our repentance, yet there will suddenly come a day of reckoning, all together.... Six market days he hath given us to provide us necessaries for our bodies, and but one hath he chosen for himself to be a day of holiness, which is the market day for the soul wherein we should provide us of comforts for the whole week. The excellency and worth of this day is unspeakable to those that sanctify it. It is the badge and livery whereby they are known to be the servants of God; to those that profane it in spending the day in worldly pleasures, drunkenness, and filthiness, it is the certain badge and livery whereby they are known to be the servants of the devil....

Therefore, dear husband, defer no time, put not off from day to day to turn unto the Lord, neither be you deceived; for God is not mocked. The longer you run on, the more you set on the score, and such as you sow, such shall you reap. For the Lord hath said, 'He that heareth my words, and doth bless himself in heart, saying, I shall have peace, although I walk according to the stubbornness of my heart, thus adding drunkenness to thirst, the Lord will not be merciful unto him, but the wrath of the Lord and his jealousy shall smoke against that man, and every curse that is written in this book shall light upon him, and the Lord shall put out his name from under

83. *the ... congregation*: church
85. *comfort*: strengthening; well-being
86. *straitly*: strictly
87. *of vocations*: our everyday work or activities
93. *all together*: all at once
96. *comforts*: spiritual refreshment
97. *unspeakable ... sanctify it*: inexpressible ... keep it sacred
98. *livery*: uniform (worn by servants)
99. *filthiness*: moral degeneracy; obscenity
104. *set ... score*: run up your tally (of misdeeds); Proverbs 22.8
104–5. *sow ... reap*: Luke 8.5–15
105–11. *He ... heaven*: paraphrasing Deuteronomy 29.19–20. The image of drunkenness signifying unrestrained will and appetite extends Caldwell's earlier complaints against her husband's carousing.
108. *jealousy*: vehement indignation

heaven'. But unto them that repent, the Lord hath said, 'When the wicked turneth away from his wickedness that he hath committed, and doth that which is lawful and right, he shall save his soul alive'. You see the judgements of God are begun already in your house. Happy shall you be if you make a holy use of them; otherwise heavier may be expected, especially if you persist. In his mercy he hath spared you, and doth yet wait for your repentance. Do not you abuse his patience any longer, lest thereby you provoke him to proceed to execution against you. But embrace his mercy which is yet a-offered unto you; for which, that you may so do, I shall not cease to pray whilst I live, to him who only is able to effect it, even the Lord of heaven, who send us joyful meeting at the day of our resurrection.

Your poor wife,
Elizabeth Caldwell.

111–13. *When ... alive*: Ezekiel 33.19

113–16. *You ... persist*: Caldwell reinscribes herself a final time as a scourge of God, thus carrying her self-transformation from criminal to victimised wife to its logical conclusion

118. *execution*: destruction

ELIZABETH CLINTON, COUNTESS OF LINCOLN
(? 1574–1632+)

FROM *THE COUNTESS OF LINCOLN'S NURSERY*

(1622)

Introduction

Thomas Lodge, a contemporary writer and physician, praises Elizabeth Clinton in his Preface to *The Countess of Lincoln's Nursery* for uniting three qualities he believes will attract readers to her work: 'Eminency, or interest in the author. Rarity in the handled matter. Brevity in the quick dispatch' (A4[r]). The last of these becomes self-evident in the course of reading Clinton's lucid and neatly organised little treatise. The first quality – her social rank – Lodge mentions not only out of respect but also because it was integral to her subject, which consists partly of reproving the 'unnatural practice' of wet-nursing. During this period it was generally only upper-class women who were able to have their children breast-fed by wet-nurses. Clinton herself, as she confesses near the end of her work, had all eighteen of her children nursed, though she came deeply to regret this decision. She now atones for her actions by publishing *The Nursery*, which positively urges all gentlewomen to recognise 'the duty of nursing due by mothers to their own children'. In this case she hopes her 'eminency' will lend greater weight to her claims than if she were simply like the vast majority of Englishwomen who had no choice in the matter.

The 'Rarity' that Lodge mentions may be less obvious but is an aspect of Clinton's work which may surprise readers. For despite its cosy-sounding title and well-mannered refutation of common prejudices against breast-feeding, *The Countess of Lincoln's Nursery* takes a radical stand against what is essentially an upper-class fashion and protests its attendant exploitation of working-class women. Only richer women could afford wet-nursing because of the high cost, while poorer ones were tempted to neglect their own children for the sake of regular employment and good wages. Clinton argues that while working women may seem content to become wet-nurses, they are effectively 'estranged' from their own children and may take the resulting frustration out on their charges in the form of casual neglect or active mistreatment. *The Nursery* therefore urges better-off women to adopt a responsible attitude towards both their own children and the needy women of their communities whom they employ. There is also a sense that as privileged women they ought to be magnanimous enough to recognise an inherent natural equality in maternal affection and not attempt to disrupt it. This undercurrent of universality emerges throughout the first section of her work as Clinton develops arguments from biblical and natural history. The four exemplary matriarchs she cites – Eve, Sarah, Hannah, and Mary – were all initially devalued in their societies because of their gender, social status, and/or barrenness. Eventually, however, they were divinely favoured with children whom they chose to nurse themselves. Doing so, Clinton argues, represented their fulfilment of a covenant with God for being heard and empowered. She sees breast-feeding as a similar opportunity for all women to confirm their spiritual links with the unfolding power of creation and to glory in a uniquely female heritage.

Though a few Renaissance divines and physicians had written on breast-feeding in the contexts of proper female conduct and gynaecology (with virtually all – like Lodge in his Preface – approving of breast-feeding and condemning wet-nursing), their advice was consistently ignored by most noble and gentry families. Within these discourses *The Countess of Lincoln's Nursery* is also 'rare' because its author is female and can therefore draw upon practical knowledge of delivering and caring for children, whereas male commentators could rely only on received theories, since childbirth and child-rearing were exclusively female responsibilities during this period. This situation was slowly beginning to change, however, as new seventeenth-century medical practitioners became professionalised and male physicians began to displace women from their traditional roles as family and village health-givers (Smith 1976a: 98; Clark 1919: 259–63). Though Clinton does not refer explicitly to these developments, her advocacy of breast-feeding arises out of a historical context in which women felt increasingly anxious about losing personal control over various related areas of healthcare such as midwifery.

Much of the pressure on upper-class women to avoid nursing their own children was created by husbands who disliked the practice (for reasons of decorum and/or because it meant abstaining from sexual intercourse – see n. to ll. 208–9 below). Clinton appears to attest this situation when she explains that although she may have wanted to nurse her own children, she had been 'overruled by another's authority'. If this 'authority' was her husband, the writing and publication of *The Nursery* in 1622 may be related to his death two years earlier. Clinton also attributes women's unwillingness to breast-feed to the lack of active nursing mothers amongst English gentry families. Here she supplies a role model in her daughter-in-law Bridget Fiennes, who had become Countess of Lincoln when Clinton's son Theophilus succeeded to the title in 1619. Clinton (now Dowager) dedicates *The Nursery* to the new Countess and celebrates the psychological benefits and maternal well-being which accompany the 'giving the sweet milk of your own breasts to your own child'.

Editions:

The Countess of Lincoln's Nursery (1622). STC 5432, reel 984. *The Female Spectator*, ed. Mary R. Mahl and Helene Koon (Bloomington, 1977). *The Paradise of Women*, ed. Betty Travitsky (Westport, Conn., 1981, brief excerpts). *English Women's Voices, 1540–1700*, ed. Charlotte F. Otten (Miami, 1992, excerpts).

ELIZABETH CLINTON, COUNTESS OF LINCOLN

FROM *THE COUNTESS OF LINCOLN'S NURSERY*

(1622)

Because it hath pleased God to bless me with many children, and so caused me to observe many things falling out to mothers and to their children, I thought good to open my mind concerning a special matter belonging to all childbearing women seriously to consider of, and to manifest my mind the better, even to write of this matter so far as God shall please to direct me. In sum, the matter I mean is the duty of nursing due by mothers to their own children.

In setting down whereof, I will first show that every woman ought to nurse her own child, and secondly, I will endeavour to answer such objections as are used to be cast out against this duty to disgrace the same.

The first point is easily performed. For it is the express ordinance of God that mothers should nurse their own children, and being his ordinance, they are bound to it in conscience. This should stop the mouths of all repliers. For God is most wise and therefore must needs know what is fittest and best for us to do. And to prevent all foolish fears or shifts, we are given to understand that he is also all sufficient, and therefore infinitely able to bless his own ordinance and to afford us means in ourselves (as continual experience confirmeth) toward the observance thereof.

If this (as it ought) be granted, then how venturous are those women that dare venture to do otherwise and so to refuse, and by refusing to despise, that order which the most wise and almighty God hath appointed, and instead thereof to choose their own pleasures? Oh what peace can there be to these women's consciences, unless through the darkness of their understanding they judge it no disobedience?

And then they will drive me to prove that this nursing and nourishing of their own children in their own bosoms is God's ordinance. They are very wilful or very ignorant if they make a question of it. For it is proved sufficiently to be their duty, both by God's word and also by his works.

By his word it is proved first by examples, namely the example of Eve.

2. *falling out*: that normally happen
8. *whereof*: (referring to 'duty' in line 6)
10. *cast out*: commonly made
15. *prevent ... shifts*: avoid ... evasions
19. *venturous*: dangerously bold

For who suckled her sons Cain, Abel, Seth, etc. but herself? Which she did not only of mere necessity because yet no other woman was created, but especially because she was their mother and so saw it was her duty, and because she had a true natural affection which moved her to do it gladly. Next the example of Sarah the wife of Abraham. For she both gave her son Isaac suck, as doing the duty commanded of God, and also took great comfort and delight therein as in a duty well-pleasing to herself, whence she spake of it as of an action worthy to be named in her holy rejoicing. Now if Sarah, so great a princess, did nurse her own child, why should any of us neglect to do the like, except (which God forbid) we think scorn to follow her, whose daughters it is our glory to be, and which we be only upon this condition, that we imitate her well-doing? Let us look therefore to her worthy pattern, noting withal that she put herself to this work when she was very old, and so might the better have excused herself than we younger women can, being also more able to hire and keep a nurse than any of us. . . .

But now to another worthy example, namely that excellent woman Hannah who, having after much affliction of mind obtained a son of God whom she vowed unto God, she did not put him to another to nurse, but nursed him her own self until she had weaned him and carried him to be consecrate unto the Lord, as well knowing that this duty of giving her child suck was so acceptable to God, as for the cause thereof, she did not sin in staying with it at home from the yearly sacrifice. But now women, especially of any place and of little grace, do not hold this duty acceptable to God because it is unacceptable to themselves, as if they would have the Lord to like and dislike according to their vain lusts.

To proceed, take notice of one example more, that is of the blessed Virgin. As her womb bare our blessed saviour, so her paps gave him suck.

30. *Cain . . . etc.*: Genesis 4ff

34–7. *Sarah . . . rejoicing*: 'Then Sarah said, God hath made me to rejoice; all that hear will rejoice with me. / Again she said, Who would have said to Abraham that Sarah should have given children suck? for I have borne him a son in his old age' (Genesis 21.6–7, Geneva version, 1560, which Clinton uses throughout; also below ll. 64–5). Sarah was 90 and had been barren, Abraham was 100.

39. *think scorn*: despise

42. *withal*: besides

44. *nurse*: wet-nurse

47–52. *Hannah . . . sacrifice*: 1 Samuel 1. Hannah's 'affliction of mind' was childlessness, which lowered her social status and led her husband's other wife Peninnah, who was fertile, to torment her. Her barrenness ended when she prayed fervently to God for a son – Samuel – whom she promised to dedicate to his service.

50. *consecrate*: dedicated

53. *place*: rank

Now whom shall deny the own mother's suckling of their own children to be their duty, since every godly matron hath walked in these steps before them: Eve the mother of all the living, Sarah the mother of all the faithful, Hannah so graciously heard of God, Mary blessed among women and called blessed of all ages? And who can say but that the rest of holy women mentioned in the holy scriptures did the like, since no doubt that speech of that noble dame, saying 'Who would have said to Abraham that Sarah should have given children suck?', was taken from the ordinary custom of mothers in those less corrupted times?

And so much for proof of this office and duty to be God's ordinance by his own word according to the argument of examples. I hope I shall likewise prove it by the same word from plain precepts. First from that precept which willeth the younger women to marry and to bear children; that is, not only to bear them in the womb and to bring them forth, but also to bear them on their knee, in their arms, and at their breasts. For this bearing a little before is called nourishing and bringing up. And to enforce it the better upon women's consciences, it is numbered as the first of the good works for which godly women should be well reported of. And well it may be the first; because if holy ministers or other Christians do hear of a good woman to be brought to bed and her child to be living, their first question usually is whether she herself give it suck, yea or no. If the answer be she doth, then they commend her. If the answer be she doth not, then they are sorry for her.

And thus I come to a second precept. I pray you, who that judges aright doth not hold the suckling of her own child the part of a true mother, of an honest mother, of a just mother, of a sincere mother, of a mother worthy of love, of a mother deserving good report, of a virtuous mother, of a mother winning praise for it? All this is assented to by any of good understanding. Therefore this is also a precept. As for other duties, so for this of mothers to their children, which saith 'Whatsoever things are true, whatsoever things are honest, whatsoever things are just, whatsoever things are pure, whatsoever things be worthy of love, whatsoever things be of good report, if there be any virtue, if there be any praise, think on these things, these things do, and the God of peace shall be with you'.

So far for my promise to prove by the word of God that it is his ordi-

59. *matron*: dignified married women, especially one with personal expertise in birth and child-care

61. *heard of God*: literal meaning of 'Hannah'

61–2. *blessed ... ages*: Luke 1.28

69–70. *precepts ... children*: 1 Timothy 5.14, whose context is young widows remarrying

72–3. *a little before*: i.e. 1 Timothy 5.10

77. *bed*: (safe) childbirth

84. *report*: public commendation

87–91. *Whatsoever ... you*: Philippians 4:8–9

nance that women should nurse their own children. Now I will endeavour to prove it by his works. First by his works of judgement. If it were not his ordinance for mothers to give their children suck, it were no judgement to bereave them of their milk. But it is specified to be a great judgement to bereave them hereof, and to give them dry breasts. Therefore it is to be gathered, even from hence, that it is his ordinance, since to deprive them of means to do it is a punishment of them.

I add to this the work that God worketh in the very nature of mothers, which proveth also that he hath ordained that they should nurse their own children. For by his secret operation the mother's affection is so knit by nature's law to her tender babe, as she finds no power to deny to suckle it, no not when she is in hazard to lose her own life by attending on it. For in such a case it is not said, 'let the mother fly and leave her infant to the peril', as if she were dispensed with, but only it is said, 'woe to her', as if she were to be pitied that for nature to her child she must be unnatural to herself. Now if any then, being even at liberty and in peace, with all plenty, shall deny to give suck to their own children, they go against nature and show that God hath not done so much for them as to work any good, no not in their nature, but left them more savage than the dragons and as cruel to their little ones as the ostriches.

Now another work of God, proving this point, is the work of his provision for every kind to be apt and able to nourish their own fruit. There is no beast that feeds their young with milk but the Lord (even from the first ground of the order of nature, 'Grow and multiply') hath provided it of milk to suckle their own young, which every beast takes so naturally unto: as if another beast come toward their young to offer the office of a dam unto it, they show according to their fashion a plain dislike of it, as if nature did speak in them and say it is contrary to God's order in nature (commanding each kind to increase and multiply in their own bodies and by their own

94. *judgement*: i.e. punishment

96–7. *great ... breasts*: 'O Lord, give them: what wilt thou give them? give them a barren womb and dry breasts' (Hosea 9:14)

98. *it*: breast-feeding

102. *secret*: instinctive

106. *were ... with*: absolved of responsibility

108. *plenty*: material abundance

109–12. *they ... ostriches*: Lamentations 4:3: 'Even the dragons draw out the breasts, and give suck to their young, but the daughter of my people is become cruel like the ostriches in the wilderness.' The context is the Babylonian destruction of Jerusalem, in which children being denied their mothers' breasts become symbolic of the city's calamitous desperation.

116, 130. *Grow ... multiply*: Genesis 1.22

118. *office ... dam*: service of a mother

121. *kind*: species

breasts) not to bring forth by one dam and to bring up by another. But it is his ordinance that every kind should both bring forth and also nurse its own fruit.

Much more should this work of God prevail to persuade women, made as man in the image of God, and therefore should be ashamed to be put to school to learn good nature of the unreasonable creature. In us also, as we know by experience, God provideth milk in our breasts against the time of our children's birth. And this he hath done ever since it was said to us also, 'Increase and multiply', so that this work of his provision showeth that he tieth us likewise to nourish the children of our own womb with our own breasts even by the order of nature; yea, it showeth that he so careth for and regardeth little children even from the womb that he would have them nursed by those that in all reason will look to them with the kindest affection, namely their mothers; and in giving them milk for it, he doth plainly tell them that he requires it.

Oh consider, how comes our milk? Is it not by the direct providence of God? Why provides he it, but for the child? The mothers then that refuse to nurse their own children, do they not despise God's providence? Do they not deny God's will? Do they not, as it were, say 'I see, O God, by the means thou hast put into me, that thou wouldst have me nurse the child thou hast given me. But I will not do so much for thee.' Oh impious and impudent unthankfulness, yea monstrous unnaturalness, both to their own natural fruit borne so near their breasts and fed in their own wombs, and yet may not be suffered to suck their own milk.

And this unthankfulness and unnaturalness is oftener the sin of the higher and the richer sort than of the meaner and poorer, except some nice and proud idle dames who will imitate their betters till they make their poor husbands beggars. And this is one hurt which the better rank do by their ill

127. *unreasonable creature*: animal lacking the reason that uniquely distinguishes humans

128. *against*: in anticipation of

144. *yet*: (their children)

147. *nice*: wanton (i.e. socially ambitious)

148–9. *till ... beggars*: wet-nursing was an expensive proposition. Nurses were the most highly paid domestic servants, which is why it was attractive to working-class women as employment; e.g. a wage of 8s. per four weeks was paid under poor-relief foster-care in Aldenham, Hertfordshire (Newall 1990: 126–7), while a typical private household paid 30s for eighteen months in 1650. Besides wages there were numerous extras such as christening dinners, rent, clothing and presents; one list of 120 items in 1630 included shirts, sheets, headcloths, lace stomachers, neckcloths, navel cloths, silk sleeves, lace handkerchiefs, aprons, gloves, girdles, pillows, a counterpane, and a whistle (McLaren 1985: 45).

149–50. *better ... lower*: the expense of wet-nursing generally restricted it to upper-class households, but in London some middle-class families sent their children to country nurses (McLaren 1985: 33)

example: egg and embolden the lower ones to follow them to their loss. Were it not better for us greater persons to keep God's ordinance and to show the meaner their duty in our good example? I am sure we have more helps to perform it and have fewer probable reasons to allege against it than women that live by hard labour and painful toil. . . .

And so I come to the last part of my promise, which is to answer objections made by divers against this duty of mothers to their children.

First it is objected that Rebekah had a nurse and that therefore her mother did not give her suck of her own breasts, and so good women in the first ages did not hold them to this office of nursing their own children. To this I answer that if her mother had milk and health and yet did put this duty from her to another, it was her fault, and so proveth nothing against me. But it is manifest that she that Rebekah calleth her nurse was called so either for that she most tended her while her mother suckled her, or for that she weaned her, or for that, during her nonage and childhood, she did minister to her continually such good things as delighted and nourished her up. For to any one of these the name of a nurse is fitly given, whence a good wife is called her husband's nurse. And that Rebekah's nurse was only such a one appeareth, because afterward she is not named a nurse but a maid, saying, 'Then Rebekah rose, and her maids'. . . .

Secondly it is objected that it is troublesome, that it is noisome to one's clothes, that it makes one look old, etc. All such reasons are uncomely and unchristian to be objected, and therefore unworthy to be answered. They argue unmotherly affection, idleness, desire to have liberty to gad from home, pride, foolish fineness, lust, wantonness, and the like evils. Ask Sarah, Hannah, the blessed Virgin, and any modest loving mother what trouble they accounted it to give their little ones suck? Behold most nursing mothers and they be as clean and sweet in their clothes, and carry their age, and hold their beauty, as well as those that suckle not. And most likely are they so to do because, keeping God's ordinance, they are sure of God's blessing. And it hath been observed in some women that they grew more beautiful and better favoured by very nursing their own children.

150. *egg*: egg on
156. *divers*: sundry (people)
157. *Rebecca*: another Old Testament woman who was barren until her husband Isaac (son of Sarah, above ll. 34–45) entreated the Lord on her behalf (Genesis 25:21). Her 'nurse' is mentioned at Genesis 24.59.
159. *office*: duty
164. *nonage*: minority
169. *maids*: Genesis 24.61
170. *noisome*: harmful
171. *uncomely*: improper
172. *objected*: put forward
181. *favoured*: in appearance, features

But there are some women that object fear, saying that they are so weak and so tender that they are afraid to venture to give their children suck lest they endanger their health thereby. Of these I demand why then they did venture to marry and so to bear children? And if they say they could not choose and that they thought not that marriage would impair their health, I answer that for the same reasons they should set themselves to nurse their own children because they should not choose but do what God would have them do. And they should believe that this work will be for their health also, seeing it is ordinary with the Lord to give good stomach, health, and strength to almost all mothers that take this pains with their children.

One answer more to all the objections that use to be made against giving children suck is this: that now the hardness to effect this matter is much removed by a late example of a tender young lady; and you may all be encouraged to follow after in that wherein she hath gone before you and so made the way more easy and more hopeful by that which she findeth possible and comfortable by God's blessing, and no offence to her lord nor herself. She might have had as many doubts and lets as any of you, but she was willing to try how God would enable her; and he hath given her good success, as I hope he will do to others that are willing to trust in God for his help.

Now if any reading these few lines return against me that it may be I myself have given my own children suck and therefore am bolder and more busy to meddle in urging this point, to the end to insult over and to make them to be blamed that have not done it, I answer that, whether I have or have not performed this my bounden duty, I will not deny to tell my own practice. I know and acknowledge that I should have done it, and having not done it, it was not for want of will in myself, but partly I was overruled

182. *object*: object out of

183. *venture to give*: risk giving

192. *use to be*: are habitually

194. *lady*: Elizabeth Clinton's daughter-in-law Bridget Fiennes, daughter of Viscount Say and Sele. She became Countess of Lincoln when Thomas Clinton died in January 1619 and the Clintons' eldest surviving son, Theophilus, became Earl.

197. *lord*: husband (though the original edition's 'Lord' may signify God)

198. *lets*: hindrances

199–200. *good success*: Bridget Clinton bore one son and three daughters; she died *c.* 1631

208–9. *overruled … authority*: if this 'authority' was Elizabeth Clinton's husband, who had died two years before, it could explain the timing of the *Nursery*'s publication. In a dedicatory epistle to her daughter-in-law Clinton states that it is 'the first work of mine that ever came in print', suggesting she wrote other unpublished material as well. The strong cultural pressure on upper-class families to hire wet-nurses, despite near-unanimous advice against the practice by physicians and divines, was created partly by male hostility towards public breast-feeding. Moreover, 'sexual intercourse was both forbidden and feared during lactation because it was universally thought that the milk

by another's authority, and partly deceived by some's ill counsel, and partly I had not so well considered of my duty in this motherly office as since I did, when it was too late for me to put it in execution. Wherefore, being pricked in heart for my undutifulness, this way I study to redeem my peace: first by repentance towards God, humbly and often craving his pardon for this my offence; secondly by studying how to show double love to my children, to make them amends for neglect of this part of love to them when they should have hung on my breasts and have been nourished in mine own bosom; thirdly by doing my endeavour to prevent many Christian mothers from sinning in the same kind against our most loving and gracious God.

And for this cause, I add unto my performed promise this short exhortation. Namely, I beseech all godly women to remember how we elder ones are commanded to instruct the younger to love their children. Now, therefore, love them so as to do this office to them when they are born, more gladly for love's sake than a stranger who bore them not shall do for lucre's sake. Also I pray you to set no more so light by God's blessing in your own breasts, which the holy spirit ranketh with other excellent blessings. If it be unlawful to trample under feet a cluster of grapes in which a little wine is found, then how unlawful is it to destroy and dry up those breasts in which your own child (and perhaps one of God's very elect, to whom to be a nursing father is a king's honour, and to whom to be a nursing mother is a queen's honour) might find food of sincere milk, even from God's immediate providence until it were fitter for stronger meat. I do know that the Lord may deny some women either to have any milk in their breasts at all, or to have any passage for their milk, or to have any health, or to have a right mind, and so they may be letted from this duty by want, by sickness, by lunacy, etc. But I speak not to these. I speak to you whose consciences witness against you, that you cannot justly allege any of those impediments.

would become corrupted by intercourse or a new conception and kill the child' (King 1991: 14; McLaren 1985: 27). Men paid for wet-nurses, in other words, to keep their wives sexually available.

209. *some's*: some people's

210. *did*: have

211. *pricked*: stung

223–4. *lucre's sake*: sake of material gain

224. *to … by*: no more to put to one side so indifferently

224–5. *God's … blessings*: 'And it came to pass as [Jesus] said these things, a certain woman of the company lifted up her voice, and said unto him, Blessed is the womb that bare thee, and the paps which thou hast sucked' (Luke 11.27)

226–7. *trample … found*: i.e. squander the resources of creation, alluding to Isaiah 65.8; is found = could be made from

228. *elect*: chosen for eternal salvation (referring to the Calvinist theory of election)

231. *meat*: food

234. *letted*: excused

Do you submit yourselves to the pain and trouble of this ordinance of God? Trust not other women, whom wages hires to do it, better than yourselves, whom God and nature ties to do it. I have found by grievous experience such dissembling in nurses, pretending sufficiency of milk when indeed they had too much scarcity, pretending willingness, towardness, wakefulness, when indeed they have been most wilful, most froward, and most slothful, as I fear the death of one or two of my little babes came by the default of their nurses. Of all those which I had for eighteen children, I had but two which were thoroughly willing and careful. Divers have had their children miscarry in the nurses hands; and are such mothers (if it were by the nurse's carelessness) guiltless? I know not how they should, since they will shut them out of the arms of nature and leave them to the will of a stranger, yea, to one that will seem to estrange herself from her own child to give suck to the nurse-child. This she may fain to do upon a covetous composition, but she frets at it in her mind if she have any natural affection.

Therefore be no longer at the trouble and at the care to hire others to do your own work. Be not so unnatural to thrust away your own children. Be not so hardy as to venture a tender babe to a less tender heart. Be not accessory to that disorder of causing a poorer woman to banish her own infant for the entertaining of a richer woman's child, as it were, bidding her unlove her own to love yours....

241. *towardness*: willingness

244. *eighteen*: not an unusually high number for upper-class women, who by not breast-feeding failed to benefit from the contraceptive effect of lactation, traditionally recognised since ancient times and now known to be result of the hormone prolactin. As a result, women who hired wet-nurses had 'appallingly high' fertility rates (twenty births being not uncommon), high infant mortality, and smaller achieved family size, whilst mothers who suckled their own children normally had longer birth intervals (approximately two to three years as opposed to one) and low infant mortality rates (Newall 1990: 128–31; McLaren 1985: 22–7). Clinton does not explicitly link nursing and fertility in the *Nursery*, but the difference between her own experience and her daughter-in-law's (see above ll. 197–201) implies a case in point.

246. *miscarry*: perish

247. *should*: should be

250–1. *fain ... composition*: consent to do for the sake of money

254. *hardy*: foolishly daring

less ... heart: a common perception, but difficult to gauge. There is evidence to suggest that children put out to be breast-fed were affected by the unhealthy living conditions, poverty, and intemperance of their nurses, and that some nurses neglected or sacrificed their own children in favour of their charges. But infanticide seems to have been limited almost exclusively to children of unmarried mothers (McLaren 1985: 29; Newall 1990: 129).

255. *disorder*: disruptive (social) practice

Think always that, having the child at your breast and having it in your arms, you have God's blessing there. For children are God's blessings. Think again how your babe crying for your breast, sucking heartily the milk out of it and growing by it, is the Lord's own instruction, every hour and every day that you are suckling it, instructing you to show that you are his newborn babes by your earnest desire after his word and the sincere doctrine thereof; and by your daily growing in grace and goodness thereby, so shall you reap pleasure and profit. Again, you may consider that when your child is at your breast, it is a fit occasion to move your heart to pray for a blessing upon that work and to give thanks for your child, and for ability and freedom unto that which many a mother would have done and could not, who have tried and ventured their health and taken much pains and yet have not obtained their desire. But they that are fitted every way for this commendable act have certainly great cause to be thankful. And I much desire that God may have glory and praise for every good work, and you much comfort that do seek to honour God in all things. Amen.

262. *instructing . . . you*: revealing by analogy that you yourselves
263. *after*: to follow
269. *ventured*: risked

ELIZABETH CARY, LADY FALKLAND (1585/6–1639)

FROM *THE HISTORY OF THE LIFE, REIGN, AND DEATH OF EDWARD II*

(*c.* 1627)

Introduction

Though many writers in this anthology have the distinction of being the first women to write in a particular genre in English, Elizabeth Cary can claim several firsts. Her *History of Edward II* is the first political history written by an Englishwoman, and it follows her *Tragedy of Mariam* (1613), the first original play. She is also the subject of the first biography of an English female author, *The Lady Falkland Her Life* (1643–50), written by one of her daughters (the two latter works have recently been edited by Weller and Ferguson (in Cary 1994)). Renaissance England produced many literary and historical treatments of Edward II, with most focusing on the singularly wilful and incompetent rule which led Parliament to depose him in favour of his son Edward III. Writers paid little attention to Queen Isabel except in terms of her romantic attachment to Roger Mortimer, which was seen as the understandable but still wicked response to Edward's homosexual infatuation with two court favourites, Gaveston and Spencer. Cary's *Edward II*, by contrast, is remarkable for its exceptionally full, psychologically complex, and arguably feminist portrait of Isabel. And like her *Tragedy of Mariam* it invites interpretation from a number of critical perspectives: literary, political, cultural, and biographical. These will be touched on briefly, but first something must be said about the work's authorship, since this is still the subject of some controversy.

When *The History of Edward II* was published in 1680, its title-page stated that it was 'Written by *E.F.* in the year 1627. And printed verbatim from the original'. Notwithstanding the initials *E.F.*, the work was assumed to have been written by Elizabeth Cary's husband Henry Cary, Viscount Falkland, partly because history was considered 'properly' to be a man's genre, and partly because another book about Edward II, also published in 1680 and related to *The History* in some way, was attributed to Viscount Falkland on its title-page:

> *The History of the Most Unfortunate Prince, King Edward the Second. With Choice Political Observations on Him and his unhappy Favourites, Gaveston & Spencer: Containing Several Rare Passages of those Times, Not found in other Historians. Found among the Papers of, and (supposed to be) Writ by the Right Honourable Henry Viscount Faulkland, Sometime Lord Deputy of Ireland.* [hereafter *Unfortunate Prince*]

The *Unfortunate Prince* is an octavo (a small-format book), written entirely in prose and much shorter than *The History of Edward II*, a folio (larger format book) containing both prose and verse. Many scholars now believe the octavo to be a later abridgement of the 1627 *History* intended to comment on the 1679–81 Exclusion Crisis, and therefore *not* by Viscount Falkland (who died in 1633; Stauffer 1935: 294; Lewalski 1993: 317; Woolf 1988: 440; Kennedy 1995). Donald W. Foster, however, has recently revived the alternative theory that Falkland first wrote the *Unfortunate Prince*, which Elizabeth Cary subsequently 'plagiarized' in *The History of Edward II* (1993: 164–6). Though his article is valuable in other ways, Foster offers no detailed evidence to support these claims, and he introduces a confused teleology by belittling Cary's 'excessive borrowing' from and 'tinkering with' her husband's work, while also referring to her 'deliberately appropriated' and 'rewritten' version as 'the completed text' (166–9).

It was Donald A. Stauffer in 1935 who first suggested that E.F. stood for 'Elizabeth Falkland', as Cary signed herself after her husband was made Viscount Falkland in 1620. The same initials appear at the end of *The History*'s 'Preface to the Reader':

> To out-run those weary hours of a deep and sad passion, my melancholy pen fell accidentally on this historical relation, which speaks a king, our own, though one of the most unfortunate, and shows the pride and fall of his inglorious minions.
>
> I have not herein followed the dull character of our historians, nor amplified more than they infer by circumstance. I strive to please the truth, not time; nor fear I censure, since at the worst 'twas but one month mis-spended, which cannot promise aught in right perfection.
>
> If so you hap to view it, tax not my errors; I myself confess them.
>
> 20 Feb. 1627 [= 1628]. E.F.

The pair of initials here and on the title-page, reminiscent of the 'E.C.' which identifies Cary's undisputed *Tragedy of Mariam*, constitutes the strongest evidence for her authorship, and there is now growing agreement on this and other grounds that *The History of Edward II* is hers (best summarised by Lewalski 1993: 201–3, 317–20; also Cary 1994: 12–16; Krontiris 1990: 137–40; Fischer 1985: 227).

Certain remarks in the 'Preface to the Reader' cited above point towards a consideration of the type of history represented by her work. Cary vows to avoid the 'dull' kind of sprawling chronicle written by earlier Renaissance historians (e.g. the collectively written volume that appeared under the name of Raphael Holinshed) that tended to compile all the accounts passed down by previous writers. Instead she wishes to serve 'truth' by presenting focused narratives of major characters and their most significant actions from which readers can quickly identify moral issues and political lessons. This was the new 'practical' history that looked back to the model of classical writers such as Tacitus and Livy (Lewalski 1993: 203), and also to Plutarch's *Lives* in its focus on human passions and psychology as key determinants of historical events. The result in Cary's case is what Isobel Grundy calls a 'hybrid' genre, 'highly literary, morally questioning, sometimes elaborately and sometimes stiffly rhetorical' (1988: 83). In the interests of writing vivid history, she 'amplifies' facts derived eclectically from earlier sources with dramatised orations and heightened language. The latter includes pictorial imagery, a range of colloquial and formal diction, and highly wrought metaphors, some of which occasionally become over-elaborate or confused. Her prose has a strong rhythmic sense and is sometimes scannable as blank verse with an unusually high number of feminine endings, though the shifts between prose and verse are not clear-cut except for the formal orations (Stauffer 1935: 300; see n. to l. 125ff.).

For modern readers the story of Edward II and his scandalous favourites is best known from Marlowe's *Edward II* and, more recently, from Derek Jarman's film version (1992) with its heightened attention to sexual and class politics. Cary probably wrote a verse-life of Tamburlaine *c.* 1603–10 (Cary 1994: 190), and her treatments of Edward and Gaveston are not dissimilar to Marlowe's, though neither is especially remarkable; her real interest lies in the power struggle between Spencer and Queen Isabel in the second half of Edward's reign (the focus of passages selected below). Spencer is the classic upstart courtier animated by Machiavellian expediency and overreaching ambition. His dominance of Edward probably also has topical resonances. For just as the *Unfortunate Prince* is believed to have been written to comment on the Exclusion Crisis, it is likely that Edward's indulgence of Spencer would have been read in the late 1620s as criticism of James I's devotion to his own court favourite, George Villiers, Duke of Buckingham (Lewalski 1993: 205–7, 393, Bradbrook 1982: 93; Woolf 1988 dissents). A question remains, however, as to why Elizabeth Cary would have wished to suggest such a comparison, given that she was a close friend of the Duchess of Buckingham and her Catholic-leaning circle at court (Cary 1994: 15).

While no topical analogies have been suggested for Queen Isabel, more interesting possibilities exist for reading her story in terms of Cary's own life. In this regard the 'Preface to the Reader' is again suggestive when Cary speaks of writing as a way of living through 'those weary hours of a deep and sad passion'. Less than two years before in 1626 Lady Falkland had converted to Catholicism and been abandoned by her zealously Protestant husband. He had taken away her children, cut off her financial support, and forced her to eke out an existence in a cottage outside London until close to the time of his own death seven years later. Cary was also virtually disowned by her own family. So while Weller and Ferguson are right to caution us that claims of writing for self-consolation are conventional during this period (Cary 1994: 17), it is hard to resist the Preface's invitation to regard Cary using her writing to resolve personal conflicts vicariously, here as in her other works. After a precocious childhood, she became deeply committed to philosophical, literary, and religious paths of self-expression, while at the same time finding these ambitions continually at odds with the social principles she was equally determined to fulfil in the roles of daughter, wife, Catholic, and Englishwoman. These irreconcilable loyalties created crises at several points in her life, of which the breakdown of her marriage was perhaps the most agonising. This may therefore explain Cary's decision to take up her 'melancholy pen' in order to live imaginatively through Isabel's dynamic of victimisation and independence (Beilin 1987: 153; Fischer 1985: 228; Foster 1993: 173). Cary sympathises openly with Isabel's suffering at the hands of dishonest men, while celebrating her shrewd leadership in outmanoeuvring her rivals, and she robustly defends her sexual freedom in the face of Edward's adulterous homosexuality (Krontiris 1990: 137–41). Insofar as she fulfils a role as tragic heroine, her fall comes about only at the very end when she yields to a wrathful vengeance against the defeated Spencer; yet it is notable that Cary frames Isabel's triumph in terms of the political outcome of the military campaign she has planned from France (she was the sister of the French King) and led personally in England, whereas other accounts by male writers devalue this same will to resistance by portraying it as the corollary of her sexual dalliance with Mortimer. Cary makes little mention of the latter's relationship with Isabel until after the King's deposition, when Mortimer is blackened as the prime mover behind Edward's murder. Here again Cary departs from previous accounts and minimises Isabel's guilt by withholding the violent details of Edward's death, and refers only perfunctorily to her (non-historical but traditional) penitence in later years (Lewalski 1993: 207–10, 394).

Editions:
The History of the Life, Reign, and Death of Edward II (1680). Wing F313, reel 93.
The Paradise of Women, ed. Betty Travitsky (Westport, Conn., 1981, brief excerpts).

ELIZABETH CARY, LADY FALKLAND

FROM *THE HISTORY OF THE LIFE, REIGN, AND DEATH OF EDWARD II*

(*c.* 1627)

Edward could not but know that a new president over his royal actions must make his subjects his but at a second hand; yet he is resolved of a new choice, of such a favourite as might supply and make good the room of his lost beloved Gaveston; hence sprung that fatal fire which scorched the kingdom with intestine ruin. He was put to no great trouble to seek a foreign climate; he had variety of his own, that might be easily made capable enough for such a loose employment. He had a swarm of sycophants that gaped after greatness, and cared not to pawn their souls to gain promotion; amongst these his eye fixed on Spencer, a man till then believed a naked statesman; he was young, and had a pleasing aspect; a personage though not super-excellent, yet well enough to make a formal minion.

1. *president*: sovereign; i.e. Hugh le Despencer (or Spencer) the younger, Edward II's second great favourite and counsellor after Piers Gaveston (see below). Prior to this point in *The History*, Gaveston has been captured and executed by the barons, and Edward has led a disastrous campaign against the invading Scots. He now turns to personal consolation, seeking to replace Gaveston.
2. *second hand*: i.e. once removed from direct rule
3. *room*: place
4. *Gaveston*: Edward's first and most notorious favourite and lover. Cary's portrayal of Gaveston and Edward is similar to that of Marlowe's *Edward II*. Spencer's meteoric rise to public power, his dominance of Edward and displacement of Isabel, the barons' resentment, and his ultimate fall, parallel the course of Gaveston's career. The chief difference is that Spencer's main political opponent is Queen Isabel rather than Thomas Earl of Lancaster and the barons, as it had been for Gaveston.
5. *intestine*: internal, civil

5–6. *foreign climate*: i.e. for finding a new favourite. Gaveston 'came out of Gascony', France.

7. *loose*: wanton
8. *gaped after*: were ravenous for
9. *a naked*: barely a. Historically the Despencers were noblemen, unlike Gaveston, but Cary follows early modern historians in attributing low social origins to both.

11. *formal minion*: adequate favourite, paramour. French 'mignon' has the same male sexual connotations deriving from the example of the court 'mignons' who surrounded Henri III. Cary calls him Edward's 'new *Ganymede*', alluding to the boy-god who displaces Juno's daughter Hebe as cupbearer to Jupiter and the gods. See the opening

The ladder by which he made his ascent was principally thus: he had been always conformable to the King's will, and never denied to serve his appetite in every his ways and occasions; which was virtue enough to give him wealth and title. Some others think this feat was wrought by witchcraft, and by the spells of a grave matron that was suspected to have a journeyman devil to be her loadstone: which is not altogether improbable, if we behold the progression; for never was servant more insolently fortunate, nor master unreasonably indulgent. Their passages are as much beyond belief as contrary to the rules of reason. But leaving the discourse of the cause, the King applauds his own workmanship, and dotes infinitely on the nonage of this imposture, which seeing the advantage, labours to advance it; and though in his own nature he were proud, harsh, and tyrannous, yet he clothes himself in the habit of humility, as obsequious to his master, as smooth and winning to his acquaintance, knowing that a rub might make the bowl fall short while it was running: heat of blood, and height of spirit, consult more with passion than judgement; where all sides are agreed, quick ends the bargain. Spencer must rise, the King himself avows it, and who was there durst cross their sovereign's pleasure? The resolution known, like flocks of wild geese the spawn of court corruption fly to claw him. The great ones that till now scarce knew his offspring, think it an honour to become his kinsmen: the officers of state, to win his favour, forget their oaths, and make his will their justice. Lord, how the vermin creep to this warm sunshine and count each beam of his a special favour! Such a thing is the

scene of Marlowe's *Dido Queen of Carthage*, where 'There is discovered *Jupiter* dandling *Ganymede* upon his knee'. As Gwynne Kennedy observes, Edward's homosexuality will ultimately offer Isabel 'an authoritative site from which to speak and act as an unduly wronged, neglected wife' (1995)

13–14. *will* ... *appetite*: sexual and otherwise

16. *matron*: knowledgeable woman (in witchcraft)

16–17. *journeyman devil* ... *loadstone*: devil assistant ... attractive power

18. *progression*: of Spencer's career

21. *workmanship*: i.e. in 'making' his creature

21–2. *nonage* ... *imposture*: early stage or 'adolescence' of Spencer's ambitious dissembling of superior rank and power (perhaps also, with 'dotes', alluding to his youthful physical appeal)

23. *he*: Spencer

25–6. *rub* ... *running*: obstacle might divert the bowl before reaching its mark; cf. *Hamlet*: 'To die, to sleep; / To sleep, perchance to dream - ay, there's the rub' (3.1.64-5). 'Rub' also suggests sexual contact; cf. 'heat of blood'.

26. *height of spirit*: a possible pun on male erection

30. *spawn*: offspring

30–1. *him* ... *great ones*: Spencer ... established nobles

32. *oaths*: to Edward

prologue of a beginning greatness, that it can metamorphose all but those that hate it....

Being resolved to countenance [Spencer's] will with more haste than advisement, [the King] honours the subject of his choice with the Lord Chamberlain's place, professing freely he thought him worthy, and would maintain him in it. This foreright jump going so high, made all men wonder, and soon suspect him guilty of some secret virtue. Scarce had this new great lord possession of the white staff, but he forgets his former being, and sings the right night-crow's tune of upstart greatness, and follows his predecessor's pattern to the life, but with a far more strength and cunning. He was not born a stranger or an alien, but had his birth and breeding here, where he is exalted; and though he had not so much depth to know the secrets, yet understands the plainsong of the state, and her progressions, which taught him his first lesson, that infant-greatness falls where none support it. From this principle, his first work is employed to win and to preserve an able party. To work this sure, he makes a monopoly of the King's ear; no man may gain it but by his permission, establishing a sure intelligence within the royal chamber; not trusting one, but having sundry agents, who must successively attend all motions. By this he wedgeth in his sentinels at such a distance, that none can move, but he receives the larum. The first request he makes his sovereign (who never denied him) was, that he would not pass a grant till he surveyed it; for this he makes a zealous care the cover, lest by such gift the subject might be grieved, the King abused.

38. *advisement*: wise reflection
40. *foreright*: direct
42. *white staff*: emblem of the Lord Chamberlain's office
43. *right*: self-same
night-crow's: normally a nocturnal bird of evil omen, but here signifying false merit or pride; cf. Robert Greene's famous attack on Shakespeare for his alleged borrowings from Greene and other playwrights: an 'upstart crow, beautified with our feathers' (*A Groats-worth of Wit*, 1592)
predecessor's: Gaveston's
45. *stranger*: foreigner
46. *depth*: intellectual discernment
47. *plainsong ... her*: main tune (i.e. central workings) ... the state's
50. *party*: faction
51–2. *establishing ... intelligence*: by which means he establishes ... network of informers
53. *successively*: in a prescribed order
motions: desires, inclinations
54. *at ... distance*: with such a close and complete view
receives ... larum: is immediately alerted
56. *grant*: of money or patronage

This stratagem unmasked, gave perfect knowledge: whoever leaped the horse, he held the bridle, which reined his foes up short, while friends unhorsed them, and raised as he pleased all such as bribed or sought him. To mix these serious strains with lighter objects, he feeds the current of his sovereign's vices with store of full delights, to keep him busied, whilst he might act his part with more attention. He quarrels those whom he suspects too honest, or at the least, not his more than their master's, and quickly puts them off, that there may be entry for such as he prefers his proper creatures, so that a short time makes the court all of a piece at his commandment. Those whom he feared in state would cross his workings, he seeks to win by favour or alliance; if they both fail, he tenders fairly to lift them higher by some new promotion, so he may have them sure on all occasions; and with these baits he catched the hungry planets. Such as he finds too faithful for surprisal, these he sequesters, mounting his kindred up to fill their places. The Queen, that had no great cause to like those sirens that caused her grief and did seduce her husband, he yet presumes to court with strong professions, vowing to serve her as a faithful servant. She seeing into the quality of the time, where he was powerful, and she in name a wife, in truth a handmaid, doth not oppose, but more increase his greatness, by letting all men know that she received him. To win a nearer place in her opinion, he gains his kindred places next her person; and those that were her own, he bribes to back him. The court thus fashioned, he levels at the country, whence he must gain his strength if need enforced it. Here he must have an estate, and some sure refuge; this he contrives by begging the custody of

58. *unmasked, gave*: coming into play, gave Spencer

58–9. *the horse*: i.e. into the saddle

65. *proper*: own

66. *all . . . commandment*: all united to do his bidding

68. *alliance . . . tenders fairly*: marriage . . . generously offers

70. *planets*: apparently meaning satellites to himself as their 'sun' (while not suiting the metaphor satisfactorily)

71. *surprisal . . . sequesters*: successful capture or conversion . . . removes from their offices

72. *Queen*: historically Isabella (but called Isabel in Cary and Marlowe), daughter of King Philip the Fair of France. *The History* almost always refers to her by title rather than name.
sirens: mythological monsters, part bird, part woman, whose enchanted singing lured sailors to destruction

74. *professions*: of loyalty

76. *increase*: i.e. the public perception of

79. *levels*: aims

80. *gain . . . it*: draw his strength should it become necessary

81. *estate*: historically, Despencer seized a vast number of lands and offices, including Bristol Castle and much of South Wales
refuge: stronghold

divers of the principal honours and strength of the kingdom. But these were no inheritance which might perpetuate his memory, or continue his succession. He makes a salve for this sore; and to be able to be a fit purchaser of lands by the benefit of the prerogative, he falls a-selling of titles, in which it was believed he thrived well, though he sold many more lordships than he bought manors; by this means yet he got many pretty retiring places for a younger brother, within the more fertile counties of the kingdom. This for the private, now to the public: he makes sure the principal heads of justice, that by them his credit might pleasure an old friend, or make a new at his pleasure. If in this number any one held him at too smart a distance, prizing his integrity and honour before so base a traffic, he was an ill member of state, and either silenced or sent to an Irish or Welsh employment. It is enough to be believed faulty, where a disputation is not admitted. The hare knows her ears be not horns, yet dares not venture a trial, where things must not be sentenced as they are, but as they are taken. The commanders that sway most in popular faction, as far as he durst or might without combustion, he causeth to be conferred on his friends and kindred; and above all things, he settles a sure correspondence of intelligence in all the quarters of the kingdom, as a necessary leading precedent: he fills the people's ears with rumour of foreign danger, to busy their brains from discoursing domestic errors, and sends out a rabble of spying mercuries, who are instructed to

82. *honours*: legal powers; titles, social positions
strength: legal authorities, powers; military forces or fortresses
83. *inheritance*: lineal possessions which would descend to his heirs
85. *prerogative*: royal power (of creating and selling titles)
87. *retiring*: secluded (and perhaps 'secure')
89. *sure*: personally reliable
90. *credit*: personal influence, including monetary power
91. *smart*: alertly wary
92. *was*: was regarded as
93. *Irish ... employment*: i.e. put down uprisings against English rule that regularly occurred in those countries
94. *a disputation*: any self-defence or objection
95–6. *yet ... taken*: and does not risk its abilities, in which things must be judged not as they are perceived but as they really are
97. *sway ... faction*: have under their control the greatest popular support
he: Spencer
98. *conferred on*: brought together with (as allies)
99. *settles*: establishes firmly
correspondence ... intelligence: i.e. spy-network
100. *leading precedent*: first line (of public control)
102. *mercuries*: swift news-messengers (alluding to the classical god's winged sandals and hat)

talk liberally, to taste other men's inclinations, and feel the pulses of those that had most cause to be discontented. For the ancient nobility, which was a more difficult work to reduce to conformity, laying aside the punctilios of his greatness, he strives to gain them as he won his master; but when he found them shy and nice to make his party, he slights them more and more, to show his power, and make them seek to entertain his favour. And to eclipse their power by birth and number, he finds the means to make a new creation, which gave the rabble-gentry upstart honours, as children do give nuts away by handfuls; yet still he hath some feeling of the business. Lastly, he wins the King to call his father to the court, who with the shoal of all his kin are soon exalted, while he makes all things lawful that correspond his will, or master's humour....

Ever since the breach that happened between him and the Queen concerning Mortimer, there had been a strong heart-burning, and many distasteful expressions of the ill inclination she bare him. He knew her to be a woman of a strong brain and stout stomach, apt on all occasions to trip up his heels, if once she found him reeling; and was not without some discreet suspicion that she was, as well, contriving inward practice, as she had

103. *taste*: ascertain

104. *ancient nobility*: opponents of Spencer and his predecessor Gaveston; they deeply resented each favourite's personal arrogation of royal patronage and government power

105–6. *punctilios ... greatness*: strict insistence on respecting his social rank (regardless of personal feelings)

107–8. *shy ... make*: distrustful and unwilling to join

110. *creation*: of peers

111. *still ... business*: could not put out of his mind an awareness that his actions were fraudulent

112–13. *father ... exalted*: 'to let all the world know he stood right in his master's affections, [Spencer] gets his father, himself, and Sir Andrew Harclay, a chip of the same block, made Earls of Winchester, Bristol, and Carlisle' (*History* 81). Historically, Despencer the younger became Earl of Gloucester.

115–16. *breach ... Mortimer*: Roger Mortimer, later Earl of March. In *The History* he and his father, Roger Mortimer the elder, ransack some of Spencer's properties but are protected from prosecution by Parliament, which then banishes Spencer. But eventually Spencer returns to help Edward win a civil war culminating in the battle at Boroughbridge, in which Thomas Earl of Lancaster and 22 other barons are captured and executed. This marked 'the beginning of all [Edward's] ensuing misery', according to Cary, as his 'government became hateful, and his name odious' (*History* 74). The Mortimers managed to survive this purge, however, by being imprisoned in the Tower, and it was believed they were spared because of Isabella's influence.

119. *reeling ... was*: becoming vulnerable ... Spencer was

120. *contriving ... practice*: plotting secretly

been closely forward in the instigation of her brother. To make her sure, and to pare her nails before she scratched him, he thinks occasion had presented him with a fit opportunity, which he intended not to lose without a trial; from which ground he thus expresseth his conceptions:

'Things standing as they do, royal sir, there is but one way left to right them; but how that way may like you, that I know not. You are not fit for war, if you consider your proper weakness, bare of strength or money: to seek, not sue for peace, is no dishonour, but shows a pious will to perfect goodness. A servant's care, I not deny, may work it; but this will ask instruction, time and leisure, which your condition cannot fitly limit. Such treaties, for the most part, so are settled; but 'tis with long dispute and many windings, by which we must grow worse, and they still stronger. If they once find that we pursue it hotly, they'll raise their height to win their own conditions, which may be far unfit your state and greatness. I know you love the Queen too much to spare her, and I am loathe to touch the string should cause it. But since great works are fittest for great actors, I wish to her alone this brave employment: her wisdom and her love so well united, will work (I doubt not) peace as you desire; so fair a pleader cannot be denied in that request, which chiefly made her wedlock. And since I am all yours, vouchsafe your pardon if I in reason discourse it farther: Admit that he deny, her

121. *closely forward*: secretly keen, prompt
instigation ... brother: urging of her brother, Charles IV, King of France, who, 'privately informed of the ill usage of his sister, and that the king [Edward] was wholly led by his proud minion', broke the peace by seizing several English possessions in France, and threatened to invade England to restore Isabel to her dignity (*History* 85)

124. *trial ... expresseth*: attempt ... to Edward

125ff. This speech, set in italic prose in the *History*, is one of more than 20 such orations written in blank verse with mainly feminine endings. Donald Foster believes the printers probably found the verse written this way, which was a way of saving paper (1993: 166). Some sections of the body of the text can also be scanned as unrhymed iambic pentameter, though the metre is often irregular and they are not separated from real prose (Stauffer 1935: 300). I have chosen to retain the original edition's prose presentation for ease of reading.

126. *like*: please

128. *to perfect*: perhaps a verb (= to bring nearer to perfection), rather than an adjective

130. *cannot ... limit*: will not allow for in a suitable way
treaties: i.e. for peace

132. *they*: the French

135. *touch ... string*: i.e. sound the first note (of this subject)

139. *chiefly made*: was the main motivation for; Isabella was married to Edward in 1308 for the sake of political entente between France and England

140. *he ... her*: King Charles (though confusingly, he is called John in the *History*) ... Isabel's. Gwynne Kennedy suggests to me that Cary may have changed the name to obscure contemporary parallels with Charles I.

journey sort not, you still are where you were, with some advantage: If he refuse your love, you may his sister which is then with him, where he so may keep her till things are reconciled and quarrels ended. Reason of state must master your affections, which in this act will tell you 'tis unfitting she should be here, that may inform her brother from time to time of all your secret counsels. Say that your love and her obedience tie her, and keep the scale still even, 'tis a hazard which wise men dare not trust in female weakness: admitting that her goodness do assure it, this cannot warrant yet her silent servants, who may be sent with her perhaps of purpose, or after bribed to sift and show your workings. Counsels are seldom so reserved but that they glimmer some little light that leads to their intentions; which if they fly to those they touch unacted, find swift prevention, ere their worth be valued. These things considered, I do speak it freely, 'tis fit the Queen alone should undertake it; which lessens well the charge of your great household, and brings you peace, or makes you else a freeman from those domestic cares that shake your quiet.'

This act ended, Baldock the chorus, who equally hated the Queen, seconds it with a learned approbation; and the old roost-cock, in his country language (which was the only tongue he was guilty of) tells the King briefly, he should be sure of peace at home or abroad. The King with an attentive ear hears this relation, and could not but believe his Spencer spake it; nor did he dote so much upon his wedlock, but he could be contented well to spare her, whose eyes did look too far into his pleasures. But yet his wandering soul had strange impressions, which struck him deeply with a sad prediction, and made him faintly yield but yet delay it.

143. *Reason of state*: a Machiavellian term ('*ragion' di stato*')

145. *that*: who

146–7. *keep ... even*: i.e. in terms of Isabel's supposedly divided loyalties between Edward and her brother King Charles

148. *warrant*: assure (the loyalty of)
silent: confidential

150. *sift*: probe

150–2. *Counsels ... valued*: no plan is so secret that some hint of it cannot be discovered, and if it becomes known to the intended targets, it must be quickly scotched before its full implications can occur

154. *charge*: expenses

155. *or*: (if Isabel fails and you refuse her re-entry to the country)
a freeman: legally free

157. *Baldock*: 'a mean man altogether unworthy', another of Spencer's followers and made Chancellor by him

158. *old roost-cock*: probably Spencer's father (lately created Earl of Winchester and here caricatured as an old gaffer)

165. *prediction ... yet*: foreboding ... (even when he had agreed to the plan)

This overture being come to the Queen's ear, and withal the knowledge how this gipsy had marshalled his cunning practice, and had prescribed the way for her escape, which she herself intended and in her private thoughts had laboured with the best powers of her understanding; she seemed wondrously well-pleased, and offers to undertake and to assure the business. Their several ends, far wide of one another, do kindly meet and knit in the first prologue; where craft encounters cunning, it sometimes happens one and the self-same hood doth fit the head-piece of divers actors, diversely affected; hence it proceeds the plot's more surely acted, when each side doth believe his proper issue: there is not such a cut-throat for a cozener, as that which in his own trade doth crossbite him: the bee gets honey where the spider poison; and that may kill physicians, cures their patients. Such are the qualities of statesmen's actions, that labour to contrive another's mischief, and in their own way find their own destruction. Love and jealousy, that equally possessed the Queen, being intermixed with a stronger desire of revenge, spurs her on to hasten on this journey. She saw the King a stranger to her bed, and revelling in the wanton embraces of his stolen pleasures, without a glance on her deserving beauty. This contempt had begot a like change in her, though in a more modest nature, her youthful affections wanting a fit subject to work on, and being debarred of that warmth that should have still preserved their temper, she had cast her wandering eye upon the gallant Mortimer, a piece of masculine bravery without exception; had those his inward gifts been like his outside, he had not been behind-hand in reception; but with a courtly, brave respect, full meets her glances. A silent rhetoric, sparkling love, finds quick admittance; such private trading needs few words or brokage: but his last act had mewed him in

166. *overture ... withal*: proposition ... beyond that
167. *gipsy*: cunning rogue = Spencer (*OED*'s first citation under this definition), though the word was normally applied to a deceitful or fickle woman and is in keeping with *The History*'s frequent allusions to Spencer's effeminacy
169. *laboured*: to bring about
173. *head-piece*: head (or an actor's prop?)
174. *affected*: assigned (different roles)
175. *his ... issue*: in its own action
175–6. *not ... him*: i.e. no greater villain to a cheat than another cheat who double-crosses him
177. *that*: that which
182. *stolen*: secret, furtive; i.e. pleasures which should really belong to her
186. *warmth*: i.e. of given and received love, feeling
temper: balance, good condition
189. *reception*: of her interest
191. *brokage ... last act*: agents ... see n. to ll. 115–16
191–2. *mewed ... Tower*: cooped up ... of London

the Tower, where he was fast from sight of his great mistress's love; that makes some men fools, makes others wary: had Mortimer's design been known, his head had paid for it; which Spencer's malice long and strongly aimed at, but that the Queen had begged a solemn respite, which Edward would not break at his entreaty. The cage of his restraint was strong and guarded, yet 'twas too weak to cloister his ambition, which did suspect but never feared his freedom; which he attempts, but yet was not so sure that he durst trust it. In the meantime, with a sweet correspondence, and the interchange of many amorous letters, their hearts are brought together, and their several intents perfectly known; hers, to prosecute her journey; his, to purchase his freedom, and to wait upon her, or else to lose his life if it miscarry. It was a strange adventure in the Queen, in this inquisitive and dangerous time, to hazard her honour under the fidelity of a messenger; but she was well beloved, paid liberally, and was not more careful in her election than wary in the employment; which makes things difficult in themselves, prove facile and easy. No sooner had she knowledge of the plot for his escape, but by all her best means she confirms and strengthens it, and in the meantime advances her own affairs by all ways possible: she courts her adversary with all the shows of perfect reconcilement. But new delays interpose; the King had certainly some inward motive that presaged his ruin, and that this wife of his must be the actor; which brought him slowly on to set her forward. Spencer, that by his own could judge her cunning, suspects her plea of haste and sudden kindness, and now begins to grow a little colder, till he had better sounded her intentions; which by his spies he could not so discover, but that she seemed as pure and clear as crystal.

Yet Edward would not give consent she should be a-gadding; time past away, she labours hard, but fruitless, till at length she found she was abused. Guienne must be rather lost, than she should wander. Her heart so strongly fixed upon this journey, was torn as much with anger as with sorrow: reason at length overcame her sex's weakness, and bids her rather cure than vent her passion. The opportunity thus snatched from her hopes, she seems well pleased, and glad to stay at home; no inward motion seemed to

192. *that*: that which
196. *his*: Mortimer's
197. *suspect*: expect (with knowledge of the danger)
201. *prosecute*: pursue
203. *it*: i.e. his attempt to get free
204. *under … fidelity*: in the trust
206. *election*: choice (of messenger)
211. *motive*: impression, premonition
220. *abused*: deceived
223. *vent*: utter
224. *motion*: impulse, desire

appear that might beget suspicion. Spencer, that was as cunning as a serpent, finds here a female wit that went beyond him, one that with his own weapons wounds his wisdom, and taught him not to trust a woman's lip-salve when that he knew her breast was filled with rancour. When the nap of this project was fallen off, and Spencer with the King were seeking for some other bush to stop this gap, her judgement was so fortunate as to pretend a journey of devotion to St Thomas of Canterbury; which by her jealous overseers (being a work of piety) is wholly unsuspected. All things prepared, by a faithful messenger she gives her beloved servant Mortimer knowledge of the time, and her intention. Then, with the prince her son and comfort, that must be made the stale of this great action, she fearless ventures on this holy journey. The King was well content that she should be absent, and pray to whom she would within the kingdom; her jealous eyes so watchful, had enforced him to take by stealth what now he gets in freedom. Spencer is not displeased, but well contented, that wished she would remain an absent pilgrim. A short time bringing her to the shrine of her pretensions, she makes as short a stay, but hasteth forward. Mortimer, informed the plot was now in action, puts on his practice for a present trial. Some say that with a sleeping-drink he charmed his keepers; I rather think it drink that made them sleepy: whatever 'twas, by this he stole his freedom, and slyly 'scapes away unseen, untaken. At the seaside he finds his royal mistress and the young prince prepared to go a-shipboard, the Earl of Cane and Bishop of Hereford ready to attend them; and he now comes, to make the consort perfect. All things succeeding thus fortunately, they lose no time, but embark and weigh their anchor. Winchelsey had the honour of their last farewell, that did provide them shipping. Their sails hoist up, the heavens they find propitious, the blustering winds were quiet, and Neptune bears them without a rugged brow of angry billows; a pleasing foreright gale (as kept of purpose) fills up their sails, and brings them safe to Boulogne. Thus did our pilgrims 'scape the pride and malice of him which little dreamed of this adventure: his craft and care, that taught him all those lessons of cunning greatness, here fell apparent short of all discretion, to be

227–8. *lip-salve*: flattering speech
228. *nap*: smooth sheen
230. *bush*: plug
231. *St Thomas*: the shrine of Thomas à Becket, the most famous in pre-Reformation England
232. *jealous*: suspicious, watchful
234. *prince*: Duke of Aquitaine and future Edward III
235. *stale*: decoy
242. *puts … trial*: immediately puts his anticipated plan to the test
252. *foreright*: favourably direct
253. *as … purpose*: as if ordered and kept ready
254–5. *him, his*: Spencer … Spencer's
256. *apparent*: apparently
256–7. *discretion … over-reached*: discernment … overtaken, surpassed

thus over-reached by one weak woman. For her escape, it skilled not, nor could hurt him: it was the rising son, with cause, he feared; which who would have trusted with a mother justly moved by their disorder? Where now were all his spies, his fawning agents that fed his ear with every little motion that did but crack within the kingdom? Now it thundered; they were asleep, as was their minion-master, else he would sure have seen and soon prevented so lame a project, that paced afoot so long a walk, so softly. But when the glorious power of heaven is pleased to punish man for his transgression, he takes away the sense and proper power by which he should foresee and stop his danger.

This news flies swiftly to the King, who entertains it with a sad heart, as justly it deserved. The Spencers, with the crew of their dependents, are nettled with a tale that starts their greatness; they think the plot was surely laid, that took so rightly; and in the maker's wit, condemn their judgement that led them by the hand to what they acted. Mortimer, whom Spencer deadly hated, was well allied and strong in friends and kindred; he had a cause in hand would win assistance, when that a Queen and an heir apparent backed it. . . . The King frames a letter to his Holiness, full of humility and fair obedience yet craving help, and bitterly complaining that Isabel his wife had fled his kingdom, pretending a mere voyage of devotion, and had stolen away his son, his only comfort, attended by a crew of traitorous rebels. . . .

The cardinals, that freely felt the English bounty, persuade the Pope it was both just and pious so great a misdemeanour should be questioned, that gave the Christian word so lewd example. On this flies out a present admonition to the French King, that straight he free his kingdom of this his

257–8. *skilled* ... *son*: mattered ... i.e. Prince Edward (with a pun on 'sun')
259. *moved* ... *disorder*: angered by Spencer's and his party's corrupt practices
261. *motion* ... *crack*: murmur that was uttered
262. *minion-master*: i.e. Spencer
265. *proper*: particular
269. *starts*: alarms, surprises
269–70. *surely* ... *took*: carefully pre-planned that was carried off
270. *in* ... *their*: in acknowledging ... their own
271. *they*: Isabel and her party
272. *cause*: i.e. the country's universal hatred of the Spencers
274. *his Holiness*: the pope
278. *cardinals* ... *bounty*: Edward has complained to Rome that Isabel has made a mockery of religious pilgrimage, while Spencer has bribed the cardinals to dissuade the Pope from endorsing King Charles IV of France in any plan to support Isabel against Edward
279. *misdemeanour*: offence (not necessarily minor)
280. *word*: precept, or perhaps an error for 'world'
lewd: bad
281. *straight*: immediately

sister-queen and her adherents, on pain of disobedience, interdiction. … He, nothing sorry for so fair a warrant that took him off from charge and future hazard, and yet withal would cover such unkindness, seems to lament the cause and his condition, that of necessity must yield obedience: he could not for her sake at one blow hazard the danger of himself and his whole kingdom. Not to forsake her wholly, he persuades her to entertain a peace. …

The amazed Queen, abandoned and forsaken, relates at full this far unlooked-for passage unto the Bishop, Cane, and Mortimer: their valiant hearts make good their mistress's sorrows, and tell her they would set her right without the Frenchmen, bidding her not consent to her returning, though it were soldered up with showers of kindness: she well enough did know her husband's humour, which would observe no vow, no oath, no promise: if Spencer once more seized her in his clutches, she should be surely mewed, and kept from gadding. Mortimer contains not in this strain his passion, but breaks into the bitterness of anger, taxing the French as base, unkind, perfidious, that knew not what belonged to love or valour. The Queen, that knew the danger, mildly calms him, letting him truly understand his weakness, that in such provocation might beget surprisal, when they must be sent back without prevention. Though that her heart were fired, and swollen with anger, she temporiseth so, 'twas undiscovered: a whispering murmur, muttered from the courtiers, says that she should be sent with speed for England: she feigns to make provision for her journey, yet unresolved which way to 'scape or whither; yet with this preparation she beguiled the French that had cozened her; for they had bargained to see her safe at home, and re-delivered. Being thus irresolute of means, of friends, of succour unprovided, the master failing, she attempts the servants, who sing their master's tune by rote verbatim; they cannot give her single help or comfort. … The Queen in this distraction finds, past her hope, an unexpected comfort; this heaven can do, when flesh and blood's at weakest.

282. *interdiction*: under threat of being cut off from ecclesiastical benefits, privileges
283. *took … off*: freed him
285. *cause*: i.e. Isabel's
287–8. *persuades … peace*: and to return to her husband
290. *passage*: proceeding
293. *soldered up*: secured, made fast
294. *humour*: temperament
300. *weakness*: i.e. revealing his anger to the French
301. *prevention*: any possibility of not being sent back; of being able to provide for their arrival in England
302. *temporiseth*: seems to go along with the present situation
307. *irresolute*: uncertain
308. *master*: i.e. King Charles
attempts: tries to win

Robert of Artois, a man both wise and valiant, that loved goodness for her own sake, not for fashion, at her first coming tendered her his service: he was a well-resolved steady statesman, not led by compliment or feigned professions: he had been absent during all this passage; returning, hears and pities her condition, blaming her nation's falsehood and her misfortune, which he resolves to help out with his best counsel....

Infinitely was the Queen joyed with his relation, which weighing the quality of the man that spake it, seemed justly worth embracing: she finds it was sincere, not light or verbal, which makes itself a partner of her sorrows; she doubles many thanks and gentle proffers of true requital, which her son performed when he himself was forced to leave his country. Straight she provides to follow his directions, and with a wary and secret carriage, settles herself for her intended journey; yet still gives out she meant to go for England, whither she sends a post to treat conditions, with letters smoothly writ in all submission; and courting Spencer with a world of kindness, she lets him know that she relied solely upon his love to be the mediator. Unto her royal brother she discourseth that now she understood the peace was finished which made her first a stranger to her husband, who now would hasten home to make it perfect. And to the council, which well she knew were bribed to send her back perforce if she denied it, she more and more extols and praiseth Spencer, as if 'twere he alone had wrought her welfare. The English thus abused, the French deluded, both are secure; she was providing homewards, which made the one remiss, the other careless; else she, forestalled, had found her project harder. In this her course she sees but small appearance, and few such hopes as might induce assurance; yet she resolves to hazard all and wander, rather than to return thus unprovided.

312–13. *her ... her*: its ... Isabel's

314. *compliment*: ceremonial courtesy

318. *relation*: news. Besides pledging his support, Artois suggests that Isabel try seeking help from other European rulers. This leads to the agreement with the Earl of Hainault (see n. to l. 372).

320. *light*: insincere

322. *son performed*: probably alluding to Prince Edward's marriage to Philippa, daughter of the Earl of Hainault (see l. 372 and n.)

323–4. *carriage ... gives out*: conduct, demeanour ... causes it to be known

325. *post ... treat*: messenger ... negotiate
smoothly: flatteringly

328–9. *peace ... finished*: the 'conditions' at l. 325

330. *council*: i.e. the English council

331. *perforce ... denied it*: by constraint ... broke the agreement

333. *providing*: making herself ready (to go)

336. *appearance*: semblance of certainty

337. *return*: i.e. directly to England

Could she in reason look for any assistance from strangers, when her brother had denied it? Or could she think the Germans would be faithful, when her own birthright had for gain betrayed her? Alas, she could not; yet enforced, must venture, that in her hopes could find no other refuge. Necessity, the law of laws, makes cowards valiant, and him content that hath no choice to guide him; which from the barrenest ground expects some harvest, that else in danger would despair and perish. All things prepared, and her attendants ready, she takes a solemn leave, and thanks her brother, assuring him she nothing more desired than that she might but live to quite his kindness. His answer, like his gifts, was short and little. And thus she leaves the court, in show contented: with a sad heart, a watery eye, a passion highly inflamed, she journeys forward till she came nearer where the bounders parted. . . .

Stapleton, Bishop of Exeter, who till now had faithfully followed the Queen's party, and made himself a sharer of her action, with an unnoble precedent doth now forsake her, seeing the French hopes vanished, and those remaining hopeless; examining the grounds of her adventure almost as short in hope as in assurance, he slyly steals away to his old master, which wins him grace, but lost his life and honour. Some think him from the first not sound or real, but a mere stalking-horse for Spencer's cunning: but this hath no congruity with reason. The Queen's departure unknown and unsuspected, in which he was a prime and private actor, had he at first been false, had been prevented, at least the Prince's, which had marred the project. Neither can I believe so mean or basely of that same reverend honour of his calling, that it would be a conduit-pipe to feed the stomach of such a tainted, foul, polluted cistern. By this treachery the resolutions of the Queen are fully discovered; the landscape of her travels soon surveyed, begets a more contempt than fear of danger. The coldness of the French King being understood, their flat denial yet contents not Spencer, who did expect his bargain for his money: had he had but the Prince, they had dealt fairly while he was being in their proper power. But they, to justify them-

338. *strangers*: foreigners (i.e. Artois and the Earl of Hainault)
340. *birthright*: family
343. *which*: which person
346. *quite*: repay
350. *bounders parted*: boundaries met
356. *grace*: i.e. favour from his 'old master' Edward
357. *stalking-horse*: blind, screening the real design
359. *private*: secret
360. *Prince's*: departure
362. *calling*: i.e. office as a bishop
364. *landscape*: route, plan
366. *their*: the Frenchmen's
368. *proper*: own

selves, profess it freely the Queen had gone beyond them with their cunning; they thought she had been homeward bound, as she divulged. Thus women's wit sometimes can cozen statesmen....

At Dordrecht the Prince and she with their retinue are led a-shipboard, whence they depart and steer their course for Dongport-haven, which was the place resolved on for their landing, that part being held the fittest and the readiest to give them succour. The heaven, that favoured their design, was more propitious, and from their present fear procures their safety. Spencer, being largely informed of their intentions, had made a sound provision, to give them a hotter welcome than they could withstand or look for, had their direction held as they had meant them. Scarce had they run the morning's watch, the skies grew cloudy, a sullen darkness spread all over the welkin; the blustering winds break loose with hollow roaring, and angry Neptune makes his level mountains: the watery element had no green-sickness, but curled banks of snow that sparkle fury.... Three days together tossed and tumbled, they float it out in hope without assurance; in all which time the poor distressed vessel durst neither wear a band, or bear a bonnet. The violence at length being somewhat 'suaged, and the bright sun appearing, smiling sweetly, they find themselves in view of land, but where they knew not, nor thought it fit by landing to discover. While thus irresolute they rest debating, a second doubt enforced their resolution; their victual was too short to feed their number till they could tack about for some new harbour, a fault without excuse in such employments; this made them venture forth at Harwich to try their fortune: unshipping of their men, their arms, their luggage, was long in action and with much disorder; three days are spent in this, while they are forced to make the naked sands their strength and bulwark. This made great Spencer's error most apparent; the

372. *Dordrecht ... retinue*: Dort ... Isabel's expedition consists of 300 soldiers supplied by the Earl (historically Count William) of Hainault; in return she has agreed to marry Prince Edward to the Earl's daughter Philippa. *The History* attributes this exchange to the goodwill, 'ambition of glory' and 'honest care' of the Earl (114); in fact Isabella hired mercenaries in Germany and the Low Countries with money from her daughter-in-law's marriage portion.

374. *part*: (of the country)

377. *largely*: fully

381. *welkin*: sky

382. *level*: (usual) horizontal surface
green-sickness: sickly weakness, lack of vigour

385. *band ... bonnet*: collar or fetter (implying restraint)

386. *'suaged*: assuaged, allayed

389. *victual*: food

393. *luggage*: military equipment and heavy baggage

394. *naked*: bare; unarmed, indefensible

least resistance here, or show, or larum, had sent them back to sea or else surprised them; a little strength at sea had stopped their passage, or made them lawful prize by such a purchase: but after-wits can help precedent errors, if they may be undone and then new acted....

Now this weather-beaten troop marched boldly forward, finding as yet few friends, but no resistance: whoso had seen their body might have deemed they had been come to rob some neighbour village, rather than bent to bid the King to such a breakfast. St Hamond's, an abbey of black monks, had the honour to give their long-lost mistress the first welcome: here she receives a fair and free refreshing, and yet but a faint hope of present succour, without the which she knew her case was desperate. The bruit of this strange novelty was here divulged, which like a thunder-shower, or some land-water that had drowned the marshes and overflown the level, doth make the cattle run to seek for succour: but when they knew the bent of her intentions not fixed to rifle but reform the kingdom, they come like pigeons by whole flocks to her assistance. Soon flew the news unto the grieved barons, whose itching ears attentive, longed to meet it: it doubled as it flew; and ere it touched them, three hundred Hainaults were ten thousand soldiers. They lose no time, for fear of some prevention. Henry of Lancaster, whose brother's death and proper grievance inflamed his heart with grief, his hand for vengeance, with a strong troop of friends and stout attendants, was the first great one that increased her party; while many other brave and noble spirits do second him themselves, and all their forces....

The slumbering King had slept out all the prologue of this sad tragedy, which he suspects would end in blood and mischief; as in his pleasures, in this weighty business he had relied secure on Spencer's wisdom; but now the

396. *resistance*: i.e. by the English towards Isabel's army
show ... larum: show of strength or call to battle

398. *purchase ... after-wits*: capture (i.e. by lawful piracy) ... wisdom that comes too late, in hindsight

398–9. *precedent ... if*: former ... only if

403. *breakfast*: loosely, an end to his 'slumber'
black monks: i.e. wearing black habits, members of a Benedictine order

406–7. *bruit ... novelty*: report, rumour ... new proceeding (perhaps with reference to Isabel leading an army)

408. *land-water*: inland flooding

412. *itching ... attentive*: ears 'itching' to hear some news (of means to challenge Edward)

413. *three ... Hainaults*: historically the invading army was commanded by Roger Mortimer the younger and John, brother of the Count of Hainault. Cary omits the latter and suppresses Mortimer's presence in this section of the *History* to focus attention on Isabel as leader of the expedition.

414. *prevention*: interception, obstruction

415. *brother's death*: Thomas Earl of Lancaster, executed in 1322 (see above n. to ll. 115–16)

hollow murmur of his danger thundered so loud, that he enforced, awakes, and sees nought but the face of a despairing sorrow: each day brings news of new revolt, each hour a larum, that threatened guilty souls with blood and vengeance: his startled council frighted, fainting, hopeless, fall to survey the strength of their pursuers; but while they are a-registering their forces, they are informed the storm grows strong and greater, and like a ball of snow increased by motion....

The King, with Arundel and both the Spencers, with small attendance get them hence to Bristol: his army was much less in his own kingdom than those the Queen had raised by foreign pity. This town was strong and able, well provided, and had a haven, whence in occasion they might venture further: but yet the King might have the same suspicion, which made him leave and quit the strength of London. Arundel and Winchester do undertake the city, Edward and Bristol would make good the castle; here was the refuge they resolve to stick to, which in the citizens' assurance seemed defensive.

The Queen, understanding the royal chamber was forsaken and left to the custody of the bishop her old servant that had given her the slip in her travels, quickly apprehends the advantage; addressing a fair, but mandatory letter from herself and her son to Chickwell, then Lord Mayor, to charge him so to reserve and keep the city to their use, as he expected favour, or would answer the contrary at his peril. Upon the receipt of this letter, he assembles the common council, and by a cunning-couched oration, the recorder makes known the contents; which is no sooner understood, but the general cry, that observed the tide turning, proclaim it reason to embrace the Queen's party, who was so strongly provided to reform the disorders of the kingdom....

Now is the Queen settling her remove for Bristol, where the prey remained her haggard-fancy longed for: she was unwilling to give them so

432. *haven ... in occasion*: harbour ... if necessity required

433. *yet*: now as always

434. *Arundel ... Winchester*: Edmund Fitzalan, Earl of Arundel; Hugh le Despencer the elder, Earl of Winchester

434–5. *undertake ... city*: take charge of the town lying outside the central castle

435. *Bristol*: i.e. Spencer (see n. to ll. 112–13)

436. *in ... assurance*: according to assurances given by the citizens

437. *royal chamber*: in London

438. *bishop*: Stapleton of Exeter; see above l. 351.

439. *mandatory*: commanding

444. *recorder*: magistrate appointed to set down as well as publicly announce the city council's proceedings

448. *settling*: arranging beforehand, deciding upon

449. *haggard-fancy ... for*: haggard = a wild untamed female hawk; thus, 'the object long fancied in the mind of this haggard'

much advantage, though she believed it almost impossible, as to hazard the raising of an army, or so to enable their provisions and defences, that it might adjourn the hope of making her victory perfect. She saw she had a great and royal army, well provided; but how long it would hold so she knew not, the principal strength and number consisting of the giddy commons, who like land-floods, rise and fall in an instant: they had never yet seen the face of an enemy, nor did rightly understand what it was to bear arms against the King, whom they must here behold a party. These considerations hasten her on with more expedition. All the way as she went, she is entertained with joyful acclamations: her army still grows greater, like a beginning cloud that doth forerun a shower. When she was come before this goodly city, and saw his strength, and the maiden bravery of their opposition (which gave her by a hot sally, led by the valiant Arundel, a testimony of her welcome), she then thinks that in the art of war there was somewhat more than mere imagination, and justly feared lest the royal misery would beget a swift compassion; which was more to be doubted of him in his own kingdom, since she herself had found it in a foreign country. But smiling fortune, now become her servant, scarce gives her time to think she might be hindered. The townsmen, that knew no wars but at their musters, seeing themselves begirt, the market hindered, which was their chiefest and best revenue, begin among themselves to examine the business; they saw no likelihood of any to relieve them, and daily in danger of some sad surprisal. ... The Queen, seeing a pusillanimity beyond her hopes, and a taint unlooked for, makes the use and hits them on the blind side, and answers plainly, she will have no imparlance, no discoursing; if they desired their own peace, and her assured favour, they then must entertain and follow her conditions: which if they but delayed, the next day following they should abide their chance, she would her fortune.

450. *impossible*: (not to do so in some degree)
452. *adjourn*: put off indefinitely
454. *commons*: common people
457. *behold a party*: regard as merely one side in a contest (rather than somebody commanding universal allegiance)
458. *expedition*: speed
461. *city ... his*: Bristol ... its
maiden: never before conquered
465. *doubted*: feared
466. *it*: compassion
468. *musters*: militia exercises, assemblies
469. *begirt*: surrounded
472. *pusillanimity*: faint-heartedness
taint: infecting weakness
474, 484. *imparlance*: debate, parleying before action
476–7. *abide ... would*: face their chance as she would face

A choice so short, so sharp, so peremptory, being related in the staggering city, breeds straight a supposition, not without reason: she had some certain practised plot within them, or else some way assured for to force the city. They could have been content she had their captains, since it would set them free from fear and danger; but to be actors in so foul a treason, or sacrifice their guests that came for succour, this they conceit too false and poor a baseness. No more imparlance is allowed, or will be heard, no second motion; the breach in their faint hearts is so well known that nothing is allowed but present answer: this smart proceeding melts their leaden valour, which at the first had made so brave a flourish, and brings Arundel, Winchester, and the town to her possession. . . .

The castle in itself was strong, but weakly furnished. The Queen, impatient to surprise this fortress, doth batter, undermine, and still assail it; but these were all in vain, and proved fruitless; the rampires were too strong, too well defended: she threatens and entreats, but to small purpose; here were no citizens that might betray it: alas, there needed none, as it succeeded; the proper owners wrought their own confusion; they leave their strength and closely try their fortune, which made them board a barque rode in the harbour, in hope to get away undescried.

Sir Henry Beaumont, quartered next the haven, being informed that this gadding pinnace had often attempted passage without reason, the wind contrarious and the weather doubtful, suspects that her design was great and hasty; on this he seized her and surveys her lading, which proved a prize beyond his expectation: within her hollow bulk, a cell of darkness, he finds this pair obscured, not undiscovered. The King hath gracious words, and all due reverence; but Spencer is condemned, and used with rigour. This ends the war, and gave the work perfection.

The Queen, having thus attained to the full of her desire, resolves to use

480. *practised*: ready to be deployed
481. *she . . . captains*: to yield up the King and his party to her
483. *conceit*: think
486. *smart*: brisk, vigorous, keen; clever, adept
leaden: dull, spiritless
489. *castle*: i.e. within the city, into which Edward and Spencer have retreated
491. *rampires*: ramparts
494. *proper owners*: possessors themselves (i.e. Edward and Spencer)
495. *closely*: covertly
495–6. *barque rode . . . undescried*: small ship (which) lay anchored . . . unnoticed
497. *haven*: harbour
498. *pinnace . . . without reason*: small light vessel . . . in unreasonable conditions
contrarious: adverse
500. *lading*: freight
502. *obscured, not undiscovered*: hidden (but) not undetected
hath: (from Beaumont)

it to the best advantage: ambition seized her strongly, yet resigneth to her incensed passion the precedence; her own good nature (though she might adventure) she would not trust so far to see her husband; nor did she think it fit those valiant strangers, begun the work, should view or see the captive; such sights sometimes beget as strange impressions; instantly he is conveyed to Berkeley Castle, there to remain restrained but well attended. Spencer is hardly kept, but often visited; 'twas not with pity, which befits a prisoner, but with insulting joy and base derision. Their eyes with sight, and tongues with railing, glutted, the act must follow that may stop the rancour, which gives him to the marshal locked in irons: he here receives the self-same entertainment his aged father found; alone the difference, he had a longer time and sharper sentence. All things thus ordered, the Queen removes for London, meaning to make Hereford her way, and the last journey of her condemned prisoner, that attends her each place she passeth by. A world of people do strain their wider throats to bid her welcome with yelping cries that echoed with confusion. While she thus passeth on with a kind of insulting tyranny, far short of the belief of her former virtue and goodness, she makes this poor unhappy man attend her progress, not as the ancient Romans did their vanquished prisoners, for ostentation to increase their triumph, but merely for revenge, despite, and private rancour; mounted upon a poor, lean, ugly jade, as basely furnished, clothed in a painted tabard, which was then a garment worn by condemned thieves alone, and tattered rascally, he is led through each town behind the carriage, with reeds and pipes that sound the summons to call the wondering crew together might abuse him; all the bitterest actions of disgrace were thrown upon him. Certainly this man was infinitely vicious, and deserved as much as could be laid upon him, for those many great and insolent oppressions, acted with injustice, cruelty, and blood; yet it had been much more to the Queen's honour if she had given him a quicker death, and a more honourable trial,

506ff. *ambition* ... : As Gwynne Kennedy observes, until this point in the text Isabel's only ambition has been to reclaim or correct her husband, but now she displays ignoble anger and revengeful impulses suggesting a loss of control and authority (1995)

507. *precedence*: supremacy

508. *adventure*: risk it

509. *strangers*: i.e. her Hainault allies

510. *strange*: unpredictable

512. *hardly*: harshly

513. *Their*: the Queen and her party's

515. *him*: Spencer

515–16. *he* ... *found*: Spencer's father was hastily tried and executed after Bristol fell to Isabel's army (*History* 125–6)

525–6. *private* ... *jade*: personal ... worn-out horse

526. *tabard*: a loose upper garment of coarse material, without sleeves; 'painted' = writing publicly identifying the criminal

528–9. *reeds* ... *pipes*: instruments suggesting raucous, derisory music

free from these opprobrious and barbarous disgraces, which savoured more of a savage, tyrannical disposition, than a judgement fit to command, or sway the sword of justice.

Though not by birth, yet by creation he was a peer of the kingdom, and by the dignity of his place one of the most eminent; which might (if not to him in his particular, yet in the rights due to nobility and greatness) have found some more honourable a distinction, than to be made more infamous and contemptible than the basest rogue, or most notorious cutpurse. It is assuredly (give it what title you will) an argument of a villainous disposition, and a devilish nature, to tyrannise and abuse those wretched ruins which are under the mercy of the law, whose severity is bitter enough without aggravation.... To see such a monster so monstrously used, no question pleased the giddy multitude, who scarcely know the civil grounds of reason: the recollected judgement that beheld it censured it was at best too great and deep a blemish to suit a queen, a woman, and a victor....

Her business thus dispatched, she comes to London, where she hath all the royal entertainment due to her greatness. The citizens do run and crowd to see her, that if the wheel should turn, would be as forward to make the self-same speed to see her ruin. As soon as here she had settled her affairs and made things ready, she calls a parliament, and sends forth summons for the appearance, which as soon ensued; herein she makes her husband seal the warrant, who, God knows, scarcely knew what she was doing, but lived a recluse, well and surely guarded. When this grave assembly was come together, the errors and the abuses of the kingdom are laid full open; which touched the King with a more insolent liberty than might well become the tongues of those which must yet be his subjects. Many ways of reformation for form's sake are discussed, but the intended course was fully before resolved.... The three estates *una voce* conclude the father must be deposed, and his unripe son must be invested in the royal dignity. Not a

535. *opprobrious*: shamefully insulting, degrading
543. *argument*: proof
544. *ruins*: persons brought into a pitiful state
548. *recollected ... censured*: considered, studied, finer ... unfavourably judged
552. *wheel ... forward*: of Fortune, on which the states of princes continually rise and fall ... ready, prompt
555. *appearance*: formal attendance, gathering
556. *warrant*: calling a new Parliament
559. *touched*: referred to
562. *three estates*: of Parliament – nobility, bishops, and commons
una voce: with one voice
563. *deposed ... son*: Parliament deposed Edward in 1327 and recognised his son, then aged fourteen, as Edward III. Isabella and Mortimer governed in his name to increasing public discontent until 1330, when Mortimer was arrested and executed as a traitor.

lord, bishop, knight, judge, or burgess, but that day left his memory behind him; they could not else so generally have forgot the oaths of their allegiance, so solemnly sworn to their old master, whom they had just cause to restrain from his errors, but no ground or colour to deprive him of his kingdom, who that day found neither kinsman, friend, servant, or subject to defend his interest. … [They], having received their new warrant and their royal prisoner, carry him by sudden and hasty journeys to Corfe Castle, the place that in all the world he most hated.

The historians of these times differ both in the time, place, and manner of his death; yet all agree that he was foully and inhumanely murdered, yet so, that there was no visible or apparent sign which way 'twas acted. A small tract of time discovers the actors, and shows evidently that it was done by an extremity of violence: they long escape not: though Mortimer's greatness for the present time keep them both from question and punishment, yet by the divine justice they all meet with a miserable and unpitied death; and the master workman himself in a few years after suffered an ignominious execution.

The Queen, who was guilty but in circumstance, and but an accessory to the intention, not the fact, tasted with a bitter time of repentance what it

564. *burgess*: magistrate, town official

567. *colour*: pretext; reason, excuse

569. *They*: Edward's keepers, assigned by Mortimer

571. *place … hated*: because a magician had once foretold that it would be 'to him both fatal and ominous' (*History* 154)

572–4. *historians … acted*: Cary pointedly omits mentioning any of the pitifully horrifying details of Edward's violent death recorded by other historians, or even the less explicit scene staged in Marlowe's *Edward II*. Holinshed, for example, reports that the Queen and the Bishop of Hereford first had Edward lodged 'in a chamber over a foul filthy dungeon, full of dead carrion, trusting so to make an end of him, with the abominable stench thereof'. But when this failed his keepers 'came suddenly one night into the chamber where he lay in bed fast asleep, and with heavy featherbeds or a table (as some write) being cast upon him, they kept him down and withal put into his fundmant [anus] an horn, and through the same they thrust up into his body an hot spit, or (as others have) through the pipe of trumpet, a plumber's instrument of iron made very hot, the which passing up into his entrails, and being rolled to and fro, burnt the same, but so as no appearance of any wound or hurt outwardly might be perceived. His cry did move many within the castle and town of Berkeley to compassion, plainly hearing him utter a wailful noise' (Thomas and Tydeman 1994: 369). Tina Krontiris believes (1990: 145) that the *History*'s reticence suggests Cary was repelled by cruelty, as it violated her principles of 'Christian ethics with a sense of fairness in the exercise of power … toward a powerless subject'.

579. *master workman*: called Lightborn in Marlowe's *Edward II* but unnamed in the chronicles

582. *bitter … repentance*: historically, Isabella lived comfortably into old age, devoting herself to works of charity and eventually becoming a sister of St Clare

was but to be quoted in the margent of such a story; the several relations so variously expressed of their confessions that were the actors and consenters to this deed, differ so mainly, that it may be better passed over in silence, than so much as touched; especially since if it were in that cruel manner, as is by the major part agreed on, it was one of the most inhumane and barbarous acts that ever fell within the expression of all our English stories, fitter rather to be passed over in silence, than to be discoursed, since it both dishonoureth our nation, and is in the example so dangerous.

583. *quoted … margent*: margent = margin; noticed in the marginal commentary (i.e. the 'footnotes' of history). The 'story' refers to 'the manner of [Edward's] death'; but if it is taken to mean the whole account of his reign, the statement seems odd, since Isabel is hardly marginal to Cary's text, and perhaps reveals an ambivalence about whether Isabel really is central to its account (Kennedy 1995).
relations: accounts

585. *mainly*: greatly

586. *touched*: mentioned

587. *part*: (of historians)

3

AUTOBIOGRAPHY

MARGARET, LADY HOBY (1571–1633)

FROM *THE DIARY OF MARGARET, LADY HOBY* (1599–1605)

Introduction

Lady Hoby's *Diary*, the earliest document of its kind by a female English writer, provides us with a valuable record of an Elizabethan gentlewoman's daily occupations, but it conveys this information in a rather abstemious way. For unlike many diaries which preserve a writer's most intimate thoughts so that they may be analysed later with some detachment, Lady Hoby's purpose is not self-reflection but accountability. Her *Diary* is primarily a schedule of daily religious exercises consisting of meditation, reading, and prayer. This explains why its entries seem formulaic – a kind of 'spiritual ledger' (Mendelson 1985: 186) – and tend to mention secular activities only in nondescript terms which convey little sense of her taking pleasure from either the activities themselves or the act of writing about them. Since the *Diary* is dedicated to this one, albeit deeply important, aspect of her life, we must be careful when making assumptions about the character that lies behind it (as is the case for other Renaissance women writing on religious themes). When we compare her *Diary* with a letter Lady Hoby wrote to her husband in the same period, for example, a very different personality emerges:

> Dear heart, I am not sure that I have sent you all right, because I could not find both the books so written of as you told me, but I have sent you all that is likely to be that you spake of. I pray you if you come hither by York, let John Brown buy me, or send it me by this boy, 2 pound of starch, for I have none left. ... I must needs give you thanks for the letter you writ from Linton. I will [sic] for your kindness to them. If you gave me n'other trial, yet I should confess you to be an exceeding good husband and to deserve a better wife than my wit will serve me to be, but I will draw as nigh to the high degree as I can. And so because it is late, I will commit you without more circumstances to the Lord's best protection. My mother desires to be commended unto you, and so doth myself to all my cousins. From Hackness this 6 of June, 1599. Your assured and loving wife
>
> Dame Margaret Hoby.
>
> (Hoby 1930: 268, shortened and modernised)

The graceful self-depreciation and affectionate familiarity of *this* Margaret Hoby are important to bear in mind as we listen to the more severe writer of the present work.

Since the *Diary* tends to foreground regular religious devotions against a field of 'incidental' experiences, a reader may wish to bring the latter forward and try to build up what is implied by or can be inferred from them. Entries that make passing reference to domestic tasks such as preserving fruit, making sweetmeats, distilling, and sowing seed, for example, illustrate Lady Hoby's skilful and wide-ranging involvement in the practical operation of her household. By contrast with later times, such 'hands-on' management was normal for early modern gentlewomen. In fact whenever she is not at prayer, writing the *Diary*, or making notes on sermons (either for her own or her friends' use), Lady Hoby is constantly busy supervising large numbers of servants and workmen and conducting financial business in her local village of Hackness and neighbouring towns. This assiduity ensured that estates owned by her husband and herself (she had inherited land independently as her parents' only child and heir) were run efficiently. As with other country women, such responsibilities fell mainly to her because her husband was usually absent carrying out his duties as an MP and JP in the North Riding of Yorkshire where they lived.

Margaret was the only child of Arthur Dakins and Thomasine Guy, and had grown up serving in the household of the Earl and Countess of Huntingdon, both of whom were strong Puritans who undoubtedly shaped her religious views. She had married Walter Devereux in 1589. He was the second son of the Earl of Essex and brother to Robert Devereux, who later himself became Earl as well as Queen Elizabeth's tragic favourite. The manor of Hackness, valued at £6,500, was bought for the new couple (£3,000 coming from Margaret's father, £3,000 from the Earl of Essex, and £500 from Lord Huntingdon); so when Walter Devereux died only two years later, Margaret was left a rich widow. She was immediately courted by Thomas Sidney, brother of Sir Philip Sidney and Mary Herbert, Countess of Pembroke. At this point Thomas Hoby was also a suitor, but Margaret showed little interest in him and her father decided in favour of Sidney. This second marriage did not last long either, as Sidney died in 1595, and again her hand was immediately sought by Hoby, this time successfully even though Margaret remained cool. She was urged to accept him, however, by Hoby's uncle Lord Burghley and by Lord Huntingdon, among others, who wished to see Thomas serve as a government agent in Yorkshire where a large Catholic community lived, since Hoby was known to be an 'uncompromising' Protestant (several entries in the selections presented below record his pursuit of Catholic recusants). Margaret probably also relented because she was facing a lawsuit over lands at Hackness, and Thomas's well-connected friends could provide her with support. The letter to him cited above, however, suggests that over time their relationship became companionable. Throughout her three marriages Margaret did not have any children (Hoby 1930: 4–32).

Aside from domestic and estate management, the *Diary* refers at many points to Lady Hoby's service to her community. She was regularly called upon to act as a midwife, for example, reminding us that delivering children was collectively and exclusively a female practice. She likewise organised local charitable relief and performed surgery on injured tenants and neighbours (at one point calling them her 'patients'); they in turn received her herbal drugs and medicines. She often mentions 'walking abroad' to chat with neighbours in the surrounding countryside, or receiving visitors at home, inviting them to dine or to join her in exercise and sport. From these occasional references we begin to recognise the picture of a cheerfully sociable woman, highly esteemed within a network of close local relationships. Moreover, from a wider perspective such details suggest that institutions such as the 'family' and the 'household' operated far more openly than they have done in later periods. It is true that such openness involved the risk of censure if patriarchal interests judged women to be stepping beyond their 'official' spheres, and also true that public circulation by women could always be linked to sexual impropriety (Crawford 1993a: 60). But overall Lady Hoby's leadership challenged traditional ideologies that defined social roles in terms of gender alone and tied female virtues strictly to the domestic sphere (though Lady Hoby's potentially transgressive individualism is admittedly made more socially acceptable by her fervent piety; see Wilcox 1992: 53).

Perhaps Lady Hoby's most significant public activity was her support of Puritanism, a movement gaining increasing cultural and political influence at this time. Entries record her giving spiritual counsel to neighbours (e.g. 'with a woman that was to be divorced from her husband') and supervising the instruction of servants and their children, thereby directly shaping future attitudes in her community. Like other reform-minded gentlewomen, she regularly provided patronage and hospitality to Puritan ministers and preachers, a number of whom had been or were shortly to be ejected from their livings or censored for their nonconformity. In doing so, she lent indispensable material and moral support at the local level to a sectarian movement whose national power would continue to grow until reaching its revolutionary apogee in the next generation.

Manuscript:
BL Egerton 2614 (source of extracts presented here).

Editions:
Diary of Lady Margaret Hoby, ed. Dorothy Meads (London, 1930). *The Paradise of Women*, ed. Betty Travitsky (Westport, Conn., 1981, brief excerpts from Meads). *English Women's Voices, 1540–1700*, ed. Charlotte F. Otten (Bloomington, 1992, brief excerpts from Meads).

MARGARET, LADY HOBY

FROM *THE DIARY OF MARGARET, LADY HOBY* (1599–1605)

WEDNESDAY 15 AUGUST 1599

In the morning at 6 o'clock I prayed privately: that done, I went to a wife in travail of child, about whom I was busy till 1 o'clock, about which time, she being delivered and I having praised God, returned home and betook myself to private prayer two several times upon occasion: then I writ the most part of an examination or trial of a Christian, framed by Mr Rhodes, in the doing where[of] I again fell to prayer, and after continued writing after 3 o'clock: then I went to work till after 5, and then to examination and prayer: the Lord make me thankful, who hath heard my prayers and hath not turned his face from me: then I talked with Mrs Brutnell till supper time, and after walked a little into the fields, and so to prayers, and then to bed.

FRIDAY 7 SEPTEMBER

After private prayers I writ my notes in my testament, which I gathered out of the lecture the night before: then I did eat my breakfast, then I walked

2. *travail*: labour
3. *I ... God*: probably in the form of prayers of thanksgiving for a safe birth, such as those found in the *BCP* and also in Grace Mildmay's *Book of Meditations*
4. *upon occasion*: during the course of that time
5. *examination ... Christian*: self-examination to account for one's behaviour and use of time, with the intention of avoiding idleness and sin – an important element of puritan discipline. The *Diary* serves this purpose on a daily basis.
   Mr Rhodes: Lady Hoby's chaplain and vicar of the local parish church in Hackness. He may have suggested the idea of writing the diary as a spiritual exercise. As Meads observes, however, when Rhodes was no longer resident in her household (June 1601 onwards) Lady Hoby increasingly neglects her regular schedule of devotions (or at least the diary entries become more and more brief; see Hoby 1930: 280).

7, 17. *work, wrought*: needlework, but sometimes other tasks as well, which Lady Hoby occasionally specifies

9. *Mrs Brutnell*: a neighbour, like many other people mentioned casually throughout the *Diary*
11. *notes ... testament*: comments on scriptural themes and interrelated passages, recorded in her Bible
12. *lecture*: similar to a sermon but more informal and given in the afternoon or early evening, often by a parish lay-person

abroad and talked of good things, so that I found much comfort: after I came home I writ my sermon that was preached the sabbath day before, then I went to private prayer, and so to dinner: after which I talked a little with some of my friends, and exercised my body at bowls awhile, of which I found good: then I came home and wrought till 4, then I prayed with Mr Rhodes, and after walked abroad: and when I came home I prayed privately, and soon after went to supper: after which I went to the lecture and then to bed.

THE LORD'S DAY 28 OCTOBER

After private prayers I writ notes in my testament, and did eat my breakfast: then to church: after, I came home to prayer and so to dinner: after which I talked with a woman that was to be divorced from her husband with whom she lived incestuously: then I went to church and, after catechising and sermon, I walked abroad: then I meditated of the sermons, and read and spoke to Mrs Ormstone of the chapter that was read in the morning, and so went to private prayer: after to supper, then to prayers, and soon after to bed.

MONDAY 7 JANUARY 1600

After I had praised God for my rest and was ready, I went about the house, then I returned to private prayer: after, I did eat my breakfast, and again was busy till almost dinner-time: then I prayed, dined, and after went into the town about some business: then I was in the granary receiving corn, and again took order for supper and heard one of my women read of Perkins, and after that returned to private prayer and examination: then soon after I went to supper, after that to the lecture, then to private prayer, and so to bed.

13. *abroad*: in the neighbourhood
14. *writ ... sermon*: i.e. copied out or epitomised the sermon she had heard preached the previous Sunday
24. *incestuously*: a relation with whom marriage was legally prohibited. See the *BCP*'s 'Table of Kindred and Affinity wherein whosoever are related are forbidden to marry together'. 'Divorced' may signify co-habitation rather than marriage.
    catechising: instruction in the essential principles of the Christian faith by way of formal question and answer. One such catechism is found in the *BCP*.
26. *Mrs Ormstone*: a neighbour
32. *receiving corn*: from tenants as rent
33. *took order*: discussed (with the servants) and ordered
    Perkins: William Perkins (1558–1602), popular and prolific writer of theological treatises

SATURDAY 26 JANUARY

After private prayers I went about the house and then I read of the Bible till dinner-time: after dinner I dressed up my closet and read, and, to refresh myself being dull, I played and sung to the alpharion: after, I took order for supper and the next day, and then, after I had conferred awhile with Mr Hoby, I went to private examination and prayer.

WEDNESDAY 30 JANUARY

After I had prayed privately, I dressed a poor boy's leg that came to me, and then brake my fast with Mr Hoby: after, I dressed the hand of one of our servants that was very sore cut, and after I writ in my testament notes upon James: then I went about the doing of some things in the house, paying of bills, and after I had talked with Mr Hoby, I went to examination and prayer, after to supper, then to the lecture: after that I dressed one of the men's hands that was hurt, lastly prayed, and so to bed.

FRIDAY 15 FEBRUARY

After prayer and breakfast and dressing of my patients, I went to church: then from the sermon I went to work: after to prayer and so to dinner: after dinner I talked with a neighbour touching the misdemeanours of a kinsman of mine, then I wrought some trifle I had to do till night, so the afternoon was spent without any spiritual profiting extraordinary: then I dressed my patients and after returned to private prayer and meditation when I had taken order for supper: after supper I heard public prayers, and soon after I went to bed.

38. *dressed ... closet*: decorated my private room
39. *alpharion*: 'A little-known stringed musical instrument' (*OED*, only citation 1610). In *John Aubrey and his Friends* (1963: 35) Anthony Powell quotes Aubrey's description in his manuscript papers: ''Tis as big as a lute, but flat bellyed with wire springs'.
40. *conferred*: conversed (not necessarily on a serious subject)
42. *dressed*: basic medicine and surgery were one of a country gentlewoman's main responsibilities, since physicians were either distant or unavailable. See also Lady Mildmay pp. 220–1.
43. *brake ... fast*: breakfasted
53. *extraordinary*: i.e. consciously sought-after spiritual benefit (implying no activity is without this in some degree)
55. *public*: household (family and servants)

SATURDAY 22 FEBRUARY

After private prayer I did break my fast, read of the Bible, walked to my workmen, and then was busy in the house till Mr Hoby came home: then I kept him company till dinner-time and after, all the day going about sundry things and talking of divers matters: after supper I went to public prayer, and then to private examination and prayer, and so to bed.

THURSDAY 13 MARCH

I was this day so ill with cold as I kept my chamber and had some of my neighbours, with whom I took occasion to speak of divers needful duties to be known, as of parents choosing for their children, of the charge of godfathers, and of the first instituting of them: after they were gone from me I prayed, went to supper, and then heard the lecture: after I talked with Mr Rhodes touching his match, and so went to bed, taking order for sundry things to be done the next morning.

MONDAY 24 MARCH

After private prayer I went to the church: after, I prayed, dined, and then kept company with a kinswoman of mine: then I took order for supper, dispatched some business, and after went to private prayer: then to supper and, after one o'clock after midnight when I had prayed privately, went to bed: Mr Hoby that night went to search a house for papists.

WEDNESDAY 16 APRIL

After I was awake, Mr Lister came with physic which I took presently and

57. *my*: Meads (Hoby 1930: 300) suggests this pronoun indicates Lady Hoby employed men of her own (perhaps to work on the properties she owned independently of her husband)
62. *had*: (call upon me)
64. *choosing*: marriage partners
    charge: responsibilities (towards their godchildren)
65. *first instituting*: reasons why they were instituted
67. *match*: marriage
73. *papists*: probably Roman Catholic priests, who were outlawed in England at the time and had to conceal their movements. As a local JP Sir Thomas Hoby was tireless in tracking them down.
74. *physic*: medicine

lay after it awhile, which continued me ill almost all the day that I omitted my ordinary exercises of prayer: in the afternoon a friend of mine came to me with a godly preacher, Mr Wilson, of whom I learned this, among other conferences: that religion consisted of two principal heads, which, whosoever did deny, could not be saved: the one was justification by and in Christ's righteousness: the other of life touching the true worship of God, so that whosoever were either idolaters or grounded their justification on works, did deny so far the truth in the foundation of Christian religion: after they were gone I went to private prayer and examination: after, I went to supper, then I talked with Mr Lister, and lastly went to bed.

MONDAY 2 JUNE

After private prayers I did eat and then went about the house and was busy till dinner-time: after, I prayed, dined, and after talked with a friend of mine: then I went about business, and after walked a-fishing with a friend that came to me for that purpose: after I came home and did go to private examination and prayer: after, I went to supper, then walked abroad, and, after I had heard the lecture, I went to bed.

FRIDAY 18 JULY

After private prayers I went about the house and delivered some directions to Jurden: after, I talked with my cousin Isons and about his going to York, and then I went to dinner: after, I was busy providing something to be carried to York, after I wrought, and lastly I went to private examination and prayer: after, I went to supper, then I walked abroad: after, I came in to public prayers, and after to private, where it please[d] the Lord to touch my heart with such sorrow, for some offence committed, that I hope the Lord, for his son['s] sake, hath pardoned it according to his promise, which is ever just: after, I read a paper that wrought a farther humiliation in me, I thank God.

78. *conferences*: topics discussed
79. *deny ... justification*: deny (them) ... salvation by faith in Christ's complete atonement for human sin, rather than by holy works – a fundamental Protestant belief
92. *Jurden*: a servant
97. *offence*: unexplained. Hoby's MS follows this with 'that night' crossed out
99. *paper*: legal document, formal request

SATURDAY 19 JULY

After private prayer I writ an answer to a demand Mr Hoby had given me overnight: after, I went about and then writ in my sermon book: after that I prayed and then I dined: the afternoon I wrought till almost 5 o'clock, and then I went about the house: after, I returned unto my closet and altered that a little which before I had written, and then I examined myself and prayed: after, I went to supper, then to public prayers, and lastly after private [prayers] I went to bed.

THE LORD'S DAY 3 AUGUST

After private prayers I did read and went about the house, and, after I had broken my fast, I went to the church: when I came home I prayed: after, dined: and then I talked and read to some good wives that was with me: after, I walked with Mr Hoby and prayed, and then I went again to the church, and after I read of the testament: and then I talked with Mr Rhodes, and after went to private examination and prayer, then to supper: after to public prayers, then to private, and lastly to bed.

SATURDAY 9 AUGUST

After private prayers I went about my stilling, and then returned to private prayer before dinner: after, I was busy with sweetmeat, and went about with my husband, and read of the Bible, and after returned to private meditation and prayer: after, I went to supper, then to the lecture: after, to public prayers, and, when I had prayed privately, I went to bed.

THE LORD'S DAY 14 SEPTEMBER

After private prayer I went to the church when I had read, and eaten something: after I came from thence I prayed: then I dined, and then, till church time again, I talked with Mr Jenkins, and after the sermon I writ some notes

101. *demand*: unexplained, but perhaps related to the foregoing 'offence'. Meads speculates that it may have been a request for money to be raised from mortgaging some of Lady Hoby's own property (Hoby 1930: 267).
102. *overnight*: the night before
104. *closet*: private room (and personal space)
115. *stilling*: distilling (alcohol, medicines, cosmetics)
116. *busy with*: (making)
sweetmeat: sweet food

in my commonplace book: and when I had read awhile, I went to private examination and prayer: after to supper, then to prayers, and, when I had prayed privately, I went to bed.

THURSDAY 17 OCTOBER

From thence I took my journey to London where, in the way, I was told that order was given to fetch all the stuff from York, and to give over that house there, upon which and about we had laid forth £181 which news did much touch me, so that I procured contrary directions forthwith: after I came to London I prayed, and was visited with all my cousin Cookes: then I prayed after supper and went to bed, where I was more meanly lodged, with so great cost, than to my remembrance I was ever in my life: and yet I was glad of my brother's house.

TUESDAY 28 OCTOBER [SAINTS] SIMON AND JUDE

After private prayers I went to the minster and heard one Mr Smith preach, where I heard, to my knowledge, nothing worth the noting but that *abba*, 'father', was to note out that both Jew and gentile should call God father: after I came home, I dined and was all the afternoon within, and busied myself in my chamber, writing some notes of sermons which I purpose to send Mr Rhodes: after, I talked with Mr Urpith and then prayed and went to supper: after supper I was busy awhile, and then I prayed, and so went to bed.

123. *commonplace book*: book of pithy sayings or memorable quotations; it may also have functioned as her book of meditations. See n. to l. 220.

126. *thence*: Lady Hoby has travelled from Hackness through Linton, Hull, Lincoln, and Huntington on her way to London

127. *stuff*: household goods such as furniture and utensils
give over: sell

130. *Cookes*: Sir Thomas Hoby's mother, Lady Russell (by a later marriage) was one of Sir Anthony Cooke's daughters, who were praised by contemporaries for their learning (see Lamb 1985: 107–25). These cousins, however, were the children of Lady Russell's brother, William Cooke (Hoby 1930: 272–3).

132–3. *glad of*: (being able to stay in)

133. *brother's*: Sir Edward Hoby, brother of Sir Thomas

134. *minster*: Westminster Abbey
Smith: perhaps Henry Smith (1550?–91), famous Puritan-leaning divine and prolific writer of popular sermons

135–6. *abba* ... note out: Aramaic (transliteration) ... signify

136. *father*: in a familiar or intimate sense, like 'dad'; used by Jesus to address God in Mark 14.36

138–9. *writing* ... *Rhodes*: i.e. either by letter or by scribal publication

TUESDAY 11 NOVEMBER

After private prayer I went about and read of the Bible: after, I helped my mother to wash some fine linen, my maid [Anne] France being not able: after, I strung some pearls, and then went to cast up some accounts that concerned my being at Malton: and so soon after took order for supper, and then went to private examination and prayer: after to supper, and then to bed.

THURSDAY 13 NOVEMBER

After prayers I went to dinner: after, I went to a standing to see the Queen come to London, where I read a sermon: after, I came home: being not well, I went to supper and so to bed.

MONDAY 1 DECEMBER

After I was ready and had prayed and read, I walked, set my hand to a release to my cousin Strangways of all debts and suits that I might claim anything from him, and so went to dinner: after came young Mr Theckstone, and so I went to the minster to see the monuments: after, I walke[d] and was visited by my cousin Cooke's wife, and, after they were gone, I went to reading and prayer.

SATURDAY 20 DECEMBER

After private prayer and reading I went to work, and then to prayer and so to dinner: after, I talked with Mr Betnam who dined with us, and then I went with Mrs Thornborough to the Exchange: after, I came home and prayed.

144–5. *cast up* ... *Malton*: calculate ... in Yorkshire where she owned property
148. *standing*: standing-place (on a route)
149. *read a sermon*: i.e. while waiting
151. *set* ... *to*: signed
152. *release*: written discharge
158. *Mr Betnam*: apparently the family solicitor
159. *Exchange*: the Royal Exchange, which housed vending-stalls

WEDNESDAY 7 JANUARY 1601

After private prayers I went about, and, when I dined, I went to my Lady Russell's, and there I heard of the solemnity at court: after, I went with my mother to see the glass house, and from thence to visit my Lady Shirley: and I came home and found Mr Gatts, and, when I had talked awhile with Mr Hoby, I went to private prayer and examination.

MONDAY 26 JANUARY

This day I, being not well, prayed and read in mine own chamber, and had Mr Betnam to dinner: after I had talk with Mr Betnam touching my mother's assurance, and then, being agreed that he should draw the books, Mrs Thornborough came in, and after she was gone, my aunt Cooke with her sons and daughters: after I went to prayers and so to supper.

From the 26 of January unto the 8 of February I remained weak, and so ill that I could not go out of my chamber: and upon the Lord's day in the morning, began the treason of the Earls of Essex, Southampton, and Rutland, with their associates, to appear to the view of all that were not over partially blind: from that day I remained sickly, but not so ill, till the 16th day [of February], upon which day was Captain Lee arraigned, and executed the day following for his intention to murder the Queen's majesty: the 19th day was the Earl of Southampton and Essex arraigned and con-

161–2. *Lady Russell's*: see n. to l. 130 above

162. *solemnity*: Christmas and New Year's festivities

163. *glass house*: where Venetian glass was made and sold (Hoby 1930: 276)
Lady Shirley: perhaps Frances Vavasour, who married Sir Thomas Shirley in 1591 (Hoby 1930: 276)

168. *assurance*: regarding title to her mother's property (?)
books: deeds, documents

173–4. *treason … Rutland*: Robert Devereux, Earl of Essex, Hoby's brother-in-law during her first marriage to Walter Devereux (1589–91). Essex and his associates attempted a rebellion against the government on 8 February 1601. The day before they tried to rally support at a performance of Shakespeare's *Richard II* at the Globe Theatre, and the next day marched towards the City claiming that their common enemies, Secretary of State Robert Cecil and his circle, had plotted to murder Essex. Public backing failed to materialise, however, and Essex, Southampton, Rutland and others were arrested later that day and executed on 25 February.

174. *to appear*: i.e. as truly treasonous

176. *Lee*: Thomas Lee joined the Essex rebellion at the performance of *Richard II* after earlier offering to kill Essex for the government. He was arrested on the 12th after trying to curry favour with both sides.

demned: this day, I thank God, I was better than before, so that I continued my ordinary exercises in my chamber.

FRIDAY 28 FEBRUARY

I went to the court to see my Lady Warwick, and the next day I went again to see the Queen: and the day following I trussed up our stuff to be sent into the country: the next day, being the 2nd day of March, I took my journey towards Yorkshire, and the Lord's even following I came to Mrs Terlington's house, where I stayed the Lord's day: the day after I came the water side, and the next morning, I having a fair tide, to Hull: I came that night to Linton where I, being sick, stayed there from the 10 to the 16 of March: and then I came home to Hackness where I remained very well until the 25, which night I was very sick of a fit, as I think of the stone and colic, for one hour and an half: after which time, I praise God, I having ease took good rest all the night after.

SATURDAY 4 APRIL

This day I performed my accustomed exercises, I praise God, and was almost all the afternoon in the garden sowing seed, whither Mr Bushill came to see us: after, I returned into my chamber and there read and prayed till almost I went to supper.

TUESDAY 5 MAY

After prayers I went to the church where I heard a sermon: after I came home and heard Mr Rhodes read: after dinner I went abroad, and when I was come home I dressed some sores: after, I heard Mr Rhodes read, and wrought within awhile: after, I went to see a calf at Munckman's, which

180. *exercises*: of prayer and self-examination
181. *Lady Warwick*: Anne Russell, sister-in-law of Sir Thomas Hoby's mother Lady Russell, and wife of Ambrose Earl of Warwick (Meads 1930: 278)
182. *trussed*: packed
184. *Lord's even*: Saturday evening
184–5. *Mrs Terlington's house*: near Lincoln
186. *water side*: at Barton before crossing the River Humber
187. *Linton*: where her mother lived
189. *stone … colic*: kidney- or gall-stones … intestinal spasms
199ff. *calf*: such 'abortives' and prodigies fascinated Elizabethans as estranging wonders of nature and possible divine omens

had two great heads, four ears, and had to either head a throat-pipe besides: the heads had long hairs like bristles about the mouths, such as n'other cow hath: the hinder legs had no parting from the rump but grew backward, and were no longer but from the first joint: also, the backbone was parted about the midst of the back, and a round hole was in the midst into the body of the calf: but one would have thought that to have comed of some stroke, it might get in the cow's belly: after this I came in to private meditation and prayer.

WEDNESDAY 26 AUGUST

This day in the afternoon I had a child brought to see that was born at Silpho, one Talliour['s] son, who had no fundament, and had no passage for excrements but at the mouth: I was earnestly entreated to cut the place to see if any passage could be made, but although I cut deep and searched, there was none to be found.

WEDNESDAY 23 SEPTEMBER

After a few prayers I went about the house: and after dinner I preserved some damsons Mrs Etherington sent me: after, Sara spake to me, and then I went to private prayer and praising God, who had been more kind to me than I had deserved.

THURSDAY 21 OCTOBER

After private prayer I went about the house, and before dinner Mr Stillington came, with whom after dinner I walked: writ to Mr Hoby, and lent a poor man of Scarborough 20s.: after I went to private prayer.

201. *n'other*: no other

205–6. *but ... belly*: the meaning here is not entirely clear, but 'stroke' possibly refers to a stroke of lightning which entered the cow's womb and caused her calf to be born deformed

209. *fundament*: anus

214. *Sara*: a servant

TUESDAY AND WEDNESDAY 10 AND 11 NOVEMBER

I continued well, I thank God, these days: and read some meditations of the Lady Bowes her making, as I heard.

MONDAY 5 DECEMBER

All this week following I was well, I praise God, being visited by divers that came to see Mr Hoby: by whom we heard some news, as by Mr Pollard, that the Wednesday fortnight, before which was the 4 of November, died of drunkenness one Sir Hunter Adam, minister of the Bethlehem of York: we heard also of Mr Bishop['s] marriage to Mr Cholmley's daughter, being about 14 years old and himself fifty: besides we heard of woodruffs hurt by young George Dakins, with some other things of less moment.

FRIDAY 26 DECEMBER

Was young Farley slain by his father's man, one that the young man had before threatened to kill, and for that end prosecuting him: the man, having a pike-staff in his hand, run him into the eye and so into the brain: he never spoke after: this judgement is worth noting, this young man being extraordinary profane, as once causing a horse to be brought into the church of God, and there christening him with a name, which horrible blasphemy the Lord did not leave unrevenged, even in this world, for example t'others.

220–1. *meditations ... heard*: meditations were regularly circulated by women and read in manuscript without any intention of printing them. For other instances see Lady Mildmay (above p. 208), and *The Meditations of Lady Elizabeth Delaval* (ed. Douglas G. Greene, Surtees Society vol. 190, Gateshead, 1978). Lady Bowes possibly refers to Isabel, wife of Sir William Bowes of Coventry. In 1606 she allowed nonconformist ministers deprived of their parishes to use her house to discuss separating from the Church of England. And like Lady Hoby and other gentlewomen, she patronised Puritan clerics by direct grants of money, giving them £100 (Greaves 1985: 78, 80). There is a letter of hers to Lord Zouche extant (BL Egerton MS 2812) but apparently no book of meditations.

225. *Sir*: title denoting a parish priest
Bethlehem: or Bedlam, hospital or asylum for lunatics

228. *George Dakins*: a cousin

230–1. *prosecuting ... pike-staff*: chasing (with hostile intent) ... walking staff with a metal point at the lower end

234. *christening ... name*: presumably with holy water in the baptismal font

23 MARCH 1603, WHICH DAY THE QUEEN DEPARTED THIS LIFE

Mr Hoby received letters which came from the Privy Council to the Lord President and all the justices of peace, that our Queen was sick, which wrought great sorrow and dread in all good subjects' hearts: these letters were dated the 16th of March.

26 MARCH

This day, being the Lord's day, was the death of the Queen published, and our now King James of Scotland proclaimed king to succeed her: God send him a long and happy reign. Amen.

27 MARCH

Went Mr Hoby and myself towards York, thinking to continue there until all things were established: but he received letters from the Council at York: we both returned from Linton the 29th day to Hackness, where we found all quiet, God be praised.

5 OCTOBER

Mr Hoby, my mother, and myself went to the dales this day: we had in our gardens a second summer, for artichokes bare twice, white roses, red roses: and we, having set a musk rose the winter before, it bare flowers now: I think the like hath seldom been seen: it is a great fruit year all over.

15 NOVEMBER

This day we had Mr Fairfax and his wife, Mr Skatey, Mrs Nettleton, at din-

236–7. *Lord President*: of the Privy Council. He presides at Council meetings and is responsible for reporting them to the Queen.

238. *dread*: of civil unrest in the event of a disputed succession. Contemporaries worried about this happening after Elizabeth's death, but James I succeeded to the throne peacefully

244. *established*: i.e. concerning the transfer of power to King James

251. *Nettleton*: 'and Mrs Rhodes' crossed out in the MS

ner with us: we saw the printed paper of those that died at and about London this summer, which were 31,967 from July to October.

THE LORD'S DAY 14 APRIL 1605

This day was the first day that the Common Prayer Book was read in our church.

14 MAY

This day Mr Hoby raided Fylyng [Dale] church, there to take order for recusants.

252. *printed paper*: plague-bill listing deaths. See F.P. Wilson, *The Plague in Shakespeare's London* (London, 1963)
257. *recusants*: Roman Catholics who failed to attend services in the Church of England, as they were required to do by law or face crushing fines. The degree of enforcement depended upon the zeal of the local officials.

GRACE, LADY MILDMAY (1552–1620)

FROM *AUTOBIOGRAPHY*

(*c.* 1617–20)

Introduction

Lady Mildmay's *Autobiography* was written following the death of her husband in 1617, though she had been writing long before this, setting down devotional exercises on biblical passages from her youth. Gradually these grew into a 900-page volume she called her 'Book of Meditations', a life-long record of her personal conversations with God. During this time she did not think of herself as an 'author', in the sense of somebody fashioning a story for readers whose expectations would to some extent determine her presentation of details and events. After her husband's death, however, Lady Mildmay began to conceive of her meditations as spiritual counsel to be passed on to her only child, Mary, her grandchildren, and general readers. She therefore decided to preface them with an autobiography, 'as familiar talk and communication with [my family], I being dead, as if I were alive'. Retha Warnicke describes this as an unusual step, since many male writers considered their meditations too personal to be bequeathed (1989: 64). But the same was not true of women. Besides Lady Mildmay, Elizabeth Delaval circulated her meditations (Ezell 1992), as did Katherine Parr, Mary Ward, Margaret Hoby, and others, including a Lady Bowes whom Hoby mentions reading (above p. 205). The *Autobiography* thus marks Grace Mildmay's new conception of herself as an author, since she writes not only to offer readers moral and spiritual advice but also to convince them of the sincerity of her beliefs and actions. The development of such a conscious self-image may be partly related to her newly liberated status as a widow, for she now asserts an autonomy hitherto suppressed in the roles of daughter and wife, and presents herself as an independent agent who will define herself in the negotiation between her own words and readers' responses to them. The *Autobiography* serves to validate her late-conceived desire to publish her 'Book of Meditations', and in so doing is distantly reminiscent of St Augustine prefacing *The City of God* with his *Confessions* – a combination of spiritual autobiography or personal conversion narrative with prophetic writing that subsequently became common to early modern Protestants. It likewise guarantees the transmission of a family heritage, which previously in the legal and financial realms she had been able to secure only with more protracted struggles.

In historical terms the *Autobiography* provides us with the fullest account we possess of an Elizabethan gentlewoman's upbringing and married life. It begins with an extensive list of recommended books and areas of secular and religious knowledge. Lady Mildmay recalls a rigorous but happy childhood in the care of her governess, Mrs Hamblyn, whose strict moral values and impeccable behaviour, reinforced by the example of her mother's deep piety, she values as a spiritual legacy to her children. As Mary Ellen Lamb observes, in these passages of the *Autobiography* we also receive one of the most detailed 'representations of the actual teaching offered to a young woman in the Renaissance' (1990: 200–1). This programme was conventional to Grace's sex, class, and religion: music, arithmetic, letter-writing, needlework, basic surgery and physic, and daily scripture reading – a curriculum intended to produce pious and useful domestic companions for men. While being taught to avoid such works of the devil as 'books of idle plays', she was also encouraged to write letters to various people, as well as poetry on moral themes (e.g. she and Mrs Hamblyn compose satirical stanzas upon an 'impudent' common-law couple). Literacy in fact seems to be as important to her model of education as moral discipline – a notable shift of emphasis from male writers of advice books, who dwell just as heavily on morals but hardly mention literacy because they assume their sons will automatically receive such training.

Grace was the second daughter of Sir Henry Sharrington and Ann Paggett of Lacock Abbey, Wiltshire. In 1567 at the age of fifteen she was married to Anthony Mildmay, eldest son and heir of Sir Walter Mildmay and Mary Walsingham, sister of Sir Francis Walsingham. She seems to have become a favourite of Sir Walter's since she reports that he not only overcame Anthony's reluctance towards marrying her with a combination of threats and financial inducements but also intervened successfully on her behalf in an inheritance dispute with her younger sister. This 'conspiracy', in which her sister and other family members persuaded the dying Sir Henry into altering his will to reduce Grace's share of the estate following the death of his eldest daughter, as well as their later efforts to defraud Grace of her mother's bequest, are dramatically portrayed in the *Autobiography*. Here as at other points one receives a strong impression of Lady Mildmay wishing to make known her side of the story to defend her innocence, engage her readers' sympathies, and ventilate emotions long suppressed but still potentially disturbing to her own moral standards. She also presents her life so as to reveal God's deliverance from her troubles as a reward for her constancy of faith (Warnicke 1989: 65–7).

While recalling her father-in-law with respect and affection, Lady Mildmay does not hide her disappointment with his failure to arrange the jointure he had promised her upon marriage. She also clearly believes that she and her husband were stinted of the full support Sir Walter had pledged them. And her own father, somewhat surprisingly, seems not to have provided her with a marriage portion. As Linda Pollock points out, the Mildmays' apparent lack of negotiated financial arrangements was unusual, since precisely specified contributions were normally the object of lengthy discussions between upper-class families prior to marriages (1993: 8). As in the case of other country gentlewomen of the time, the burden of managing and running the household fell on Grace, but in this case on the inadequate annual allowance of 'but £130 by year bare pension'. This led to 'many afflictions and contrary occasions which fell out betwixt me and my husband, and betwixt us and [her parents-in-law]'. Since at this point prior to her father's death she possessed no property of her own, she worried that her husband would die before providing for her widowhood, which at several points seemed likely. During this time Sir Anthony was often in attendance at court or on government business abroad. These activities caused him to go heavily into debt, thereby further heightening Grace's sense of vulnerability. Though he planned to pay off his debts upon inheriting, after Sir Walter's death the Mildmays were again disappointed of their expectations. Grace still received no jointure, while her husband was bequeathed a little over half the total estate (perhaps because Anthony had only a daughter as heir; see Warnicke 1989: 67). This led him first to seek Parliamentary redress to claim a portion of the lands entailed to his brother, and then, when his brother contested this, to sue him, this time successfully. It was only after this that the Mildmays were well off, and that what had apparently been a strained marriage became agreeable. Lady Mildmay's story not only confirms the conventional impression of a litigious age, but also speaks movingly of the distress faced by women who experienced isolation after marriage and risked penury in the absence of strictly negotiated settlements. That she forcefully articulates her moral positions towards these events and patiently justifies her actions, while at the same time depreciating her personal knowledge and accomplishments, makes her typical of many early modern women torn between confidence in the value of their convictions and fear of intruding on male-dominated areas of competence.

Manuscript:
Lady Mildmay's Journal, Northampton Central Library.

Editions:
Rachel Weigall, 'An Elizabethan Gentlewoman', *Quarterly Review* 215 (1911), pp. 119–38 (excerpts from the *Autobiography, Meditations*, and Lady Mildmay's medical receipt-books, silently emended). Linda Pollock, *With Faith and Physic* (London, 1993, excerpts from the *Meditations* and the receipt-books, and the entire *Autobiography*, modernised and re-ordered). Randall Martin, 'The *Autobiography* of Grace, Lady Mildmay', *Renaissance and Reformation* 18 (1994), pp. 33–82 (diplomatic transcript of excerpts).

GRACE, LADY MILDMAY

FROM *AUTOBIOGRAPHY*

(*c.* 1617–20)

I have found by experience I commend unto my children as approved, this to be the best course to set ourselves in, from the beginning unto the end of our lives.

That is to say, first to begin with the scriptures, to read them with all diligence and humility as a disciple continually every day in some measure, until we have gone through the whole book of God from the first of Genesis unto the last of the Revelation, and then begin again, and so over and over without weariness. To the end that our heart, soul, spirits, and whole inner man may first be seasoned with it, and receive the true stamp and lively impression thereof, whereby we may the better judge of all learning whatsoever, and be able to make true use and good application of all men's judgements and educations. And be conferred this constant resolution: never to receive any doctrine from men which proceedeth not from God, according to the truth of his word in all sanctity and true holiness. The holy sacraments, baptism and the Lord's supper, confirm within us and seal it up forever, betwixt God and our consciences never to be altered, that we are the selected people of God, to do his will, to bless his holy name, and to publish his praise, truly separated and opposed from satan, the flesh, and the world, and from all their wicked actions and conspiracies.

Also to make ourselves expert in the knowledge of the histories contained in the book of *Acts and Monuments* of the church, whereby our faithful zeal may be increased and strengthened and our hearts encouraged manfully to suffer death and to give our lives for the testimony of

1. *approved*: tried and confirmed
2. *set*: place
6. *measure*: portion
9. *man*: being
   seasoned: matured, perfected; familiarised
10. *stamp* ... *impression*: the imagery is from minting coins
12. *conferred*: added (to what has just been recommended)

15–16. *sacraments* ... *supper*: held by Protestants to be the only two sacraments warranted by the Gospels; Catholics retained the other traditional five (confirmation, penance, extreme unction, holy orders, and matrimony)

22. *Acts and Monuments*: the popular *Book of Martyrs* by Protestant John Foxe (1563, and many reprintings)

the truth of God, wherein we are thus confirmed and sealed by the death and blood of Christ.

Also to make ourselves expert in the understanding and knowledge of the chronicles of the land, what matters of moment have passed from the beginning under the government of our royal and anointed princes, whereby we may be instructed to imitate and to follow the good examples of true and faithful subjects, and to have their worthy acts and exploits in memory, which are registered for the same end, and also whereby we may avoid and shame all treasons and treacherous attempts, and all unfaithful combinations with plotters and devisors of evil. For the danger of their society is great; many honourable houses of antiquity and renown and ancient names have been utterly subverted thereby, and rooted out as if they had never been, and the innocent and ignorant persons not made acquainted with their purposes and intents have been brought in question being seen but to frequent their companies, supposing at the least that they could not but see or hear somewhat thereof.

Also to be well instructed in the statutes and laws of this land is very profitable and necessary, whereby they may keep themselves within the compass thereof without controlment or running into danger.

Also the wise and witty sentences of the philosophers, being heathen men without the knowledge of God, are worthy books to be used sometimes for recreation. For they exhort unto virtue and dehort from vice, whereby the excellent gifts of God may be magnified in them.

28. *chronicles ... land*: books of national history and geography such as Raphael Holinshed's *Chronicles* (1577)

32. *registered*: recorded

35. *their society*: following or being associated with them

39. *being ... but*: merely being noticed

40. *supposing*: referring to those who call into question such 'innocent and ignorant persons'; thus, 'they who watch such persons suppose that at the very least they must have seen or heard something treasonous'

42. *statutes ... laws*: not only criminal laws but also those relating to marital and property rights, as illustrated by Lady Mildmay's inheritance disputes and the legal conflicts of other early modern women such as Lady Anne Clifford

44. *controlment*: actual restraints

45. *sentences ... philosophers*: commonplaces or pithy sayings gathered from classical authors into handy collections, rather than whole original works. There is no certain evidence that Lady Mildmay knew Latin or Greek.

47. *recreation*: i.e. in (strictly limited) leisure time; the corollary is that only the Bible is worthy of serious, applied study. Many male commentators warned women readers against the dangers of 'pagan' values in classical literature.
dehort: advise against

These said exercises will establish substance of good matter in the mind, and prepare noble men and gentlemen of good worth for worthy and great employments, and make them wise and able to undergo whatsoever great business they shall take in hand, to the advancement of the Gospel and comfort of the whole commonwealth. A mind thus furnished will think all times ill bestowed in books of idle plays and of all such fruitless and unprofitable matter, which will pervert and carry the mind from all goodness, and is an introduction unto all evil. It is the virtue of the mind which maketh the man, or the woman, without the which they appear as blocks which have eyes and see not, like images set up, in whom is no counsel nor forecasting of perils; such cannot but stumble upon every inconveniency, and be buffeted on every side for want of wisdom. Which wisdom is gotten by continual exercise and well spending the time (as is above said), which should be the labour of a man's whole life, for every day bringeth forth new experience.

All these things coming into my mind, I thought good to set them down to my daughter and her children, as familiar talk and communication with them, I being dead, as if I were alive. And I do therewithal heartily pray them to accept thereof, and of the whole book of my meditations, which hath been the exercise of my mind from my youth until this day, even with the zeal of my heart by the sweet conference with God, and his holy spirit, and faith in Jesus Christ, who brought them all into my mind and gave them to me from time to time, being all unto me as Jacob's pillar, even true testimonies to my soul and conscience of the love and gracious presence of God which never forsook me in all my days. Whereby I am encouraged steadfastly to believe that he will be the same God unto me forever. And though I think none can take that measure of comfort in these meditations which I myself may do, yet whosoever read them may make good use of them, especially seeing they

49. *substance*: a solid foundation, or wealth

58. *blocks*: compare *Julius Caesar*: 'You blocks, you stones, you worse than senseless things!' (1.1.35)
images: statues or carvings, e.g. of saints, to which Puritans strongly objected as idolatrous

59. *forecasting of*: spiritual power of prophesying

63. *new experience*: which can be understood as divinely ordained

66. *I ... alive*: as if I were dead but still able to speak to them
therewithal: in addition

67–8. *book ... meditations*: the substantial manuscript volume, written intermittently over the course of Lady Mildmay's lifetime, that follows the *Autobiography*

72. *Jacob's pillar*: set up to mark the place where God reveals to Jacob in a dream ('Jacob's ladder') that the land at Bethel will be Israel's future inheritance (Genesis 28.10–22)

77–8. *they ... scriptures*: Lady Mildmay's original MS contains copious marginal references to biblical texts, though some of these may have been added by later readers

shall find every point of doctrine confirmed and approved by the scriptures. Which if it please them to peruse, they shall find that profit and consolation therein which they could not have imagined....

It is certain that there is a foundation and ground of many great ensuing evils, that is to say, when the nobility and great personages have no regard nor forecast what governors they set over their children, nor what servants they appoint to attend upon them. Whereby it cometh to pass too often and too universally, that the minds of children are tainted and corrupted even from their infancy, and made capable of every lewd and evil conversation, and are made impudent and bold, without all shame, and so stiff-necked and perverse therein, that no counsel, example, or reproof can restrain them. Many gentlemen and their wives are desirous to place their sons and daughters in honourable services, but they take no care to furnish their minds with true religion and virtue, and other good parts fit for such preferment. But if they were put off and not received into services for want of better education, every one would endeavour to amend that fault, lest their children should lie upon their hands unpreferred, whereas otherwise they would be sought for and enquired after, and whosoever should retain them would think themselves happy.

I had experience of a gentlewoman, niece unto my father, and brought up by my mother from her childhood, whom afterward she trusted to be governor over her own children. She proved very religious, wise, and chaste, and all good virtues that might be in a woman were constantly settled in her; for from her youth she made good use of all things that ever she did read, see, or hear, and observed all companies that ever she came in, good or bad, so that she could give a right censure and true judgement of most things, and give wise counsel upon any occasion. And she could apprehend, and contrive any matter whatever

83. *forecast ... governors*: forethought ... tutors

86. *lewd*: wicked

87–8. *all ... stiff-necked*: any ... stubborn, wilful (common biblical phrase)

89–90. *Many ... services*: it was customary for children to be sent from the age of seven or eight to serve in the households of better-off or higher-ranking relations, partly for good breeding and partly in the hope of making socially advantageous marriages

92, 95. *preferment, unpreferred*: advancement in social rank or to a position in life

92. *they*: sons and daughters

93. *education ... one*: in religious and moral virtue ... parent

98. *gentlewoman*: a Mrs Hamblyn (Weigall 1911: 119)

101. *chaste*: sexually and/or morally pure

102. *constantly settled*: resolutely fixed

103. *observed*: learned by observing

104. *censure*: opinion

106. *contrive*: come to understand

propounded unto her most judiciously, and set her mind down in writing, either by letters indited or otherwise, as well as most men could have done. She had also good knowledge in physic and surgery. She was of an excellent quick spirit, and pleasantly conceited, so that she won my eldest sister and me to be in love with her, and to delight in all her speeches and actions; for her mirth was very savoury and full of wit, and in her sadness she uttered forth nothing but wisdom and gravity. She scoffed at all dalliance, idle talk, and wanton behaviour appertaining thereto, with a touch of a caveat to take heed thereof. She counselled us when we were alone, so to behave ourselves as if all the world did look upon us, and to do nothing in secret whereof our conscience might accuse us, and by any means to avoid the company of servingmen, or any other of like disposition, whose ribald talk, idle gestures, and evil suggestions were dangerous for our chaste ears and eyes to hear and behold, lest the innocency and virginity of our tender hearts should be stained. And further she advised us to deal truly and faithfully in all things, both in word and deed, in small matters and in great, and to beware of all lies, and of oaths, and of reporting of news, to hear much and speak little, seeming to be ignorant in some things rather than to boast of the knowledge which we have not, and thereby to discover our folly, and give occasion to be laughed at.

I delighted so much in her company that I would sit with her all day in her chamber, and, by my good will, would never go from her, embracing always her rebukes and reproofs. And when she did see me idly disposed, she would set me to cipher with my pen, and to cast up and prove great sums and accounts, and sometimes set me to write a supposed letter to this or that body concerning such and such things, and other times set me to read Dr Turner's *Herbal,* and in Bartholomew

108. *indited … otherwise*: dictated or penned herself
109. *physic*: healing, medicine
110. *conceited*: ingenious, imaginative
112. *savoury*: pleasantly edifying, spiritually delightful
113. *sadness*: serious moods
115. *touch … caveat*: hint of a warning
119. *ribald*: scurrilous, base
124. *reporting … news*: gossiping
126. *discover*: reveal
131. *cipher*: practise arithmetic
131–2. *cast … prove*: calculate and verify
133. *body*: person
134. *Dr Turner's*: William Turner, *A New Herbal* (1551, enlarged 1562, 1568), describes various properties and uses of herbs for remedies, cookery, etc.
134–5. *Bartholomew Vigo*: Joannes de Vigo, *The most excellent Works of Surgery*, trans. Bartholomew Traheron (1543) and/or *This Little Practice of Joannes de Vigo in Medicine* (1550)

Vigo, and other times set me to sing psalms, and sometimes set me to do some curious work (for she was an excellent workwoman in all kinds of needle work, and most curiously she would perform it). And when I was not with her, she would be sure to be with me at my heels to see where and with whom I was, and what I did or spake, such was her honest and faithful care to perform the trust which my mother reposed in her.

She gave me warning of a gentlewoman who frequented my father's house, to take heed of her, for that she was of a subtle spirit, full of words and questions, and of an undermining disposition, a busybody, and a meddler in matters which concerned her not, neither regarding what hurt or trouble might redound to many thereby, nor how my reputation might be brought in question by conversing with her, for she sought much into my company. (And surely this counsel which she gave me was very sweet, and good to be observed, for in mine own experience I have found the danger very great. For such a busybody as this, of whom this godly gentlewoman hath spoken, hath not let to speak to me of things by them committed worthy of blame concerning other men, and then at her pleasure report that it was I that spoke them to her.)

Also there was a gentleman of great account sitting at my father's table, who spent all the dinnertime in arguments and much talk, wandering in his discourses. So when dinner was done she asked me if I did not observe the same, and how he gloried in his own wit and to hear himself speak, and how his words were many but little true substance of matter, so that if he were so wise (as he took himself to be) she would judge him to be the wisest man in the kingdom.

Also there was a man and a woman both married but not man and wife, of impudent behaviour one towards another; which when she beheld, she asked me if I did not think it a monstrous spectacle to behold, and wished me to make one staff and she would make another, until there were four or five verses made thereupon, which she performed all herself, very wittily and sharp against such licentious behaviour. And this she did for mine instruction, to take heed of the like, and to abhor and despise the same. Also she advised me to avoid such company by all means possible, and to take heed of whom I received any gifts, as a book, wherein might be written some words whereby I might betray myself unawares, or gloves, apples, or such like;

136. *curious*: delicate, intricate

150–1. *let ... them*: refrained ... i.e. the 'other men'

157–8. *true ... matter*: real weight of true meaning

160–1. *married ... wife*: a common-law couple

161. *impudent*: shameless, immodest

163. *staff*: stanza (of verse)

164. *verses ... performed*: stanzas ...composed

for that wicked companions would ever present treacherous attempts, which afterwards I found true in some sort, and remembered her counsel. Also that I should ever carry with me a modest eye, a chaste ear, a silent tongue, and a considerate heart, wary and heedful of myself in all my words and actions....

And further I have thought good to call to mind the extraordinary love and favour of [my father-in-law Sir Walter Mildmay] towards myself in my tender youth. Which love was such that he desired me of my father to marry with his eldest son. His son, being then more willing to travel to get experience of the world than to marry so soon, was unwilling to give ear thereunto. But his father told him, if he did not marry me, he should never bring any other woman into his house. Upon which importunity of his father, he was content, and entered into communication with him what jointure he would make me, and what allowance he would give for our maintenance in his own time. His father answered him again by earnest protestations and vow in the presence of the lady his good mother, saying, 'Dost thou distrust me Anthony? Here I speak it before God, if thou marry with this woman, I will give thee all that I have, and whatsoever else I can procure shall be thine. And further if I do not, your mother shall be a witness against me in heaven', expressing the same with tears, which moved the hearts of himself and his mother to weep also. Whereupon he yielded unto his father, and the marriage was concluded betwixt him and me upon the trust of his fidelity and good hope that he would never alter his mind nor break his said oath and vow, the consummation of that marriage being the seal of that bond.

My father-in-law gave me this posy in my wedding ring: *Maneat inviolata fides*; that is to say, let thy faith remain inviolate, which in the very instant of my marriage I received most religiously, with a full resolution (by the grace of God) to perform the same unto the end of my life,

171. *treacherous*: deceptive

177. *Sir Walter Mildmay*: *c*. 1520–89, MP from 1545 and Chancellor of the Exchequer from 1566 until his death, founder of Emmanuel College, Cambridge. He gained a reputation for being an able and upright minister in Elizabeth I's government.

179. *eldest son*: Anthony Mildmay, d.1617, married to Grace in 1567, knighted in 1596

181–2. *But ... house*: Pollock speculates that the marriage was political, since Sir Walter and Grace's father had been commissioned to audit the royal mint, and her sister Ursula had married Sir Ralph Sadleir, another auditor (1993: 8)

184. *jointure*: financial settlement which remained under the wife's control rather than passing, as the rest of her wealth did, into her husband's hands upon marriage; it provided her with long-term independent security, particularly in the event of being widowed and/or her husband dying intestate (Erickson 1993: 25–6).

187, 192. *his, himself, his*: Anthony's

197. *posy*: inscribed motto

wherein he bound me unto his son as he had before bound himself unto him upon that condition of our marriage.

After which, we lived with him almost twenty years, receiving no more maintenance from him but £130 by year bare pension to pay our servants' wages, and to apparel ourselves, and to defray all other charges whatsoever, which could not by any means possible suffice in any competency to our necessities. For my husband followed Queen Elizabeth her court, and was appointed by her majesty to go forth with ambassadors that went about any special business, and was employed divers times therein for his own experience, whereby he might be the better enabled to serve his prince and country at opportunities and all occasions; all which he did upon his own charge without craving any allowance from the Queen or from any else, keeping men and horses answerable to such a course of life as well at home as abroad. Which was a strange thing how he could do this without running himself so far in debt that all or a very great part of his father's whole estate could not have been able to discharge the same. But God, who can make a little go far, put into his mind to remember a time to spare and a time to spend, which he did observe in all his expenses, wherein God reserved a blessing for the future times; yet could he not but be in debt, which he was.

And when his father died, not long before his death, he divided his land almost equally betwixt him and his second brother, and likewise his plate and household stuff, and left him no money, or that not much, and therewithal bound his portion of land by a perpetuity, and made me no jointure. Neither did he leave any sufficient portion for the prefer-

204. *bare pension*: basic (perhaps 'poor') allowance

210–12. *experience* ... *occasions*: Anthony was ambassador to France 1596–97, aided Sir Edward Montague in putting down a rebellion at Newton Field, and maintained cavalry against the Spanish in the Netherlands (Henry Roberts, *Fame's Trumpet Sounding*, 1589, 'The honorable life and death of the most famous and noble Counsellor Sir Walter Mildmay knight [in verse]', (A4^{r-v}).

224. *plate*: gold or silver domestic utensils and objects
left ... *much*: besides the bulk of his father's property, Anthony received £200 in money, and £400 in plate; his brother Humphrey received the same amount of money but £300 in plate (Lehmberg 1964: 304–5)

225. *bound* ... *perpetuity*: restricted it legally so that no part could be sold or willed to anybody but a male family heir

226–7. *Neither* ... *daughter*: portion = marriage settlement or cash dowry; child = grandchild, Grace's daughter Mary, b.1582. Lady Mildmay's meaning hinges on what she considers to be 'sufficient': Mary received '£667, a gold chain, and a diamond ring worth £30' (Lehmberg 1964: 305). Such a marriage portion was not large for an upper-class only child; the norm was between £1,000 and £5,000 (Erickson 1993: 87). Lady Anne Clifford, admittedly one of the richest heiresses in England, received a por-

ment of his only child and daughter. My husband finding himself so straitened that he could make me no jointure, nor give his daughter any portion, nor make any states good unto his tenants but only for his own life for fines received, nor pay his debts, nor ransom himself if he should be taken prisoner by some extraordinary occasion, he sought to enlarge himself by the Parliament, and propounded all these said points to that honourable court. Where they were received as things most reasonable and fitting to be yielded unto, both in nature and conscience. But his brother would not by any means be persuaded to give his consent that the least tittle thereof should be granted unto him, though less than one half of my husband's land would have satisfied all his demands, and his brother might have confirmed the residue of his land to himself and his posterity by the Parliament. By which obstinacy and evil nature of his brother, the Parliament dismissed the cause, and left off to take consideration of it, leaving it to the law, and he constrained to remain still in his wants. Then he, being thus provoked, adventured to set himself at liberty by cutting off the entail and perpetuity; which he did perform by the law of the land, and according to the law of God, in that thereby he was enabled and did provide for me and for my daughter, and discharged all his debts, to the good contentment of us and many other....

The lady [Sir Walter's] wife was also a virtuous woman and dutiful to her husband, in all chastity, obedience, love, and fear towards him as ever I did know any, and she instructed me likewise to become a faithful wife unto her son. Whereof there was great proof made in all their time by many afflictions and contrary occasions which fell out betwixt me and my husband, and betwixt us and them.

My husband was much from me in all that time, and I spent the best

tion of £17,000 upon her first marriage. In any event, all or most of Mary Mildmay's inheritance seems to have gone towards paying off her father's debts.

228. *straitened*: restricted

229. *states*: estates, parcels of land

230. *fines*: rent

231–2. *enlarge ... Parliament*: appeal to Parliament for the legal right to alter the terms of his father's will

236. *him*: Anthony

239. *his*: Anthony's

243. *cutting ... entail*: legally breaking the settlement which bequeaths property in a strict order of lineal inheritance

244. *law ... God*: i.e. in the courts of equity, which provided legal remedies based on claims of good faith and moral conscience

248. *wife*: Mary Walsingham, d.1598

254–5. *husband ... solitariness*: a common situation among upper- and upper-middle-class early modern women, as the diaries of Lady Hoby, Lady Anne Clifford and others attest

part of my youth in solitariness, shunning all opportunities to run into company, lest I might be enticed and drawn away by some evil suggestions to stain mine unspotted garment, and so be robbed of mine innocency, for I durst put no confidence in myself for mine own defence. And some great personages, ladies of mine acquaintance, would persuade me to go with them to the court, to feasts, marriages, and plays, saying that it was pity my youth should be swallowed up without all pleasure or delight in the world. Mine answer was that God had placed me in this house, and if I found no comfort here, I would never seek it out of this house, and this was my certain resolution.

And as I gave myself wholly unto God, in the sincerity of my heart so he received me graciously, and preserved me in safety, and directed and prospered me in all my ways, and left me not comfortless but put into my mind many good delights wherein I spent my time almost continually. First in divinity every day as my leisure would give me leave, and the grace of God permit and draw me. I did read a chapter in the books of Moses, another in one of the prophets, one chapter in the gospels, and another in the Epistles to the end of the Revelation, and the whole psalms appointed for the day, ending and beginning again, and so proceeded in that course. Wherein I found that as the water pierceth the hard stone by often dropping thereupon, so the continual exercise in the word of God made a deep impression in my stony heart, with an aptness to incline unto the will of God, and to delight in the meditation thereof upon every occasion of thoughts arising in my mind, or upon whatsoever mine eye did behold or mine ear did hear, applying the same as I was directed by the spirit of God. Which said course was the only stability of my mind, and my stay and comfort in all the troubles and calamities of my whole life.

Also every day I spent some time in playing on my lute, and setting songs of five parts thereunto, and practised my voice in singing of psalms, and in making my prayers to God, and confessing any sins, which were ever ready to meet me in every thought and to turn me away from God and from all goodness. ... Also every day I spent some time in the *Herbal* and books of physic, and in ministering to one or other by

261. *all*: any

265–7. *And ... ways*: unlike many seventeenth-century autobiographies, Lady Mildmay's is not in the form of a 'conversion narrative' tracing a person's religious attitude to a definitive spiritual experience (Graham 1989: 3); rather, it testifies to a lifetime process of spiritual and human education (Warnicke 1989: 56)

270–1. *books ... Moses*: the Pentateuch, or first five books of the Old Testament, whose authorship was traditionally ascribed to Moses

273. *appointed*: in the table of daily readings in the *BCP*

284. *of ... parts*: in five-part harmony

288. *Herbal*: see n. to l. 134

the directions of the best physicians of mine acquaintance, and ever God gave a blessing thereunto. Also every day I spent some time in works of mine own invention, without sample of drawing or pattern before me, for carpet or cushion work, and to draw flowers and fruits to their life with my plummet on paper. All which variety of exercises did greatly recreate at my mind; for I thought of nothing else but that I was doing in every particular one of these said exercises. And though I was but meanly furnished to be excellent in any one of these exercises, yet they did me good, in as much as I found in myself that God wrought with me in all.

And further, betwixt the time of my father-in-law his death and the cutting off of the said perpetuity, our daughter was to be given in marriage, and her father had no portion to give her, whereupon I gave her all my present possession of mine own inheritance, being the flower and best part of my whole portion, my husband having his life in it also. Then was there nothing left unto me for my security but the other part of my portion of inheritance contained in my mother's jointure which was questionable and to be recovered with much suits in law after her death. … My husband, in a due consideration thereof, and in his good nature and thankful mind unto me for my extraordinary love to his daughter, thus to dispossess myself for her sake (and his own of so great a portion, whereby I might have put myself into great want and disgrace in mine age), made great haste to break and cut off his perpetuity, fearing he should not live to perform the same. At which time when he went up to London about this business and finished it; I knew nothing thereof, but at that very instant I made means unto him, that he would be pleased to repair the parsonage at Oundell wherein I had my life, that I might have an house to go unto and to convey my stuff upon any sudden occasion that might befall me (for my husband was then very sickly); with this resolution, to spend my whole life in that place in the most private manner possible, and never to have lived with my daugh-

290. *works*: needlework

291. *sample*: model or example

293. *plummet*: chalk (or possibly lead) pencil or pen

296. *meanly furnished*: minimally instructed

300. *marriage*: in 1599 to Sir Francis Fane, created 1st Earl of Westmorland at the coronation of Charles I in 1625

302. *inheritance*: income-generating lands bequeathed to Grace by her natal family as her jointure

306. *questionable*: because contested by her sister; see below l. 378ff.

310–11. *I … age*: had Anthony died before he freed up his father's inheritance by breaking the entailment or Grace won the settlement dispute with her sister

319. *most … possible*: i.e. without any intention of remarrying, which would otherwise have been a normal expectation, though only one-third of early modern female adults

ter or to be beholding unto her or to any other friend whosoever, with great contentation of mind, and mortification to the world without repentance of whatsoever I had given, wishing it much more with the abundance of God's blessing therewith to my daughter, and to her worthy and honourable husband who deserved the same, and their children....

And further I must not let slip out of my mind what God had done for me in my own particular inheritance, whereunto I was lawfully born. My father Sir Henry Sharrington of Lacock in Wiltshire, Knight, had only three daughters then living, and upon our marriages he divided his land into three parts, and entailed the same unto us with a perpetuity. It happened that our eldest sister died without children that lived, and her part was to be divided betwixt me and my younger sister according to the words in the conveyance and according to the articles of the covenants of our marriage so intended. Yet notwithstanding, when my father died he was persuaded to alter his mind, and to forget that my sister and I proceeded both from one father and from one mother, and that I had ever been his obedient and loving daughter, and that I had never provoked him to displeasure by any misdemeanour toward him any way. But God did behold mine innocency, and my natural and faithful heart to my father, and forgat it not according unto the scriptures. ... For my father lying on his deathbed did before a judge, by name Judge Meade, revoke his said former conveyance and established another, wherein he gave my sister two third parts of his best land and gave me but one third part of his worst land. And I coming to visit my father, not thinking to find him so near his end (for his great danger in his sickness was kept from me), I was brought into his chamber upon a sudden, at the very instant when the judge was there, and those accompanying him were plotters and workers of this unjust alter-

were married at any given time (Erickson 1993: 100). Upon his death, Sir Anthony left her sole executrix (Warnicke 1989: 65).

328. *Lacock*: Lacock Abbey, the family seat

331. *eldest sister*: Ursula

332. *younger sister*: Olivia. During the seventeenth century approximately 20 per cent of families had only female children, who thus became potential heiresses of any freehold land (Erickson 1993: 63).

333. *conveyance*: will

335. *he ... mind*: perhaps because Olivia was the only daughter by 1581 to have had a child; 'Ursula had died childless and Grace, fourteen years after her marriage, had no offspring' (Pollock 1993: 14)

338. *misdemeanour*: misconduct, evil deed

348. *were*: that were

ation. And upon the sight of me they scattered one from another and put away the books and parchments. As soon as I had done my duty to my father I was carried out of his presence into another room, where there came to me my mother, my sister, and mine uncle my mother's brother, one after another, to persuade me and to comfort me in my sorrow for my father, that he was my good father and loved me, and that all his care was for me more than for my sister, wherein I was innocent and suspected no injury towards me, my conscience bearing me witness that I never deserved the same.

At which time I desired to watch with my father and to lie in the house, but I could not be permitted thereunto until they had effected all that business in hand; and after that, I lay in the house and was entertained in all kindness as though there had been no such matter and all well with me. And I entreated them to put my father in mind to be good unto his old servants, and to the nearest of his blood and kindred who stood in need thereof, and also to remember some friends of his to whom he was beholding for many kindnesses, which friends also combined themselves against me in this conspiracy. Wherein they requited me evil for good, and hatred for my good will, whereof God was witness, and turned his loving countenance towards me.

And when my father drew nearer and nearer towards his end, the pangs of death appearing in his face, and I kneeling down by his bedside weeping at the view thereof, he looked sternly upon me and shook me hard by the hand, saying, 'Oh Grace, Grace, Grace. I pray God bless thee. Thou shalt have much trouble with thy land, I tell thee, but I pray God you mayest well overcome it.' These were his last words to me, wherein, assuredly, the blessing of God was included.

And sometime in his fit of the stone, he was heard to say, 'Oh that it were to do again'.

After my father was dead, my sister came to me and said, 'My father hath set out our portions, and the books are drawn that each of us may take our part, which is, you have only that third which was mine, and I have that part which was given unto you, with that other part also which was allotted unto our eldest sister; and I would my brother Mildmay would come and take his part'. And I answered her, that I thought he would not lose his part for want of taking it when he did see his time. Then further I asked her, 'And is it so indeed that my father

352. *mother*: Ann Paggett
358. *watch with*: sit in attendance on
362–3. *to ... servants*: i.e. remember them in his will
376. *stone*: gall- or kidney-stone
379. *books*: last will and testament
382. *brother*: in-law – Anthony
383. *would ... part*: on behalf of Grace, as her husband was legally required to do

has dealt thus with me who never offended him willingly, but ever sought to please him in all things with as much duty and love as any child he had? If God moved him thereunto without any indirect dealings by your husband, yourself, or any other friends for you, then the will of God be done. I beseech him to give his blessing therewithal, and my small portion shall content me as well as your great portion shall content you. But if you have laboured my father, by all means, to work and bring to pass this unnatural wrong towards me, I commit my whole cause into the hand of God, and do most earnestly desire him to be judge betwixt you and me, and to right and defend my cause.' Then went I into a place by myself alone, and poured out my heart to God with abundance of tears, confessing mine unworthiness of the least part; and after I had committed my care unto God, my mind was satisfied and never troubled after.

And after the funeral was ended, my father-in-law Sir Walter Mildmay caused diligent search to be made whether that said last conveyance were lawfully returned into the court of record and enrolled there, and it was found that my father did not live out the time to make out that his last deed good in law; whereupon there was exceptions taken thereunto, and the matter was so effectually followed, that within the very next term after that last conveyance was made, it received an absolute overthrow by law, and the first conveyance stood good in his former force.

Then when they did see this part of their hope frustrate, they gave it out that they had another string to their bow, which was that my father had made a lease of that land contained in that last conveyance, unto my said sister for a thousand years. Whereupon my father-in-law instantly called those words in question. And some reasonable time after my sister's first husband died, she assured herself and was married to her second husband, by whose means she was fallen into great trouble. Whereupon she was constrained to make suit to my father-in-law as to her only friend on whom she did wholly rely, and he performed all things to do her good, and helped her out of her troubles, and was unto his dying day her most faithful friend, notwithstanding he had heard of the speeches betwixt her and her first husband a little before his death;

390. *therewithal*: at the same time

402. *record*: where documents are formally recorded as valid legal evidence; probably a probate court in the case of a will

403–4. *make … law*: by signing the deed and properly registering it

406. *term*: law term

407. *his*: its

414. *assured*: betrothed

415. *trouble*: unhappiness, but not explained

420–1. *speeches … he*: against Grace … the first husband

for he persuaded her to be content, and to give me leave to enjoy my portion equally with her, forasmuch as there was enough for us both, saying, it was pity I should be wronged, for that I had not deserved it, or words to this effect. Whereunto she answered, 'Doth thy heart fail thee now? I will be drawn in pieces with wild horses before ever I will yield to her.' But howsoever her mind was then in this her trouble, she gave consent that this said lease for a thousand years should to come a trial in law; and so the suit proceeded, and the said lease received a judgement, and was cancelled by order of law.

Yet when my father-in-law was dead, they gave it out that they hoped to bring the matter about to another trial, and to overthrow that judgement after my mother's death. And when my mother was dead, my sister fortified the house to keep me out by force, and kept her possession of all the lands, but only that part of mine contained in my mother's jointure which my husband held by force against her. My husband also told her that it were good for us both to end this chargeable course in the beginning; whereunto she answered that she would be torn in pieces with wild horses before she would give over. But after a whole year's expenses and charges in this business, God did put it into my sister's mind to yield unto an equal partition and dividing of our portion betwixt us, which was performed accordingly to both our great contents, all strife ended, natural love revived and confirmed, with all well-wishing to each other and our posterity as to ourselves, even from our hearts. All which was the work of God expressly. For who could have reconciled us in love and peace but God? Even the same God which worketh all things for the best for his children....

THE AUTHOR'S MEDITATION UPON HER* CORPSE

Let me behold my corpse which lieth folden in cerecloths, leaded and coffined here before me yet unburied, and consider: he was as I am, and as he is, I shall be. His candle is put out, his fire is quenched, and he hath made his bed in the dark. The grass is mown, the seed falleth into the earth and shall rise again....

This my corpse was a man with whom I lived almost fifty years, his

436. *chargeable*: expensive legal

444. *expressly*: directly, definitely. As Warnicke observes (1989: 66), though Lady Mildmay's certainty of God's vindication 'helped her to overcome the struggles of a lifetime', it was nonetheless her religion that defined the subordinate roles of daughter and wife which often caused her difficulties.

* *Her, my*: Anthony's, but also with a sense of Grace ultimately sharing the same fate

447. *cerecloths*: a winding-sheet for wrapping a dead body, sometimes waxed
leaded: corpses were often also encased in lead

faithful wife, in all which time I have observed an extraordinary favour of God towards him divers ways, wherein appeared the love, mercy, and protection of God over him. He hath passed through and amongst an army of men, very many of whom died of the plague, and he escaped; he was twice in danger to have been drowned upon the seas. In running at tilt he had a splinter of a lance ran far into the midst of his forehead; another time he was stricken on the head with a bullet, both being very dangerous escapes. By the sickness of his body he was often in danger and escaped. If he should have died in any one of these hazards, myself had been utterly undone touching [my] worldly estate, and my child much prejudiced, wherein God preserved him to be a blessed helper unto me.

He suffered some prejudice, by God's permission, touching the disposing of his inheritance, wherein by order of law he prevailed against his adversaries. Which recovery was effected by God's own hand in his great love and mercy, neither did ever any great suit or matter of importance go against him. He never carried malice in his heart towards any. He was charitable and of a compassionate mind; he would soon forget a wrong, and seek to be reconciled; for I have known when he had spoken bitter words in his anger to the great offence of them to whom he spake, at the same instant he hath called for them and entreated them to take it in the best part, and bear with him, and that every rash word which he spake in his anger was not from his heart, nor of evil meaning.

He was not covetous nor worldly, he loved hospitality and bounty; he was of a free heart and good nature, he was not treacherous but faithful in all things, nor he never deceived any trust. He was very well instructed from his tender youth in the grounds of his faith in Jesus Christ and in his truth, and he was more sincere in his own heart before God than he made show of to the world. Neither did he justify himself; for he would often confess his own errors and defects which he found in himself betwixt him and God, and desired earnestly oftentimes that the thoughts of his heart might be turned away from them, and that he might never apprehend them more, which was an assured token of his election, and that he was a blessed man, unto whom the Lord imputed not his sin.

458. *at tilt*: tilting matches were a fashionable recreation at the court of Elizabeth I

462. *undone*: i.e. before the point at which the Mildmays had secured their financial positions and various inheritances

463. *prejudiced*: disadvantaged by lacking a proper dowry

465. *prejudice*: disadvantage

477. *bounty*: liberality

487. *election ... imputed*: predestined by God for eternal salvation ... reckoned (against him)

I carried always that reverent respect towards him, in regard of my good conceit, which I ever had of the good parts which I knew to be in him, that I could not find in my heart to challenge him for the worst word or deed which ever he offered me in all his life; as to say, 'Why spoke you this?', or 'Why did you that?', but in silence passed over all such matters betwixt us, so that we are parted in all love and Christian charity, until our happy meeting in heaven.

So long as this my corpse is above the earth, I cannot but think upon him in this manner, and beseech the Lord to enable me to perform the trust which in his lifetime he reposed in me, to the honour of God, and the comfort of my neighbour, and so rest at the Lord's good pleasure to follow him in my happy end, and blessed departure out of this changeable world to eternal bliss in the everlasting kingdom of heaven.

489–90. *reverent ... conceit*: revered ... consideration (of him)
498. *trust*: towards their daughter in matters of care and inheritance

MARY WARD (1585–1645)

FROM *THE AUTOBIOGRAPHICAL PAPERS* (1617–26)

Introduction

Mary Ward was a Catholic reformer who founded communities of religious women throughout Europe dedicated to local charitable work and female education. At a time when schools for girls in England were virtually non-existent, and Catholic colleges on the Continent were open only to boys, Ward opened the first free public school for English and local Catholic girls in Saint-Omer, France in 1609. The school followed a liberal-arts programme reminiscent of the humanist curriculum boys had long enjoyed, and thus educated girls for either secular or religious lives rather than training them exclusively for the novitiate as other convent schools did (Orchard 1985: 7). After initial success in Saint-Omer, she founded schools in Liège, Rome, Naples, Perugia, Cologne, Trier and elsewhere; in England her school was not permanently settled until 1686 owing to religious persecution and the civil war.

Mary Ward also reconceptualised vocational possibilities for Catholic women but achieved only limited practical success in her lifetime owing to opposition from male Church officials. Since the Middle Ages women wishing to follow a religious life had had only one option: to enter a cloistered order organised around a daily schedule of contemplative offices. Ward's new order – the Institute of the Blessed Virgin Mary – was non-monastic and non-cloistered, and it ran public schools in conjunction with its religious houses. Its members were apostolic (or publicly active) 'militant virgins', dressed soberly but in ordinary clothes rather than habits, and serving their communities through teaching and active pastoral care. Like the Jesuits, whose vows and spirituality Ward closely adopted as a model for the Institute, her 'galloping girls' were also self-governing (under a mother-general) and answerable directly to the pope rather than to local male clerics as other female religious communities were. This radically new thinking inevitably clashed with traditional ideas about proper feminine conduct and restricted public roles, while also challenging received theories about women's 'natural' inability to develop the same intellectual and spiritual capacities as men. Similar complaints were levelled against the Institute's schools: if girls received the same education as boys they might prove to possess those powers declared impossible by social and religious authorities (Brennan 1985: 97).

Mary Ward has left us a large number of writings pertaining to her life and Institute. Among these is a limited *Autobiography* (1600–9) which covers her formative years as a girl in England, her early religious life in France, and most importantly, the two visionary experiences in 1609 which led her to leave the traditional Poor Clares and begin establishing a new non-enclosed order. Ward began to write down these events intermittently from 1617 onwards at the suggestion of her confessor Father Roger Lee. She has also left behind some fragmentary autobiographical papers, most of which retell experiences recorded in the *Autobiography* but some of which provide additional information about events occurring after them. In all, these various writings do not amount to a full story but represent the outline of a complete life Ward never managed to finish. Moreover, the *Autobiography* has come down to us in Italian, having been translated from Ward's original English close to the time of its composition in 1624–26 by her secretary Elizabeth Cotton for use by the Institute's Italian members. It has been translated back into English by Sister Immolata Wetter, who compiled and edited all of Ward's now widely scattered papers in Rome in the 1970s as a series of nine *Letters of Instruction* for use by current members of the Institute. They are the only complete printed source of Mary Ward's writings, and I am grateful for permission to present some of this material here.

Since the autobiographical material tells only part of Ward's story, it will be useful to summarise her life briefly. She was the eldest child of Marmaduke Ward and Ursula Wright of Mulwith, Yorkshire. During the last quarter of the sixteenth century a large number of Catholics lived in this county; they were declared recusants for refusing to attend Church of England services and subject to crushing fines and imprisonment (Rowlands 1985: 150–6). After Pope Pius V published the bull *Regnans in excelsis* (1570) excommunicating Elizabeth I and calling on all Catholics to dethrone her, government persecutions intensified, especially if local commissioners happened to be keen Protestants. Unfortunately for Yorkshire Catholics, one of these was the Earl of Huntingdon, President of the Council in the North 1572–99. During the 1580s and 1590s he and his officials (e.g. Margaret Hoby's husband) imprisoned many of Ward's family and friends. Moreover, since Catholic husbands often conformed publicly to try to shield their families, it was their wives who became responsible for safeguarding (outlawed) Catholic priests, organising household religious services, educating children in the faith, and aiding local persecuted families (Rowlands 1985: 156–66; Orchard 1985: 5). In effect Catholic wives such as Ursula Ward and Grace Babthorpe (in whose household Mary spent five years of her late childhood) assumed many of the pastoral functions normally exercised by priests. The activities of these women closely resembled the kind of public service Ward later envisioned for the women of her Institute. As the *Autobiography* partly attests, the young Mary Ward was strongly influenced by, and eventually became an expatriate representative of, the efforts of a strong network of Catholic Englishwomen who struggled to resist government-imposed religious conformity (Cover 1993: 27–9).

In 1606 Ward travelled to Saint-Omer to become a lay-sister with the Poor Clares but remained unconvinced that this represented her true vocation. She left the existing order in 1607 to found a separate house of Poor Clares for Englishwomen. Despite its institutional success, this work still proved personally unfulfilling, and on 2 May 1609 she experienced the first of three important visions that convinced her that her real calling lay in founding a non-traditional community of publicly active religious women. She therefore left the Poor Clares and returned with several followers to Saint-Omer to set up an informal community and to open her school for girls. In September of the same year she returned to London to work amongst Catholics and seek support for her plans. Several months later she experienced the second of her spiritual illuminations, the so-called 'gloria vision'. This revealed to her that the 'new way' lay in adopting the 'mixed life' of the Jesuits, consisting of self-governing pastoral and teaching functions. This decision was confirmed by a third major vision in 1611, and a fourth in 1615. After receiving local encouragement from the Bishop of Saint-Omer and founding a second house at Liège, Ward received provisional approval for her Institute from Pope Paul V in Rome in 1616, and then travelled on foot across the Alps to open schools and religious houses elsewhere in Europe. She was briefly arrested when she returned to England in 1619, and then went back to Italy to settle for a time in Rome. By 1631 the Institute numbered 300 members, and was teaching more than 500 pupils in its free schools (Rowlands 1985: 170).

Well before this, however, the unorthodox nature of her Institute had begun to attract strong opposition, especially from Jesuits. Besides its members' uncloistered and self-directing freedom, their refusal to wear recognisable habits provoked complaints about transgressing fixed social roles: 'They sometimes dress like noble ladies and drive abroad in fine carriages; and sometimes like servants' (Byrne 1985: 75). They were also accused of siphoning off rich girls from traditional enclosed orders. And when one priest predicted that the fervour of Institute members would decline because they were 'but women', Ward objected:

> Fervour is a will to do well, that is, a preventing grace of God and a gift given gratis by God which we could not merit. It is true fervour doth many times grow cold, but what is the cause? It is because we are imperfect women, and love not verity ... The verity of our Lord remaineth forever. It is not *veritas hominum*, verity of men, nor verity of women, but *veritas Domini* [of the Lord], and this verity women may have as well as men. If we fail, it is for want of this verity and not because we are women! (Wetter 1970 VI: 12; Cover 1993: 82)

Nonetheless, despite their determination to assert an equality of vocation with their Jesuit colleagues (excepting preaching and sacramental functions), the Institute was suppressed by a series of official Church measures between 1628 and 1631. Ward and certain colleagues remained in Rome under the protection of Pope Urban VIII, and only in some places did her various communities manage to continue operating informally. When she travelled to Munich in 1631 she was arrested and gaoled on heresy charges but eventually released. She returned to England in 1639 to found a school openly in London under the patronage of Queen Henrietta Maria. During the civil war this school moved to Yorkshire. Ward died there in 1645 and was buried in a Protestant churchyard by a minister who was '"honest enough to be bribed"' (Orchard 1985: 15). The Institute's rules were officially allowed in 1703, though Ward herself was not recognised as its foundress until 1909, and full recognition came only in 1978, by which time her order's schools and colleges for women were operating on five continents.

Manuscript:
Sister Immolata Wetter, 'Letters of Instruction', 9 vols (Rome: Institutum Beatae Mariae Virginis, 1970–75) [privately circulated typescripts].

MARY WARD

FROM *THE AUTOBIOGRAPHICAL PAPERS* (1617–26)

When I was about 15 years old I had a religious vocation, which grace by the mercy of God has been so continuous that not for one moment since then have I had the least thought of embracing a contrary state. My parents, though otherwise extraordinary pious, would not for any consideration give their consent, for I was the eldest child and much loved, especially by my father. I was therefore obliged to remain in England six years and some months longer. During that time many of what the world esteems fortunate opportunities happened [to] me, against which, when nothing in me could prevail, God himself took the matter in hand, and freed me by means considered by many more divine than human.

In those six years and as many months or more, living in the house of a relation of my mother (in great measure because the retirement was more to my taste), I practised much prayer, some few fasts, and some austerities and internal and external mortifications (as far as I recollect on all occasions that served) and acts of humility, such as that, to those who did not know me, I appeared to be one of the domestics of the house.... I delighted in

1. *15 years*: Ward was brought up by her parents and, between the ages of five and ten, her grandparents Robert and Ursula Wright. She records elsewhere that her grandmother, 'noted and esteemed for her great virtue', had been imprisoned for fourteen years for her beliefs (Wetter 1970 I: 6) and her mother fined £80 on four counts of recusancy in 1591–92 (Cover 1993: 26). Many of her other relations and family friends suffered similarly.
   vocation: i.e. calling to become a member of a Catholic religious order
6. *six years*: from *c.* 1599/1600 to 1606, before she left for France
8. *opportunities*: Mary Ward received four offers of marriage during these years
12. *relation*: Sir Ralph Babthorpe. His wife Grace had been imprisoned for recusancy between *c.* 1593 and 1594 (Cover 1993: 27).

12–13. *because ... taste*: elsewhere in her autobiographical papers Ward explains this as the result of her parents' removal to a colder climate and their fears for her weak health (Wetter 1970 I: 11)

13–14. *austerities ... mortifications*: self-denying acts to subject the appetites and passions

reading spiritual books, particularly those which treated of monastic life, and I spent much time by day and sometimes by night in this employment.

The divine goodness (perhaps to prevent in me a less useful exercise of the affections, with which I abounded) gave me at that time such light as to the beauty and perfection of the religious state, that in all that I have since seen or read in this kind, I have never seen anything exceed, if it equalled, the same. But this affection to the religious life was in general, for I had no inclination to any order in particular, only I was resolved within myself to take the most strict and secluded, thinking and often saying that, as women did not know how to do good except to themselves (a penuriousness which I resented enough even then), I would do in earnest what I did.

Of all the virtues to which I was drawn with the greatest affection was chastity, but I did not aspire to take the vow then, fearing lest the devil should tempt me extremely and I should not have the courage to consult upon it or ask advice. I frequented the sacraments with extraordinary fervour, confession alone was rather difficult to me, no otherwise than from my too great bashfulness and extreme repugnance to hear myself speak against myself, although in those years I did not find much to say.

From my exterior, and my application to the exercises most fitting for that state, it was generally known that I was resolved to leave England for that purpose. For this reason my father came in person to the place where I was and most peremptorily prohibited me from departing out of England

17. *spiritual books*: Ward elsewhere mentions two in particular: *The Rules of a Christian Life* (probably Robert Southwell's *A Short Rule of the Good Life,* 1596–79), and Lorenzo Scupoli's *The Spiritual Conflict* (1589, trans. John Gerard 1598). The first was a popularised lay-version of Ignatius Loyola's *Spiritual Exercises* (see n. to ll. 184–5 below), the second advocated the ascetic life for women in religious orders (Wetter 1970 II: 2; Cover 1993: 37–42).
18. *this employment*: besides the books mentioned above, Ward read the Vulgate, church fathers, and accounts of martyrs, having been taught by her grandmother to read Latin, a language later emphasised in her schools. Like other English Catholic girls, Ward received little formal instruction other than through reading (Cover 1993: 37).
19. *prevent*: forestall
23. *affection ... life*: 'I liked to keep company most with those of the house that I thought to be most virtuous, amongst whom there was especially one, a maid of great virtue (and in years) who looked to the chapel and such like businesses, with whom I loved to be ... for by some speeches of hers I found myself moved to love a religious life' (Wetter 1970 I: 11–12)
26. *penuriousness*: want of what is desired
31. *sacraments*: a contemporary writer reports there were two masses each morning in the Babthorpe household, with Evensong at 4.00 p.m. and Matins and Litanies at 9.00 p.m.; Sundays and holy days included sermons and catechism (Cover 1993: 33)
36. *state*: religious life

without his leave and express order, to which command I made no resistance either by word or sign (for I loved him extremely, and had not the heart to say anything to him which would grieve him); but at the same moment I was most firmly resolved to observe nothing less than this precept, but to set out immediately....

Setting forth then upon the so greatly desired journey, and not yet out of England, a great obscurity darkened my mind and doubts rose up within me as to where, and in what religious order, I should have to settle, and in this darkness and disquiet of soul I crossed the sea and arrived at Saint-Omer in Flanders, where I went immediately to the College of the Fathers of the Company of Jesus of the English nation to treat with them concerning the monasteries of the city, etc.

At my first word, one of these said that the religious of St Clare of that town had heard of my coming with the intention of choosing a severe order, and were expecting me with much anxiousness, and had already assigned me a place. This was not within the enclosure, he said, because they could no longer admit foreigners within, but outside with those who spent themselves in the humble duty of begging for the enclosed (according to the custom of that country). The father added that enclosed and unenclosed were the same order and had the same rule, only the latter added the charity of supporting the enclosed with their labours, etc. (which I afterwards experienced to be the contrary, the rules being very different and the way of life and exercises quite diverse; but the father spoke as he had heard). In conclusion he expressed his admiration of the providence of God in ordaining circumstances to coincide with the great desire of the nuns to accept me so quickly, never having seen me, affirming that it certainly was the will of God and my true vocation. Which words 'will of God' so pierced my heart that I had no inclination to say or think of anything else: I stood silent for

43. *immediately*: by 1606 Ward had reached 21 and was therefore legally free to make her own decisions; however, she must have eventually obtained her parents' permission since they arranged for her journey to the Continent

44–5. *not* ... *England*: en route from Yorkshire. Ward spent part of spring 1606 in Canterbury with a family friend, Mrs Catherine Bentley, whose mother Mrs Lucy Roper was the granddaughter of Sir Thomas More. Ward says she was 'to go overseas as one of [Mrs Bentley's] daughters' (Wetter 1970 I: 14, 16).

47. *Saint-Omer*: in France (at that time part of the Spanish Netherlands), and College (St Omer) for educating English Catholic boys founded by the Jesuit Robert Persons in 1593

49. *Company*: i.e. the Jesuits
treat: discuss

51. *religious* ... *St Clare*: the Poor Clares

54. *place*: as a lay-sister, not a regular professed nun

56. *enclosed*: women who had taken solemn religious vows and were required to remain within the nunnery at all times

a while feeling an extreme repugnance to their offer, but reasoning within myself that the rules [being] the same and the place offered me being only more abject and contemptible, this disinclination and repugnance could only come from pride....

The first day after my arrival I was invited by those holy nuns to live with them, which I did, remaining there one month or more before taking the habit (as the provincial made a difficulty about receiving me for the service of the enclosed, judging perhaps that I was not fit for the practices). The people of the city likewise protested at it, asking the abbess why she did not receive me within. But she answered that my humility was such that I absolutely insisted on serving the enclosed; which devotion, God knows, was far from my thoughts, although his divine majesty made use of their customs and manner of living on this occasion for my great good and to dispose my soul for still greater. The real cause, however, of the nuns' desire I should be outside was that some time before, some of the out-sisters had given disedification causing dishonour and loss to the convent, so much so that one of the choir nuns had been obliged privately to break her enclosure in order to superintend the out-sisters until someone satisfactory could be found for such a post. And the idea of the nuns was that a person endowed by God with gifts of nature, inspired by him to renounce fortune and favour in the world, urged to leave her native land and parents in the best years of her life, and drawn to serve him in retirement and solitude, should, and rightly so, give an example in all religious exercises, especially in matters concerning chastity. In fact the reputation I had for modesty was beyond the ordinary.

This conceit the nuns had of me made them determine, when my noviceship should be finished, to give me the government of those outside; which had I known, assuredly I should never have entered, having even then, as I remember, a very different idea as to the qualities necessary to govern well; and as to the affection I might have to such an office, I can with truth say that from my first vocation to religion (which was, as I have said, about the age of fifteen) until now, I was never capable of any, as one might who leaves a position honourable in the esteem of the world, stable as belonging to her state of life, and who could feel an exaltation in promotion to titles or superiority and offices in religion....

I remained in the monastery nearly a year, during the whole of which time the same distress continued, rather with augmentation than otherwise; but through the special grace of God, they did not cause any impediment in the exact observance of the rules and customs practised there during these months, too long to state now. For the present I will only say (as well as I can) just what is necessary to understand better what I have said and still

73. *provincial*: head of the religious order in a particular province

82. *disedification*: words or actions unbecoming to the order

82–3. *loss ... privately*: in terms of donations ... personally, perhaps secretly

have to say. Two months after my entrance ... my confessor declared for certain that this was not my vocation etc; which opinion of his amazed me and forced me to turn to God with increased love, which I did, feeling persuaded that he would not deceive me nor could he be deceived.... Towards the end of this year of probation, on the feast of St Gregory the Great (my particular advocate), sitting in silence at work with the nuns, I recited privately certain prayers in honour of that saint, entreating him that as on earth he loved and helped the English, so now in heaven he would help and protect one of that nation, betaking myself to him that I might live and die in the will of God, and in the state which should most please his divine majesty, etc.; which short devotion I had not finished when I was called to receive the blessing of the Father General of that order who happened to be there (as I remember to have heard accidently); who after having given me his blessing, spoke to me in private and counselled me, with demonstration of great affection, to think well what I ought to do, that the time of my profession drew near, that I was still free and fit to serve God in any state or religion, but having once made my profession, I should be obliged to remain, and should have to content myself with he means of perfection which I found there; to which as far as I recollect, I did not say a word in reply, but making my reverence and showing signs of gratitude, I took my leave, returning to my work and devotions to St Gregory, when I found myself full of astonishment at the words of the Father General, never having spoken with or even seen him before. Suddenly I was enkindled with a vehement desire to procure a monastery for the English of this order; but not being able otherwise to moderate this vehemence and place myself in indifference before speaking or doing anything for that purpose, I retired myself alone, and earnestly entreated our lord God that nothing I might do in this business should have other success than that which he willed and which should be the most acceptable to him, praying our most Blessed Lady and other saints to be witnesses that my desire were no other but to do and have done his divine will. And so not being able further to restrain myself, I went in all haste to entreat the said Father General, that in this visitation of his,

108. *confessor*: Fr George Keynes S.J. of the English seminary at St Omer, and the same who advised her to enter the Poor Clares as a lay-sister (above l. 51ff; Wetter 1970 II: 20)

112. *year*: 1607

112–13. *feast ... advocate*: 12 March; Pope Gregory the Great (540–604) sent the first missionaries to England

113. *work*: needlework

119. *Father General*: Fr Andrea de Soto (Wetter 1970 II: 20)

120. *accidently*: incidently

125. *perfection*: spiritual perfection, as a lay-sister

131. *monastery ... order*: i.e. a separate house of English Poor Clares

he would put two monasteries into one and give one of them to the English; but I could not find the Father, who had returned to his convent. And this my simplicity appeared not to displease God, who afterwards showed more appropriate means, and concurred with them to the entire fulfilment of the good desired. . . .

A few days later I left the convent.

Putting on a secular dress, without further delay I applied myself to secure a habitation and all else to found a monastery of St Clare for the English. In that work God knows I did little, but his divine majesty supplied all my deficiencies in such a manner, that in the space of two years, a little more or less, a convenient site was found, a spacious monastery and church built, English nuns of that order taken out of other monasteries to preside in it, and persons of fitting qualities and talents admitted to probation.

During these two years I suffered extreme aridity without any intermission, and without any cause, but I believed most firmly that I had wholly lost the spirit of devotion and the sensible sweetness that I used to feel, through some unknown negligence of mine in the divine service; which thought caused me great grief, and sometimes fear whether I should be saved or not, but this never with doubt or mistrust in the divine mercy – only I feared myself, lest I should thus fall away for ever. By an especial grace this fear was nevertheless always accompanied by a firm resolution, followed by acts when the occasion occurred, that although I might never see God, yet I would serve him until death, and especially I would do all that was possible in me to carry out his work, which it appeared to me he had placed in my hands. And from these sufferings and the above-named acts

140. *put . . . one*: if this is not an error (meaning creating two *out of* one), it may refer to separate parts of the order outside and within the convent, each following different rules, which Ward hoped to unify when an English house was established

145. *later*: between the time of this revelation and leaving the order Ward 'turned to God, my only help, who without delay . . . favoured me with frequent and clear lights, accompanied with peace and strength of soul far more than I had ever before experienced, showing me that this was not my vocation'. She also consulted the mother-superior of the out-sisters, the only person to whom she had confided her difficulties, who advised her to become a regular enclosed nun (Wetter 1970 II: 9–11).

150. *monastery . . . church*: in Gravelines, actually later than is suggested here, in September 1609. The community operated until the French Revolution, when it moved to England.

151–2. *English . . . probation*: the Bishop of Saint-Omer obtained permission from Pope Paul V for the new community, with five choir nuns and two lay-sisters coming from the existing Poor Clares in November 1608 (Wetter 1970 II: 21). Other women soon followed from England.

153. *aridity*: lack of spiritual devotion, interest

155. *sensible*: capacity for physical well-being, emotional sensitivity

161. *acts*: of devotion

sprang great love and desire to labour without reward, that giving me most satisfaction which was done unseen....

At that time I confessed to that Father of the Company through whose advice I entered the first monastery.... This Father was truly of great goodness of life and no less solicitous for the progress of my soul, but he guided my conscious entirely by the way of fear; for instance, that I ought to hate myself, to fear the judgements of God, to tremble at the pains of hell, in all of which I was most inept.... I could not sensibly hate the enemy of all good, much less myself, whom I loved too well. To labour through love even death appeared to me to be easy, but fear with me made but little impression. Hell I was resolved, by the assistance of God's grace, never to merit, and of the doings there I could form no conception as vivid as the Father wished. Finding myself so differently disposed from what he required (and which I therefore with all diligence sought to be) was, I believe, in a great measure the cause of that aridity and those doubting thoughts. Perhaps he did this that the good success of the business I had in hand might not cause me injury, and whichsoever way, through his merits it proved, as I hope, for my profit....

As a beginning, both the religious taken from the other monastery to govern the new one, as well and those still seculars, made the *Spiritual Exercises* for the space of a month; which that they might make them with more profit, I procured that Father Baldwin of the Company of Jesus, then Provincial of the English Mission, should assign some father in the College of that nation in the city to aid in grounding them in spiritual things; he nominated Father Roger Lee, of happy memory (a man truly apostolic and much illumined and favoured by God), who charitably accepted the burden; and when the said exercises commenced, I among the rest began also to confess to him, whose aid to the great profit of my soul I was so happy as to have for ten years together.

172. *sensibly*: in any physical sense

183. *beginning*: November–December 1608

183–4. *religious ... seculars*: professed Poor Clares ... lay-sisters, among whom was Mary's sister Frances (Wetter 1970 II: 21)

184–5. *Spiritual Exercises*: manual of devotional practices formulated by St Ignatius Loyola (1491–1556). They were the spiritual rationale of the Jesuits, founded by Loyola in 1534 as a non-monastic priestly order bound by vows of poverty, chastity, and obedience to the Holy See. Besides having the Jesuits undertake the spiritual direction of her community, Ward later adopted their educational and charitable mission as the model for her Institute. Ignatian meditative techniques also influenced early seventeenth-century English Metaphysical poets; see L. Martz, *The Poetry of Meditation* (1954).

188. *city*: Gravelines

193. *ten years*: Lee died in December 1615, so the period is actually closer to seven years. He urged Ward to write down the mystical and life experiences which led to formation of her Institute; she wrote intermittently from 1617 onwards (Wetter 1970 I: 4).

Having passed four or five months in this place and at these exercises, and enjoying great peace of mind and interior consolation, I was sitting at work among the other nuns on the day of St Athanasius, the second of May about ten o'clock of the forenoon, being employed making cords of St Francis for the use of the religious (and reciting privately, as I was accustomed to do at each one that I made, the litanies of our most Blessed Lady, that whoever should wear that cord might never commit mortal sin), when there happened to me a thing of such a nature, that I knew not, and never did know, how to explain. It appeared wholly divine, and came with such force that it annihilated and reduced me to nothing; my strength was extinguished, and there was no other operation in me but that which God caused; the sight intellectually of what was done and what was to be fulfilled in me, I willing or not willing, of this only was I conscious. The suffering was great because far beyond my powers, and the consolation was greater to see that God willed to make use of me in what pleased him more. Here it was shown me that I was not to be of the order of St Clare; some other thing I was to do, what, or of what nature, I did not see nor could I guess, only that it was to be a good thing, and what God willed.

The bell for examen was rung as usual before eating, which was to my content, for thus I had time to be alone to return to myself in order that the others might not see any difference in me, etc. But what I say bears no proportion to what passed on this occasion, and is in no way to my satisfaction, nor will it be to those who read it: may God supply what is wanting as far as it will be to his service.

The next day, the feast of the Invention of the Holy Cross, I sought to speak to the above-named Father Roger Lee, upon whose counsel I then depended, and begged him to receive what I had to tell him under the seal of confession, but he would not be content to do so. I argued and would by all means tell it thus, saying that things were of that nature that he could not properly keep them from his superiors if not thus heard, and that once known, it would immediately follow that, where now I was loved and praised by all, in one half hour I should not have a single friend, nor would

When the Jesuits opposed her desire to adopt their Society's '*matter and manner*' as the basis for her female-run order (below l. 331 and n.), Lee trod a fine line between obedience to his superiors and support for Ward's plans (Cover 1993: 93).

196. *second … May*: 1609

197. *cords*: belts or girdles worn round the waist

204–5. *no … caused*: Ward says elsewhere that the experience lasted for 'half an hour or more' (Wetter 1970 V: 9)

212. *examen*: time dedicated to examining one's conscience

218. *Invention*: discovery, reputedly by Helena, mother of the Emperor Constantine, in AD 326 and later a church festival (3 May)

there be a person who would not condemn and despise me, and more (which I believe I also felt the most) he himself would have his part in this suffering (as afterwards most minutely happened). But with all this he would not yield, so that I related to him what had passed in the manner he desired, which from prudence and for my greater trial he appeared to disapprove and oppose with a certain severity unusual to him, exhorting me to a more than ever exact observance of the rules and regulations of the place where I was, which I did with a very good will. I loved what I possessed most sensibly and before all things that I knew – so much so that when I was left to my own nature and human defects, I wept to remember that I was not to be in that order. And so desirous was I of a quiet life, and so good for nothing, that I found myself already wearied out with the little labour taken in that foundation. At the same time I was in everything too human, and sometimes even fearful of being deceived, and of believing that to be good which was not so. All which were motives to cause me to remain there with all content for further trial, and so six or seven more months passed. In this time many things happened which, not to be tedious to the one who reads it, I omit.

The time drew near when all those not yet formally clothed were to again put on their secular dress, and to appear in their own rank and condition at the new monastery in the city of Gravelines, and there solemnly to receive the habit, among whom I was to be one. But in those seven months I saw more and more that God did not desire this, though I remained entirely ignorant of that which his divine majesty willed from me; and seeing that I had to return to live in the world, to prevent the deceits of the devil and to dispose my soul entirely for the divine service, on Palm Sunday I made a vow of chastity, with the leave and approval of the above mentioned Father, and then took leave of these dear friends with much feeling on both sides. To the end that this foundation might not suffer on account of my departure (the conceit of the people being more placed in me than was fitting), the report was spread (with my consent) that my constitution was too weak to support such austerity (which nevertheless was not in the least the motive

228. *minutely*: precisely

233. *possessed*: i.e. the place and conditions of the order in which she was living

234. *sensibly*: intensely

245. *rank … condition*: i.e. signifying their secular status

251–2. *Palm … chastity*: this actually took place on 12 April 1609, just prior to the first vision on the feast of St Athanasius, 2 May 1609 (Wetter 1970 II: v). As Ruth Liebowitz observes, seventeenth-century female religious activists viewed the task of preserving their virginity while working in the world as a heroic challenge; this new 'militant virginity' was more valuable than 'the cloistered virtue of their contemplative sisters' (1979: 134).

255. *conceit … me*: i.e. the townspeople of Gravelines having a more confident understanding of me

of my leaving). There was, however, some appearance of its being so to the public and to those who did not know the contrary. . . .

At that time I made a vow with the consent of my confessor to be a religious, but not of any order in particular, not being able to incline towards one more than another, and finding in none of them anything which appealed to me. Then in obedience to my confessor, without any inclination on my part, I made another vow to enter the Order of St Teresa should he so command me.

Afterwards for good reasons and with his consent, I returned to England for some months with the intention of trying to do good to others, and, as far as I can judge, I did not spend that time ill, nor did I neglect to do as much as possible for the cause I went over to serve. My few labours were not altogether in vain; divers now living holily in various religious orders say that they left the world in great part through my conversation. Various other good things happened then, which it appears better to omit, because I do not know how to explain myself without so many words, and those unapt. The following, nevertheless, I ought not to leave out.

One morning, making my meditation coldly and not at all to my satisfaction, at the end of it I resolved to assist a person to be accepted in some convent who much desired to become a nun, but wanting a portion could not otherwise enter. And then going to dress myself according to the fashion of the country and other circumstances, whilst I adorned my head at the mirror, something very supernatural befell me, similar to that already related on the day of St Athanasius but more singular, and, as it appears to me, with greater impetuosity, if greater there could be. I was abstracted out of my whole being, and it was shown to me with clearness and inexpressible certainty that I was not to be of the Order of St Teresa, but that some other thing was determined for me, without any comparison more to the glory of God than my entrance into that holy religion. I did not see what the assured good thing would be, but the glory of God which was to come through it showed itself inexplicably and so abundantly as to fill my soul in such a way that I remained for a good space without feeling or hearing any-

264. *Order . . . Teresa*: founded by Carmelite reformer and mystic Teresa of Avila in 1567

266. *Afterwards*: October 1609

I . . . England: to London, where she and her companions were forced to move from house to house to avoid arrest (Cover 1993: 28)

277. *portion*: women gave a sum of money called a dowry upon entering a convent, and the accumulated capital providing interest became a convent's main source of income. Dowries also released fathers from future material responsibility for their postulant daughters. Men objected to self-ruled non-enclosed female communities such as Mary Ward's partly on the grounds that women could, according to canon law, recover their dowries if they decided to return to secular life, and/or make support or inheritance claims on their families (Liebowitz 1979: 141).

thing but the sound, 'Glory, glory, glory'. By accident I was then alone, therefore what external changes this and similar things cause I cannot say; but from the internal feeling and bodily disturbance they must be remarkable; my knowledge fails as to their continuance; all appears to last but a moment, even at those times when afterwards I made a computation and found it to have been about two hours.

On this occasion a good deal of time passed before I recovered, but returning to myself found my heart full of love for this thing, accompanied by such glory that not yet can I comprehend what it was. And seeing for certain that I was not to be of the Order of St Teresa, remembering also the vow which I had made [for] being of that order if my confessor should command me, I felt great fear of offending God in these two contraries, or of adhering to one or the other side. To resist that which now had been operated in me I could not, and to have a will in opposition to the vow I ought not. In this conflict, giving myself to pray, I protested to God freely that I had not and would not admit on this occasion any other will than his. As a testimony and sign, that my mind and will were totally to do his without exception, I put on a haircloth, which I have forgotten for how long a time I wore, but I believe for some continuance; for I well recollect through this and other corporal penances, done for this end during the months that I remained in England, I did no little injury to my health, especially being occupied at that time with some fervour in winning and aiding others, observing (according to my knowledge) the circumstances requisite and suitable to the said business and to my condition. Such a labour is only too honourable, but nevertheless painful enough, if not undertaken for him to whom we owe all, and through the help of whose grace alone it is fitly and perseveringly feasible.

My purposed time of stay in England expired, I returned to St Omer. Divers followed with intention to be religious where I should be, living together there. Great instance was made by divers spiritual and learned men

290. *Glory*: 'a central tenet of Ignatian spirituality': the goal of learning to discern the values of Christ in one's life and in service to one's neighbour (Cover 1993: 85–7). Following this 'gloria vision', Mary Ward's movement towards Jesuit spirituality and practice became clearer (Wetter 1970 II: 22).

307. *haircloth*: shirt or vest made of hair; enduring its discomfort was a traditional act of penance

317ff. The main thread of Mary Ward's story now switches from the *Autobiography*, which ends at this point, to a biographical letter in English to Monsignor Albergati, Papal Nuncio (= ambassador) in Lower Germany, written in the spring of 1621. The letter summarises events in the *Autobiography* and goes on to describe Mary Ward's third major vision in 1611, which is presented here.

318–19. living together: as an informal community, without vows or a rule

that we would take upon us some rule already confirmed; several rules were procured by our friends both from Italy and France, and we earnestly urged to make choice of some of them. They seemed not that which God would have done, and the refusal of them caused much persecutions, and the more because I denied all and could not say what in particular I desired or found myself called to.

About this time, in the year 1611 I fell sick in great extremity. Being somewhat recovered (by a vow made to go in pilgrimage to our Blessed Lady of Sichem), and being alone in some extraordinary repose of mind, I heard distinctly, not by sound of voice but intellectually understood, these words: '*Take the same of the Society*'; *so understood as that we were to take the same both in matter and manner, that only excepted which God by diversity of sex hath prohibited*. These few words gave so great light in that particular Institute, comfort and strength, and changed so the whole soul, as that [it was] impossible for me to doubt but that they came from him whose words are works.

My confessor resisted, all the Society opposed; divers institutes were drawn by several persons, some of which were approved and greatly commended by the last Bishop, Blasius of Saint-Omer, our so great friend, and some other divines; these were offered us; there was no remedy but to refuse them, which caused infinite troubles. Then would they needs [have] that at least we should take the name of some order confirmed, or some new one, or any we could think of, so not that of Jesus. This the Fathers of the Society urged exceedingly (and that do still every day more than others), telling us

320. *some rule*: the orders in Belgium and France that received Englishwomen during this period followed Augustinian, Benedictine, Dominican, Franciscan, and Teresean rules (Cover 1993: 75). These were all cloistered, contemplative communities under the authority of a local bishop, provincial of a male order, or prior of a male monastery (Liebowitz 1979: 136–42).
confirmed: by the pope

328. *Sichem*: in Belgium

330. *same ... Society*: *same* = the heritage of Ignatius Loyola (Wetter 1970 V: 13), and in terms of authority = self-governance. The Jesuits' independence led to disputes with civil authorities even in Catholic countries.

331. *matter... manner*: when Ward presented her final plan to Gregory V for approval in 1622, 85 per cent of it was taken verbatim from the Jesuit *Formula Instituti* or rule. The scope of her Institute was to be equally world-wide, and its mission concerned with active work in society at large (Cover 1993: 96).
only excepted: the major exceptions were the priesthood, administration of the sacraments, and preaching, whose reservation to men Ward and her colleagues did not question

334. *him*: God

342. *so ... Jesus*: until it was suppressed in 1628–31, the Institute was called 'The Mothers of the Society of Jesus'

that to any such name we may take what constitutions we will, even theirs in substance if otherwise we will not be satisfied, but by no means will they [permit] that we observe that form which their constitutions are written in, which, say they, are not essential or needful. The neglect of these offers did and do cause extreme troubles, especially for the first seven years. While my confessor (whom I had tried myself to obey) lived, they urged him in many things to say as they said, though against his own judgement and knowledge, (as often I understood); neither would he yield to them in all. One time in particular they urged him so much about the name as that he made answer to divers grave fathers that if the case were his, they durst not urge any change.

Concerning the name, I have twice in several years understood, in as particular [a] manner as these other things I have recounted, that the denomination of these must be of Jesus. And thrice I think more often of the inconveniences [that] would happen to both parts, if ours should have any dependency of the Fathers of the Society.

I beseech all those (even for our Lord's love) that should read these my faults and the goodness of God towards me (notwithstanding my unworthiness), that they judge not of anything there according to their own affections, but determine of all as the truth is, distinguishing the great and true difference between God's preventing grace, his immeasurable goodness and the means afforded me to be wholly his, and my continual falls, unspeakable negligences, and imperfect concurrence with all such his favours as yourselves will judge and notice with me; so shall you do justice giving God what is his, and me my deserts, who asks no other recompense or wage, etc., as accountable of anything they could do for me, besides those that the readers of these would endeavour henceforward to become lovers of truth and workers of justice. Which petition, who grants and proceeds accordingly, verity itself will free them from errors, rectify their judgements, perfect their knowledge, endow them with true wisdom, make them able to discern things as they are in themselves, the difference between trifles and matters of importance, what is to be done or not done in all.

360ff. This final paragraph derives from an autobiographical fragment written in English after Ward experienced a further vision in 1615 which strengthened her call to an apostolic life

363. *affections*: inclinations, predispositions

364. *preventing*: preceding

LADY ANNE CLIFFORD (1590–1676)

FROM *THE DIARY OF LADY ANNE CLIFFORD* (1616–19)

Introduction

Lady Anne Clifford was the daughter of Lady Margaret Russell and George Clifford, 3rd Earl of Cumberland and 13th Baron Clifford. As their eldest surviving child, Anne was heir to the Clifford barony and its extensive lands and buildings in the north-west of England by virtue of original writs issued in the reign of Edward II that entailed the family title and estates to direct heirs, male or female. When George Clifford died in 1605, however, he willed this property to his brother Francis and his succeeding male heirs, with reversion to Anne only if the male line failed. During her eleven years as a widow, Margaret Clifford sued to recover her daughter's inheritance, and when she died Anne continued her struggle. Yet court judgements went against her, and she was put under great pressure by her husband, Richard Sackville Earl of Dorset, as well as by the King and other powerful men, to sign away her rights to the Clifford lands in return for a cash settlement. She steadfastly refused to do this, however, or to recognise the courts' decisions as binding. Her resistance preserved her lineal claim, so that when her uncle's son, Henry, 5th Earl of Cumberland, died in 1643 without male heirs, she at last became Baroness Clifford. After delays caused by the civil war, she travelled north from London in 1649 to take possession of her Westmorland properties. She lived there as virtual ruler of the region for the remaining 27 years of her life, undertaking ambitious rebuilding programmes, founding almshouses, chronicling her family's history, and convening local courts of justice – virtually unprecedented for a Renaissance woman – as High Sheriffess of Westmorland and Lady of the Honour of Skipton in Craven.

The 1616–19 *Diary* (or *Knole Diary*, from the name of the family seat where Lady Anne lived during her first marriage, 1609–24) is one of four autobiographical documents dating from separate periods of her life (extensively reproduced in Clifford 1992). All four were intended in varying degrees to justify Lady Anne's legal entitlement to her inheritance, and to demonstrate her stewardship of the family property afterwards. The *Knole Diary* was written at the time of the events it describes, although the document we now possess is an eighteenth-century copy of the lost original. It contains a higher proportion of intimate detail and self-revelation than most other domestic diaries by early modern women such as Margaret Hoby (Lewalski 1993: 140–1). It actually opens with a section of reminiscences for the year 1603 (perhaps based on an earlier contemporary diary) in which Lady Anne as a young girl recalls the funeral of Queen Elizabeth and surrounding events. The succeeding sections, 1616–19, contain marginal notes (here presented as footnotes) which she added in hindsight; these expand on information in the main entries and mark notable public events, thereby situating Lady Anne's personal life within a larger historical context.

Lady Anne's three other autobiographical manuscripts were written or dictated after she became Baroness Clifford. As a result, when they look back to past events they do so with the knowledge of her ultimate triumph, and therefore tend to be more self-assured, even masterful, than the *Knole Diary*. The first of these is a brief *Life* contained within *A Summary of the Lives of the Veteriponts, Cliffords, and Earls of Cumberland*, a précis of her Books of Record (see below) copied by Henry Fisher in 1727. Since this *Life* narrates events up to 1649, it provides essential information about her second, largely unhappy, marriage to Philip Herbert, Earl of Montgomery and Pembroke, from 1630 to 1650. In a section which is worth quoting in full for its candid portrait of both her marriages, Lady Anne sums up the difficulties she had with her husbands, affirms her belief that Providence guided events towards her rightful succession, distinguishes her separate destiny as head of the Cliffords from her husbands' family interests, and notes the contribution of books and moral wisdom to her sense of personal autonomy:

> I must confess with unexpressible thankfulness that, through the goodness of almighty God and the mercies of my saviour Christ Jesus redeemer of the world, I was born a happy creature in mind, body, and fortune, and that those two lords of mine, to whom I was afterwards by the divine providence married, were in their several kinds worthy noblemen as any then were in this kingdom. Yet was it my misfortune to have contradictions and crosses with them both: with my first lord about the desire he had to make me sell my rights in the lands of my ancient inheritance for money, which I never did nor never would consent unto, insomuch as this matter was the cause of a long contention betwixt us, as also for his profuseness in consuming his estate, and some other extravagancies of his; and with my second lord because my youngest daughter [by Lady Anne's first marriage], the Lady Isabella Sackville, would not be brought to marry one of his younger sons, and that I would not relinquish my interest I had in 5000 pounds, being part of her [marriage] portion, out of my lands in Craven. Nor did these [two husbands] want divers malicious ill-willers to blow and foment the coals of dissension betwixt us, so as in both their lifetimes the marble pillars of Knole in Kent, and Wilton in Wiltshire [the Pembroke family seat], were to me oftentimes but the gay arbour of anguish, insomuch as a wise man that knew the insides of my fortune would often say, that I lived in both these my lords' great families as the river of Roan, or Rodamus, runs through the lake of Geneva, without mingling any part of its streams with that lake. For I gave myself wholly to retiredness as much as I could, in both those great families, and made good books and virtuous thoughts my companions, which can never discern affliction nor be daunted when it unjustly happens; and by a happy genius I overcame all those troubles (Psalm 62), the prayers of my blessed mother helping me therein. (BL Harl. MS 6177 fol. 63^{r-v})

Lady Anne began dictating her third diary in 1650. This *Kendal Diary* runs from 1649 to 1676 and comprises the third volume of her Books of Record, a vast genealogical chronicle of the Cliffords initiated by Margaret Clifford and continued by Lady Anne to support her legal position (Clifford 1992: xii). Unlike the *Knole Diary*, it is more an official record of family landmarks, visits, and improvements by Lady Anne to her numerous properties than a journal of daily experience. The fourth diary, still in private hands, records events during the last months of Lady Anne's life and recaptures some of the intimate character of the *Knole Diary*.

The selections presented below are from this earliest *Diary*. Near the beginning and end of its entries Lady Anne records two profound losses she suffered in 1616 and 1619 respectively: the deaths of her mother, and of Queen Anne. Lady Anne became very close to her mother during her childhood when her father spent much of his time at sea; after he returned permanently he and his wife lived separately because he kept several mistresses. (The conflicted circumstances of her parents' relationship were to anticipate many aspects of Lady Anne's two marriages.) When her father died, Anne's mother became her guardian to protect her fortunes from male interference, and she began legal action to recover her daughter's alienated lands. Her mother's solicitude, love of learning, and spiritual guidance made Lady Anne come to value her matrilineal heritage as much as the landowning one she derived through her father (Lewalski 1993: 133–6; this duality is complexly represented in the Great Picture of Anne and her parents at Appleby Castle, reproduced and discussed in Williamson 1922: 334–45, and Lamb 1992). Lady Anne was also supported by Queen Anne in refusing to renounce her ancestral property rights, and she received further help and advice from the wider network of women at court.

The *Knole Diary* is chiefly concerned, however, with the inheritance dispute that led to two climactic interviews with King James, during which a settlement with her uncle was imposed on her but she successfully managed to resist signing away her rights. Though understated, her accounts of these two meetings do not fail to convey the extraordinary strength of will she demonstrated in confronting two intimidating displays of patriarchal power. Her adversaries on these occasions included her husband, who throughout the years of the *Diary* is shown threatening, cajoling, harassing, and isolating his wife in order to force her consent to an agreement he favoured because it represented an opportunity of paying off the debts he had run up in gaming and amusements; he also wished to keep in good favour with James, and had little imaginative interest in the Clifford heritage. Overall, as Lady Anne pointedly observes, the Earl of Dorset lived a life of pleasure-seeking entirely different from her own, and this situation she had no alternative but to accept. Yet despite all their rancour and disagreements, the *Diary* also records moments of companionship between them, so that Lady Anne was able to observe in a letter of 20 November 1615 to her mother:

> My Lord ... is a very kind, loving, and dear father, and in everything I will commend him, saving in this business of my land, wherein I think some evil spirit works, for in this he was as violent as possible. (Williamson 1922: 152)

When the subject of her lands (or the Earl of Dorset's favourite attendant Matthew) were not under discussion, Lady Anne seems to have been capable of genuine fondness for her husband, even though their relationship was always dominated by his concerns and meant continual sublimation of her resentment and disappointments. Identification with her family history and defence of her rightful inheritance, on the other hand, created a nucleus of resistance in her life which neither her husband nor anyone else could ever shatter. It was these guiding principles as well as a tenacious conviction that a daughter was as worthy as a son to inherit lineal property and offices, that ultimately defined her identity.

Manuscript:
Centre for Kentish Studies, Maidstone, Sackville Collection U269 F48/1–3 (currently lost).

Editions:
The Diary of the Lady Anne Clifford, ed. Vita Sackville-West (London, 1923). *The Diaries of Lady Anne Clifford*, ed. D.J.H. Clifford (Stroud, Glouc. and Wolfeboro Falls, N.H., 1990; rev. edn 1992).

LADY ANNE CLIFFORD

FROM: *THE DIARY OF LADY ANNE CLIFFORD* (1616–19)

1616

FEBRUARY

All the time I stayed in the country I was sometimes merry and sometimes sad, as I had news from London.

Upon the 8th day of February I came to London, my Lord Bishop of St David's riding with me in the coach and Mary Neville. This time I was sent for up by my lord about the composition with my uncle of Cumberland.

Upon the 16th my Lady Grantham and Mrs Newton came to see me – the next day, she told me, the Archbishop of Canterbury would come to [see] me, and she persuaded me very earnestly to agree to this business, which I took as a great argument of her love. My cousin Russell came to me the same day and chid me and told me of all my faults and errors in this business – he made me weep bitterly; then I spoke a prayer of Owen's and went to see my Lady Wotton at Whitehall, where we walked five or six turns but spoke nothing of this business, though her heart and mine were

1. *the country*: at Knole, the family seat in Sevenoaks, Kent
2. *news*: in particular about her efforts to recover the Clifford family lands (estimated total size, 90,000 acres; see Clifford 1992: 3), from her uncle Francis, who had been willed them by Lady Anne's father and succeeded him as 4th Earl of Cumberland in 1605, even though the original writ dating back to Edward II stipulated that they were to pass to direct male or female heirs. See the 'composition' l. 5.
3. *Bishop*: Richard Milbourne
4. *Mary Neville*: cousin and goddaughter of Lady Anne's husband, Richard Sackville, Earl of Dorset

4–5. *sent for up*: *sic*. similarly below at l. 243

5. *composition*: agreement, by which Lady Anne was to receive a cash settlement in exchange for renouncing her ancestral claims to the Barony of Clifford and its lands. The *Knole Diary* in large part records her struggle to resist this arrangement.
7. *Canterbury*: George Abbot, formerly domestic chaplain to the Sackville family
8. *business*: i.e. the 'composition' with her uncle
9. *Russell*: Francis, later 4th Earl of Bedford
11. *prayer* ... *Owen's*: unidentified

full of it – from hence I went to the Abbey at Westminster where I saw the Queen of Scots, her tomb and all the other tombs, and came home by water, where I took an extreme cold.

Upon the 17th my Lord Archbishop of Canterbury, my Lord William Howard, my Lord Roos, my cousin Russell, my brother Sackville, and a great company of men of note were all in the gallery at Dorset House, where the Archbishop took me aside and talked with me privately one hour and half, and persuaded me both by divine and human means to set my hand to their arguments. But my answer to his lordship was that I would do nothing till my lady and I had conferred together. Much persuasion was used by him and all the company, sometimes terrifying me and sometimes flattering me, but at length it was concluded that I should have leave to go to my mother and send an answer by the 22nd of March next, whether I will agree to the business or not, and to this prayer my Lord of Canterbury and the rest of the lords have set their hands.

Next day was a marvellous day to me through the mercy of God, for it was generally thought that I must either have sealed to the arguments or else have parted with my lord.

MARCH

Upon the 20th in the morning my Lord William Howard with his son, my cousin William Howard, and Mr John Dudley came hither to take the answer of my mother and myself, which was a direct denial to stand to the judges' award. The same day came Sir Timothy Whittington hither, who did all he could do to mitigate the anger between my Lord William Howard and my mother, so as at last we parted all good friends, and it was agreed upon my men and horses should stay, and we should go up to London together after Easter.

15. *Queen of Scots*: Mary, who claimed the English throne by descent from Margaret Tudor, daughter of Henry VII, but was imprisoned on charges of plotting against Elizabeth I. Lady Anne mentions her several times, perhaps associating her story of disinheritance with her own. Anne's father was a witness at Mary's execution in 1587 (Clifford 1992: 11).
    by water: i.e. down the Thames
18. *brother Sackville*: Edward Sackville, Lady Anne's brother-in-law
21. *means*: of persuasion
23. *my lady*: Anne's mother, Margaret (Russell) Clifford, Dowager Countess of Cumberland
35. *judges' award*: Lady Anne and her mother tried to recover the Clifford lands in an earlier suit before the Court of Common Pleas (Williamson 1922: 87). The judgement went against them, and Anne was told to surrender the land-rights in return for a cash award (the 'composition' and 'business' above).

APRIL

Upon the 11th I came from London to Knole where I had but a cold welcome from my lord. My lady Margaret met me in the outermost gate and my lord came to me in the drawing chamber.

Upon the 12th I told my lord how I had left those writings which the judges and my lord would have me sign and seal behind with my mother.

Upon the 13th my lord and Thomas Glenham went up to London.

Upon the 17th came Tom Woodyatt from London, but brought me no news of my going up, which I daily look for.[1]

Upon the 18th Baskett came hither and brought me a letter from my lord to let me know this was the last time of asking me whether I would set my hand to this award of the judges.

Upon the 19th I returned my lord for answer that I would not stand to the award of the judges, what misery soever it cost me. This morning the Bishop of St David's and my little child were brought to speak to me.

MAY

Upon the 2nd came Mr Legge and told divers of the servants that my lord would come down and see me once more, which would be the last time that I should see him again.

Upon the 3rd came Baskett down from London and brought me a letter from my lord, by which I might see it was his pleasure that the child should go the next day to London, which at the first was somewhat grievous to me, but when I considered that it would both make my lord more angry with me and be worse for the child, I resolved to let her go. After, I had sent for

[1] Upon the 17th my Mother sickened as she came from prayers, being taken with a cold chillness in the manner of an ague, which afterwards turned to great heats and pains in her side, so as when she was opened, it was plainly seen she had an imposthume.

43. *12th ... my lord*: Lady Anne has returned to Knole after a visit to London ... Lord Dorset, her husband

45. *Thomas Glenham*: Dorset's gentleman-servant

47 n. 1. *ague ... opened ... imposthume*: shivering fever ... in an autopsy ... abscess

48. *Baskett*: Peter Baskett, listed in a 1613–14 Catalogue of the Dorset household at Knole as a 'Gentleman of the [Earl's] Horse' (Clifford 1992: 274)

53. *child*: Margaret Sackville, b.1614

54. *Legge*: Edward Legge, steward (Knole Catalogue)

58–9. *child ... London*: i.e. to be separated from Lady Anne

61. *child ... go*: she left six days later

Mr Legge and talked with him about that and other matters, and wept bitterly.[2]

Upon the 8th I dispatched a letter to my mother.

Upon the 9th I received a letter from Mr Bellasis, how extreme ill my mother had been, and in the afternoon came Humphrey Godding's son with letters that my mother was exceeding ill, and as they thought, in some danger of death – so as I sent Rivers presently to London with letters to be sent to her, and certain cordials and conserves. At night was brought me a letter from my lord to let me know his determination was, the child should go live at Horsley, and not come hither any more, so as this was a very grievous and sorrowful day to me.

Upon the 10th Rivers came from London and brought me word from Lord William that she was not in such danger as I feared.

All this time my lord was in London, where he had all and infinite great resort coming to him. He went much abroad to cocking, to bowling alleys, to plays and horse races, and [was] commended by all the world. I stayed in the country, having many times a sorrowful and heavy heart, and being condemned by most folks because I would not consent to the agreement, so as I may truly say, I am like an owl in the desert.

Upon the 15th my lord came down from London and my cousin Cecily Neville; my lord lying in Leslie Chamber and I in my own.

Upon the 18th, being Saturday, in the morning my lord and I having

[2] My Lady Margaret lay in the Great Dorset House, for now my lord and his whole company was removed from the Lesser Dorset House where I lay when I was first married.

63 n. 2. *Lady Margaret ... Great Dorset House*: Lady Anne's daughter ... in London

64. *dispatched ... mother*: living in Westmorland on her jointure estate

71. *Horsley*: West Horsley, Surrey, where Lady Anne's sister-in-law Lady Cecily (Sackville) Compton had a house

hither: to Knole; i.e. Lady Anne was to be sent away to a smaller house

74. *William*: William Howard

76. *resort*: number of visitors

76–7. *abroad ... world*: Dorset spent vast sums on these amusements and went heavily into debt. One of the reasons he urged his wife to exchange the Clifford lands for cash was that he would receive the money in her name.

76. *cocking*: cock-fighting

81–2. *Cecily Neville*: sister of Lady Anne's father-in-law, and daughter of Lady Frances Abergavenny, who wrote prayers in prose and verse for Thomas Bentley's *Monument of Matrons* (1582)

much talk about these businesses, we agreed that Mr Marsh should go presently down to my mother and that by him I should write a letter to persuade her to give over her jointure presently to my lord, and that he would give her yearly as much it was worth.

Upon the 22nd Mr Davis came down from London and brought me word that my mother was very well recovered of her dangerous sickness; by him I writ a letter to my lord that Mr Amherst and Mr Davy might confer together about my jointure to free it from the payment of debts and all other incumbrances.

Upon the 24th my Lady Somerset was arraigned and condemned at Westminster Hall, where she confessed her fault and asked the King's mercy, and was much pitied by all beholders.[3]

Upon the 29th Kendal came and brought me the heavy news of my mother's death, which I held as the greatest and most lamentable cross that could have befallen me. Also he brought her will along with him, wherein she appointed her body should be buried in the parish church of Alnwick,

[3] Upon the 24th, being Friday, between the hours of 6 and 9 at night, died my dear mother at Brougham, in the same chamber where my father was born, 13 years and two months after the death of Queen Elizabeth, and ten years and seven months after the death of my father, I being then 26 years old and five months, and the child two years old, wanting a month.

84–7. *agreed ... worth*: why Lady Anne should have 'agreed' to propose this arrangement is unclear, since Dorset would have then been able to sell the jointure property (perhaps to the Earl of Cumberland, as some evidence suggests; see Williamson 1922: 93–4)

84. Marsh: Christopher Marsh, Lady Anne's secretary and later steward of her Westmorland estates. He helped to compile her voluminous Books of Record which were partly intended – like the present *Diary* – to bolster her legal right to the Clifford inheritance.
presently: immediately

86. *jointure*: land settled on her by her husband for her widowhood

90. *Amherst ... Davy*: Queen's serjeant and bencher of Gray's Inn ... a family lawyer

91–2. *jointure ... incumbrances*: Dorset had evidently mortgaged part of his wife's jointure to raise money

93–5. *Somerset ... beholders*: Frances Howard, cousin to Richard Sackville and wife of Robert Carr, Earl of Somerset and favourite of James I. She divorced Robert Devereux, Earl of Essex, in 1613 in order to marry Carr. They were later both accused of poisoning Carr's secretary Thomas Overbury who had objected to their marriage. Lady Somerset confessed to the murder, but her husband maintained his innocence. Both were found guilty but avoided execution because of James's protection.

95 n. 3. *Brougham*: Brougham Castle, near Penrith, in Westmorland, part of the Clifford estates

99. *Alnwick*: in Northumberland (pronounced 'Annick'). Lady Anne subsequently arranged for a memorial chapel to be built there.

which was a double grief to me when I considered her body should be carried away and not interred at Skipton; so as I took that as a sign that I should be dispossessed of the inheritance of my forefathers.

JUNE

Upon the 4th Marsh and Rivers came from London and gave me to understand how my lord, by the knowledge and consent of Sir William Howard and the advice of his learned counsel, had sent a letter down into Westmorland to my lady's servants and tenants to keep possession for him and me, which was a thing I little expected but gave me much contentment, for I thought my lord of Cumberland had taken possession of the jointure quietly.

Upon the 8th being Saturday Rivers and Mr Burridge were sent down into Westmorland from the Council for restoring the possession of Appleby Castle as it was at my lady's decease.

At this time my lord desired to have me pass my rights of the lands of Westmorland to him and my child, and to this end he brought my Lord William Howard to persuade me, and then my lord told me I should go presently to Knole; and so I was sent away upon half an hour's warning, leaving my cousin Cecily Neville and Willoughby behind me at London, and so went down alone with Katherine Baxton about 8 o'clock at night, so as it was 12 before we came to Knole.

101. *carried ... Skipton*: Skipton Castle in Craven, West Yorkshire, was another Clifford property. Lady Anne was born there on 30 January 1590. Clifford (1992: 36) suggests this was a codicil to the original will.

104–7. *my ... me*: the jointure lands belonging to Lady Anne's mother would now pass legally to her uncle, the Earl of Cumberland. The Earl of Dorset believed, however, that if he took possession immediately the lands might be claimed for his wife. He sent representatives to Westmorland for this purpose and Lady Anne travelled to Brougham Castle (see above), but the Earl of Cumberland's men had arrived before them (reported below ll. 143–4). Following this positive gesture on his wife's behalf, Dorset also tried to persuade her to sign over her 'rights of the lands of Westmorland' to him in the event of her death, with their daughter Margaret as heir to both of them.

111. *Council*: Privy Council

116. *so ... warning*: the reason for this dispute is unclear

117. *Willoughby*: perhaps a daughter of William, Lord Willoughby and his wife Lady Frances Manners who was one of Lady Anne's gentlewomen at the time (Williamson 1922: 89)

118. *Baxton*: apparently her gentlewoman

Upon the 17th came down Dr Layfield, Ralph Conniston and Baskett, Dr Layfield bringing with him the conveyance which Mr Walter had drawn, and persuaded me to go up and set my hand to it, which I refused because my lord had sent me down so suddenly two days before.

Upon the 19th my lord came down for me and Dr Layfield with him, when my lord persuaded me to consent to his business and assured me how kind and good a husband he would be to me.

Upon the 20th my lord and I, Dr Layfield and Katherine Baxton went up to London, and the same day I passed (by fine before my Lord Hobart) the inheritance of Westmorland to my lord if I had no heirs of my own body, and upon the 21st, being Friday, my lord wrote his letters to my Lord William and gave directions to Mr Marsh to go with them, and that the possession of Brougham Castle should be very carefully looked to; the same day he went to Horsley to see the child at his sister's.[4]

JULY

Upon the 1st, Lord Hobart came to Dorset House, where I acknowledged a fine to him of a great part of my thirds in my lord's land, but my lord gave me his faithful word and promise that in Michaelmas term next he would make me a jointure of the full thirds of his living. About one o'clock I set

[4] About this time I went into the Tiltyard to see my Lord Knolles, where I saw Lady Somerset's little child, being the first time I ever saw it.

120. *Dr Layfield*: Fellow of Trinity College Cambridge and Rector of St Clement Danes, London (Williamson 1922: 40). Margaret Clifford wrote a brief autobiographical letter to him using the trope of the seven ages of woman, portraying her life as subject to constant and usually negative changes in fortune (reproduced in Williamson 1920: 285–8).

Conniston: Margaret Clifford's servant (Williamson 1922: 147–8)

121. *conveyance*: over the rights to her lands

128. *fine* ... *Lord Hobart*: deed ... probably the informal title of Chief Justice Sir Henry Hobart (Williamson 1922: 97)

131. *William*: Howard

133. *sister's*: see n. to l. 71.

n. 4. *Tiltyard*: near Whitehall Palace and the Banqueting House, used for tournaments and masques

135. *fine* ... *land*: deed legally relinquishing her common-law claim to a third of her husband's estate in the event of being widowed; such claims were often contested by male relations, however, whereas jointures made during a husband's lifetime were more secure (see l. 91)

forward on my journey. My lord brought me down to the coach side where we had a loving and kind parting.[5]

Upon the 17th I rid into Whinfell park, and there I willed the tenants that were carrying of hay at Billian Town that they should keep the money in their own hands till it were known who had a right to it.

Upon the 29th I sent my folks into the park to make hay, where, they being interrupted by my uncle Cumberland's people, two of my uncle's people were hurt by Mr Kidd, the one in the leg, the other in the foot, whereupon complaint was made to the judges at Carlisle, and a warrant sent forth for the apprehending of all my folks that were in the field at that time, to put in surety to appear at Kendal at the assizes.

AUGUST

Upon the 1st day came Baron Bromley and Judge Nichols to see me as they came from Carlisle, and ended the matter about the hurting of my uncle's men, and have released my folks that were bound to appear at the assizes.

Upon the 4th my cousin John Dudley supped here and told me that I had given very good satisfaction to the judges and all the company that was with them.

Upon the 22nd I met my lord at Appleby Town's end where he came with a great company of horses, Lord William Howard, he, and I riding in the coach together, and so we came that night to Brougham. There came with him Thomas Glenham, Coventry, Grosvenor, Grey Dick, etc, etc. The

[5] About this time Acton, my lord's footman, lost his race to my Lord Salisbury, and my lord lost 200 twenty-shilling pieces by betting on his side.

141. *carrying of*: gathering. The tenants bringing in hay evidently expected Lady Anne to succeed to her mother's jointure lands rather than the Earl of Cumberland.

143. *the park*: not necessarily Whinfell park mentioned above

148. *put ... to*: ensure that they
assizes: county court sessions, usually held twice a year

149. *Baron Bromley*: Sir Edward Bromley, Puisne Baron of the Exchequer (Williamson 1922: 99)

158. *Grosvenor, Grey Dick*: perhaps a misreading of the Mr Graverner named as a gentleman usher in the Knole Catalogue. Likewise Grey Dick may refer to two people, since the Catalogue lists a Mr Gray and several Richards (Clifford 1992: 274).

same night Prudence, Bess, Penelope, and some of the men came hither, but the stuff was not yet come, so as they were fain to lie three or four in a bed.[6]

Upon the 24th in the afternoon I dressed the chamber where my lady died, and set up the green velvet bed, where the same night we went to lie there.

SEPTEMBER

Upon the 11th Mr Sandford went to London, by whom I sent a very earnest letter to my lord that I might come up to London.[7]

Upon the 21st was the first day I put on my black silk grogram gown. Upon the same day came Rivers down to Brougham and brought me word that I could not go to London this winter.

Upon the 31st I rid into Whinfield in the afternoon. This month I spent in working and reading. Mr Dumbell read a great part of the *History* of the Netherlands.

NOVEMBER

Upon the 1st I rose betimes in the morning and went up to the Pagan Tower to my prayers, and saw the sun rise.

Upon the 9th I sat at my work and heard Rivers and Marsh read Montaigne's *Essays*, which book they have read almost this fortnight.

[6] Upon Saturday my lord showed me his will, whereby he had given all his land to the child saving £3,500 per annum to my brother Sackville, £1,500 per annum which is appointed payment of his debts, and my jointure excepted, which was a matter I little expected.

[7] Upon the 18th died my Lady Margaret's old beagle.

159–60. *Prudence, Penelope ... stuff*: maids (Knole Catalogue) ... bedding and room furnishings, which were normally carried with the household when it travelled

160 n. 6. *brother*: brother-in-law

my ... excepted: i.e. any of her husband's debts were not to be paid from Lady Anne's jointure

161–2. *dressed ... died*: i.e. took down the black hangings that had been put up when her mother died, and furnished it normally

166. *grogram*: coarse

170. *working*: needlework

History: perhaps Edward Grimestone's *General History of the Netherlands* (1608)

175. *Essays*: probably the edition trans. by John Florio, 1603, as Lady Anne's father had forbidden her to learn any foreign languages (Williamson 1922: 66)

DECEMBER

Upon the 9th I set out from Brougham Castle towards London. About 3 o'clock in the afternoon we came to Roses. All this day I rode on horseback on Rivers's mare, 27 miles that day.

Upon the 18th I alighted at Islington where my lord, who came in my Lady Withypoll's coach which he borrowed, my Lady Effingham the widow, my sister Beauchamp and a great many more, came to meet me, so that we were in all ten or eleven coaches, and so I came to Dorset House where the child met me in the gallery. The house was well dressed up against I came.

All this time of my being at London I was much sent to and visited by many, being unexpected that ever matters should have gone so well with me and my lord, everybody persuading me to hear and make an end, since the King had taken the matter in hand so as now.

Upon the 27th I dined at my Lady Elizabeth Gray's lodgings at Somerset House where I met my Lady Compton and Lady Fielding and spoke to them about my coming to the King. Presently after dinner came my lord thither and we went together to my Lady Arundel's, where I saw all the pictures and statues in the lower rooms.

1617

JANUARY

Upon New Year's Day, presently after dinner, I went to the Savoy to my Lady Carey's; from thence she and I went to Somerset House to the Queen

176. *set ... London*: on 19 November King James sent for her to appear with her husband and uncle to settle the dispute over the Clifford lands

177. *Roses*: castle at Bowes, Yorkshire. The coach was left there and Lady Anne continued on horseback.

180. *Withypoll*: the wife of either Sir Edmund Withypoll or Sir William Withypoll

181. *Beauchamp*: Frances Devereux, cousin to Richard Sackville and wife of William, Lord Beauchamp

183. *the child*: Lady Anne had not seen her daughter since her mother's death

183–4. *against I came*: in anticipation of my coming

186. *being unexpected*: never expecting

192–3. *Arundel's ... statues*: Alathea Talbot, wife of Thomas Howard, 2nd Earl of Arundel, whose collections of art in the galleries of Arundel House in London became famous

194. *Savoy*: palace between the Strand and the River Thames, west of Somerset House, originally built in the thirteenth century

where I met Lady Derby, my Lady Bedford, my Lady Montgomery, and a great deal of company that came along with the King and the Prince. My Lady Arundel had much talk with me about the business and persuaded me to yield to the King in all things. From Somerset House we went to Essex House to see my Lady of Northumberland. From thence I went to see my Lady Rich, and so came home. After supper I went to see my sister Beauchamp and stayed with her an hour or two, for my lord was at the play at Whitehall that night.[8]

Upon the 6th being Twelfth Day, I went about 4 o'clock to the court with my lord. I went up with my Lady Arundel and ate a scrambling supper with her and my Lady Pembroke at my Lord Duke's lodgings. We stood to see the masque in the box with my Lady Ruthven.

Upon the 8th we came from London to Knole. This night my lord and I had a falling out about the land.

Upon the 9th I went up to see the things in the closet and began to have Mr Sandys's book read to me about the government of the Turks, my lord sitting the most part of the day reading in his closet.

Upon the 10th my lord went up to London upon the sudden, we not knowing it till the afternoon.

Upon the 16th I received a letter from my lord that I should come up to London the next day because I was to go before the King on Monday next. Upon the 17th when I came up, my lord told me I must resolve to go to the King the next day.

Upon the 18th being Saturday, I went presently after dinner to the Queen to the drawing chamber, where my Lady Derby told the Queen how my business stood, and that I was to go to the King; so she promised me she would do all the good in it she could. When I had stayed but a little while there, I was sent for out, my lord and I going through my Lord

[8] As the King passed by he kissed me. Afterwards the Queen came out into the drawing chamber, where she kissed me and used me very kindly. This was the first time I ever saw the King, Queen or Prince since they came out of the north.

196. *Bedford*: Lucy, Countess of Bedford, celebrated as a literary patron
202. *play*: unknown, but on the 5th she saw John Fletcher's *The Mad Lover*
205. *scrambling*: hurried and brief
207. *masque ... Ruthven*: Ben Jonson's *Vision of Delight* ... probably one of the daughters of William, Earl of Gowrie (Williamson 1922: 106–7)
210. *closet*: private room
211. *Mr Sandys's ... Turks*: George Sandys, *A Relation of a Journey begun A.D. 1610* (1615)
221. *she*: the Queen

Buckingham's chamber, who brought us into the King, being in the drawing chamber. He put out all that were there, and my lord and I kneeled by his chair side, when he persuaded us both to peace, and to put the whole matter wholly into his hands, which my lord consented to, but I beseeched his Majesty to pardon me, for that I would never part from Westmorland while I lived, upon any condition whatsoever. Sometimes he used fair means and persuasions, and sometimes foul means, but I was resolved before so as nothing would move me. From the King we went to the Queen's side, and brought my Lady St John to her lodging, and so we went home. At this time I was much bound to my lord, for he was far kinder to me in all these businesses than I expected and was very unwilling that the King should do me any public disgrace.[9]

Upon the 19th my lord and I went to the Court in the morning, thinking the Queen would have gone to the chapel, but she did not, so my Lady Ruthven and I and many others stood in the closet to hear the sermon. I dined with my Lady Ruthven. Presently after dinner she and I went up to the drawing chamber where my [Dowager] Lady Dorset, my Lady Montgomery, my Lady Burghley, persuaded me to refer these businesses to the King.

Upon the 20th, I and my lord went presently after dinner to the court; he went up to the King's side about his business, I went to my aunt Bedford in her lodging, where I stayed in Lady Ruthven's chamber till towards 8 o'clock, about which time I was sent for up to the King into his drawing chamber, when the door was locked and nobody suffered to stay here but

[9] The Queen gave me warning not to trust my matters absolutely to the King, lest he should deceive me.

224. *Buckingham's*: Lady Anne had witnessed George Villiers being created Earl of Buckingham on 5 January

225. *all*: everybody else

by: on either side of

227. *matter*: James sided with the Earl of Cumberland in wishing to see Lady Anne surrender her rights to the Clifford barony and lands

230. *before*: beforehand

233–4. *bound ... expected*: Dorset may have tried to sooth the King after Lady Anne's defiance

241. *Lady Burghley*: wife of Thomas Cecil, Lord Burghley

247. *suffered*: allowed

my lord and I, my uncle Cumberland, my cousin Clifford, my Lords Arundel, Pembroke, Montgomery [and] Sir John Digby. For lawyers there were my Lord Chief Justice Montagu and Henry Yelverton, the King's solicitor, Sir Randal Crewe that was to speak for my lord and I. The King asked us all if we would submit to his judgement in this case. My uncle Cumberland, my cousin Clifford and my lord answered they would, but I never would agree to it without Westmorland, at which the King grew in a great chafe, my Lord of Pembroke and the King's solicitor speaking much against me. At last when they saw there was no remedy, my lord, fearing the King would do me some public disgrace, desired Sir John Digby would open the door, who went out with me and persuaded me much to yield to the King. My Lord Hay came to me, to whom I told in brief how this business stood. Presently after my lord came from the King, when it was resolved that if I would not come to an agreement, there should be an agreement made without me. We went down, Sir Robert Douglas, and Sir George Chaworth bringing us to the coach. By the way my lord and I went in at Worcester House to see my lord and lady, and so came home this day. I may say I was led miraculously by God's providence, and next to that, I trust all my good to the worth and nobleness of my lord's disposition, for neither I nor anybody else thought I should have passed over this day so well as I have done.

Upon the 28th at this time I wore a plain green flannel gown that William Punn made me, and my yellow taffety waistcoat. Rivers used to read to me in Montaigne's *Essays* and Moll Neville in *The Fairie Queene*.

Upon the 30th Mr Amherst the preacher came hither to see me, with whom I had much talk. He told me that now they began to think at London

248. *Clifford*: Henry, son of Lady Anne's uncle Francis and later 5th Earl of Cumberland in 1641. He died without male heirs in 1643, and Anne finally succeeded to the Clifford title.

249. *Pembroke*: Philip Herbert, Lady Anne's second husband, 1630–50

250–1. *Henry ... solicitor*: i.e. solicitor-general. James appointed him attorney-general in the following year.

255. *chafe*: rage

262. *went down*: to Knole

266. *worth ... disposition*: when it became apparent that Lady Anne was not going to yield, Dorset again seems to have relented somewhat and defended her before the King

270. *taffety*: taffeta

270–1. *Rivers ... Queene*: Louise Schleiner notes Lady Anne's tendency to have romances read to her by women and more 'serious' works by men (1992: 7)

that I had done well in not referring this business to the King, and that everybody said God had a hand in it.[10]

FEBRUARY

Upon the 7th, presently after dinner Mr Oberton and I had a great deal of talk, he telling me how much I was condemned in the world, and what strange censures most folks made of my courses. So as I kneeled down to my prayers and desired God to send a good end to these troublesome businesses, my trust being wholly in him that always helped me.

Upon the 12th the child had a bitter fit of her ague again, insomuch I was fearful of her that I could hardly sleep all night. So I beseeched God almighty to be merciful to me and spare her life. Rivers came down presently from London and told me that the judges had been with the King divers times about my business, but as yet the award is not published, but it is thought that it will be much according to the award that was formerly set down by the judges. He told me that he had been with Lord William, who, as he thought, did not well like the agreement, considering how he had heretofore shown himself in the business.[11]

[10] All this time of my being in the country there was much ado at London about my business, in so much that my lord, my uncle Cumberland, my cousin Clifford with the Chief Justice and the Council, [disputed] of both sides on divers times with the King about it, and that the King hearing it go so directly for me, he said there was a law in England to keep me from the land. There was during this time much cock-fighting at the court, where my lord's cocks did fight against the King's. Although this business was somewhat chargeable to my lord, yet it brought him into great grace and favour with the King, so as he useth him very kindly, and speaketh very often to him and better of him than of any other man. My lord grew very great with my Lord of Arundel.

[11] My sister Compton and her husband were now upon terms of parting, so as they left Horsley, she lying in London; it was agreed she should have a £100 a year, and he to take the child from her.

275 n. 10. *of both*: on both
so ... me: i.e. Lady Anne's right to inherit was legally unassailable
cock-fighting ... King's: Dorset and James shared an interest in this sport
chargeable: expensive

278. *strange*: unheard of; ignorant

283. *presently*: immediately

286–7. *formerly ... judges*: see above l. 35

288–9. *considering ... business*: William Howard initially sided against Lady Anne but later came to defend her position. His reversal presumably explains the 'coldness' which grew between him and Lord Dorset (l. 294 n. 12).

289 n. 11. *sister*: sister-in-law (see n. to l. 71)

After supper the child's nose bled, which I think was the chief cause she was rid of her ague.

Upon the 13th the King made a speech in the Star Chamber about duels and combats, my lord standing by his chair where he talked with him all the while, being in extraordinary grace and favour with the King.[12]

Upon the 16th my lord came hither from London before dinner, and told me how the whole state of my business went and how things stood at court.[13]

Upon the 21st the child had an extreme fit of the ague, and the doctor sat by her all the afternoon and gave her a salt powder to put in her beer.

Upon the 22nd, Baskett went up with the great horses to my lord because my lord intended to ride a day's journey with the Prince. Legge came down and brought me word that the King would make a composition and take a course to put me from my rights to the lands, so as if I did not consider of it speedily, it would be too late, and how bitter the King stood against me. My sister Compton sent to borrow 77 pounds, so I sent her ten twenty-shilling pieces.

Upon the 27th I spent my time in working and hearing Mr Rose read the Bible, and walking abroad. My lord writ me word that the King had referred the drawing and perfecting the business to the solicitor. My soul was much troubled and afflicted to see how things go, but my trust is still in God, and [to] compare things past with things present, and read over the chronicles.

MARCH[14]

The 14th I made an end of my Irish stitch cushion. This afternoon Baskett came from London and told me that my lord and my uncle were agreed and

[12] My Lord did nothing so often come to Lord William as heretofore, the friendship between them grew cold, my lord beginning to harbour some ill opinion of him.

[13] He told me the Earl of Buckingham was sworn of the Privy Council, and that Lord Willoughby's brother, Mr H. Bertie, was put into the Inquisition at Ancona.

[14] About this time the curtain in the child's room was let up to let in the light, which had been close shut up for three weeks or a month before.

About this time the King and my Lord Chancellor delivered the seals to Sir Francis Bacon, and he was Lord Keeper.

305–6. *borrow ... pieces*: Lady Anne probably lent her as much as she was able, since her husband controlled her allowance

309. *perfecting*: concluding

311–12. *read ... chronicles*: i.e. for historical analogies to the present situations, as well as identifying her place at the end of the extensive Clifford lineage

n. 14. *seals to ... was*: seals of office to ... became

the writings sealed. The King set forward this day on his journey to Scotland, the Queen and Prince going with him to Theobalds.[15]

The 27th my lord told me he had acknowledged no statutes, and that the matter was not so fully finished, but there was a place left for me to come in.

The 28th I walked abroad with my lord in the park and the garden, where he spake to me much of this business with my uncle. I wrought much within doors and strived to set as merry a face as I could upon a discontented heart, for I might easily perceive that Matthew and Lindsay had got a great hand of my lord and were both against me. Yet by this means they put Lord William clean out of all grace and trust with my lord, which I hope may be the better hereafter for me and my child, knowing that God often brings things to pass by contrary means.

APRIL

The 4th my lord told me he had as yet passed no fines and recoveries of my land, but that my uncle Cumberland had acknowledged statutes for the payment of the money, and that all the writings were left with my Lord Keeper and Lord Hobart till 21st next term, at which time they were fully to be concluded on. This was strange news to me, for I thought all matters had been finished.

[15] The 14th being Friday, my uncle Cumberland and my cousin Clifford came to Dorset House, where my lord and they signed and sealed the writings, and made a final conclusion of my business, and did what they could to cut me off from my right, but I referred my cause to God.

Upon this Friday or Saturday died my Lord Chancellor Egerton, Lady Derby's husband.

316. *Theobalds*: royal summer residence in Hertfordshire north of London. Also l. 493 below.

317. *acknowledge ... statues*: signed no legal instrument which would extinguish his wife's rights to the Clifford barony

321. *wrought*: at needlework

323. *Matthew*: Caldicott, named in the Knole Catalogue, Lord Dorset's favourite attendant and hostile to Lady Anne for reasons perhaps alluded to below at ll. 448–9. He may be one of the 'malicious ill-willers' she refers to in the passage from the *Life* quoted in the Introduction (above p. 246). Lindsay may have been another attendant.

324. *great ... of*: advantage, power over

328. passed ... recoveries: handed over no legal deeds to, or transferences of the rights in

329. *statutes*: the King's directions regarding the judges' award

The 5th, my lord went up to my closet and said how little money I had left, contrary to all they had told him. Sometimes I had fair words from him and sometimes foul, but I took all patiently, and did strive to give him as much content and assurance of my love as I could possibly; yet I told him that I would never part with Westmorland upon any condition whatever.

Upon the 6th after supper, because my lord was sullen and not willing to go into the nursery, I made Mary bring the child to him into my chamber, which was the first time she stirred abroad since she was sick.

The 16th my lord and I had much talk about these businesses, he urging me still to go to London to sign and seal, but I told him that my promise was so far passed to my mother and to all the world that I would never do it, whatever became of me and mine.

Upon the 17th in the morning, my lord told me he was resolved never to move me more in these businesses, because he saw how fully I was bent.

The 18th, being Good Friday, I spent most of the day in hearing Kate Buckin read the Bible and a book of the preparation to the sacrament.

The 19th I signed 33 letters with my own hand, which I sent by him to the tenants in Westmorland. The same night my lord and I had much talk of, and persuaded me to, these businesses, but I would not, and yet I told him I was in perfect charity with all the world. All this Lent I ate flesh and observed no day but Good Friday.

The 20th being Easter day, my lord and I and Tom Glenham and most of the folk received communion by Mr Rand, yet in the afternoon my lord and I had a great falling out, Matthew continuing still to do me all the ill offices he could with my lord. All this time I wore my white satin gown and my white waistcoat.

The 23rd, Lord Clanricarde came hither. After they were gone, my lord and I and Tom Glenham went to Mr Lane's house to see the fine flowers that is in the garden. This night my lord should have lain with me, but he and I fell out about matters.

The 25th being Friday I came to keep my fish days, which I intend to keep all the year long. After dinner I had a great deal of talk with Richard Dawson that served my lady, he telling me all the names, how the pos-

334. *closet*: private room

334–6. *said … foul*: Dorset seems to have used the decision that Lady Anne would henceforward be receiving a smaller allowance to renew pressure on her to sign the award (Williamson 1922: 114)

349. *to … sacrament*: to receive Easter communion

350–1. *letters … Westmorland*: perhaps explaining to them why she had been prevented from claiming her lands

353–4. *Lent … day*: Lent is the 40-day fast before Easter in which fish rather than meat was eaten ('fish days' below). Fridays are also a traditional fast day.

356. *Mr Rand*: the chaplain

366. *my lady*: Lady Anne's mother

session of Brougham Castle was delivered to my uncle of Cumberland's folks, and how Mr Worleigh and all my people are gone from home except John Ruvy, who kept all the stuff in the Baron's Chamber, the plate being already sent to Lord William Howard's.

The 26th I spent the evening in working and going down to my lord's closet, where I sat and read much in the Turkish *History* and Chaucer.

MAY

The 17th, the steward came from London and told me my lord was much discontented with me for not doing this business, because he must be fain to buy land for the payment of the money, which will much encumber his estate.

Upon the 18th Mr Wolrich came hither to serve me, he bringing me news that all in Westmorland was surrendered to my uncle Cumberland.

The 24th we set up a great many of the books that came out of the north in my closet, this being a sad day, with me thinking of the troubles I have passed. I used to spend much time with Mr Wolrich in talking of my dear mother and other businesses in the north. This time my lord's mother did first of all sue out of her thirds, which was an increase of trouble and discontent to my lord.

The 25th my Lord St John's tailor came to me hither to take measure of me and to make me a new gown. In the afternoon my cousin Russell wrote me a letter to let me know how my lord had cancelled my jointure he made upon me last June when I went into the north, and by these proceedings I may see how much my lord is offended with me, and that my enemies have the upper hand of me. I am resolved to take all patiently, casting all my care upon God.

The 27th I wrote a letter to my lord to let him know how ill I took his cancelling my jointure, but yet told him I was content to bear it with patience, whatsoever he thought fit.

JUNE

The 3rd Mr Heardson came hither in the morning and told me that many did condemn me for standing out so in this business, so on the other side

372. *Turkish History*: probably Richard Knolles's *General History of the Turks* (1603)

373. *steward*: Mr Legge

382–3. *my ... thirds*: Anne Sackville, Lord Dorset's stepmother. Her common-law entitlement to a third of her deceased husband's lands would have been in Dorset's control. Evidently she wanted a larger allowance and a more legally reliable jointure from him.

many did commend me in regard that I have done that which is both just and honourable. This night I went into a bath.

The 8th, being whit Sunday, we all went to church, but my eyes were so blubbered with weeping that I could scarce look up, and in the afternoon we again fell out about Matthew. After supper we played at barley-break upon the bowling green.

The 9th I wrote a letter to the Bishop of London against Matthew. The same day Mr Hodgson came home, who had been with my cousin Russell at Chiswick, and told me what a deal of care he had about me; and my cousin Russell and my cousin George sent me word that all my businesses would go on well, but they could not find that the business or agreement was fully concluded, in regard there was nothing had passed the Great Seal.

The 30th still working and being extremely melancholy, and sad to see things go so ill with me, and fearing my lord would give all his land away from the child.

JULY

The 1st still working and sad.

The 2nd received a letter from Sir George Rivers, who sent me word that my lord was setting his land upon his brother.

The 9th, Marsh brought me the King's award. The 10th and 11th I spent

401. *we again ... Matthew*: writing to the Bishop of London was an unusual step because Matthew was a layman, and suggests that Lady Anne was lodging a moral complaint against him. See n. to ll. 448–9.
barley-break: game usually involving three couples, one of whom stands in the middle of a playing area (called 'hell') and tries to catch the others while they try to exchange partners. Philip Sidney uses the game as an extended metaphor in *Lamon's Tale*, published at the end of the 1593 *Arcadia*'s First Ecologues.

410–11. *land ... child*: inheritance from their daughter Margaret

414. *setting ... brother*: willing his land to ... Edward Sackville

415. *King's award*: commanding that Lady Anne and her husband were to convey all the Clifford lands to the Earl of Cumberland under the Great Seal, with reversion to her if the male line failed, and that they were to receive £20,000 in four instalments, the last £3,000 to be paid when Lady Anne signed over her rights. This she refused to do, so the total received was £17,000. Because this sum was raised from the Clifford estates and went largely to pay Dorset's debts, when she eventually inherited she was short of money (Williamson 1922: 120–1; Lewalski 1993: 128).

in perusing that and other writings, the award being as ill for me as possible.[16]

The 12th Mr Davis came hither, to whom I showed the award, desiring him to make an abstract of it to send down to the tenants. Presently after my lord came down hither, he being something kinder to me than he was, out of pity in regard he saw me so much troubled.

AUGUST

The 4th in the morning my lord went to Penshurst but would not suffer me to go with him, although my Lord and Lady Lisle sent a man on purpose to desire me to come. He hunted and lay there all night, there being my Lord of Montgomery, my Lord Hay, my Lady Lucy, and a great deal of other company; yet my lord and I parted reasonable good friends, he leaving with me his grandmother's wedding ring.

The 12th and 13th I spent most of the time in playing at glecko and hearing Moll Neville read the *Arcadia*.

SEPTEMBER

The 29th my lord came home to Knole from his long journey. At this Michaelmas did my lord receive four thousand pounds of my uncle the Earl of Cumberland, which was the first penny that I received of my portion.

[16] About this time there was a great stir about my Lady Hatton's daughter – my brother Sackville undertaking to carry her away with men and horses. And he had another squabble about a man that was arrested in Fleet Street. After this he went to the Spa and left my sister Sackville to keep my sister Beauchamp company.

417 n. 16. *daughter ... horses*: perhaps an elopement
Spa: probably the Spa in Germany

419. *send down*: to Westmorland

422–3. *Penshurst ... Lisle*: seat of Robert Sidney, Viscount Lisle, and Barbara Gamage, parents of Lady Dorothy Sidney and Lady Mary (Sidney) Wroth (see below p. 398). Lady Anne did later visit Penshurst on the 19th.

428. *glecko*: card game for two or three players

429. *Arcadia*: prose romance by Sir Philip Sidney

430. *journey*: from meeting the King at Woodstock and visiting friends at Bath and other places (Williamson 1922: 124)

431. *Michaelmas*: St Michael's day, 29 September

432. *portion*: of the King's award (above l. 415)

NOVEMBER

The 4th I carried Lady Rich to dine with me to Mrs Watson's, where we met my cousin Russell and my cousin George and had an extreme great feast. From thence I went to the court where the Queen sent for me into her own bedchamber, and here I spake to the King.[17] He used me very graciously and bid me go to his attorney, who should inform him more of my desires. All the time of my being in London I used to sup privately and to send to Mr Davis to confer privately about my said business.

The 5th I carried Mr Davis to Gray's Inn to the attorney, when I told him his Majesty's pleasure. From thence I went to Mr Walton's lodgings to entreat his advice and help in this business, and so I came down this night to Knole.

DECEMBER

The 10th. My lord went to Buckhurst where all country gentlemen met him with their greyhounds. All the officers of the house went to Buckhurst where my lord kept great feastings till the 13th, at which time all the gentlemen went away. Sir Thomas Parker was there; my brother Sackville and he had much squabbling. From this day to the 20th my lord lived privately at Buckhurst having no company with him but Matthew.

[The 28th] Now I had a great desire to have all my father's sea voyages written, so I did set Jones to enquire about these matters.[18]

[17] The 4th day King James kissed me when I was with him, and that was the first time that ever I was so near King James as to touch him.

[18] About this time Lady Rich was brought to bed of her first son at Baynard's Castle, and in a little while after fell sick of the small-pox.

About his time died Jem Robins's man, but he left his master no remembrance, for they was fallen out.

434. *cousin George*: Sir Edward George

436 n. 17. *kissed . . . him*: Lady Anne may have forgotten the occasion mentioned at l. 203 n. 8

440. *Gray's Inn*: one of the Inns of Court in London for students of common law

448–9. *From . . . Matthew*: Lewalski suggests this implies a homosexual relationship (1993: 147); this may explain the personal crisis recorded on 8–9 June and Lady Anne's letter to the Bishop of London. The effect of the letter was Matthew's attempted reconciliation with her on 11 August 1617 through the chaplain Mr Rand (Clifford 1992: 61). If Lewalski is right, however, this entry suggests the problem had not ended.

450–1. *father's . . . written*: George Clifford, 3rd Earl of Cumberland, outfitted private ships which over time made twelve expeditions, some for exploration but most for plundering Spanish and Portuguese treasure ships. He also helped found the East India Company. The records of his voyages are extant and discussed in Williamson 1920.

1619[*]

JANUARY

The 2, 3, 4, 5, I sat up and had many ladies come to see me, and much other company, and so I passed the time.

My lord went often to the court and abroad, and on Twelfth Eve lost 400 pieces playing with the King.

FEBRUARY[19][†]

The 2nd my lord went to Buckhurst, meaning to lie there private a fortnight or thereabouts.

The 8th Lady Woolton sent Mr Page to see me, and that day I made pancakes with my women in the great chamber.

The 10th Wat Conniston began [to] read St Austin, *Of the City of God*, to me, and I received a letter from Mr Davis with another enclosed in it of Ralph Conniston, whereby I perceived things went in Westmorland as I would have them.[20]

My lord should have gone to London on the 24th of this month but I entreated him to stay here until the 25th, because on that day ten years ago I was married, which I kept as a day of jubilee to me.

MARCH

The 2nd the Queen died at Hampton Court between two and three in the morning. The King was then at Newmarket. Legge brought me the news of

[19] About this time Lord Willoughby caused my cousin Clifford to come before the Lords of the Council about northern business, so as the spleen increased between them more and more, and bred faction in Westmorland, in which I held to be a very good matter for me.

[20] My Lady of Suffolk at Northampton House about this time had the small-pox, which spoiled that good face of hers which had brought to others much misery, and to herself greatness which ended with much unhappiness.

* *1619*: There are no diaries for 1618.

† n. 19. *Clifford … business*: relations between the Westmorland gentry and tenants and Lady Anne's uncle became strained after the latter took full possession of the Clifford estates. Lady Anne viewed this local discontent as a vindication of her rights.

460. *Austin*: Augustine

461. *of*: from

468. *King … Newmarket*: where Lady Anne reports that on 20 February he had 'an extreme fit of the [gall]stone' which prevented him from returning to London immediately and led to postponement of the Queen's funeral until May (see below)

her death about four in the afternoon, I being in my bedchamber at Knole where I had the first news of my mother's death about the same hour. (Legge told me my lord was about to take some physic of Mr Smith, and as he could not come from London these four or five days yet.) She died in the same room that Queen Jane, Harry VIII's wife died in, the Prince was there when the pangs of death came upon her, but went into another chamber some half an hour before she died.[21]

The 17th my lord went to Buckhurst to search for armour and provision which should be laid up by the papists. This day I made an end of my lady's book, *In Praise of a Solitary Life*.

The 26th Good Friday after supper I fell in a great passion of weeping in my chamber, and when my lord came in I told him I found my mind so troubled as I held not myself fit to receive the communion this Easter, which all this Lent I intended to have done.

The 27th in the morning I sent for Mr Rand and told him I found not myself fit to receive the communion. The next day when my lord heard I had told Mr Rand so much, he sent for him and told him the communion should be put off both for him and the household, except any of them should receive at the church.

The 28th Easter Day Mr Rand preached in the chapel, but there was no communion in the house, but at the church. In the afternoon I began to repent that I had caused the communion to be put off till Whit Sunday, my lord protesting to me that he would be a very good husband to me, and, that I should receive no prejudice by releasing my thirds.

APRIL

Saturday 24th my lord went to Theobalds to see the King, who used him very graciously. This night my cousin Clifford came out of the north, where matters went more to my content and less to his than were expected.

Tuesday the 27th I put on my new black mourning nightgown and those

[21] Most of the great ladies about the town put themselves in mourning and did watch the Queen's corpse at Denmark House, which lay there with much state.

The Queen Dowager of Denmark was alive when her daughter Queen Anne of England died.

471. *and as*: so

473. *Queen Jane*: Jane Seymour, Henry VIII's third wife and mother of Edward VI

475 n. 21. *Most ... state*: Lady Anne travelled to London to take her turn at the watch

477–8. *my ... Life*: probably *The Praise of Solitariness*

492. *releasing ... thirds*: relinquishing her common-law rights to a third of her husband's estate during her lifetime in the event of being widowed. Dorset had perhaps been pressuring his wife to do this.

white things that Nan Horn made for me. This day Mr Orfuir brought me two of the tenants of Westmorland, who craved my assistance against my uncle Cumberland.

MAY

The 8th John and Richard Dent were before the Chancellor, my cousin Clifford and John Taylor being present, where the Chancellor told them that fr[om] tenants' rights he meant utterly to break them, willing them to be good tenants to my uncle Cumberland, whereat the poor men were much perplexed and troubled, but I gave them the best comfort and encouragement I could.

The 13th I was one of the mourners at the Queen's funeral.[22] I attended the corpse from Somerset House to the Abbey at Westminster. My lord was also one of the earls that mourned. I went all the way hand in hand with my Lady Lincoln; after the sermon, and, all the ceremonies ended, my lord, myself and the Earl of Warwick and his Lady came home by barges. Being come home I went to my sister Beauchamp to show her my mourning attire. At the funeral I met with my old Lady Pembroke and divers others of my acquaintance, with whom I had much talk. My cousin Clifford was also a mourner and bare the banner after the lords. When all the company was gone and the church door shut up, the Dean of Westminster, the Prebends, Sir Edward Zouch, who was Knight Marshal, came up a private way and buried the corpse at the east end of Henry VII chapel about 7 o'clock at night. There was 180 poor women mourners.

[22] The 13th. It is just 13 years and a month since my father's funeral was kept and solemnised in the church at Skipton, as Queen Anne's body was this night buried in the Abbey church at Westminster.

498–9. *two ... Cumberland*: see next entry

500–5. *John ... could*: Lady Anne could not legally defend her tenants, who had quarrelled with her uncle's son and been brought before the Lord Chancellor, Sir Francis Bacon, but she gave them moral support and money (below ll. 522–3). The fact they sought her help indicates they preferred to regard her as their true landlady.

509. *Lady Lincoln*: Elizabeth Clinton, Countess of Lincoln (see above p. 148ff.)

510. *home*: to her London residence, Dorset House

511–12. *my ... Pembroke*: Mary (Sidney) Herbert, Dowager Countess of Pembroke (p. 311ff.) and mother of Philip Herbert, Lady Anne's second husband

515. *Prebends*: canons receiving stipends from Westminster Abbey

518. *180 ... mourners*: to whom alms would have been distributed

The 15th I went by water to the Savoy to my Lord Carew, and spoke to him very earnestly in behalf of Peter Coolinge and his son for a gunner's place in Carlisle, and received a reasonable good answer from him.

The 17th my lord and I and all the household came down to Knole. I took my leave also of the two tenants and gave them gold and silver.[23]

The 24, 25, 26 and 27th I went abroad with my brother Sackville, sometimes early in the morning and sometimes after supper, he and I being kind and having better correspondence than we have had.

The 31st I stayed at home and was sad and melancholy.[24]

JUNE[25]

The 6th, Sunday, I heard neither sermon or prayers because I had no coach to go to church. All this week I spent at my work and sometimes riding abroad. My cousin Mary read Ovid's *Metamorphoses* to me.

[23] After I came out of town, my Lord Chancellor had the tenants before him and willed them to yield to my uncle Cumberland, at which time he gave Mr Davis bad words.

[24] The 27th my lord and my brother Sackville and I, Moll Neville and Mr Longworth, rid abroad on horseback in Whitby Wood and did not sup till 8 or 9 o'clock. After supper my lord and I walked before the gate, where I told him how good he was to everybody else and how unkind to me. In conclusion he promised me in a manner that he would make me a jointure of four thousand pounds a year, whereof part should be of that land he has assured to my uncle Cumberland.

This term there was great expectation that my Lord and Lady Suffolk and that faction would be proceeded against in the Star Chamber, but at their suit it was put off till Michaelmas term. This term Lord William Howard put a bill into the Star Chamber against Sir William Hatton and others of my cousin Clifford's faction. This term my lord kept an exceeding great table, at dinner and had much company. He had often cocking, and sometimes with the King at Greenwich, and won a great deal of money....

About this time my cousin Mary made an end of reading Parson's *Resolutions* to me.

[25] The 1st my sister Beauchamp took her journey to Glenham, where she intends to sojourn this two or three years, so as her household is dispersed. Only some necessary attendants remain, and Mrs Batten came into Kent.

523 n. 23. *he ... words*: perhaps over Lady Anne's intervention in the Earl of Cumberland's disputes with his Westmorland tenants (Williamson 1922: 136)

527 n. 24. *jointure ... year*: Dorset did not fulfil this promise until 10 July 1623, close to the time of his death (Williamson 1922: 142)

Lord ... Suffolk: Thomas Howard, Earl of Suffolk and Lord Treasurer from 1614, and his wife Catharine Knevet were tried for embezzlement in July 1618, fined £7,000 and imprisoned for one month in the Tower (Clifford 1992: 81)

Resolutions: Robert Parsons, *A Book of Christian Exercise, appertaining to Resolutions* (1584 and many reissues)

The 24th my lord received the last payment of my portion which was £6,000, so as he hath received in all £17,000. John Taylor required of my lord an acquittance, which he refused to give in regard he had delivered in the statutes, which were a sufficient discharge.

OCTOBER

Upon the 18th at night the fire dog played with fire, so as I took cold with standing in the window.

NOVEMBER

Upon the 24th Sir Francis Slingsby came hither to me and read to me in the sea papers about my father's voyages.

The 28th though I kept my chamber altogether, yet methinks the time is not so tedious to me as when I used to be abroad. About this time I received letters from Mr Davis by which I perceived how ill things were likely to go in Westmorland, especially with Mr Hilton and Michael Brunstall.[26]

[26] About this time of my lord's being at London he kept a great table, having a great company of lords and gentlemen that used to dine with him. All this winter my Lady Margaret's speech was very ill, so as strangers cannot understand her. Besides she was so apt to take a cold, and so out of temper, that it grieved me to think of it. I verily believe all these inconveniences proceed from some distemper in her head. . . .

The 29th November was the last time my lord came to my Lady Penniston at her mother's lodgings in the Strand.

The 30th my Lord and Lady Suffolk came out of the Tower.

533. *acquittance*: perhaps meaning Lady Anne's final signature (see above n. to l. 415)

535. *fire ... fire*: weather condition similar to aurora borealis, producing a fiery sky (Clifford 1992: 80)

537. *Slingsby*: captain on Lady Anne's father's expeditions in 1593, 1597, and 1598 (Williamson 1920: 21, 118, 171)

538. *sea papers*: the book Lady Anne began to have compiled on 28 December 1617

542 n. 26. *Margaret's ... ill*: she had difficulty learning how to speak clearly

Lady Penniston: Lord Dorset's mistress. Their open affair in London kept Lady Anne from regularly visiting the court (Williamson 1922: 126). She also resisted receiving Lady Penniston and her husband at Knole, but records one visit on 24 August 1619 (Clifford 1992: 79). The present entry may mark her knowledge of the end of the affair.

DECEMBER

The 2nd Wat Conniston made an end of reading a book called *Leicester's Commonwealth*, in which there's many things concerning the arraignment and death [of] the Queen of Scots, which was all read to me.

The 14th Wat Conniston began to read the book of Josephus.

The 15th my lord and I, by Mr Amherst's directions set our hands to a letter of attorney for Ralph Conniston to receive those debts which were due of my lady of the tenants, and this day he went on his journey to the north.

543–4. *Leicester's Commonwealth*: 1584, an attack on Robert Dudley, Earl of Leicester, erroneously attributed to Robert Parsons

546. *Josephus*: ancient Jewish historian (*c.* 37–100), author of *The Jewish War* and *Antiquities of the Jews*. His *Works* were translated by Thomas Lodge in 1602. For further discussion of Lady Anne's reading, especially those books depicted in her Great Picture at Appleby Castle, see Williamson 1922: 340–5, and Lewalski 1993: 137–40. Lamb 1992 in particular assesses the empowering effect of Lady Anne's reading on her sense of autonomy.

4

VERSE

ISABELLA WHITNEY (*fl.* 1567–78)

FROM *A SWEET NOSEGAY, OR PLEASANT POSY (1573)* AND *THE LAMENTATION OF A GENTLEWOMAN UPON THE DEATH OF HER LATE-DECEASED FRIEND, WILLIAM GRUFFITH* (1578)

Introduction

Isabella Whitney's poetry possesses a distinctiveness stemming from the author's virtually unique status as a non-aristocratic woman writing creatively within an overwhelmingly male literary culture. She must have needed extraordinary resources of self-motivation and confidence simply to compose and publish original verse in the absence of any contemporary role models; the only woman to do so at this time besides herself was the Queen – an exception in every sense. Whitney is also the first Englishwoman who writes and publishes in the hope of earning money (of which she claims to have had urgent need), she experiments with a variety of verse-forms while seeking to please the tastes of a popular readership, and she produces imaginative and often playful poetry at a time when only devotional literature or translations of men's texts were considered acceptable pursuits for female writers. Seen in this light, Whitney is remarkably pioneering. And while modern readers may be tempted to judge her work on the basis of its apparently modest poetic skill and sometimes plaintive tone, it is essential to bear in mind that by the standards of the day her writing is intelligently conceived, artfully varied, and even fashionable. Poetry composed in the 1560s and 1570s differs considerably in style and aim from that written in the following decades. During this later period authors were more self-conscious about seeking metrical and metaphoric innovation as advertisements of personal genius, and as a result traditional literary history has tended to privilege their work as more 'genuinely' Elizabethan. But in imitating the customary forms and language of her time, Whitney's poetry is no less historically representative.

Her two previously known works, as well as one recently attributed to her by Robert J. Fehrenbach (1981, 1985) and the present writer (1996), are diverse in subject and approach. *The Copy of a Letter, lately written in metre, by a young Gentlewoman to her unconstant Lover* (1567) consists of verse-epistles composed in ballad form by Whitney and two male writers arguing conventionally on opposite sides of the theme of sexual infidelity. *A Sweet Nosegay, or Pleasant Posy* (1573) is entirely by Whitney and more technically ambitious and varied, and we may suppose that Richard Jones, printer of both collections, agreed to publish it after the acceptable reception of *The Copy of a Letter*. In an Epistle to the Reader Whitney discloses the personal circumstances under which she apparently wrote this work: after becoming unemployed as a servant and falling ill, she finds solace in reading Sir Hugh Plat's *Flowers of Philosophy* (1572), a collection of neo-Senecan moral precepts. She decides to versify some of these, partly with a view to presenting her work to her former employer to try to regain her lost position. But clearly the speaker also enjoys adopting the unconventional female role of moral teacher, as this and later sections reveal, and she pays careful attention to her readers' potential responses, as Tina Krontiris observes (1992: 42). *A Sweet Nosegay*'s opening section of 110 'philosophical flowers' is followed by a series of *Familiar Epistles* addressed to various relations and friends, with several accompanying replies. These reveal Whitney experimenting with different metres, stanza lengths, and rhyme schemes, and collectively they imitate private exchanges of verse-letters amongst contemporary aristocratic readers and writers. This part of Whitney's volume is the most biographically revealing (supposing that she and the poetic persona can be equated – an assumption that must be made with caution here, and even more so elsewhere), with most of her own epistles taking the form of complaints about her distressed circumstances.

Isabella was the sister of Geoffrey Whitney, author of a well-known emblem-book, *A Choice of Emblems* (1586). She was probably born within a few years of him (*c.* 1548) in Cheshire at Coole Pilate near Nantwich, where the Whitneys were an established gentry family. As a girl she left the country for London, where she tells us she was 'bred', evidently serving in the household of a 'virtuous lady', probably as her attendant or companion (such a position would be compatible with Whitney's social background). She tells us later that her parents lived in Smithfield for a time and were alive when she wrote *A Sweet Nosegay*. In the *Familiar Epistles* selected here she imagines herself living in the country writing to Geoffrey, to a second brother, Brooke, also in service, to two unnamed younger sisters employed as domestics, and to a married sister, Anne Baron. Being poor, unwell, and compelled by unemployment to leave London, the author reaches out for family support while bolstering her sense of self-esteem by offering them moral counsel and practical guidance; at times she sounds like later writers of mothers' advice books such as Elizabeth Grymeston and Dorothy Leigh. Despite the adverse conditions under which she ostensibly writes, she seems to relish talking knowledgeably about such matters. Yet as Ann Rosalind Jones observes (1987: 63–8), Whitney is likewise careful to suggest that this activity is merely temporary prior to becoming settled in her own household as a wife. Rhetorically, such conformist views serve her own interests, for by upholding traditional gendered roles in a domestic hierarchy, she safeguards her 'irregular' status as an independent female poet.

Whitney further develops her personal voice, while at the same time extending the rationale of using writing to offset her personal losses, in a final section of *A Sweet Nosegay* subtitled *The Manner of her Will*, a fictional last 'will and testament' to the City of London. Her farewell 'bequests' are a inventory of contemporary London streets, trades, goods, and buildings, the selection and arrangement of which seem to be telling. For while her descriptions of plentiful food and rich clothing in the first half of the poem seem genuinely festive, with only occasional tinges of irony, those in the second half suggest an element of censure as she makes a tour of city prisons, focusing particularly on those for debtors (and therefore, she hints, people in the same straits as herself potentially). Given the prevailing misery of Elizabethan gaols and the fact that Whitney mentions few other buildings, her poem's tone inevitably darkens as her identification with the destitute and marginalised deepens. But while her images are occasionally grim, she never entirely gives up a certain cheerful affection for the city, of whose teeming public spaces she is proud to display her personal knowledge.

If it is the threat of death or loss of bodily health and sexual power that provide many early modern women with the pretext they need to write about desires and ideas normally forbidden in public discourse, as Wendy Wall (1991) has argued, then Whitney reprises *A Sweet Nosegay*'s permissive context of personal misfortune in a third work, *The Lamentation of a Gentlewoman upon the Death of her Late-Deceased Friend, William Gruffith, Gentleman,* which appeared in Thomas Proctor's miscellany, *A Gorgeous Gallery of Gallant Inventions* (1578; Fehrenbach 1981, 1983). Ostensibly written to mourn Gruffith's death and to challenge the adequacy of an inferior tribute to him, this elegy also gradually asserts Whitney's legitimacy as a female writer and social critic. While initially recalling the plangent language of Ovid's *Heroides*, in which various classical heroines lament their betrayal by faithless lovers (Jones 1990a: 43–52), Whitney's speaker invokes a different situation in which a woman mourns the loss of a close male friend who is not a relation or her husband. Displaying such feelings apparently aroused public hostility, and in response she protests the devaluation of female grief and male–female love outside patriarchally regulated family or marital contexts. In addition, Whitney's speaker defends her ability to express herself in print and to influence public opinion by presenting herself as the authentic custodian of Gruffith's memory. She thereby manoeuvres him into 'speaking' on behalf of their shared professional aspirations. This is a strategy reminiscent of *The Manner of her Will*, but this time taken from a position of greater strength, with the author managing to benefit from a genuine personal legacy that empowers her own vocation as a writer.

Editions:
A Sweet Nosegay, or Pleasant Posy (1573). STC 25440, reel 1048. *The Flowers of Philosophy* (1572) by Hugh Plat and *A Sweet Nosegay* (1573) and *The Copy of a Letter* (1567) by Isabella Whitney, ed. Richard J. Panofsky (New York, 1982, facsimiles). Betty Travitsky, 'The "Wyll and Testament" of Isabella Whitney', *English Literary Renaissance* 10 (1980), pp. 76–94. Thomas Proctor *et al.*, *A Gorgeous Gallery of Gallant Inventions* (1578). STC 20402, reel 1114. Proctor, *A Gorgeous Gallery*, ed. Hyder E. Rollins (1926; repr. New York, 1971).

ISABELLA WHITNEY

CERTAIN FAMILIAR EPISTLES AND FRIENDLY LETTERS FROM *A SWEET NOSEGAY, OR PLEASANT POSY* (1573)

TO HER BROTHER GEOFFREY WHITNEY

Good brother, when a vacant time
  Doth cause you hence to ride,
And that the fertile fields do make
  You from the city bide,
Then cannot I once from you hear?
  Nor know I how to send,
Or where to harken of your health;
  And all this would be kenned,
And most of me, for why I least
  Of fortune's favour find,
No yielding year she me allows,
  Nor goods hath me assigned.
But still to friends I must appeal,
  And (next our parents dear)
You are and must be chiefest staff
  That I shall stay on here.

1. *vacant*: unoccupied
2. *hence*: away (from London)
3. *fertile fields*: possibly referring to the Whitney family property in Cheshire, of which Geoffrey was the head
8. *kenned*: known
9. *for why*: because

9–12. *least … assigned*: in the Epistle to the Reader the author describes herself as 'harvestless', 'serviceless' (i.e. without employment), and 'subject unto sickness', all professed reasons for writing *A Sweet Nosegay*. Yet if we know something about Whitney's life, these invite speculation about the extent to which the writer's complaints are biographical, fictional, or some combination of both. In the *Familiar Epistles* Whitney writes not only for help and sympathy but also to recover a measure of self-worth by representing herself as an affectionate, quasi-maternal elder sister and worldly-wise counsellor.

16. *stay*: rely on

Wherefore, mine own good brother, grant
   Me when that you are here
To see you oft, and also hence
   I may have knowledge where
A messenger to hark unto,
   That I to you may write
And eke of him your answers have,
   Which would my heart delight.
Receive of me, and eke accept
   A simple token here:
A smell of such a nosegay as
   I do for present bear
Unto a virtuous lady, which
   Till death I honour will;
The loss I had of service hers,
   I languish for it still.

Your loving (though luckless) sister,
Isabella Whitney.

TO HER BROTHER BROOKE WHITNEY

Good brother Brooke, I often look
   To hear of your return,
But none can tell if you be well
   Nor where you do sojourn;
Which makes me fear that I shall hear
   Your health appaired is,
And oft I dread that you are dead,
   Or something goeth amiss.
Yet when I think you cannot shrink
   But must with master be,
I have good hope, when you have scope,

23, 25. *eke*: also

28–9. *present ... lady*: implying Whitney intended making a gift of her work to the gentlewoman she had once served in the hope of regaining her position. Authors sought to advance their careers and secure adequate income from publication by presenting copies to potential patrons or by dedicating works to them (e.g. Whitney's dedicatee is her childhood friend George Mainwaring; see also Aemilia Lanyer's multiple dedications in *Salve Deus Rex Judaeorum*).

6. *appaired*: deteriorated

10. *master*: suggesting that Brooke, like Isabella and her younger sisters (see below), was serving in a gentle household

You will repair to me.
And so the fear and deep despair
That I of you then had,
I drive away, and wish that day
Wherein we may be glad.
Glad for to see: but else for me
Will be no joy at all;
For on my side no luck will bide,
Nor happy chance befall,
As you shall know; for I will show
You more when we do speak
Than will I write or yet recite
Within this paper weak.
And so I end and you commend
To him that guides the skies,
Who grant you health, and send you wealth,
No less than shall suffice.

Your loving sister,
Isabella Whitney.

AN ORDER PRESCRIBED BY ISABELLA WHITNEY TO TWO OF HER YOUNGER SISTERS SERVING IN LONDON

Good sisters mine, when I shall further from you dwell,
Peruse these lines, observe the rules, which in the same I tell.
So shall you wealth possess and quietness of mind,
And all your friends to see the same a treble joy shall find.

1 In mornings when you rise, forget not to commend
Yourselves to God, beseeching him from dangers to defend
Your souls and bodies both, your parents and your friends,
Your teachers and your governors. So pray you that your ends
May be in such a sort as God may pleased be:
To live to die, to die to live, with him eternally.

2 Then justly do such deeds as are to you assigned;
All wanton toys, good sisters now, exile out of your mind.

15. *wish*: wish for

1. *sisters*: probably signifies those mentioned in Geoffrey Whitney's will (1600): 'sister Evans' and 'sister M. D. Colly' (married names; 'M.' may signify 'Mistress'), and 'sister Margery' (first name) (Whitney 1886: lxxxiii)
12. *wanton toys*: idle, perhaps amorous, fancies

I hope you give no cause whereby I should suspect;
But this I know, too many live that would you soon infect
If God do not prevent, or with his grace expel.
I cannot speak or write too much because I love you well.

3 Your business soon dispatch, and listen to no lies,
Nor credit every feigned tale that many will devise.
For words they are but wind, yet words may hurt you so,
As you shall never brook the same if that you have a foe.
God shield you from all such as would by word or bill
Procure your shame, or never cease till they have wrought you ill.

4 See that you secrets seal, tread trifles underground;
If to rehearsal oft you come, it will your quiet wound.
Of laughter be not much, nor over solemn seem,
For then be sure they'll count you light or proud will you esteem.
Be modest in a mean, be gentle unto all,
Though cause they give of contrary, yet be to wrath no thrall.
Refer you all to him that sits above the skies;
Vengeance is his, he will revenge; you need it not devise.

5 And sith that virtue guides where both of you do dwell,
Give thanks to God, and painful be to please your rulers well.
For fleeting is a foe, experience hath me taught,

13. *suspect*: imagine some bad behaviour
14. *infect*: corrupt with evil habits. Avoidance of infection is a governing trope of *A Sweet Nosegay*, based on the belief that exposure to pleasant, healthful smells (or figuratively, sound ethical precepts) will expel noxious ones. Whitney's 110 'flowers' of sententious advice, which precede the *Familiar Epistles*, thus act as a kind of inoculation against the various kinds of metropolitan 'contagion' – physical, moral, and social – that *The Manner of her Will* later catalogues.
15. *prevent*: forestall
18. *credit*: believe
19. *For ... wind*: proverbial (Tilley W833)
20. *brook*: endure
21. *bill*: public writing defaming somebody
23. *trifles*: rumours, malicious talk
24. *rehearsal*: repetition (i.e. spreading 'trifles')
26. *light*: frivolous
27. *in a mean*: with moderation
30. *Vengeance ... revenge*: proverbial (Tilley V24), based on Psalm 94.1 and Romans 12.19
31. *virtue ... dwell*: i.e. you live in an upright household
32. *painful*: diligent
33. *fleeting*: unreliable, changeable

The rolling stone doth get no moss, yourselves have heard full oft.
Your business being done, and this my scroll perused,
The day will end; and that the night by you be not abused,
I something needs must write: take pains to read the same
(Henceforth my life as well as pen shall your examples frame).

6 Your masters gone to bed, your mistresses at rest,
Their daughters all with haste about to get themselves undressed,
See that their plate be safe, and that no spoon do lack,
See doors and windows bolted fast for fear of any wrack.
Then help, if need there be, to do some household thing;
If not to bed, referring you unto the heavenly king,
Forgetting not to pray as I before you taught,
And giving thanks for all that he hath ever for you wrought.
Good sisters when you pray, let me remembered be,
So will I you, and thus I cease till I yourselves do see.
Isabella Whitney.

TO HER SISTER MISTRESS ANNE BARON

Because I to my brethren wrote,
  And to my sisters two,
Good sister Anne, you this might wote,
  If so I should not do
To you or ere I parted hence;
You vainly had bestowed expense.

Yet it is not for that I write,
  For nature did you bind
To do me good, and to requite

34. *The ... moss*: i.e. it is better to be usefully occupied than idle. Proverbial (Tilley S885).
35. *scroll*: letter
38. *my ... frame*: I shall draw upon my own personal experiences as well as knowledge from books
42. *wrack*: mishap, danger

3. *wote*: find out about
5. *or ere*: before
6. *You ... expense*: this does not follow easily from the previous lines. The sense may be that Anne would waste her money writing to Isabella if the latter did not notify Anne of her imminent departure from London.
7. *not*: not only
8. *nature*: natural bonds of kinship

Hath nature me inclined.
Wherefore, good sister, take in 'gree
These simple lines that come from me.

Wherein I wish you Nestor's days
In happy health to rest,
With such success in all assays
As those which God hath blest.
Your husband with your pretty boys
God keep them free from all annoys.

And grant if that my luck it be
To linger here so long
Till they be men, that I may see
For learning them so strong.
That they may march amongst the best
Of them which learning have possessed.

By that time will my aged years
Perhaps a staff require,
And quakingly, as still in fears,
My limbs draw to the fire;
Yet joy I shall them so to see
(If any joy in age there be).

Good sister so I you commend
To him that made us all,
I know you housewifery intend,
Though I to writing fall.
Wherefore no longer shall you stay
From business, that profit may.

11. *'gree*: degree = 'relation' (to 'nature'). The sense of this stanza is: 'consider my writing motivated by genuine natural affection rather than by the mere necessity of treating you the same way I have treated our other sisters by writing'.

13. *Nestor's*: famous for longevity. In Homer's *Iliad* he had outlived two generations yet remained mentally and physically vigorous.

15. *assays*: events, occasions; trials, tests

18. *annoys*: troubles

25–8. *aged . . . fire*: as Panofsky observes (1982: xviii) this is probably fictionalising. As the eldest sister, Isabella was presumably close in age to her brother Geoffrey, who in 1573 was between 25 and 28

36. *business*: being occupied (by domestic affairs)

Had I a husband or a house,
  And all that longs thereto,
Myself could frame about to rouse
  As other women do.
But till some household cares me tie
My books and pen I will apply.

Your loving sister,
Isabella Whitney.

39. *frame ... rouse*: adapt (myself) to become active

ISABELLA WHITNEY

THE MANNER OF HER WILL, AND WHAT SHE LEFT TO LONDON
FROM *A SWEET NOSEGAY, OR PLEASANT POSY*
(1573)

The author, though loathe to leave the city, upon her friend's* procurement† is constrained to depart. Wherefore she feigneth as she would die, and maketh her will and testament as followeth: with large legacies of such goods and riches which she most abundantly hath left behind her, and thereof maketh London sole executor to see her legacies performed.

A COMMUNICATION WHICH THE AUTHOR HAD TO LONDON BEFORE SHE MADE HER WILL

The time is come, I must depart
   From thee, ah famous city;
I never yet, to rue my smart,
   Did find that thou hadst pity.
Wherefore small cause there is that I
   Should grieve from thee to go;
But many women, foolishly
   Like me and other mo,
Do such a fixed fancy set
   On those which least deserve,
That long it is ere wit we get
   Away from them to swerve.
But time with pity oft will tell
   To those that will her try,

* *friend's*: or perhaps plural, as the original reads 'Friendes'

† *procurement*: prompting, arrangement, perhaps because the narrator was in debt and being threatened by creditors, which she alludes to below, ll. 181–92

3. *rue ... smart*: recall sorrowfully my adverse fortune

7–12. *But ... swerve*: Whitney adapts the usual Petrarchan scenario in which a male lover finds it difficult to distance himself from a mistress whom he believes to be unfaithful or unworthy yet cannot stop desiring

8. *mo*: more

Whether it best be more to mell,
Or utterly defy.
And now hath time me put in mind
Of thy great cruelness,
That never once a help would find
To ease me in distress.
Thou never yet wouldst credit give
To board me for a year,
Nor with apparel me relieve
Except thou payed were.
No, no, thou never didst me good
Nor ever wilt, I know.
Yet am I in no angry mood
But will, or ere I go,
In perfect love and charity
My testament here write,
And leave to thee such treasury
As I in it recite.
Now stand aside and give me leave
To write my latest will,
And see that none you do deceive
Of that I leave them till.

THE MANNER OF HER WILL, AND WHAT SHE LEFT TO LONDON AND TO ALL THOSE IN IT, AT HER DEPARTING

I whole in body and in mind,
But very weak in purse,

15. *mell*: compromise or temporise with

27–9. *angry … charity*: conflicting motivations that apparently inform the contradictory tones marking Whitney's descriptions of London life: wry and satirical, even bitter, as well as light-hearted and generous. Such shifts may suggest a tension between a rhetorical persona and the author's personal feelings.

28. *or ere*: before

34. *latest*: last

36. *leave … till*: leave to them

1–4. *I … worse*: witty inversion of the standard opening formula of contemporary wills. Compare that of Isabella's brother (1600):

I Geoffrey Whitney of Ryle's Green in the County of Cheshire, gentleman, being sick in body but of sound and perfect memory, thanks be to God, therefore make and set down with my own hand this my last will and testament (Whitney 1886: lxxxiii).

Do make and write my testament
  For fear it will be worse.
And first I wholly do commend
  My soul and body eke
To God the Father and the Son,
  So long as I can speak.
And after speech, my soul to him
  And body to the grave,
Till time that all shall rise again
  Their judgement for to have.
And then I hope they both shall meet
  To dwell for aye in joy,
Whereas I trust to see my friends
  Released from all annoy.
Thus have you heard touching my soul
  And body, what I mean;
I trust you all will witness bear
  I have a steadfast brain.

And now let me dispose such things
  As I shall leave behind,
That those which shall receive the same
  May know my willing mind.
I first of all to London leave,
  Because I there was bred,
Brave buildings rare, of churches store,
  And Paules to the head.
Between the same, fair streets there be
  And people goodly store;
Because their keeping craveth cost,
  I yet will leave him more.

6. *eke*: also

14. *aye*: ever

15. *Whereas*: when

26. *bred*: but not necessarily born there. The Whitney family property was in Cheshire, although she states below (ll. 217–18) her parents lived in Smithfield, north-west of London, for some time. In accordance with the customary practice of serving as a maidservant or gentlewoman's attendant in a prominent household, Isabella would have left home as a girl or young teenager.

27, 30, 35, 73. *store*: many – a favourite word (e.g. see *Lamentation* l. 37) whose associations of abundance resonate against Whitney's apparent personal situation of material and emotional need

28. *Paules*: = Paul's (original two-syllable spelling). 'to the head' = 'to its top'.

32. *him*: London

First for their food, I butchers leave,
  That every day shall kill;
By Thames you shall have brewers store
  And bakers at your will.
And such as orders do observe
  And eat fish thrice a week,
I leave two streets full fraught therewith;
  They need not far to seek.
Watling Street and Canwick Street
  I full of woollen leave,
And linen store in Friday Street,
  If they me not deceive.
And those which are of calling such
  That costlier they require,
I mercers leave, with silk so rich
  As any would desire.
In Cheap, of them they store shall find,
  And likewise in that street,
I goldsmiths leave with jewels such

33. *butchers*: were typically found in Eastcheap

37–8. *orders* ... *week*: the Elizabethan government sought to build up the navy by strengthening the fisheries, so in 1563 it passed an act increasing from two to three the number of fast-days on which eating meat was forbidden (Wednesday, Friday, Saturday). Invalids were exempt, and certain butchers were granted special licences to supply their needs. As Whitney's conditional phrasing suggests, however, the strictness of observance varied.

39. *two streets*: there are, as Travitsky (1980: 85) suggests, a range of possibilities: New and Old Fish Streets, Stock Fishmongers Row, Friday Street, Billingsgate, Bridge Street, and Knightrider Row

41. *Watling Street*: runs south-east of St Paul's Churchyard through Bridge Row to Canwick (or Candlewick) Street. In his *Survey of London* John Stow observes: 'The inhabitants [of Watling Street] are wealthy drapers, retailers of woollen cloths, both broad and narrow, of all sorts, more than in any one street of this city' (1603; 1971 I: 346). Canwick, earlier inhabited by candlemakers, was also known for its cloth-dealers.

43. *Friday Street*: runs south between Cheapside and Cannon Street

47. *mercers*: dealers in drapery, velvet, and silks

49. *Cheap*: Cheapside, runs east from the north-east corner of St Paul's Churchyard. The Mercers' Company Hall was found west of Bow Church (below l. 78). (I am indebted for much of my information about early modern London public places to Edward H. Sugden, *A Topographical Dictionary to the Works of Shakespeare and His Fellow Dramatists*, Manchester, 1925.)

51. *goldsmiths*: Goldsmiths' Row lay in Cheapside between Bread Street and Bow Church

As are for ladies meet,
And plate to furnish cupboards with
Full brave there shall you find,
With purl of silver and of gold
To satisfy your mind;
With hoods, bongraces, hats or caps
Such store are in that street
As, if on t'one side you should miss,
The t'other serves you feat.
For nets of every kind of sort
I leave within the Pawn,
French ruffs, high purls, gorgets, and sleeves
Of any kind of lawn.
For purse or knives, for comb or glass,
Or any needful knack,
I by the Stocks have left a boy
Will ask you what you lack.
I hose do leave in Birchin Lane
Of any kind of size,
For women stitched, for men both trunks

52. *meet*: suitable
54. *brave*: fine
55. *purl*: thread used for embroidery or trimming borders
57. *hoods*: head-covering often taking the form of a pointed arch with falling material split at the shoulders into two front lappets and a curtain behind
bongraces: shades worn on the front of women's bonnets to protect one's face from the sun
60. *feat*: becomingly
61. *nets*: hairnets, worn under bonnets and hoods
62. *Pawn*: covered arcade or upper walk of the Royal Exchange on Lombard Street, selling a variety of fabrics
63. *French ruffs*: pleated or layered linen collar worn to frame the head; they were stiffened with starch, wire frames, or 'setting-sticks' (stays)
high purls: another kind of ruff or band
gorgets: wimples to cover the neck and breast
sleeves: were often different in colour and fabric from the main body of the garment, and elaborately designed
64. *lawn*: fine linen
67. *Stocks*: market in the centre of the City taking its name from the stocks originally standing there. It occupied the site of the present Mansion House.
69. *hose*: stockings, leggings
Birchin Lane: running north from Lombard Street to Cornhill, known for its drapers and second-hand clothes dealers
71. *stitched* ... *trunks*: embroidered ... padded-out and/or rounded hose worn above the knee

And those of Gascoyne guise.
Boots, shoes, or pantables good store
St Martin's hath for you;
In Cornwall, there I leave you beds
And all that longs thereto.
For women shall you tailors have,
By Bow the chiefest dwell;
In every lane you some shall find
Can do indifferent well.
And for the men few streets or lanes
But body-makers be,
And such as make the sweeping cloaks
With guards beneath the knee.
Artillery at Temple Bar
And dags at Tower Hill;
Swords and bucklers of the best
Are nigh the Fleet until.

Now when thy folk are fed and clad
With such as I have named,
For dainty mouths and stomachs weak
Some junkets must be framed.
Wherefore I 'pothecaries leave,
With banquets in their shop,

72. *Gascoyne*: wide, often bag-like breeches
73. *pantables*: pantofles – slippers, overshoes
74. *St Martin's*: probably St Martin-le-Grand at the east end of St Martin's Lane, notorious for its cheap clothes and boots
75. *Cornwall*: Travitsky (1980: 87) says this refers to a 'Cornwallish ground' in Vintry Ward, but Stow's *Survey of London* does not mention it. It may be a printer's error for 'Cornhill' where there was a large established market.
78. *Bow*: Church of St Mary le Bow, between Bread Street and Bow Lane. To be born within the sound of its bells designated a true cockney.
80. *indifferent*: tolerably
82. *body-makers*: tailors
84. *guards*: ornamental borders
85. *Temple Bar*: gate marking the boundary between Westminster and the City of London, at the west end of Fleet Street
86. *dags*: large pistols
88. *nigh ... until*: close towards the Fleet
92. *junkets*: dish made from sweetened curds and cream, or more generally, any sweet delicacy
93. *'pothecaries*: apothecaries, who sold spices, drugs, and perishable foods
94. *banquets*: not usually a festive dinner in the modern sense but an after-dinner meal consisting of fruit, sweetmeats and wine

Physicians also for the sick,
  Diseases for to stop.
Some roisters still must bide in thee
  And such as cut it out,
That with the guiltless quarrel will
  To let their blood about.
For them I cunning surgeons leave,
  Some plasters to apply,
That ruffians may not still be hanged
  Nor quiet persons die.
For salt, oatmeal, candles, soap,
  Or what you else do want,
In many places shops are full;
  I left you nothing scant.
If they that keep what I you leave
  Ask money when they sell it,
At Mint there is such store it is
  Unpossible to tell it.
At Steelyard store of wines there be
  Your dulled minds to glad,
And handsome men that must not wed
  Except they leave their trade.
They oft shall seek for proper girls
  (And some perhaps shall find),
That needs compels or lucre lures
  To satisfy their mind.
And near the same I houses leave
  For people to repair
To bathe themselves, so to prevent

97. *roisters*: swaggerers, loud bullies
98. *cut it out*: flaunt themselves, show off
101. *cunning*: skilful
108. *scant*: scarce
111. *Mint*: the mint located in the Tower
112. *tell*: count
113. *Steelyard*: or Stillyard, a hall in Upper Thames Street for Hanse merchants (a commercial and political league of northern German towns) who were reputed for selling strong Rhine wines
115–16. *And ... trade*: according to the Statute of Artificers (1563) regulating apprentices, men had to remain single during their seven-year terms, which normally began at the age of fourteen
119. *needs*: emotional or sexual
122. *repair*: resort

Infection of the air.
On Saturdays I wish that those
Which all the week do drug
Shall thither trudge to trim them up
On Sundays to look smug.
If any other thing be lacked
In thee, I wish them look,
For there it is (I little brought
But nothing from thee took).

Now for the people in thee left,
I have done as I may,
And that the poor, when I am gone,
Have cause for me to pray,
I will to prisons portions leave
(What though but very small),
Yet that they may remember me,
Occasion be it shall.
And first the Counter they shall have,
Lest they should go to wrack,
Some coggers and some honest men
That sergeants draw aback.
And such as friends will not them bail,
Whose coin is very thin,
For them I leave a certain Hole
And little ease within.
The Newgate once a month shall have
A sessions for his share,

124. *Infection ... air*: notably, it was believed, the plague
126. *drug*: obsolete form of 'drudge'
128. *smug*: smart, gay
141. *Counter*: two debtors' prisons, one called Poultry and the other Bread, after the streets in which they were located. There were four levels of cells, depending on what prisoners could afford to pay. For those without money, the worst was 'the Hole' (below l. 147), where prisoners held out a basket through the grating to collect food from passers-by.
142. *wrack*: ruin; ironic, since being sent to the Counter often followed bankruptcy
143. *coggers*: cheats, gamblers
148. *little ease*: with a pun on the name of an infamous cramped cell that allowed the prisoner neither fully to stand nor sit
149. *Newgate*: prison for those guilty of criminal or treasonable offences, located northwest of St Paul's Churchyard, east of Old Bailey
150. *sessions*: normally presided over by a Justice of the Peace

Lest, being heaped, infection might
  Procure a further care.
And at those sessions some shall 'scape
  With burning near the thumb,
And afterward to beg their fees
  Till they have got the sum.
And such whose deeds deserveth death,
  And twelve have found the same,
They shall be drawn up Holborn hill
  To come to further shame.
Well, yet to such I leave a nag
  Shall soon their sorrows cease,
For he shall either break their necks
  Or gallop from the press.
The Fleet not in their circuit is,
  Yet if I give him nought,
It might procure his curse ere I
  Unto the ground be brought.
Wherefore I leave some Papist old
  To underprop his roof,
And to the poor within the same,
  A box for their behoof.
What makes you standers-by to smile
  And laugh so in your sleeve?
I think it is because that I
  To Ludgate nothing give.

151. *heaped*: crowded

154. *burning*: branding, common punishment for petty and/or lower-class offenders

155–6. *beg ... sum*: convicts could become 'professed beggars' (i.e. licensed to beg) to enable them to raise money to pay their fines

158. *twelve*: members of a jury

159. *Holborn hill*: a procession of condemned prisoners from Newgate typically rode past St Sepulchre's up Giltspur Street, across Smithfield and down Cow Lane to the bottom of Holborn, and from there up to Tyburn for execution

163. *either ... necks*: by going slowly but surely

164. *press*: executions were popular spectator events

165. *Fleet*: prison near Ludgate Hill east of Fleet Ditch, for those found guilty in Star Chamber or Chancery

169. *Papist*: Roman Catholics were subject to crushing fines for failing to attend Church of England services (= recusancy)

172. *box*: presumably a money-box to collect alms for prisoners. But an additional sense, 'blow', seems appropriate since London gaols were extremely violent.

176. *Ludgate*: prison for debtors and bankrupts west of St Paul's

I am not now in case to lie,
  Here is no place of jest;
I did reserve that for myself
  If I my health possessed
And ever came in credit so
  A debtor for to be.
When days of payment did approach,
  I thither meant to flee,
To shroud myself amongst the rest
  That choose to die in debt.
Rather than any creditor
  Should money from them get
(Yet 'cause I feel myself so weak
  That none me credit dare),
I here revoke and do it leave
  Some bankrupts to his share.
To all the bookbinders by Paul's,
  Because I like their art,
They every week shall money have
  When they from books depart.
Amongst them all my printer must
  Have somewhat to his share;
I will my friends these books to buy
  Of him, with other ware.
For maidens poor, I widowers rich
  Do leave, that oft shall dote,
And by that means shall marry them
  To set the girls afloat.
And wealthy widows will I leave
  To help young gentlemen,
Which when you have, in any case,
  Be courteous to them then,
And see their plate and jewels eke
  May not be marred with rust,

177. *case*: a position to
181. *came ... so*: became so honoured as (and an ironic pun with 'debtor')
190. *credit*: believe, and in a financial sense
193. *Paul's*: i.e. St Paul's Churchyard, walled precinct around the cathedral containing houses and shops, especially booksellers
197. *my printer*: Richard Jones, publisher of popular literature and pamphlets, with an apparent specialty in women writers. He printed all of Whitney's work, as well as Jane Anger's *Protection for Women* with Thomas Orwin in 1589. See Fehrenbach 1981.
204. *afloat*: fully 'launched' towards prosperity
210. *rust*: tarnish

Nor let their bags too long be full,
  For fear that they do burst.
To every gate under the walls
  That compass thee about,
I fruit-wives leave to entertain
  Such as come in and out.
To Smithfield I must something leave,
  My parents there did dwell;
So careless for to be of it
  None would account it well.
Wherefore it thrice a week shall have
  Of horse and neat good store,
And in his spital, blind and lame
  To dwell for evermore.
And Bedlam must not be forgot,
  For that was oft my walk;
I people there too many leave
  That out of tune do talk.
At Bridewell there shall beadles be,
  And matrons that shall still
See chalk well chopped, and spinning plied,
  And turning of the mill.
For such as cannot quiet be
  But strive for house or land,

215. *fruit-wives*: fruit-sellers

217. *Smithfield*: north-west beyond the City walls in an area bounded by Holborn, Aldergate Street and Charterhouse Street. It was known for its horse-market, and for Bartholomew Fair (24 August, memorably caricatured in Jonson's play of the same name). More grimly, Smithfield was also the place where witches and heretics were burnt at the stake, especially Protestants during the reign of Queen Mary. Their sufferings are recorded at length by John Fox in *Acts and Monuments of these Latter and Perilous Days* (1563 – better known as the *Book of Martyrs*).

222. *neat*: oxen

223. *spital*: Hospital of St Bartholomew

225. *Bedlam*: Hospital of St Mary of Bethlehem, at one time a priory but in Whitney's day a lunatic asylum. As she attests, Londoners visited it to watch the ravings of the mad for 'amusement'.

229. *Bridewell*: on the west side of Fleet Ditch and the Thames. A former royal palace often used by Henry VIII, but later given to the City of London by Edward VI. It became a workhouse for the poor and unemployed and then a prison for women, hence the references to 'matrons' and seemingly 'domestic' forms of work/punishment in the following lines.

beadles: officers or guards

231. *chalk*: or perhaps 'limestone'

At th'Inns of Court I lawyers leave
  To take their cause in hand.
And also leave I at each Inn
  Of Court or Chancery,
Of gentlemen, a youthful rut
  Full of activity;
For whom I store of books have left
  At each bookbinder's stall,
And part of all that London hath
  To furnish them withal.
And when they are with study cloyed,
  To recreate their mind,
Of tennis courts, of dancing schools
  And fence, they store shall find.
And every Sunday at the least,
  I leave, to make them sport,
In divers places players, that
  Of wonders shall report.

Now London have I for thy sake
  Within thee and without,
As comes into my memory,
  Dispersed round about
Such needful things as they should have
  Here left now unto thee;

239. *rut*: company, with an association of being sexually active (literally, a company of female deer dedicated to one stag)

248. *fence*: fencing

251. *divers … players*: Richard Burbage had built the first permanent public playhouse – The Theatre – in Shoreditch as early as 1567. Before The Curtain (1577) and others were founded during the remainder of the century (most famously the Globe in 1599), companies regularly performed in the yards of large London inns until these locations were forbidden by the City authorities, who objected to plays as the 'occasion of frays and quarrels, evil practices of incontinency … inveigling and alluring of maids, specially orphans and good citizens' children under age, to privy and unmeet contracts, the publishing of unchaste, uncomely, and unshamefast speeches and doings, withdrawing of the Queen's Majesty's subjects from divine service on Sundays and holy days … unthrifty waste of the money of the poor and fond [silly] persons, sundry robberies by picking and cutting of purses, uttering of popular, busy, and seditious matters, and many other corruptions of youth and other enormities …' (1574, Act of London Common Council, E.K. Chambers, *The Elizabethan Stage*, Oxford, 1923, IV, 273–4).

When I am gone, with conscience
Let them dispersed be.
And though I nothing named have
To bury me withal,
Consider that above the ground
Annoyance be I shall.
And let me have a shrouding sheet
To cover me from shame,
And in oblivion bury me
And never more me name.
Ringings nor other ceremonies
Use you not for cost,
Nor at my burial make no feast;
Your money were but lost.
Rejoice in God that I am gone
Out of this vale so vile,
And that, of each thing left such store
As may your wants exile,
I make thee sole executor
Because I loved thee best,
And thee I put in trust to give
The goods unto the rest.
Because thou shalt a helper need
In this so great a charge,
I wish good fortune be thy guide, lest
Thou shouldst run at large.
The happy days and quiet times
They both her servants be,
Which well will serve to fetch and bring
Such things as need to thee.
Wherefore, good London, not refuse
For helper her to take.
Thus being weak and weary both
An end here will I make.
To all that ask what end I made
And how I went away,
Thou answer may'st like those which here
No longer tarry may.

259. *with*: on your
261–2. *named ... me*: i.e. for burial costs
264. *Annoyance ... shall*: I shall trouble you further (?)
265. *shrouding sheet*: winding sheet, for wrapping corpses before burial
284. *run ... large*: at length (or altogether) run short
290. *her*: i.e. (good) fortune

And unto all that wish me well
Or rue that I am gone,
Do me commend and bid them cease
My absence for to moan.
And tell them further, if they would
My presence still have had,
They should have sought to mend my luck
Which ever was too bad.
So fare thou well a thousand times,
God shield thee from thy foe;
And still make thee victorious
Of those that seek thy woe.
And though I am persuade that I
Shall never more thee see,
Yet to the last I shall not cease
To wish much good to thee.
This 20 of October, I,
In Anno Domini
A thousand five hundred seventy three,
(As almanacs descry),
Did write this will with mine own hand
And it to London gave
In witness of the standers-by;
Whose names (if you will have)
Paper, Pen, and Standish were
At that same present by,
With Time who promised to reveal
So fast as she could hie
The same, lest of my nearer kin
From anything should vary.
So finally I make an end;
No longer can I tarry.

Finis by Isabella Whitney.

298. *rue*: regret
309. *persuade*: *sic* for 'persuaded'
316. *descry*: observe
321. *Standish*: inkpot or stand
324–5. *So ... same*: hie = dispatch, apparently meaning, 'as fast as I could sell my work'

ISABELLA WHITNEY

THE LAMENTATION OF A GENTLEWOMAN UPON THE DEATH OF HER LATE DECEASED FRIEND, WILLIAM GRUFFITH,* GENTLEMAN

(1578)

With poet's pen I do not press to write,
Minerva's mate I do not boast to be,
Parnassus mount (I speak it for no spite)
Can cure my cursed cares, I plainly see:
  For why my heart contains as many woes
  As ever Hector did amongst his foes.

Each man doth moan when faithful friends be dead,
And paint them out as well as wits do serve.

* William Gruffith: unidentified. There is no reason, as Rollins observes (1971: 204), for linking him to the Elizabethan printer William Griffith, but he may be the W.G. who contributed an afterpiece to Whitney's *Copy of a Letter*, which was published, like *A Sweet Nosegay* and *A Gorgeous Gallery*, by Richard Jones.

1–4. *I ... see*: self-disabling gestures and denial of artistic ambition are conventional opening gambits associated with the 'modesty topos' (E. Curtius, *European Literature and the Latin Middle Ages,* London, 1953). They were employed by both male and female writers in this period, though for women modesty was never merely a dispensable convention.

1. *press*: attempt, or in a stronger sense, entreat urgently
2. *Minerva's*: goddess of wisdom and the liberal arts, especially writing
3. *Parnassus*: mountain seat of the nine classical Muses
4. *Can*: *cannot* seems to be implied. See ll. 119–20.
5. *For why*: because
6. *Hector*: greatest of the Trojan heros. When he was being tracked down by Achilles during the fall of Troy, Minerva tricked him into thinking his brother Deiphobus was coming to his rescue. Hector recognised the deception too late, and when he died the Greeks mutilated his body, but the extremity and pathos of his suffering confirmed his heroism, and his funeral concludes *The Illiad*. Whitney's comparison suggests that, despite the liability of her gender (like the fact of Hector's ultimate defeat), she seeks renown from the same kind of self-authorising passion.

8. *paint ... out*: depict vividly

But I, a maid, am forced to use my head
To wail my friend, whose faith did praise deserve.
  Wit wants to will: alas, no skill I have;
  Yet must I needs deplore my Gruffith's grave.

For William white, for Gruffith green, I wore,
And red long since did serve to please my mind;
Now black, I wear, of me not used before;
In lieu of love, alas, this loss I find.
  Now must I leave both white and green and red,
  And wail my friend who is but lately dead.

Yet hurtful eyes do bid me cast away
In open show this careful black attire,
Because it would my secret love bewray,
And pay my pate with hatred for my hire;
  Though outwardly I dare not wear the same,
  Yet in my heart a web of black I frame.

9–10. *But … deserve*: the contrast is between men, whose cultural right to define 'wit' and educational privileges allow them to celebrate their departed friends as casually as their varying abilities permit, and women who lack these advantages and so must be extraordinarily inventive simply to obtain a hearing

10. *wail*: bewail

11. *Wit … will*: wit is lacking in proportion to will

12. *deplore*: grieve deeply over

13–17. *William … red*: gender decorum prohibits the author from recalling her friend's physical features in the way a male poet might itemise his mistress's body (in a Petrarchan *blazon*) and so disclose his own desires. Instead Whitney imagines clothing whose colours encode her feelings for Gruffith. White represents chastity and devotion, while green denotes love and joy; together both colours suggest youth and virtue. Red signifies courage as well as passion, whereas black represents constancy as well as mourning.

19–22. *hurtful … hatred*: see l. 125. Whitney complains that social custom forbids women the wearing of mourning apparel or displays of intense public grief for men who are not husbands or brothers. The implication is that deep male–female love has no legitimacy outside patriarchally regulated marriage or kinship ties.

20. *careful*: literally, full of care, anxiety

21. *bewray*: reveal

22. *pay … pate*: bring hatred (i.e. social hostility) on my head

24. *web … frame*: frame = produce; perhaps alluding to Penelope, figure of wifely devotion, who is traditionally represented spinning while she waits at home for her husband Odysseus to return from his adventures in Homer's *Odyssey*

You ladies all, that pass not for no pain,
But have your lovers lodged in your laps,
I crave your aids to help me mourn amain;
Perhaps yourselves shall feel such careful claps,
    Which God forbid that any lady taste,
    Who shall by me but only learn to waste.

My wits be weak an epitaph to write,
Because it doth require a graver style;
My phrase doth serve but rudely to recite
How lover's loss doth pinch me all this while,
    Who was as pressed to die for Gruffith's sake,
    As Damon did for Pythias undertake.

But William had a worldly friend in store,
Who writ his end to small effect, God knows;
But 'I' and 'H', his name did show no more,
Rhyme rough it is (the common sentence goes);

25. *pass ... pain*: do not circulate socially in order to avoid the pain (of a reputation for promiscuity)
26. *lodged ... laps*: harboured in your breast or skirts (i.e. securely and secretly), or perhaps more explicitly sexual: lap = female pudendum. See ll. 76–7.
27. *amain*: with all (your) strength
28. *claps*: strokes of misfortune
29. *taste*: experience
30. *waste*: experience loss (of a lover)
32. *graver*: serious, solemn, with puns on 'engraver' (with 'epitaph' above) and (burial) 'grave'
33. *rudely*: roughly, inelegantly
36. *Damon ... Pythias*: proverbial for fast friendship, although Whitney reverses the usual order. When Damon was condemned to death by the tyrant Dionysius, Pythias remained as his pledge when Damon was permitted to leave temporarily to settle his affairs. Damon returned on time, however, and Dionysius was so impressed by the friends' mutual trust that he freed him. The story derived from Sir Thomas Elyot's *The Governor* (1531) and subsequently became a popular subject of street ballads as well as a play by Richard Edwards (*c.*1565).
37. *in store*: among his acquaintance
39. *'I' and 'H'*: possibly Jasper Heywood, as Rollins speculates (1971: 205). His name appears on the title-page as one of the contributors to Richard Edwards's *Paradise of Dainty Devices* (1576), a popular miscellany on which *A Gorgeous Gallery* was modelled. The reference to Damon and Pythias (see n. to l. 36) just before I.H. is mentioned may possibly provide a clue to his identity through Edwards.
40. *Rhyme rough*: doggerel verse, perhaps with puns on 'ruff' = vainglorious, blockhead (*OED* first citation 1606)

It hangs at Paul's as every man goes by,
One rhyme too low, another ramps too high.

He praised him out as worldly friends do use,
And uttered all the skill that God had sent.
But I am she that never will refuse,
But as I am, so will I still be bent:
No blasts shall blow my linked love awry,
O would the Gods, with Gruffith I might die!

Then had it been that I, poor silly dame,
Had had no need to blot this scratched scroll,
Then virgin's fist had not set forth the same,
How God hath gripped my Gruffith's sacred soul;
But woe is me, I live in pinching pain,
No wight doth know what sorrows I sustain.

Unhappy may that drowsy day be named
Wherein I first possessed my vital breath,
And eke I wish that day that I was framed,
Instead of life I had received death:

41. *Paul's*: St Paul's cathedral, where books were sold and writers posted their work for public reading
42. *ramps*: climbs awkwardly
43. *worldly*: superficial, as opposed to the intimate relationship enjoyed by the writer and Gruffith
44. *uttered ... sent*: ironic recollection of l. 8, 'as well as wits do serve'
45. *refuse*: decline challenging (I.H. as a rival); abandon (her friend, when inferior tributes detract from his reputation); undervalue (her own critical powers). In this and the next line Whitney implicitly states her responsibility both to her own calling as a poet and to her friend's memory. There is a tension – characteristic of the poem overall – between her will to self-determination and personal expression, and submission to social conventions within which she must live.
46. *bent*: accepting (of misfortune, and of the self-disabling role society compels her to adopt); resolved (not to devalue her relationship with Gruffith)
47. *linked love*: also l. 105. The possible images are of a couple arm-in-arm, which denotes fortitude, hand-in-hand, which suggests tenderness and devotion, or, with 'blasts', of a storm-tossed ship (a conventional Petrarchan image).
49. *silly*: weak, deserving of pity
54. *wight*: person
55. *drowsy*: dull, uneventful
57. *eke*: also

Then with these woes I needed not to waste,
Which now, alas, in every vein I taste.

Some Zoilus sot will think it lightly done
Because I moan my mate and lover so,
Some Momus match this scroll will overrun;
But love is lawless, every wight doth know.
Sith love doth lend me such a friendly scope,
Disdainful dogs I may despise, I hope.

Wherefore I do attempt so much the more
By this good hope to show my slender art,
And mourn I must (who, never marked before),
What fretting force do hold each heavy heart;
But now I see that Gruffith's greedy grave
Doth make me feel the fits which lovers have.

My mournful muse, good ladies, take in worth,
And spare to speak the worst, but judge the best;
For this is all that I dare publish forth;
The rest recorded is within my breast,
And there is lodged forever to remain,
Till God doth grant, by death, to ease my pain.

And when that death is come to pay her due,
With all the pains that she can well invent,
Yet to my Gruffith will I still be true,
Hap death, hold life, my mind is fully bent:

59. *waste*: be consumed

61. *Zoilus*: fourth-century BC sophist and biting critic

62. *mate ... lover*: like 'friend', may imply either a marriage(able) partner or a non-sexual companion in Elizabethan usage. Whitney mixes these terms interchangeably throughout the poem, thereby keeping the exact nature of her relationship with Gruffith ambiguous, and avoiding the reductive labelling which accompanies being identified as a maid or mistress.

63. *Momus match ... overrun*: equal of Momus, god of jests and satire ... read hastily

69. *marked*: i.e. by loss or grief

70. *force do*: treated as a plural

75–6. *this ... breast*: the second line suggests the writer does not mean publishing at all times, but in this case only

82. *Hap ... life*: whether death comes (by chance) or life remains

Before I will our secret love disclose,
To Tantal's pains my body I dispose.

So live I shall, when death hath spit her spite,
And Lady Fame will spread my praise, I know,
And Cupid's knights will never cease to write
And cause my name through Europe for to flow:
And they that know what Cupid can prevail,
Will bless the ship that floats with such a sail.

If I had part of Pallas' learned skill,
Or if Calliope would lend her aid,
By tract of time, great volumes I would fill,
My Gruffith's praise in wailing verse to spread;
But I, poor I, as I have said before,
Do wail to want Minerva's learned lore.

By help, I hope, these ragged rhymes shall go,
Entitled as lovers' lines should be,
And 'scape the chiding chaps of every foe,
To praise that man who was best liked of me.
Though death hath shaped his most untimely end,
Yet for his praise my tristive tunes I send,

In hope the gods, who guide the heav'ns above,
His buried corpse alive again will make,

84. *Tantal's*: Tantalus offended the gods and was punished in hell with an insatiable thirst. He was placed up to the chin in a pool of water which receded whenever he tried to drink.

88. *flow*: issue forth

91. *Pallas'*: Minerva. See ll. 2 above and 96 below.

92. *Calliope*: Muse of epic poetry, and thus promoter of 'great volumes' (in both senses of the word). Renaissance conventions considered epic inappropriate for women writers; in his commendatory Epistle to Whitney's *Sweet Nosegay* (1573), for example, Thomas Berrie praises the author for choosing moral philosophy as her subject over epic or tragedy (another proscribed genre): 'She doth not write the brute or force in arms, / Nor pleasure takes, to sing of others' harms' ($B1^r$).

96. *want*: lack

98. *Entitled*: bearing an author's name
as ... be: i.e. anonymously

99. *chaps*: jaws

102. *tristive*: sorrowful

And have remorse of lady's linked love,
As once they did for good Admetus' sake;
   Or change him else into some flower to wear,
   As erst they did transform Narcissus fair.

So should I then possess my former friend,
Restored to life, as Alcest was from hell:
Or else the gods some fragrant flower would send,
Which for his sake, I might both wear and smell;
   Which flower out of my hand shall never pass,
   But in my heart shall have a sticking place.

But woe is me, my wishes are in vain;
Adieu delight, come crooked cursed care!
To bluntish blocks I see I do complain,
And reap but only sorrow for my share;
   For well I know that gods nor sprites can cure
   The pains that I for Gruffith do endure.

Since wailing no way can remedy me,
To make an end I therefore judge it best,
And drink up all my sorrow secretly,
And as I can, I will abide the rest.
   And sith I dare not mourn to open show,
   With secret sighs and tears my heart shall flow.

105. *remorse of*: compassion on

106–10. *Admetus* ... *Alcest*: Admetus was Alcestis's husband. When he was dying, Apollo obtained longer life for him from the Fates provided he could find somebody to die in his place. Alcestis agreed, thereby saving her husband. She was brought back from hell by Heracles, however, who had been entertained cheerfully by Admetus despite his grief. Alcestis subsequently became a type of female conjugal devotion. Moreover, as Margaret Arnold points out to me, in the Renaissance version of this story Heracles became allegorised as a Christ-figure, wrestling with Death to 'resurrect' Alcestis. By daring to write about her close relationship with Gruffith, Whitney reverses traditional gender roles and represents herself as a female Heracles (as well as venturing into the prohibited realm of 'heroic' poetry seemingly declined at ll. 93–4 but invoked by the comparison to Hector in l. 6). She thereby defies 'death' (cf. ll. 79–82, 85) and rescues Gruffith and herself from cultural and literary oblivion.

108. *Narcissus*: beautiful youth who fell in love with his own image, and ultimately died in frustration at being unable to approach his own reflection. The gods changed him into the flower of the same name.

119. *sprites*: variant form of 'spirits'

Some busy brain perhaps will ask my name,
Disposed much some tidings for to mark:
That dare I not, for fear of flying fame,
And eke I fear lest biting bugs will bark.
  Therefore farewell, and ask no more of me,
  For as I am, a lover will I die.

128. *tidings*: information
129. *That*: i.e. disclosing my name
  flying: fleeting, transient
130. *bark*: sound not confined exclusively to dogs during this period. Whitney playfully inverts the expression 'his bark is worse than his bite'.

MARY (SIDNEY) HERBERT, COUNTESS OF PEMBROKE (1561–1621)

FROM *THE PSALMS* (*c.* 1586–1599), AND *A DIALOGUE BETWEEN TWO SHEPHERDS, THENOT AND PIERS, IN PRAISE OF ASTRAEA* (1602)

Introduction

When Lord Denny decided to attack Mary Wroth, the Countess of Pembroke's niece, for satirising his family in Wroth's prose romance *Urania*, he believed the precedent set by the Countess's earlier writings would serve as a damning comparison. He wrote to Wroth telling her to avoid 'lascivious tales and amorous toys' such as the *Urania*, and instead to imitate her 'virtuous and learned aunt, who translated so many godly books, and especially the holy Psalms of David'. Denny was wrong about the Countess (as I shall explain in a moment), but his patronising remarks were typical of prevailing attitudes which held that translation of religious texts, rather than original composition, was the only proper pursuit for women writers. From the late fifteenth century onwards humanist scholars had promoted the benefits of educating (upper-class) women and encouraging them to write; but in practice the new potential for female self-assertion made many male authorities anxious. To contain the freedom opened up by learning formerly available only to men, and also to uphold traditional feminine virtues of piety and obedience, educated women were steered away from writing fiction and poetry towards classical and religious translation. The result was that sixteenth-century Englishwomen wrote and occasionally published far more translations, nearly all of religious texts, than original works, and of those female translators virtually none went on to create works of their own – unlike men, for whom the widespread activity of translation was often a genuine apprenticeship prior to fully independent literary careers. Translation thus permitted educated women only limited opportunities for creative autonomy. It kept them under intellectual control, since their writing remained artistically subordinate to male-authored compositions, and also within approved social boundaries, since they were dependent on fathers or male relations first for their educations and then for support and public approval of their work (Hannay 1985: 8–10; Lamb 1985: 124).

One woman who succeeded better than most in negotiating these cultural cross-currents – Lord Denny's opinions notwithstanding – was Mary (Sidney) Herbert, Countess of Pembroke. Her *Psalms* were neither literal translations nor quaint works of piety, but innovative re-creations of biblical texts constituting strikingly original poems. Though not published until 1823, they circulated extensively in manuscript and gave contemporary writers such as John Donne, George Herbert, and Henry Vaughan suggestive new models for English poetry. As Donne declared in 'Upon the Translation of the Psalms', they 'tell us why, and teach us how to sing' (Rathmell 1963: ix). The Countess of Pembroke also managed to go beyond customary restraints by translating works from diverse genres (Robert Garnier's *Marc Antonie,* 1592; Petrarch's *Triumph of Death*; and Philippe du Plessis-Mornay's *Discourse of Life and Death,* 1592), and composing original verse of her own. She was also the most celebrated literary patron in late-Elizabethan England. As a result of these multiple activities she became the first Englishwoman to establish a recognised literary reputation for herself (Beilin 1987: 121; Lewalski 1979: 241).

Elizabethan readers would certainly not have considered the Countess's originality disabled by her text's sacred origins. Traditionally the biblical Psalms were considered to have been inspired by God and written by David. Later versions in other languages were believed to manifest the same divine primacy: they were re-revelations of the eternal power of creation, and in this sense were as 'original' as David's Hebrew texts – particularly if the new translations were considered to possess extraordinary poetic and affective power, as were the Countess's (Lewalski 1979: 246, 275–6).

Contemporaries would also have read her *Psalms* as sectarian documents. Among the scholarly sources she consulted were Clement Marot's earlier French translations, commentaries by Théodore de Bèze and John Calvin, and the Geneva Bible – ideologically all strongly Protestant works. The last of these was dedicated to Queen Elizabeth in the hope of persuading her to promote reformist policies; Marot and de Bèze offered their work to the French King for similar reasons. Mary Sidney followed in this tradition of veiled political advice by presenting Queen Elizabeth with a copy of her Psalms in 1599, prefaced by two dedicatory poems (reproduced in Sidney 1977: 88–95). In one, 'Even Now that Care which on thy Crown Attends', she quietly urges Elizabeth to support Continental Protestantism, a cause which the powerful Sidney and Dudley families had long championed but which Elizabeth resisted (Hannay 1989: 24–5; the Countess's translation of *A Discourse* (1592) by the French Huguenot Plessis-Mornay – also dedicated to Elizabeth – was likewise motivated). The second poem, 'To the Angel Spirit of the Most Excellent Sir Philip Sidney', was a lament for her brother, who had died fighting the Spanish in the Netherlands in 1586 and subsequently became celebrated in England and on the Continent as a Protestant martyr. The poem daringly hints that Elizabeth failed to provide adequate support for the military campaign Philip had promoted and was thus indirectly responsible for his death (Hannay 1985: 149–56). The *Psalms* also acquired Protestant overtones during the sixteenth century because religious reformers made them a central text symbolising their struggles and sufferings, and exemplifying their new focus on individual unmediated spirituality. Protestant readers accordingly tended to identify the psalmist's voice with their own, so that when Psalm 82's speaker cries out for justice against corrupt magistrates, for example, the situation would have carried strong memories of recent political persecution for Elizabethan reformers (Hannay 1989: 30).

The *Psalms* may also be judged original poems on the basis of their innovative verse-forms and imaginative appeal; collectively they represent 'a landmark in the development of the English religious lyric' (Waller 1986b: 162). Following her brother's death in 1586, the Countess began to edit Philip's translations of Psalms 1–43 but gradually went further to compose her own more technically varied and intellectually searching versions of the remaining 107 psalms. She read every Protestant text and commentary available in English, French, and Latin; and while not reading Hebrew herself, she perhaps consulted somebody who did for advice on the original texts (Hannay 1994: 16). This research meant that instead of producing literal translations or relying too heavily on her brother's models, she sought independently to capture each psalm's underlying doctrinal or allegorical meaning in her attention to verbal detail (Rathmell 1963: xii). This is not to underestimate the degree to which Philip's legacy – not only his psalms but also works such as *Astrophil and Stella* – guided Mary's poetic development, nor to which his increasingly legendary status (fostered in part by the publication of the *Arcadia* in 1590 as well as commemorative accounts of his life promoted by the Countess) facilitated public acceptance of her literary authority as a woman. Nor should one ignore the devaluing effects of being 'Sister to that Incomparable Sidney', such as the tendency of later readers to discount her own contributions to the 'Sidneian Psalms' (Lamb 1990: 115–18; Waller 1990: 336–8). In terms of personal recognition, being 'Sidney's sister' was decidedly a mixed blessing. Nonetheless, comparisons between the Countess's work and preceding psalm translations – including those by earlier women such as Anne Lock and Queen Elizabeth – reveal the extent to which she created personally distinctive poems. Over 23 years she experimented with a huge variety of verse-forms, with the result that most psalms present unique combinations of line and stanza lengths (amongst the sixteen MS versions of her psalms, there are 164 distinct stanzaic forms, and 94 metrical patterns; (see Sidney 1977: 37). Her frequent use of short lines not only departs from previous religious prosody but also serves to heighten the dramatic action of a poem, as in Psalm 139 (15–21) where the juxtaposition of long and short lines evokes the speaker's oscillating physical movements. Overall the Countess's experiments with metre and rhythm constituted part of her self-education as a poet, while for later writers they opened up 'a new aesthetic consciousness of the possibilities for imitation' (Lewalski 1979: 245).

Perhaps the most remarkable feature of her *Psalms* is their vivid evocation of material experiences and individualised voices. In the Hebrew original and in literal translations, the language of the Psalms is fairly non-specific. While conveying a full range of human emotions, it tends to draw on general phenomena in nature and society for its metaphors, thereby creating transhistorical poems of universal appeal. By contrast Mary Sidney particularises her images, basing them on closely observed physical features. In Psalm 139, for example, she conveys a sense of the ubiquity of the divine in the material world at lines 50–6 by depicting a foetus being fashioned in the womb (Fisken 1985: 177). Here one also notices another prominent feature of Sidney's *Psalms*: her tendency to elaborate on an original biblical image when it pertains to female realms of experience (a related instance is the image of an aborted embryo in Psalm 58, ll. 22–4). Her diction often draws on colloquial and/or spoken forms of speech, so that her speakers' voices become more inflected and passionate, as for example in the agitated rhythms and abrupt questions of God in Psalm 50. Such carefully nuanced details, appearing in characteristically 'packed, concise' lines and sharpened by the Countess's taste for irony and paradox, explain why her work anticipates that of Metaphysical poets in the next generation (Rathmell 1963: xii; Freer 1972: 105).

Given that Sidney's translations of the *Psalms* have been seen as cunning ventriloquism in which she cloaks her self-conscious artistry within generically acceptable, male-authorised discourse (handmaid, as it were, to God, David, and Philip), her *Dialogue between Two Shepherds, Thenot and Piers, in Praise of Astraea* presents a contrasting, highly sceptical view of literary art. Ostensibly it is a poem praising Elizabeth I written for a projected 1599 state visit (which never took place) to Wilton, the Pembroke family seat. It takes the form of a debate between two shepherds, Thenot and Piers, that questions the capacity of human (and therefore fallible) language to represent eternal truths. This theme goes back to Augustine and Plato, and had recently been explored in Philip Sidney's *Apology for Poetry*. The Countess's poem, however, puts forward an extreme position, perhaps for the sake of clarity (Hannay 1990: 165). Thenot's view is that of the aspiring, Neoplatonic artist: by praising Astraea – a figure for Elizabeth – with all the 'eloquence' he can muster, he hopes to achieve a perfect expression of her divine nature (part of the poem's fun lies in Thenot's inept versifying and mixed diction). Piers, on the other hand, puts forward the ancient objection that poetry is a form of lying. He is likewise an advocate for Protestant plain speech, intensely suspicious of rhetoric in all senses of the word, and a believer in the theoretically absolute separation of human language as metaphor and allegory, and divine truth. Poetry, in Piers's view, is not art aspiring to enlightenment, but a prophetic instinct utterly dependent on God's grace, and thus untransmittable by human symbolic languages. To know Astraea truly, in his terms, is to contemplate her virtues in spiritual silence.

Though its particular bearing on the validation of female experience is very different from the *Psalms*, in terms of the Countess's literary career the *Dialogue* adds another distinctive voice to her repertoire. Overall the latter created an idealised public image of manifold accomplishment which allowed her successfully to circumvent traditional injunctions to female self-subordination (Brennan 1988: 82; Hannay 1994: 2–8).

Manuscripts:
The multiple MSS of the Sidney *Psalms* are discussed in Sidney 1962, Rathmell 1963, Sidney 1977, and Kinnamon 1992. My texts are based on MS A (Penshurst, Viscount De L'Isle), and consult MSS B and C (Bodleian MS Rawl. poet. 24 and 25).

Editions:
The Psalmes of David, begun by ... Sir Philip Sidney ... and ... The Countess of Pembroke (Chiswick, 1823). *The Psalms of Sir Philip Sidney and the Countess of Pembroke*, ed. J.C.A. Rathmell (New York, 1963). *The Triumph of Death and Other Unpublished and Uncollected Poems by Mary Sidney, Countess of Pembroke*, ed. G.F.

Waller (Salzburg, 1977). *The Female Spectator*, ed. Mary R. Mahl and Helene Koon (Bloomington, 1977, brief excerpts from the Psalms, and 'Even Now that Care which on thy Crown Attends'). Francis Davison, *A Poetical Rhapsody* [containing *A Dialogue Between Two Shepherds*] (1602). STC 6373, reel 643. Sidney 1977. *The Paradise of Women*, ed. Betty Travitsky (Westport, Conn., 1981, brief excerpts).

MARY (SIDNEY) HERBERT, COUNTESS OF PEMBROKE

FROM THE PSALMS

(*c.* 1586–99)

PSALM 50

The mighty God, the ever-living lord,
    All nations from earth's uttermost confines
Summoneth by his pursuivant, his word,
    And out of beauty's beauty, Zion shines.
God comes, he comes with ear and tongue restored,
    His guard huge storms, hot flames his ushers go;
And called, their appearance to record,
    Heav'n hasteth from above, earth from below.

He sits his people's judge and thus commands:
    'Gather me hither that beloved line,
Whom solemn sacrifices, holy bands,
    Did in eternal league with me combine
Then when the heav'ns subsigned with their hands,

Psalm 50: 'Because the church is alway full of hypocrites, which do imagine that God will be worshipped with outward ceremonies only, without the heart ... therefore the Prophet [David, traditional author of the Psalms] doth reprove this gross error, and pronounceth the name of God to be blasphemed where holiness is set in ceremonies. For he declareth the worship of God to be spiritual, whereof are two principal parts, invocation and thanksgiving' (Geneva Bible heading). Using volatile syntax and conversational diction, Sidney creates a personalised dramatic monologue: 'The God imaged in [this psalm] ... speaks to us in our own language to make us understand His will' (Fisken 1985: 171).

3. *pursuivant*: herald or messenger empowered to execute warrants issued by the monarch or state

4. *beauty's beauty*: i.e. manifested beauty from the ultimate source of all beauty. Compare Geneva Bible: 'Out of Zion, *which is* the perfection of beauty, hath God shined'. Zion = the citadel of Jerusalem, later signifying the city itself, and spiritually the heavenly city of God (Hebrews 12.22).

5–6. *God ... go*: 'As when God gave his law in Mount Sinai [Exodus 19], he appeared terrible with thunder and tempest, so will he appear terrible to take account for the keeping thereof' (Geneva Bible note)

11. *bands*: covenants

13. *subsigned*: signed, attested

That God in justice eminently reigns,
Controlling so, as nothing countermands
What once decreed, his sacred doom contains.

You then, my folk, to me your God attend;
Hark, Israel, and hear thy people's blame:
Nor want of sacrifice doth me offend,
Nor do I miss thy altar's daily flame;
To me thy stall no fatted bull shall send.
Should I exact one he-goat from thy fold,
I that as far as hills, woods, fields extend,
All birds and beasts in known possession hold?

Suppose me hungry; yet to beg thy meat
I would not tell thee that I hungry were;
Myself may take: what needs me then entreat,
Since earth is mine and all that earth doth bear?
But do I long the brawny flesh to eat
Of that dull beast that serves the ploughman's need?
Or do I thirst, to quench my thirsty heat,
In what the throats of bearded cattle bleed?

Oh no: bring God of praise a sacrifice,
Thy vowed debts unto the highest pay;
Invoke my name, to me erect thy cries,
Thy praying plaints, when sorrow stops thy way.
I will undo the knot that anguish ties,
And thou at peace shalt glorify my name'.
Mildly the good, God schooleth in this wise,
But this sharp check doth to the godless frame:

'How fits it thee my statutes to report,
And of my covenant in thy talk to prate,
Hating to live in right-reformed sort,
And leaving in neglect what I relate?

16. *doom*: judgement
18. *blame*: charge, accusation; reproof
19. *Nor*: neither
25. *meat*: food
29. *brawny*: meaty
32. *what … bearded cattle*: whatever … goats
36. *plaints … way*: lamentations … ability to speak
39. *wise*: manner
44. *what I relate*: i.e. God's words

See'st thou a thief? thou grow'st of his consort;
  Dost with adult'rers to adult'ry go?
Thy mouth is slander's ever-open port,
  And from thy tongue doth nought but treason flow.

Nay, ev'n thy brother thy rebukes disgrace,
  And thou in spite defam'st thy mother's son;
And for I wink a while, thy thoughts embrace:
  "God is like me, and doth as I have done".
But lo, thou see'st I march another pace
  And come with truth thy falsehood to disclose;
Thy sin, revived, upbraids thy blushing face,
  Which thou long dead in silence didst suppose.

Oh lay up this in marking memory,
  You that are wont God's judgements to forget:
In vain to others for release you fly
  If once on you I griping fingers set.
And know the rest: my dearest worship I
  In sweet perfume of offered praise do place;
And who directs his goings orderly,
  By my conduct shall see God's saving grace'.

PSALM 52

Tyrant, why swell'st thou thus
  Of mischief vaunting,

45. *consort*: company
48. *treason*: Geneva Bible = 'deceit'
51. *wink*: shut my eyes, seem not to see *embrace*: seize upon (the apparent situation)
56. *Which ... suppose*: i.e. sin ... presume (to remain)
57. *marking*: observant
60. *griping*: (tightly) grasping
62. *place*: i.e. value

Psalm 52: 'David describeth the arrogant tyranny of his adversary Doeg, who by false surmises [= allegations] caused Ahimelech with the rest of the priests to be slain [1 Samuel 22] ... In this psalm is lively set forth the kingdom of Antichrist' [= figure for the Pope for Protestants] (Geneva Bible). As Margaret Hannay observes of the Psalms' Reformation readership, 'Any psalm which spoke of the persecution of the godly, the righteous, or of Israel (automatically defined as the true [i.e. reformed] Church) was read as though it spoke of Protestants' (1989: 32–3). Lewalski (1979: 241) compares the dramatic opening lines of this psalm to those of John Donne's poems.

1. *swell'st*: grow arrogant, proud
2. *Of ... vaunting*: as a result of ... boasting

Since help from God to us
Is never wanting?

Lewd lies thy tongue contrives,
Loud lies it soundeth;
Sharper than sharpest knives
With lies it woundeth.

Falsehood thy wit approves,
All truth rejected;
Thy will all vices loves,
Virtue neglected.

Not words from cursed thee
But gulfs are poured;
Gulfs wherein daily be
Good men devoured.

Think'st thou to bear it so?
God shall displace thee;
God shall thee overthrow,
Crush thee, deface thee.

The just shall fearing see
These fearful chances,
And laughing shoot at thee
With scornful glances.

Lo, lo, the wretched wight
Who God disdaining,
His mischief made his might,
His guard his gaining.

I as an olive tree
Still green shall flourish;

5. *Lewd*: vile
14. *gulfs*: whirlpools; voracious appetites
25. *wight*: person
27. *might*: empowerment, bodily strength
28. *guard … gaining*: protective escort, but perhaps with an added undercutting sense of a trimming or border (as on a garment) which is merely ornamental … reward
29. *I*: (But) I

God's house the soil shall be
My roots to nourish.

My trust on his true love
Truly attending,
Shall never thence remove,
Never see ending.

Thee will I honour still,
Lord, for this justice;
There fix my hopes I will
Where thy saints' trust is.

Thy saints trust in thy name,
Therein they joy them;
Protected by the same,
Nought can annoy them.

PSALM 58

And call ye this to utter what is just,
You that of justice hold the sov'reign throne?
And call ye this to yield, O sons of dust,
To wronged brethren every man his own?
Oh no: it is your long malicious will
Now to the world to make by practice known,
With whose oppression you the balance fill,
Just to yourselves, indifferent else to none.

But what could they, who ev'n in birth declined
From truth and right to lies and injuries?

Psalm 58: '[David] describeth the malice of his enemies, the flatterers of Saul, who both secretly and openly sought his destruction, from whom he appealeth to God's judgment ... ' (Geneva Bible)

2. *You ... throne*: 'The counsellors of Saul, who under pretence of consulting for the common wealth [= public good], conspire my death, being an innocent' (Geneva Bible)
3. *dust*: the Geneva version reads 'men': the Countess's more concrete word emphasises humanity's beginning (Genesis 2.7) and end in 'dust'
5. *long*: enduring
7. *balance*: pan of the balance or scales
9. *they*: they do

9–10. *who ... injuries*: alluding to the Calvinist doctrine of election, according to which God has predestined individual human souls as either wicked or godly

To show the venom of their cankered mind
  The adder's image scarcely can suffice;
Nay scarce the aspic may with them contend,
  On whom the charmer all in vain applies
His skilfull'st spells, aye missing of his end,
  While she self-deaf and unaffected lies.

Lord crack their teeth, Lord crush these lions' jaws,
  So let them sink as water in the sand;
When deadly bow their aiming fury draws,
  Shiver the shaft ere past the shooter's hand.
So make them melt as the dishoused snail,
  Or as the embryo, whose vital band
Breaks ere it holds, and formless eyes do fail
  To see the sun, though brought to lightful land.

O let their brood, a brood of springing thorns,
  Be by untimely rooting overthrown
Ere bushes waxed, they push with pricking thorns,
  As fruits yet green are oft by tempest blown.
The good with gladness this revenge shall see
  And bathe his feet in blood of wicked one,
While all shall say: 'The just rewarded be;
  There is a God that carves to each his own'.

11. *show*: represent
13. *aspic*: asp, poisonous snake
15. *aye ... end*: always ... intent, goal
16. *she self-deaf*: the asp refusing to listen
21. *melt ... dishoused*: be dissolved ... evicted from a house. *OED's* first citation.
22. *vital band*: life-sustaining (i.e. umbilical) cord. Rathmell observes that the 'image of the stillborn embryo has an immediacy that is certainly not present in the formal metaphor of the "untimely frute" that we find in both the Geneva and the Bishops' Bible' (1963: xxi)
26. *untimely*: prematurely
27. *waxed ... with*: fully grown they thrust out. As Waller observes (Sidney 1977: 198), in fashioning this image of a budding thornbush uprooted by a whirlwind, the Countess turned from the Geneva to the Coverdale (*BCP*) wording: 'Or e'er your thorns be sharp, the wrath shall take them away quick, like a stormy wind'.
29. *good*: good person
32. *carves ... own*: creates each person according to his or her (predestined) nature. Waller notes (1979: 216) that the energetic image makes more explicit what the Countess's sources alluded to in marginal notes but left implicit in their translated texts: election theology's emphasis on an absolute gulf between the godly and the wicked, and the incapacity of each for self-transformation. Certain phrases in other psalms carry similar ideological meanings; e.g. 'right-reformed sort', 'God's saving grace' (50: 43, 64); 'free grace' (59: 43).

PSALM 59

Save me from such as me assail;
 Let not my foes,
O God, against my life prevail;
 Save me from those
Who make a trade of cursed wrong
And, bred in blood, for blood do long.

Of these one sort do seek by slight
 My overthrow;
The stronger part with open might
 Against me go;
And yet, thou God, my witness be,
From all offence my soul is free.

But what if I from fault am free?
 Yet they are bent
To band and stand against poor me,
 Poor innocent.
Rise, God, and see how these things go,
And rescue me from instant woe.

Rise, God of armies, mighty God
 Of Israel;
Look on them all who spread abroad
 On earth do dwell,
And let thy hand no longer spare
Such as of wicked malice are.

When golden sun in west doth set,
 Returned again
As hounds that howl their food to get,
 They run amain

Psalm 59: 'David being in great danger of Saul, who sent [men to his house] to slay him in his bed, prayeth unto God, declareth his innocency and their fury, desiring God to destroy all those that sin of malicious wickedness ... ' (Geneva Bible)

15. *band*: unite

21–2. *them* ... *dwell*: i.e. 'the heathen' or 'the reprobate who maliciously persecute his church' (Geneva v. 5 and marginal note)

25–30. Rathmell observes that the varying line lengths in this and other stanzas of this psalm 'ingeniously reflects the restless movement' of menacing, ravenous hounds (1963: xviii)

28. *amain*: with full force, violently

The city through from street to street,
With hungry maw some prey to meet.

Night elder grown, their fittest day,
    They babbling prate,
How my lost life extinguish may
    Their deadly hate.
They prate and babble void of fear,
For, 'Tush', say they, 'who now can hear?'

Ev'n thou canst hear, and hearing, scorn
    All that they say;
For them (if not by thee upborne)
    What props do stay?
Then will I, as they wait for me,
O God my fortress, wait on thee.

Thou ever me with thy free grace
    Prevented hast;
With thee my prayer shall take place
    Ere from me past,
And I shall see who me do hate,
Beyond my wish, in woeful state.

For fear my people it forget,
    Slay not outright,
But scatter them and so them set
    In open sight,
That by thy might they may be known
Disgraced, debased, and overthrown.

No witness of their wickedness
    I need produce
But their own lips, fit to express
    Each vile abuse:
In cursing proud, proud when they lie,
O let them dear such pride aby.

30. *maw*: stomach
31. *Night … grown*: grown (powerful in evil) during the preceding night
40. *stay*: support
44. *prevented*: have gone before
45. *place*: effect, be realised
60. *aby*: pay the penalty for

At length in rage consume them so
  That naught remain;
Let them all, being quite forego,
  And make it plain
That God, who Jacob's rule upholds,
Rules all all-bearing earth enfolds.

Now thus they fare: when sun doth set,
  Returned again
As hounds that howl their food to get,
  They run amain
The city through from street to street,
With hungry maws some prey to meet.

Abroad they range and hunt apace
  Now that, now this,
As famine trails a hungry trace;
  And though they miss,
Yet will they not to kennel hie,
But all the night at bay will lie.

But I will of thy goodness sing,
  And of thy might,
When early sun again shall bring
  His cheerful light;
For thou, my refuge and my fort,
In all distress dost me support.

My strength doth of thy strength depend;
  To thee I sing:

62. *naught*: nothing
63. *Let ... forego*: abandon ... foregone
65. *rule*: law
75. *trails ... trace*: scents ... path
78. *at bay*: in a state of manic barking
83. *fort*: fortress, stronghold
85–6. *My ... sing*: sing = speak in verse, make poetry: the Countess appears to merge her voice with that of the psalmist – albeit with an element of gender irony, since a Geneva note reads: '[God's power] which didst use the policy of a weak woman to confound the enemy's strength, as 1 Samuel 19.12'. This refers to the story of Michal, Saul's daughter, who is given by him to be David's wife in exchange for one hundred Philistine foreskins. Michal helps David escape murderers sent by Saul by letting him out 'through a window', placing an effigy of him in their bed as a decoy, and then telling his pursuers he is ill. Like Michal, Sidney is also God's agent as reinterpreter of David's psalms, substituting metaphors from her own experience in order to 'sing' divine truth.

Thou art my fort, me to defend;
My God, my king,
To thee I owe, and thy free grace,
That free I rest in fearless place.

PSALM 73

It is most true that God to Israel
(I mean to men of undefiled hearts)
Is only good, and nought but good imparts.
Most true, I see, albe almost I fell
From right conceit into a crooked mind,
And from this truth with straying steps declined.
For lo, my boiling breast did chafe and swell
When first I saw the wicked proudly stand,

88. *My … king*: compare George Herbert, 'Jordan 1': 'I envy no man's nightingale or spring, / Nor let them punish me with loss of rhyme, / Who plainly say, My God, my King'

89. *owe*: am indebted

Psalm 73: 'The Prophet teacheth by his example that neither the worldly prosperity of the ungodly nor yet the affliction of the good ought to discourage God's children, but rather ought to move us to consider our Father's providence … ' (Geneva Bible)

1–6. Rivkah Zim (1987: 201) compares these lines with Philip Sidney's *Astrophil and Stella* 5:

> It is most true that eyes are formed to serve
> The inward light, and that the heavenly part
> Ought to be king, from whose rules who do swerve,
> Rebels to nature, strive for their own smart,
> It is most true, what we call Cupid's dart
> An image is, which for ourselves we carve;
> And, fools, adore in temple of our heart
> Till that good god make church and churchman starve.
> True, that true beauty virtue is indeed,
> Whereof this beauty can be but a shade,
> Which elements with mortal mixture breed;
> True, that on earth we are but pilgrims made,
> And should in soul up to our country move;
> True, and yet true that I must Stella love.

4. *albe*: although

5. *conceit*: understanding

6. *declined*: turned away

Prevailing still in all they took in hand,
And sure no sickness dwelleth where they dwell;
Nay, so they guarded are with health and might,
It seems of them death dares not claim his right.

They seem as privileged from others' pain:
The scourging plagues which on their neighbours fall
Torment not them, nay touch them not at all.
Therefore with pride, as with a gorgeous chain,
Their swelling necks encompassed they bear,
All clothed in wrong, as if a robe it were;
So fat become, that fatness doth constrain
Their eyes to swell; and if they think on aught,
Their thought they have, yea have beyond their thought.
They wanton grow, and, in malicious vein,
Talking of wrong, pronounce as from the skies,
So high a pitch their proud presumption flies.

Nay, heav'n itself, high heav'n escapes not free
From their base mouths; and in their common talk
Their tongues no less than all the earth do walk.
Wherefore ev'n godly men, when so they see
Their horn of plenty freshly flowing still,
Leaning to them, bend from their better will;
And thus they reasons frame: 'How can it be
That God doth understand? that he doth know,
Who sits in heav'n, how earthly matters go?'
See here the godless crew, while godly we
Unhappy pine, all happiness possess:
Their riches more, our wealth still growing less.

9. *still*: always
16. *chain*: necklace
20. *aught*: anything
22. *wanton*: insolent in their triumphant prosperity, reckless; unmanageable; merciless; self-indulgent
24. *So ... flies*: compare *Richard II*: 'How high a pitch his resolution soars!' (I.i.109)
27. *walk*: move rapidly (over any topic whatsoever)
29. *horn ... plenty*: cornucopia, superabundance (and following ll. 25–7, perhaps recalling the principle from Renaissance rhetoric of copiousness in persuasive words, which explains why the godly 'lean to them' against their better judgement). *OED*'s first citation.
31. *they*: the ungodly
35. *pine*: suffer; waste away

Nay, ev'n within myself, myself did say:
In vain my heart I purge, my hands in vain
In cleanness washed, I keep from filthy stain,
Since thus afflictions scourge me every day,
Since never a day from early east is sent
But brings my pain, my check, my chastisement.
And shall I then these thoughts in words bewray?
O let me, Lord, give never such offence
To children thine that rest in thy defence.
So then I turned my thoughts another way,
Sounding, if I this secret's depth might find;
But cumbrous clouds my inward sight did blind.

Until at length nigh weary of the chase,
Unto thy house I did my steps direct:
There, lo, I learned what end these did expect,
And what but that in high but slipp'ry place
Thou didst them set; whence, when they least of all
To fall did fear, they fell with headlong fall.
For how are they in less than moment's space
With ruin overthrown? with frightful fear
Consumed so clean, as if they never were,
Right as a dream, which waking doth deface?
So, Lord, most vain thou dost their fancies make,
When thou dost them from careless sleep awake.

Then for what purpose was it? to what end
For me to fume with malcontented heart,
Tormenting so in me each inward part?
I was a fool (I can it not defend)
So quite deprived of understanding might,
That as a beast I bare me in thy sight.
But as I was, yet did I still attend,
Still follow thee, by whose upholding hand,
When most I slide, yet still upright I stand.
Then guide me still, then still upon me spend

43. *bewray*: reveal
49. *nigh*: nearly (completely)
51. *these*: the ungodly
52. *what ... that*: nonetheless how
57. *clean*: utterly
58. *Right as ... deface*: exactly like ... obliterate
65. *understanding might*: the power of understanding
66. *beast*: i.e. creature lacking reason

The treasures of thy sure advice, until
Thou take me hence into thy glory's hill.

O what is he will teach me climb the skies?
With thee, thee good, thee goodness to remain?
No good on earth doth my desires detain.
Often my mind and oft my body tries
Their weak defects; but thou, my God, thou art
My endless lot and fortress of my heart.
The faithless fugitives who thee despise
Shall perish all, they all shall be undone
Who leaving thee to whorish idols run.
But as for me, nought better in my eyes
Than cleave to God, my hopes in him to place,
To sing his works while breath shall give me space.

PSALM 82

Where poor men plead at princes' bar
(Who gods, as God's vicegerents, are),
The God of gods hath his tribunal pight,
Adjudging right
Both to the judge and judged wight:

73. *O ... skies*: compare *Astrophil and Stella* 31.1: 'With how sad steps, O moon, thou climb'st the skies' (Zim 1987: 201)
76. *tries*: experiences
78. *endless lot*: everlasting condition or destiny (signifying purposeful determination, though the implied metaphor of casting lots suggests an arbitrary process)

Psalm 82: 'The Prophet [David], declaring God to be present among the judges and magistrates, reproveth their partiality, and exhorteth them to do justice. But seeing none amendment, he desireth God to undertake the matter and execute justice himself' (Geneva Bible). Margaret Hannay argues that Elizabethan Protestants would have read this psalm's clamorous imperatives and images of the suffering poor in terms of Protestant persecutions under Mary I (1989: 32–5).

1. *bar*: court of justice
2. *vicegerents*: = deputies, implying a hierarchy of two courts: an imperfect worldly one, and a divine supreme one; 'while poor men plead "at Princes barre", the judges themselves are being judged by God'. The implication – considered dangerously subversive in the sixteenth century – is that obedience by subjects is not absolute but conditional upon kings and magistrates ruling justly (Hannay 1989: 33–5).
3. *pight*: ordered, set in place, or more literally 'pitched'
5. *wight*: person

'How long will ye just doom neglect?
How long', saith he, 'bad men respect?
You should his own unto the helpless give,
   The poor relieve,
Ease him with right, whom wrong doth grieve.
You should the fatherless defend,

You should unto the weak extend
Your hand to loose and quiet his estate,
   Through lewd men's hate
Entangled now in deep debate.

This should you do; but what do ye?
You nothing know, you nothing see;
No light, no law; fie, fie, the very ground
   Becomes unsound,
So right, wrong, all your faults confound.

Indeed to you the style I gave
Of gods and sons of God, to have;
But err not, Princes, you as men must die;
   You that sit high
Must fall, and low, as other lie'.

Since men are such, O God, arise,
Thyself most strong, most just, most wise;

8. *own*: rights, justice (following the sense of the Geneva version), or possessions, property (i.e. God's material creation)

13. *loose ... quiet ... estate*: set free, redeem, absolve ... acquit, make peaceful its condition, class ... fortune or possessions

15. *deep debate*: 'entangled in litigation' (Hannay 1989: 33)

18. *No ... law*: 'an extraordinarily concise statement of [Théodore de] Bèze's interpretation, one which draws on the law as lamp (Psalm 119), and also on the New Testament's association of God with light. The ungodly judges turn their backs on God's law and oppress the poor' (Hannay 1989: 34).

18–19. *fie ... unsound*: while the Geneva gloss merely generalises, 'all things are out of order', the full sense of its translation is, 'they remain impassive and oblivious, even in the face of "all the foundations of the earth" being moved'

21. *style*: 'title of honour' (Geneva), form of address

24–5. *You ... lie*: Hannay suggests the Countess departs from her sources in not threatening the evil judges with divine wrath: 'she leaves them lying dead, awaiting burial' (1989: 35). Vengeance may be implied, however, by the final stanza's invocation.

Of all the earth king, judge, disposer be,
  Since to decree
Of all the earth belongs to thee.

PSALM 134

You that Jehovah's servants are,
Whose careful watch, whose watchful care,
  Within his house are spent,
  Say thus with one assent:
  Jehovah's name be praised.
  Then let your hands be raised
    To holiest place,
    Where holiest grace
      Doth aye
        Remain;
      And say
        Again
  Jehovah's name be praised.
Say last unto the company
  Who tarrying make
  Their leave to take:
All blessings you accompany
From him in plenty showered,
Whom Zion holds embowered,
  Who heav'n and earth of nought hath raised.

29. *decree*: command, order authoritatively; appoint; judge

Psalm 134: '[David] exhorteth the Levites, watching in the temple, to praise the Lord' (Geneva Bible)

2. *careful … care*: this chiasmus, a characteristic structure of the psalms, anticipates the vertical shape of the entire poem. watch = night guard.
15. *tarrying*: waiting
19. *embowered*: secluded, sheltered, as in a bower (Philip Sidney's coinage, according to the *OED*)
20. *of nought*: from nothing

PSALM 139

O Lord in me there lieth nought
  But to thy search revealed lies:
    For when I sit
    Thou markest it,
  No less thou notest when I rise;
Yea, closest closet of my thought
  Hath open windows to thine eyes.

Thou walkest with me when I walk,
  When to my bed for rest I go,
    I find thee there
    And everywhere;
  Not youngest thought in me doth grow,
No not one word I cast to talk,
  But yet unuttered thou dost know.

If forth I march, thou go'st before,
  If back I turn, thou com'st behind;
    So forth nor back
    Thy guard I lack,
  Nay on me too thy hand I find.
Well I thy wisdom may adore,
  But never reach with earthy mind.

To shun thy notice, leave thine eye,
  O whither might I take my way?
    To starry sphere?
    Thy throne is there.
  To dead men's undelightsome stay?
There is thy walk, and there to lie
  Unknown, in vain I should assay.

Psalm 139: 'David, to cleanse his heart from all hypocrisy, showeth that there is nothing so hid which God seeth not, which he confirmeth by the creation of man. After declaring his zeal and fear of God, he protesteth to be enemy to all them that condemn God' (Geneva Bible).

4. *markest*: observe
6. *closet*: private space
12. *youngest*: *OED*'s first citation, signifying earliest, most youthful; perhaps also 'the latest'
13. *cast*: utter forth
21. *reach*: grasp, attain
26. *dead ... stay*: i.e. in hell
28. *assay*: attempt

O sun, whom light nor flight can match,
Suppose thy lightful flightful wings
Thou lend to me,
And I could flee
As far as thee the ev'ning brings;
Ev'n led to west he would me catch,
Nor should I lurk with western things.

Do thou thy best, O secret night,
In sable veil to cover me,
Thy sable veil
Shall vainly fail;
With day unmasked my night shall be,
For night is day, and darkness light,
O father of all lights, to thee.

Each inmost piece in me is thine:
While yet I in my mother dwelt,
All that me clad
From thee I had.
Thou in my frame hast strangely dealt:
Needs in my praise thy works must shine,
So inly them my thoughts have felt.

Thou, how my back was beam-wise laid,
And raft'ring of my ribs, dost know;
Know'st every point
Of bone and joint,
How to this whole these parts did grow,
In brave embroid'ry fair arrayed,
Though wrought in shop both dark and low.

Nay fashionless, ere form I took,
Thy all and more beholding eye

35. *western things*: i.e. point on the horizon where the sun sets. Compare Geneva Bible: 'in the uttermost parts of the sea'.

37, 38. *sable*: black

44–56. *While ...low*: Fisken notes that the Countess's image of a developing foetus unites physical and spiritual growth, and that while she borrowed the idea of embroidery wrought in a dark shop from commentaries by Calvin and de Bèze, she added the vivid physical images of assembled back and ribs (1985: 177–8)

47. *strangely*: wondrously

49. *inly*: inwardly

55. *arrayed*: clothed, dressed

My shapeless shape
Could not escape:
All these time framed successively
Ere one had being, in the book
Of thy foresight enrolled did lie.

My God, how I these studies prize,
That do thy hidden workings show!
Whose sum is such,
No sum so much,
Nay summed as sand they sumless grow.
I lie to sleep, from sleep I rise,
Yet still in thought with thee I go.

My God, if thou but one wouldst kill,
Then straight would leave my further chase
This cursed brood
Inured to blood,
Whose graceless taunts at thy disgrace
Have aimed oft, and hating still
Would with proud lies thy truth outface.

Hate not I them, who thee do hate?
Thine, Lord, I will the censure be.
Detest I not
The cankered knot
Whom I against thee banded see?
O Lord, thou know'st in highest rate
I hate them all as foes to me.

Search me, my God, and prove my heart,
Examine me, and try my thought;
And mark in me
If aught there be
That hath with cause their anger wrought.
If not (as not) my life's each part,
Lord safely guide from danger brought.

72. *straight*: immediately
79. *will*: desire
81. *cankered knot*: corrupted (literally ulcerated) company. A typically Elizabethan phrase, the kind with which the Countess stamped her versions of the psalms as contemporary poems.
82. *banded*: grouped together
85. *prove*: test
86. *try*: refine
90. *as not*: nothing (opposite of 'aught' = anything)

MARY (SIDNEY) HERBERT, COUNTESS OF PEMBROKE

A DIALOGUE BETWEEN TWO SHEPHERDS, THENOT AND PIERS, IN PRAISE OF ASTRAEA†*

(1602)

THENOT I sing divine Astraea's praise,
O Muses! Help my wits to raise
And heave my verses higher.
PIERS Thou needst the truth but plainly tell,
Which much I doubt thou canst not well,
Thou art so oft a liar.

THENOT If in my song no more I show
Than heav'n, and earth, and sea do know,
Then truly I have spoken.
PIERS Sufficeth not no more to name,
But being no less, the like, the same,
Else laws of truth be broken.

THENOT Then say, she is so good, so fair,
With all the earth she may compare,
Not Momus' self denying.
PIERS Compare may think where likeness holds,

* *Thenot*.. .*Piers*: stock names of shepherds in pastoral poetry. Thenot recalls the figure who appears in the February, April, and November eclogues of Spenser's *Shepherd's Calendar*, in which he offers wise advice to Colin. Here, however, his role is reversed, as he learns 'the insufficiency of human "conceit" and [poetic] language'. Piers, who appears in Spenser's May and October eclogues, was often the spokesman for Protestant plain speech and values, as here (Beilin 1987: 141; Sidney 1977: 209).

† *Astraea*: virgin goddess of justice who fled the earth at the end of the golden age (see also n. to l. 41), and allegorical figure representing Elizabeth I in poetry and civic pageantry

2. *Muses*: nine classical goddesses who inspire poets and musicians
8. *know*: acknowledge, manifest
10. *Sufficeth*: (It) suffices
11. *being* ... *same*: a cryptic line, perhaps meaning 'she being nothing less than the whole world, you cannot accurately represent her other than by depicting it in total'
15. *Momus*: god of satire; i.e. public detractors, cynics
16. *Compare* ... *holds*: comparisons may legitimately be used to represent literal or physical likenesses

Nought like to her the earth enfolds –
I looked to find you lying.

THENOT Astraea sees with wisdom's sight,
Astraea works by virtue's might,
And jointly both do stay in her.
PIERS Nay, take from them her hand, her mind;
The one is lame, the other blind.
Shall still your lying stain her?

THENOT Soon as Astraea shows her face,
Straight every ill avoids the place,
And every good aboundeth.
PIERS Nay, long before her face doth show,
The last doth come, the first doth go.
How loud this lie resoundeth!

THENOT Astraea is our chiefest joy,
Our chiefest guard against annoy,
Our chiefest wealth, our treasure.
PIERS Where chiefest are, three others be,
To us none else but only she.
When wilt thou speak in measure?

THENOT Astraea may be justly said
A field in flow'ry robe arrayed,
In season freshly springing.
PIERS That spring endures but shortest time,
This never leaves Astraea's clime.
Thou liest, instead of singing.

17. *Nought*: (But) nothing
22. *take ... them*: imagine them (wisdom and virtue) to be
23. *one ... other*: virtue ... wisdom
28. *face*: i.e. physical presence or representation
32. *annoy*: annoyance, trouble
36. *measure*: moderation; regular metre
41. *clime*: climate. At the close of the golden age perpetual spring ended and the cycle of the seasons began. Again Piers contrasts the inadequacy of any symbolic or material comparison – which is subject to change and thereby able to distort – to represent the immutable Astraea. Queen Elizabeth's personal motto was *semper eadem*, 'ever the same'.
42. *singing*: speaking in (regular) verse, making (the right kind of) poetry

THENOT As heavenly light that guides the day,
Right so doth thine each lovely ray
That from Astraea flyeth.
PIERS Nay, darkness oft that light enclouds,
Astraea's beams no darkness shrouds.
How loudly Thenot lieth!

THENOT Astraea rightly term I may
A manly palm, a maiden bay,
Her verdure never dying.
PIERS Palm oft is crooked, bay is low,
She still upright, still high doth grow.
Good Thenot leave thy lying.

THENOT Then Piers, of friendship, tell me why
My meaning true, my words should lie,
And strive in vain to raise her?
PIERS Words from conceit do only rise,
Above conceit her honour flies;
But silence, nought can praise her.

50. *A ... bay*: i.e. androgynous, and therefore superior to the limitations of a single sex; the palm was associated with feminine graces as well as military victory, and the bay (or laurel) tree with masculine virtue and poetic gifts
51. *verdure*: flourishing greenness
55. *of friendship*: for friendship's sake
56. *meaning*: idea or object signified
58. *conceit*: human mental (and poetic) invention (with a pejorative implication that such metaphorical means of representation are always fanciful and misleading)
59. *Above*: i.e. beyond
60. *But silence*: except for being itself, not materially or poetically expressed in any way

ANNE DOWRICHE (?–1638)

FROM *THE FRENCH HISTORY*

(1589)

Introduction

As its title-page announces, *The French History* is 'A lamentable discourse of three of the chief and most famous bloody broils [= tumults] that have happened in France for the Gospel of Jesus Christ' during the sixteenth-century wars of religion. The first of these 'broils' was an attack on a reformist prayer-meeting in 1557, the second the trial and execution of Annas Burgeus, a Protestant senator, and the third, presented here, the murder of the Huguenot leader Gaspard de Coligny. His death preceded the massacre of French Protestants on St Bartholomew's Day (24 August) 1572. Dowriche's *History* is therefore anything but a neutral account, but we should bear in mind that she was writing for an English audience who would have shared her point of view. After being horrified by the St Bartholomew's Day atrocities in which 30–50,000 people died across France, Protestant reformers in 1589 had reason to feel vindicated. The massacre's arch-villain, Henry, Duke of Guise, had been assassinated in the previous year, the same in which England had repulsed the Armada of the greatest Catholic power in Europe, Spain. With the then-Protestant Henry of Navarre positioned to inherit the French throne, God's justice on behalf of French and English reformers seemed to be ascendant.

Into this charged atmosphere Dowriche issued her verse-narratives based upon *The Three Parts of Commentaries containing the whole and perfect discourse of the Civil Wars of France* by Jean de Serres, translated into English by Thomas Tymme (1574). Book Ten of this volume, the section covering the events of St Bartholomew's Day, was not actually written by de Serres, however, but by François Hotman, whose *True and Plain Report of the Furious Outrapes of France* (1573) was also used by Christopher Marlowe for his *Massacre at Paris* (*c.* 1592). Like Marlowe, Dowriche telescopes Hotman's details to a single plot-line: the conspiracy to lure de Coligny and other Huguenot leaders into a false sense of security prior to their 'butcherly murder' in Paris, where they had gathered for the royal marriage of Henry of Navarre and Margaret de Valois which was intended to reconcile Protestant and Catholic factions. Dowriche produces a clear, vigorous story enlivened by impassioned speeches, in which her use of alternating verses of six and seven feet moves the reader along more quickly than the older chronicle-form of steady fourteeners.

The French History's narrator is an Englishman who in the opening scene encounters a 'godly French exile' while strolling in the woods. After explaining his distress, the latter agrees to recount his country's miseries, 'in verse', to his sympathetic listener. Dowriche's adoption of a male persona may be intended to veil her gender, just as the disclosure of her male source-writer in her Epistle to the Reader may serve to extenuate her act of independent creativity. Yet the degree to which these opening moves 'completely [disguise] the knowledge and ability of a woman to write so public a narrative poem' (Beilin 1987: 103) is uncertain. The encounter between English and French story-tellers is patently an artful contrivance, of a kind used without apology by many Elizabethan writers and entirely conformable to contemporary standards of composition. As such it may actually draw attention to Dowriche's skill in transforming her rather flat prose-source 'to the better liking' of her readers. Similarly, although in a Dedicatory Epistle she urges her brother to value the poem for its content rather than its style, forestalling possible objections to the latter by reminding him 'that it is a woman's doing' (A2^{r-v}), these self-disabling gestures are arguably swept aside, perhaps knowingly, by the poem's elaborate fictive reconstructions and conspicuous artistry, as seen in Part Three by the introduction of Satan as a character and by Catherine de Medici's theatrically resonant 'Machiavel' speech.

Though we possess few facts about the author's life, her work suggests an acquaintance with humanist models of historical writing. Structurally these consisted of narratives that focused on key episodes and prominent personalities brought to life by emotionally charged speeches and dialogue. The aim was to produce imaginatively engaging history out of which readers could identify precepts for moral conduct and political action. The episodic format of such histories relied for unity more on thematic than documentary patterning, and in *The French History* Dowriche selects events to create a dramatic narrative of martyrdom leading to divine vengeance. The concluding section of her volume consists of 'The Judgement of the Lord against this bloody and perjured King of France, Charles the 9th [1574]'. This event looks beyond the text to the Duke of Guise's death in the year preceding its publication in 1589.

Anne was the daughter of Sir Richard Edgecombe and Margaret Lutterall. She is described as 'under age' in her father's will of 1560, but by 1580 she married Hugh Dowriche, rector of Honiton, Devon from 1587. He wrote a religious pamphlet, *The Gaoler's Conversion*, in 1596, to which Anne contributed commendatory verses. In her own volume she writes a dedication and some acrostic verses to her brother Piers (or Peter), who was sheriff of Devon. She has been wrongly identified as the Anne who later married Richard Trefusis, but this was actually her niece. She died at Petherwyn, Cornwall in 1638.

Editions:
The French History (1589). STC 7159, reel 289. *The Paradise of Women*, ed. Betty Travitsky (Westport, Conn., 1981, brief excerpts).

ANNE DOWRICHE

FROM *THE FRENCH HISTORY*

(1589)

[PART] THREE

THE BLOODY MARRIAGE, OR BUTCHERLY MURDER, OF THE ADMIRAL* OF FRANCE AND DIVERS OTHER NOBLE AND EXCELLENT MEN, AT THE MARRIAGE OF MARGARET,† THE KING'S OWN SISTER, UNTO PRINCE HENRY,‡ SON TO THE QUEEN§ OF NAVARRE, COMMITTED THE 24 OF AUGUST¶ IN THE CITY OF PARIS, ANNO 1572.

Now have you heard before of faggot, fire, and sword
Enhanced by Satan for to quell God's truth and blessed word.
But now I must begin such treason to unfold
As former times for cruelty, and ages new and old,
Have never seen the like in Christendom, till now
When sacred faith by flattery, and oath of princely vow
By treason, did contrive to shed the guiltless blood
Of them which now by peace did seek to do their country good.
For when the Lord did send his truth into the land,
He raised up some noble men to take this cause in hand.
Among the which, as chief and sovereign of the field,
There was Prince Henry of Navarre, with such as would not yield

* *Admiral*: Gaspard de Coligny (1519–72), Colonel-General of the French Infantry, Admiral of France, and defender of religious toleration for Huguenots, of whom he was perhaps the most celebrated martyr

† *Margaret*: de Valois, daughter of Catherine de Medici (the 'Mother Queen' at l. 57 below) and Henry II (1519–59), brother of the reigning king, Charles IX (1550–74)

‡ *Henry*: later King of Navarre, and future King of France. He remained a Protestant until 1593 when he was offered the French throne on the condition that he convert. He decided 'Paris was worth a Mass'.

§ *Queen*: Jeanne (Joan) established Protestantism as the state religion of Navarre in 1570

¶ *24 of August*: the St Bartholomew's Day massacre of Huguenots, and climax of the political rivalry between the house of Guise and de Coligny. The latter's death actually occurred the day before, following the failed assassination attempt against him on the 22nd.

10. *cause*: i.e. the Protestant cause

Unto the Guisian race, the Prince of Condé next,
The Admiral and d'Andelot, with others that were vexed
By bloody Guise's band, who daily did invent
How to oppress the word of truth, which Christ had thither sent.
But whenas Satan saw by words and dealings plain
That many princes were in arms this truth for to maintain,
It galled him to the heart, that where he did devise
To choke the word, that even there the more it did arise.
He summons all his mates these matters to debate,
How they might choke this springing seed before it were too late.
Where all within a round they come without delay,
To whom this bloody captain then these words began to say:
'There is a subtle vein that feeds this cankered sore,
For now the deeper it is lanced it riseth still the more.
We see that fire and sword cannot at all prevail,
We see that all our bloody broils their courage cannot quail.
We see how noble men their forces daily bend
To counter-cross our planted plots, this cause for to defend.
Two civil wars are past, the third is now in hand;
We see how stoutly they are bent our forces to withstand.
Therefore we must devise to play some other part,
Or else in vain we take in hand these princes to subvert.
Now lend your listening ears and mark what I shall say,

13. *Guisian*: politically powerful Catholic family from Lorraine. Henry, 3rd Duke of Guise, became its head after the assassination of his father, François, in 1563. Henry suspected de Coligny's involvement (wrongly) and sought revenge, ultimately plotting his murder as well as the St Bartholomew's Day massacre. His uncle Charles was Cardinal of Rheims (here called Cardinal of Lorraine).
Prince of Condé: son of Louis de Condé, militant Calvinist and anti-Guisian who died in 1569

14. *d'Andelot*: François, brother of de Coligny

17ff. *Satan*: this fanciful counsel-speech creates a dramatic point of departure for events leading to de Coligny's death, which Dowriche streamlines from Hotman's more complex account into an unambiguous story of conspiracy and entrapment. Figuratively, Satan may represent Machiavelli, who was widely believed to have inspired the events leading to St Bartholomew's Massacre, and whose name and the devil's had become synonymous (*viz.* 'Old Nick') in the context of the decades-old legend that had grown up around Machiavelli's writings.

20. *word*: gospel

22. *springing*: sprouting

31. *Two . . . third*: first war of religion 1562, second 1567. The third war (1568–70) so ravaged the country that Charles IX was forced to seek peace with de Coligny and the Huguenots and to invite them to help oppose the Spanish in the Netherlands (see notes to ll. 61–3, 75–87 below).

A secret thing I have bethought which here I will bewray:
You must make show, as though you loved to live at ease;
As weary of these broils, you must entreat to have a peace.
The King as chiefest man this play must first begin,
By loving letters, words and cheer at first to bring them in.
And look what they mislike, the King must raze it out,
And yield to all things they request to put them out of doubt.
The King must show such face to them above the rest
As though he did unfeignedly of all men love them best.
The worst of all their band the King must entertain
With such goodwill that no mistrust in any may remain.
And he must make them know as though of late he felt
Some prick in conscience for the cause against the which he dealt,
And that he will forgive all quarrels that are past,
In hope that this their new goodwill with love might ever last;
And he must make complaint as though he did of late
Mislike the dealings of the Guise, and such as they do hate,
And then the Guises must awhile from court retire;
For thus you shall entrap them all, and have your full desire.
The King must yield to all that they request or crave,
And he must grant for to confirm the thing that they would have.
The Mother Queen in this must also play her part,
That no suspect of treason may remain within their heart.
And here you must give out as though you would employ
Their service in some foreign wars which doth your state annoy,

36. *bewray*: betray
38. *broils*: violent quarrels
40. *bring ... in*: entrap them
41. *look what*: if anything
51–8. 'and to take from [the Admiral] all occasion of distrust upon his adversaries, or of otherwise suspecting of the King's or Queen Mother's affection towards him, first, all the Guisians of a set purpose departed the court' (Hotman, *A True and Plain Report of the Furious Outrages of France,* 1573, in de Serres, *Three Parts of Commentaries* (1574), bk 10, B1[r])
57. *Mother Queen*: Catherine de Medici (1519–89), daughter of Laurence Duke of Urbino, wife of Henry II, and regent during her son Charles IX's minority. Despite being reviled by Protestant propagandists for her court intrigues and Catholic alliances, she promoted many of the edicts granting Huguenots greater rights. But like de Coligny himself she was often caught between extremists on both sides. Modern historians have shifted some of the blame for the St Bartholomew's Day massacre, traditionally ascribed to her and the Guisians, on to the fanaticism of the Parisian mobs (though see n. to l. 341 below).

As if you would not trust the weight of such affairs
To any man but them alone, whose faith and watchful cares
You long have tried; and so you may your plot prepare
By these and suchlike feigned things to trap them in your snare.
If this prevail not, then I stand in fearful doubt
What practice next to put in ure to have them rooted out.
Now therefore say your mind if thus it be not best
To cut them off, that so again we all may live in rest.'
  The council did agree this was the only way,
And every man did give his word this sentence to obey,
And that they would devise such things to put in ure
As best might fit this cursed plot and make the same most sure.
Which Satan hearing rose, and thanked them with his heart,
That they to him so willing were, and so they did depart.
  Then presently the King in post a message sent
Unto the Admiral, to whom he showed his good intent,
Which was that he was loath more civil wars to have,
And that he greatly did desire his subjects for to save.
'I will', said he, 'forget, yea pardon and release
All former griefs, so that you will now yield to have a peace,
Which might be now to me a cause of passing joy,
For that I mean in foreign wars your service to employ;
And first we do require that we may join our band,
Against the man that causeth all these troubles in our land.
Our armies being joined, we may the stronger go
Against the Duke of Alva, whom we know to be our foe.
Great matters move our mind against the King of Spain,
For he hath taken Florida and late our sister slain.'
  With lies of like device the godly to betray,

61–3. *As … tried*: Charles appointed de Coligny to conduct the French military campaign in support of the Protestant Prince of Orange against the Spanish, who were occupying the Netherlands

66, 71. *ure*: use

75–87. 'the King sent messengers to the Admiral to signify … that the armies of both parties joined together should go into the Low Countr[ies] against the Duke of Alva' (Hotman, A3v)

87. *King of Spain*: Philip II (1556–98)

88. *Florida*: '[Charles] signified further that he had great causes of quarrels against the King of Spain, and this principally: that he had invaded and held by force … an island of the new-found world called Florida, which had been taken by the French' (Hotman, A3v)

late … slain: 'one Albeny late returned out of Spain had informed the King … that King Philip a few months before had poisoned his wife, the French King's sister (Hotman, A4r)

Requesting him most earnestly that he would come away,
And that he should obtain what safety he would crave,
Yea, for his surety there, that he his faith and oath should have.
The message being done, the Admiral as wise,
Within himself did half suspect the plot of this device.
And though that many things did some suspicion bring,
Yet all things else he doubted more than falsehood in the King.
He thought the promise sure, and firmly did believe
No treason could be meant whereas the King his word did give.
The Admiral, as one that was devoid of fear
And willing for to hear of peace, unto the King gave ear.
So now the civil broils, which many did intend,
By this device were pacified and brought unto an end.
It cannot be expressed what shows of friendly mind
Both in the King and courtiers all the Admiral doth find.
His friends likewise, which had the gospel long professed,
As County Rochefoucault and eke Theligny with the rest,
Like grace and favour found; which made them so rejoice,
That to consent unto the King they all did give their voice.
And if in former wars the Admiral had lost
Either castles, houses, towns or farms whatever it should cost,
The King commanded straight for to restore them all,
And all things else which he of right of any man could call.
And those whom he perceived the Admiral to love,
He blinded them with great rewards, suspicion to remove.
Besides, he did command out of his purse to give
To him an hundred thousand pounds his losses to relieve.
And when as it did chance his brother for to die,
The Cardinal Chatillon, the King then presently
The fruits and profits all of livings all one year
Unto the Admiral he gave his charges to forwear.
Yet not content with this, one thing above the rest

90. *away*: together (with him)

92. *surety*: guarantee

93. *wise*: knowing

94–5. 'The Admiral hearing these things was marvellously troubled; for albeit he doubted not of the King's fidelity, yet therewithal many things fell into his mind to be considered: as the power of the Cardinal and the rest of the Guisians, who were well known to have been at all times most affectionate to the King of Spain ... ' (Hotman, A3^{v})

103–30. this passage follows Hotman (B2^{r-v}) closely

106. *County ... Theligny*: Count Theligny, de Coligny's son-in-law

112. *call*: claim

119. *livings*: ecclesiastical properties or benefices

120. *forwear*: spend

The King most friendly did, the which the godly liked best:
He wrote to Philibert the Duke of Savoie then,
That he should cease for to molest or grieve those godly men,
The which in former wars the gospel did defend,
And that to such he should leave off his rigour to extend.
And that the Admiral might no misliking find,
He did by gentle means appease the Duke of Guise's mind;
He tried to make them friends, and brought the same to pass,
Although it on the Guise's part a feigned friendship was.
The Cardinal likewise, that was their greatest foe,
To choose a pope made them believe to Rome that he would go.
So all things being done, t'abandon all suspect,
What they misliked the King would seem the same for to reject.
So that about the King they only credit win
Which did defend the gospel, and which lately were come in.
But nothing did prevail to put them out of doubt
So much as one thing, which as now the King did go about,
Which was, that he did wish his sister for to match
Unto Prince Henry of Navarre, by this in hope to catch
Them all within his snare; for this he did conclude
Not for good will, but mere deceit the godly to delude.
Which match the king would have consummate out of hand,
'That so it might remain', said he, 'a sure and perfect band
Of that unfeigned love and inward hearty care,
Which we to those that love the truth and gospel now do bear.'
Which made them all rejoice and quite cast off their fear,
When in the King they did behold such love and friendly cheer.
Yet some did here allege that conscience did restrain
The Prince to match with her, which yet did seem for to remain
In love with popish rites; to which the King replied
That he to ease those scruples all such order would provide
Which they should not mislike; for he would there dispense
With all such rites and orders as might breed the least offence.

126. *rigour*: harsh treatment

133. *suspect*: suspicion

134. *they*: i.e. the Admiral's party

139–41. *sister ... snare*: 'But there was none greater and more assured token of public peace and quietness than this: that the King purposed to give his sister Margaret in marriage to the Prince Henry' (Hotman, B2^{v})

141–6. *for ... bear*: 'Which marriage the King declared ... should be the most strait bond of civil concord and the most assured testimony of his good will to those of the [Protestant] religion' (Hotman, B3^{r})

149–55. this follows Hotman (B3^{r}) closely

150. *Prince ... her, which*: Henry ... Margaret, who

152. *order*: of ceremonies

Which courtiers all mislike and openly repined,
Much doubting lest unto the truth the King had been inclined.
The Admiral again was much confirmed besides
By other signs, not doubting now their falsehoods and their slides.
The godly did rejoice to see the King so bent,
Not thinking of the treachery and treason that they meant.
  So, matters being passed and parties all agreed,
In Paris town to have them joined by both it was decreed.
The Queen of Navarre now (a rare and virtuous dame)
With others to the Prince's court in full assurance came;
Where having stayed awhile, she took her leave to ride
To Paris for this solemn fast the better to provide.
The King, to like effect, by message did request
The Admiral that he would go to Paris there to rest,
And see that nothing want for that appointed day,
And that himself would after come and make no long delay.
And that he might not fear the malice and the rage
That Paris men did bear to him, he said he would assuage
The same himself; and so he presently did write
To Marcel, Provost of the town (perceiving well their spite)
That he should entertain and use in friendly wise
The Admiral and all his train, that nothing might arise
Which might offend his mind or burst to any flame;
For if there did, he swore he would most fiercely plague the same.
The King and Queen, also unto the like effect,
Unto the Duke of Anjou did their letters now direct,
So that the Admiral, not doubting any foe,
Resolved himself and did provide to Paris for to go.
Where being come, he found the King and all the rest
With friendly welcomes, so as more he could not well request
But whilst that every man was busy to provide
Within the court, most suddenly the Queen of Navarre died.

156. *doubting*: fearing
158. *slides*: slippery dealings
164. *Prince's*: Henry's
171–3. *And ... himself*: '[The King assured] him that there was now no cause for him to fear the threatenings and mad outrages of the Parisians. For in as much as the same town is above all other given to superstitions, and is with seditious preachings of monks and friars daily enflamed to cruelty, it is hard to express how bitterly they hated the Admiral and the professors of that religion' (Hotman, B3^{v})
179. *Queen*: i.e. Catherine de Medici
180. *Duke of Anjou*: brother of Charles IX and later King Henry III
185. *provide*: for the wedding
186–8. 'Joan Queen of Navarre ... died in the court at Paris of a sudden sickness, being about the age of forty and three years, where as the suspicion was great that she died

Which afterward was known (as some have plainly said)
That by a pair of gloves perfumed this treason was conveyed.
Which lewd and sinful deed was now no sooner done,
But that the kingdom of Navarre descended to her son.
Here many did rejoice in hope of perfect rest,
Yet this unequal bloody match the Guises did detest.
  That dismal day is come, the marriage must begin,
Where were assembled solemnly the chief of every kin.
And for because the Mass their minds might grieve no more,
The marriage was solemnised before the great church door
Of Paris, with such words as both were well content.
Which done, into the church the bride in solemn manner went
To hear a Popish Mass, both she and all her train;
Her husband walked without the door till she returned again.
Then home at last they go with mirth and passing joy;
They little thought this pleasant day would end with such annoy.
And now begins the plays, the dancings and the sport,
Which were performed by lusty youths that thither did resort.
The King and nobles all in pleasures are so mad,
That for to talk of great affairs no leisure could be had.
And now the Admiral from court had gone his way,
Had not some causes of the church enforced him to stay.
  Now from the wedding night five days are come and past,
Whenas the King and senate were contented at the last
In council for to sit such matters to decide,
As best might fit their feigned wars in Flanders to provide.

of poison, and her body being for that cause opened by the physicians, there were no tokens of poison espied. But shortly after, by the detection of one A. P., it hath been found that she was poisoned with a venomed smell of a pair of perfumed gloves, dressed by one Renat the King's apothecary, an Italian ... which could not be espied by the physicians which did not open the head nor looked into the brain' (Hotman, C1[r]). Modern historians say Joan died of consumption.

189. *lewd*: wicked

191. *rest*: peace

194. *kin*: family

195. *for because*: in order that

200. *without*: outside

201. *passing*: extreme

204. *lusty*: vigorous

205–6. 'But so great was the preparation of plays, so great was the magnificence of banquets and shows, and the King so earnestly bent to those matters, that he had no leisure not only for weighty affairs, but also not so much as to take his natural sleep' (Hotman, C1[v])

208. *causes ... church*: petitions and complaints against the mistreatment of Huguenots

210. *Whenas*: when

Which ended, near about the middle of the day
As every man unto his house did take his ready way,
The Admiral himself, with other nobles mo
Along the streets (not doubting hurt) in pleasant talk to go,
A harquebus was shot from other side the street,
Which charged was with bullets two the Admiral to greet.
Which cursed blow did wound and strike this noble man,
That thorough both his valiant arms the leaden pellets ran.
Which done, although the wound did touch him somewhat near,
Yet nothing daunted with the stroke, he said with wonted cheer,
'From yonder house it came, go look who is within,
What vile unworthy treachery is this they do begin?'
And therewithal he sent in haste unto the King
Such as might show unto his grace this bad and shameful thing.
The message being done (the King as then did play
At tennis with the Duke of Guise), he fiercely threw away
His racket in a rage, as though it grieved his heart
That thus the Admiral was hurt, and straight he did depart
Unto his castle, where a while he did remain
Close with his brother of Navarre till he might hear again
More certain news; but now the matter was too plain
That this assault was surely made by one of Guise's train.
Now whilst these grievous wounds the surgeons had in cure,
He sent Theligny to the King (because he was not sure
Whe'r he should live or die) for to desire his grace
That he would now vouchsafe to come unto that simple place
Where he did lie, for that he had a secret thing
To tell him which did much concern the safety of the King.
Which was no sooner said, the King was well content,
And with the man the message came, without delay he went.
They went likewise, that sought the Admiral to kill,
The Mother Queen with all her mates, no doubt for great good will.
Which all no sooner did within the door appear,
But that the King saluted him with sweet and friendly cheer:

215. *mo*: more
217. *harquebus*: large early form of musket
220. *thorough*: through
221. *near*: mortally
232. *brother*: brother-in-law (Henry of Navarre)
236. *He*: the Admiral
237. *Whe'r*: whether
238. *vouchsafe*: condescend
239, 266. *secret*: private
246. *saluted*: greeted

'Alas, my dearest friend, how cam'st thou to this place,
Where wounded now I see thee lie, me thinks in heavy case?
What arrant villain wrought this lewd and sinful act?
Would God I knew the wicked wretch that did commit the fact.
For though, my Admiral, the hurt be done to thee,
Yet the dishonour of the fact and shame redounds to me.
Both which I will revenge, by death of God I swear,
As like in France was never seen, to make such wretches fear.'
Such speeches had the King, and questions many more
Concerning judges, health and grief, and how he felt his sore.
To which the Admiral with mild and quiet mind
Such answer gave as moved them much such patience for to find
In him that had received such cause of deadly ire;
Who did request but only that the King would straight enquire
Upon the fact, 'which was I surely know', said he,
'Procured by the Duke of Guise, for great goodwill to me.
Which deed the Lord revenge as he shall think it best;
For if I die, I hope by faith with Christ to be in rest.'
The rest he did desire a while to stand away,
For that he had some secret thing unto the King to say.
Which done, he thus began: 'O King, this life to save
Is not the thing, I thank the Lord, that I do greatly crave.
For this I know is true, we all must pay a death
To God our maker, which hath lent this use of lively breath.
But to your majesty the great goodwill I bear
Is it which now, above the rest, doth most increase my care.
To see you now beset with such as wish no good
Unto your health, your crown and life, and such as seek the blood

248. *heavy case*: grave condition

250, 252, 261. *fact*: deed

256. *he*: the Admiral

265. *he ... away*: 'Then the King's brethren and their mother withdrawing themselves a while ... ' (Hotman, C3v)

269–70. *we ... maker*: proverbial (Tilley G237)

273ff. *To see ...*: Dowriche appeals to the sympathies of her English readers by focusing on a foreign power's threat to national sovereignty – a timely theme in the year after the Armada. She has the Admiral downplay religious strife as the main cause of the preceding civil wars, and she substitutes an earlier more provocative remark by Hotman for the vague warnings he makes at this point: 'And such a multitude is there begun to be of Italians commonly throughout all France, specially in the court, since the administration of the realm was committed to the Queen Mother, that many do commonly call it France-Italian, and some term it a colony, and some a common sink, of Italy' (C2r). This shift of emphasis on to Italian political hegemony sets the scene for the Queen Mother's 'Machiavel' speech (below 341ff.).

Of you and of your friends to spill your noble race,
That so they may in future time your princely stock deface,
And so at length engraft a strange Italian weed,
Which may in France most surely choke the prince's royal seed –
This is the only mark to which they do aspire;
This is the only wood, O King, that doth maintain the fire
Of these your civil wars, although they do pretend
Religion and some other thing; this is the chiefest end
Of all their drift. Therefore, O King, beware thy time,
Mark this eclipse, whilst yet ye see the moon is in her prime.
I say the less because I know your grace is wise;
You shall in time most plainly see this plot of their device.
Your wisdom doth perceive, I hope, whom I do mean,
For of the same, with grief before, I heard you oft complain.
For though that I do lie here wounded as you see,
The chiefest treason they intend is not alone to me
But to your noble grace, whose death they daily crave,
Whose life by treason, long ere this and now, desire to have.
I know when God shall take this frail and wretched life,
Some will not stick to say that I was cause of all the strife.
But God that is above and you my witness be,
How dear the safeguard of my prince, and peace, hath been to me.
God grant you see in time your friends from fleering foe,
That still in safety you may reign devoid of grief and woe.
Now I can say no more, but God preserve your grace,
And shield you from your feigned friends which bear a double face.
And this amidst your mirth I pray remember still,
That they that seek to have my life, do bear you no goodwill.'
Which said, the King did give such speech as he thought best;
And then in loud and solemn words in hearing of the rest
He did with friendly cheer request the Admiral
Unto his court for to remove, whatever should befall.
And others spake likewise unto the same intent;
His simple meaning could not see the treason that was meant.
But yet upon advice his friends did think it best,
Not knowing what may there betide, the King he should request
That he would them assign some of his grace's guard
Before his gates both night and day to keep their watch and ward.

275. *spill*: destroy
279. *mark*: goal
294. *stick*: scruple
297. *fleering*: contemptuous
308. *His ... meaning*: the Admiral's trusting nature
312, 322. *ward*: guard

The motion being made, the King was well content,
And said to this their good device he gladly gave consent,
And that he would provide to have it surely known
That of his life he made account no less than of his own,
And that he would preserve with care more tenderly
The Admiral than he would keep the apple of his eye,
For that he did admire the valour of his mind,
Who little thought in mortal man such courage for to find.
The Duke of Anjou then commanded out of hand
One Cossin, captain of the guard, to ward with prince's band
The gates and streets wherein the Admiral did lie;
Which was no sooner said but was performed presently.
This Cossin that was set with watch to ward the gate
Was one that did the Admiral in heart most deadly hate.
And farther, for to put the matter out of doubt,
They did consent that he should have his trusty friends about
The place where he did lie, which came of no goodwill
But hoping rather all by this the easier for to kill.
And this among the rest a bloody practice was,
Which cloaked guile to Satan's art too soon was brought to pass.
  But here the prologue ends, and here begins the play,
For bloody minds resolved quite to use no more delay.
The Mother Queen appears now first upon the stage,
Where like a devilish sorceress with words demure and sage,
The King she calls aside with other trusty mates
Into a close and secret place, with whom she now debates
The great desire she had to quit them all from care,
In planting long a bloody plot, which now she must declare:
  'O happy light', quoth she, 'O thrice most happy day,

318. *apple ... eye*: Dowriche replaces Hotman's banal 'ball of his eye' with a better known phrase from Deuteronomy 32.10.

321. *out of hand*: without premeditation

324. *presently*: right away

328–9. *he ... he*: Cossin ... de Coligny

336. *demure*: grave, serious

339. *quit*: rid

341ff. 'In this memorable fictional appearance, Catherine de Medici may be the first female character created by a woman writer of this period' (Beilin 1987: 106). As Dowriche's metaphor of prologue and play suggests, her speech is a mine of Machiavellian commonplaces reminiscent of Elizabethan stage villains such as Richard of Gloucester in *3 Henry VI* and *Richard III*. In Marlowe's *Jew of Malta* (*c.* 1592), 'Machiavel' himself appears as a Prologue to announce that his spirit has transmigrated from the recently dead Duke of Guise to the play's villain, Barabbas. Dowriche anticipates Shakespeare and Marlowe, however, and alludes by marginal notes in the original edition to her

Which thus hath thrust into our hands our long-desired prey.
We have them all in hold, we have the chiefest fast;
And those for whom we waited long we have them all at last.
Why should we longer stay? what can we farther crave?
What, are not all things come to pass which we do long to have?
Doth not our mightiest foe lie wounded in his bed,
Not able now to help himself, which others long hath led?
The captains captive are, the King of Navarre sure;
The Prince of Condé with the rest, that mischief did procure,
Are close within our walls, we have them in a trap;
Good fortune, lo, hath brought them all and laid them in our lap.
By force or flight to save their lives it is too late,
If we (to cut off future fear and cause of all debate)
Do take the proffered time, which time is only now;
And wisdom matched with policy our dealings doth allow.
We need not fear the spot of any cruel fame,
So long as we may feel some ease or profit by the same.
For wisdom doth allow the prince to play the fox,

source: Innocent Gentillet's *Discours ... Contre Nicholas Machiavel, Florentin* (1576) transl. into English in 1577 (see Martin 1997). See n. to l. 355. In Hotman's account, Catherine de Medici states the pros and cons of the situation more dispassionately. Modern historians observe that she agreed to the murder of de Coligny when the Guises' first assassination attempt failed and an investigation promised by the King (the vague 'judges' at l. 256) threatened to reveal her complicity. She saved herself by persuading Charles to order the Huguenot leaders' deaths.

344. *those*: Henry of Navarre's marriage to Margaret de Valois brought a large number of Protestant leaders to Paris, partly for the purpose of petitioning the King (see above l. 208).

350. *mischief*: i.e. policy of seeming reconciliation

355. *Do ... now*: 'The Queen Mother was a good scholar of that devil of Florence, Machiavel, of whom she learned many bad lessons, as this: 1. That a prince must not care to be accounted cruel, so that any profit come by it' (original marginal note keyed to maxim 8 in Gentillet's *Contre-Machiavel*, transl. 1577 (printed 1602) 2K2[v])

356. *policy*: an Elizabethan 'buzz-word' associated with the new *realpolitik* ascribed to Machiavelli

357. *cruel fame*: future infamy

359–60. *For ... ox*: alluding to one of the most famous passages in Machiavelli's *The Prince*: 'So, as a prince is forced to know how to act like a beast, he should learn from the fox and the lion; because the lion is defenceless against traps and a fox is defenceless against wolves. Therefore one must be a fox in order to recognize traps, and a lion to frighten off wolves. Those who simply act like lions are stupid. So it follows that a prudent ruler cannot, and should not, honour his word when it places him at a disadvantage' (trans. George Bull (Harmondsworth, 1961), pp. 99–100).

And lion-like to rage, but hates the plainness of an ox.
What though ye do forswear? what though ye break your faith?
What though ye promise life and yet repay it with their death?
Is this so great a fault? Nay, nay, no fault at all;
For this we learn we ought to do, if such occasions fall:
Our masters do persuade a king to cog and lie
And never keep his faith, whereas his danger grows thereby.
Cut off, therefore, the head of this infectious sore,
So may you well assure yourselves this bile will rise no more.
The captains being slain, the soldiers will be faint;
So shall we quickly on the rest perform our whole intent.
Pluck up, therefore, your spirits, and play your manly parts,
Let neither fear nor faith prevail to daunt your warlike hearts.
What shame is this that I, a woman by my kind,
Need thus to speak or pass you men in valour of the mind?
For here I do protest, if I had been a man,
I had myself before this time this murder long began.
Why do you doubting stand, and wherefore do you stay?
If that you love your peace or life, procure no more delay.
We have them in our hands within our castle gates,
Within the walls of Paris town the masters and their mates.
This is the only time this matter to dispatch;
But being fled, these birds are not so easy for to catch.
The town of Paris will most gladly give consent,
And three score thousand fighting men provide for this intent.
So shall we quickly see the end of all our strife,
And in a moment shall dispatch these rebels of their life.
But if we stand in fear and let them 'scape our hand,
They will procure in time to come great trouble in our land;
For if the Admiral his strength receive again,
Can any doubt but that he will be mindful of his pain?
It is a simple thing for princes to believe
That new goodwill an ancient hate from galled hearts can drive.
Therefore if we permit these rebels to retire,

364. *fall*: present themselves
365. *masters*: i.e. political mentors such as Machiavelli
cog: cheat
366. *whereas*: whenever (it happens)
371. *spirits*: one syllable: sp'rits
372. *faith*: conscience
373. *kind*: nature
374. *pass*: surpass
391. *simple*: naïve, foolish
392. *galled*: rancorous

We soon shall see by wars again our country set on fire.
This is a woman's mind, and thus I think it best;
Now let us likewise hear, I pray, the sentence of the rest.'
  This counsel of them all was liked passing well,
And in respect of present state, all others did excel.
Some doubting, mused long which were the better way,
The King of Navarre and the Prince of Condé for to slay,
Or else to save their lives in hope they would recant,
Because the proof of perfect years they both as yet did want.
But here they did prevail (as God no doubt would have)
Who thought it best in this assault these princely youths to save,
Because they were in hope that when those imps should see
Their mates tormented thus, they would most willingly agree
To bow where they would bind, to go where they would call,
And to forswear their former faith would make no doubt at all.
But all the rest remain condemned for to die,
Which cruel verdict must be put in practice presently,
The night that should ensue then next without delay,
Beginning ere the same were spent, long time before the day.
The Duke of Guise was thought the fittest of the train
To take in hand this bloody plot to have the godly slain.
Concluding thus, they go each one unto his place,
The godly doubting nothing less than this so heavy case.

  Here is the first part played, and here I do lament
My slender skill wants fitted phrase the sequel to depaint.
The Duke in office put, begins for to prepare,
So that in troops the armed men ran bustling here and there
With noise and threat'ning words, as though some tumult were
Preparing now in every street, which made the wisest fear
What would ensue. At length the Admiral did hear
This tumult, and not knowing how the truth for to enquire,

397. *passing*: extremely
398. *state*: of affairs
399. *doubting*: undecided
402. *proof*: experience, achievement
405. *imps*: children
407. *bow ... bind*: submit obediently instead of continuing to resist
   go ... call: obey ... command
410. *presently*: immediately
412. *ere*: before
417–18. a 'bridging' passage typical of sixteenth-century historical writing; its expression of modesty is not gender-specific
418. *fitted ... depaint*: suitable, furnished ... depict

He sent unto the King to know the full intent,
Why in the night in riot-wise these armed people went
Thus raging in the streets, and whe'r it were his will?
If so he would not fear, but rest in hope of safety still.
  The King returned word, and willed him not to fear:
For this was done by his advice, yet not in everywhere,
But in some certain ways these armed men were set,
The foolish rage of lewd attempts by this in hope to let.
  O lewd and filthy lie! unseemly for a King;
What Turk or devil could devise a more unworthy thing?
For when the Duke of Guise had all in order set,
And nothing rested which might seem their purpose for to let,
He Marcel calls in haste, and wills him have a care
That all the masters of the streets ere midnight did repair
Unto the council hall, where they should hear at large
Great matters from the King himself of strange and special charge
The message being done, they all without delay
Assembled were, to know the thing the Guises had to say.
Where Provost Carron rose with stomach stout and bold,
And, guarded with a Guisian troop, this bloody message told:
  'My friends', quoth he, 'give ear and mark what I shall say:
The King's intent is presently this night without delay
Those rebels to destroy, which now these latter years
Bore arms against his grace; which though they be his peers,
Yet will he quite pull up and root the lawless race
Of them that long have sought by force his dealings to disgrace.
And what a happy time, I pray, my mates, is this;
When fast within our city walls the captain closed is
That fiercely brewed the broil of this our doubtful strife,
And many times hath put us all in danger of our life.
Their trust, by treason trained, is cause of this deceit;
O happy she that wrought the mould of this so cunning feat.
Their friends will prove their foes, sweet pleasures will have pain,
And being here they are not like to see their homes again.
Their chambers prisons are, their beds shall be their grave;
And ere the day appear we must a glorious conquest have.

430. *his*: the King's
432, 436. *let*: hinder
436. *rested*: remained
438. *ere*: by
443. *Carron*: the new 'Provost of the Merchants (which is the highest dignity in Paris)' (Hotman, B3[v])
stomach: proud arrogance
455. *trained* ... *cause of*: lured ... reason for

Be strong therefore, my friends, make sharp the fatal knife;
For of these rebels ere the day not one shall 'scape with life.
Their leader and their guide lies wounded in his bed,
And therefore, as the chiefest foe, we'll first have off his head.
And when we have dispatched the rebels we have here,
We'll likewise ransack all the land of like that shall appear.
This is the King's intent, this is his grace's mind,
To do this feat let him in us a willing courage find;
And for a token when this murder shall begin,
The warlike trumpet shall not sound, nor banner shall be seen,
But tocsin shall be heard this bloody news to bring;
For then begin, whenas you hear this palace bell to ring:
The badge which you shall bear by which you shall be known,
Shall be a linen cloth of white made fast about the brawn
Of left side arm, and eke a cross upon your cap
Of white likewise; and these keep fast whatever chance may hap.
And this is all, my friends, that I have now to say,
Come follow me and let's begin and use no more delay.'
  This while the Duke of Guise did show his whole intent
Unto the captains of the guard, and bade them give consent
With courage to perform so great and famous act;
Which service as the case did stand, they might not long protract.
Now shortly after this the Duke with many more,
Accompanied with the Chevalier and armed men great store,
Came posting to the gate which Cossin took to keep;
Woe worth the time when they did trust the wolf to guard the sheep!
The Admiral knew well the tumult of this rout,
Yet this nor anything could make his valiant heart to doubt;
For though he had but few, scarce ten within the place,
Yet nothing could at all prevail to make him doubt his case.
  For oft he would repeat the King's assured love
Approved by so many signs, as you have heard above:
'What though the commons rise? what though the tumult rage?
When they shall see the prince's guard, their malice will assuage.
I know the King will not by treason false his faith,
Though for the same there might ensue the hazard of his death.
The oath that he hath sworn so oft to keep the peace,
No Christian conscience can assent at all for to release.
His mother gave her faith, his brothers sware likewise,

475. *eke*: also
484. *Chevalier*: 'the bastard son of King Henry [II]'
485. *posting*: speedily
486. *trust … sheep*: proverbial (Tilley W602)
494. *prince's*: King's

The public records of the land do witness this device.
What band may surer be? what more may you desire?
What can we farther wish? and yet if more you do require,
The Queen of England is a witness of the same,
The Prince of Orange and the states that from the Germans came;
This royal match likewise my heart doth well assure
That such a seal of perfect love forever will endure;
Which marriage lately made with counsel grave and good,
The King will not permit to be so soon defiled with blood.
For what would strangers say if such things should befall?
But such things Lord be far from us, and Lord preserve us all!
What would the future age of imps as yet unborn,
What would all nations think if we by trust should be forlorn?
The stout and constant mind, and honour of the King,
Will never give consent I know to do so lewd a thing.'
  Thus whilst among the rest the case he did debate,
His trusty keeper Cossin came and knocked at his gate.
Who was no sooner come within the outward door,
But that there came in after him of armed men great store.
Then after went the lords, the nobles, and the rest
For to dispatch this noble man, whom they did most detest.
And those whom Cossin found within to lie or stand,
He slew them with a partisan which he had in his hand.
Which woeful news whenas the Admiral perceived,
'Woe worth the time', quoth he, 'that I by trust have been deceived.
Well, now the time is come, I may no longer doubt;
Come lend your help my friends, I pray, from bed to lift me out.
To Christ my only hope my soul I do betake,
And in this place from off my couch this life I will forsake.'
Then standing on his feet, his nightgown on his back,
'Shift for yourselves my friends', quoth he, 'that you go not to wrack,
And have no care for me; for I am well content
This life to yield unto the Lord, which he to me hath lent. . . .
Now let these traitors come, the fear of death is past;
And fainting flesh that did rebel hath yielded at the last.
Now doth my soul rejoice, my heart most gladly say;

501. *band*: or bond

502–3. *and ... same*: with de Coligny acting as ambassador, France had entered into a league with England and the Prince of Orange against Spain. Similar treaties had been made with Saxony and Brandenburg; 'And of all those leagues, the first and principal condition was that the liberty of religion should continue' (Hotman, B1^{v}).

509. *strangers*: foreigners

522. *partisan*: spear with pointed, double-edged blade

530. *wrack*: destruction

Thou son of God, my saviour come, my Christ now come thy way!
For here again to thee my soul I do commend,
And to thy poor afflicted church, O Lord, thy mercy send.
So shall they be at rest, so shall they praise thy name;
Let not these tyrants longer, Lord, thy servants put to shame.
Lest they do proudly brag, and say within their heart,
Where is the God whom they do serve, that now should take their part.
Come quickly Lord, therefore, and make no more delay
To end these fierce and bloody broils; Amen, Amen, I say.'
  By this came up the stairs, ere ended were his words,
One Benvise and two other mates with targets and with swords.
The chamber broken up, this Benvise swearing came
With sword drawn to the Admiral and asking for his name:
'Art thou the Admiral?' The man not much appalled,
With quiet mind gave answer thus 'indeed so am I called'.
Then seeing Benvise bend his naked sword to slay,
'My friend', quoth he, 'that bloody blade I pray thee for to stay,
And have respect unto my age and weak estate,
To which by treason wrought by trust I have been drawn of late.'
But beastly Benvise would to this no answer give,
But swearing, to this noble man his pointed sword let drive
And thrust him to the heart; but yet not fully dead,
With force he laid a mighty blow and strake him on the head.
With that came Attin in with pistol in his hand
And shot him in the wounded breast, yet did he stoutly stand;
Till Benvise came again with third repeated wound
And slashed him on the thigh; which done, he fell unto the ground
Where he gave up the ghost. The bloody Guise that stayed
This while within the lower court, with lifted voice now said,
'Ho Benvise, hast thou done?' Who straightway did reply,
'Yea sir, this happy deed is done, and that most perfectly.'
Then said the Duke of Guise, 'Come throw him down to me,
That whe'r it be the same or not, we here may quickly see;
For now our Chevalier will think it but a lie,
Except at window throwen out he see him with his eye.'
Then Benvise with his mates to put them out of doubt,
Took up this bloody corpse and so from window cast him out.

541–2. *Lest ... part*: paraphrasing Psalm 79.10: 'Wherefore should the heathen say, where is their God?'

546. *Benvise*: 'a German, brought up in the house of the Duke of Guise' (Hotman D2[r])
targets: type of small shield

553. *estate*: condition

559. *Attin*: 'a Picard, a retainer and familiar of the Duke d'Aumale [= François, former Duke of Guise]' (Hotman, D2[r])

Where from his wounded head sprang out so fresh a flood,
That vizard-like his face was all imbrued with gory blood,
Whereby they could not well at first discern his face
Till that the Duke of Guise himself, first kneeling in the place,
Had with his napkin wiped the clotted blood away,
And searching viewed every part; he rose without delay,
And crying to his crew devoid of fear and shame,
'It's he, my friends, I know him well; trust me it is the same.'
The Duke descending then from out the stately gates,
With bloody heart and cursed mouth he cried unto his mates:
'O happy luck that we so good beginnings have,
Lo, fortune frames her willing hand to give that we do crave.
And sith it pleased the fates at first such hap to send,
It gives me cause of future hope to see some happy end.
Come on my valiant hearts, so place your warlike bands,
That marching forward to the rest, not one may 'scape our hands.
This is the King's decree, this hath he given out;
We do no more than he commands, to put you out of doubt;
Let pity take no place till rebels all be rid,
Thus saith the King; fear not therefore to do what he doth bid.
Let nothing now prevail to daunt your hardy mind;
No, though with tears they pity crave, let them no mercy find.
Have no remorse unto the young ne yet the old;
Without regard to anyone, to kill them all be bold.
Now sanctify your swords, and bathe them in the blood
Of these religious rebels, which do mean the King no good.
So shall we quickly find a path to perfect peace,
So shall we see assured means at length to live at ease;
For if we can recount the troubles that are past,
Then happy time wherein we may dispatch them all at last.'
Which said, he bade in haste the tocsin for to ring,
Which sounding bell appointed was the fatal news to bring
Whenas this raging rout, this murder, should begin;
Which they performed as though they had no men but monsters been,
And therewithal devise a larum for to raise,
Pretending with some solemn lie the people for to please.
So now the trumpets sound this lie and shameful thing:
That certain traitors were in arms about to kill the King.

574. *vizard-like ... blood*: bloodied as if wearing a visor. imbrued = stained, dyed
577. *napkin*: handkerchief
595. *ne*: nor
607. *larum*: call to arms
610. italicised in the original edition

Here one among the rest from Rome that lately came
(Desirous by some valiant act perhaps to get a name)
Cut off the bleeding head imbrued with reeking blood
Of that most worthy Admiral, in hope to do some good,
And sent it straight to Rome as Lorraine had required,
A present welcome to the Pope, which he had long desired.
His hands cut off by some, by some his secret parts,
Declares what hate to shining light lies hid in blinded hearts.
His hacked and mangled corpse by space of certain days
Was dragged by rascals all along the streets and filthy ways.
At length this rustic rage, as fury thought it meet,
At common gallows of the town did hang him by the feet.
Thus came this noble man to this unworthy death,
Thus do the Papists learn to break the vow of plighted faith.

The Admiral being slain, they likewise murdered most cruelly not only all such friends, physicians, preachers, and all other that were found hidden in the Admiral's lodging, but also as many as were suspected to be of that religion within the town or anywhere else, were lamentably put to the sword....

611–16. 'Then a certain Italian of [the Duke of] Gonzague's band cut off the Admiral's head and sent it preserved with spices to Rome to the Pope and the Cardinal of Lorraine' ($D2^v$)

621. *rustic*: rough, boorish

AEMILIA LANYER (1569–1645)

FROM *SALVE DEUS REX JUDAEORUM*

(1611)

Introduction

Aemilia Lanyer's title seems at first to advertise her work as conventional both in genre (a religious meditation) and in subject (a passion narrative). But such expectations soon recede as unforeseen and extraordinary elements begin to emerge. The volume's title-page summarises its contents thus:

1 The Passion of Christ
2 Eve's Apology in Defence of Women
3 The Tears of the Daughters of Jerusalem
4 The Salutation and Sorrow of the Virgin Mary
With divers other things not unfit to be read

The second of these hints at the boldly feminist viewpoint Lanyer will adopt to reinterpret scripture, while the 'other things' in fact constitute over half her entire book. They consist of nine dedications in verse and prose to Queen Anne and prominent court women, as well as verses 'To all Virtuous Ladies in General' and a prose-letter 'To the Virtuous Reader'. The main narrative 'Salve Deus Rex Judaeorum' (Hail God King of the Jews) then follows, a poem of 230 eight-line stanzas. The first section announced by the title-page, 'The Passion of Christ', does not begin until stanza 42, however, while the fourth ends at stanza 147. Framing this sequence are verses addressed to Margaret Clifford, née Russell, Dowager Countess of Cumberland, whom Lanyer honours as the poem's chief reader for her Christian virtues and fortitude. The volume concludes with 'The Description of Cookham', a 210-line poem in rhyming couplets which pays farewell to the estate where the Countess of Cumberland lived whilst separated from her husband and which Lanyer had visited as her guest. On the final page a brief *envoie* 'To the Doubtful Reader' explains how the book's title occurred to Lanyer in a dream (see opening note to 'Salve Deus'). *Salve Deus Rex Judaeorum* is therefore a multifaceted collection of original poems and prose, mingling devotional and personal interests. Overall it represents Lanyer as a complex author possessing considerable artistic ambition, who like other women of the age wrote not insincerely on devotional themes to sanction more controversial explorations of gender and social relations.

The multiple dedications seek support from Queen Anne and members of her circle, many of whom Lanyer had known from the days of Queen Elizabeth when she had cut a minor figure at court and been financially better off. Her father Baptista Bassani had been an Italian musician at the English court, and when he died in 1576 he bequeathed Aemilia a dowry of £100 as well as rental income from three houses to be shared with her elder sister (Lanyer 1993: xvii). Of her mother Margaret Johnson we know only that she was buried at St Botolph's, Bishopsgate in 1587 (Lanyer 1993: xviii). According to Simon Forman, the astrologer and physician whose records of Lanyer's visits between 1597 and 1600 provide most of our biographical information about her, she was raised (and likely served) in the household of Susan Wingfield, Countess of Kent, to whom Lanyer addresses one of her opening dedicatory poems. It was here that Lanyer undoubtedly received her formal education. As a young woman she became the mistress of Henry Cary Lord Hunsdon, the Lord Chamberlain, who was 45 years her senior and patron of Shakespeare's acting company. (On the basis of this and other slender links A.L. Rowse asserts that Lanyer was the so-called 'Dark Lady' of Shakespeare's sonnets. His evidence is too weak and his reasoning too speculative to support such a claim, though his text of *Salve Deus* is generally reliable.) Forman tells us that Lanyer received an annual allowance of £40 from Hunsdon, besides rich gifts and access to the social life of Elizabeth's court. Her life changed dramatically on 18 October 1592, however, when she was married off to Alphonso Lanyer, a court musician, to cover up bearing Hunsdon a child (named Henry after his father). Later, after several miscarriages she also gave birth to a daughter, Odillya, who died after only nine months in 1599. During the early years of their marriage Alphonso Lanyer served as a volunteer on expeditions to Ireland and Spain, but he did not gain a secure income until 1604 when King James granted him a minor monopoly on charges for the weighing of hay and grain coming into London. When he died in 1613, income from this patent was claimed by his natal family, which meant that over the next 25 years Aemilia was repeatedly forced to sue and petition for her share. Prior to 1609 she spent time with Margaret Clifford, Countess of Cumberland, and her daughter Anne at Cookham, a royal manor leased to Margaret's brother where she lived while estranged from her husband (Lewalski 1993: 216). We do not know the circumstances under which Lanyer was associated with the Cliffords, but the 'Description' claims that she experienced a religious conversion at Cookham and that it was the Countess who first put her in mind of writing 'Salve Deus'. The 'Description' also mentions Anne Clifford's marriage to Richard Sackville, Earl of Dorset, which took place on 25 February 1609; so *Salve Deus* must have been completed sometime between then and its entry in the Stationers' Register on 2 October 1610, since the 'Description' was written after the main poem. Lanyer addresses the Countess of Cumberland as her most hopeful patron at a time when her personal fortunes had declined and she had lost her tenuous foothold at court. As Katherine Duncan-Jones observes, re-establishing such contacts may also have become important to Lanyer as her son Henry approached marriageable age; for Hunsdon was first cousin to the Queen (or her half-brother, as some thought), and Lanyer may have seen herself as 'a conduit for royal blood, and so fully entitled to a place among her aristocratic patronesses' (1994: 23).

That Lanyer was methodical in her appeal to the powerful circle of women she had once known, targeting dedicatees individually (from whom she could typically expect to receive £2–3 in acknowledgement; see Bradbrook 1982: 92), is demonstrated by the fact that copies of her volume were originally issued with different combinations of dedications, some dropped and some retained according to the rank and disposition of the receiver (Lanyer 1993: xlvii–l, and Lewalski 1993: 321–2). One copy now in the Victoria and Albert Museum was bound with special care in a sumptuous vellum-cover edition bearing the Prince of Wales's device, apparently being intended for presentation to him either directly or through the Countess of Cumberland, since her signature appears on the flyleaf (Lewalski 1993: 321). Another copy deposited at Williams College and once owned by Thomas Jones, Archbishop of Dublin, is inscribed as the 'gift of Mr Alphonso Lanyer' and dated 8 November 1610 – although the pro-female epistle 'To the Virtuous Reader' as well as most of the other dedications to women have been removed (Lewalski 1993: 322; Lanyer 1993: xlviii–l). In the end, however, the precarious financial circumstances of Lanyer's later life suggest that these several appeals fell on deaf ears.

The dedication 'To the Virtuous Reader' (presented below) joins the other prefatory material in actualising a female audience to support Lanyer's public authorship in the face of potential hostility from male readers, especially towards her polemical readings of scripture. It widens her female audience beyond a small group of upper-class women to include 'all virtuous ladies and gentlewomen of this kingdom' and, near the end, 'all good Christians and honourable-minded men'. Yet this dedication also begins by acknowledging that female solidarity and virtue, of the kind Lanyer will celebrate throughout her volume, is sometimes more notional than real, since certain women play into the hands of their male detractors by denigrating other women and forgetting their achievements. Such amnesia amounts to misogyny, Lanyer argues, since men also routinely forget what their public roles and very lives owe to women. By doing so they commit the same errors as those men who knew and experienced Jesus but blinded themselves to his divine nature by persecuting him and his disciples. Misogyny and rejection of Christ therefore have similar origins in human maleness; for as Lanyer will show in her main poem, women responded utterly differently to his suffering, and were virtually alone in discerning his extraordinary spiritual gifts. The latter part of Lanyer's letter goes on to defend women in terms resembling the rhetorical *querelle des femmes*, which Rachel Speght would soon enter against Joseph Swetnam (Lewalski 1993: 225; above p. 126ff.). Lanyer issues an implied call to political action by citing several Old Testament women who changed the course of ancient Jewish history through their courage, wit, and integrity, and she recalls the favour Christ showed to women in his various actions, and by choosing them as custodians of his salvational message.

Lanyer's central 'Salve Deus' poem expands on these ideas, opening with an address praising the Countess of Cumberland for her attention to inward moral virtues rather than outward physical beauty. This renders her a fit subject to meditate faithfully on Christ's humanity. In a conventional gesture of literary modesty, Lanyer also depreciates her aspirations as the poem's narrator by recalling Icarus's fate, while praying for divine illumination to avoid comparable failure as she presses forward.

The passion story itself falls into three sections, the first dealing with Christ's betrayal by his male apostles in the garden of Gethsemene, and the second his arraignment before male authorities – Caiaphas, Pilate, and Herod – to whom Lanyer addresses conventional complaints (the excerpt presented below begins with Pilate). A speech by Pilate's wife petitioning for justice on Christ's behalf strikes a more unusual note, however, and one feels Lanyer's sympathies quickening as Pilate's wife goes on to mount a passionate defence of Eve based on the argument that what she unselfishly offered Adam was shared wisdom from the tree of knowledge while being innocent of the disastrous consequences. Adam on the other hand foresaw what was to ensue, and by turning against Eve after the fall he became 'the prototype of all men who ever thereafter denounced women for [Eve's] act of generosity and sustenance' (McGrath 1991: 105). Eve and her daughters are therefore guilty of misplaced love at most, whereas Adam's sons are responsible for the sad legacy of violence and injustice in succeeding ages, a reflexive recrimination that is epitomised by the torments Pilate, Herod, and their creatures inflict upon Christ, and that women continue to experience in her own time (e.g. the Countess of Cumberland, harassed and abandoned by her philandering husband, and Lanyer, discarded by Lord Hunsdon).

The third section of 'Salve Deus' rejoins the biblical account of Christ's procession to Calvary, the crucifixion, and the drama of the empty tomb. Lanyer also apostrophises the grieving Daughters of Jerusalem, who were hailed and blessed by Christ for their distress on his behalf, unlike the men to whom he responded with silence. She then merges her voice with that of Mary as they both focus on the cross as an object of sorrowful meditation. Conspicuous by his absence at this point is John the 'disciple whom Jesus loved', who kept a vigil with the three Marys at the crucifixion and whom Jesus commanded from the cross to care for his mother (John 19.25–7). If Lanyer excludes him so as to concentrate on the responses of women, she does not neglect 'honourable-minded' men altogether, since she singles out Joseph of Arimathaea, who begged Pilate to recover and bury Christ's body. Lanyer praises him for possessing the kind of faithful insight otherwise displayed only by women such as the two Marys, who subsequently go to anoint Jesus's body and become the first witnesses to his resurrection. Lanyer concludes the title poem by once again addressing the Countess of Cumberland and rejoicing in the mercies she has received by remaining true to Christ, by which she gains spiritual ascendancy over various conventionally heroic women of history such as Cleopatra.

Like other Renaissance meditations 'Salve Deus' is formally designed to elicit a strong emotional response towards passion scenes brought to life in rhetorically heightened descriptions and speeches, the reader's active sympathy being a sign of grace. But the poem also clearly puts forward a challenging social thesis within this framework. In Lanyer's reading the passion seems less representative of Christ's atonement for universal human sin than a revelatory indictment of ubiquitous male cruelty and patriarchal oppression, which in a sense remain unredeemed because men continue to tyrannise women (Lamb 1993: 4). Jesus, on the other hand, displays the love, nurturing functions, and healing actions traditionally associated with women, and he shares their experiences of marginalisation and injustice. In gender terms he therefore becomes androgynous – a not untraditional formulation – since his bond with women enables them to see beyond his outward maleness to the non-belligerent behaviour he mandates to both sexes but which men tend to extinguish in themselves and others. Christ therefore affirms women's authentic subjectivity, and in meditating upon his ordeal Lanyer's women readers are in effect gazing at themselves (McGrath 1991: 109). This reciprocal process is signalled by Lanyer's recurring image of herself as a servant holding up a mirror before her readers wherein they may see both Jesus and their true natures, undistorted by traditional constructions of male scholars who depreciate the role played by biblical women as active agents of God's will, or who portray them as passive bystanders or handmaidens (McGrath 1992: 344). Lanyer thus offers women a new way of dignifying themselves using Christ as their model of personhood, newly reclaimed as both 'female' and divine.

The 'Description of Cookham' has been called a country-house poem, but this is misleading since its atmosphere and content are different from works such as Ben Jonson's 'To Penshurst' (considered to be the first English example of the genre but which may actually post-date Lanyer's poem). The tone of 'Cookham' is tristfully elegiac rather than celebratory, as Lanyer pays farewell to the natural beauties of an estate Margaret Clifford and her daughter Anne have been forced to leave. Lanyer's vision is one of displacement, mutability, and loss of female friendship rather than Jonson's portrait of a bountiful household sustained by patriarchal benevolence (Lewalski 1993: 216, 235). 'Cookham' represents wider society only in an indirect or limited way, since no human figures are mentioned other than the Countess, her daughter and Lanyer. One's dominant impression is of a bittersweet personal recollection of former happiness moving irrevocably towards desolation, which Lanyer conveys primarily through an extended pathetic fallacy as the property's flora and fauna mimic the psychological drama of human parting.

Like 'Salve Deus', the 'Description of Cookham' combines elements from various genres: classical poetry of retirement celebrating an escape from the corrupt city to an idyllic rural setting; topographical poetry, influenced by early modern interest in map-making and local history; and pastoral valedictions, exemplified by Virgil's first *Eclogue* (Lewalski 1993: 235). 'Cookham' is a *locus amoenus* whose most prominent natural landmark – like its Edenic archetype – is a 'stately tree' situated on a green hill overlooking the estate, under which the three women gather to meditate on the 'beauty, wisdom, grace, love [and] majesty' of nature and its creator. When the Countess takes leaves of this spot for the last time she bestows a kiss upon the tree which Lanyer subsequently 'steals' by kissing the tree herself. Her gesture is coyly sentimental, as Lewalski notes (1993: 240), but since it claims a certain freedom and even equality with the Countess, its audacity may also suggest a more ambivalent relationship with her. Lanyer's 'theft' may betray some of the resentment she elsewhere openly expresses about the class-divide between herself and the Countess and her daughter, in whose 'sports' she is no longer able to 'bear a part' because of Anne's recent marriage to the Earl of Dorset.

If 'The Description of Cookham' represents a bid for a position in Lady Anne's newly formed household (thereby adding to our sense of the entire volume as a plea for patronage), the challenge implicit in her 'stolen' kiss may also hint at the 'darker side' of such relationships: the feelings of humiliation created by differences in rank, and the 'powerlessness of a patronized writer' grudging the need to beg for assistance (Lamb 1993: 10–11). One might even go so far as to say that, within the personal context of the Countess's estrangement from her adulterous husband and Cookham as a female refuge, the tree suggests an ideal 'lover'. In this case Lanyer's kiss may appear even more disruptive, insofar as her role as a 'rival' reconstructs the unharmonious triangle that was a real-life feature of the Countess's marriage.

On the other hand, the tree may represent a very different kind of 'dear lover': Christ the bridegroom, whom Lanyer urges Margaret Clifford in the main poem to receive into her own 'soul's pure bed'. The tree masculine's nature, its 'kingly' prospects, its outspread arms, 'the Tree' as a traditional name for the Cross, and the correspondence between the women's grouped presence and that of three Marys, all function to carry over associations of the crucified Christ from the title poem to 'Cookham'. If the situation is read this way the tree/Tree becomes a spiritual nexus for the women, perhaps one which bridges the social inequality that divides them, or simply dissolves traditional notions of worth based on class and ancestry (though in view of Lanyer's hopes for patronage such implications seem ill-advised in the presence of *Salve Deus*'s other dedicatees, particularly Anne, who derived a deep sense of her identity from her noble heritage). As 'Cookham' concludes by lamenting the devastation wrought by the enforced departure of the Countess and her daughter, the reader is reminded of the persistent undercurrent of brokenness in 'Salve Deus', in which Christ's passion seems not so much to anticipate joyful triumph as to offer spiritual consolation for the patriarchally engendered conflicts women such as Margaret and Anne Clifford experienced during much of their lives.

Editions:
Salve Deus Rex Judaeorum (1611). STC 15227, reel 1929. *The Poems of Shakespeare's Dark Lady*, ed. A.L. Rowse (London, 1978). *The Poems of Aemilia Lanyer Salve Deus Rex Judaeorum*, ed. Susanne Woods (New York, 1993). *The Female Spectator*, ed. Mary R. Mahl and Helene Koon (Bloomington, 1977, excerpts). *The Paradise of Women*, ed. Betty Travitsky (Westport, Conn., 1981, brief excerpts). *Kissing the Rod*, ed. Germaine Greer *et al.* (New York, 1988, 'The Description of Cookham').

AEMILIA LANYER

FROM *SALVE DEUS REX JUDAEORUM*

(1611)

TO THE VIRTUOUS READER

Often have I heard that it is the property of some women not only to emulate the virtues and perfections of the rest, but also, by all their powers of ill-speaking, to eclipse the brightness of their deserved fame. Now, contrary to this custom, which men I hope unjustly lay to their charge, I have written this small volume or little book for the general use of all virtuous ladies and gentlewomen of this kingdom, and in commendation of some particular persons of our own sex, such as for the most part are so well known to myself and others that I dare undertake Fame dares not to call any better. And this have I done to make known to the world that all women deserve not to be blamed, though some, forgetting they are women themselves and in danger to be condemned by the words of their own mouths, fall into so great an error as to speak unadvisedly against the rest of their sex. Which if it be true, I am persuaded they can show their own imperfection in nothing more, and therefore could wish (for their own ease, modesties, and credit) they would refer such points of folly to be practised by evil-disposed men, who forgetting they were born of women, nourished of women, and that if it were not by the means of women, they would be quite extinguished out of the world and a final end of them all, do like vipers deface the wombs wherein they were bred, only to give way and utterance to their want of discretion and goodness. Such as these were they that dishonoured Christ, his apostles and prophets, putting them to shameful deaths. Therefore we are not to regard any imputations that they undeservedly lay upon us, no other-

1. *property*: particular quality
   emulate: envy, feel a grudge against
3. *their*: i.e. 'the rest' of women, l. 2
6–7. *some ... persons*: chiefly Margaret (Russell) Clifford, Dowager Countess of Cumberland, in the main poem, and both her and her daughter Anne (Clifford) Sackville, Countess of Dorset, in 'The Description of Cookham'
13. *imperfection*: i.e. as fallen human beings
14. *ease*: relief (from 'ill-speaking' and 'condemnation')
   modesties: sense of shame from, or aversion to, disrepute
19. *want*: lack
22. *regard*: give heed to
22–3. *no ... than*: except

wise than to make use of them to our own benefits, as spurs to virtue, making us fly all occasions that may colour their unjust speeches to pass current. Especially considering that they have tempted even the patience of God himself, who gave power to wise and virtuous women to bring down their pride and arrogance: as was cruel Sisera by the discreet counsel of noble Deborah, judge and prophetess of Israel, and resolution of Jael, wife of Heber the Kenite; wicked Haman by the divine prayers and prudent proceedings of beautiful Esther; blasphemous Holofernes by the invincible courage, rare wisdom, and confident carriage of Judith; and the unjust judges by the innocency of chaste Susanna; with infinite others, which for brevity sake I will omit. As also in respect it pleased our Lord and saviour Jesus Christ, without the assistance of man, being free from original and all other sins, from the time of his conception till the hour of his death, to be begotten of a woman, born of a woman, nourished of woman, obedient to a woman; and that he healed women, pardoned women, comforted women – yea, even when he was in his greatest agony and bloody sweat, going to be crucified, and also in the last hour of his death, took care to dispose of a woman; after his resurrection appeared first to a woman, sent a woman to declare his most glorious resurrection to the rest of his disciples. Many other examples I could allege of divers faithful and virtuous women who have in

24. *fly*: flee

24–5. *colour ... current*: lend a pretence of legitimacy and common acceptance to their unjust opinions

27–9. *Sisera ... Kenite*: Judges 4. Inspired by God, Deborah joined Barek in leading the Israelites in battle against the more powerful Canaanites under Sisera. The Israelites were victorious, but Sisera escaped on foot to the tent of Jael, wife of Heber, whose Kenites were minor allies of the Canaanites. Jael feared Israel's vengeance (especially their anticipated rape of Kenite women); so after welcoming Sisera she killed him while he was asleep, thereby saving the Kenites and vanquishing Israel's enemy. Deborah's song in Judges 5 recasts Jael's story as a heroic combat with Sisera (*Women's Bible Commentary* 1992: 69–70).

29–30. *Haman ... Esther*: Esther 5–7. By shrewd diplomacy Esther saved the Jews of the Persian Empire by turning the Persian king, Ahasuerus, against his vizier Haman, leader of Israel's enemies the Amalekites. Haman had threatened to destroy Israel, but Ahasuerus had him hanged.

30–1. *Holofernes ... Judith*: Judith 8–16. Judith was a young widow who saved Israel when it seemed doomed to destruction by King Nebuchadnezzar's army. Relying on piety, wisdom, and physical allure, she gained access to the tent of Nebuchadnezzar's general Holofernes and, when he had become drunk after banqueting, cut off his head.

31–2. *unjust ... Susanna*: in the Apocryphal History of Susanna two judges surprise her in a garden while she is bathing and threaten to accuse her of unchastity if she does not lie with them. Susanna refuses and is later brought to trial, but she is saved by the prophet Daniel who exposes the judges as liars.

38. *agony ... sweat*: from the Litany, *BCP*

all ages not only been confessors, but also endured most cruel martyrdom for their faith in Jesus Christ. All which is sufficient to enforce all good Christians and honourable-minded men to speak reverently of our sex, and especially of all virtuous and good women. To the modest censures of both which, I refer these my imperfect endeavours, knowing that according to their own excellent dispositions they will rather cherish, nourish, and increase the least spark of virtue where they find it by their favourable and best interpretations, than quench it by wrong constructions. To whom I wish all increase of virtue, and desire their best opinions.

*SALVE DEUS REX JUDAEORUM**

[1]

Now when the dawn of day 'gins to appear,
And all your wicked counsels have an end
To end his life, that holds you all so dear
(For to that purpose did your studies bend),
Proud Pontius Pilate must the matter hear,
To your untroths, his ears he now must lend:
  Sweet Jesus bound, to him you led away,
  Of his most precious blood to make your prey.

[2]

Which, when that wicked caitiff did perceive,
By whose lewd means he came to this distress,
He brought the price of blood he did receive,
Thinking thereby to make his fault seem less;

43. *confessors*: Christians persecuted and possibly tortured (but not killed) for publicly declaring their religious faith

* *Salve … Judaeorum*: Hail God King of the Jews, alluding to the inscription 'This is Jesus the King of the Jews' affixed to the cross (Matthew 27.37). In a postscript, 'To the Doubtful Reader', Lanyer claims the words came to her in a dream years before she wrote *Salve Deus* and had been forgotten, but she recalled them after writing the poem. As Lewalski observes, this sequence hints at a supernatural inspiration for her work (and her vocation as a poet) while preserving a sense of independent creativity, since Lanyer claims she added the title after finishing the poem (1993: 218).

1.2–4. *your … your*: in the preceding stanzas the narrator has been recounting Christ's trial before Caiaphas and the Sanhedrin, respectively chief priest and Jewish supreme council

1.5. *Pontius Pilate*: Roman governor of Judaea AD 26–36

2.1. *caitiff*: wretch = Judas, who betrayed Jesus for 30 pieces of silver. He hanged himself after failing to return the money (Matthew 27.3–5).

2.2. *lewd*: vile

And with these priests and elders did it leave,
Confessed his fault, wherein he did transgress:
    But when he saw repentance unrespected,
    He hanged himself, of God and man rejected.

[3]

By this example, what can be expected
From wicked man, which on the earth doth live,
But faithless dealing, fear of God neglected?
Who for their private gain cares not to sell
The innocent blood of God's most dear elected,
As did that caitiff wretch, now damned in hell:
    If in Christ's school, he took so great a fall,
    What will they do that come not there at all?

[4]

Now Pontius Pilate is to judge the cause
Of faultless Jesus, who before him stands;
Who neither hath offended prince, nor laws,
Although he now be brought in woeful bands:
O noble governor, make thou yet a pause,
Do not in innocent blood imbrue thy hands,
    But hear the words of thy most worthy wife,
    Who sends to thee, to beg her saviour's life.

[5]

Let barbarous cruelty far depart from thee,
And in true justice take affliction's part;
Open thine eyes, that thou the truth mayst see,

2.7. *unrespected*: unrecognised (perhaps also 'disdained')

3.4. *Who*: either refers to 'wicked man' in l. 2, or starts a new idea: 'Those people who . . .'

3.5. *elected*: chosen

3.7. *in . . . school, he*: as a disciple, Judas

4.1. *cause*: legal case

4.4. *bands*: bondage

4.6. *imbrue*: stain

4.7. *thy . . . wife*: Pilate's wife pleads on Christ's behalf after being warned in a dream that he is a 'just' or righteous man. This detail occurs only in Matthew (27.19) and is characteristic of that gospel's emphasis on virtuous but socially powerless people being vindicated in the face of opposition from those in authority (*Women's Bible Commentary* 1992: 261–2). Lanyer's poem shares this perspective, justifying women's identification with Christ when he is being persecuted by men, and thus presenting his passion as an archetype of women's victimisation by men.

Do not the thing that goes against thy heart,
Condemn not him that must thy saviour be,
But view his holy life, his good desert.
  Let not us women glory in men's fall,
  Who had power given to overrule us all.

[6]

Till now your indiscretion sets us free
And makes our former fault much less appear;
Our mother Eve, who tasted of the tree,
Giving to Adam what she held most dear,
Was simply good, and had no power to see,
The after-coming harm did not appear:
  The subtle serpent that our sex betrayed,
  Before our fall so sure a plot had laid.

[7]

That undiscerning ignorance perceived
No guile or craft that was by him intended;
For had she known, of what we were bereaved,
To his request she had not condescended.
But she, poor soul, by cunning was deceived,
No hurt therein her harmless heart intended:
  For she alleged God's word, which he denies
  That they should die, but even as gods, be wise.

[8]

But surely Adam cannot be excused;
Her fault, though great, yet he was most to blame;
What weakness offered, strength might have refused,
Being lord of all, the greater was his shame:
Although the serpent's craft had her abused,
God's holy word ought all his actions frame,
  For he was lord and king of all the earth,
  Before poor Eve had either life or breath.

6.1. 'Eve's apology' (marginal note in early editions)
indiscretion: lack of discernment (in being able to find fault with Jesus)

6.2. *fault*: the fall into temptation in Eden

6.7. *subtle*: crafty

7.1. *ignorance*: innocence, state of being unaware

7.2. *him*: the serpent

7.7. *alleged … word*: cited (as her authority), 'Ye shall not eat of [the fruit of the tree] … lest ye die' (Genesis 3.3)
he: the serpent

8.3. *weakness … strength*: i.e. Eve … Adam

[9]

Who being framed by God's eternal hand,
The perfect'st man that ever breathed on earth,
And from God's mouth received that strait command,
The breach whereof he knew was present death:
Yea, having power to rule both sea and land,
Yet with one apple won to lose that breath
  Which God had breathed in his beauteous face,
  Bringing us all in danger and disgrace.

[10]

And then to lay the fault on patience back,
That we, poor women, must endure it all;
We know right well he did discretion lack,
Being not persuaded thereunto at all;
If Eve did err, it was for knowledge sake,
The fruit being fair persuaded him to fall:
  No subtle serpent's falsehood did betray him;
  If he would eat it, who had power to stay him?

[11]

Not Eve, whose fault was only too much love,
Which made her give this present to her dear,
That what she tasted, he likewise might prove,
Whereby his knowledge might become more clear;
He never sought her weakness to reprove
With those sharp words, which he of God did hear:
  Yet men will boast of knowledge, which he took
  From Eve's fair hand, as from a learned book.

[12]

If any evil did in her remain,
Being made of him, he was the ground of all;

9.1. *Who*: Adam
9.3. *strait*: strict
9.4. *present*: immediate
9.7. *breathed ... face*: 'God also made the man of the dust of the ground, and breathed in his face the breath of life' (Genesis 2.7)
10.1. *patience back*: the back of patience (Eve and women generally)
10.6. *fair*: outwardly attractive
11.3. *prove*: try, test
11.6. *sharp ... hear*: 'Hast thou eaten of the tree, whereof I commanded thee that thou shouldest not eat?' (Genesis 3.11)

If one of many worlds could lay a stain
Upon our sex and work so great a fall
To wretched man, by Satan's subtle train,
What will so foul a fault amongst you all?
  Her weakness did the serpent's words obey,
  But you in malice God's dear son betray.

[13]

Whom, if unjustly you condemn to die,
Her sin was small to what you do commit;
All mortal sins that do for vengeance cry,
Are not to be compared unto it:
If many worlds would altogether try,
By all their sins the wrath of God to get,
  This sin of yours surmounts them all as far
  As doth the sun, another little star.

[14]

Then let us have our liberty again,
And challenge to yourselves no sovereignty;
You came not in the world without our pain,
Make that a bar against your cruelty;
Your fault being greater, why should you disdain
Our being your equals, free from tyranny?
  If one weak woman simply did offend,
  This sin of yours, hath no excuse, nor end.

[15]

To which, poor souls, we never gave consent,
Witness thy wife, O Pilate, speaks for all;

12.3. *one … worlds*: one act involving multiple realms of being (?)
13.3. *mortal sins*: wilful and serious moral offences, bringing risk of eternal damnation
13.5. *worlds*: ages of human life
13.6. *get*: provoke
14.2. *challenge*: lay (exclusive) claim as due
14.7. *simply*: by herself only; without dishonest intent
15.1–2. *we … all*: since the narrator uses the second person elsewhere in the poem, there is no distinct closure to the speech by Pilate's wife; the narrator's voice gradually re-emerges through it, drawing strength from the defence of Eve and the prophetic warnings to Pilate, to construct a widely inclusive female viewpoint
15.2. *speaks … all*: the warnings of Pilate's wife represent an occasion for women to give wise advice to men, and therefore, insofar as the effects of the crucifixion are potentially of the same magnitude as the Fall, for reversing the blame for the latter which is

Who did but dream, and yet a message sent,
That thou shouldst have nothing to do at all
With that just man; which, if thy heart relent,
Why wilt thou be a reprobate with Saul?
  To seek the death of him that is so good,
  For thy soul's health to shed his dearest blood.

[16]

Yea, so thou mayst these sinful people please,
Thou art content against all truth and right,
To seal this act, that may procure thine ease
With blood, and wrong, with tyranny and might;
The multitude thou seekest to appease,
By base dejection of this heavenly light,
  Demanding which of these that thou should'st loose,
  Whether the thief or Christ, King of the Jews.

[17]

Base Barabbas the thief they all desire,
And thou more base than he, perform'st their will;
Yet when thy thoughts back to themselves retire,
Thou art unwilling to commit this ill:
Oh that thou couldst unto such grace aspire,
That thy polluted lips might never kill
  That honour, which right judgement ever graceth,
  To purchase shame, which all true worth defaceth.

[18]

Art thou a judge, and asketh what to do
With one, in whom no fault there can be found?
The death of Christ wilt thou consent unto,
Finding no cause, no reason, nor no ground?
Shall he be scourged, and crucified too?
And must his miseries by thy means abound?

traditionally attributed to Eve's transgression and Adam's wrongful acceptance of her authority. As Lamb observes (1993: 5), Lanyer reinterprets the biblical account to make Pilate's failure to listen to his wife one of the main causes of the crucifixion.

15.6. *Saul*: St Paul initially persecuted Jesus's disciples in the years following the crucifixion but was later converted on the road to Damascus when he saw a blinding light and heard the words 'Saul, Saul, why persecutest thou me?' (Acts 9.4)

16.6. *dejection*: casting down; humiliation

17.1. *Barabbas*: prisoner whom Pilate released instead of Christ (Mark 15.6–15)

17.3. *back … retire*: withdraw into reflection

18.6. *abound*: increase

Yet not ashamed to ask what he hath done,
When thine own conscience seeks this sin to shun.

[19]

Three times thou ask'st, what evil hath he done?
And say'st, thou find'st in him no cause of death,
Yet wilt thou chasten God's beloved son,
Although to thee no word of ill he saith?
For wrath must end what malice hath begun,
And thou must yield to stop his guiltless breath.
This rude tumultuous rout doth press so sore,
That thou condemnest him thou shouldst adore.

[20]

Yet Pilate, this can yield thee no content,
To exercise thine own authority,
But unto Herod he must needs be sent,
To reconcile thyself by tyranny:
Was this the greatest good in justice meant,
When thou perceiv'st no fault in him to be?
If thou must make thy peace by virtue's fall,
Much better 'twere not to be friends at all.

[21]

Yet neither thy stern brow nor his great place,
Can draw an answer from the holy one:
His false accusers, nor his great disgrace,
Nor Herod's scoffs; to him they are all one:
He neither cares, nor fears his own ill case,
Though being despised and mocked of every one:
King Herod's gladness gives him little ease,
Neither his anger seeks he to appease.

[22]

Yet this is strange, that base impiety
Should yield those robes of honour which were due;
Pure white, to show his great integrity,
His innocency, that all the world might view;

19.3. *chasten*: discipline, punish

20.3. *Herod*: or Antipas, ruler of Galilee under the Romans (4 BC–AD 39) and son of Herod the Great, appointed king of the Jews by the Romans in 40 BC. Jesus was sent to Herod for questioning because he was a Galilean (Luke 23.6ff.).

20.4. *reconcile thyself*: (1) ease Pilate's moral doubts/troubled conscience; (2) become friendly with his former enemy, Herod, for disparaging Christ's claims (Luke 23.12)

Perfection's height in lowest penury,
Such glorious poverty as they never knew:
  Purple and scarlet well might him beseem,
  Whose precious blood must all the world redeem.

[23]

And that imperial crown of thorns he wore,
Was much more precious than the diadem
Of any king that ever lived before
Or since his time; their honour's but a dream
To his eternal glory, being so poor,
To make a purchase of that heavenly realm;
  Where God with all his angels lives in peace,
  No griefs, nor sorrows, but all joys increase.

[24]

Those royal robes, which they in scorn did give,
To make him odious to the common sort,
Yield light of Grace to those whose souls shall live
Within the harbour of this heavenly port;
Much do they joy, and much more do they grieve,
His death, their life, should make his foes such sport:
  With sharpest thorns to prick his blessed face,
  Our joyful sorrow, and his greater grace.

[25]

Three fears at once possessed Pilate's heart:
The first Christ's innocence, which so plain appears;
The next, that he which now must feel this smart,
Is God's dear son, for any thing he hears;
But that which proved the deepest wounding dart,
Is people's threatenings, which he so much fears,
  That he to Caesar could not be a friend,
  Unless he sent sweet Jesus to his end.

[26]

Now Pilate thou art proved a painted wall,
A golden sepulchre with rotten bones,
From right to wrong, from equity to fall;
If none upbraid thee, yet the very stones
Will rise against thee, and in question call
His blood, his tears, his sighs, his bitter groans:

22.7. *Purple . . . scarlet*: royal colours, in which Herod dressed Christ to ridicule his claims to authority (below 24.1–2)

All these will witness at the latter day,
When water cannot wash thy sin away.

[27]

Canst thou be innocent, that 'gainst all right
Wilt yield to what thy conscience doth withstand?
Being a man of knowledge, power, and might,
To let the wicked carry such a hand,
Before thy face to blindfold heaven's bright light,
And thou to yield to what they did demand?
Washing thy hands, thy conscience cannot clear,
But to all worlds this stain must needs appear.

[28]

For lo, the guilty doth accuse the just,
And faulty judge condemns the innocent,
And wilful Jews to exercise their lust,
With whips and taunts against their Lord are bent;
He, basely used, blasphemed, scorned, and curst,
Our heavenly king to death for us they sent:
Reproaches, slanders, spittings in his face,
Spite doing all her worst in his disgrace.

[29]

And now this long-expected hour draws near,
When blessed saints with angels do condole;
His holy march, soft pace, and heavy cheer,
In humble sort to yield his glorious soul,
By his deserts the foulest sins to clear;
And in th'eternal book of heaven to enroll
A satisfaction till the general doom,
Of all sins past, and all that are to come.

[30]

They that had seen this pitiful procession,
From Pilate's palace to Mount Calvary,
Might think he answered for some great transgression,

26.8. *water ... away*: alluding here and below to Pilate's act of publicly washing his hands to signify his innocency after releasing Jesus to be crucified (Matthew 27.24)

28.3. *lust*: pleasure

28.8. *Spite ... her*: one of the few places where Lanyer genders Christ's opposition as feminine, albeit here an abstract quality

29.4. *sort*: manner

29.7. *general doom*: last judgement

Being in such odious sort condemned to die;
He plainly showed that his own profession
Was virtue, patience, grace, love, piety;
   And how by suffering he could conquer more
   Than all the Kings that ever lived before.

[31]

First went the crier with open mouth proclaiming
The heavy sentence of iniquity,
The hangman next, by his base office claiming
His right in hell, where sinners never die,
Carrying the nails, the people still blaspheming
Their maker, using all impiety;
   The thieves attending him on either side,
   The sergeants watching, while the women cried.

[32]

Thrice happy women that obtained such grace
From him whose worth the world could not contain;
Immediately to turn about his face,
As not remembering his great grief and pain,
To comfort you whose tears poured forth apace
On Flora's banks, like showers of April's rain:
   Your cries enforced mercy, grace and love
   From him, whom greatest princes could not move

[33]

To speak one word, nor once to lift his eyes
Unto proud Pilate, no nor Herod king,

31.1–3. *crier ... hangman*: details deriving from seventeenth-century executions

31.7. *thieves attending*: the two criminals crucified with Christ

32.1ff. 'The tears of the daughters of Jerusalem' (marginal note). Jesus speaks freely to these women – in contrast to his silence towards his male accusers – telling them not to weep for him but for themselves and their children (Luke 23.28). They provide one model for the emotional responses of Lanyer's female readers, who will hope to be similarly blessed. Historically the daughters of Jerusalem may have represented professional mourners, introduced anachronistically by Luke to prefigure Jerusalem's destruction by the Romans in ad 70. They are different from the 'great multitude of ... [Galilean] women' who accompany Christ in Luke 23.27, though Lanyer, like her contemporaries, did not distinguish between the two groups (Luke, incidentally, also adds 'of people and' to v. 27 from a source which originally identified only women following Jesus; see Women's Bible Commentary 1992: 290).

32.6. *Flora's*: Roman goddess of spring and flowers

32.7. *enforced*: brought forth

By all the questions that they could devise,
Could make him answer to no manner of thing;
Yet these poor women, by their piteous cries
Bid move their lord, their lover, and their king,
To take compassion, turn about, and speak
To them whose hearts were ready now to break.

[34]

Most blessed daughters of Jerusalem,
Who found such favour in your saviour's sight,
To turn his face when you did pity him;
Your tearful eyes, beheld his eyes more bright,
Your faith and love unto such grace did climb,
To have reflection from this heavenly light:
Your eagles' eyes did gaze against this sun,
Your hearts did think, he dead, the world were done.

[35]

When spiteful men with torments did oppress
The afflicted body of this innocent dove,
Poor women, seeing how much they did transgress,
By tears, by sighs, by cries entreat, nay prove,
What may be done among the thickest press,
They labour still these tyrants' hearts to move;
In pity and compassion to forbear
Their whipping, spurning, tearing of his hair.

[36]

But all in vain, their malice hath no end,
Their hearts more hard than flint, or marble stone;
Now to his grief, his greatness they attend,
When he, God knows, had rather be alone;
They are his guard, yet seek all means to offend:
Well may he grieve, well may he sigh and groan,
Under the burden of a heavy cross,
He faintly goes to make their gain his loss.

[37]

His woeful mother waiting on her son,
All comfortless in depth of sorrow drowned;

34.7. *eagles' ... sun*: proverbially, eagles could look into the sun without blinking
35.5. *press*: crowds
36.1. *their*: the 'tyrants''
36.5. *offend*: i.e. transgress against those in authority
37.1ff. 'The sorrow of the virgin Mary' (marginal note)

Her griefs extreme, although but new begun,
To see his bleeding body oft she swooned;
How could she choose but think herself undone,
He dying, with whose glory she was crowned?
None ever lost so great a loss as she,
Being son and father of eternity.

[38]

Her tears did wash away his precious blood,
That sinners might not tread it under feet
To worship him, and that it did her good
Upon her knees, although in open street,
Knowing he was the Jesse flower and bud
That must be gathered when it smelled most sweet:
Her son, her husband, father, saviour, king,
Whose death killed death, and took away his sting.

[39]

Most blessed virgin, in whose faultless fruit
All nations of the earth must needs rejoice,
No creature having sense, though ne'er so brute,
But joys and trembles when they hear his voice,
His wisdom strikes the wisest persons mute;
Fair chosen vessel, happy in his choice,
Dear mother of our Lord, whose reverend name
All people blessed call, and spread thy fame.

[40]

For the almighty magnified thee,
And looked down upon thy mean estate;
Thy lowly mind, and unstained chastity,
Did plead for love at great Jehovah's gate,
Who sending swift-winged Gabriel unto thee,
His holy will and pleasure to relate;

37.4. *swooned*: fainted

38.5. *Jesse flower*: alluding to the traditional depiction of Christ as the topmost flower on a family tree originating with Jesse, father of the royal house of David

39.1. *fruit*: i.e. of her womb (= Christ)

40.1ff. 'The salutation of the virgin Mary' (marginal note), alludes to the song of Mary, or Magnificat (Luke 1.46–55) in which she praises God for choosing her to bear the Messiah, and, insofar as Mary's female status allies her with the socially disenfranchised, proclaims their liberation from oppression

40.5. *Gabriel*: angel who announces to Mary she has been chosen by God to give birth to Christ (Luke 1.26–38). Lanyer's succeeding stanzas retell the story of their encounter.

To thee most beauteous queen of womankind,
The angel did unfold his maker's mind.

[41]

He thus began: 'Hail Mary full of grace,
Thou freely art beloved of the Lord,
He is with thee, behold thy happy case.'
What endless comfort did these words afford
To thee that saw'st an angel in the place
Proclaim thy virtue's worth, and to record
Thee blessed among women: that thy praise
Should last so many worlds beyond thy days.

[42]

Lo, this high message to thy troubled spirit,
He doth deliver in the plainest sense;
Says, thou shouldst bear a son that shall inherit
His father David's throne, free from offence,
Calls him that holy thing, by whose pure merit
We must be saved; tells what he is, of whence,
His worth, his greatness, what his name must be,
Who should be called the son of the most high.

[43]

He cheers thy troubled soul, bids thee not fear,
When thy pure thoughts could hardly apprehend
This salutation, when he did appear;
Nor couldst thou judge, whereto those words did tend;
His pure aspect did move thy modest cheer
To muse, yet joy that God vouchsafed to send
His glorious angel, who did thee assure
To bear a child, although a virgin pure.

42.4. *offence*: sin

42.5. *Calls ... thing*: paraphrase of Luke 1.35: 'therefore also that holy thing which shall be born of thee shall be called the Son of God'. The same verse tells of Jesus's conception by the holy spirit (below 46.3-4), which as Amy-Jill Levine notes is grammatically neuter in New Testament Greek but feminine in Hebrew and Jesus's native Aramaic. The combination of this originally feminine spirit and Jesus's lack of a human father indicates an archetypal family structure not ruled or defined by male headship (*Women's Bible Commentary* 1992: 254).

[44]

Nay more, thy son should rule and reign forever;
Yea, of his kingdom there should be no end;
Over the house of Jacob, heaven's great giver
Would give him power, and to that end did send
His faithful servant Gabriel to deliver
To thy chaste ears no word that might offend:
  But that this blessed infant born of thee,
  Thy son, the only son of God should be.

[45]

When on the knees of thy submissive heart
Thou humbly didst demand, how that should be?
Thy virgin thoughts did think, none could impart
This great good hap, and blessing unto thee;
Far from desire of any man thou art,
Knowing not one, thou art from all men free:
  When he to answer this thy chaste desire,
  Gives thee more cause to wonder and admire.

[46]

That thou a blessed virgin should remain,
Yea, that the Holy Ghost should come on thee
A maiden mother, subject to no pain,
For highest power should overshadow thee:
Could thy fair eyes from tears of joy refrain,
When God looked down upon thy poor degree?
  Making thee servant, mother, wife, and nurse
  To heaven's bright king, that freed us from the curse.

[47]

Thus being crowned with glory from above,
Grace and perfection resting in thy breast,
Thy humble answer doth approve thy love,
And all these sayings in thy heart do rest:

44.3. *house of Jacob*: Israel
45.6. *Knowing … free*: being free from sexual relations with men liberates you from male possession and authority
46.3. *subject … pain*: of labour, perhaps also of sexual intercourse, Lanyer's extension of a traditional reading in which the passage describing the holy spirit 'overshadowing' Mary is taken to mean impregnating her yet leaving her sinless
46.6. *poor degree*: low social status
46.8. *curse*: original sin
47.3. *approve*: verify

Thy child a lamb, and thou a turtle dove,
Above all other women highly blessed;
  To find such favour in his glorious sight,
  In whom thy heart and soul do most delight.

[48]

What wonder in the world more strange could seem,
Than that a virgin could conceive and bear
Within her womb a son, that should redeem
All nations on the earth, and should repair
Our old decays: who in such high esteem,
Should prize all mortals, living in his fear
  As not to shun death, poverty and shame,
  To save their souls, and spread his glorious name.

[49]

And partly to fulfil his father's pleasure,
Whose powerful hand allows it not for strange,
If he vouchsafe the riches of his treasure,
Pure righteousness to take such ill exchange;
On all iniquity to make a seizure,
Giving his snow-white weed for ours in change:
  Our mortal garment in a scarlet dye,
  Too base a robe for immortality.

[50]

Most happy news, that ever yet was brought,
When poverty and riches met together,
The wealth of heaven, in our frail clothing wrought
Salvation by his happy coming hither:
Mighty messiah, who so dearly bought
Us, slaves to sin, far lighter than a feather:

47.5. *turtle dove*: symbol of steadfast love

48.5. *Our ... decays*: originally sinful human nature

49.2. *allows ... not*: does not regard it as

49.6–7. *snow-white ... dye*: 'These are they, which came out of great tribulation, and have washed their long robes and have made their long robes white in the blood of the Lamb' (= Christ's sacrifice; Revelation 7.14). weed = garment. Scarlet can also suggest intemperate passion and (in view of the references to mock-royal clothes above 22.7) love of wielding power over others.

50.3. *frail clothing*: i.e. in mortal human flesh

50.5. *bought*: redeemed

50.6. *lighter*: morally and wilfully unstable, frivolous

Tossed to and fro with every wicked wind,
The world, the flesh, or devil gives to blind.

[51]

Who on his shoulders our black sins doth bear
To that most blessed, yet accursed, cross;
Where, fastening them, he rids us of our fear,
Yea for our gain he is content with loss,
Our ragged clothing scorns he not to wear,
Though foul, rent, torn, disgraceful, rough and gross,
Spun by that monster Sin, and weaved by Shame,
Which grace itself, disgraced with impure blame.

[52]

How canst thou choose, fair virgin, then but mourn,
When this sweet offspring of thy body dies,
When thy fair eyes beholds his body torn,
The people's fury, hears the women's cries;
His holy name profaned, he made a scorn,
Abused with all their hateful slanderous lies,
Bleeding and fainting in such wondrous sort,
As scarce his feeble limbs can him support.

[53]

Now Simon of Cyrene passeth them by,
Whom they compel sweet Jesus' cross to bear
To Golgotha, there do they mean to try
All cruel means to work in him despair:
That odious place, where dead men's skulls did lie,
There must our Lord for present death prepare:
His sacred blood must grace that loathsome field,
To purge more filth than that foul place could yield.

[54]

For now arrived unto this hateful place,
In which his cross erected needs must be,
False hearts and willing hands come on apace,
All pressed to ill, and all desire to see:
Graceless themselves, still seeking to disgrace,
Bidding him, if the son of God he be,

50.8. *blind*: deceive
52.7. *wondrous sort*: admirable, or miraculous, way
53.1. *Simon of Cyrene*: passer-by whom the Romans compelled to carry Christ's cross to Golgotha (Matthew 27.32)
54.1ff. 'Christ's death' (marginal note)

To save himself, if he could others save,
With all th'opprobrious words that might deprave.

[55]

His harmless hands unto the cross they nailed,
And feet that never trod in sinners' trace;
Between two thieves, unpitied, unbewailed,
Save of some few possessors of his grace,
With sharpest pangs and terrors thus appaled,
Stern Death makes way, that Life might give him place:
His eyes with tears, his body full of wounds,
Death, last of pains, his sorrows all confounds.

[56]

His joints disjointed, and his legs hang down,
His alabaster breast, his bloody side,
His members torn, and on his head a crown
Of sharpest thorns, to satisfy for pride:
Anguish and pain do all his senses drown,
While they his holy garments do divide:
His bowels dry, his heart full fraught with grief,
Crying to him that yields him no relief.

[57]

This with the eye of faith thou maist behold,
Dear spouse of Christ, and more than I can write;
And here both grief and joy thou maist unfold
To view thy love in this most heavy plight,
Bowing his head, his bloodless body cold;
Those eyes wax dim that gave us all our light,
His countenance pale, yet still continues sweet,
His blessed blood wat'ring his pierced feet.

[58]

O glorious miracle without compare!
Last but not least which was by him effected;

54.8. *deprave*: vilify (him)
55.2. *trace*: path
55.5. *appaled*: used to make pale with fear, or enfeeble
56.7. *bowels*: internal organs generally
56.8. *Crying ... relief*: 'My God, my God, why hast thou forsaken me?' (Matthew 27.46)
57.1. *thou*: 'To my Lady [Margaret] of Cumberland' (marginal note)
57.8–58.1. *His ... miracle*: 'one of the soldiers with a spear pierced his side, and forthwith came there out blood and water' (John 19.34)

Uniting death, life, misery, joy and care,
By his sharp passion in his dear elected.
Who doth the badges of like liveries wear,
Shall find how dear they are of him respected.
  No joy, grief, pain, life, death was like to his,
  Whose infinite dolours wrought eternal bliss.

[59]

What creature on the earth did then remain,
On whom the horror of this shameful deed
Did not inflict some violent touch or strain,
To see the Lord of all the world to bleed?
His dying breath did rend huge rocks in twain,
The heavens betook them to their mourning weed:
  The sun grew dark, and scorned to give them light,
  Who durst eclipse a glory far more bright.

[60]

The moon and stars did hide themselves for shame,
The earth did tremble in her loyal fear,
The temple veil did rend to spread his fame,
The monuments did open everywhere;
Dead saints did rise forth of their grave, and came
To divers people that remained there
  Within that holy city; whose offence,
  Did put their maker to this large expense.

[61]

Things reasonable and reasonless possessed
The terrible impression of this fact;
For his oppression made them all oppressed,
When with his blood he sealed so fair an act,
In restless misery to procure our rest;
His glorious deeds that dreadful prison sacked:
  When death, hell, devils, using all their power,
  Were overcome in that most blessed hour.

58.5. *liveries*: clothes or badge worn by servants; uniforms

59.1ff. 'The terror of all creatures at that instant when Christ died' (marginal note)

59.5–60.7. *His* ... *city*: Matthew 27.51–3; Mark 15.33

59.8. *durst eclipse*: the sense seems to be 'durst *not* eclipse', or the line may be a rhetorical question

60.3. *temple*: the holiest Jewish sanctuary in Jerusalem, destroyed by the Romans in AD 70

61.2. *impression* ... *fact*: mark ... deed

61.6. *prison*: i.e. hell

[62]
Being dead, he killed death, and did survive
That proud insulting tyrant: in whose place
He sends bright immortality to revive
Those whom his iron arms did long embrace;
Who from their loathsome graves brings them alive
In glory to behold their saviour's face:
Who took the keys of all death's power away,
Opening to those that would his name obey.

[63]
O wonder, more than man can comprehend,
Our joy and grief both at one instant framed,
Compounded: contrarieties contend
Each to exceed, yet neither to be blamed.
Our grief to see our saviour's wretched end,
Our joy to know both death and hell he tamed:
That we may say, O death where is thy sting?
Hell, yield thy victory to thy conquering king.

[64]
Can stony hearts refrain from shedding tears,
To view the life and death of this sweet saint?
His austere course in young and tender years,
When great endurements could not make him faint:
His wants, his pains, his torments, and his fears,
All which he undertook without constraint,
To show that infinite goodness must restore
What infinite justice looked for, and more.

[65]
Yet, had he been but of a mean degree,
His sufferings had been small to what they were;
Mean minds will show of what mean moulds they be;
Small griefs seem great, yet use doth make them bear:
But ah! 'tis hard to stir a sturdy tree;
Great dangers hardly puts great minds in fear:
They will conceal their griefs which mighty grow
In their stout hearts until they overflow.

62.4. *his*: death's
63.7. O . . . *sting*: 1 Corinthians 15.55
65.4. *use* . . . *bear*: habit . . . bearable

[66]

If then an earthly prince may ill endure
The least of those afflictions which he bare,
How could this all-commanding king procure
Such grievous torments with his mind to square,
Legions of angels being at his lure?
He might have lived in pleasure without care:
  None can conceive the bitter pains he felt,
  When God and man must suffer without guilt.

[67]

Take all the sufferings thoughts can think upon,
In every man that this huge world hath bred;
Let all those pains and sufferings meet in one,
Yet are they not a mite to that he did
Endure for us: Oh let us think thereon,
That God should have his precious blood so shed:
  His greatness clothed in our frail attire,
  And pay so dear a ransom for the hire.

[68]

Lo, here was glory, misery, life and death,
An union of contraries did accord;
Gladness and sadness here had one berth,
This wonder wrought the passion of our Lord,
His suff'ring for all the sins of all th'earth;
No satisfaction could the world afford,
  But this rich jewel, which from God was sent,
  To call all those that would in time repent.

[69]

Which I present, dear Lady, to your view,
Upon the cross deprived of life or breath,
To judge if ever lover were so true,
To yield himself unto such shameful death:
Now blessed Joseph doth both beg and sue,
To have his body who possessed his faith,
  And thinks, if he this small request obtains,
  He wins more wealth than in the world remains.

66.4. *square*: reconcile
66.5. *lure*: call
67.8. *hire*: temporary use (of human nature)
69.5. *Joseph*: 'a rich man of Arimathaea' who obtained Pilate's permission to recover Christ's body (Matthew 27.57; John 19.38)

[70]

Thus honourable Joseph is possessed
Of what his heart and soul so much desired,
And now he goes to give that body rest,
That all his life, with griefs and pains was tired;
He finds a tomb, a tomb most rarely blessed,
In which was never creature yet interred;
There this most precious body he encloses,
Embalmed and decked with lilies and with roses.

[71]

Lo, here the beauty of heaven and earth is laid,
The purest colours underneath the sun,
But in this place he cannot long be stayed,
Glory must end what horror hath begun;
For he the fury of the heavens obeyed,
And now he must possess what he hath won:
The Marys do with precious balms attend,
But being come, they find it to no end.

[72]

For he is ris'n from death t'eternal life,
And now those precious ointments he desires
Are brought unto him by his faithful wife
The holy church; who in those rich attires
Of patience, love, long suffering, void of strife,
Humbly presents those ointments he requires:
The oils of mercy, charity and faith,
She only gives that which no other hath.

71.7. *Marys*: Mary Magdalene and Mary the mother of James (Matthew 27.56), who kept a vigil at Jesus's tomb as they had with his mother during his crucifixion, and were the first witnesses to the resurrection, reporting it to the male disciples

71.7–72.8. *balms ... hath*: anointing symbolically defines the relationship between the crucifixion and the spiritual lives of Christ's followers (including Lanyer's seventeenth-century readers). Her metaphor recalls the two Marys' burial observances (their anointing of Jesus's body after his death) as well as the the anointing of his head by a woman (traditionally identified as Mary Magdalene) in prophetic recognition of his divine mission. The latter event marks the start of the passion story just prior to the point at which Lanyer begins her narrative. Anointing thus becomes a gendered sign-action characteristic of the female disciples, beginning with Mary Magdalene and continuing with her spiritual sisters, 'as the true disciples in the passion narrative' (Fiorenza 1992: xiv).

72.1ff. 'Christ's resurrection' (marginal note)

72.8. *only*: alone

[73]

These precious balms do heal his grievous wounds,
And water of compunction washeth clean
The sores of sins, which in our souls abounds;
So fair it heals, no scar is ever seen;
Yet all the glory unto Christ redounds,
His precious blood is that which must redeem;
  Those well may make us lovely in his sight,
  But cannot save without his powerful might.

[74]

This is that bridegroom that appears so fair,
So sweet, so lovely in his spouses' sight,
That unto snow we may his face compare,
His cheeks like scarlet, and his eyes so bright
As purest doves that in the rivers are
Washed with milk, to give the more delight;
  His head is likened to the finest gold,
  His curled locks so beauteous to behold

[75]

Black as a raven in her blackest hue;
His lips like scarlet threads, yet much more sweet

73.1ff. 'A brief description of his [i.e. Christ's] beauty upon [in the manner of] the Canticles' (marginal note). Canticles = the Song of Songs, traditionally ascribed to Solomon, but containing the only female speakers in the Bible unmediated by male narrators. The book is a collection of often openly erotic love poems, mainly between a woman and her male suitor, that has traditionally been interpreted metaphorically as representing the relationship between God and Israel, or Christ and his Church. The book's speakers include the daughters of Jerusalem; so Lanyer's allusion to this book is related to the mourning daughters of Jerusalem (32.1ff.) and suggests a continuous identification with Christ by multiple women speakers as they trace the passion story's emotional trajectory from lamentation to celebration. Lanyer suggests that their voices merge collectively here, following the practice of the Song of Songs itself, to establish a powerfully gendered vision of Christ's spiritual witnesses. Mueller (1994: 222) further observes that Lanyer also 'understands her Christ' because his 'thoroughly feminized' demeanour and language mirrors the norms of proper female behaviour prescribed in conduct books and doctrinal tracts by Renaissance male authors. But see also n. to 74.3ff.

74.1–2. *bridegroom ... spouses'*: the spiritual relationship between Christ and members of the Church (including men) is traditionally described in terms of a mystical union or marriage

74.3ff. the physical comparisons are reminiscent of conventional metaphors used in Petrarchan love poetry

Than is the sweetest honey dropping dew,
Or honeycombs, where all the bees do meet;
Yea, he is constant, and his words are true,
His cheeks are beds of spices, flowers sweet;
  His lips like lilies, dropping down pure myrrh,
  Whose love before all worlds we do prefer.

THE DESCRIPTION OF COOKHAM

Farewell, sweet Cookham, where I first obtained
Grace from that grace where perfect grace remained,
And where the muses gave their full consent,
I should have power the virtuous to content;
Where princely palace willed me to indite
The sacred story of the soul's delight.
Farewell, sweet place, where virtue then did rest,
And all delights did harbour in her breast;
Never shall my sad eyes again behold
Those pleasures which my thoughts did then unfold.
Yet you, great lady, mistress of that place,
From whose desires did spring this work of grace,

75.8. love ... worlds: worlds = conditions of life or existence; but the original spelling allows this also to be read as 'world's' = world's love, and thus: 'Whose (divine) form of love before all worldly or human forms ...'

Lanyer's passion narrative ends here. The remainder of the title poem returns to the opening address praising the virtues of the Countess of Cumberland.

1. *Cookham*:: in Berkshire near Maidenhead, 'it has extensive frontages on the Thames, rich woodlands, lush meadows, picturesque scattered hamlets, and high hills in the west' (Lewalski 1993: 234). The village is now best known through the work of twentieth-century British painter Stanley Spencer (who does not appear to have known Lanyer's poem).
2. *Grace ... grace ... grace*: all capitalised in the original edition; the middle word could refer to Margaret Clifford (the 'great lady' at l. 11) or to Cookham itself
3. *muses*: nine sisters of classical myth who inspired poets, musicians, and other artists
4. *power*: i.e. in composing poetry
5. *princely palace*: the house was owned by the Crown and leased by Margaret Clifford's brother William Russell; this may be why Lanyer pays so little attention to it and instead focuses on the natural features of the estate (Lewalski 1993: 216)
   indite: write
6. *sacred story*: Christ's passion as related in the main poem

Vouchsafe to think upon those pleasures past
As fleeting worldly joys that could not last,
Or as dim shadows of celestial pleasures,
Which are desired above all earthly treasures.
Oh how, me thought, against you thither came
Each part did seem some new delight to frame!
The house received all ornaments to grace it,
And would endure no foulness to deface it.
The walks put on their summer liveries,
And all things else did hold like similes:
The trees with leaves, with fruits, with flowers clad,
Embraced each other, seeming to be glad,
Turning themselves to beauteous canopies
To shade the bright sun from your brighter eyes;
The crystal streams with silver spangles graced,
While by the glorious sun they were embraced;
The little birds in chirping notes did sing,
To entertain both you and that sweet spring,
And Philomela with her sundry lays,
Both you and that delightful place did praise.
Oh how, me thought, each plant, each flower, each tree
Set forth their beauties then to welcome thee:
The very hills right humbly did descend,
When you to tread upon them did intend,
And as you set your feet, they still did rise,
Glad that they could receive so rich a prize.
The gentle winds did take delight to be
Among those woods that were so graced by thee,
And in sad murmur uttered pleasing sound,
That pleasure in that place might more abound.
The swelling banks delivered all their pride,
When such a phoenix once they had espied.
Each arbour, bank, each seat, each stately tree,

12. *desires*: near the beginning of *Salve Deus* Lanyer apologises for not writing 'Those praiseful lines of that delightful place [Cookham]', as Margaret Clifford had asked her to do. This passage indicates that 'Cookham' was written after the title poem.
21. *liveries*: uniforms
31. *Philomela*: was changed into a nightingale (or a swallow accordingly to some authorities) after being raped and having her tongue cut out by her brother-in-law Tereus. He imprisoned her, but she was able to weave her story in a tapestry which she smuggled out to her sister Procne, who took revenge on Tereus by killing his son Itys and serving up his flesh. 'lays' = songs.
32. *delightful place*: = *locus amoenus* of classical and later literary tradition
44. *phoenix*: mythical Arabian bird that came back to life after being burnt in a pyre, and thus a symbol of resurrection, but here a more general compliment

Thought themselves honoured in supporting thee.
The pretty birds would oft come to attend thee,
Yet fly away for fear they should offend thee;
The little creatures in the burrow by
Would come abroad to sport them in your eye,
Yet fearful of the bow in your fair hand,
Would run away when you did make a stand.
Now let me come unto that stately tree,
Wherein such goodly prospects you did see:
That oak that did in height his fellows pass
As much as lofty trees, low growing grass;
Much like a comely cedar straight and tall,
Whose beauteous stature far exceeded all.
How often did you visit this fair tree,
Which, seeming joyful in receiving thee,
Would like a palm tree spread his arms abroad,
Desirous that you there should make abode;
Whose fair green leaves, much like a comely veil,
Defended Phoebus when he would assail;
Whose pleasing boughs did yield a cool fresh air,
Joying his happiness when you were there;
Where, being seated, you might plainly see
Hills, vales, and woods, as if on bended knee
They had appeared, your honour to salute,
Or to prefer some strange unlooked-for suit;
All interlaced with brooks and crystal springs:
A prospect fit to please the eyes of kings;
And thirteen shires appeared all in your sight:
Europe could not afford much more delight.
What was there then but gave you all content,
While you the time in meditation spent

47. *to attend*: pronounced 't'attend'

51. *bow ... hand*: perhaps evoking an image of Diana, goddess of hunting and chastity

57–61. *cedar ... palm*: associated with spiritual celebration: 'The righteous shall flourish like a palm tree, and shall grow like a cedar in Lebanon' (Psalm 92.12). Solomon used cedars to build the temple in Jerusalem (1 Kings 5–6), which in turn became an Old Testament type for Christ.

64. *Defended Phoebus*: blocked the sun

70. *prefer*: present, put forward
strange ... suit: the courtly metaphor seems to turn negative, as this phrase suggests unwanted attention, whereas the sense overall appears to be of positive, welcome devotion

73. *thirteen*: an exaggeration, but Lewalski notes that the number figuratively suggests Adam and Eve's view of the whole world from paradise (1993: 238)

Of their creator's power, which there you saw,
In all his creatures held a perfect law;
And in their beauties did you plain descry,
His beauty, wisdom, grace, love, majesty.
In these sweet woods how often did you walk,
With Christ and his apostles there to talk,
Placing his holy writ in some fair tree,
To meditate what you therein did see:
With Moses you did mount his holy hill,
To know his pleasure, and perform his will;
With lovely David you did often sing,
His holy hymns to heaven's eternal king,
And in sweet music did your soul delight,
To sound his praises, morning, noon, and night;
With blessed Joseph you did often feed
Your pined brethren, when they stood in need.
And that sweet lady sprung from Clifford's race,
Of noble Bedford's blood, fair strem of Grace,
To honourable Dorset now espoused,
In whose fair breast true virtue then was housed,
O what delight did my weak spirits find
In those pure parts of her well-framed mind;
And yet it grieves me that I cannot be
Near unto her, whose virtues did agree

83–4. *Placing ... see*: one of several points where Lanyer relates 'The Description of Cookham' symbolically to events in 'Salve Deus', here specifically the crucifixion. Christ is figured by 'holy writ', while 'fair tree' (and later Cookham's 'great tree') alludes to 'the Cross', often called 'the Tree'. The three women recall the three Marys who stood by the cross. The crucified Christ is thereby invoked metonymically through the Writ/Tree image. Furthermore when we recall that Lanyer urges Margaret Clifford to meditate upon the passion with the 'eye of faith' ('Salve Deus', 57.1) and that her narrative contains few actual depictions of Jesus, she seems to reveal a Protestant sensibility that regards the graphic visual imagery found in Catholic meditative practices as potentially idolatrous.

85–6. *his*: God's

87–8. *David ... hymns*: the Psalms, traditionally ascribed to David (Lanyer states in her dedication poem to Mary Sidney that she knew the latter's widely circulated translation of the Psalms)

91–2. *Joseph ... need*: Joseph was sold by his brothers into service in Egypt but nonetheless prospered, amassing large stores of grain. When famine struck, his 'pined' (= starved) brothers were forced to plead with him for food, which he provided (Genesis 37, 42–5).

93–5. *lady ... Dorset*: Lady Anne Clifford (above p. 245ff.), daughter of Lady Margaret (Russell) Clifford, and wife of Richard Sackville, 3rd Earl of Dorset

With those fair ornaments of outward beauty,
Which did enforce from all both love and duty.
Unconstant fortune, thou art most to blame,
Who casts us down into so low a frame
Where our great friends we cannot daily see,
So great a difference is there in degree.
Many are placed in those orbs of state,
Parters in honour, so ordained by fate,
Nearer in show, yet farther off in love,
In which the lowest always are above.
But whither am I carried in conceit?
My wit too weak to conster of the great.
Why not? although we are but born of earth,
We may behold the heavens, despising death;
And loving heaven that is so far above,
May in the end vouchsafe us entire love.
Therefore, sweet memory, do thou retain
Those pleasures past, which will not turn again;
Remember beauteous Dorset's former sports,
So far from being touched by ill reports,
Wherein myself did always bear a part,
While reverend love presented my true heart;
Those recreations let me bear in mind,
Which her sweet youth and noble thoughts did find;
Whereof deprived, I evermore must grieve,
Hating blind fortune, careless to relieve.
And you, sweet Cookham, whom these ladies leave,
I now must tell the grief you did conceive
At their departure, when they went away
How every thing retained a sad dismay;

106. *degree*: social rank

108. *parters*: dividers, distributors; or perhaps an error for 'partners'

109. *show ... love*: superficial appearance (of honour) ... true desire (for honour)

110. *lowest ... are above*: in social status ... i.e. upper-class people value real honour less than people beneath them in rank, who are their true superiors. Lanyer's inversion of the social hierarchy follows naturally from the main poem's focus on Christ being supported by and in turn empowering those members of society such as women who have traditionally been excluded from positions of authority. Yet Lanyer recognises that such comments may offend her aristocratic readers (and potential patrons); so in the next line she breaks off, perhaps to give the impression of musing rather than speaking 'seriously'.

112. *conster*: construe = explain, or interpret

119. *Dorset's*: i.e. Anne Clifford's

Nay, long before, when once an inkling came,
Me thought each thing did unto sorrow frame:
The trees that were so glorious in our view,
Forsook both flowers and fruit, when once they knew
Of your depart; their very leaves did wither,
Changing their colours as they grew together.
But when they saw this had no power to stay you,
They often wept, though speechless could not pray you,
Letting their tears in your fair bosoms fall,
As if they said, why will ye leave us all?
This being vain, they cast their leaves away,
Hoping that pity would have made you stay;
Their frozen tops, like age's hoary hairs,
Shows their disasters, languishing in fears;
A swarthy rivelled rind all over spread,
Their dying bodies half alive, half dead.
But your occasions called you so away,
That nothing there had power to make you stay;
Yet did I see a noble grateful mind,
Requiting each according to their kind,
Forgetting not to turn and take your leave
Of these sad creatures, powerless to receive
Your favour, when with grief you did depart,
Placing their former pleasures in your heart,
Giving great charge to noble memory,
There to preserve their love continually;
But specially the love of that fair tree,
That first and last you did vouchsafe to see,
In which it pleased you oft to take the air
With noble Dorset, then a virgin fair,
Where many a learned book was read and scanned
To this fair tree; taking me by the hand,
You did repeat the pleasures which had passed
Seeming to grieve they could no longer last;
And with a chaste yet loving kiss took leave,
Of which sweet kiss I did it soon bereave,

138. *pray you*: beg you to stay
141. *vain*: futile
143. *age's*: old age's
145. *swarthy ... rind*: dark (suggesting discoloration) wrinkled or shrivelled bark
146. *Their*: the trees'
147. *occasions*: responsibilities
166–8. *bereave ... happiness*: by 'stealing' the Countess's kiss, Lanyer appropriates a gesture that would regularly be exchanged only between social equals. The phrasing hints

Scorning a senseless creature should possess
So rare a favour, so great happiness.
No other kiss it could receive from me,
For fear to give back what it took of thee;
So I, ingrateful creature, did deceive it
Of that which you vouchsafed in love to leave it;
And though it oft had given me much content,
Yet this great wrong I never could repent,
But of the happiest made it most forlorn,
To show that nothing's free from fortune's scorn,
While all the rest, with this most beauteous tree,
Made their sad consort, sorrow's harmony.
The flowers that on the banks and walks did grow,
Crept in the ground, the grass did weep for woe.
The winds and waters seemed to chide together,
Because you went away they knew not whither;
And those sweet brooks that ran so fair and clear,
With grief and trouble wrinkled did appear.
Those pretty birds that wonted were to sing,
Now neither sing nor chirp nor use their wing,
But with their tender feet on some bare spray,
Warble forth sorrow, and their own dismay.
Fair Philomela leaves her mournful ditty,
Drowned in dead sleep, yet can procure no pity.
Each arbour, bank, each seat, each stately tree,
Looks bare and desolate now for want of thee,
Turning green tresses into frosty grey,
While in cold grief they wither all away.
The sun grew weak, his beams no comfort gave,
While all green things did make the earth their grave;
Each briar, each bramble, when you went away,

at a muted revenge against fortune for its mistreatment of her (above ll. 103–6), and perhaps even against the Countess herself, insofar as Lanyer must supplicate for Clifford patronage.

178. *consort*: music (or a company of musicians)

193–6. *frosty ... grave*: Katherine Duncan-Jones points out to me that these 'wintry conceits' may allude to a local topographical feature, 'Winter Hill', the highest viewpoint near Cookham

195–6. *sun ... grave*: the pathetic fallacy Lanyer deploys throughout this section is a generic feature of literary elegies (e.g. the 'Doleful Lay of Clorinda', possibly by Mary Sidney). Within the scriptural context of *Salve Deus* it also recalls the gospel accounts of natural phenomena during the crucifixion ('*Salve Deus*', stanzas 59–60, 'The terror of all creatures at that instant when Christ died').

Caught fast your clothes, thinking to make you stay.
Delightful Echo, wonted to reply
To our last words, did now for sorrow die.
The house cast off each garment that might grace it,
Putting on dust and cobwebs to deface it.
All desolation then there did appear,
When you were going whom they held so dear.
This last farewell to Cookham here I give;
When I am dead thy name in this may live,
Wherein I have performed her noble hest,
Whose virtues lodge in my unworthy breast,
And ever shall, so long as life remains,
Tying my heart to her by those rich chains.

199. *wonted*: accustomed

201–2. *house ... it*: the metaphorical gesture of mourning perhaps relates to the passion detail of the veil of the temple being rent (above 'Salve Deus', 60.3)

207. *her*: the Countess of Cumberland's

LADY MARY WROTH (*c.* 1586–1651/3)

SELECTED SONNETS AND SONGS FROM *PAMPHILIA TO AMPHILANTHUS* AND *THE COUNTESS OF MONTGOMERY'S URANIA* (1621), AND EXCERPTS FROM *LOVE'S VICTORY* (after 1621)

Introduction

Mary Wroth, née Sidney, was heir to the most celebrated literary legacy in Elizabethan England. Her uncle Sir Philip Sidney had written three or four seminal works – *Astrophil and Stella*, the *Old Arcadia* and the *New Arcadia*, and *A Defence of Poetry* – and he was memorialised as the ideal Renaissance courtier, soldier, and poet following his premature death in 1586. Wroth's father Sir Robert Sidney, later Viscount Lisle, succeeded his brother Philip as Governor of Flushing and held various diplomatic and court posts. His interest in estate husbandry is known from Ben Jonson's 'To Penshurst', while his poetry (rediscovered only in the 1970s) considerably influenced Wroth's own style and verse-forms (Kelliher and Duncan-Jones 1975: 107–16). Her aunt Mary (Sidney) Herbert, Countess of Pembroke, had been the most prominent literary patron of the late-Elizabethan age, and her pioneering reputation as a female author and translator created an enabling precedent for her niece's career (Hannay 1991b: 15–34). Yet, like her aunt, Wroth found that working in the shadow of the dominantly male Sidney tradition could foster as well as derogate from recognition of her achievement. While being a Sidney undoubtedly helped her overcome traditional prejudices against female authors and secure a public readership (Quilligan 1990: 307–8), contemporary interest in her work sometimes owed more to her famous background than to a clear appreciation of her own talents. Her connections likewise probably shielded her from social disapproval after a long-standing affair with her cousin William Herbert, Earl of Pembroke, resulted in the birth of two illegitimate children. But when she was attacked for satirising members of the Denny and Hay families in the *Urania*, Wroth's adversary Lord Denny tried to turn her Sidneian heritage against her, advising her to avoid writing original compositions and instead to follow the example of her 'virtuous and learned aunt', who had made a celebrated translation of the Psalms.

A desire to perpetuate her family's literary tradition partly explains Wroth's decision to write in genres previously chosen by her uncle: pastoral romance (with the *Urania* modelled on Philip Sidney's *Arcadia*), the sonnet sequence (*Pamphilia to Amphilanthus* on *Astrophil and Stella*) and pastoral drama (*Love's Victory* much more loosely on *The Lady of May*). All three genres were traditionally associated with female readers while serving as the means for exploring male desires and ambitions. Though Wroth's works adhere to many of the conventions of each genre, she is not merely an imitator. Her significance lies in the fact that she reassesses each one's male-oriented assumptions from female perspectives.

The *Urania*, dedicated to Wroth's friend Susan, Countess of Montgomery, is a vast work of prose fiction with intermingled songs and poems. Through multiple characters and adventures it develops themes of love, deception, and self-realisation. Less traditionally, its focus on personal relationships between men and women foregrounds female yearnings for self-assertion and transcendence, as well as 'psychic, familial, gender, and broader social contradictions' experienced by early modern women (Waller 1991: 413). Such concerns come to light most clearly in the deep, frustrated passion of Pamphilia ('all-loving' and heroically constant) for Amphilanthus ('lover of two' and chronically unfaithful, though admirable in some other ways). The *Urania* also devotes comparatively little time to matters of chivalry and court politics which occupy an important place in the *Arcadia* and Renaissance romance generally. Wroth probably began writing the First Part of her work around 1618. It was published hastily, perhaps against her wishes, in 1621, with a continuation nearly as long remaining in manuscript (perhaps owing to the row with Lord Denny).

Pamphilia to Amphilanthus is a Petrarchan-style sonnet sequence of the kind made popular by *Astrophil and Stella* in the late sixteenth century. It was published with the *Urania* in 1621, though parts of it were being read in manuscript by Wroth's circle of friends at least as far back as 1613, and the Folger manuscript contains several poems not printed in 1621. Wroth received many tributes from contemporary writers for her work (listed fully in Wroth 1983: 17–22), including Ben Jonson, who dedicated *The Alchemist* to her in 1612 and claimed that reading her sonnets had made him 'a better lover and a much better poet'. Certain characters and themes in the *Urania* inform the slender narrative development in Wroth's sequence of 103 sonnets and songs, with the main fact being Pamphilia's unrequited love for the unfaithful Amphilanthus. Furthermore, scattered hints in both the *Urania* and the poems suggest an identification of the former with Wroth and the latter with her lover William Herbert, who was known at court as a notorious womaniser.

The sequence falls roughly into two halves. The first half follows the Petrarchan tradition of sonnets ordered into groups of six, each followed by a song; the last sonnet (48, or P55 following Roberts's through-numbering) is signed 'Pamphilia'. The second half contains three or four discrete groups of poems, including a crown of fourteen sonnets (modelled on her father's incomplete crown), in which the last line of each sonnet supplies the first of the one that follows. In the Folger manuscript but not the 1621 printed edition (the copy-text used here) the final sonnet of this half (P103) also ends with the signature 'Pamphilia'.

Paul Salzman has noted how the *Urania* recalls medieval romance in its proliferation of intertwining subsidiary stories (1991: xv). In this and other ways, Wroth seems to be returning to the origins of her chosen genres and attempting to reconstruct them according to female values and experiences (Lewalski 1993: 252). This is true of *Pamphilia to Amphilanthus*, which not only recalls Petrarch's original poems addressed to Laura, but also reworks certain conventions of late English Petrarchanism, as exemplified by *Astrophil and Stella*. Such reworkings become apparent in several ways. Although Wroth reverses the sexes of her poet-speaker and beloved – a bold departure in itself – Pamphilia does not woo or write about Amphilanthus using the aggressively self-regarding complaints and exquisite flattery that Astrophil does to Stella. Physically, Amphilanthus is barely present in Wroth's sequence, and when Pamphilia describes him she usually refers only to his eyes or heart using stylised Petrarchan images and metaphors suggestive of Platonic attraction. There are no blazons of the beloved's body, and no fetishising projections of the speaker's sexual desires on to it, following the customary practice of male poet-speakers addressing their mistresses. Pamphilia appears to suppress the erotic dimension of her desires in conformity with traditional cultural injunctions to female modesty (though as Kelliher and Duncan-Jones observe, in Robert Sidney's sequence the speaker's passions also lack the 'carnality' of *Astrophil*; 1975: 117). The result in many of her poems is a quality of despairing passivity and melancholy introspection reminiscent of her father's work. Furthermore, Amphilanthus is virtually silent as well as physically absent: he speaks only four words (in sonnet P71, not included here). This situation also departs from *Astrophil and Stella*, but in this case it arguably leads Pamphilia towards a positive assertion of selfhood, and may also represent an instance of Wroth reverting to Petrarch's example. For as Gordon Braden has observed (1990: 253–5), when Petrarch imagines Laura refusing his attentions, his thwarted desire reveals itself in at least two ways: it leaves him speechless, and it leads him to repackage his physical desire as Platonic virtue. When Laura refuses his advances, her chastity and self-control prompt Petrarch to shift his sexual urges towards spiritual union and metaphysical enlightenment. This is rather different from Sidney's Astrophil, who is not rebuffed nearly to the same degree. When he propositions Stella directly at several points she responds verbally and physically (Braden 1990: 256–8). In terms of the narrative action, Astrophil is not always fully in control because his dialogue with Stella becomes an external event which allows for the possibility of her acting on her own impulses when she speaks to or touches him. Petrarch by contrast remains tongue-tied, Laura inscrutable and absent, and so any reciprocal love they exchange occurs monologically, in signs he invents from his internalised image of her, rather than through public speech. Petrarch's feelings and desires remain a conversation with himself, between a private interior voice and Laura as an imagined presence. His self-sovereignty is never threatened.

This contrast between Petrarch and Astrophil provides a touchstone for Pamphilia, who adopts a position closer to that of Petrarch in choosing to commune silently and chastely with an imagined Amphilanthus. She thus avoids being mastered by his desires, or estranged by the male-empowering rhetoric of courtly love. There is one point at which Pamphilia does consider emulating Amphilanthus's carefree promiscuity (Song P75), but this is an exception; everywhere else the terms of Pamphilia's complaints remain wholly oriented to her personal desire for constancy (the same alternatives are debated in a lighter key in some of the Songs from the *Urania*, selected below). By turning inward and using the Petrarchan strategy of fully internalising Amphilanthus's presence, her sense of subjectivity remains authoritatively private, untroubled by the will of a male other.

Pamphilia's cultivation of solitude bears some resemblance to the later circumstances of Wroth's personal history. From the time of her (largely unhappy) marriage to Sir Robert Wroth in 1603 until 1614 she had been an active member of Queen Anne's inner circle, appearing in the Queen's first masque, *The Masque of Blackness*, in 1605, and in *The Masque of Beauty* three years later. During this time she gained public recognition as a patron and poet; it was also the period of her affair with William Herbert. When her husband died in 1614, he left her with crushing debts of £23,000 which she spent much of the rest of her life trying to pay off. Wroth retired from the court but continued to correspond with friends and occasionally to return to public life to participate in events such as the Queen's funeral in 1619 (Wroth 1983: 22–7). Her diminished role in court life reprised earlier experiences of her father and uncle. Sir Robert Sidney had been virtually exiled for over fifteen years as English Governor of Flushing, and during Elizabeth's reign he was unable to gain employment at court (his situation improved under James, but not to the point of exercising significant power). Much of his poetry bears signs of the anguish he felt during long periods of absence from his wife and family. Sir Philip Sidney's promotion of militant Protestantism, as well as his high-minded theories about the moral and social uses of poetry, found little support from Elizabeth and led to a personally disappointing public career. From this perspective Mary Wroth's distancing from court activities followed the general trajectory of Sidneian involvement in national affairs: as the seventeenth century advanced they were left to nurture past glories and largely private virtues apart from the political mainstream.

Though residual in this context, from another perspective Pamphilia's self-authenticating inwardness may have reminded contemporary readers of Calvinist ideas of grace and election that had become a regular part of Jacobean religious consciousness, and which by extension shaped the development of early modern subjectivity. Calvinist thought urged believers to become rigorously self-scrutinising and to view the world and its works with suspicion. These reactions were based on a belief in the radical incompatibility of divine truth and human endeavour, and a rejection of any agency claiming to mediate between the two: the internal divinely conferred resources of mercy and grace alone united these separate realms. Previous generations of the Sidney–Dudley family had championed such beliefs, which in their non-extreme forms became widely integrated in Jacobean religious culture (Doerksen 1994). They are evident in works such as the Countess of Pembroke's *Dialogue Between Thenot and Piers* as well as the spiritual diaries of many seventeenth-century women. Wroth's poems suggest that Pamphilia comes to recognise a similar kind of profound division between worldly (especially patriarchally implicated) agencies and her own internally validated destiny. The resulting scepticism not only asserts itself against the gender exclusions of Petrarchan poetics but also questions the refiguring capacity of any symbolic language deriving from masculine literary or court culture. Contemporary readers may have related the anti-world Wroth creates within her poems to renascent *con-*

temptus mundi ('contempt of the world') attitudes fostered by election theology that were to find their most characteristic expression several decades later in the works of John Bunyan (Delameau 1990: 140, 536–43). During the course of Wroth's sequence Pamphilia expresses disillusionment with human relationships and social contact (also evident in the *Urania*, and possibly reflective of Wroth's personal experience of the Jacobean court; (see Wroth 1977: 5). She likewise becomes dissatisfied with writing about love as a Petrarchanised psychodrama and instead comes to embrace the purely unmediated value of constancy. Her poems contain few topical allusions to people or events (Masten 1991: 67) or to the material realities of women's everyday lives (perhaps because even 'women's culture' was always hedged by male control; by contrast Pamphilia pointedly refers to masculine recreations in order to disparage them) (Fienberg 1991: 180; Jones 1991: 145–6). Nor does Pamphilia invoke her beloved as an agent of spiritual deliverance as Petrarch does Laura (MacArthur 1989: 14–15). Any quality of transcendence readers may detect in her poems (critics read Pamphilia's evolving situation with varying degrees of optimism) must derive from powers within her, as she gradually works her way towards a regenerate self-consciousness.

If Mary Wroth presents characters who struggle to realise women's choices and visions, and through them explores the problem of patriarchal restrictions on female agency, as Waller and others suggest (1991: 403), *Love's Victory* situates such initiatives within a more fanciful world of pastoral comedy in which its female characters achieve greater liberty of mobility, speech, and action than in her other works. Venus and Cupid, who appear in the Prologue and *entractes* and observe the action throughout, subject four pairs of lovers to a period of misunderstanding and thwarted passions so they will be forced to acknowledge Venus's sovereignty over affairs of the human heart. Each couple represents a different kind of love-relationship, whose tensions are heightened by the involvement of several additional lover-rivals and stock characters. Most of the main figures also appear in the Vale of Tempe episode of the Second Part of the *Urania*; but whereas in Wroth's romance the shepherds are disguised royal personages, in *Love's Victory* the shepherds are 'real' and interact amongst themselves and with the foresters on a fairly equal footing (though perhaps not with the virtual flattening of cultural, gender, or class hierarchies that Lewalski sees in the play; 1993: 297–300).

Love's Victory exists in two manuscript versions, never originally published: one an unfinished draft (Huntington), the other a complete five-act play (Penshurst, recently reproduced and edited by Michael Brennan, 1988). We have no evidence that Wroth's play was ever acted, but if it was it would probably have been staged in a private house before a small audience. Pastoral comedy in general had a wide currency in the early seventeenth century, and women were known not only as favourite readers of the genre but also writers and spectators. Queen Henrietta Maria, for example, acted in a pastoral she had written herself, at Somerset House in 1626 (Wroth 1983: 57).

There is no single source for the play, but Philip Sidney's quasi-dramatic entertainment *The Lady of May* bears some similar features: comic rustics, gentle social and aesthetic rivalries between the shepherds and the foresters, intermingled songs and duets, and contests or games. The latter occur in each of the play's first four acts, where they provide some of its liveliest moments and eventually lead to the potion-induced 'death' and resuscitation of Philisses and Musella in Act Five. (The game of confessions in Act Three is selected for presentation below, as well as the opening dialogue between Venus and Cupid.) All the features mentioned above originated in Virgil's *Eclogues*, the *locus classicus* of Renaissance pastoral lyric, while the pastoral drama closest to Wroth's is probably Tasso's *Aminta*, translated by Abraham Fraunce and dedicated to Mary Sidney in *The Countess of Pembroke's Ivychurch* (1591). But *Love's Victory* is more comical and lyrical than Tasso, and like Shakespeare's *As You Like It* its conflicts arise from personal anxieties and misdirected passions rather than grim treachery and violence; it is likewise distinguished by strong friendships among women and confident female agency (Lewalski 1993: 299–307). Moreover, Renaissance pastoral, again taking its cue from Virgil where urban concerns and topical issues were encoded in rural *otium*, usually afforded male writers a means of commenting allusively on court politics. This dimension is largely absent from Wroth's play, which prefers to concentrate, as her other works do, on the personal realms of the human psyche and emotions, albeit here in a holiday spirit.

Manuscripts:
Pamphilia to Amphilanthus, Folger Library MS V.a.104. *Love's Victory*, Penshurst MS, Viscount De L'Isle; Huntington Library MS HM 600.

Editions:
The Countess of Montgomery's Urania (1621, containing *Pamphilia to Amphilanthus*). STC 26051, reel 980. *Pamphilia to Amphilanthus*, ed. G.F. Waller (Salzburg, 1977). *The Poems of Lady Mary Wroth*, ed. Josephine A. Roberts (Baton Rouge and London, 1983). *Love's Victory*, ed. Michael Brennan (London, 1988). *The Paradise of Women*, ed. Betty Travitsky (Westport, Conn., 1981, brief excerpts). *Kissing the Rod*, ed. Germaine Greer *et al.* (New York, 1988, excerpts).

LADY MARY WROTH

FROM *PAMPHILIA TO AMPHILANTHUS*

(1621)

SONNET 1 (P1)

When night's black mantle could most darkness prove,
And sleep, death's image, did my senses hire
From knowledge of myself, then thoughts did move
Swifter than those most swiftness need require.
In sleep, a chariot drawn by winged desire
I saw, where sat bright Venus, Queen of Love,
And at her feet her son, still adding fire
To burning hearts which she did hold above;
But one heart flaming more than all the rest
The goddess held, and put it to my breast:
'Dear son, now shoot', said she, 'thus must we win'.
He her obeyed, and martyred my poor heart;
I waking hoped as dreams it would depart,
Yet since, O me, a lover I have been.

1. *mantle ... prove*: cover ... create

2. *sleep*: Pamphilia's dream is reminiscent of Petrarch's *Triumph of Love*, in which the speaker experiences a vision of love's power (Wroth 1983: 85). It likewise recalls the opening sonnet of Dante's *Vita Nuova*, but with a twist: instead of the speaker imagining that his burning heart is offered to and eaten by the lady, Pamphilia dreams that Venus and Cupid implant a flaming heart in her breast, thereby awakening her to love (Fienberg 1991: 184–5). This means that Amphilanthus's desires do not kindle Pamphilia's love, which is already present in her own body (Lewalski 1993: 252–3). *hire*: temporarily withdraw

5. *chariot ... desire*: in conventional representations Venus's chariot was drawn by doves; e.g. in *Astrophil and Stella*, 'Sweet kiss ... coupling doves, guides Venus' chariot right' (79.1–4)

9–10. *heart ... held*: The image of Venus holding a flaming heart appears on the title-page of Wroth's *Urania* and later atop one of the three towers marking the entrance to the Throne of Love (Salzman 1991: 58–60)

12. *martyred ... heart*: conventional image conveying the lover's pangs; e.g. *Astrophil and Stella* 20

SONNET 8 (P9)

Led by the power of grief, to wailings brought,
By false conceit of change fallen on my part,
I seek for some small ease by lines, which bought,
Increase the pain; grief is not cured by art.
Ah! how unkindness moves within the heart
Which still is true, and free from changing thought;
What unknown woe it breeds, what endless smart
With ceaseless tears, which causelessly are wrought.
It makes me now to shun all shining light,
And seek for blackest clouds me light to give,
Which to all others only darkness drive;
They on me shine, for sun disdains my sight.
Yet though I dark do live, I triumph may,
Unkindness, nor this wrong, shall love allay.

SONNET 19 (P22)

Come darkest night, becoming sorrow best,
Light leave thy light, fit for a lightsome soul;

2. *conceit*: notion, perhaps 'imaginary fancy'
change: i.e. in the beloved's affections; cf. 'unkindness' l. 5
3. *lines ... bought*: (writing) verse ... bartered, exchanged
5. *moves*: causes anger, exasperation
6. *still*: ever
7. *smart*: pain
8. *causelessly*: without provocation (i.e. for the 'unkindness')
9–12. *shun ... sight*: The light/night paradoxes originated with Petrarch and became very common in Elizabethan sonnets; e.g. *Astrophil and Stella* 33, 89, 91, 96–9:

Thought, with good cause thou lik'st so well the night,
Since kind or chance gives both one livery,
Both sadly black, both blackly darkened be,
Night barred from sun, thou from thy own sun's light.
(96.1–4)

11. *drive*: yield
13–14. *Yet ... allay*: the turn at the end of this sonnet, like others in the first half of the sequence, marks a moment of intense 'struggle between passionate surrender and self-affirmation' that leads to Pamphilia's 'determination to love as an individual choice' (Wroth 1983: 44)
14. *allay*: overthrow, destroy

1–2. *night ... light*: Pamphilia frequently invokes 'Night and its qualities – blackness, coldness, absence, grief – as valued female companions, identifying Night especially as her

Darkness doth truly suit with me oppressed,
Whom absence power doth from mirth control.
The very trees with hanging heads condole
Sweet summer's parting, and of leaves distressed
In dying colours, make a grief-full role,
So much, alas, to sorrow are they pressed.
Thus of dead leaves her farewell carpet's made,
Their fall, their branches, all their mournings prove
With leaveless naked bodies, whose hues vade
From hopeful green to wither in their love.
If trees and leaves for absence mourners be,
No marvel that I grieve, who like want see.

SONNET 22 (P25)

Like to the Indians scorched with the sun,
The sun which they do as their god adore,

alter ego' (Lewalski 1993: 254–5; Jones 1991: 146). Also compare Wroth's opening quatrain with that of Robert Sidney's Sonnet 30:

Absence, I cannot say thou hid'st my light,
Not darkened, but for aye set is my sun;
No day sees me, not when night's glass is run;
I present, absent am; unseen in sight. . . .

becoming = befitting, adorning

4. *absence . . . control*:: absence overrules the power of (or drains the strength from) mirth

5ff. The image of mournful autumn trees shedding carpets of leaves is reminiscent of Shakespeare's Sonnet 73 ('That time of year thou mayst in me behold') and Robert Sidney's Sonnet 31.1–4:

Forsaken woods, trees with sharp storms oppressed,
Whose leaves once hid the sun, now strew the ground,
Once bred delight, now scorn, late used to sound
Of sweetest birds. . . .

condole = grieve

9. *her*: i.e. summer's (but as often in Wroth's sonnets, the feminine pronoun suggests the speaker's identification with the emotional state of the thing or person being described)

11. *vade*: fade, decay

14. *like . . . see*: like (summer) feel absence, (and thus) see (things in the same way)

1. *Indians*: the references to Indians, blackness, and night may allude to Wroth's participation in Ben Jonson's *Masque of Blackness* (1605), commissioned by Queen Anne (Wroth 1983: 99; Lewalski 1993: 254). Jones relates Wroth's images of darkness and mourning to her (partly self-imposed) exile from court and loss of royal favour (1991: 144–6).

So am I used by love; for evermore
I worship him, less favours have I won.
Better are they who thus to blackness run,
And so can only whiteness' want deplore,
Than I, who pale and white am with grief's store,
Nor can have hope but to see hopes undone.
Besides their sacrifice received in sight
Of their chose saint, mine hid as worthless rite,
Grant me to see where I my off'rings give,
Then let me wear the mark of Cupid's might
In heart, as they in skin of Phoebus' light,
Not ceasing off'rings to love while I live.

SONNET 23 (P26)

When everyone to pleasing pastime hies –
Some hunt, some hawk, some play, while some delight
In sweet discourse, and music shows joy's might –
Yet I my thoughts do far above these prize.
The joy which I take is that, free from eyes
I sit and wonder at this daylike night,
So to dispose themselves, as void of right,

3–4. *love ... him*: Cupid
6. *whiteness' ... deplore*: bewail or mourn lack of whiteness
7. *store*: abundance, fulness
10. *chose*: *sic*
worthless rite: puns on worth/Wroth and rite/write/right
13. *Phoebus'*: the sun's

1. *hies*: goes
2. *play*: at cards or dice
4. *Yet ... prize*: Fienberg observes that by rejecting court pastimes devised by men, Pamphilia focuses on the pleasures of her own imagination and poetry, thereby substituting a process of self-invention and authentication (1991: 176; also Jones 1991: 146). Masten, however, reads such 'privatization' in this and related sonnets (e.g. 38) less optimistically, as a 'withdrawal into an interiorized corporeal space' and 'a withdrawal from public signification', resulting in an embryonic subjectivity that as yet exists only as an absence (1991: 70–82).
5. *eyes*: (others') eyes; i.e. as an object, gazed upon
6. *wonder*: marvel deeply
7. *themselves*: i.e. 'everyone' else
void of right: oblivious of a just appreciation (of what really is valuable and brings 'true pleasure')

And leave true pleasure for poor vanities.
When others hunt, my thoughts I have in chase,
If hawk, my mind at wished end doth fly;
Discourse, I with my spirit talk, and cry
While others music choose as greatest grace.
O God, say I, can these fond pleasures move?
Or music be but in sweet thoughts of love?

SONNET 38 (P43)

What pleasure can a banished creature have
In all the pastimes that invented are
By wit or learning, absence making war
Against all peace that may a biding crave?
Can we delight but in a welcome grave,
Where we may bury pains, and so be far
From loathed company, who always jar
Upon the string of mirth that pastime gave?
The knowing part of joy is deemed the heart;
If that be gone what joy can joy impart,
When senseless is the feeler of our mirth?
No, I am banished and no good shall find,
But all my fortunes must with mischief bind,
Who but for misery did gain a birth.

8. *vanities*: idle, worthless pastimes
9. *chase*: active pursuit (there is a shift in emphasis from the external object which draws hunters, thereby exercising a certain power over them, to the internally determining subject of 'my thoughts')
13. *these ... pleasures*: i.e. hunting, hawking, etc; fond = trivial

1. *banished*: suggesting banishment from royal favour, and thus possibly alluding to Wroth's departure from the Jacobean court, as well as the speaker's rejection by the beloved
4. *biding*: dwelling, refuge. The original spelling could also represent 'bidding'.
7. *jar*: play discordantly
7–8. *loathed ... gave*: the speaker contrasts two kinds of pastimes: diversions and entertainment, and those leading to inward reflection and self-knowledge (ll. 2–3). Jones argues that the latter are part of Pamphilia's cultivation of melancholy apartness, which according to NeoPlatonic theory signified genius and divine fury and aimed at self-sufficiency in the face of the instability, triviality, and disappointments of court-life and amorous intrigues (1991: 144–8, and see next sonnet).
10. *joy ... joy*: joy can the source of joy
14. *but for ... did*: were it not for ... would

SONNET 39 (P45)

If I were giv'n to mirth, 'twould be more cross
Thus to be robbed of my chiefest joy;
But silently I bear my greatest loss,
Who, used to sorrow, grief will not destroy.
Nor can I as those pleasant wits enjoy
My own framed words, which I account the dross
Of purer thoughts, or reckon them as moss,
While they, wit-sick, themselves to breath employ.
Alas, think I, your plenty shows your want;
For where most feeling is, words are more scant;
Yet pardon me: live, and your pleasure take,
Grudge not if I, neglected, envy show;
'Tis not to you that I dislike do owe,
But, crossed myself, wish some like me to make.

SONNET 40 (P46)

It is not love which you poor fools do deem
That doth appear by fond and outward shows

1. *cross*: affliction, misfortune

5–6. *Nor ... words*: i.e. fashionable male courtier-poets, who view composing love-verses as a rhetorical game to exhibit their personal desires; also a conventional Petrarchan conceit, that writing poetry in some sense makes the beloved present and thus consoles the male writer-lover; e.g. *Astrophil and Stella* 1.1: 'Loving in truth, and fain in verse my love to show'. Also 34, 50.

6. *framed*: contrived

7. *moss*: excrescence (i.e. something superficially outward)

9. *plenty*: abundance (of ready, 'witty' words)
want: lack (of deep feelings)

12. *Grudge not*: do not become envious

14. *crossed*: troubled, afflicted
make: regard, consider. The speaker contrasts two versions of her self: one genuine, defined by the interior space of her private thoughts and emotions; the other unauthentic ('*like* me'), swayed by the wills of others including Amphilanthus, and by the lure of Petrarchan discourse which she discovers is unsuited to a female speaking position or her own feelings. Masten (1991: 72–3 and *passim*) discusses these distinctions within the framework of 'the inauthentic theatricality of stock Petrarchanism'.

1. *poor fools*: addressed to an imagined company of conventional (male) lovers who exult in displaying their desires publicly in witty, rhetorically coded ways

Of kissing, toying, or by swearings, gloze;
O no, these are far off from love's esteem.
Alas, they are not such that can redeem
Love lost, or winning, keep those chosen blows;
Though oft with face and looks love overthrows,
Yet so slight conquest doth not him beseem.
'Tis not a show of sighs or tears can prove
Who loves indeed, which blasts of feigned love
Increase, or die as favours from them slide;
But in the soul true love in safety lies,
Guarded by faith which to desert still hies;
And yet kind looks do many blessings hide.

SONNET 45 (P52)

Good now be still, and do not me torment
With multitude of questions; be at rest,
And only let me quarrel with my breast,
Which still lets in new storms my soul to rent.
Fie, will you still my mischiefs more augment?
You say I answer cross: I that confessed
Long since; yet must I ever be oppressed
With your tongue-torture which will ne'er be spent?
Well then, I see no way but this will fright

3. *toying*: amorous dalliance
swearings, gloze: oaths or protestations, speciously express
6. *winning ... blows*: winning (love, imagined as Cupid armed with arrows), maintain his (pleasantly) desirable shots or strokes
8. *him beseem*: become, suit him (Cupid)
11. *favours ... them*: i.e. from the beloved ... the lovers
12. *true love*: alluding to the NeoPlatonic idea of binary love represented by two Cupids, one earthly, physical, and blind (described above), the other heavenly, spiritual, and clear-sighted. Compare the 'true love' and 'nobler course' of *Astrophil and Stella* 62. To this conventional distinction Wroth adds the notion of private retirement ('desert' = wild, uninhabited place; deserted condition, desolation).
safety: i.e. from volatile or mutable earthly love (as above)
13. *still hies*: always resorts

1. *Good*: the speaker addresses an impatient, vexing interlocutor in a dramatic monologue reminiscent of poems by Donne or Herbert. See also *Astrophil and Stella* 14 and 21.
4. *rent*: rend, tear apart
8. *spent*: exhausted

That devil speech: alas, I am possessed!
And mad folks senseless are of wisdom's right;
The hellish spirit, absence, doth arrest
All my poor senses to his cruel might;
Spare me then till I am myself, and blessed.

SONNET 6 (SECOND SERIES; P68)

My pain, still smothered in my grieved breast,
Seeks for some ease, yet cannot passage find
To be discharged of this unwelcome guest;
When most I strive, more fast his burdens bind,
Like to a ship on Goodwins cast by wind:
The more she strive, more deep in sand is pressed,
Till she be lost; so am I in this kind
Sunk and devoured and swallowed by unrest.
Lost, shipwrecked, spoiled, debarred of smallest hope,
Nothing of pleasure left, save thoughts have scope,
Which wander may; go then my thoughts and cry:
Hope's perished, love tempest-beaten, joy lost,
Killing despair hath all these blessings crossed;
Yet faith still cries, love will not falsify.

10ff. *alas* …: Compare Astrophil's 5th Song, in which he 'revenges' himself by projecting various evil personas on Stella: 'A witch I say thou art, though thou so fair appear … Alas, that I am forced such evil of thee to say! / I say thou art a devil, though clothed in angel's shining' (74, 80–1)

11. *right*: claims

5. *Goodwins*: the metaphor comparing a lover's emotional state to a wandering ship propelled by her or his own sighs is Petrarchan. Wroth makes it more topical by referring to the Goodwin Sands, a shoal off the Kentish coast. See *The Merchant of Venice* 3.1.4–6: 'Goodwins … a very dangerous flat, and fatal, where the carcasses of many a tall ship lie buried'.

6. *she*: cf. Sonnet 19.9 and n.
pressed: weighed down, oppressed

9. *spoiled*: destroyed, ruined, plundered

14. *falsify*: prove (hopes, expectations) to be ill-founded; counterfeit, make false representations or statements. By suddenly projecting her personal beliefs of hope and constancy into the poem, the speaker evades the finality set up by the Goodwins metaphor, and extends rather than reverses the emotional strivings represented by the immobilised ship.

SONG 3 (P93)

'Come merry spring delight us,
For winter long did spite us,
In pleasure still persever,
Thy beauties ending never,
  Spring and grow
  Lasting so,
With joys increasing ever.

Let cold from hence be banished
Till hopes from me be vanished,
But bless thy dainties growing
In fulness freely flowing:
  Sweet birds sing,
  For the spring
All mirth is now bestowing'.

Philomel in this arbour
Makes now her loving harbour,
Yet of her state complaining,
Her notes in mildness straining,
  Which though sweet,
  Yet do meet
Her former luckless paining.

As Lewalski observes (1993: 258), in songs from the last half of *Pamphilia to Amphilanthus* the speaker ventriloquises various lovers' voices using different metrical and stanzaic forms. This song begins as a celebration of seasonal change from winter to spring expressive of hopeful love.

9. *hopes ... vanished*: i.e. turned to certainties
10. *thy*: spring's
17. *state*: i.e. present emotional condition
18. *mildness straining*: i.e. straining to sound calm, self-possessed, but her tune 'falsifies' her words
20. *meet*: encounter, come face to face with
21. *former ... paining*: Philomel was raped and had her tongue cut out by Tereus, who fell in love with her after marrying Procne. In prison Philomel depicted her sufferings on a tapestry which she sent to Procne, who disguised herself and smuggled Philomel out. Procne went on to kill her son Itys to deprive Tereus of an heir and then to serve his flesh to him. The gods turned Philomel into a swallow, and Procne into a nightingale (or vice-versa in some versions). Thus, even though Philomel wishes to forget past misfortune, the memory of her 'former luckless paining' uncontrollably undercuts her will.

SONNET 7 (FOURTH SERIES; P101)

No time, no room, no thought or writing can
Give rest or quiet to my loving heart,
Or can my memory or fancy scan
The measure of my still-renewing smart.
Yet would I not, dear love, thou shouldst depart,
But let my passions as they first began
Rule, wound, and please; it is thy choicest art
To give disquiet which seems ease to man.
When all alone I think upon thy pain,
How thou dost travail our best selves to gain,
Then hourly thy lessons I do learn,
Think on thy glory which shall still ascend
Until the world come to a final end,
And then shall we thy lasting power discern.

SONNET 8 (FOURTH SERIES; P102)

How glow-worm-like the sun doth now appear:
Cold beams do from his glorious face descend,
Which shows his days and force draw to an end,
Or that to leave-taking, his time grows near.
This day his face did seem but pale though clear;
The reason is, he to the north must lend

This and the next poem fall into the sequence's last section of nine Sonnets analysing 'the course of a love threatened by jealousy' (Lewalski 1993: 262)

1–2. *No … heart*: see n. to sonnet 39.5–6
room: position, authority, or employment; assigned or appropriate place

3. *fancy scan*: imaginative fantasy or love judge, discern, comprehend; analyse metrically (as if it were verse, and, by extension, transform into verse)

5. *would*: desire

7. *art*: i.e. Pamphilia's creative stimulus does not derive from the conventional formulas of (male-oriented) Petrarchan love-poetry, or the external will of Amphilanthus, but in love as a manifestation of her personal desires

10. *travail*: labour

4. *leave-taking … time*: i.e. late December, before the winter solstice. Roberts draws attention to the resemblance between Wroth's image of the winter sun and Donne's 'A Nocturnal upon St Lucy's Day' (Wroth 1983: 142).

6–8. *north … dear*: compare *Astrophil and Stella* 8.5–8:
But [Love] finding these North climes too coldly him embrace,
Not used to frozen clips, he strave to find some part
Where with most ease and warmth he might employ his art.
At length he perched himself in Stella's joyful face ….

His light, and warmth must to that climate bend,
Whose frozen parts could not love's heat hold dear.
Alas if thou, bright sun, to part from hence
Grieve so, what must I hapless? who, from thence
Where thou dost go, my blessing shall attend;
Thou shalt enjoy that sight for which I die,
And in my heart thy fortunes do envy;
Yet grieve, I'll love thee, for this state may mend.

SONNET 9 (P103)

My muse, now happy, lay thyself to rest,
Sleep in the quiet of a faithful love,
Write you no more, but let these fancies move
Some other hearts, wake not to new unrest.
But if you study, be those thoughts addressed
To truth, which shall eternal goodness prove,
Enjoying of true joy the most and best,
The endless gain which never will remove.
Leave the discourse of Venus and her son
To young beginners, and their brains inspire
With stories of great love, and from that fire
Get heat to write the fortunes they have won,
And thus leave off; what's past shows you can love,
Now let your constancy your honour prove.

10. *from thence*: i.e. from (here to) there

8. *remove*: depart

9–14. *Leave ... prove*: Lewalski observes that Pamphilia does not end her sequence with the usual Petrarchan 'palinode or repudiation of earthly love' but chooses to adopt a '(revised) neo-Platonic perspective' that reconceptualises love as inner fidelity to a self-defined longing, rather than turbulent other-centred passions projected as factitious images of Venus and Cupid (1993: 262). Quilligan likewise reads Pamphilia's final sonnets as an 'act of willful self-definition' in defiance of both Petrarchan poetics and pressures to conform to the norms of seventeenth-century wifehood (1990: 323). Roberts, Beilin, and Paulissen, on the other hand, assign constancy a spiritual value and see this transformation leading towards transcendant, possibly Christian, love (Wroth 1983: 49; Beilin 1987: 240–2; Paulissen 1982: 95 and *passim*).

SONNET (F3)

Eyes, can you tell me where my heart remains?
  Have you not seen it in these lovely eyes?
  With pride show you the place it there retains,
  And baby-like still pastime as it lies?
Or can you in that blessed breast surprise
  The runaway, when it new triumph gains,
  To lodge where greatest hearts for mercy cries?
  Have you not seen it there joy at their pains?
If neither, where? where lives it? where abides
  This careless spirit who from me closely slides
  And heartless leaves me? Oh, alas I know,
It is petitioning for pity's place,
  Where love hath purest and still-during grace;
  Thus while I thought it soared, it creeps below.

1–4. *Eyes ... lies*: The topos of lovers' eyes mutually reflecting each others' exchanged hearts (represented as a playful baby Cupid, or runaway; see below) is Petrarchan and was common amongst Elizabethan sonnet writers; e.g. *Astrophil and Stella* 11.9–10: 'So when thou [Love] saw'st, in nature's cabinet, / Stella, thou straight look'st babies in her eyes'. The related image of the migrating heart became another common conceit (Wroth 1983: 102). See *Astrophil and Stella* Song 10.41–2.

Pamphilia's sparing and stylised physical descriptions of Amphilanthus defer to the social taboos of Wroth's time, which prohibited women from expressing sexual desire openly, and thus uphold traditional female virtues of modesty and chastity.

4. *pastime*: entertain itself

14. *Thus ... below*: see *Astrophil and Stella* 70.1–2: 'My muse may well grudge at my heavenly joy, / If still I force her in sad rhymes to creep'

LADY MARY WROTH

FROM *THE COUNTESS OF MONTGOMERY'S URANIA*

(1621)

SONG (U13)

Love what art thou? A vain thought
In our minds by fancy wrought;
Idle smiles did thee beget,
While fond wishes made the net
Which so many fools have caught.

Love what art thou? Light and fair,
Fresh as morning, clear as th'air;
But too soon thy evening change
Makes thy worth with coldness range,
Still thy joy is mixed with care.

Love what art thou? A sweet flower,
Once full blown, dead in an hour;
Dust in wind as staid remains
As thy pleasure, or our gains,
If thy humour change to lour.

Love what art thou? Childish, vain,
Firm as bubbles made by rain,
Wantonness thy greatest pride;
These foul faults thy virtues hide,
But babes can no staidness gain.

Love what art thou? Causeless cursed,
Yet alas these not the worst,

One of the concluding eclogues of Book One of the Urania, sung by a shepherdess who had 'fallen out with Love, or [had] some great quarrel to him' (I.i.143; Wroth 1983: 156)

2. *fancy*: love, amorous inclinations; imagination
9. *range*: roam, rove
13. *staid*: calm
15. *lour*: frown, scowl
20. *staidness*: peacefulness, rest

Much more of thee may be said;
But thy law I once obeyed,
Therefore say no more at first.

SONG (U14)

Who can blame me if I love,
Since love before the world did move?
When I loved not, I despaired,
Scarce for handsomeness I cared;
Since so much I am refined,
As new-framed of state and mind,
Who can blame me if I love,
Since love before the world did move?

Some in truth of Love beguiled,
Have him blind and childish styled;
But let none in these persist,
Since so judging judgement missed.
Who can blame me etc?

Love in chaos did appear
When nothing was, yet he seemed clear;
Nor when light could be descried,
To his crown a light was tied.
Who can blame me etc?

Love is truth and doth delight,
Whereas honour shines most bright;
Reason's self doth love approve,
Which makes us ourselves to love.
Who can blame me etc?

Could I my past time begin,
I would not commit such sin
To live an hour and not to love,
Since love makes us perfect prove.
Who can blame me etc?

Sung by a 'spruce' Cypriot shepherd to mollify Amphilanthus after he takes umbrage at an earlier song mocking love (I.i.144–5; Wroth 1983: 157)

2. *move*: urge, incite (i.e. love is equated with God, the first 'mover' of the spheres (cf. p. 418 n. 1))

12. *judgement*: (competent) judgement

13. *etc*: = continuation of the two-line refrain which begins the song

SONG (U28)

The joy you say the heav'ns in motion try
  Is not for change, but for their constancy;
Should they stand still, their change you then might move,
  And serve your turn in praise of fickle love.
That pleasure is not but diversified,
  Plainly makes proof your youth, not judgement, tried.
The sun's renewing course yet is not new,
  Since 'tis but one set course he doth pursue;
And though it feigned be that he hath changed,
  'Twas when he from his royal seat hath ranged.
His glorious splendour, free from such a stain,
  Was forced to take new shapes, his end to gain;
And thus indeed the sun may give you leave
  To take his worst part, your best to deceive.
And whereof he himself hath been ashamed,
  Your greatness praiseth, fitter to be blamed.
Nothing in greatness loves a strange delight;
  Should we be governed then by appetite?
A hungry humour, surfeiting on ill,
  Which glutton-like with cramming will not fill.
No serpent can bring forth so foul a birth
  As change in love, the hatefull'st thing on earth.
Yet you do venture this vice to commend,

1. *you*: Nicholarus, who had written amorous verses to the speaker, wife of Polydorus, commending 'variety in love' (I.i.316–19; Wroth 1983: 168)
   heav'ns in motion: referring to the pre-Copernican conception of the universe as a series of nine concentric, moving spheres; = 'they' l. 3
   try: exhibit
3. *move*: cite as evidence
5. *That … not but*: that (you claim) … without exception
6. *your … tried*: you were ruled by youthful ignorance rather than your better, more mature, judgement
9. *feigned … he*: fabled … strictly the sun-god Apollo, though here applied loosely to Zeus or Jove
11. *stain*: i.e. the charge of mutability
12. *new shapes*: e.g. as recorded in Ovid's *Metamorphoses* and elsewhere in classical myth
14. *worst part*: Zeus usually transformed himself as a cover to seduce or abduct mortal women
16. *greatness*: illustrious authority (spoken ironically)
    fitter: (though it is) fitter
17. *strange*: ignorant
19. *humour*: disposition, fancy

  As if of it you patron were or friend.
Foster it still, and you shall true man be
  Who first for change lost his felicity.
Rivers, 'tis true, are clearest when they run,
  But not because they have new places won;
For if the ground be muddy where they fall,
  The clearness with their change doth change with all.
Lakes may be sweet, if so their bottoms be;
  From roots, not from the leaves, our fruit we see.
But love too rich a prize is for your share,
  Some little idle liking he can spare
Your wit to play withal; but true love must
  Have truer hearts to lodge in, and more just.
While this may be allowed you for love's might,
  As for day's glory framed was the night,
That you can outward fairness so affect
  Shows that the worthier part you still neglect,
Or else your many changings best appears,
  For beauty changeth faster than the years;
And that you can love greatness makes it known
  The want of height in goodness of your own.
'Twas not a happiness in ancient time
  To hold plurality to be no crime,
But a mere ignorance, which they did mend
  When the true light did glorious lustre lend.
And much I wonder you will highly rate
  The brutish love of nature, from which state
Reason doth guide us, and doth difference make
  From sensual will, true reason's laws to take.
Were't not for reason, we but brutish were,
  Nor from the beasts did we at all differ;

25. *Foster ... still*: continue to foster it
27. *Rivers ... run*: run = flow quickly. Proverbial (Tilley W103).
31. *sweet*: fresh, clean
35. *play withal*: amuse (himself) therewith
true love: i.e. of the rational soul
37. *this*: i.e. 'idle liking'
for: to demonstrate
39. *affect*: love; aspire to
44. *height*: noble aspirations
45. *happiness*: happy, fitting situation
46. *plurality*: i.e. of lovers
48. *true light*: i.e. Christianity (dispelling 'pagan' ignorance, sensuality)
52. *take*: prefer, accept

Yet these you praise, the true style opinion,
By which truth's government is shrewdly gone.
Honour by you esteemed a title; true,
A title cannot be claimed by change as due;
It is too high for such low worth to reach:
Heav'n gifts bestow'th as to belong to each.
And this true love must in revenge bestow
On you, his sacred power with pain to know:
A love to give you, fickle, loose, and vain,
Yet you with ceaseless grief seek to obtain
Her fleeting favours, while you wailing prove,
Merely for punishment, a steady love;
Let her be fair but false, great, disdainful,
Chaste but to you, to all others gainful;
Then shall your liberty and choice be tied
To pain, repentance, and (the worst sin) pride.
But if this cannot teach you how to love,
Change still, till you can better counsel prove;
Yet be assured, while these conceits you have,
Love will not own one shot (you say) he gave.
His are all true, all worthy: yours unjust;
Then, changing you, what can you from him trust?
Repentance true felt, oft the gods doth win.
Then in your wane of love, leave this foul sin;
So shall you purchase favour, banish shame,
And with some care obtain a lover's name.

55. *style opinion*: name (for such views is actually) self-conceited, misguided belief
56. *shrewdly gone*: wrongly overthrown
60. *to … each*: each person deserves
65. *prove*: experience yourself
66. *for*: (your own)
67. *great*: of high rank
68. *but … gainful*: only … yielding, promiscuous
72. *prove*: find
73. *conceits*: fanciful notions
76. *trust*: believe in, be certain of
78. *wane*: declining authority, decreasing vigour

LADY MARY WROTH

FROM *LOVE'S VICTORY*

(after 1621)

[ACT I]

*[Enter] Venus, and Cupid with her, in her temple,**
her Priests attending her.

VENUS Cupid, methinks we have too long been still
And that these people grow to scorn our will.
Mercy to those ungrateful breeds neglect,
Then let us grow our greatness to respect.
Make them acknowledge that our heav'nly power
Cannot their strength but even themselves devour.
Let them not smile and laugh (because thine eyes
Are covered as if blind) or love despise.
No, thou that scarce shalt from thine eyes take off
Which gave them cause on thee to make this scoff.
Thou shalt discern their hearts and make them know
That humble homage unto thee they owe.
Take thou the shaft, which headed is with steel,
And make them bow, whose thoughts did lately reel.
Make them thine own, thou, who didst me once harm,
Cannot forget the fury of that charm.

* *Temple*: perhaps in Cyprus, where a cult of Venus is described in Ovid's *Metamorphoses*. Wroth departs from Tasso's *Aminta* and other Renaissance pastorals in having Venus initiate the action and dominate Cupid, rather than the other way round; the change emphasises female agency in the supernatural realm (Lewalski 1993: 96). Wroth may also have been influenced by Ben Jonson, who used Cupid as a commentator and participant in several masques as well as *Cynthia's Revels* (1600; Wroth 1983: 54).

4. *grow*: develop

6. *Cannot*: Can not only

14. *reel*: run riot

15. *who … harm*: alluding to the story of Cupid and Psyche. Venus became jealous of Psyche's great beauty and sent Cupid to make her fall in love with some ugly creature, but Cupid became her lover instead. After Psyche broke Cupid's command not to attempt to look at him during his nocturnal visits, he abandoned her and she later died after performing great feats searching the earth for him. She was ultimately brought to heaven, however, at Cupid's request.

Wound them but kill them not, so may they live
To honour thee, and thankfulness to give.
Shun no great cross which may their crosses breed,
But yet let blessed enjoying them succeed.
Grief is sufficient to declare thy might,
And in thy mercy glory will shine bright.

CUPID Mother, I will no cross, no harm forbear
Of jealousy for loss, of grief or fear
Which may, my honour touched, again repair,
But with their sorrows will my glory rear.
Friends shall mistrust their friends, lovers mistake,
And all shall for their folly woes partake.
Some shall love much, yet shall no love enjoy,
Others obtain when lost is all their joy.
This will I do, your will and mind to serve,
And to your triumph will these rights preserve.

VENUS Then shall we have again our ancient glory,
And let this called be love's victory.
Triumphs upon their travails shall ascend,
And yet most happy ere they come to end.

CUPID Joy and enjoying on some shall be set,
Sorrow on others caught by Cupid's net.

[Venus and Cupid stand apart]

19. *Shun*: omit
cross ... crosses: misfortune ... vexations
20. *enjoying*: possession (of happiness, of each other); enjoyment of their own wills
21. *Grief*: experience of grief
25. *my ... repair*: if my honour is sullied, be changed back or remedied
26. *rear*: rise
30. *obtain*: obtain love
32. *rights preserve*: claims, powers (referring to Venus's 'will' and 'mind') endure, remain. The original spelling 'Rights' may also signify 'rites'; hence, 'rites contribute'.
35. *travails*: toils

[ACT III, 125ff.]

[Enter] Dalina, Climaena, Simaena, Phyllis. [Venus and Cupid watch the action unobserved]

DALINA Now w'are alone let every one confess
Truly to other what our lucks have been,
How often liked and loved, and so express
Our passions past. Shall we this sport begin?
None can accuse us, none can us betray
Unless ourselves our own selves will bewray.
PHYLLIS I like this. But will each one truly tell?
CLIMAENA Trust me, I will. Who doth not, doth not well.
SIMAENA I'll plainly speak. But who shall be the first?
DALINA I can say least of all, yet I will speak.
A shepherd once there was, and not the worst
Of those were most esteemed, who sleep did break
With love, forsooth, of me. I found it thought
I might have him at leisure – liked him not.
Then was there to our house a farmer brought,

[Act III]: The action to this point involves four pairs of lovers: Musella and Philisses, traditionally virtuous lovers who survive a period of misunderstanding; Simaena and Lissius, less experienced and more emotionally volatile lovers, swayed by jealousy and pride respectively; Silvesta and the Forester, Neoplatonic lovers who have chosen chaste love; Dalina and Rustic, who delight in physical love. There are also three independent rival lovers: Climaena, a foreigner who loves Lissius; Phyllis who loves Philisses; and Lacon who loves Musella.

In Act I Philisses rejects the love of Silvesta in favour of Musella, but in Act II he begins to suspect that the latter loves Lissius instead of him. Lissius protests to Philisses that he loves only Simaena, Philisses's sister, and they vow to help each other in their respective suits. At the beginning of Act III, Musella accuses Silvesta of adopting chastity merely because she was earlier rejected by Philisses. Musella confesses her love for Philisses, but fears his jealousy.

39. *Dalina*:: instigator of all the games or contests in each of the first four acts that serve to reveal the characters and their desires. The game of confessions played here was originally proposed in Act I but rejected; 'As the play progresses, the protagonists choose to face truths they feared earlier, and as a result they become stronger … the women are now able to speak of their varied pasts' (Swift 1989: 182).
40. *other … lucks*: one another … fortunes
42. *sport*: diversion, amusement, probably with a connotation of amorousness
44. *bewray*: betray
50. *were … who*: who were … whose
52. *liked*: yet I liked

Rich and lively, but those bought not his lot
For love. Two jolly youths at last there came
Which both me thought I very well could love.
When one was absent, t'other had the name,
In my staid heart he present did most move.
Both at one time in sight I scarce could say
Which of the two I then would wish away.
But they found how to choose, and as I was
Like changing, like uncertain, let me pass.

SIMAENA I would not this believe if other tongue
Should this report, but think it had been wrong.
But since you speak this, could not you agree
To choose someone, but thus unchosen be?

DALINA Truly, not I. I plainly tell the truth,
Yet do confess 'twas folly in my youth.
The next that comes this fault I'll mend and have,
I will no more be foolish or delay,
Since I do see the lads will labour save.
One answer rids them, I'll no more say nay.
But if he say, 'Dalina, will you love?'
And 'thank you' I will say, 'if you will prove'.
The next go on and tell what you have done.

SIMAENA I am next, and have but losses won,
Yet still I constant was, though still rejected.
Loved and not loved I was, liked and neglected.
Yet now some hopes remains when love thought dead
Proves like the spring's young bud when leaves are fled.

PHYLLIS Your hap's the better, would mine were as good,
Though I as long as you despised stood.
For I have loved, and loved but only one,
Yet I, disdained, could but receive that moan
Which others do for thousands. So unjust
Is love to those who in him most do trust.
Nor did I ever let my thoughts be shown

54–5. *lot / For*: prize in the absence of
57. *name*: distinction, honour
58. *staid ... present*: calm ... being present
59. *Both*: if both were
62. *Like ... like*: ever ... in the same way
63. *other*: some other
69. *have*: referring to 'The next'
74. *And ... prove*: A ... put (your love) to the test
77. *still*: ever
81. *hap's*: good fortune is

But to Musella who all else hath known;
Which was, long time I had Philisses loved
And ever would, though he did me despise.
For then, though he had ever cruel proved,
From him not me the fault must needs arise.
And if Simaena thus your brother dear
Should be unkind, my love shall still be clear.

SIMAENA 'Tis well resolved. But how liked she your choice?
Did she or blame or else your mind commend?

PHYLLIS Neither she seemed to dislike or rejoice,
Nor did commend I did this love intend,
But smiling told me 'twere best to be advised,
Comfort it were to win, but death despised.

SIMAENA I do believe her. But Climaena yet
Hath nothing said; we must not her forget.

CLIMAENA Why, you have said enough for you and me.
Yet for your sakes I will the order keep,
Who though a stranger here by birth I be,
And in Arcadia ever kept my sheep,
Yet here it is my fortune with the rest
Of you to like, and loving be oppressed.
For since I came I did a lover turn,
And turn I did indeed when I loved here.
Since for another I in love did burn,
To whom I thought I had been held as dear,
But was deceived. When I for him had left
My friends and country, was of him bereft
And all, but that you kindly did embrace
And welcome me into this happy place,
Where for your sakes I meant to keep some sheep,
Not doubting ever to be more deceived.
But now, alas, I am anew bereaved
Of heart. Now time it is myself to keep
And let flocks go, unless Simaena please
To give consent, and so give me some ease.

SIMAENA Why, what have I to do with whom you love?

CLIMAENA Because 'tis he who doth your passion prove.

89. *Philisses*: lover of Musella and distant anagram of Philip Sidney (like Astrophil of *Astrophil and Stella*, and Philisides of the *Arcadia*). Musella recalls Stella, who was widely believed to represent Sidney's lover Lady Penelope Rich, née Devereux.

96. *or … or*: either … or

105. *stranger*: foreigner

114. *was*: I was

124. *he … prove*: Lissius … know

SIMAENA The lesser need I fear the winning of his love,
Since all my faith could never so much move.
Yet can he not so cruel ever be
But he may live my misery to see.

CLIMAENA And when his eyes to love shall open be,
I trust he will turn pity unto me
And let me have reward which is my due.

SIMAENA Which is your due? What pity's due to you?
Dream you of hope? O you too high aspire.
Think you to gain by kindling an old fire?

CLIMAENA My love will be the surer when I know
Not love alone, but how love to bestow.

SIMAENA You make him yet for all this but to be
The second in your choice; so was not he
In mine, but first and last, of all the chief,
That can to me bring sorrow or relief.

CLIMAENA This will not win him. You may talk and hope,
But in love's passages there is large scope.

SIMAENA 'Tis true, and you have scope to change and choose,
To take and dislike, like and soon refuse.

CLIMAENA My love as firm is to him as is thine.

SIMAENA Yet mine did ever rise, never decline;
No other moved in me the flames of love.
Yet you dare hope as much as I to move;
Folly indeed is proud and only vain,
And you his servant feeds with hope of gain.

CLIMAENA I love him most.

SIMAENA I love him best. Can you
Challenge reward, and cannot say you're true?

CLIMAENA In this you wrong me. False I have not been,
But changed on cause.

SIMAENA Well now you hope to win
This second. Yet I, like those, lose no time.
But can you think that you can this way climb
To your desires? This shows you love have tried
And that you can both choose and choice divide.
But take your course and win him if you can,
And I'll proceed in truth as I began.

DALINA Fie, what a life is here about fond love!
Never could it in my heart thus much move.
This is the reason men are grown so coy,

142. *passages*: proceedings
147. *other*: other person
157. *tried*: tested

When they perceive we make their smiles our joy.
Let them alone and they will seek and sue,
But yield to them and they'll with scorn pursue.
Hold a while off, they'll kneel and follow you
And vow and swear, yet all their oaths untrue.
Let them once see you coming, then they fly,
But strangely look, and they'll for pity cry.
And let them cry; there is no evil done.
They gain but that which you might else have won.

SIMAENA Is this your counsel? Why, but now you said
Your folly had your loves and good betrayed,
And that hereafter you would wiser be
Than to disdain such as have left you free.

DALINA 'Tis true, that was the course I meant to take,
But this must you do, your own ends to make.
I have my fortunes lost, yours do begin,
And to cross those could be no greater sin.
I know the world, and hear me, this I advise,
Rather than too soon won, be too precise.
Nothing is lost by being careful still,
Nor nothing so soon won as lover's ill.

[Enter Lissius]

Here Lissius comes. Alas, he is love-strook.
He's even now learning love without the book.

LISSIUS Love, pardon me, I know I did amiss
When I thee scorned, or thought thy blame my bliss.
Oh pity me, alas I pity crave.
Do not set trophies on my luckless grave.
Though I, poor slave and ignorant, did scorn
Thy blessed name, let not my heart be torn
With thus much torture. Oh but look on me
Take me a faithful servant unto thee.

[Climaena accosts Lissius]

CLIMAENA Dear Lissius, my dear Lissius, fly me not.
Let not both scorn and absence be my lot.

LISSIUS Pray let me go, you know I cannot love.
Do not thus far my patience strive to move.

CLIMAENA Why, cruel Lissius, wilt thou never mend

170. *strangely*: distantly, reservedly
174. *good*: well-being
182. *precise*: fastidious, choosy
185. *strook*: struck
188. *blame*: injury, hurt
190. *trophies*: emblems or memorials; garlands (signifying triumph)

But still increase thy frowns for my sad end?
LISSIUS Climaena, 'tis enough that I have said.
Be gone and leave me. Is this for a maid
To follow and to haunt me thus? You blame
Me for disdain but see not your own shame.
Fie, I do blush for you. A woman woo?
The most unfitting'st, shameful'st thing to do.
CLIMAENA Unfit and shameful? Ay, indeed 'tis true,
Since suit is made to hard, relentless you.
Well, I will leave you and restore the wrong
I suffer for my loving you so long.
No more shall my words trouble you, nor I
E'er follow more, if not to see me die.

Exit [Climaena]

LISSIUS Farewell, you now do right. This is the way
To win my wish; for when I all neglect
That seek me, she must needs something respect
My love the more, and what though she should say
I once denied her, yet my true-felt pain
Must needs from her soft breast some favour gain.
DALINA Lissius is taken; well said, Cupid, now
You partly have performed your taken vow.
Of all our shepherds I ne'er thought that he
Would of thy foolish troop a follower be.
But this it is a goddess to despise
And thwart a wayward boy that wants his eyes.
Come, let's not trouble him, he is distressed
Enough. He need not be with us oppressed.
SIMAENA I'll stay and ask him who 'tis he doth love.
DALINA Do not a pensive heart to passion move.
SIMAENA To passion? Would I could his passion find
To answer my desire and grieved mind.
DALINA Stay then and try him, and your fortune try.
It may be he loves you. *[To Phyllis]* Come, let's go by.

Exit [Dalina and Phyllis]

LISSIUS O sweet Simaena, look but on my pain.
I grieve and curse myself for my disdain.

209. *restore*: amend

212. *if*: if it is only

214. *neglect*: avoid

219–20. *Cupid ... vow*: As Michael G. Brennan notes (Wroth 1988: 236), Cupid, watching the action, 'would presumably react with pleasure ... to Dalina's invocation'.

223. *goddess*: i.e. Venus

224. *wayward ... eyes*: i.e. blind Cupid

Now but have pity, love doth make me serve,
And for your wrong and you I will reserve
My life to pay, your love but to deserve,
And for your sake I do myself preserve.

SIMAENA Preserve it not for me. I seek not now
Nor can I credit this or any vow
Which you shall make. I was too long despised
To be deceived. No, I will be advised
By reason now. My love shall no more blind
Me nor make me believe more than I find.

LISSIUS Believe but that, and I shall have the end
Of all my pain and wishes. I pretend
A virtuous love; then grant me my desire,
Who now do waste in true and faithful fire.

SIMAENA How can I this believe?

LISSIUS My faith shall tell
That in true love I will all else excel.
But then will you love me as I do you?

SIMAENA I promise may, for you cannot be true.

LISSIUS Then you will promise break.

SIMAENA Not if I find
That as your words are, so you'll make your mind,

LISSIUS Let me nor speech nor mind have when that I
In this or any else do falsify
My faith and love to you.

SIMAENA Then be at rest,
And of my true affection be possessed.

LISSIUS So, dear Simaena, be of me and mine.
Now do my hopes and joys together shine.

SIMAENA Nor let the least cloud rise to dim this light,
Which love makes to appear with true delight.

[*Exeunt*].

Venus and Cupid [come forward]

CUPID Is not this pretty? Who doth free remain
Of all this flock that waits not in our train?
Will you have yet more sorrow? Yet more woe?
Shall I another bitter arrow throw?
Speak, if you will, my hand now knows the way
To make all hearts your sacred power obey.

VENUS 'Tis pretty, but 'tis not enough. Some are
Too slightly wounded; they had greater share

246. *pretend*: offer
255. *nor ... nor*: neither ... nor
264. *waits ... train*: serves in attendance ... body of followers, retinue

In scorning us. Lissius too soon is blessed
And with too little pain hath got his rest.
Scarce had he learned to sigh before he gained,
Nor shed a tear ere he his hopes obtained.
This easy winning breeds us more neglect,
Without much pain few do love's joys respect;
Then are they sweetest purchased with felt grief;
To floods of woe sweet looks gives full relief.
A world of sorrow is eased with one smile,
And heart-wounds cured when kind words rule the while;
That foregone, wailings in forgotten thought
Shall wasted lie disdained, once dearly bought.
One gentle speech more heals a bleeding wound
Than balms of pleasure, if from other ground.
Strike then to favour him, and let him gain
His love and bliss by love's sweet pleasing pain.

CUPID That shall be done, nor had he this delight
Bestowed but for this greater harm and spite.
You shall before this act be ended see
He doth sufficiently taste misery.
'Tis far more grief from joy to be down-thrown
Than joy to be advanced to pleasure's throne.

VENUS Let me see that, and I contented am. . .

284. *if . . . ground*: if they derive . . . sources
287–8. *had . . . for*: would he ever have this delight conferred on him were it not for
290. *taste*: experience
292. *advanced*: (from grief)

RACHEL SPEGHT (*c.* 1597–1630+)

A DREAM, FROM *MORTALITY'S MEMORANDUM* (1621)

Introduction

One of the main obstacles faced by early modern women who wished to gain access to restricted areas of knowledge was the lack of enabling precedents. A possible first step was to redefine existing social metaphors in order to sanction greater female activity in roles traditionally reserved to men. But prevailing cultural attitudes made such a project difficult, since social and legal values based on historical custom and precedent were highly, even jealously, esteemed, partly in reaction to the disconnection many people felt as public institutions underwent radical changes during the sixteenth and seventeenth centuries. Nonetheless, for some women attempting to rewrite patriarchal language and invent pro-female metaphors was an essential part of the process of reconceiving themselves as legitimate authors and subjects, possessed of the ability to speak freely with power and authority.

Rachel Speght's *Dream*, which precedes her verse-meditation on death, *Mortality's Memorandum*, represents one such attempt at cultural reconstruction. She presents her story as a quest for knowledge in which the female narrator travels from uneducated 'native' intelligence to rational self-awareness. Along the way personified attributes and symbolic events map her journey towards overcoming internal feelings of inadequacy and external voices of disapproval. Such conflicts may reflect Speght's personal history to some degree, because in *A Muzzle for Melastomus* (1615) she tells us that her own education had been equally precarious. As in the *Dream*, which comes to the narrator in the threshold period of waking consciousness just before dawn, Speght was able to read only in the brief intervals when she was not obliged to perform regular household tasks which otherwise occupied most of her waking hours: 'that little smattering in learning which I have obtained [was] only the fruit of such vacant hours as I could spare from affairs befitting my sex' ('Certain Queries to the Baiter of Women', Epistle to the Reader, F1^{r}).

Acquiring knowledge under such conditions must have been a situation shared by many women of her background. In a society that restricted formal female education almost entirely to private tutoring for a small minority of upper- and middle-class women (and even then, as in Speght's case, as something secondary to everyday domestic duties and social obligations), the *Dream* can be read as an Everywoman story. Speght universalises her narrator's experiences by allegorising them, inviting contemporary female readers to identify their lives with her own. At the same time Speght deepens the *Dream*'s cultural resonance by mapping it on to a central Western myth: Eve's desire for knowledge in Eden. Her combination results in a rewriting of Eve's story and the creation of a new paradigm (Beilin 1987: 11–12). Whereas tradition has it that Eve was banished from the garden paradise after being misled by Satan into seeking forbidden knowledge, the *Dream*'s narrator reverses this sequence: Eve gradually casts off Ignorance while being guided onward by Thought, Experience, Age, and her own 'labours'. Her goal is 'Erudition's garden': rational Knowledge and Truth, both conceived as ways of reclaiming the divine element in human nature that was obscured by the fall into original sin.

A Dream suggests that learning has practical uses as well. For as Speght's earlier pamphlet-debate with Joseph Swetnam demonstrated, knowledge is empowering, which explains why patriarchal culture seeks to restrict it; unfettered, it generates female prophets who may question a society's established hierarchies and values. Speght illustrates this point through her narrator's encounters with two enemies on her journey. One is Dissuasion, whose gender remains unidentified, in contrast with the *Dream*'s friendly entities who are all explicitly feminine. Dissuasion puts forward conventional objections based on alleged female inferiority but is easily routed by the narrator's guardian virtues. The second enemy is Swetnam, personified as a 'full-fed beast'. The narrator credits herself with first 'Muzzling' this creature, but ultimately leaves him to be finished off by two other pamphlet-writers who clashed with him in 1617, Esther Sowernam and Constantia Munda (both probably men using female pseudonyms). The fact that the narrator distances herself from their challenges to Swetnam suggests that she regarded their full-volume 'defences' as too other-defined and self-regarding – and perhaps too close to male stereotypes of shrewishness. She therefore hastens on her way towards a more serene rationality. In the end her only true enemy is Death, which has recently claimed her mother. But having glimpsed a vision of Truth through Knowledge, she can put her theoretical tools of wisdom to public use by exposing 'the nature of this mortal foe'. Her main poem (not presented here) continues to celebrate the virtues of self-possession supported by Christian faith and reason that she upheld in her earlier defence, and reaffirms here.

Editions:
Mortality's Memorandum, with A Dream Prefixed (1621). STC 23057, reel 1220. *The Paradise of Women*, ed. Betty Travitsky (Westport, Conn., 1981, brief excerpts). *Kissing the Rod*, ed. Germaine Greer *et al.* (London, 1988, excerpts from *A Dream*).

RACHEL SPEGHT

FROM *MORTALITY'S MEMORANDUM, WITH A DREAM PREFIXED, IMAGINARY IN MANNER, REAL IN MATTER* *

(1621)

THE DREAM

When splendent Sol, which riseth in the east,
Returning thence took harbour in the west;
When Phoebus laid her head in Titan's lap,
And creatures sensitive made haste to rest;
When sky which erst looked like to azure blue
Left colour bright and put on sable hue,

Then did Morpheus close my drowsy eyes
And stood as porter at my sense's door,
Diurnal cares excluding from my mind,
Including rest, the salve for labours sore.
Night's greatest part in quiet sleep I spent;
But nothing in this world is permanent.

For ere Aurora spread her glitt'ring beams
Or did with robes of light herself invest,
My mental quiet sleep did interdict
By entertaining a nocturnal guest:

* *Imaginary ... Matter*: i.e. an allegorical fiction

1. *Sol*: the sun

3. *Phoebus ... her*: either this is right (= Apollo, the sun god) and 'her' is mistaken for 'his', or (less likely) Phoebus represents an error for Phoebe, the Titaness who represented the moon; her husband was the Titan Coeus

4. *sensitive*: living

6. *sable*: black

7. *Morpheus*: god of sleep

9. *Diurnal*: daily

13. *Aurora*: goddess of dawn

15. *did interdict*: was restrained or interrupted (Speght may be thinking of the underlying Latin meaning, to interpose; *OED* does not cite an instance of this intransitive use of the verb)

A Dream which did my mind and sense possess
With more than I by pen can well express.

At the appointment of supernal power,
By instrumental means methought I came
Into a place most pleasant to the eye,
Which for the beauty some did Cosmos name,
Where stranger-like on everything I gazed,
But wanting wisdom was as one amazed.

Upon a sudden, as I gazing stood,
Thought came to me and asked me of my state,
Enquiring what I was and what I would,
And why I seemed as one disconsolate.
To whose demand I thus again replied,
'I, as a stranger in this place abide.

The haven of my voyage is remote,
I have not yet attained my journey's end;
Yet know I not, nor can I give a guess,
How short a time I in this place shall spend;
For that high power which sent me to this place,
Doth only know the period of my race.

The reason of my sadness at this time
Is 'cause I feel myself not very well.
Unto you I shall much obliged be,
If for my grief a remedy you'll tell.'
Quoth she, 'if you your malady will show,
My best advice I'll willingly bestow'.

'My grief', quoth I, 'is called Ignorance,
Which makes me differ little from a brute;
For animals are led by nature's lore,
Their seeming science is but custom's fruit;
When they are hurt they have a sense of pain,
But want the sense to cure themselves again.

19. *supernal*: heavenly
20. *instrumental means*: effective or efficient means (of the dream)
22. *Cosmos*: universal harmony, or more literally, order (as opposed to chaos)
36. *period*: limit
41. *she*: i.e. Thought (either *mens* or *cogitatio*, and like most of the personifications here, gendered feminine)
46. *science ... custom's*: knowledge ... instinct's or habit's

And ever since this grief did me oppress,
Instinct of nature is my chiefest guide
I feel disease, yet know not what I ail,
I find a sore, but can no salve provide;
I hungry am, yet cannot seek for food,
Because I know not what is bad or good.

And sometimes when I seek the golden mean,
My weakness makes me fail of mine intent,
That suddenly I fall into extremes,
Nor can I see a mischief to prevent,
But feel the pain when I the peril find,
Because my malady doth make me blind.

What is without the compass of my brain,
My sickness makes me say it cannot be;
What I conceive not, cannot come to pass,
Because for it I can no reason see.
I measure all men's feet by mine own shoe,
And count all well which I appoint or do.

The pestilent effects of my disease
Exceed report, their number is so great;
The evils, which through it I do incur,
Are more than I am able to repeat.
Wherefore, good Thought, I sue to thee again
To tell me how my cure I may obtain.'

Quoth she, 'I wish I could prescribe your help;
Your state I pity much and do bewail;
But for my part, though I am much employed,
Yet in my judgement I do often fail.
And therefore I'll commend unto your trial
Experience, of whom take no denial.

For she can best direct you, what is meet
To work your cure and satisfy your mind.'
I thanked her for her love and took my leave,
Demanding where I might Experience find.
She told me if I did abroad enquire,
'Twas likely Age could answer my desire.

58. *see ... prevent*: foresee a mistake in order to avoid it
61. *without*: beyond

I sought, I found, she asked me what I would.
Quoth I, 'your best direction I implore,
For I am troubled with an irksome grief'.
Which when I named, quoth she, 'declare no more,
For I can tell as much as you can say,
And for your cure I'll help you what I may.

The only medicine for your malady,
By which and nothing else your help is wrought,
Is Knowledge, of the which there is two sorts,
The one is good, the other bad and naught;
The former sort by labour is attained,
The latter may without much toil be gained,

But 'tis the good which must effect your cure.'
I prayed her then that she would further show
Where I might have it. 'That I will', quoth she,
'In Erudition's garden it doth grow;
And in compassion of your woeful case,
Industry shall conduct you to the place.'

Dissuasion, hearing her assign my help
(And seeing that consent I did detect),
Did many remoras to me propose,
As dullness and my memory's defect,
The difficulty of attaining lore,
My time and sex, with many others more.

Which when I heard, my mind was much perplexed,
And, as a horse new come into the field
Who with a harquebus at first doth start,
So did this shot make me recoil and yield.
But of my fear when some did notice take,
In my behalf they this reply did make.

'First', quoth Desire, 'Dissuasion, hold thy peace,
These oppositions come not from above.'
Quoth Truth, 'they cannot spring from reason's root,

104. *detect*: reveal
105. *remoras*: obstacles
106–8. *dullness ... sex*: insofar as *A Dream* can be read as Speght's 'intellectual autobiography' (Shepherd 1985: 58), each of these is associated with typical male objections to female learning, which Speght may have encountered herself
111. *harquebus*: large early form of musket

And therefore now thou shalt no victor prove'.
'No', quoth Industry, 'be assured this,
Her friends shall make thee of thy purpose miss.

For with my sickle I will cut away
All obstacles that in her way can grow,
And by the issue of her own attempt,
I'll make thee *labor omnia vincet* know.'
Quoth Truth, 'and sith her sex thou dost object,
Thy folly I by reason will detect.

Both man and woman of three parts consist,
Which Paul doth body, soul, and spirit call,
And from the soul three faculties arise,
The mind, the will, the power. Then wherefore shall
A woman have her intellect in vain,
Or not endeavour Knowledge to attain?

The talent God doth give must be employed,
His own with vantage he must have again;
All parts and faculties were made for use,
The God of Knowledge nothing gave in vain.
'Twas Mary's choice our Saviour did approve,
Because that she the better part did love.

Cleobulina and Demophila,
With Telesilla, as historians tell,
(Whose fame doth live, though they have long been dead)
Did all of them in poetry excel.

124. *labor ... vincet*: work overcomes everything

127–8. *man ... spirit*: 1 Thessalonians 5.23

133–4. *talent ... again*: alluding to the parable of talents in Luke 19 (or alternatively Matthew 25; see n. to Epistle Dedicatory ll. 4–5)

137–8. *Mary's ... love*: presumably Mary Magdalene, identified with the unnamed woman in Mark 14 who displays her prophetic recognition of Jesus's messianic role by anointing his head with an expensive ointment. The meaning of her action eludes the male disciples, who see it as wasteful expense, but Jesus commends her loving gesture, saying it will be remembered throughout the world. Judas's betrayal of Jesus for money immediately follows.

139. *Cleobulina*: sixth-century BC Greek female poet celebrated for solving riddles
Demophila: eight-century BC sibyl (prophet) of Cumae (Beilin 1987: 307), the earliest Greek settlement in Italy

140. *Telesilla*: fifth-century BC Greek lyric poet famous for arming the women of Argive after the men had been defeated in battle by the Lacedemonians

A Roman matron that Cornelia hight,
An eloquent and learned style did write.

Hypatia in astronomy had skill,
Aspasia was in rhet'ric so expert
As that Duke Pericles of her did learn;
Arete did devote herself to art,
And by consent (which shows she was no fool)
She did succeed her father in his school.

And many others here I could produce,
Who were in science counted excellent;
But these examples, which I have rehearsed
To show thy error, are sufficient.'
Thus having said, she turned her speech to me,
That in my purpose I might constant be.

'My friend', quoth she, 'regard not vulgar talk,
For dunghill-cocks at precious stones will spurn,
And swine-like natures prize not crystal streams,
Condemned mire and mud will serve their turn.
Good purpose seldom oppositions want,
But constant minds Dissuasion cannot daunt.

Shall every blast disturb the sailor's peace?
Or boughs and bushes travellers affright?
True valour doth not start at every noise;
Small combats must instruct for greater fight.
Disdain to be with every dart dismayed;
'Tis childish to be suddenly afraid.

If thou didst know the pleasure of the place
Where Knowledge grows, and where thou mayst it gain,

143. *Cornelia*: daughter of Scipio Africanus and widow of Sempronius Gracchus; her letters were praised by Cicero for their eloquence. She refused offers of remarriage in order to devote herself to managing her estate and educating her children.

145. *Hypatia*: Alexandrian famous for her writings on algebra

146. *Aspasia*: celebrated fifth-century BC intellectual who taught eloquence at Athens, to Socrates amongst others. Her talents and charms attracted King ('Duke') Pericles, who was satirised for accepting her political advice after she became his mistress.

148. *Arete*: philosopher of Cyrene, 337 BC

154. *sufficient*: four syllables

158. *spurn*: oppose contemptuously

159. *swine-like … streams*: proverbial (Tilley P165)

Or rather knew the virtue of the plant,
Thou would'st not grudge at any cost or pain
Thou canst bestow to purchase for thy cure
This plant, by which of help thou shalt be sure.

Let not Dissuasion alter thy intent;
'Tis sin to nip good motions in the head.
Take courage, and be constant in thy course,
Though irksome be the path which thou must tread.
Sick folks drink bitter medicines to be well,
And to enjoy the nut men crack the shell.'

When Truth had ended what she meant to say,
Desire did move me to obey her will,
Whereto consenting I did soon proceed
Her counsel and my purpose to fulfill;
And by the help of Industry my friend,
I quickly did attain my journey's end.

Where being come, Instruction's pleasant air
Refreshed my senses, which were almost dead,
And fragrant flowers of sage and fruitful plants
Did send sweet savours up into my head,
And taste of science appetite did move
To augment theory of things above.

There did the harmony of those sweet birds
(Which higher soar with Contemplation's wings
Than barely with a superficial view
Denote the value of created things)
Yield such delight as made me to implore,
That I might reap this pleasure more and more.

And as I walked wand'ring with Desire,
To gather that for which I thither came
(Which by the help of Industry I found),
I met my old acquaintance, Truth by name,
Whom I requested briefly to declare
The virtue of that plant I found so rare.

180. *enjoy … shell*: proverbial (Tilley K19)
189–91. *sage … savours … taste of science*: word-play related to Latin root *sapere* meaning to taste or savour and its derivative *sapiens* meaning wisdom (= 'science')
192. *theory*: mental contemplation

Quoth she, 'by it God's image man doth bear,
Without it he is but a human shape
Worse than the Devil (for he knoweth much);
Without it who can any ill escape?
By virtue of it evils are withstood;
The mind without it is not counted good.

Who wanteth Knowledge is a scripture fool;
Against the Ignorant the prophets pray,
And Hosea threatens judgement unto those
Whom want of Knowledge made to run astray.
Without it thou no practic good canst show
More than by hap, as blind men hit a crow.

True Knowledge is the window of the soul,
Through which her objects she doth speculate;
It is the mother of faith, hope, and love;
Without it who can virtue estimate?
By it, in grace thou shalt desire to grow;
'Tis life eternal God and Christ to know.

Great Alexander made so great account
Of Knowledge that he oftentimes would say
That he to Aristotle was more bound
For Knowledge, upon which Death could not prey,
Than to his father Philip for his life,
Which was uncertain, irksome, full of strife.'

This true report put edge unto Desire,
Who did incite me to increase my store,
And told me 'twas a lawful avarice
To covet Knowledge daily more and more.
This counsel I did willingly obey,
Till some occurrence called me away

211. *scripture fool*: one who mouths passages from the Bible without any critical understanding of their significance or context (Speght's historicising scriptural analysis in *A Muzzle for Melastomus* demonstrates the wise approach; above p. 126ff.)

213–14. *Hosea ... astray*: Hosea 5, condemning Israel's blasphemous worship of Canaanite gods

216. *hap*: accident

218. *speculate*: contemplate mentally; observe closely

223–5. *Alexander ... bound*: Aristotle tutored Alexander the Great in the liberal arts. Since the latter went on to conquer the world, some Renaissance humanists celebrated him as an example of the value of such an education.

And made me rest content with that I had,
Which was but little, as effect doth show,
And quenched hope for gaining any more,
For I my time must otherways bestow.
I therefore to that place returned again
From whence I came, and where I must remain.

But by the way I saw a full-fed beast,
Which roared like some monster, or a devil,
And on Eve's sex he foamed filthy froth,
As if that he had had the falling evil;
To whom I went to free them from mishaps,
And with a *Muzzle* sought to bind his chaps.

But, as it seems, my mood out-ran my might,
Which when a self-conceited creature saw,
She passed her censure on my weak exploit,
And gave the beast a harder bone to gnaw;
Haman she hangs, 'tis past he cannot shun it;
For Esther in the preter tense hath done it.

And yet her enterprise had some defect,
The monster surely was not hanged quite;
For as the child of prudence did conceive,

244. *falling evil*: epilepsy

246. *Muzzle . . . chaps*: Speght's *Muzzle for Melastomus* (1617); the beast is Swetnam; chaps = jaws

247. *mood . . . might*: Speght deliberately avoided a slanging match with Swetnam, preferring to argue away his claims calmly and rationally with textual evidence. Her choices are therefore consciously gendered, and she commends the same approach to her female readers (see above p. 129).

248–52. *self-conceited . . . it*: Speght's *Muzzle* was followed in 1617 by Esther Sowernam's *Esther hath Hanged Haman* (alluding to the Old Testament heroine) and Constantia Munda's *Worming of a Mad Dog*. Sowernam criticised Speght's 'slender' answers, while both she and Munda attacked Swetnam with abandon. 'Esther' and 'Constantia' were almost certainly men who knew that sensational claims and inflammatory rhetoric were more profitable in this 'debate' serving male commercial interests. Speght may have known the real identity of her 'colleagues' (she was forced to deny charges of her work being ghost-written) and in any case wished to differentiate her approach.

252. *preter*: past

255. *child of prudence*: Constantia Munda = elegant constancy or perseverance. 'Her' *Worming of a Mad Dog* bore the alternative title *A sop for Cerberus the Jailer of Hell*. Cerberus was the triple-headed dog guarding the entrance to the classical underworld. In Virgil's *Aeneid*, Aeneas throws him a sop (= liquid-soaked bread) to distract him.

His throat not stopped, he still had power to bite.
She therefore gave to Cerberus a sop,
Which is of force his beastly breath to stop.

But yet if he do swallow down that bit,
She otherways hath bound him to the peace,
And like an artist takes away the cause,
That the effect by consequence may cease.
This frantic dog, whose rage did women wrong,
Hath Constance wormed to make him hold his tongue.

Thus leaving them I passed on my way,
But ere that I had little further gone,
I saw a fierce insatiable foe
Depopulating countries, sparing none
Without respect of age, sex, or degree;
It did devour, and could not daunted be.

Some feared this foe, some loved it as a friend;
For though none could the force of it withstand,
Yet some by it were sent to Tophet's flames,
But others led to heavenly Canaan land.
On some it seized with a gentle power,
And others furiously it did devour.

The name of this impartial foe was Death,
Whose rigour whilst I furiously did view,
Upon a sudden, ere I was aware,
With piercing dart my mother dear it slew;
Which when I saw, it made me so to weep
That tears and sobs did rouse me from my sleep.

But when I waked I found my dream was true,
For Death had tane my mother's breath away,
Though of her life it could not her bereave,
Sith she in glory lives with Christ for aye;

260. *peace*: with a pun on 'piece' = 'bit'

261. *artist*: person who acts in a practical manner (as opposed to a theorist)

264. *wormed*: cut out the tendon in a dog's tongue that was believed to make it rabid (= 'rage')

273. *Tophet's flames*: retributive pyre for Israel's enemies the Assyrians (Isaiah 30.33)

284. *tane*: taken

286. *aye*: ever

Which makes me glad, and thankful for her bliss,
Though still bewail her absence, whom I miss.

A sudden sorrow pierceth to the quick,
Speedy encounters fortitude doth try;
Unarmed men receive the deepest wound,
Expected perils time doth lenify;
Her sudden loss hath cut my feeble heart
So deep, that daily I endure the smart.

The root is killed; how can the boughs but fade?
But sith that Death this cruel deed hath done,
I'll blaze the nature of this mortal foe
And show how it to tyrannize began.
The sequel then with judgement view aright,
The profit may and will the pains requite.
Esto Memor Mortis

292. *lenify*: soothe
297. *blaze*: publish
301. *Esto Memor Mortis*: Let the reader be mindful of death

TEXTUAL NOTES

The following list records substantive or debatable departures from the original printed sources or manuscripts.

MARGARET TYLER, EPISTLE TO THE READER, FROM *THE MIRROR OF PRINCELY DEEDS AND KNIGHTHOOD*

2 *indeed*] in deede A3^r
106 *prize*] price A4^v

ANNE DOWRICHE, EPISTLE TO THE READER, FROM *THE FRENCH HISTORY*

28 *considered, so*] considered. So A4^r

RACHEL SPEGHT, EPISTLE DEDICATORY, FROM *MORTALITY'S MEMORANDUM*

15 *right's sake*] rights sake A2^v

ELIZABETH JOCELIN, EPISTLE DEDICATORY, FROM *THE MOTHER'S LEGACY*
MS = BL ADD. MS 27467 1624 = 1ST PRINTED EDN

4 *from* 1624] for MS
44 I 1624] omitted MS
55 *is* – 1624] is? MS
85 *ubique* 1624] *ubiq* MS

KATHERINE PARR, FROM *THE LAMENTATION OF A SINNER*

41 *withstood*] withstande A7^v
106 *thee*] the D3^v

139 *deceiveth*] disc . . . veth D6^{v} (letters obscured)
254 *understood*] understande F4^{v}

JANE ANGER, FROM *JANE ANGER HER PROTECTION FOR WOMEN*

199 *is no constancy*] is ‸ constancy C1^{r}

ELIZABETH GRYMESTON, FROM *MISCELLANEA, MEDITATIONS, MEMORATIVES*

ch. 3, l. 57 *waning*] wauing C1^{r}
ch. 9, l. 4 *papyrionibus*] *papilionibus* D3^{r}
ch. 17, l. 46 *vitare*] *vicare* E8^{v} (3rd edn = *vitare*)

RACHEL SPEGHT, FROM *A MUZZLE FOR MELASTOMUS*

'To Joseph Swetnam'

6 *roving*] roaring B1^{v} (uncorrected)

A Muzzle

45 *its*] it C2^{v}

ELIZABETH CLINTON, COUNTESS OF LINCOLN, FROM *THE COUNTESS OF LINCOLN'S NURSERY*

41–2 *to her worthy*] to our worthy B2^{v}
102 *is so*] it so B4^{v}

MARGARET, LADY HOBY, FROM *THE DIARY OF MARGARET, LADY HOBY* MS = BL EGERTON MS 2614

225 *Bethlehem*] Betheme MS
256 *raided*] reed MS

MARY WARD, *THE AUTOBIOGRAPHICAL PAPERS* (FROM THE *LETTERS OF INSTRUCTION*, TRANSLATIONS AND TRANSCRIPTIONS OF MARY WARD'S WRITINGS BY SISTER IMMOLATA WETTER IBVM, 1970, PRIVATELY CIRCULATED)

53 *anxiousness*] anxiety II:5
94 *have*] had II:6
163 *in*] to II:12
185 *Exercises‸ for*] Exercises each for II:14
285 *any*] all II:18
304 *God freely*] God, so liberal II:19
327 *go*] send V:10

ISABELLA WHITNEY, FROM *A SWEET NOSEGAY, OR PLEASANT POSY*

'To Geoffrey Whitney'

14 *And (next … dear)*] (and … deare,) C6^{v}

The Manner of her Will

* *friend's*] Friendes E2^{r}
239 *rut*] roote C7^{r}

The Lamentation upon the death of William Gruffith

51 *same*] fame P3^{v}
69 *(who, never … before),*] (who) neuer … before, P3^{v}
98 *lines*] lyues P4^{r}
111 *fragrant*] flagrant P4^{r}

MARY (SIDNEY) HERBERT, COUNTESS OF PEMBROKE, FROM *THE PSALMS* MSa = VISCOUNT DE L'ISLE, PENSHURST; MSb = BODLEIAN MS RAWL. POET 25

Ps 58.5 *Oh no:*] No MSa; O MSb
Ps 58.28 *oft*] of MSa
Ps 59.32 *They*] Their MSa
Ps 73.52 *what‸ but*] what? but MSa

Thenot and Piers

55 *friendship,*] friendship‸ B6^{r}

ANNE DOWRICHE, FROM *THE FRENCH HISTORY*, PART THREE

13 *race, ... next,*] race; ... next; F2^{v}
161 *passed*] past F4^{v}
253 *revenge,*] reuenge‸ G2^{r}
272 *care.*] care: G2^{r}
276 *deface,*] deface. G2^{v}
278 *seed* –] seede. G2^{v}
283 *thy*] by G2^{v}
557 *heart;*] heart: H3^{v}

AEMILIA LANYER, FROM *SALVE DEUS REX JUDAEORUM*

'To the Virtuous Reader'

27 *Sisera*] *Cesarus* f3^{v}
30 *Esther*] *Hester* f3^{v}
37 *healed women,*] healed woman f3^{v}

'Salve Deus Rex Judaeorum'

5.2 *affliction's*] afflictions C4^{v}
20.7 *virtue's*] Virtues D2^{v}
22.5 *Perfection's*] Perfections D3^{r}
34.7 *eagles'*] Eagles D4^{v}
72.1 *ris'n*] rize F1^{r}
74.2 *spouses'*] Spouses F1^{v}
74.8 *behold‸*] behold; F1^{v}

'To Cookham'

162 *tree;*] tree, H4^{v}

LADY MARY WROTH, FROM *PAMPHILIA TO AMPHILANTHUS*

The copy-text is the edition of 1621 (except for Sonnet F3)
Sonn 1 (P1) 11 *shoot*] shut 4A1^{r}
Song (U28) 58 *be*] not in 1621 R3^{r}
68 *Chaste but to you, to all others gainful;*] Chast, but to you, to all others, gainefull, R3^{r}

RACHEL SPEGHT, *A DREAM*, FROM *MORTALITY'S MEMORANDUM*

96 *gained*,] gain'd. B1^{v}
99 *it.*] it, B1^{v}
207 *Devil* (*for ... much*);] Deuill; for ... much; B3^{v}
234 *away*‸] away. B3^{v}
298 *began*] begun C1^{r}

BIBLIOGRAPHY

Allot, Robert (1970), *Englands Parnassus* [1600, facsimile reprint], Amsterdam: Theatrum Orbis Terrarum Ltd.

Amussen, Susan D. (1985), 'Gender, Family and the Social Order, 1560–1725', *Order and Disorder in Early Modern England*, ed. Anthony Fletcher and John Stevenson, Cambridge: Cambridge Univ. Press, pp. 196–205.

(1988), *An Ordered Society: Gender and Class in Early Modern England*, Oxford: Basil Blackwell.

Bacon, Francis (1968), *Essayes* [1597, facsimile reprint], Amsterdam, N.Y.: Da Capo Press.

Baines, Barbara (1978), *Three Pamphlets on the Jacobean Antifeminist Controversy*, Delmar, N.Y.: Scholars' Facsimiles and Reprints.

Bainton, Roland (1973), *Women of the Reformation in France and England*, Boston: Beacon Press.

Bale, John (1849), *Select Works of John Bale, D.D. Containing The Examinations of . . . Anne Askew*, ed. Henry Christmas, Parker Society, Cambridge: Cambridge Univ. Press.

Beechey, Veronica (1979), 'On Patriarchy', *Feminist Review* 3, pp. 66–82.

Beilin, Elaine V. (1981), 'The Onely Perfect Vertue: Constancy in Mary Wroth's *Pamphilia to Amphilanthus*', *Spenser Studies* 2, pp. 229–45.

(1987), *Redeeming Eve: Women Writers of the English Renaissance*, Princeton: Princeton Univ. Press.

(1990), 'Writing Public Poetry: Humanism and the Woman Writer', *Modern Language Quarterly* 51, pp. 249–71

(1991), 'Anne Askew's Dialogue with Authority', *Contending Kingdoms*, ed. Marie-Rose Logan and Peter L. Rudnytsky, Detroit: Wayne State Univ. Press, pp. 313–22.

Bell, Maureen, George Parfitt, and Simon Shepherd (eds) (1990), *A Biographical Dictionary of English Women Writers 1580–1720*, London: Harvester Wheatsheaf.

Belsey, Catherine (1985), *The Subject of Tragedy*, London and New York: Methuen.

Benson, Pamela Joseph (1992), *The Invention of Renaissance Women*, University Park, Penn.: Pennsylvania State Univ. Press.

Bornstein, Diane (ed.) (1980), *The Feminist Controversy of the Renaissance*, Delmar, N.Y.: Scholars' Facsimiles and Reprints. Bowles, W.L. and J.G. Nichols (1835), *Annals and Antiquities of Lacock Abbey*, London: Bowyer Nichols and Son.

Boxer, Marilyn J. and Jean H. Quataert (eds) (1987), *Connecting Spheres: Women in the Western World, 1500 to the Present*, New York: Oxford Univ. Press.

Brackett, Virginia (1994), 'Elizabeth Cary, Drayton, and *Edward II*', *Notes and Queries* 239, pp. 517–19.

(1995), '*The Countesse of Lincolne's Nurserie* as Inspiration for Anne Bradstreet', *Notes and Queries* 240, pp. 364–6.

Bradbrook, M.C. (1982), Review of *The Paradise of Women*, ed. Betty Travitsky, *Tulsa Studies in Women's Literature* 1, pp. 89–93.

Braden, Gordon (1990), 'Unspeakable Love: Petrarch to Herbert', *Soliciting Interpretation: Literary Theory and Seventeenth-Century English Poetry*, ed. Elizabeth D. Harvey and Katharine Eisaman Maus, Chicago: Univ. of Chicago Press, pp. 253–72.

Brennan, Margaret (1985), 'Women and Theology: Singing of God in an Alien Land', *The Way*, Supplement 53 on Mary Ward, pp. 93–103.

Brennan, Michael G. (1982), 'The date of the Countess of Pembroke's Translation of the Psalms', *Review of English Studies* 33, pp. 434–6.

(1988), *Literary Patronage in the English Renaissance: The Pembroke Family*, London and New York: Routledge.

Byrne, Lavinia (1985), 'Mary Ward's Vision of the Apostolic Religious Life', *The Way*, Supplement 53 on Mary Ward, pp. 73–84.

Cary, Elizabeth (1994), *The Tragedy of Mariam, the Fair Queen of Jewry, with The Lady Falkland Her Life*, ed. Barry Weller and Margaret Ferguson, Berkeley: Univ. of California Press.

Chambers, Mary Catherine Elizabeth (1882), *The Life of Mary Ward (1585–1645)*, 2 vols, London: Burns & Oates.

Clark, Alice (1919), *Working Life of Women in the Seventeenth Century*, London: Frank Cass & Co. [reprinted 1968, 1982].

Clifford, Anne (1923), *The Diary of the Lady Anne Clifford*, ed. Vita Sackville-West, London: William Heinemann Ltd.

(1992), *The Diaries of Lady Anne Clifford*, ed. D.J.H. Clifford, Stroud, Gloucestershire and Wolfeboro Falls, N.H.: Alan Sutton.

Collinson, Patrick (1983), 'The Role of Women in the English Reformation Illustrated by the Life and Friendships of Anne Locke', *Godly People: Essays on English Protestantism and Puritanism*, London: Hambledon Press, pp. 273–87.

Cover, Jeanne (1993), 'The Significance of Mary Ward's Spirituality and Practice for Moral Theology Today', Toronto: unpublished Ph.D. thesis, Univ. of Toronto.

Crandall, Coryl (ed.) (1969), *Swetnam the Woman-Hater: The Controversy and the Play*, West Lafayette, Ind.: Purdue Univ. Studies.

Crawford, Patricia (1993a), 'Public Duty, Conscience, and Women in Early Modern England', *Public Duty and Private Conscience Festschrift for G.E. Aylmer*, ed. John Morrill, Paul Slack, and Daniel Woolf, Oxford: Clarendon Press, pp. 57–76.

(1993b), *Women and Religion in England 1500–1720*, London and New York: Routledge.

Cressy, David (1980), *Literacy and the Social Order: Reading and Writing in Tudor and Stuart England*, Cambridge: Cambridge Univ. Press.

Cunnington, C. Willett and Phillis Cunnington (1970), *Handbook of English Costume in the Sixteenth Century*, London: Faber and Faber.

Davis, John F. (1983), *Heresy and Reformation in the South-East of England, 1520–1559*, London: Royal Historical Society.

Davis, Natalie Zemon (1980), 'Gender and Genre: Women as Historical Writers 1400–1820', *Beyond Their Sex: Learned Women of the European Past*, ed. Patricia H. LaBalure, New York: New York Univ. Press, pp. 153–82.

Delameau, Jean (1990), *Sin and Fear* [1983], trans. Eric Nicholson, New York: St Martin's Press.

Dickens, A.G. (1959), *Lollards and Protestants in the Diocese of York 1509–1558*, London: Oxford Univ. Press.

(1989), *The English Reformation*, 2nd edn, London: B.T. Batsford Ltd.

Doerksen, Daniel W. (1994), 'Preaching Pastor versus Custodian of Order: Donne, Andrewes, and the Jacobean Church', *Philological Quarterly* 73, pp. 417–29.

Dolan, Frances E. (1994a), '"Gentlemen, I have one thing more to say": Women on Scaffolds in England, 1563–1680', *Modern Philology* 92, pp. 157–78.

(1994b), *Dangerous Familiars: Representations of Crime in England 1550–1700*, Cornell: Cornell Univ. Press.

Duncan-Jones, Katherine (1985), Review of *The Poems of Lady Mary Wroth*, ed. J. Roberts, *Review of English Studies* 36, pp. 565–6.

(1986), Review of *Silent But For the Word*, *Times Literary Supplement* 13 June 1986, p. 636.

(1992), private communication.

(1994), Review of *The Poems of Aemilia Lanyer*, ed. Susanne Woods, *Times Literary Supplement*, 19 August, p. 23.

Elizabeth, Queen of England (1964), *The Poems of Elizabeth I*, ed. Leicester Bradner, Providence, R.I.: Brown Univ. Press.

Elton, G.R. (1985), 'History According to St Joan', *American Scholar* 54, pp. 549–55.

Emerson, Kathy Lynne (1984), *Wives and Daughters: The Women of Sixteenth-Century England*, Troy, N.Y.: Whitson Publishing Co.

Erickson, Amy Louise (1993), *Women and Property in Early Modern England*, London and New York: Routledge.

Ezell, Margaret J.M. (1987), *The Patriarch's Wife: Literary Evidence and the History of the Family*, Chapel Hill: Univ. of North Carolina Press.

(1992), 'Elizabeth Delaval's Spiritual Heroine: Thoughts on Redefining Manuscript Texts by Early Women Writers', *English Manuscript Studies 1100–1700*, vol. 3, ed. Peter Beal and Jeremy Griffiths, London and Toronto: British Library and Univ. of Toronto Press, pp. 216–37.

(1993), *Writing Women's Literary History*, Baltimore and London: Johns Hopkins Univ. Press.

Fairfield, Leslie F. (1976), *John Bale: Mythmaker of the English Reformation*, West Lafayette, Ind.: Purdue Univ. Press.

Farrell, Kirby, Elizabeth Hageman, and Arthur Kinney (eds) (1990), *Women in the Renaissance: Selections from English Literary Renaissance*, Amherst: Univ. of Massachusetts Press.

Fehrenbach, Robert J. (1981), 'Isabella Whitney and the Popular Miscellanies of Richard Jones', *Cahiers Elisabéthains* 19, pp. 85–7.

(1983), 'Isabella Whitney, Sir Hugh Plat, Geoffrey Whitney, and "Sister Eldershae"', *English Language Notes* 21, pp. 7–11.

Ferguson, Moira (1985), *First Feminists: British Women Writers 1578–1799*, Bloomington: Indiana Univ. Press.

Ferguson, Margaret W., Maureen Quilligan, and Nancy J. Vickers (eds) (1986), *Rewriting the Renaissance*, Chicago: Univ. of Chicago Press.

Fienberg, Nona (1991), 'Mary Wroth and the Invention of Female Poetic Subjectivity', *Reading Mary Wroth*, ed. Naomi J. Miller and Gary Waller, Knoxville: Univ. of Tennessee Press, pp. 175–90.

Findley, Sandra and Elaine Hobby (1981), 'Seventeenth-Century Women's Autobiography', *Literature and Power in the Seventeenth Century: Proceedings of the Essex Conference on the Sociology of Literature, July 1980*, ed. Francis Barker *et al.*, Colchester: Univ. of Essex Press, 1981.

Fiorenza, Elisabeth Schüssler (1992), *In Memory of Her A Feminist Theological Reconstruction of Christian Origins* [1983], New York: Crossroad Publishing Co.

Fischer, Sandra K. (1985), 'Elizabeth Cary and Tyranny, Domestic and Religious', *Silent But For the Word*, ed. Margaret P. Hannay, Kent, Ohio: Kent State Univ. Press, pp. 225–37.

Fisher, Sheila and Janet E. Halley (eds) (1989), *Seeking the Woman in Late Medieval and Renaissance Writings*, Knoxville: Univ. of Tennessee Press.

Fisken, Beth Wynne (1985), 'Mary Sidney's *Psalmes*: Education and Wisdom', *Silent But For the Word*, ed. Margaret P. Hannay, Kent, Ohio: Kent State Univ. Press, pp. 166–83.

(1990), '"To the Angell Spirit ...": Mary Sidney's Entry into the "World of Words"', *The Renaissance Englishwoman in Print*, ed. Anne M. Haselkorn and Betty S. Travitsky, Amherst: Univ. of Massachusetts Press, pp. 263–75.

Fletcher, Anthony (1995), *Gender, Sex and Subordination in England, 1500–1800*, New Haven and London: Yale Univ. Press.

Fletcher, Anthony and John Stevenson (eds) (1985), *Order and Disorder in Early Modern England*, Cambridge: Cambridge Univ. Press.

Fletcher, B.Y. and C.W. Sizemore (1981), 'Elizabeth Grymeston's *Miscelanea, Meditations, Memoratives*: Introduction and Selected Text', *Library Chronicle* 45, pp. 53–83.

Foster, Donald W. (1993), 'Resurrecting the Author: Elizabeth Tanfield Cary', *Privileging Gender in Early Modern England*, ed. Jean R. Brink, Kirksville, Mo: Northeast Missouri State Univ., pp. 144–73.

Foxe, John (1843), *The Acts and Monuments of John Foxe*, 8 vols, ed. George Townsend, London.

Fox-Genovese, Elizabeth (1978/80), 'For Feminist Interpretation', *Union Seminary Quarterly Review* 35, pp. 5–14.

Freeman, Arthur (1991), Review of *Lady Mary Wroth's Love's Victory*, ed. Michael G. Brennan, *The Library* 13.2, pp. 168–73.

Freer, Coburn (1972), *Music for a King: George Herbert's Style and the Metrical Psalms*, Baltimore and London: Johns Hopkins Univ. Press.

(1987), 'Mary Sidney: Countess of Pembroke', *Women Writers of the Renaissance and Reformation*, ed. Katherine Wilson, Athens: Univ. of Georgia Press, pp. 481–521.

Goreau, Angeline (1985), *The Whole Duty of a Woman: Female Writers in Seventeenth-Century England*, New York: Dial.

Graham, Elspeth (1989), Introduction, *Her Own Life: Autobiographical Writings by Seventeenth-Century English women*, ed. E. Graham *et al.*, London and New York: Routledge, pp. 1–27.

Greaves, Richard (1985), 'Foundation Builders: The Role of Women in Early English Nonconformity', *Triumph Over Silence: Women in Protestant History*, ed. R. Greaves, Westport, Conn.: Greenwood Press, pp. 75–92.

Greer, Germaine *et al.* (eds) (1988), *Kissing the Rod: An Anthology of Seventeenth-Century Women's Verse*, London: Virago Press.

Grundy, Isobel (1988), 'Falkland's *History of ... King Edward II*', *Bodleian Library Record* 13, pp. 82–3.

(1992), 'Women's History? Writings by English Nuns', *Women Writing, History, 1640–1740*, ed. I. Grundy and Susan Wiseman, Athens, Ga: Univ. of Georgia Press, pp. 126–38.

Hageman, Elizabeth and J.A. Roberts (1984), 'Recent Studies in Women Writers of Tudor England and the Seventeenth Century', *English Literary Renaissance* 14, pp. 409–39.

Hannay, Margaret P. (1985), '"Doo What Men May Sing": Mary Sidney and the Tradition of Admonitory Dedication', *Silent But For the Word*, ed. M. Hannay, Kent, Ohio: Kent State Univ. Press, pp. 149–65.

(1989), '"Princes You As Men Must Dy": Genevan Advice to Monarchs in the *Psalmes* of Mary Sidney', *English Literary Renaissance* 19, pp. 22–41.

(1990a), *Philip's Phoenix: Mary Sidney, Countess of Pembroke*, New York: Oxford Univ. Press.

(1990b), '"This Moses and This Miriam": The Countess of Pembroke's Role in the Legend of Sir Philip Sidney', *Sir Philip Sindey's Achievements*, ed. M.J.B. Allen, Dominic Baker Smith, Arthur F. Kinney, New York: AMS, pp. 217–26.

(1991a), '"Wisdome the wordes": Psalm Translation and Elizabethan Women's Spirituality', *Religion and Literature* 23, pp. 65–82.

(1991b), '"Your vertuous and learned Aunt": The Countess of Pembroke as a Mentor to Mary Wroth', *Reading Mary Wroth*, ed. Naomi J. Miller and Gary Waller, Knoxville: Univ. of Tennessee Press, pp. 15–34.

(1993), '"Unlock my lipps": the *Miserere mei Deus* of Anne Vaughan Lok and Mary Sidney Herbert, Countess of Pembroke', *Privileging Gender in Early Modern England*, ed. Jean R. Brink, Kirksville, Mo: Sixteenth Century Journal Publishers, pp. 19–36.

(1994), '"My song might good acceptance find": The Countess of Pembroke's Literary [A]vocation', Seminar on Renaissance women writers, Shakespeare Association Meeting.

Harvey, Elizabeth D. (1992), *Ventriloquized Voices: Feminist Theory and English Renaissance Texts*, London and New York: Routledge.

Haselkorn, Anne M. and Betty S. Travitsky (eds) (1990), *The Renaissance Englishwoman in Print*, Amherst: Univ. of Massachusetts Press.

Haugaard, William P. (1969), 'Katherine Parr: The Religious Convictions of a Renaissance Queen', *Renaissance Quarterly* 22, pp. 348–59.

Hazlitt, W.C. (1874), *Prefaces. Dedications. Epistles Selected from Early English Books 1540–1701*, London [reprints Epistle to Elizabeth Grymeston's *Miscellanea*].

Heertum, Cis van (1987), 'A Hostile Annotation of Rachel Speght's *A Mouzell for Melastomus* (1617)', *English Studies* 68, pp. 490–6.

Henderson, Katherine and Barbara McManus (eds) (1985), *Half Humankind: Contexts and Texts of the Controversy about Women in England, 1540–1640*, Urbana and Chicago: Univ. of Illinois Press.

Hill, Bridget (1987), 'A Refuge from Men: The Idea of a Protestant Nunnery', *Past and Present* 117, pp. 107–30.

Hobby, Elaine (1988), *Virtue of Necessity: English Women's Writing 1649–1688*, London: Virago Press.

(1992), '"Discourse so unsavoury": Women's Published Writings of the 1650s', *Women, Writing, History 1640–1940*, ed. Isobel Grundy and Susan Wiseman, Athens: Univ. of Georgia Press, pp. 16–32.

Hoby, Lady Margaret (1930), *Diary of Lady Margaret Hoby 1599–1605*, ed. Dorothy M. Meads, London: George Routledge.

Hogrefe, Pearl (1972), 'The Legal Rights of Tudor Women and their Circumvention by Men and Women', *Sixteenth Century Journal* 3, pp. 97–105.

Holmes, Martin (1975), *Proud Northern Lady: Lady Anne Clifford, 1590–1676*, London and Chichester: Phillimore & Co. Ltd.

Hooper, Wilfrid (1915), 'Tudor Sumptuary Laws', *English Historical Review* 30, pp. 433–49.

Howard, Jean E. (1991), 'Feminism and the Question of History: Resituating the Debate', *Women's Studies* 19, pp. 149–57.

Huber, Elaine C. (1985), *Women and the Authority of Inspiration*, New York: Univ. Press of America.

Hughey, Ruth and Philip Hereford (1934), 'Elizabeth Grymeston and Her *Miscellanea*', *The Library* 15, 4th series, pp. 61–91.

Hull, Suzanne W. (1982), *Chaste, Silent and Obedient*, San Marino: Huntington Library.

Hutson, Lorna (1992), 'Why the lady's eyes are nothing like the sun', *Women, Texts and Histories 1575–1760*, ed. Clare Brant and Dianne Purkiss, London and New York: Routledge, pp. 13–38.

(1994), 'Contextualizing Women's Writings in the 1570s: Isabella Whitney and the "Elizabethan Prodigals"', *The Usurer's Daughter*, London and New York: Routledge, pp. 116–28

Ingram, Martin (1990), *Church Courts, Sex and Marriage in England 1570–1640*, Cambridge: Cambridge Univ. Press.

Jones, Ann Rosalind (1981), 'Writing the Body: Toward an Understanding of *L'écriture feminine*', *Feminist Studies* 7, pp. 247–63.

(1987), 'Nets and Bridles: Early Modern Conduct Books and Sixteenth-Century Women's Lyrics', *The Ideology of Conduct*, ed. Nancy Armstrong and Leonard Tennenhouse, London and New York: Methuen, pp. 39–72.

(1990a), *The Currency of Eros: Women's Love Lyric in Europe, 1545–1620*, Bloomington and Indianapolis: Indiana Univ. Press.

(1990b), 'Counterattacks on "the Bayter of Women": Three Pamphleteers of the Early Seventeenth Century', *The Renaissance Englishwoman in Print*, ed. Anne M. Haselkorn and Betty S. Travitsky, Amherst: Univ. of Massachusetts Press, pp. 45–62.

(1991), 'Designing Women: The Self as Spectacle in Mary Wroth and Veronica Franco', *Reading Mary Wroth*, ed. Naomi J. Miller and Gary Waller, Knoxville: Univ. of Tennessee Press, pp. 135–53.

Jordan, Constance (1990), *Renaissance Feminism: Literary Texts and Political Models*, Ithaca: Cornell Univ. Press.

Kahin, Helen Andrews (1947), 'Jane Anger and John Lyly', *Modern Language Quarterly* 8, pp. 31–5.

Kay, Dennis (1990), *Melodious Tears: The English Elegy from Spenser to Milton*, Oxford: Clarendon Press.

Kelliher, Hilton and Katherine Duncan-Jones (1975), 'A Manuscript of Poems by Robert Sidney: Some Early Impressions', *British Library Journal* 1, pp. 107–44.

Kelly-Gadol, Joan (1977), 'Did Women Have a Renaissance?', *Becoming Visible: Women in European History*, ed. Renate Bridenthal and Claudia Koonz, Boston: Houghton Mifflin, pp. 137–64.

Kelso, Ruth (1978), *Doctrine of the Lady in the Renaissance* (1956), Urbana, Chicago and London: Univ. of Illinois Press.

Kennedy, Gwynne (1995), 'Reform of Rebellion?: The Limits of Female Authority in Elizabeth Cary's *The History of the Life, Reign, and Death of Edward II*', *The Rhetoric of Politics*, ed. Patricia Sullivan and Carole Levin, Albany: SUNY Press, pp. 205–22.

King, John (1982), *English Reformation Literature: The Tudor Origins of the Protestant Tradition*, Princeton: Princeton Univ. Press.

(1985), 'Patronage and Piety: The Influence of Catherine Parr', *Silent But For the Word*, ed. Margaret P. Hannay, Kent, Ohio: Kent State Univ. Press, pp. 43–60.

King, Margaret (1991), *Women of the Renaissance*, Chicago: Univ. of Chicago Press.

Kinnamon, Noel (1992), 'The Sidney Psalms: The Penhurst and Tixall Manuscripts', *English Manuscript Studies 1100–1700*, vol. 3, ed. Peter Beal and Jeremy Griffiths, London: British Library and Toronto: Univ. of Toronto Press, pp. 139–61.

Klein, Joan Larsen (1992), *Daughters, Wives and Widows: Writings by Men About Women and Marriage in England 1500–1640*, Urbana and Chicago: Univ. of Illinois Press.

Knott, John R. (1993), *Discourses of Martyrdom in English Literature 1563–1694*, Cambridge: Cambridge Univ. Press.

Krontiris, Tina (1990), 'Style and Gender in Elizabeth Cary's *Edward II*', *The Renaissance Englishwoman in Print*, ed. Anne M. Haselkorn and Betty S. Travitsky, Amherst: Univ. of Massachusetts Press, pp. 137–53.

(1992), *Oppositional Voices Women as Writers and Translators of Literature in the English Renaissance*, London and New York: Routledge.

Lamb, Mary Ellen (1985), 'The Cooke Sisters: Attitudes toward Learned Women in the Renaissance', *Silent But For the Word*, ed. Margaret P. Hannay, Kent, Ohio: Kent State Univ. Press, pp. 107–25.

(1986), 'The Countess of Pembroke and the Art of Dying', *Women in the Middle Ages and the Renaissance*, ed. Mary Beth Rose, Syracuse: Syracuse Univ. Press, pp. 207–26.

(1990), *Gender and Authorship in the Sidney Circle*, Madison: Univ. of Wisconsin Press.

(1992), 'The Agency of the Split Subject: Lady Anne Clifford and the Uses of Reading', *English Literary Renaissance* 22, pp. 347–68.

(1993), 'Constructing Women Readers in Aemilia Lanyer's *Salve Deus Rex Judaeorum*', seminar paper on Early Modern Women Writers, Shakespeare Association Meeting.

Lanyer, Aemilia (1978), *The Poems of Shakespeare's Dark Lady: Salve Deus Rex Judaeorum*, ed. A.L. Rowse, London: Jonathan Cape.

(1993), *The Poems of Aemilia Lanyer Salve Deus Rex Judaeorum*, ed. Susanne Woods, New York: Oxford Univ. Press.

Laslett, P. and R. Wall (eds) (1972), *Household and the Family in Past Time*, Cambridge: Cambridge Univ. Press.

Latz, Dorothy L. (1989), *'Glow-worm Light': Writings of the 17th Century English Recusant Women From Original Manuscipts*, Salzburg: Institut für Anglistik und Amerikanistik.

Lehmberg, Stanford E. (1964), *Sir Walter Mildmay and Tudor Government*, Austin: Univ. of Texas Press.

Levin, C. (1980), 'Women in the Book of Martyrs as Models of Behaviour in Tudor England', *International Journal of Women's Studies* 4: ii, pp. 196–207.

Levine, Mortimer (1982), 'The Place of Women in Tudor Government', *Tudor Rule and Revolution*, ed. Delloyd J. Guth and John W. McKenna, Cambridge: Cambridge Univ. Press, pp. 109–26.

Lewalski, Barbara K. (1979), *Protestant Poetics and the Seventeenth-Century Religious Lyric*, Princeton, Princeton Univ. Press.

(1987), 'Lucy, Countess of Bedford: Images of a Jacobean Courtier and Poetess', *Politics of Discourse: The Literature and History of Seventeenth-Century England*, ed. Kevin Sharpe and Steven N. Zwicker, Berkeley: Univ of California Press, pp. 52–77.

(1991), 'Re-Writing Patriarchy and Patronage: Margaret Clifford, Anne Clifford, and Aemilia Lanyer', *Yearbook of English Studies* 21, pp. 87–106.

(1993), *Writing Women in Jacobean England*, Cambridge, Mass.: Harvard Univ. Press.

Liebowitz, Ruth P. (1979), 'Virgins in the Service of Christ: The Dispute over an Active Apostolate for Women During the Counter-Reformation', *Women of Spirit: Female Leadership in the Jewish and Christian Traditions*, ed. Rosemary Ruether and Eleanor McLaughlin, New York: Simon & Schuster, pp. 131–52.

Linthicum, M.C. (1936), *Costume in the Drama of Shakespeare and his Contemporaries*, Oxford: Clarendon Press.

Love, Harold (1993), *Scribal Publication in Seventeenth-Century England*, Oxford: Clarendon Press.

Lucas, R. Valerie (1990), 'Puritan Preaching and the Politics of the Family', *The Renaissance Englishwoman in Print*, ed. Anne M. Haselkorn and Betty S. Travitsky, Amherst: Univ. of Massachusetts Press, pp. 224–40.

MacArthur, Janet (1989), '"A *Sydney*, Though Un-Named": Lady Mary Wroth and her Poetical Progenitors', *English Studies in Canada* 15, pp. 12–20.

Mackerness, E.D. (1946), 'Margaret Tyler: An Elizabethan Feminist', *Notes and Queries* 190, 3rd series, pp. 112–13.

Maclean, Ian (1980), *The Renaissance Notion of Woman*, Cambridge: Cambridge Univ. Press.

Magnusson, A. Lynne (1989), '*Jane Anger Her Protection, Boke His Surfeit*, and *The French Academie*', *Notes and Queries* 234, pp. 311–14.

(1991), '"His Pen with My Hande": Jane Anger's Revisionary Rhetoric', *English Studies in Canada* 17, pp. 269–81.

(1993), 'Nicholas Breton Reads Jane Anger', *Renaissance Studies* 7, pp. 291–300.

Mahl, Mary R., and Helene Koon (1977), *The Female Spectator*, Bloomington: Indiana Univ. Press.

Marquis, Paul A. (1995), 'Oppositional Ideologies of Gender in Isabella Whitney's *Copy of a Letter*', *The Modern Language Review* 90, pp. 314–24.

Marshall, Sherrin (ed.) (1989), *Women in Reformation and Counter-Reformation Europe Public and Private Worlds*, Bloomington and Indianapolis: Indiana Univ. Press.

Martin, Randall (1993), 'A Catholic Oldcastle', *Notes and Queries* 238, pp. 185–6.

(1994), 'The Autobiography of Grace, Lady Mildmay', *Renaissance and Reformation* 18, pp. 33–81.

(1996), 'Isabella Whitney's "Lamentation upon the Death of William Griffith"', *EMLS* (PURL http://oclc.org./emls/iemls/work).

(1997), 'Anne Dowriche's *The French History* and Innocent Gentillet's *Contre-Machiavel*', *Notes and Queries* (forthcoming March).

Mason, Mary G. (1980), 'The Other Voice: Autobiographies of Women Writers', *Autobiography: Essays Theoretical and Critical*, ed. James Olney, Princeton: Princeton Univ. Press, pp. 207–35.

Masten, Jeff (1991), ' "Shall I turne blabb?": Circulation, Gender, and Subjectivity in Mary Wroth's Sonnets', *Reading Mary Wroth*, eds. Naomi J. Miller and Gary Waller, Knoxville: Univ. of Tennessee Press, pp. 67–87.

May, Steven W. (1992), 'The Countess of Oxford's Sonnets: a Caveat', *English Language Notes* 29, pp. 9–19.

McConica, James Kelsey (1965), *English Humanists and Reformation Politics*, Oxford: Clarendon Press.

McGrath, Lynette (1991), 'Metaphoric Subversions: Feasts and Mirrors in Amelia Lanier's *Salve Deus Rex Judaeorum*', *Literature, Interpretation, Theory* 3, pp. 101–13.

(1992), ' "Let Us Have Our Libertie Againe": Amelia Lanier's 17th-Century Feminist Voice', *Women's Studies* 20, pp. 331–48.

McLaren, Dorothy (1985), 'Marital Fertility and Lactation 1570–1700', *Women in English Society 1500–1800*, ed. Mary Prior, London and New York: Methuen, pp. 22–53.

McLaren, Margaret Anne, (1990), 'An Unknown Continent: Lady Mary Wroth's Forgotten Pastoral Drama, "Loves Victorie" ', *The Renaissance Englishwoman in Print*, eds Anne M. Haselkorn and Betty S. Travitsky, Amherst: Univ. of Massachusetts Press, pp. 276–94.

Mendelson, Sara (1981), 'Women in Seventeenth-Century England: Three Studies', Oxford: unpublished D.Phil. thesis.

(1985), 'Stuart Women's Diaries and Occasional Memoirs', *Women in English Society 1500–1800*, ed. Mary Prior, London and New York: Methuen, pp. 181–210.

Mildmay, Herbert A. St John (1913), *A Brief Memoir of the Mildmay Family*, London and New York: privately printed.

Mildmay, Sir Walter (1983), *The Statutes of Sir Walter Mildmay Kt*, trans. Frank Stubbings, Cambridge: Cambridge Univ. Press.

Miller, Naomi (1989), ' "Not much to be marked": Narrative of the Woman's Part in Lady Mary Wroth's *Urania*', *Studies in English Literature* 29, pp. 121–37.

(1990), 'Rewriting Lyric Fictions: The Role of the Lady in Lady Mary Wroth's *Pamphilia to Amphilanthus*', *The Renaissance Englishwoman in Print*, ed. Anne M. Haselkorn and Betty S. Travitsky, Amherst: Univ. of Massachusetts Press, pp. 295–310.

Monson, Craig A. (ed.), *The Crannied Wall: Women, Religion, and the Arts in Early Modern Europe*, Ann Arbor: Univ. of Michigan Press.

More, Gertrude (1937), *The Writings of Dame Gertrude More*, ed. Dom. Benedict Weld-Blundell, London: R. & T. Washbourne.

Mueller, Janel (1984), *The Native Tongue and the Word: Developments in English Prose Style 1380–1580*, Chicago: Univ. of Chicago Press.

(1988), 'A Tudor Queen Finds Voice: Katherine Parr's *Lamentation of a Sinner*', *The Historical Renaissance*, ed. Heather Dubrow and Richard Strier, Chicago and London: Univ. of Chicago Press, pp. 15–47.

(1994), 'The Feminist Poetics of Aemilia Lanyer's "*Salve Deus Rex Judaeorum*" ', *Feminist Measures: Soundings in Poetry and Theory*, ed. Lynn Keller and Cristianne Miller, Ann Arbor: Univ. of Michigan Press, 208–36.

Newall, Fiona (1990), 'Wet nursing and Child Care in Aldenham, Hertfordshire, 1595–1726', *Women as Mothers in Pre-Industrial England*, ed. Valerie Fildes, London and New York: Routledge, pp. 122–38.

Newsom, Carol A. and Sharon H. Ringe (eds) (1992), *The Women's Bible Commentary*, London: SPCK, Louisville, Ky: Westminster/John Knox Press.

Nyquist, Mary (1987), 'The Genesis of Gendered Subjectivity in the Divorce Tracts and in *Paradise Lost*, *Re-membering Milton*, ed. M. Nyquist and Mary Ferguson, London: Methuen, pp. 99–127.

Orchard, Emmanuel (1985), *Mary Ward: Once and Future Foundress*, London: Catholic Truth Society.

Otten, Charlotte F. (1992), *English Women's Voices, 1540–1700*, Miami: Florida International Univ. Press.

Panofsky, Richard J. (ed.) (1982), *Sir Hugh Plat's Flowers of Philosophy and Isabella Whitney's A Sweet Nosegay*, New York: Scholars' Facsimiles and Reprints.

(1983), 'Love Poetry of Isabella Whitney, a Woman Author of the English Renaissance', *New Mexico Highlands Unversity Journal* 6, pp. 1–8

Paulissen, May Nelson (1982), *The Love Sonnets of Lady Mary Wroth: A Critical Introduction*, Salzburg: Institut für Anglistik und Amerikanistik.

Pollock, Linda (1993), *With Faith and Physic*, London: Collins & Brown.

Poole, Kristen (1995), '"The fittest closet for all goodness": Authorial Strategies of Jacobean Mothers' Manuals', *Studies in English Literature* 35, pp. 69–88.

Powell, Anthony (1963), *John Aubrey and his Friends*, London: Mercury Books.

Powell, C.L. (1972), *English Domestic Relations 1487–1653* [1917], New York: Russell & Russell.

Prescott, Anne Lake (1989), 'King David as a "Right Poet": Sidney and the Psalmist', *English Literary Renaissance* 19, pp. 131–51.

Prior, Mary (ed.) (1985), *Women in English Society 1500–1800*, London and New York: Methuen.

Purkiss, Diane (1992), 'Material Girls: The Seventeenth-Century Woman Debate', *Women, Texts and Histories 1575–1760*, ed. Clare Brant and D. Purkiss, London and New York: Routledge, pp. 69–101.

Quilligan, Maureen (1990), 'The Constant Subject: Instability and Authority in Wroth's *Urania* Poems', *Soliciting Interpretation: Literary Theory and Seventeenth-Century English Poetry*, ed. Elizabeth D. Harvey and Katharine Eisaman Maus, Chicago and London: Univ. of Chicago Press, pp. 307–335.

Rappaport, Steve (1989), *Worlds Within Worlds: Structures of Life in Sixteenth-Century London*, Cambridge: Cambridge Univ. Press.

Rathmell, J.C.A. (ed.) (1963), *The Psalms of Sir Philip Sidney and the Countess of Pembroke*, New York: New York Univ. Press.

Reay, Barry (1985), *Popular Culture in Seventeenth-Century England*, London: Croom Helm, 1985.

Redworth, Glyn (1990), *In Defence of the Church Catholic: The Life of Stephen Gardiner*, Oxford: Basil Blackwell.

Roberts, Josephine A. (1982), 'The Biographical Problem of *Pamphilia to Amphilanthus*', *Tulsa Studies in Women's Literature* 1, pp. 43–54.

Rollins, Hyder E. (ed.) (1971), *A Gorgeous Gallery of Gallant Inventions* [1578], New York.

Rose, Mary Beth (1986), 'Gender, Genre, and History: Seventeenth-Century Englishwomen and the Art of Autobiography', *Women in the Middle Ages and the Renaissance*, ed. M.B. Rose, Syracuse: Syracuse Univ. Press, pp. 245–78.

Rowlands, Marie B. (1985), 'Recusant Women 1560–1640', *Women in English Society 1500–1800*, ed. Mary Prior, London and New York: Methuen, pp. 149–80.

Salzman, Paul (1978), 'Contemporary References in Mary Wroth's *Urania*', *Review of English Studies* 24, pp. 178–81.

(1991), *An Anthology of Seventeenth-Century Fiction*, Oxford: Oxford Univ. Press [reproduces Book 1 of Mary Wroth's *Urania*].

Sankovitch, Tilde (1986), 'Inventing Origin of Authority: The Difficult Enterprise', *Women in the Middle Ages and the Renaissance*, ed. Mary Beth Rose, Syracuse: Syracuse Univ. Press, pp. 227–43.

Schleiner, Louise (1992), 'Margaret Tyler, Translator and Waiting Woman', *English Language Notes* 29, pp. 1–8.

(1994), *Tudor & Stuart Women Writers*, Bloomington and Indianapolis: Indiana Univ. Press.

Schwoerer, Lois G. (1984), 'Seventeenth-Century English Women Engraved in Stone?', *Albion* 16, pp. 389–403.

Shattock, Joanne (1993), *The Oxford Guide to British Women Writers*, Oxford: Oxford Univ. Press.

Shepherd, Simon (ed.) (1985), *The Women's Sharp Revenge*, New York: St Martin's Press.

Showalter, Elaine (1982), 'Feminist Criticism in the Wilderness', *Writing and Sexual Difference*, ed. Elizabeth Abel, Chicago: Chicago Univ. Press.

Sidney, Mary (Herbert), Countess of Pembroke (1977), *The Triumph of Death and Other Unpublished and Uncollected Poems*, ed. G.F. Waller, Salzburg: Institut für Anglistik und Amerikanistik.

Sidney, Sir Philip (1973), *An Apology for Poetry*, ed. Geoffrey Shepherd, Manchester: Manchester Univ. Press.

(1962), *The Poems of Sir Philip Sidney*, ed. William A. Ringler, Oxford: Clarendon Press.

Sidney, Robert (1984), *The Poems of Robert Sidney*, ed. P.J. Croft, Oxford: Clarendon Press.

Sizemore, Christine, W. (1976), 'Early Seventeenth-Century Advice Books: The Female Viewpoint', *South Atlantic Bulletin* 41, pp. 41–8.

(1981), 'Attitudes Toward the Education and Roles of Women: Sixteenth-Century and Seventeenth-Century Advice Books', *University of Dayton Review* 15, pp. 57–67.

Smith, Hilda (1976a, 1976b), 'Gynaecology and Ideology in Seventeenth-Century England'; 'Feminism and the Methodology of Women's History', *Liberating Women's History*, ed. Bernice A. Carroll, Urbana: Univ. of Illinois Press, pp. 97–114, 369–84.

(1982), *Reason's Disciples: Seventeenth-Century English Feminists*, Urbana: Univ. of Illinois Press.

Smith, Rosalind (1994), 'The Sonnets of the Countess of Oxford and Elizabeth I: Translations from Desportes', *Notes and Queries* 239, pp. 446–50.

Spender, Dale (1989), *British Women Writers: An Anthology from the Fourteenth Century to the Present*, New York: Peter Benrick Books.

Squire, J.C. (ed.) (1921), *A Book of Women's Verse*, Oxford: Clarendon Press.

Stauffer, Donald A. (1935), 'A Deep and Sad Passion', *Essays in Dramatic Literature: The Parrott Presentation Volume*, ed. Hardin Craig, Princeton: Princeton Univ. Press, pp. 289–314.

Steen, Sara Jayne (1994), 'Recent Studies in Women Writers of the Seventeenth Century, 1604–1674', *English Literary Renaissance* 24, pp. 243–74.

Steinberg, Theodore L. (1995), 'The Sidneys and the *Psalms*', *Studies in Philology* 92, pp. 1–17.

Stone, Lawrence (1965), 'The Educational Revolution in England, 1560–1640', *Past and Present* 28, pp. 41–80.

(1977), *The Family, Sex and Marriage in England 1500–1800*, New York: Harper and Row.

Stow, John (1971), *A Survey of London* [1603], ed. C.L. Kingsford, 2 vols, Oxford: Clarendon Press.

Strype, John, (1822), *Ecclesiastical Memorials*, 3 vols, Oxford: Clarendon Press.

Sugden, Edward H. (1925), *A Topographical Dictionary to the Works of Shakespeare and his Fellow Dramatists*, Manchester: Manchester Univ. Press.

Swetnam, Joseph (1989), *The Arraignment of Lewd, Idle, Froward and Unconstant Women: A Critical Edition*, ed. F.W. Van Heertum, Nijmegen: The Cicero Press.

Swift, Carolyn (1989), 'Feminine Self-Definition in Lady Mary Wroth's *Loves Victorie*', *English Literary Renaissance* 19, pp. 171–88.

Teague, Frances (1987), 'Elizabeth I', *Women Writers of the Renaissance and Reformation*, ed. Katharina M. Wilson, Athens and London: Univ. of Georgia Press, pp. 522–47.

Thomas, Keith (1958), 'Women and the Civil War Sects', *Past and Present* 13, pp. 42–62.

Thomas, Vivien, and William Tydeman (eds) (1994), *Christopher Marlowe: The Plays and their Sources*, London and New York: Routledge.

Todd, Barbara J. (1985), 'The Remarrying Widow: A Stereotype Reconsidered', *Women in English Society*, ed. Mary Prior, London and New York: Methuen, pp. 54–92.

(1989), *British Women Writers: A Critical Reference Guide*, New York: Continuum.

Travitsky, Betty S. (1980), 'The "Wyll and Testament" of Isabella Whitney', *English Literary Renaissance* 10, pp. 76–94.

(ed.) (1981), *The Paradise of Women: Writings by English Women of the Renaissance*, Westport, Conn.: Greenwood Press.

and Adele F. Seeff (eds) (1994), *Attending to Women in Early Modern England*, Newark: Univ. of Delaware Press.

Trevor-Roper, Hugh (1987), 'Lucius Cary, 2nd Viscount Falkland', *Catholics, Anglicans and Puritans: Seventeenth Century Essays*, London: Secker & Warburg.

Trollope, Edward (1862), 'Anne Askew, the Lincolnshire Martyr', *Associated Architectural Societies' Reports and Papers* 6, pp. 117–34.

Wall, Alison D. (ed.) (1983), *Two Elizabethan Women: Correspondence of Joan and Maria Thynne*, Devizes: Wiltshire Record Society.

Wall, Wendy (1991), 'Isabella Whitney and the Female Legacy', *English Literary History* 58, pp. 35–62.

(1993a), *The Imprint of Gender: Authorship and Publication in the English Renaissance*, Ithaca, N.Y.: Cornell Univ. Press.

(1993b), 'Our Bodies/Our Texts? Renaissance Women and the Trails of Authorship', *Anxious Power: Reading, Writing, and Ambivalence in Narrative by Women*, ed. Carol V. Singley and Susan Elizabeth Sweeney. Albany: State Univ. of New York Press, pp. 51–71.

Waller, Gary F. (1979), *Mary Sidney, Countess of Pembroke: A Critical Study of Her Writings and Literary Milieu*, Salzburg: Institut für Anglistik und Amerikanistik.

(1986a), '"This Matching of Contraries": Calvinism and Courtly Philosophy in the Sidney Psalms', *Essential Articles for the Study of Sir Philip Sidney*, ed. Arthur F. Kinney, Hamden, Conn.: Archon Books, pp. 411–23.

(1986b), *English Poetry of the Sixteenth Century*, London: Longmans.

(1990), 'The Countess of Pembroke and Gendered Reading', *The Renaissance Englishwoman in Print*, ed. Anne M. Haselkorn and Betty Travitsky, Amherst: Univ. of Massachusetts Press, pp. 327–45.

(1991), 'Mother/Son, Father/Daughter, Brother/Sister, Cousins: The Sidney Family Romance', *Modern Philology* 88, pp. 401–14.

(1993), *The Sidney Family Romance: Mary Wroth, William Herbert, and the Early Modern Construction of Gender*, Detroit: Wayne State Univ. Press.

Warnicke, Retha M. (1983), *Women of the English Renaissance and Reformation*, Westport, Conn.: Greenwood Press.

(1989), 'Lady Mildmay's Journal: A Study in Autobiography and Meditation in Reformation England', *Sixteenth Century Journal* 20, pp. 55–68.

(1993), 'Private and Public: The Boundaries of Women's Lives in Early Stuart England', *Privileging Gender in Early Modern England*, ed. Jean R. Brink, Kirksville, Mo: Sixteenth Century Journal Publishers, pp. 123–40.

Weigall, Rachel (1911), 'An Elizabethan Gentlewoman: The Journal of Lady Mildmay', *Quarterly Review* 215, pp. 119–38.

Wetter, Immolata (1970), *Letters of Instruction*, 9 vols, Rome: Institutum Beatae Mariae Virginis [Mary Ward's writings].

White, Helen C. (1944), *Social Criticism in Popular Religious Literature of the Sixteenth Century*, New York: Macmillan.

Whitney, Geoffrey (1886), *Whitney's Choice of Emblemes* [1586], ed. Henry Green, London: Lovell Reeve & Co.

Wiesner, Merry E. (1986), 'Women's Defense of Their Public Role', *Women in the Middle Ages and the Renaissance*, ed. Mary Beth Rose, Syracuse: Syracuse Univ. Press, pp. 1–27.

Wilcox, Helen (1992), 'Private Writing and Public Function: Autobiographical Texts by Renaissance Englishwomen', *Gloriana's Face*, ed. S.P. Cerasano and Marion Wynne-Davies, New York: Harvester Press, pp. 47–62.

Willen, Diane (1989), 'Women and Religion in Early Modern England', *Women in Reformation and Counter-Reformation Europe*, ed. Sherrin Marshall, Bloomington and Indianapolis: Indiana Univ. Press, pp. 140–65.

Williams, F.B. (1962), 'The Literary Patronesses of Renaissance England', *Notes and Queries* 207, pp. 364–6.

Williams, Neville (1964), *Thomas Howard Fourth Duke of Norfolk*, London: Barrie and Rockliff.

Williamson, George C. (1920), *George, Third Earl of Cumberland (1558–1605)*, Cambridge: Cambridge Univ. Press.

(1922), *Lady Anne Clifford Countess of Dorset, Pembroke and Montgomery. 1590–1676*, Kendal: Titus Wilson and Son.

Wilson, Katharina (ed.) (1987), *Women Writers of the Renaissance and Reformation*, Athens: Univ. of Georgia Press.

Woodbridge, Linda (1984), *Women and the English Renaissance*, Urbana and Chicago: Univ. of Illinois Press.

(1991), Review of *The Renaissance Englishwoman in Print* and *The Paradise of Women*, 2nd edn, *Shakespeare Quarterly* 42, pp. 376–9.

Woods, Susanne (1994), 'Aemilia Lanyer and Ben Jonson: Patronage, Authority, and Gender', *Ben Jonson Journal* 1, pp. 15–30.

Woolf, D.R. (1988), 'The True Date and Authorship of Henry, Viscount Falkland's *History of the Life, Reign and Death of King Edward II*', *Bodleian Library Record* 12, pp. 440–52.

Wright, Louis B. (ed.) (1962), *Advice to a Son: Precepts of Lord Burghley, Sir Walter Raleigh, and Francis Osborne*, Ithaca: Cornell Univ. Press.

Wrightson, Keith (1982), *English Society 1580–1680*, New Brunswick, N.J.: Rutgers Univ. Press.

Wroth, Lady Mary (1977), *Pamphilia to Amphilanthus*, ed. G.F. Waller, Salzburg: Institut für Anglistik und Amerikanistik.

(1983), *The Poems of Lady Mary Wroth*, ed. Josephine A. Roberts, Baton Rouge: Louisiana State Univ. Press.

(1988), *Love's Victory (The Penshurst Manuscript)*, ed. Michael G. Brennan, London: The Roxburghe Club.

(1995), *The First Part of The Countess of Montgomery's Urania*, ed. Josephine A. Roberts, Binghamton, N.Y.: Medieval & Renaissance Texts & Studies.

Youngs, Frederic A. (1976), *The Proclamations of the Tudor Queens*, Cambridge: Cambridge Univ. Press.

Zeigler, Georgianna M. (1994), 'Recent Studies in Women Writers of Tudor England, 1485–1603', *English Literary Renaissance* 24, pp. 229–42.

Zim, Rivkah (1987), *English Metrical Psalms Poetry as Praise and Prayer, 1535–1601*, Cambridge: Cambridge Univ. Press.